D1605291

K
A Common Law Approach
to Contracts

ASPEN CASEBOOK SERIES

K
A Common Law Approach
to Contracts

Tracey E. George

Professor of Law and Professor of Political Science
Director, Cecil D. Branstetter Litigation & Dispute Resolution Program
Vanderbilt University Law School

Russell Korobkin

Professor of Law
Faculty Director, Negotiation & Conflict Resolution Program
UCLA School of Law

Wolters Kluwer
Law & Business

Published by Wolters Kluwer Law & Business in New York.

Wolters Kluwer Law & Business serves customers worldwide with CCH, Aspen Publishers, and Kluwer Law International products. (www.wolterskluwerlb.com)

To contact Customer Service, e-mail customer.service@wolterskluwer.com,
call 1-800-234-1660, fax 1-800-901-9075, or mail correspondence to:

Wolters Kluwer Law & Business
Attn: Order Department
PO Box 990
Frederick, MD 21705

Printed in the United States of America.

1 2 3 4 5 6 7 8 9 0

ISBN 978-1-4548-0285-3

Library of Congress Cataloging-in-Publication Data

George, Tracey E., 1967-
  K : a common law approach to contracts / Tracey E. George, Russell Korobkin.
    p. cm.
  Includes index.
  ISBN 978-1-4548-0285-3
1. Contracts — United States. 2. Standardized terms of contract — United States. 3. Common law — United States. I. Korobkin, Russell. II. Title.
  KF801.G46 2012
  346.7302′2 — dc23

                                                                      2012008849

Certified Chain of Custody
Promoting Sustainable Forestry
www.sfiprogram.org
SFI-01042

SFI label applies to the text stock

About Wolters Kluwer Law & Business

Wolters Kluwer Law & Business is a leading global provider of intelligent information and digital solutions for legal and business professionals in key specialty areas, and respected educational resources for professors and law students. Wolters Kluwer Law & Business connects legal and business professionals as well as those in the education market with timely, specialized authoritative content and information-enabled solutions to support success through productivity, accuracy and mobility.

Serving customers worldwide, Wolters Kluwer Law & Business products include those under the Aspen Publishers, CCH, Kluwer Law International, Loislaw, Best Case, ftwilliam.com and MediRegs family of products.

CCH products have been a trusted resource since 1913, and are highly regarded resources for legal, securities, antitrust and trade regulation, government contracting, banking, pension, payroll, employment and labor, and healthcare reimbursement and compliance professionals.

Aspen Publishers products provide essential information to attorneys, business professionals and law students. Written by preeminent authorities, the product line offers analytical and practical information in a range of specialty practice areas from securities law and intellectual property to mergers and acquisitions and pension/benefits. Aspen's trusted legal education resources provide professors and students with high-quality, up-to-date and effective resources for successful instruction and study in all areas of the law.

Kluwer Law International products provide the global business community with reliable international legal information in English. Legal practitioners, corporate counsel and business executives around the world rely on Kluwer Law journals, looseleafs, books, and electronic products for comprehensive information in many areas of international legal practice.

Loislaw is a comprehensive online legal research product providing legal content to law firm practitioners of various specializations. Loislaw provides attorneys with the ability to quickly and efficiently find the necessary legal information they need, when and where they need it, by facilitating access to primary law as well as state-specific law, records, forms and treatises.

Best Case Solutions is the leading bankruptcy software product to the bankruptcy industry. It provides software and workflow tools to flawlessly streamline petition preparation and the electronic filing process, while timely incorporating ever-changing court requirements.

ftwilliam.com offers employee benefits professionals the highest quality plan documents (retirement, welfare and non-qualified) and government forms (5500/PBGC, 1099 and IRS) software at highly competitive prices.

MediRegs products provide integrated health care compliance content and software solutions for professionals in healthcare, higher education and life sciences, including professionals in accounting, law and consulting.

Wolters Kluwer Law & Business, a division of Wolters Kluwer, is headquartered in New York. Wolters Kluwer is a market-leading global information services company focused on professionals.

To Chris and Elliot
—TEG

To Sarah and Jessica
—RK

Summary of Contents

Contents

Chapter 4.   Contract Interpretation 251

Chapter 5.   Defining Performance Obligations: Conditions and Excuses   373

Chapter 7.   Alternative Bases for Liability: Non-Contract Claims 589

Preface

The purpose of this book is — in conjunction with the guidance provided by your Contracts professor — to teach you the method of legal reasoning. The law of contracts provides the raw material for this endeavor.

This is, of course, the classic goal of the document known as a law school "casebook," but we think that this goal has too often become obscured over the course of the last generation. Contracts textbooks, like those in many other fields, have tended to evolve and expand into longer and more sophisticated discourses on contract law and related theory, inching closer and closer to the model of the "hornbook" that provides a detailed and comprehensive description of the law and further away from the casebook model.

Many of these are impressive works of scholarship, but we believe that what contracts textbooks have become is not the tool best suited for a contracts course as it is usually taught in the modern American law school. As a first-year course now often taught in one semester, Contracts must help you learn to read judicial opinions, distinguish material from immaterial facts, and apply holdings from one case to others that bear substantial similarities but also notable differences. At root, this means that first and foremost, Contracts is a course in analogical reasoning, the fundamental skill of lawyering. Learning the details of contract law, per se, is a worthy objective — and you will learn a great deal of law in the course — but this is clearly the secondary objective.

It is our view, embodied in this casebook, that many prominent features of contemporary casebooks do not advance the goal of teaching the lawyerly skill of analogical reasoning and can often hinder the pursuit of that goal. Many Contracts texts include excerpts of law journal articles that provide normative theories of law. These can be illuminating for more advanced scholars, but they are rarely helpful to first-year law students, who are focused on understanding and applying precedent rather than critiquing it. To the extent that scholarly articles are more doctrinal in nature and carefully distinguish between case precedents, they sometimes model analogical reasoning, but we believe this is something that the classroom instructor can do, using these materials, in a way that makes a stronger impression.

Nearly all Contracts texts include extended note material that often follows primary cases and describes holdings of various courts on related issues. This type of material can give students the false impression that the law always — or even just usually — provides a clear, determinate answer to the question of what is the proper resolution of any dispute that arises. Such material only fuels the sometimes frantic quest of the new law student to learn the "rule" or the "black letter law," as if identifying and memorizing said "law" is sufficient to make him or her a competent lawyer. As you will learn in this course, the critical skill to master as a first-year law student is how to apply rules of law to new and unfamiliar fact patters.

Textual passage that provide string cites of relevant judicial opinions or that pose a long series of hypothetical questions — yet another standard feature of Contracts textbooks — are not necessarily harmful to your goal of learning the fundamental method of legal reasoning, but they are usually distracting and, at best, wasted space. Professors lack the time to discuss more than a small fraction (if any) of these tidbits in class, and students balancing a series of challenging courses lack the time to chase down and read all the cited opinions or to carefully think through all of the rapid-fire hypotheticals. As a result, you would quickly learn to largely ignore these materials.

You will quickly notice that this book contains none of these items. Each section is limited to three types of materials, which best promote the teaching and learning of the method of legal reasoning. Each section begins with a brief narrative that states a basic, fundamental proposition of contract law and provides some guidance as to the second order doctrinal issues that the fundamental proposition raises. This is followed by a set of edited judicial opinions, from which you, with guidance from your instructor, should tease out ways in which judges have dealt with these issues. In some situations, cases that deal with just slightly different issues are juxtaposed to illustrate the fault lines of contract doctrine. In others, cases that (arguably) deal with the same issue but reach different outcomes are juxtaposed to illustrate the conflict. Finally, each section concludes with a small number of discussion problems. These are designed to include enough factual detail that you can analyze them from the perspective of the opposing parties and the judge while, at the same time, being brief enough that you can carefully think through the problems in light of the preceding judicial opinions when preparing for class. These problems simulate (albeit in somewhat briefer form) the type of fact patterns that you will be expected to analyze during your final exam, and the opportunity to discuss and debate these in class will give you practice making exactly the form of argument your professor will expect you to make on the final exam. All of the problems present summarized facts from real cases, which allows your professor the opportunity, if he or she feels it is appropriate, to reveal how courts actually resolved the disputes in question following class debate.

In addition to believing that most contemporary contracts casebooks include too much of the wrong type of material for first-year law students, we also believe that most casebooks include too much material, period, given the ever-shortening number of contact hours allowed for the course. Nearly all other Contracts casebooks include chapters on the topics of assignment and third-party beneficiaries. Most Contracts casebooks attempt to teach many provisions of Article 2 of the Uniform Commercial Code (which applies specifically to contracts for the sale of goods) in addition to the fundamental rules and principles of the common law of contracts. Some also attempt to incorporate study of international sales law as exemplified by the Convention on International Sale of Goods. More recently, some casebooks have begun to emphasize the skill of contract drafting.

There is no question that these are all topics that a commercial lawyer should know, but we believe that attempting to teach these subjects in first-year contracts course distracts from building the fundamental skills that all lawyers need to learn regardless of their practice area. We believe — as does your professor, as evidenced by the fact that he or she has chosen from many alternatives to assign this book — that it is better for law students to study these topics in advanced courses rather than shoe-horning them into the basic contracts course and diluting the training in analogical reasoning that should be the primary pedagogical goal. This book contains only a few brief interactions with the Uniform Commercial Code — just enough, we believe, to teach students its scope and illustrates a few points of contrast with common law principles. The other peripheral topics do not appear at all. The result is a relatively lean text that can be read and taught cover to cover, or nearly so, in the time allotted for your contracts course.

TEG
RK

March 2012

Acknowledgments

Although we like to think we bring some unique insights to the material that follows and the accompanying teacher's manual, our views about the substance of contract law and how to best teach it are highly derivative of those who have both taught and assisted us over the years. We owe a particular intellectual debt to Charles Calleros, Barbara Fried, Bob Gordon, Bill Henning, and Dick Speidel, who taught us contracts as students at Stanford Law School and/or shared their teaching notes with us when we first started teaching the subject ourselves in the 1990s. We have studied from or taught out of the *Cases and Materials on Contracts* (now by Allen Farnsworth, William Young, Carol Sanger, Richard Brooks, and Neal Cohen), and *Studies in Contract Law* (now by Ian Ayres and Richard E. Speidel). And we have benefitted greatly from from the research assistance provided by UCLA law students George Chapman, Brad Flood, Michael LaPlante, Paul McReynolds, Mary Mooney, Nick Palatucci, Isaac Silverman, Jonathon Townsend, and Vanderbilt law students Patricia Duffy, Jinghui Lim, Victoria McCoy, Weslynn Reed, Deborah Yang, and Geraldire Young. Chris Guthrie deserves credit for the book's title. If you find it too clever, blame him. Sarah and Jessica, Chris and Elliot, provided support and inspiration, and helped us to keep the whole thing in perspective.

K

A Common Law Approach to Contracts

Introduction

Imagine that Tracey pays careful attention to every word spoken by her contracts professor while Russell is easily distracted and frequently gazes out the window. They contemplate making a deal for Tracey to tutor Russell in contract law for three hours and for Russell to pay Tracey $75, a transaction that both believe would make them better off than they otherwise would be. They face the problem, however, that one of them would have to perform first. Why should Tracey be sure that Russell actually will pay if she tutors him first? And why should Russell be confident that, if he pays in advance, Tracey will then perform her obligation or perform it competently? Even if it were possible for them to perform their obligations at the same time, one or both parties might be wary of relying on the representations made by the other concerning the qualities of the goods or services being exchanged. If the contract called for Tracey to provide Russell with a copy of her class notes, Russell would only be comfortable handing over the money if he could be certain about the quality of the notes. Tracey assures him that they are thorough and complete, but why should Russell trust this claim?

For most significant transactions to occur, at least one party (and usually both parties) must *trust* the other to fulfill one or more promises. Trust may arise from an existing relationship between the parties or from the parties' ongoing economic incentives. Perhaps you trust your Uncle William to keep his promises to you because he has demonstrated in the past that he is a man of his word. You might trust your classmate to keep a promise because doing so is consistent with the norms of your law school community. You might trust the local dry cleaner to thoroughly launder your shirts after you pay her because the risks to her reputation were she to fail to satisfy her commitment would far outweigh the few dollars she might hope to save. But norms and reputational incentives are only a partial—and sometimes unpredictable—basis for securing trust. And, when transacting parties are strangers and do not share social ties, these informal methods often provide little assistance.

Contract law assures performance and thus promotes exchange, thereby facilitating commerce. It is a standardized and reliable mechanism for the creation and maintenance of trust. After creating an agreement called a "contract"—often represented in law school with the letter "K"—people suddenly, and almost magically, become willing to trust complete strangers to keep their promises to provide valuable goods or services or to pay thousands or even millions of dollars, sometimes far in the future! The main reason contract law succeeds is that the government stands ready to enforce contracts, using force if necessary. Without the institution of contract law, the $15 trillion dollar annual United States economy, not to mention the $60 trillion dollar global economy, could not function efficiently, if at all. And the same system that allows the global economy to run smoothly also can protect you if your uncle lets you down, your classmate breaks a promise, or your dry cleaner returns your shirt dirty.

In light of the importance of contracts and contract law to society generally, it should come as no surprise that contract law is critically important to most lawyers as well. Transactional lawyers earn their living negotiating, drafting, and advising clients on the content and design of contracts, with one eye focused on the treatment that the law would give those contracts if a dispute were to arise later. For litigators, contract disputes make up the largest single category of civil disputes in state courts (where 95 percent of all litigation takes place)—as high as 51 percent, according to one recent study. And even litigators who do not handle contract disputes settle most of their cases out of court, a procedure that requires entering into a contract. Criminal lawyers settle most of their disputes through plea bargains, which are also contracts. Few legal careers require no familiarity with contracts, contract principles, or contract law.

American contract law has two features that are particularly important to understand as you begin your study. First, contract law is a "common law" subject, meaning that judicial opinions, rather than written statutes, are the primary source of legal authority. While many legislatures have adopted statutes concerning contract law in the modern age, the statutes frequently draw or build on the foundation of common law. Even if a contract dispute is governed by a statute, prior judicial interpretations of that statute will govern its interpretation in later cases.

Judges resolve disputes concerning contracts and contract law by interpreting and applying the reasoning of prior judicial decisions, thereby continuously honing and developing the law over time. The preceding decisions of equal or higher courts in a particular jurisdiction are binding on judges. The opinions of courts in other jurisdictions or of lower courts in the same jurisdiction are not binding, but they often have "persuasive" authority. Through the constant sifting of precedent, our modern law of contracts reflects distinctive aspects of American history and culture as well as its British roots. Understanding the contours of the law requires reading, interpreting, and reasoning from established case law.

Second, contract law is predominantly a matter of state rather than national law. Hence, there is no *single* body of contract law, and there can thus be no single authoritative statement of what the law is. Rest assured that contract law is quite similar across the country, but subtle differences still do exist from state to state. Understanding the subject of contract law requires accepting that the law you will study is *generally* the law everywhere but *not exactly* the law anywhere.

You will learn the law of contracts primarily by reading the edited judicial opinions that appear in this book. A secondary source of information is the Restatement (Second) of Contracts, adopted by the non-profit American Law Institute in 1979, which replaced the original Restatement of Contracts (adopted in 1932). The text in this book introducing each set of judicial opinions includes references to the appropriate sections of the Restatement (Second) of Contracts, which we will refer to simply as "the Restatement" (or cite as Rest. (2d) Contracts). You can locate all of the sections of the Restatement cited in this casebook easily and conveniently in the separate statutory supplement designed as a companion to this book. Alternatively, you may choose to access the complete Restatement in print or online.

The Restatement is a text written by a panel of learned scholars, judges, and lawyers that, for the most part, attempts to explain the rules of contract law clearly and concisely. It is not itself law, which is to say that the rules described in the Restatement do not bind courts in any jurisdiction. Courts often rely on the Restatement, however, and in some cases courts have explicitly adopted the text of sections of the Restatement as the law of their jurisdiction. To make matters more confusing, where there is variation across jurisdictions, the rule that appears in the Restatement is sometimes the rule followed by the majority of jurisdictions and is sometimes the rule that the Restatement's adopters found more normatively desirable, regardless of how widely followed it was at the time of the document's drafting. Thus, without conducting independent research, you cannot be sure that the law in your jurisdiction is exactly as presented in the Restatement.

The text will also occasionally direct you to Article 2 of the Uniform Commercial Code ("UCC") as well. UCC Article 2 sets forth rules governing contracts for the sale of goods; it is inapplicable to other types of contracts, most notably contracts for services or for real property. Like the Restatement, the UCC itself is technically not law but rather a text drafted by a group of experts. Unlike the Restatement, the UCC was drafted to be a model statute. Legislatures in every jurisdiction except Louisiana have enacted all (or almost all) of Article 2 as law. Thus, for the purposes of this course, you should treat the UCC as statutory law. Although there are many subtle variations between the UCC and the common law of contracts that can be important to commercial lawyers, the law of Article 2 is reasonably consistent with the common law of contracts in most cases. We specifically direct you to the UCC only when its approach provides a major departure from common law rules.

The core competency of lawyers is the ability to discern a legal rule and apply it to new facts. Your professor will often ask whether you can "distinguish" between two cases with similar but slightly different fact patterns—that is, whether the differences justify the imposition of a different rule or lead to a different result as a consequence of applying the same rule. This type of analysis, critical to legal reasoning, requires you to judge the appropriateness of a proposed analogy between two non-identical cases, based on a fundamental (but often unstated) premise of law that like cases should be treated alike.

You will begin to conduct this analysis by deriving the legal rules, or doctrine, from the assigned cases, with the help of the Restatement and (sometimes) the UCC. These materials will provide you with sufficient raw material to analyze a new set of facts in many instances. That is, a rule announced in the context of one case may clearly apply with equal force to a different set of facts, such that knowing the rule announced in the first case will enable you to predict the outcome of the second. Assume, for example, that a 17-year-old promises to purchase a boat from Bass Boat Shops and then changes her mind and refuses to complete the transaction. The store sues for breach of contract, and the court rules for the 17-year-old defendant on the ground that contracts with minors are unenforceable. If another case were to arise in which a 16-year-old promises to purchase karate lessons and then refuses to follow through, you could be confident that a court would again rule for the defendant, since the rule—which has everything to do with the age of the purchaser and nothing to do with boats—clearly applies to the second case as well as to the first. The two cases are different in some respects, as any pair of cases will be, but they are legally *indistinguishable*.

In other situations, however, the rule alone will not enable you to predict whether similar cases would be treated the same. Suppose in the new fact pattern a 16-year-old promises to purchase karate lessons and the karate teacher, an adult, later refuses to perform. In a lawsuit brought by the would-be karate student against the adult, who will prevail? To resolve this question, you would need to understand not just the applicable rule as stated by the court in the boat case, but the philosophical or policy *principle* that underlies the rule. In order to correctly predict that the court will find that the karate contract enforceable and therefore rule for the student, you would need to understand that the principle underlying the doctrine is paternalism; that is, that the rule exists to protect minors on the theory that they are not mature enough to decide for themselves whether contracting is in their best interest. Because the adult karate teacher does not need the protection of the law, the principle would not be served by refusing to enforce the contract against him. Thus, this karate hypothetical is distinguishable from the boat case because the person seeking to avoid enforcement of the contract is the adult rather than the minor. As this example hopefully demonstrates, understanding law at a theoretical level is not a rarefied pursuit relevant only to academic lawyers cloistered in an ivory tower but is a practical necessity for any lawyer who wishes to effectively advise and advocate on behalf of clients seeking solutions to their real-world problems.

All complex fields of law are animated by a variety of principles. In contract law, you will find that the following principles are often relevant, with the first trio often competing for dominance and the second trio often justifying important exceptions to general sets of rules:

- Autonomy: The law should enable people to exercise free choice.
- Efficiency: The law should support the allocation of resources to the people who value them most in order to increase total social welfare.

- Integrity: The law should encourage people to keep their commitments.
- Paternalism: The law should protect those who cannot protect themselves.
- Administrability: The law should not require judges to make decisions they are ill-equipped to make well or can make only at high cost.
- Social Justice: The law should favor those who have less wealth or opportunity.

At some point during the semester, identifying and understanding the basic legal rules of almost any area of law will become much easier than it will be at the outset, but understanding the principles behind those rules will remain challenging. This task requires deep subject-area knowledge and a significant amount of experience and wisdom. Sometimes judges describe governing principles in their opinions, but more often lawyers must infer them from more subtle cues and/or the mastery of a large body of law.

When the outcomes of a case are deeply contested—by judges, by scholars, or by students in a contracts class—the reason is often that one or more core principles are at odds, and each plausible outcome would reinforce one or more principles while undermining others. In such situations, your intuition as to what outcome would be more "just" or "fair" will often depend on which competing principle you believe is or should be primary. If you are outraged to learn that the 17-year-old boat-buyer can break his promise to deliver payment with impunity, for example, it might be because you place a higher value on the principles of autonomy or integrity than the principle of paternalism in this context.

If you understand the principles at stake in difficult cases, not only will you be better able to predict outcomes of new cases, you will be better equipped to advocate for either side in a dispute. Consider, for example, an issue that will arise in your study of the doctrine of mutual assent in Chapter 2: If you believe that a party who utters words that *appear* to indicate willingness to enter into a contract should be excused from performing if she subjectively did not *intend* to enter into a contract, you probably think the principle of autonomy should take priority over the principles of efficiency and administrability. On the one hand, to hold a party to an obligation that she did not wish to make would undermine her autonomous control of her destiny. On the other hand, to not hold her to an apparent commitment would reduce the incentive for people to rely on the apparent commitments of others, which would undermine the principle of efficiency by reducing the number of welfare-increasing transactions that would actually take place. In addition, it would be difficult for judges or juries to accurately determine the intent of an actor, since intentions are not themselves observable, so the principle of administrability counsels for resolving disputes based on observable actions rather than subjective states of mind.

Your ability to understand the law, predict outcomes, and advocate for parties will also be improved if you understand jurisprudential conflicts that frequently arise in factually distinct situations. Three such dichotomies are especially important to recognize because they recur throughout various substantive areas of contract law, although none are unique to the field of contract law: dispositional versus precedential effects of judicial decisions; rules versus standards; and text versus context.

(1) *Dispositional vs. precedential effects of judicial decisions.*   Every judicial decision resolves an actual dispute between two or more parties and also serves as precedent for future disputes. In some cases, a decision that will strike you as reaching a "just" or "fair" result as between the two parties will create incentives for future contracting parties that seem undesirable, thus creating a tension. For example, in the Chapter 6 case of *White v. Benkowski,* the Benkowskis breach a contract to supply well-water to their neighbors by maliciously turning the water off for short periods of time. The question before the court is whether to award the Whites damages sufficient to *punish* the Benkowskis, rather than merely damages sufficient to *compensate* the Whites. On the one hand, you might believe that the Benkowskis' outrageous behavior justifies punishment. On the other hand, severely punishing the Benkowskis might discourage other people (who are well-meaning but fear being mistaken for being malicious) from agreeing to share well-water with their neighbors, or it might encourage such people to overinvest in equipment to make sure there are no accidental disruptions to service, no matter how minor. Resolving the case requires the court to favor either the dispositional or precedential effect of its ruling, although the judge does not explicitly frame the choice in this way.

(2) *"Rules" vs. "Standards."*   Statements of legal doctrine can take different forms. If the law provides a clear outcome that follows from one or more triggering facts, the law may be referred to as a "rule." (We should note that, somewhat confusingly, the word "rule" also is used to refer to law generally.) In contrast, if the law requires a legal decision maker to apply a broad criterion or set of criteria to a set of facts in order to resolve a dispute, this is sometimes called a "standard." If the law provides that contracts with minors are voidable by the minor, this is an example of a simple "rule": a judge need only determine whether the person seeking to avoid enforcement of a contract is above or below the age of majority to resolve a dispute. If the law provides that contracts with minors are voidable if they are unfair to the minor, this exemplifies a "standard": to apply the law to resolve a dispute, the judge must consider and weigh a range of fact-specific circumstances. Rules provide predictability and promote administrability, but standards offer the promise of a closer fit between judicial outcomes and principles the law seeks to advance. Whether you believe that a mature 17-year-old who wishes to avoid enforcement of a contract to purchase a boat at the market price should prevail might depend on your preference for the benefits of rules or the benefits of standards.

(3) *Text vs. Context.*   When interpreting contracts, courts might give priority to the usual and ordinary meaning of the words that make up the agreement, or they might place substantial weight on the contextual features of transaction, such as the nature of the negotiations between the parties that led to the contract, customary norms of the industry in which the contracting parties operate, or the prior relationship between the parties. This tension bears a relationship to the tension between rules and standards, as relying on text has rule-like benefits of promoting

predictability and administrability, whereas taking account of context increases administrative costs and reduces predictability but offers the potential to better reflect the actual intention of the contracting parties. The Chapter V case of *In re Soper's Estate* illustrates what can be at stake in the choice between text and context. Ira Soper deserted but never divorced his wife Adele and entered into a legally invalid marriage with Gertrude, who was unaware of Adele. He later purchased an insurance policy payable to his "wife." When Soper died, Adele and Gertrude both sought payment from the insurance company. Fidelity to text would suggest Adele, Soper's only legal wife, was the proper beneficiary, but context clearly indicates that both Soper and the insurance company intended that the money go to Gertrude.

* * *

This book will provide you with the materials necessary to learn the basics of contract law. The various aspects of contract law doctrine are interrelated so that to understand any one aspect of the doctrine it is useful to understand others as well. Of course, it is impossible to study the entirety of contract law simultaneously—some portions must come early in the course, some later. To a certain extent, then, the ordering of materials reflects the taste of the authors, and different casebooks approach the basic doctrinal issues in different orders. With that said, the pages that follow provide you with a tour of contract law doctrine organized in the fashion that we find most logical for the purpose of building a coherent, overall understanding of the material: Chapters 1, 2, and 3 concern the formation and enforceability of contracts; Chapters 4 and 5 concern the construction and interpretation of rights and duties under contracts; Chapter 6 addresses the remedies available to a contracting party when her counterpart breaches his duties; and Chapter 7 addresses rules closely related to, but not actually a part of, contract law.

Chapter 1 considers the nature of a "promise," the fundamental core of contract. In it, you will consider the difference between promises and utterances, such as predictions, opinions, or statements of present intention, that share superficial similarities with promises. You also will consider the question of who should decide if a promise has been made, and from whose perspective the question should be considered.

Chapter 2 concerns the notion of "bargain," by tradition also a necessary ingredient of a legally binding contract. This chapter is subdivided into the elements of consideration, which is the obligation exchanged for the promise, and mutual assent, which is the manifestation of consent of both parties to the terms of agreement.

Even if parties have formed a contract according to the requirements of Chapters 1 and 2, that contract might be unenforceable in a court of law if it is not properly documented, involves a party lacking the legal capacity to contract, is procured through improper behavior on the part of one party, or in its substance exceeds the broad parameters in which the law allows parties to operate. Chapter 3 surveys these topics.

Chapter 4 assumes that the parties have entered into an enforceable contract. It considers the rules of interpretation and, in some cases, construction, on which courts rely to determine the duties of contracting parties.

Contractual duties can be absolute in nature, but they can also be contingent on certain facts or the occurrence of future events. Chapter 5 evaluates the doctrines of conditions and excuses, according to which parties can be relieved of contractual duties in specified circumstances.

Contracts have the ability to facilitate trust because of the promise of state action in case of breach. Chapter 6 addresses the question of what remedies a contracting party is entitled to when his counterpart breaches a contract. This chapter considers whether remedies should seek to compensate the non-breaching party or to punish the breaching party, whether compensatory remedies should take the form of court-ordered performance or the payment of money, and how courts conceptualize the amount of money necessary to adequately compensate a non-breaching party.

In some circumstances, parties suffer harms that resemble harms suffered when a contract is breached, but without the existence of a contract. Chapter 7 considers the potential for recovery under the law when a promise is broken but the element of bargain is lacking ("promissory estoppel") and when a benefit is conferred by one party on another with the expectation of compensation but without a promise of compensation ("quasi-contract").

We hope that you find your coming immersion into the specific field of contract law and the more general subject of legal reasoning enjoyable, challenging, and rewarding!

Chapter 1

Promise

The Restatement begins by describing a [contract as "a promise or set of promises for the breach of which the law gives a remedy, or the performance of which the law in some way recognizes as a duty," thus establishing the centrality of promises to the law of contract.] Rest. (2d) Contracts §1. But what is a promise? Like Supreme Court Justice Potter Stewart famously said about obscenity,[1] you might think you know a promise when you see it. While your intuition usually would be correct in relatively clear cases, the line between promise and non-promise often is hazy. Statements best described as "opinions," "predictions," or "statements of present intent" can appear quite similar to promises, even though they fail to communicate the notion of commitment to act or warranty necessary for a promise. See Rest. (2d) Contracts §2.

Thus, we begin our study of contract law by considering what is and is not a promise, what legal actor should make the determination in the case of dispute, and from whose perspective and based on what evidence that legal actor should address the question. In addition to shedding light on these issues, the New Hampshire Supreme Court's decision in *Hawkins v. McGee*, one of the most famous cases in contract law, also introduces the issue of what remedies a court should award to the victim of a breach of contract. This question will be considered in depth in Chapter 4.

---

1. Jacobellis v. Ohio, 378 U.S. 184, 197 (1964) (Stewart, J., concurring) ("[U]nder the First and Fourteenth Amendments criminal laws in this area are constitutionally limited to hard-core pornography. I shall not today attempt further to define the kinds of material I understand to be embraced within that shorthand description; and perhaps I could never succeed in intelligibly doing so. But I know it when I see it.").

HAWKINS
v.
McGEE

Supreme Court of New Hampshire
84 N.H. 114
1929

Assumpsit against a surgeon for breach of an alleged warranty of the success of an operation. Trial by jury. Verdict for the plaintiff. The writ also contained a count in negligence upon which a nonsuit was ordered, without exception.

[handwritten: suit was not allowed by judge to go to jury / maybe not sufficient evidence]

. . .

[handwritten margin: disposition]

The court . . . found that the damages were excessive, and made an order that the verdict be set aside, unless the plaintiff elected to remit all in excess of $500. The plaintiff having refused to remit, the verdict was set aside "as excessive and against the weight of the evidence," and the plaintiff excepted.

The foregoing exceptions were transferred by Scammon, J. The facts are stated in the opinion.

Branch, J.

1. The operation in question consisted in the removal of a considerable quantity of scar tissue from the palm of the plaintiff's right hand and the grafting of skin taken from the plaintiff's chest in place thereof. The scar tissue was the result of a severe burn caused by contact with an electric wire, which the plaintiff received about nine years before the time of the transactions here involved. There was evidence to the effect that before the operation was performed the plaintiff and his father went to the defendant's office, and that the defendant, in answer to the question, "How long will the boy be in the hospital?" replied, "Three or four days, not over four; then the boy can go home and it will be just a few days when he will go back to work with a good hand." Clearly this and other testimony to the same effect would not justify a finding that the doctor contracted to complete the hospital treatment in three or four days or that the plaintiff would be able to go back to work within a few days thereafter. The above statements could only be construed as expressions of opinion or predictions as to the probable duration of the treatment and plaintiff's resulting disability, and the fact that these estimates were exceeded would impose no contractual liability upon the defendant. The only substantial basis for the plaintiff's claim is the testimony that the defendant also said before the operation was decided upon, "I will guarantee to make the hand a hundred per cent perfect hand or a hundred per cent good hand." The plaintiff was present when these words were alleged to have been spoken, and, if they are to be taken at their face value, it seems obvious that proof of their utterance would establish the giving of a warranty in accordance with his contention.

[handwritten margin: counter]

The defendant argues, however, that, even if these words were uttered by him, no reasonable man would understand that they were used with the intention of entering "into any contractual relation whatever," and that they could reasonably be understood only "as his expression in strong language that he believed and expected that as a result of the operation he would give the plaintiff a very good hand." It may be conceded, as the defendant contends, that, before the question of the making of a contract should be submitted to a jury, there is a preliminary question of law for the trial court to pass upon, i.e. "whether the words could possibly have the meaning imputed to them by the party who founds his case upon a certain interpretation," but it cannot be held that the trial court decided this question erroneously in the present case. It is unnecessary to determine at this time whether the argument of the defendant, based upon "common knowledge of the uncertainty which attends all surgical operations," and the improbability that a surgeon would over contract to make a damaged part of the human body "one hundred per cent perfect," would, in the absence of countervailing considerations, be regarded as conclusive, for there were other factors in the present case which tended to support the contention of the plaintiff. There was evidence that the defendant repeatedly solicited from the plaintiff's father the opportunity to perform this operation, and the theory was advanced by plaintiff's counsel in cross-examination of defendant that he sought an opportunity to "experiment on skin grafting," in which he had had little previous experience. If the jury accepted this part of plaintiff's contention, there would be a reasonable basis for the further conclusion that, if defendant spoke the words attributed to him, he did so with the intention that they should be accepted at their face value, as an inducement for the granting of consent to the operation by the plaintiff and his father, and there was ample evidence that they were so accepted by them. The question of the making of the alleged contract was properly submitted to the jury.

2. The substance of the charge to the jury on the question of damages appears in the following quotation: "If you find the plaintiff entitled to anything, he is entitled to recover for what pain and suffering he has been made to endure and for what injury he has sustained over and above what injury he had before." To this instruction the defendant seasonably excepted. By it, the jury was permitted to consider two elements of damage: (1) Pain and suffering due to the operation; and (2) positive ill effects of the operation upon the plaintiff's hand. Authority for any specific rule of damages in cases of this kind seems to be lacking, but, when tested by general principle and by analogy, it appears that the foregoing instruction was erroneous.

"By 'damages,' as that term is used in the law of contracts, is intended compensation for a breach, measured in the terms of the contract." Davis v. New England Cotton Yarn Co., 77 N.H. 403. The purpose of the law is "to put the plaintiff in as good a position as he would have been in had the defendant kept his contract." 3 Williston Contracts §1338; Hardie-Tynes Mfg. Co. v. Easton Cotton Oil Co., 150 N.C. 150. The measure of recovery "is based upon what the defendant should have given the plaintiff, not what the plaintiff has given the defendant or otherwise expended." 3 Williston Contracts §1341. "The only losses that can be said fairly to come within the terms of a contract are such as the parties must have had in mind when the contract was made, or such as they either knew or ought to have known would probably result from a failure to comply with its terms." Davis, supra; Hurd v. Dunsmore, 63 N.H. 171.

The present case is closely analogous to one in which a machine is built for a certain purpose and warranted to do certain work. In such cases, the usual rule of damages for breach of warranty in the sale of chattels is applied, and it is held that the measure of damages is the difference between the value of the machine, if it had corresponded with the warranty and its actual value, together with such incidental losses as the parties knew, or ought to have known, would probably result from a failure to comply with its terms. Hooper v. Story, 155 N.Y. 171, 179, 49 N.E. 773. . . .

The rule thus applied is well settled in this state. "As a general rule, the measure of the vendee's damages is the difference between the value of the goods as they would have been if the warranty as to quality had been true, and the actual value at the time of the sale, including gains prevented and losses sustained, and such other damages as could be reasonably anticipated by the parties as likely to be caused by the vendor's failure to keep his agreement, and could not by reasonable care on the part of the vendee have been avoided." Union Bank v. Blanchard, 65 N.H. 21. . . . We therefore conclude that the true measure of the plaintiff's damage in the present case is the difference between the value to him of a perfect hand or a good hand, such as the jury found the defendant promised him, and the value of his hand in its present condition, including any incidental consequences fairly within the contemplation of the parties when they made their contract. 1 Sutherland, Damages (4th Ed.) §92. Damages not thus limited, although naturally resulting, are not to be given.

The extent of the plaintiff's suffering does not measure this difference in value. The pain necessarily incident to a serious surgical operation was a part of the contribution which the plaintiff was willing to make to his joint undertaking with the defendant to produce a good hand. It was a legal detriment suffered by him which constituted a part of the consideration given by him for the contract. It represented a part of the price which he was willing to pay for a good hand, but it furnished no test of the value of a good hand or the difference between the value of the hand which the defendant promised and the one which resulted from the operation.

It was also erroneous and misleading to submit to the jury as a separate element of damage any change for the worse in the condition of the plaintiff's hand resulting from the operation, although this error was probably more prejudicial to the plaintiff than to the defendant. Any such ill effect of the operation would be included under the true rule of damages set forth above, but damages might properly be assessed for the defendant's failure to improve the condition of the hand, even if there were no evidence that its condition was made worse as a result of the operation.

It must be assumed that the trial court, in setting aside the verdict, undertook to apply the same rule of damages which he had previously given to the jury; and, since this rule was erroneous, it is unnecessary for us to consider whether there was any evidence to justify his finding that all damages awarded by the jury above $500 were excessive.

3. Defendant's requests for instructions were loosely drawn, and were properly denied. A considerable number of issues of fact were raised by the evidence, and it would have been extremely misleading to instruct the jury in accordance with defendant's request No. 2, that "the only issue on which you have to pass is whether or not there was a special contract between the plaintiff and the defendant to

produce a perfect hand." Equally inaccurate was defendant's request No. 5, which reads as follows: "You would have to find, in order to hold the defendant liable in this case, that Dr. McGee and the plaintiff both understood that the doctor was guaranteeing a perfect result from this operation." If the defendant said that he would guarantee a perfect result, and the plaintiff relied upon that promise, any mental reservations which he may have had are immaterial. The standard by which his conduct is to be judged is not internal, but external. . . .

New trial.

Problems

1. A Promise to Marry? Joseph Ellis repeatedly expressed his intention to marry his beloved, Fanny Guggenheim, and told her, "I swear to you, and God is my witness, I will never marry any other girl but you." Guggenheim responded: "I won't swear, because we don't know what might happen; but I promise you I will never marry any other man, but will wait for you." The wedding never took place, and when Ellis married another woman, Guggenheim sued for breach of contract. Did Ellis make, and then break, a promise?

2. AstroTurf Scraps. Major Mat Company, a maker of faux-grass golf tee mats for golf ball driving ranges, purchased a large quantity of leftover turf scraps, or "remnants," from Monsanto Company, the maker of AstroTurf ground covering for athletic playing fields. Happy with the results but concerned that Monsanto might not be able to meet its future requirements, the head of Major Mat inquired about the possibility of buying Monsanto's entire scrap supply. The Monsanto official brushed off the inquiry, responding that "[w]e have so many remnants there's no way you could buy our entire supply." When Major Mat pressed him, saying that "we're concerned with keeping a constant supply of remnants because we are going to be doing what we're doing in large numbers," the Monsanto representative responded, "[Y]ou can rest assured that we will have an unending supply of remnants." When Major Mat said that it hoped Monsanto would not decide to manufacture and market its own golf tee mats, Monsanto said not to worry—that Monsanto was a supplier of products, not a fabricator.

Several years later Monsanto began to manufacture its own golf mats, offered fewer remnants for sale to Major Mat, and doubled its prices for those remnants. Major Mat sued, alleging that Monsanto broke its promise. Who should prevail? Who should decide, judge or jury?

3. Ligation Litigation. After a difficult second pregnancy, Carolyn Clevenger requested that her gynecologist perform tubal ligation surgery that would prevent her from becoming pregnant. To ensure that Clevenger understood the seriousness of the procedure, the doctor warned, "As long as you know it's a permanent thing. This is it. There is no reversal. You are not going to have any more children." The surgery was performed non-negligently, but Clevenger became pregnant again several months later and subsequently gave birth to a healthy child. Shortly thereafter, she sued for breach of contract. Did the gynecologist promise Clevenger that she would not become pregnant? Again, who should decide?

Chapter 2

Contract Formation: Consideration and Mutual Assent

Although necessary, the existence of a promise is not a sufficient basis for a contractual obligation. In the language of the Restatement, "the formation of a contract requires a bargain in which there is a manifestation of mutual assent to the exchange and a consideration." Rest. (2d) Contracts §17. If either mutual assent or consideration is lacking, then there is no contract. This chapter explores these independent prerequisites.

A. CONSIDERATION

Recall that the Restatement begins by defining contract as a legally enforceable promise. Rest. (2d) Contracts §1. This not only establishes the centrality of promise to contract, it also implies that not all promises are enforceable by the courts under contract law. Which promises enjoy this privileged status? We begin by learning how the American legal system has attempted to distinguish between enforceable and unenforceable promises by studying the doctrine of consideration.

1. Bargained-for Exchange and Gratuitous Promises

In his landmark work on jurisprudence, *The Common Law* (1881), Oliver Wendell Holmes described the concept of consideration:

> [I]t is the essence of a consideration, that, by the terms of the agreement, it is given and accepted as the motive or inducement of the promise. Conversely, the promise must be made and accepted as the conventional motive or inducement for furnishing the consideration. The root of the whole matter is the relation of reciprocal conventional inducement, each for the other, between consideration and promise.

Holmes's view influenced the drafters of the Restatement, who incorporated the concept of reciprocal inducement by observing that consideration for a promise requires both (a) a performance (or a promise of a future performance) and (b) that the performance be "bargained for" by the promisor. Rest. (2d) Contracts §71; see also §§72, 73, 79 & 81. In understanding what precisely is necessary to satisfy the consideration requirement, it is useful to contrast a promise made for consideration with a gratuitous promise—that is, a promise offered as a gift, with no performance (or promise of a performance) on the part of the recipient required.

The following quartet of cases, read together, help to illustrate what the law requires for the satisfaction of both the performance element and the bargain element of the consideration requirement.

HAMER
v.
SIDWAY

Court of Appeals of New York
124 N.Y. 538
1891

This action was brought upon an alleged contract.

The plaintiff presented a claim to the executor of William E. Story, Sr., for $5,000 and interest from the 6th day of February, 1875. She acquired it through several mesne assignments from William E. Story, 2d. The claim being rejected by the executor, this action was brought. It appears that William E. Story, Sr., was the uncle of William E. Story, 2d; that at the celebration of the golden wedding of Samuel Story and wife, father and mother of William E. Story, Sr., on the 20th day of March, 1869, in the presence of the family and invited guests he promised his nephew that if he would refrain from drinking, using tobacco, swearing and playing cards or billiards for money until he became twenty-one years of age he would pay him a sum of $5,000. The nephew assented thereto and fully performed the conditions inducing the promise. When the nephew arrived at the age of twenty-one years and on the 31st day of January, 1875, he wrote to his uncle informing him that he had performed his part of the agreement and had thereby become entitled to the sum of $5,000. The uncle received the letter and a few days later and on the sixth of February, he wrote and mailed to his nephew the following letter:

"BUFFALO, Feb. 6, 1875.
"W.E. STORY, Jr.:

"DEAR NEPHEW—Your letter of the 31st ult. came to hand all right, saying that you had lived up to the promise made to me several years ago. I have no doubt but you have, for which you shall have five thousand dollars as I promised you. I had the money in the bank the day you was 21 years old that I intend for you, and you shall have the money certain. Now, Willie I do not intend to interfere with this money in any way till I think you are capable of taking care of it and the sooner that time comes the better it will please me. I would hate very much to have you start out in some adventure that you thought all right and lose this money in one year. The first five thousand dollars that I got together cost me a heap of hard work. . . . All the money I have saved I know just how I got it. It did not come to me in any mysterious way, and the reason I speak of this is that money got in this way stops longer with a fellow that gets it with hard knocks than it does when he finds it. Willie, you are 21 and you have many a thing to learn yet. This money you have earned much easier than I did besides acquiring good habits at the same time and you are quite welcome to the money; hope you will make good use of it. I was ten long years getting this together after I was your age.

"Truly Yours,
"W.E. STORY.
"P.S.—You can consider this money on interest."

The nephew received the letter and thereafter consented that the money should remain with his uncle in accordance with the terms and conditions of the letters. The uncle died on the 29th day of January, 1887, without having paid over to his nephew any portion of the said $5,000 and interest.

PARKER, J.

The question which provoked the most discussion by counsel on this appeal, and which lies at the foundation of plaintiff's asserted right of recovery, is whether by virtue of a contract defendant's testator William E. Story became indebted to his nephew William E. Story, 2d, on his twenty-first birthday in the sum of five thousand dollars. The trial court found as a fact that "on the 20th day of March, 1869, * * * William E. Story agreed to and with William E. Story, 2d, that if he would refrain from drinking liquor, using tobacco, swearing, and playing cards or billiards for money until he should become 21 years of age then he, the said William E. Story, would at that time pay him, the said William E. Story, 2d, the sum of $5,000 for such refraining, to which the said William E. Story, 2d, agreed," and that he "in all things fully performed his part of said agreement."

The defendant contends that the contract was without consideration to support it, and, therefore, invalid. He asserts that the promisee by refraining from the use of liquor and tobacco was not harmed but benefited; that that which he did was best for him to do independently of his uncle's promise, and insists that it follows that unless the promisor was benefited, the contract was without consideration.

A contention, which if well founded, would seem to leave open for controversy in many cases whether that which the promisee did or omitted to do was, in fact, of such benefit to him as to leave no consideration to support the enforcement of the promisor's agreement. Such a rule could not be tolerated, and is without foundation in the law. The Exchequer Chamber, in 1875, defined consideration as follows: "A valuable consideration in the sense of the law may consist either in some right, interest, profit or benefit accruing to the one party, or some forbearance, detriment, loss or responsibility given, suffered or undertaken by the other." Courts "will not ask whether the thing which forms the consideration does in fact benefit the promisee or a third party, or is of any substantial value to anyone. It is enough that something is promised, done, forborne or suffered by the party to whom the promise is made as consideration for the promise made to him." . . .

Pollock, in his work on contracts, . . . says: "The second branch of this judicial description is really the most important one. Consideration means not so much that one party is profiting as that the other abandons some legal right in the present or limits his legal freedom of action in the future as an inducement for the promise of the first."

Now, applying this rule to the facts before us, the promisee used tobacco, occasionally drank liquor, and he had a legal right to do so. That right he abandoned for a period of years upon the strength of the promise of the testator that for such forbearance he would give him $5,000. We need not speculate on the effort which may have been required to give up the use of those stimulants. It is sufficient that he restricted his lawful freedom of action within certain prescribed limits upon the faith of his uncle's agreement, and now having fully performed the conditions imposed, it is of no moment whether such performance actually proved a benefit to the promisor, and the court will not inquire into it, but were it a proper subject of inquiry, we see nothing in this record that would permit a determination that the uncle was not benefited in a legal sense. Few cases have been found which may be said to be precisely in point, but such as have been support the position we have taken.

In *Shadwell v. Shadwell*, an uncle wrote to his nephew as follows:

> "MY DEAR LANCEY—I am so glad to hear of your intended marriage with Ellen Nicholl, and as I promised to assist you at starting, I am happy to tell you that I will pay to you 150 pounds yearly during my life and until your annual income derived from your profession of a chancery barrister shall amount to 600 guineas, of which your own admission will be the only evidence that I shall require.

> "Your affectionate uncle,
> "CHARLES SHADWELL."

It was held that the promise was binding and made upon good consideration. . . .

The cases cited by the defendant on this question are not in point. . . . In *Vanderbilt v. Schreyer* (91 N.Y. 392), the plaintiff contracted with defendant to build a house, agreeing to accept in part payment therefor a specific bond and mortgage. Afterwards he refused to finish his contract unless the defendant would guarantee its payment, which was done. It was held that the guarantee could not be enforced for want of consideration. For in building the house the plaintiff only did that which he had contracted to do. And in *Robinson v. Jewett* (116 N.Y. 40), the court simply held that "The performance of an act which the party is under a legal obligation to perform cannot constitute a consideration for a new contract." . . .

The order appealed from should be reversed and the judgment of the Special Term affirmed, with costs payable out of the estate. All concur. Order reversed and judgment of Special Term affirmed.

MILLS
v.
WYMAN

Supreme Judicial Court of Massachusetts
3 Pick. 207
1825

[handwritten annotation: common law action for breach of contract/ promise]

This was an action of *assumpsit* brought to recover a compensation for the board, nursing, & c., of Levi Wyman, son of the defendant, from the 5th to the 20th of February, 1821. The plaintiff then lived at Hartford, in Connecticut; the defendant, at Shrewsbury, in this county. Levi Wyman, at the time when the services were rendered, was about 25 years of age, and had long ceased to be a member of his father's family. He was on his return from a voyage at sea, and being suddenly taken sick at Hartford, and being poor and in distress, was relieved by the plaintiff in the manner and to the extent above stated. On the 24th of February, after all the expenses had been incurred, the defendant wrote a letter to the plaintiff, promising to pay him such expenses. *[handwritten annotation: however, services were already rendered]*

. . .

PARKER C.J.

General rules of law established for the protection and security of honest and fair-minded men, who may inconsiderately make promises without any equivalent, will sometimes screen men of a different character from engagements which they are bound in *foro conscientiæ* to perform. This is a defect inherent in all human systems of legislation. The rule that a mere verbal promise, without any consideration, cannot be enforced by action, is universal in its application, and cannot be departed from to suit particular cases in which a refusal to perform such a promise may be disgraceful.

The promise declared on in this case appears to have been made without any legal consideration. The kindness and services towards the sick son of the defendant were not bestowed at his request. The son was in no respect under the care of the defendant. He was twenty-five years old, and had long left his father's family. On his return from a foreign country, he fell sick among strangers, and the plaintiff acted the part of the good Samaritan, giving him shelter and comfort until he died. The defendant, his father, on being informed of this event, influenced by a transient feeling of gratitude, promises in writing to pay the plaintiff for the expenses he had incurred. But he has determined to break this promise, and is willing to have his case appear on record as a strong example of particular injustice sometimes necessarily resulting from the operation of general rules.

It is said a moral obligation is a sufficient consideration to support an express promise; and some authorities lay down the rule thus broadly; but upon examination of the cases we are satisfied that the universality of the rule cannot be supported, and that there must have been some preexisting obligation, which has become inoperative by positive law, to form a basis for an effective promise. The cases of debts barred by the statute of limitations, of debts incurred by infants, of debts of bankrupts, are generally put for illustration of the rule. Express promises founded on such preexisting equitable obligations may be enforced; there is a good consideration for them; they merely remove an impediment created by law to the recovery of debts honestly due, but which public policy protects the debtors from being compelled to pay. In all these cases there was originally a *quid pro quo*; and according to the principles of natural justice the party receiving ought to pay; but the legislature has said he shall not be coerced; then comes the promise to pay the debt that is barred, the promise of the man to pay the debt of the infant, of the discharged bankrupt to restore to his creditor what by the law he had lost. In all these cases there is a moral obligation founded upon an antecedent valuable consideration. These promises therefore have a sound legal basis. They are not promises to pay something for nothing; not naked pacts; but the voluntary revival or creation of obligation which before existed in natural law, but which had been dispensed with, not for the benefit of the party obliged solely, but principally for the public convenience If moral obligation, in its fullest sense, is a good substratum for an express promise, it is not easy to perceive why it is not equally good to support an implied promise. What a man ought to do, generally he ought to be made to do, whether he promise or refuse. But the law of society has left most of such obligations to the *interior* forum, as the tribunal of conscience has been aptly called. Is there not a moral obligation upon every son who has become affluent by means of the education and advantages bestowed upon him by his father, to relieve that father from pecuniary embarrassment, to promote his comfort and happiness, and even to share with him his riches, if thereby he will be made happy? And yet such a son may, with impunity, leave such a father in any degree of penury above that which will expose the community in which he dwells, to the danger of being obliged to preserve him from absolute want. Is not a wealthy father under strong moral obligation to advance the interest of an obedient, well disposed son, to furnish him with the means of acquiring and maintaining a becoming rank in life, to rescue him from the horrors of debt incurred by misfortune? Yet the law will uphold him in any degree of parsimony, short of that which would reduce his son to the necessity of seeking public charity.

Without doubt there are great interests of society which justify withholding the coercive arm of the law from these duties of imperfect obligation, as they are called; imperfect, not because they are less binding upon the conscience than those which are called perfect, but because the wisdom of the social law does not impose sanctions upon them.

. . .

These principles are deduced from the general current of decided cases upon the subject, as well as from the known maxims of the common law. The general position, that moral obligation is a sufficient consideration for an express promise, is to be limited in its application, to cases where at some time or other a good or valuable consideration has existed.

For the foregoing reasons we are all of opinion that the nonsuit directed by the Court of Common Pleas was right, and that judgment be entered thereon for costs for the defendant.

LANGER
v.
SUPERIOR STEEL CORP.
Superior Court of Pennsylvania
105 Pa. Super. 579
1932

BALDRIGE, J.

This is an action of assumpsit to recover damages for breach of a contract. The court below sustained questions of law raised by defendant, and entered judgment in its favor.

The plaintiff alleges that he is entitled to recover certain monthly payments provided for in the following letter:

"August 31, 1927.
"Mr. Wm. F. Langer,

"Dear Sir: As you are retiring from active duty with this company, as Superintendent of the Annealing Department, on August 31, we hope that it will give you some pleasure to receive this official letter of commendation for your long and faithful service with the Superior Steel Corporation.
"The Directors have decided that you will receive a pension of $100.00 per month as long as you live and preserve your present attitude of loyalty to the Company and its Officers and are not employed in any competitive occupation. We sincerely hope that you will live long to enjoy it and that this and the other evidences of the esteem in which you are held by your fellow employees and which you will today receive with this letter, will please you as much as it does us to bestow them.

"Cordially yours,
"[Signed] Frank R. Frost,
"President."

The defendant paid the sum of $100 a month for approximately four years when the plaintiff was notified that the company no longer intended to continue the payments.

issue

The issue raised is whether the letter created a gratuitous promise or an enforceable contract. It is frequently a matter of great difficulty to differentiate between promises creating legal obligations and mere gratuitous agreements. Each case depends to a degree upon its peculiar facts and circumstances. Was this promise supported by a sufficient consideration, or was it but a condition attached to a gift? . . . It was held in Presbyterian Board of Foreign Missions v. Smith, 209 Pa. 361, 363, 58 A. 689, that "a test of good consideration is whether the promisee, at the instance of the promisor, has done, forborne, or undertaken to do anything real, or whether he has suffered any detriment, or whether, in return for the promise, he has done something that he was not bound to do, or has promised to do some act, or has abstained from doing something." . . .

rule

The plaintiff, in his statement, which must be admitted as true in considering the statutory demurrer filed by defendant, alleges that he refrained from seeking employment with any competitive company, and that he complied with the terms of the agreement. By so doing, has he sustained any detriment? Was his forbearance sufficient to support a good consideration? Professor Williston, in his treatise on Contracts, §112, states: "It is often difficult to determine whether words of condition in a promise indicate a request for consideration or state a mere condition in a gratuitous promise. An aid, though not a conclusive test in determining which construction of the promise is more reasonable, is an inquiry whether the happening of the condition will be a benefit to the promisor. If so, it is a fair inference that the happening was requested as a consideration. . . . In case of doubt where the promisee has incurred a detriment on the faith of the promise, courts will naturally be loath to regard the promise as a mere gratuity, and the detriment incurred as merely a condition."

rule

It is reasonable to conclude that it is to the advantage of the defendant if the plaintiff, who had been employed for a long period of time as its superintendent in the annealing department, and who, undoubtedly, had knowledge of the methods used by the employer, is not employed by a competitive company; otherwise, such a stipulation would have been unnecessary. That must have been the inducing reason for inserting that provision. There is nothing appearing of record, except the condition imposed by the defendant, that would have prevented this man of skill and experience from seeking employment elsewhere. By receiving the monthly payments, he impliedly accepted the conditions imposed, and was thus restrained from doing that which he had a right to do. This was a sufficient consideration to support a contract.

The appellee refers to Kirksey v. Kirksey, 8 Ala. 131, which is also cited by Professor Williston in his work on Contracts, §112, note 51, as a leading case on this subject under discussion. . . . In that case, . . . there was no benefit to be derived by the promisor, as in the case at bar, and therefore a good consideration was lacking.

. . .

Judgment is reversed, and the defendant is hereby given permission to file an affidavit of defense to the merits of the plaintiff's claim.

IN RE GREENE
U.S. District Court, S.D.N.Y.
45 F.2d 428
1930

WOOLSEY, J.

prior judge

The petition for review is granted, and the order of the referee is reversed.

I. The claimant, a woman, filed proof of claim in the sum of $375,700, based on an alleged contract, against this bankrupt's estate. The trustee in bankruptcy objected to the claim. A hearing was held before the referee in bankruptcy and testimony taken.

The referee held the claim valid and dismissed the objections. The correctness of this ruling is raised by the trustee's petition to review and the referee's certificate.

II. For several years prior to April 28, 1926, the bankrupt, a married man, had apparently lived in adultery with the claimant. He gave her substantial sums of money. He also paid $70,000 for a house on Long Island acquired by her, which she still owns.

Throughout their relations the bankrupt was a married man, and the claimant knew it. The claimant was well over thirty years of age when the connection began. She testified that the bankrupt has promised to marry her as soon as his wife should get a divorce from him; this the bankrupt denied. *potential Contract 1*

The relations of intimacy between them were discontinued in April, 1926, and they then executed a written instrument under seal which is alleged to be a binding contract and which is the foundation of the claim under consideration.

In this instrument, which was made in New York, the bankrupt undertook (1) to pay to the claimant $1,000 a month during their joint lives; (2) to assign to her a $100,000 life insurance policy on his life and to keep up the premiums on it for life, the bankrupt to pay $100,000 to the claimant in case the policy should lapse for nonpayment of premiums; and (3) to pay the rent for four years on an apartment which she had leased. *potential Contract 2 + 3*

It was declared in the instrument that the bankrupt had no interest in the Long Island house or in its contents, and that he should no longer be liable for mortgage interest taxes, and other charges on this property.

The claimant on her part released the bankrupt from all claims which she had against him.

The preamble to the instrument recites as consideration the payment of $1 by the claimant to the bankrupt, "and other good and valuable consideration."

The bankrupt kept up the several payments called for by the instrument until August, 1928, but failed to make payments thereafter. . . .

IV. A contract for future illicit cohabitation is unlawful. There is consideration present in such a case, but the law strikes the agreement down as immoral. Williston on Contracts, §1745.

Here the illicit intercourse had been abandoned prior to the making of the agreement, so that the above rule is not infringed. This case is one where the motive which led the bankrupt to make the agreement on which the claim is based was the past illicit cohabitation between him and the claimant.

The law is that a promise to pay a woman on account of cohabitation which has ceased is void, not for illegality, but for want of consideration. The consideration in such a case is past.

The mere fact that past cohabitation is the motive for the promise will not of itself invalidate it, but the promise in such a case, to be valid, must be supported by some consideration other than past intercourse. Williston on Contracts, §§148, 1745.

The problem in the present case, therefore, is one of consideration, not of illegality, and it is clear that the past illicit intercourse is not consideration.

The cases dealing with situations where there is illegitimate offspring or where there has been seduction are of doubtful authority, for the doctrine that past moral obligation is consideration is now generally exploded. But these cases and others speaking of expiation of past wrong, cited by the referee, are not in point.

Here there was not any offspring as a result of the bankrupt's union with the claimant; there was not any seduction shown in the sense in which that word is used in law. . . . There was not any past wrong for which the bankrupt owed the claimant expiation—volenti non fit injuria. . . .

V. The question, therefore, is whether there was any consideration for the bankrupt's promises, apart from the past cohabitation. It seems plain that no such consideration can be found, but I will review the following points emphasized by the claimant as showing consideration:

(1) The $1 consideration recited in the paper is nominal. It cannot seriously be urged that $1, recited but not even shown to have been paid, will support an executory promise to pay hundreds of thousands of dollars.

(2) "Other good and valuable consideration" are generalities that sound plausible, but the words cannot serve as consideration where the facts show that nothing good or valuable was actually given at the time the contract was made.

(3) It is said that the release of claims furnishes the necessary consideration. So it would if the claimant had had any claims to release. But the evidence shows no vestige of any lawful claim. Release from imaginary claims is not valuable consideration for a promise. In this connection, apparently, the claimant testified that the bankrupt had promised to marry her as soon as he was divorced. Assuming that he did—though he denies it—the illegality of any such promise, made while the bankrupt was still married, is so obvious that no claim could possible arise from it, and the release of such claim could not possibly be lawful consideration.

(4) The claimant also urges that by the agreement the bankrupt obtained immunity from liability for taxes and other charges on the Long Island house. The fact is that he was never chargeable for these expenses. He doubtless had been in

the habit of paying them, just as he had paid many other expenses for the claimant; but such payments were either gratuitous or were the contemporaneous price of the continuance of his illicit intercourse with the claimant.

It is absurd to suppose that, when a donor gives a valuable house to a donee, the fact that the donor need pay no taxes or upkeep thereafter on the property converts the gift into a contract upon consideration. The present case is even stronger, for the bankrupt had never owned the house and had never been liable for the taxes. He furnished the purchase price, but the conveyance was from the seller direct to the claimant.

(5) Finally, it is said that the parties intended to make a valid agreement. It is a non sequitur to say that therefore the agreement is valid.

A man may promise to make a gift to another, and may put the promise in the most solemn and formal document possible; but, barring exceptional cases, such, perhaps, as charitable subscriptions, the promise will not be enforced. The parties may shout consideration to the housetops, yet, unless consideration is actually present, there is not a legally enforcible contract.

What the bankrupt obviously intended in this case was an agreement to make financial contribution to the claimant because of his past cohabitation with her, and, as already pointed out, such an agreement lacks consideration.

The presence of the seal would have been decisive in the claimant's favor a hundred years ago. Then an instrument under seal required no consideration, or, to keep to the language of the cases, the seal was conclusive evidence of consideration. In New York, however, a seal is now only presumptive evidence of consideration on an executory instrument. This presumption was amply rebutted in this case, for the proof clearly shows, I think, that there was not in fact any consideration for the bankrupt's promise contained in the executory instrument signed by him and the claimant.

An order in accordance with this opinion may be submitted for settlement on two days' notice.

Problems

1. Las Vegas Dreaming. One night, Mary Iacono had a dream about winning on a Las Vegas slot machine. Her friend of 35 years, Carolyn Lyons, considered this a good omen, and invited Iacono to join her on a trip to Las Vegas. Lyons agreed to pay for all the expenses of the trip, including providing money for gambling, and to split any gambling winnings 50-50. Iacono accepted the invitation.

At Caesar's Palace, they started playing the slot machines. After losing $47, Lyons wanted to leave to see a show. Iacono begged Lyons to stay, and Lyons agreed on condition that Lyons, not Iacono, put coins into the machine. (As Iacono had advanced rheumatoid arthritis and was wheelchair bound, Lyons felt that Iacono took too long to put coins into the machine.)

Iacono led Lyons to a dollar slot machine that looked like the one in Iacono's dream. Lyons put a coin into the machine and it paid $1,908,064. Is Iacono entitled to half of the winnings?

2. A Domestic Partnership. Virginia Sigler and Helen Mariotte were close companions who had lived together in Mariotte's home since 1949. Sigler paid a modest rent, and they shared food expenses. Mariotte suffered a stroke in 1976 and required round-the-clock care. On August 1, 1976, Sigler told Mariotte's son that she would care for Mariotte if Mariotte were released from the hospital and sent home. Mariotte returned home, and, because her care was a two-person job, Mariotte's son hired a live-in health aide to help Sigler. The aide received room and board plus $85 per week. In December 1977, Sigler asked for the same compensation as the health aide. The son refused to pay any weekly salary, but offered room and board. Sigler continued to care for Mariotte, stopped paying rent, and accepted food reimbursement from the son. On June 15, 1979, Mariotte signed a document in front of witnesses that read "I, Helen Mariotte, instruct whoever is in charge of my estate to pay Virginia Sigler on the basis of $85 per week, plus room and board effective August 1, 1976." Later that year, Mariotte's condition worsened, and her son was appointed guardian and conservator of her estate. He moved her to a nursing home in September 1979 and sold her house. Sigler filed a claim with the estate for reimbursement for room and board from August 1976 to December 1977 and for $85 per week from August 1976-September 1979. What result?

3. A Paternity Promise. Gloria Schumm, a film "bit" player, was pregnant and claimed that Wallace Beery, a married movie star, was the father. Beery promised to pay Schumm's medical expenses and to provide for the child until he reached the age of majority if Schumm promised not to bring a paternity suit and to give the child Beery's first name (Wallace or Wally) but Schumm's surname. Schumm agreed. After little Wally Schumm was born, Beery refused to make any payments, contending that he had only entered into the agreement to prevent damage to his reputation and questioning whether he was in fact the father. Beery died shortly thereafter, and Schumm brought suit against his estate. Was their agreement supported by consideration?

4. In Consideration of One Cent. When Theresa Schnell died, her will left $200 each to J.B. Nell, Wendelin Lorenz, and Donata Lorenz. However, because she owned all of her property jointly with her husband Zacharias, all of her property reverted to her husband upon her death and her estate had no assets. Zacharias wrote out an agreement promising to give $200 to Nell and both Lorenzes in recognition of his wife's testamentary intent, the love and affection he bore his deceased wife, and her contribution to their joint property, and "in consideration of one cent, received" and their promise not to make any claims based on Theresa's will. They all signed and sealed the document. Is Zacharias's promise enforceable?

2. Conditional Promises

Promises exchanged for consideration can be described as conditional promises: the provision of the performance that serves as consideration is also the condition that must be satisfied. For example, in *Hamer v. Sidway*, when William Story, Sr. promises to pay his nephew $5,000 if young Willie refrains from bad behavior, the condition of the uncle's obligation to pay is that the nephew forbears from vice. In *Langer v. Superior Steel Corp.*, the condition of the company's payment of a monthly pension is that Langer does not obtain employment with a competitor.

The conditional nature of a promise does not necessarily indicate the presence of consideration, however, because the promisee's satisfaction of the condition might not induce the promisor's promise. That is, even where the promisor states a condition on her promise, the promisor might not be bargaining for the fulfillment of the condition. In some circumstances, a condition might indicate the manner by which the promisee may collect a promised gift. In other instances, a condition might restrict the scope of a gift promise without inducing the promise. *Kirksey v. Kirksey* explores the first of these two distinctions, while *Allegheny College v. National Chautauqua County Bank of Jamestown* explores the second.

KIRKSEY
v.
KIRKSEY

Supreme Court of Alabama
8 Ala. 131
1845

Error to the Circuit Court of Talladega.

ASSUMPSIT by the defendant, against the plaintiff in error. The question is presented in this Court, upon a case agreed, which shows the following facts:

The plaintiff was the wife of defendant's brother, but had for some time been a widow, and had several children. In 1840, the plaintiff resided on public land, under a contract of lease, she had held over, and was comfortably settled, and would have attempted to secure the land she lived on. The defendant resided in Talladega county, some sixty, or seventy miles off. On the 10th October, 1840, he wrote to her the following letter:

> "Dear sister Antillico—Much to my mortification, I heard, that brother Henry was dead, and one of his children. I know that your situation is one of grief, and difficulty. You had a bad chance before, but a great deal worse now. I should like to come and see you, but cannot with convenience at present. . . . I do not know whether you have a preference on the place you live on, or not. If you had, I would advise you to obtain your preference, and sell the land and quit the country, as I understand it is very unhealthy, and I know society is very bad. If you will come down and see me, I will let you have a place to raise your family, and I have more open land than I can tend; and on the account of your situation, and that of your family, I feel like I want you and the children to do well."

Within a month or two after the receipt of this letter, the plaintiff abandoned her possession, without disposing of it, and removed with her family, to the residence of the defendant, who put her in comfortable houses, and gave her land to cultivate for two years, at the end of which time he notified her to remove, and put her in a house, not comfortable, in the woods, which he afterwards required her to leave.

A verdict being found for the plaintiff, for two hundred dollars, the above facts were agreed, and if they will sustain the action, the judgment is to be affirmed, otherwise it is to be reversed.

ORMOND, J.

The inclination of my mind, is, that the loss and inconvenience, which the plaintiff sustained in breaking up, and moving to the defendant's, a distance of sixty miles, is a sufficient consideration to support the promise, to furnish her with a house, and land to cultivate, until she could raise her family. My brothers, however think, that the promise on the part of the defendant, was a mere gratuity, and that an action will not lie for its breach. The judgment of the Court below must therefore be reversed, pursuant to the agreement of the parties.

ALLEGHENY COLLEGE
v.
NATIONAL CHAUTAUQUA COUNTY BANK OF JAMESTOWN
Court of Appeals of New York
246 N.Y. 369
1927

CARDOZO, C.J.

The plaintiff, Allegheny College, is an institution of liberal learning at Meadville, Pennsylvania. In June 1921, a "drive" was in progress to secure for it an additional endowment of $1,250,000. An appeal to contribute to this fund was made to Mary Yates Johnston of Jamestown, New York. In response thereto, she signed and delivered on June 15, 1921, the following writing:

> "Estate Pledge,
> "Allegheny College Second Century Endowment
> "Jamestown, N.Y., June 15, 1921.
>
> "In consideration of my interest in Christian Education, and in consideration of others subscribing, I hereby subscribe and will pay to the order of the Treasurer of Allegheny College, Meadville, Pennsylvania, the sum of Five Thousand Dollars; $5,000.
>   "This obligation shall become due thirty days after my death, and I hereby instruct my Executor, or Administrator, to pay the same out of my estate. This pledge shall bear interest at the rate of . . . per cent per annum, payable annually, from . . . till paid. The

proceeds of this obligation shall be added to the Endowment of said Institution, or expended in accordance with instructions on reverse side of this pledge.

"Name MARY YATES JOHNSTON,
"Address 306 East 6th Street,
"Jamestown, N.Y.
"Dayton E. McClain Witness
"T.R. Courtis Witness
"to authentic signature."

On the reverse side of the writing is the following indorsement:

"In loving memory this gift shall be known as the Mary Yates Johnston Memorial Fund, the proceeds from which shall be used to educate students preparing for the Ministry, either in the United States or in the Foreign Field.
"This pledge shall be valid only on the condition that the provisions of my Will, now extant, shall be first met.
"MARY YATES JOHNSTON."

The subscription was not payable by its terms until thirty days after the death of the promisor. The sum of $1,000 was paid, however, upon account in December, 1923, while the promisor was alive. The college set the money aside to be held as a scholarship fund for the benefit of students preparing for the ministry. Later, in July, 1924, the promisor gave notice to the college that she repudiated the promise. Upon the expiration of thirty days following her death, this action was brought against the executor of her will to recover the unpaid balance.

The law of charitable subscriptions has been a prolific source of controversy in this State and elsewhere. We have held that a promise of that order is unenforcible like any other if made without consideration. . . . On the other hand, though professing to apply to such subscriptions the general law of contract, we have found consideration present where the general law of contract, at least as then declared, would have said that it was absent. . . .

A classic form of statement identifies consideration with detriment to the promisee sustained by virtue of the promise. Hamer v. Sidway, 124 N.Y. 538; Anson, Contracts [Corbin's ed.], p. 116; 8 Holdsworth, History of English Law, 10. So compendious a formula is little more than a half truth. There is need of many a supplementary gloss before the outline can be so filled in as to depict the classic doctrine. "The promise and the consideration must purport to be the motive each for the other, in whole or at least in part. It is not enough that the promise induces the detriment or that the detriment induces the promise if the other half is wanting." Wisc. & Mich. Ry. Co. v. Powers, 191 U.S. 379, 386; McGovern v. City of N.Y., 234 N.Y. 377, 389; Walton Water Co. v. Village of Walton, 238 N.Y. 46, 51; 1 Williston, Contracts, §139; Langdell, Summary of the Law of Contracts, pp. 82-88. If A promises B to make him a gift, consideration may be lacking, though B has renounced other opportunities for betterment in the faith that the promise will be kept.

. . .

The promisor wished to have a memorial to perpetuate her name. She imposed a condition that the "gift" should "be known as the Mary Yates Johnston Memorial Fund." The moment that the college accepted $1,000 as a payment on account, there was an assumption of a duty to do whatever acts were customary or reasonably necessary to maintain the memorial fairly and justly in the spirit of its creation. The college could not accept the money, and hold itself free thereafter from personal responsibility to give effect to the condition. Dinan v. Coneys, 143 N.Y. 544, 547; Brown v. Knapp, 79 N.Y. 136; Gridley v. Gridley, 24 N.Y. 130; Grossman v. Schenker, 206 N.Y. 466, 469; 1 Williston, Contracts, §§90, 370. More is involved in the receipt of such a fund than a mere acceptance of money to be held to a corporate use. Cf. Martin v. Meles, 179 Mass. 114, citing Johnson v. Otterbein University, 41 Ohio St. 527, 531, and Presb. Church v. Cooper, 112 N.Y. 517. The purpose of the founder would be unfairly thwarted or at least inadequately served if the college failed to communicate to the world, or in any event to applicants for the scholarship, the title of the memorial. By implication it undertook, when it accepted a portion of the "gift," that in its circulars of information and in other customary ways, when making announcement of this scholarship, it would couple with the announcement the name of the donor. The donor was not at liberty to gain the benefit of such an undertaking upon the payment of a part and disappoint the expectation that there would be payment of the residue. If the college had stated after receiving $1,000 upon account of the subscription that it would apply the money to the prescribed use, but that in its circulars of information and when responding to prospective applicants it would deal with the fund as an anonymous donation, there is little doubt that the subscriber would have been at liberty to treat this statement as the repudiation of a duty impliedly assumed, a repudiation justifying a refusal to make payments in the future. Obligation in such circumstances is correlative and mutual. A case much in point is N.J. Hospital v. Wright (95 N.J.L. 462, 464), where a subscription for the maintenance of a bed in a hospital was held to be enforcible by virtue of an implied promise by the hospital that the bed should be maintained in the name of the subscriber. Cf. Bd. of Foreign Missions v. Smith, 209 Penn. St. 361. A parallel situation might arise upon the endowment of a chair or a fellowship in a university by the aid of annual payments with the condition that it should commemorate the name of the founder or that of a member of his family. The university would fail to live up to the fair meaning of its promise if it were to publish in its circulars of information and elsewhere the existence of a chair or a fellowship in the prescribed subject, and omit the benefactor's name. A duty to act in ways beneficial to the promisor and beyond the application of the fund to the mere uses of the trust would be cast upon the promisee by the acceptance of the money. We do not need to measure the extent either of benefit to the promisor or of detriment to the promisee implicit in this duty. "If a person chooses to make an extravagant promise for an inadequate consideration it is his own affair." 8 Holdsworth, History of English Law, p. 17. It was long ago said that "when a thing is to be done by the plaintiff, be it never so small, this is a sufficient consideration to ground an action." Sturlyn v. Albany, 1587, Cro. Eliz. 67, quoted by Holdsworth, *supra;* cf. Walton Water Co. v. Village of Walton, 238 N.Y. 46, 51. The longing for posthumous remembrance is an emotion not so weak as to justify us in saying that its gratification is a negligible good.

We think the duty assumed by the plaintiff to perpetuate the name of the founder of the memorial is sufficient in itself to give validity to the subscription within the rules that define consideration for a promise of that order. When the promisee subjected itself to such a duty at the implied request of the promisor, the result was the creation of a bilateral agreement. Williston, Contracts, §§60-a, 68, 90, 370; Brown v. Knapp, *supra;* Grossman v. Schenker, *supra;* Williams College v. Danforth, 12 Pick. 541, 544; Ladies Collegiate Inst. v. French, 16 Gray, 196, 200. There was a promise on the one side and on the other a return promise, made, it is true, by implication, but expressing an obligation that had been exacted as a condition of the payment. A bilateral agreement may exist though one of the mutual promises be a promise "implied in fact," an inference from conduct as opposed to an inference from words. Williston, Contracts, §§90, 22-a; Pettibone v. Moore, 75 Hun, 461, 464. We think the fair inference to be drawn from the acceptance of a payment on account of the subscription is a promise by the college to do what may be necessary on its part to make the scholarship effective. The plan conceived by the subscriber will be mutilated and distorted unless the sum to be accepted is adequate to the end in view. Moreover, the time to affix her name to the memorial will not arrive until the entire fund has been collected. The college may thus thwart the purpose of the payment on account if at liberty to reject a tender of the residue. It is no answer to say that a duty would then arise to make restitution of the money. If such a duty may be imposed, the only reason for its existence must be that there is then a failure of "consideration." To say that there is a failure of consideration is to concede that a consideration has been promised since otherwise it could not fail. No doubt there are times and situations in which limitations laid upon a promisee in connection with the use of what is paid by a subscriber lack the quality of a consideration, and are to be classed merely as conditions. Williston, Contracts, §112; Page, Contracts, §523. "It is often difficult to determine whether words of condition in a promise indicate a request for consideration or state a mere condition in a gratuitous promise. An aid, though not a conclusive test in determining which construction of the promise is more reasonable is an inquiry whether the happening of the condition will be a benefit to the promisor. If so, it is a fair inference that the happening was requested as a consideration." Williston, *supra*, §112. Such must be the meaning of this transaction unless we are prepared to hold that the college may keep the payment on account, and thereafter nullify the scholarship which is to preserve the memory of the subscriber. The fair implication to be gathered from the whole transaction is assent to the condition and the assumption of a duty to go forward with performance. DeWolf Co. v. Harvey, 161 Wis. 535; Pullman Co. v. Meyer, 195 Ala. 397, 401; Braniff v. Baier, 101 Kan. 117; cf. Corbin, Offer & Acceptance, 26 Yale L. J. 169, 177, 193; McGovney, Irrevocable Offers, 27 Harv. L. R. 644; Sir Frederick Pollock, 28 L. Q. R. 100, 101. The subscriber does not say: I hand you $1,000, and you may make up your mind later, after my death, whether you will undertake to commemorate my name. What she says in effect is this: I hand you $1,000, and if you are unwilling to commemorate me, the time to speak is now.

. . .

The judgment of the Appellate Division and that of the Trial Term should be reversed, and judgment ordered for the plaintiff as prayed for in the complaint, with costs in all courts.

KELLOGG, J. (dissenting).

The Chief Judge finds in the expression "In loving memory this gift shall be known as the Mary Yates Johnston Memorial Fund" an offer on the part of Mary Yates Johnston to contract with Allegheny College. The expression makes no such appeal to me. Allegheny College was not requested to perform any act through which the sum offered might bear the title by which the offeror states that it shall be known. The sum offered was termed a "gift" by the offeror. Consequently, I can see no reason why we should strain ourselves to make it, not a gift, but a trade. Moreover, since the donor specified that the gift was made "In consideration of my interest in Christian education, and in consideration of others subscribing," considerations not adequate in law, I can see no excuse for asserting that it was otherwise made in consideration of an act or promise on the part of the donee, constituting a sufficient *quid quo pro* to convert the gift into a contract obligation. To me the words used merely expressed an expectation or wish on the part of the donor and failed to exact the return of an adequate consideration. . . .

POUND, CRANE, LEHMAN and O'BRIEN, JJ., concur with CARDOZO, C.J.; KELLOGG, J. dissents in opinion, in which ANDREWS, J., concurs.

Judgment accordingly.

Problems

1. The Million Dollar Wheel. Visitors to the Tropicana Hotel and Casino could join Tropicana's Diamond Club at no charge by providing their name and contact information. Tropicana offered Diamond Club members one free spin on the casino's "Million Dollar Wheel" each day. Tropicana promised to pay $1 million to the Diamond Club member if the pointer on the wheel landed on the grand prize space. Rena Gottlieb enrolled in the club and took her spin on the wheel. According to Gottlieb, the pointer landed on the grand prize and thus she was entitled to $1 million, but the casino contended that the pointer actually landed on a different space entitling Gottlieb only to two show tickets. Gottlieb sued Tropicana for breach of contract. Tropicana sought summary judgment on the ground that there was no consideration for its promise and, therefore, no enforceable contract regardless of how the court resolved the factual question of what happened concerning the spin. Who should prevail on the summary judgment motion?

2. Make a Wish. Janis Carlisle, owner of Wishing Well Preschool, performed bookkeeping work for her husband Thomas Carlisle's construction firm, T & R Excavating, from 1988 until 1992. She received no compensation for the work at the time.

In 1992, Ms. Carlisle purchased property to build a new facility for the preschool. When it came time for the construction work, T & R presented a proposal to Ms. Carlisle, offering to compensate her for her prior services, which she accepted. It stated:

> We hereby propose to do all of the excavation and site work at the above new Location. The total amount budgeted for this portion of the new building is $69,800.00. All labor, equipment costs, overhead, and profit, necessary for the completion of this project, totaling $40,000.00 will be provided at no cost to Wishing Well Preschool, Inc. The $29,800.00 allotted for materials will be billed to Wishing Well Preschool, Inc. at T & R Excavating's cost.

Did the parties have an enforceable contract?

3. Pick of the Litter. Matthew and Beth McCutcheon gave Gina Bono a "show potential" dog, Doozie, for free, on the condition that they would get second pick of Doozie's first litter of puppies. Is this agreement an enforceable contract?

3. Illusory Promises

A promise of a future performance can be consideration for another party's promise (or present performance), even if the obligation to provide that future performance is expressly conditioned on the occurrence of an event that is not certain to occur. For example, an insurance company's promise to pay to rebuild a homeowner's house *if* the house is destroyed by fire serves as consideration for the homeowner's present payment of a cash premium, even though the condition required for the performance to come due—that a fire destroys the homeowner's house—is unlikely to come to pass. The insurance company's promise is consideration, notwithstanding the fact that it will collect the premium but probably not actually have to provide any performance in return, because of the possibility that the company will be obliged to act.

If the occurrence of a condition of performance is entirely within the discretion of the promisor, however, the element of commitment can be so entirely absent that a promise, though cloaked in the language of obligation, does not constitute consideration. See Rest. (2d) Contracts §77. For example, if the insurer were to promise that, in return for the premium, it would rebuild the homeowner's house in case of a fire "if the company elects to do so," the promise would not constitute consideration for the premium because the insurance company is not actually promising to rebuild the house, or any other performance. If such "illusory" promises constituted consideration, the legal distinction between bargained-for exchanges and gratuitous promises would disintegrate because gifts could be transformed into bargains simply by having the recipient make a sham promise.

The distinction between a real promise and an illusory one can be difficult to draw, however. Even if a party's words lack an expression of commitment, the surrounding circumstances might imply an obligation (or the expectation of one). In each of the following quartet of cases, one party's promise appears to suggest substantial discretion over whether to perform. The courts must, therefore, determine whether the alleged contract includes implied limitations on that party's freedom of action sufficient to satisfy the performance element of the consideration requirement. The court's analysis may be complicated by the fact that, in some situations, both parties benefit if one party retains substantial control over its future behavior.

STRONG
v.
SHEFFIELD

Court of Appeals of New York
144 N.Y. 392
1895

ANDREWS, C.J.

[Benjamin Strong sold his business to his niece Louisa Sheffield's husband, Gerardus, on credit, keeping a promissory note for the amount due that was payable on demand. Subsequently, Strong asked Louisa to guarantee the payment of the debt in return for him forbearing from demanding immediate payment from Gerardus. Two years later, he sued Louisa for the amount due.]

. . . It is undisputed that the demand note upon which the action was brought was made by the husband of the defendant and indorsed by her at his request and delivered to the plaintiff, the payee, as security for an antecedent debt owing by the husband to the plaintiff. The debt of the husband was past due at the time, and the only consideration for the wife's indorsement, which is or can be claimed, is that as part of the transaction there was an agreement by the plaintiff when the note was given to forbear the collection of the debt, or a request for forbearance, which was followed by forbearance for a period of about two years subsequent to the giving of the note. There is no doubt that an agreement by the creditor to forbear the collection of a debt presently due is a good consideration for an absolute or conditional promise of a third person to pay the debt, or for any obligation he may assume in respect thereto. Nor is it essential that the creditor should bind himself at the time to forbear collection or to give time. If he is requested by his debtor to extend the time, and a third person undertakes in consideration of forbearance being given to become liable as surety or otherwise, and the creditor does in fact forbear in reliance upon the undertaking, although he enters into no enforcible agreement to do so, his acquiescence in the request, and an actual forbearance in consequence thereof for a reasonable time, furnishes a good consideration for the collateral undertaking. In other words, a request followed by performance is sufficient, and mutual promises at the time are not essential, unless it was the understanding that the promisor was not to be bound, except on condition that the other party entered into an immediate and reciprocal obligation to do the thing requested. *Morton v. Burn*, 7 A. & E. 19; *Wilby v. Elgee*, L.R., 10 C.P. 497; *King v. Upton*, 4 Maine, 387; Leake on Con. p. 54; Am. Lead. Cas. vol. 2, p. 96 et seq. and cases cited. The general rule is clearly, and in the main accurately, stated in the note to *Forth v. Stanton* (1 Saund. 210, note b). The learned reporter says: "And in all cases of forbearance to sue, such forbearance must be either absolute or for a definite time, or for a reasonable time; forbearance for a little, or for some time, is not sufficient." The only qualification to be made is that in the absence of a specified time a reasonable time is held to be intended. *Oldershaw v. King*, 2 H. & N. 517; *Calkins v. Chandler*, 36 Mich. 320. The note in question did not in law extend the payment of the debt. It was payable on demand, and although being payable with interest it was in form consistent with an intention that payment should not be immediately demanded, yet there was nothing on its face to prevent an immediate suit on the note against the maker or to recover the original debt. *Merritt v. Todd*, 23 N.Y. 28; *Shutts v. Fingar*, 100 id. 539.

In the present case the agreement made is not left to inference, nor was it a case of request to forbear, followed by forbearance, in pursuance of the request, without any promise on the part of the creditor at the time. The plaintiff testified that there was an express agreement on his part to the effect that he would not pay the note away, nor put it in any bank for collection, but (using the words of the plaintiff) "I will hold it until such time as I want my money, I will make a demand on you for it." And again: "No, I will keep it until such time as I want it." Upon this alleged agreement the defendant indorsed the note. It would have been no violation of the plaintiff's promise if, immediately on receiving the note, he had commenced suit upon it. Such a suit would have been an assertion that he wanted the money and would have fulfilled the condition of forbearance. The debtor and the defendant, when they became parties to the note, may have had the hope or expectation that forbearance would follow, and there was forbearance in fact. But there was no agreement to forbear for a fixed time or for a reasonable time, but an agreement to forbear for such time as the plaintiff should elect. The consideration is to be tested by the agreement, and not by what was done under it. It was a case of mutual promises, and so intended. We think the evidence failed to disclose any consideration for the defendant's indorsement, and that the trial court erred in refusing so to rule.

The order of the General Term reversing the judgment should be affirmed, and judgment absolute directed for the defendant on the stipulation, with costs in all courts.

WOOD
v.
LUCY, LADY DUFF-GORDON

Court of Appeals of New York
222 N.Y. 88
1917

CARDOZO, J.

The defendant styles herself "a creator of fashions." Her favor helps a sale. Manufacturers of dresses, millinery and like articles are glad to pay for a certificate of her approval. The things which she designs, fabrics, parasols and what not, have a new value in the public mind when issued in her name. She employed the plaintiff to help her to turn this vogue into money. He was to have the exclusive right, subject always to her approval, to place her indorsements on the designs of others. He was also to have the exclusive right to place her own designs on sale, or to license others to market them. In return, she was to have one-half of "all profits and revenues" derived from any contracts he might make. The exclusive right was to last at least one year from April 1, 1915, and thereafter from year to year unless terminated by notice of ninety days. The plaintiff says that he kept the contract on his part, and that the defendant broke it. She placed her indorsement on fabrics, dresses and millinery without his knowledge, and withheld the profits. He sues her for the damages, and the case comes here on demurrer.

The agreement of employment is signed by both parties. It has a wealth of recitals. The defendant insists, however, that it lacks the elements of a contract. She says that the plaintiff does not bind himself to anything. It is true that he does not promise in so many words that he will use reasonable efforts to place the defendant's indorsements and market her designs. We think, however, that such a promise is fairly to be implied. The law has outgrown its primitive stage of formalism when the precise word was the sovereign talisman, and every slip was fatal. It takes a broader view to-day. A promise may be lacking, and yet the whole writing may be "instinct with an obligation," imperfectly expressed. If that is so, there is a contract.

The implication of a promise here finds support in many circumstances. The defendant gave an exclusive privilege. She was to have no right for at least a year to place her own indorsements or market her own designs except through the agency of the plaintiff. The acceptance of the exclusive agency was an assumption of its duties. We are not to suppose that one party was to be placed at the mercy of the other. Many other terms of the agreement point the same way. We are told at the outset by way of recital that "the said Otis F. Wood possesses a business organization adapted to the placing of such indorsements as the said Lucy, Lady Duff-Gordon has approved." The implication is that the plaintiff's business organization will be used for the purpose for which it is adapted. But the terms of the defendant's compensation are even more significant. Her sole compensation for the grant of an exclusive agency is to be one-half of all the profits resulting from the plaintiff's efforts. Unless he gave his efforts, she could never get anything. Without an implied promise, the transaction cannot have such business "efficacy as both parties must have intended that at all events it should have." But the contract does not stop there. The plaintiff goes on to promise that he will account monthly for all moneys received by him, and that he will take out all such patents and copyrights and trademarks as may in his judgment be necessary to protect the rights and articles affected by the agreement. It is true, of course, that if he was under no duty to try to market designs or to place certificates of indorsement, his promise to account for profits or take out copyrights would be valueless. But in determining the intention of the parties, the promise has a value. It helps to enforce the conclusion that the plaintiff had some duties. His promise to pay the defendant one-half of the profits and revenues resulting from the exclusive agency and to render accounts

monthly, was a promise to use reasonable efforts to bring profits and revenues into existence. For this conclusion, the authorities are ample. . . .

The judgment of the Appellate Division should be reversed, and the order of the Special Term affirmed, with costs in the Appellate Division and in this court.

CUDDEBACK, MCLAUGHLIN and ANDREWS, JJ., concur; HISCOCK, Ch. J., CHASE and CRANE, JJ., dissent.

REHM-ZEIHER CO. v. F. G. WALKER CO.

Court of Appeals of Kentucky
156 Ky. 6
1913

CARROLL, J.

The appellant, a corporation, in the years 1908, 1909, 1910, 1911, and 1912, and prior thereto, was engaged in the business of selling whisky; that is to say, it purchased from distillers certain brands and quantities of whisky, and then sold the whisky so bought to the trade. The appellee, during the years named, and prior thereto, owned and operated a distillery. In 1908 the parties entered into the following contract: "This contract made and entered into this November 17, 1908, by and between the F. G. Walker Company, party of the first part, and the Rehm-Zeiher Company, party of the second part. The party of the first part has this day sold to the party of the second part 2,000 cases of old Walker whisky put up under a private brand, to be delivered during the years 1909, 3,000 cases to be delivered during the year 1910, 4,000 cases to be delivered during the year 1911, and 5,000 cases to be delivered during the year 1912, at the following prices: Quarts bottled in bond, $6.70; pints bottled in bond, $7.20; half pints bottled in bond, $7.70. Should the party of the first part lose by fire the whisky with which this bottling is to be done or the bottling room during the life of this contract, then they are to be held excusable for not filling same. If for any unforeseen reason the party of the second part find that they cannot use the full amount of the above-named goods, the party of the first part agrees to release them from the contract for the amount desired by party of the second part."

In 1912 the appellant brought this suit against the appellee to recover damages for its failure to furnish 2,596 cases of the 4,000 cases of whisky it was provided in the contract should be furnished in 1911. The petition averred that during the year 1911 the appellant demanded that the appellee furnish to it 4,000 cases of old Walker whisky, but that in violation of its contract the appellee only furnished 1,044 cases, and refused to furnish the remainder, to its damage in the sum of

$6,798, which sum it averred was the loss it sustained by the failure of the appellee to furnish the 2,596 cases it failed and refused to furnish.

. . .

It appears without contradiction that in 1909 the appellant only ordered and received 786 cases of the 2,000 called for by the contract, and that in 1910 it only ordered and received 1,200 cases of the 3,000 cases called for by the contract, and that the appellee did not demand or request that it should take in either of these years the full number of cases specified in the contract or any greater number than it did take. It further appears that in the early part of 1911 whisky advanced in price, and the appellee refused to deliver to the appellant whisky it ordered. After this, however, the appellee, upon request, furnished to the appellant 1,044 cases of the 1911 whisky; but in September, 1911, it peremptorily refused to furnish any more, and thereupon this suit was brought.

O.E. Rehm, president of the appellant corporation, testified that his company had been in business since 1904, and that in 1908 he and R.H. Edelen, president of the F.G. Walker Company, had several conversations relating to the subject of the Walker Company furnishing to his firm certain quantities of whisky, and that following these conversations Edelen, in November, 1908, prepared and presented to him the written contract heretofore quoted. He further testifies that, when Edelen brought the contract to him, "He said, 'Read this; I believe you could use this whisky.' I said, 'That is too much whisky for us; we are a young firm just building up our trade, and I don't believe we can use it.' After I told him it was too much whisky, he said, 'You don't have to take it all if you can't use it; you are a growing firm; your business will increase that much.' And I signed it. . . . Q. You signed the contract with the understanding you didn't have to use the whisky if you didn't need it, didn't you? A. The contract states that. Q. You could use as little or as much as you wanted; was that the understanding with which you signed this contract? A. That is what the contract states. Q. If you did not sell any, you did not need to take any whisky? A. We were going to sell it. Q. You expected to try to sell it? A. Yes, sir. Q. Did you understand you were obligated to take 2,000 cases during 1909? A. That is, if we could not sell that, we were not obligated. Q. Well, now, during the year 1909 how much of this whisky did you buy? A. The figures there will show. Q. Is that all you ordered that year? A. Yes, sir. Q. That is all you wanted to buy that year? A. Yes, sir. Q. That is all you would have to buy that year? A. All we sold. Q. What reason prevented you from taking the other 1,214 case that year? A. Did not sell them. Q. Was that because you did not want them? A. Did not sell them. Q. That was the unforeseen reason that was referred to in this contract? A. Yes, sir."

. . .

There is a line of cases holding that, where, for example, A. and B. enter into a contract by which A. agrees to furnish to B. all the coal that B. will require in the operation of an established factory, the contract is not lacking in mutuality, as B. may require A. to furnish him all the coal he needs to operate his factory, and A. may insist that B. shall take from him all the coal he needs for this purpose.

An illustration of this class of cases is Crane v. Crane, 105 Fed. 869, where the court said: "It is within legal competency for one to bind himself to furnish another with such supplies as may be needed during some certain period for some certain business or manufacture, or with such commodities as the purchaser has already bound himself to furnish another. Reasonable provision in business requires that such contracts, though more or less indefinite, should be upheld. Thus a foundry may purchase all the coal needed for the season, or a furnace company its requirements in the way of iron, or a hotel its necessary supply of ice. . . . In all these cases contracts looking towards the future, and embodying subject-matter necessarily indefinite in quantity, have been upheld; but it will be observed that, although the quantity under contract is not measured by any certain standard, it is capable of an approximately accurate forecast. The capacity of the furnace, the needs of the railroad, or the requirements of the hotel are, within certain limits, ascertainable by the vendor."

. . .

The facts of this case, however, do not bring it within the scope of the principle announced in these cases. The contract does not specify the brand or name under which the whisky was to be sold, nor does it appear from the evidence that the Rehm-Zeiher Company had established any ascertainable volume of trade of that would fix with any reasonable degree of certainty the quantity of whisky necessary to supply the demand for this brand.

. . .

If the contract had specified that the Rehm-Zeiher Company only obliged to take so much of the whisky as it "desired to take," or as it "pleased to take," it would not any more certainly have given the company the right to exercise its pleasure as to how much whisky it would take than do the words "unforeseen reason." The unforeseen reason that would excuse the company from only taking so much of the whisky as it desired to take, if any, left the amount it should take entirely to its discretion. The contract places no limitation whatever upon the meaning of the words "unforeseen reason," so that any reason that the company might assign for not taking the whisky would relieve it of any obligation to do so. It was not necessary that the reason should be a good reason or a reasonable reason.

If the Walker Company had sought by a suit to compel the Rehm-Zeiher Company to take in any of the years the amount of whisky specified in the contract, or any part of it, it is clear that the Rehm-Zeiher Company could have defeated this suit by pleading that some unforeseen reason had arisen that justified them in not taking any of the whisky, and therefore they were not obliged to do so. If, as we think, the contract was nonenforceable by the Walker Company, either in whole or in part, it was certainly lacking in such mutuality of obligation as rendered it nonenforceable by the Rehm-Zeiher Company.

. . .

Some importance seems to be attached to the circumstance that the Walker Company furnished in 1909, 1910, and 1911 a part of the whisky mentioned in the contract, for which the Rehm-Zeiher Company paid the prices agreed upon. We do not think, however, that this circumstance is entitled to any controlling weight in determining the rights of the parties in the present litigation. The Walker Company were not obliged to furnish any whisky in the years named, nor was the Rehm-Zeiher Company obliged to take any, and the mere fact that the Walker Company voluntarily chose to furnish some of the whisky did not deny to it the privilege of refusing at its election to furnish the remainder of the whisky. In other words, its conduct in furnishing part of the whisky did not affect in any manner the rights of the parties to the contract, or amount to an election on the part of the Rehm-Zeiher Company to accept unconditionally the terms of the contract. In short, the obstacle in the way of the Rehm-Zeiher Company in this case is that they are seeking to enforce a contract that was never at any time binding upon them. Their acceptance of a part of the whisky provided for in the contract in the years 1909 and 1910 did not oblige them to take any of it in the subsequent years.

. . .

Upon the whole case our conclusion is that the judgment of the lower court was correct, and it is affirmed.

MATTEI
v.
HOPPER

Supreme Court of California (En Banc)
51 Cal. 2d 119
1958

SPENCE, J.

. . . Plaintiff was a real estate developer. He was planning to construct a shopping center on a tract adjacent to defendant's land. For several months, a real estate agent attempted to negotiate a sale of defendant's property under terms agreeable to both parties. After several of plaintiff's proposals had been rejected by defendant because of the inadequacy of the price offered, defendant submitted an offer. Plaintiff accepted on the same day.

The parties' written agreement was evidenced on a form supplied by the real estate agent, commonly known as a deposit receipt. Under its terms, plaintiff was required to deposit $1,000 of the total purchase price of $57,500 with the real estate agent, and was given 120 days to "examine the title and consummate the purchase." At the expiration of that period, the balance of the price was "due and payable upon tender of a good and sufficient deed of the property sold." The concluding paragraph of the deposit receipt provided: "Subject to Coldwell Banker & Company obtaining leases satisfactory to the purchaser." This clause and the 120-day period were desired by plaintiff as a means for arranging satisfactory leases of the shopping center buildings prior to the time he was finally committed to pay the balance of the purchase price and to take title to defendant's property.

Plaintiff took the first step in complying with the agreement by turning over the $1,000 deposit to the real estate agent. While he was in the process of securing the leases and before the 120 days had elapsed, defendant's attorney notified plaintiff that defendant would not sell her land under the terms contained in the deposit receipt. Thereafter, defendant was informed that satisfactory leases had been

obtained and that plaintiff had offered to pay the balance of the purchase price. Defendant failed to tender the deed as provided in the deposit receipt.

Initially, defendant's thesis that the deposit receipt constituted no more than an offer by her, which could only be accepted by plaintiff notifying her that all of the desired leases had been obtained and were satisfactory to him, must be rejected. Nowhere does the agreement mention the necessity of any such notice. Nor does the provision making the agreement "subject to" plaintiffs securing "satisfactory" leases necessarily constitute a condition to the existence of a contract. Rather, the whole purchase receipt and this particular clause must be read as merely making plaintiff's performance dependent on the obtaining of "satisfactory" leases. Thus a contract arose, and plaintiff was given the power and privilege to terminate it in the event he did not obtain such leases.

However, the inclusion of this clause, specifying that leases "satisfactory" to plaintiff must be secured before he would be bound to perform, raises the basic question whether the consideration supporting the contract was thereby vitiated. When the parties attempt, as here, to make a contract where promises are exchanged as the consideration, the promises must be mutual in obligation. *rule* In other words, for the contract to bind either party, both must have assumed some legal obligations. Without this mutuality of obligation, the agreement lacks consideration and no enforceable contract has been created. . . . Or, if one of the promises leaves a party free to perform or to withdraw from the agreement at his own unrestricted pleasure, the promise is deemed illusory and it provides no consideration. . . . Whether these problems are couched in terms of mutuality of obligation or the illusory nature of a promise, the underlying issue is the same consideration.

While contracts making the duty of performance of one of the parties conditional upon his satisfaction would seem to give him wide latitude in avoiding any obligation and thus present serious consideration problems, such "satisfaction" clauses have been given effect. They have been divided into two primary categories and have been accorded different treatment on that basis. First, in those contracts where the condition calls for satisfaction as to commercial value or quality, operative fitness, or mechanical utility, dissatisfaction cannot be claimed arbitrarily, unreasonably, or *objective standard* capriciously . . . , and the standard of a reasonable person is used in determining whether satisfaction has been received. . . .

This multiplicity of factors which must be considered in evaluating a lease shows that this case more appropriately falls within the second line of authorities dealing with "satisfaction" clauses, being those involving fancy, taste, or judgment. Where the question is one of judgment, the promisor's determination that he is not satisfied, when made in good faith, has been held to be a defense to an action on the contract. . . .

Moreover, the secondary authorities are in accord with the California cases on the general principles governing "satisfaction" contracts. "It has been questioned whether an agreement in which the promise of one party is conditioned on his own or the other party's satisfaction contains the elements of a contract whether the agreement is not illusory in character because conditioned upon the whim or caprice of the party to be satisfied. Since, however, such a promise is generally considered as requiring a performance which shall be satisfactory to him in the exercise of an honest judgment, such contracts have been almost universally upheld." (Williston, Contracts (rev. ed. 1936); see also Corbin, Contracts (1951)). "A promise conditional upon the promisor's satisfaction is not illusory since it means more than that validity of the performance is to depend on the arbitrary choice of the promisor. His expression of dissatisfaction is not conclusive. That may show only that he has become dissatisfied with the contract; he must be dissatisfied with the performance, as a performance of the contract, and his dissatisfaction must be genuine."

We conclude that the contract here was neither illusory nor lacking in mutuality of obligation because the parties inserted a provision in their contract making plaintiff's performance dependent on his satisfaction with the leases to be obtained by him.

The judgment is reversed.

Problems

1. A Forestalled Foreclosure. Joseph Kahn had begun foreclosure proceedings on a past-due debt secured by a mortgage on a property located in Lynn, Massachusetts. Sarah Waldman, who held a second mortgage on the property, wished to take over Kahn's first mortgage. Waldman asked Kahn to forbear from foreclosing and promised that, in return, she would make payments on the note owed to Kahn. Kahn terminated the foreclosure proceeding, and Waldman made payments to Kahn for several months. When she then failed make a payment, Kahn foreclosed. Was their agreement supported by consideration?

2. A Right to Refuse. Telesat Cablevision, a cable operator, entered into an agreement with Johnson Enterprises of Jacksonville (JEJ), a contractor, for the construction of cable systems. The agreement provided a detailed price list, including per-foot labor prices for underground and aerial cable construction, hourly rates for the use of equipment and supplemental personnel, and prices for materials provided. A key provision of the agreement, "Non Exclusive Contract; Right of First Refusal," stated that Telesat may employ other contractors to do similar work,

> [p]rovided, however, before [Telesat] may offer any major work to other contractors, [Telesat] shall offer such work to [JEJ] and, unless such work is declined by [JEJ] or the parties mutually agree that [JEJ] cannot reasonably perform such additional work in a workmanlike and timely manner, then such work shall be performed by [JEJ] in accordance with this Agreement.

If JEJ accepted work offered by Telesat, the compensation would be governed by the price list. This agreement had a term of two years and was signed by both parties. Is it a valid contract?

3. Click & Clack. The General Services Administration (GSA) solicited bids for a contract to maintain the government's vehicle fleet at the White Sands Missile Range. GSA provided potential bidders with estimates of its expected needs, including the rate at which it had replaced vehicles in the past. Technical Assistance International (TAI) submitted a bid and was awarded the contract.

The GSA ended up replacing vehicles at more than twice the expected rate, resulting in decreased requirements for maintenance and repair work by TAI and, consequently, less income for TAI under the contract. The GSA accelerated the replacement rate due to several factors, including changes in other GSA fleets, changes in procurement policy made by the Office of Management and Budget, and so on, all of which were unrelated to the TAI contract.

TAI requested an adjustment in contract terms. The GSA refused. TAI sued in the Court of Federal Claims (which has jurisdiction over a government contract like this one), asserting that the GSA breached the contract. What is the likely outcome?

B. MUTUAL ASSENT

1. The Theory of Mutual Assent

Legally enforceable obligations arising under contract law can be distinguished from those that arise under tort law or criminal law by their voluntary nature. We generally hold people liable in tort for acting negligently and punish them for breaking criminal laws without asking whether they consented to being responsible. Contractual obligations, by contrast, are freely undertaken. To ensure voluntariness, the law requires that both parties must provide "assent" for a contract to be formed. See Rest. (2d) Contracts §§18-20. But what words or conduct are sufficient to show that a party has assented to being bound to a contract?

A foundational question, explored in the first two cases that follow, *Embry v. Hargadine, McKittrick Dry Goods Company* and *Lucy v. Zehmer,* is whether we measure assent by the subjective intentions of individuals or the objectively reasonable understanding of their words and actions. According to a distinguished proponent of the objective approach, Judge Learned Hand:

> A contract is an obligation attached by the mere force of law to certain acts of the parties, usually words, which ordinarily accompany and represent a known intent. If, however, it were proved by twenty bishops that either party, when he used the words, intended something else than the usual meaning which the law imposes upon them, he would still be held, unless there were some mutual mistake, or something else of the sort.

Hotchkiss v. National City Bank of New York, 200 F. 287, 293 (S.D.N.Y. 1911). A subjective analysis would best protect the autonomy of individuals to enter (or not to enter) into contracts, but an objective perspective best protects parties' reliance on a counterpart's words and actions and encourages clarity of communication.

Arguably the most difficult problem raised by the mutual assent requirement is determining at what point the parties' progress in negotiations moves past expressions of interest and even tentative agreements to expressions of commitment necessary for a binding contract. Rest. (2d) Contracts §§26, 27. *Empro Manufacturing Co. v. Ball-Co Manufacturing Inc.* and *International Casings Group, Inc. v. Premium Standard Farms, Inc.* explore this elusive distinction.

Finally, even when both parties express a clear desire to create a contract, the terms of their purported agreement can be too indefinite or uncertain for courts to identify a contractual obligation. *Joseph Martin, Jr., Delicatessen v. Schumacher* provides an example of this problem. Ask yourself both whether this case was decided correctly according to the principles of the Restatement and whether a different outcome would have been warranted under the UCC if the agreement had concerned the sale of goods. Rest. (2d) Contracts §§33, 34; U.C.C. §2-305.

EMBRY — *appellant*
v.
HARGADINE, McKITTRICK DRY GOODS CO. — *respondent*
St. Louis Court of Appeals, Missouri
127 Mo. App. 383
1907

GOODE, J.

. . . The appellant was an employee of the respondent company under a written contract to expire December 15, 1903, at a salary of $2,000 per annum. His duties were to attend to the sample department of respondent, of which he was given complete charge. It was his business to select samples for the traveling salesmen of the company, which is a wholesale dry goods concern, to use in selling goods to retail merchants. Appellant contends that on December 23, 1903, he was re-engaged by respondent, through its president, Thos. H. McKittrick, for another year at the same compensation and for the same duties stipulated in his previous written contract. On March 1, 1904, he was discharged, having been notified in February that, on account of the necessity of retrenching expenses, his services and that of some other employees would no longer be required. The respondent company contends that its president never re-employed appellant after the termination of his written contract, and hence that it had a right to discharge him when it chose. . . . Appellant testified: That several times prior to the termination of his written contract on December 15, 1903, he had endeavored to get an understanding with McKittrick for another year, but had been put off from time to time. That on December 23d, eight days after the expiration of said contract, he called on McKittrick, in the latter's office, and said to him that as appellant's written employment had lapsed eight days before, and as there were only a few days between then and the 1st of January in which to seek employment with other firms, if respondent wished to retain his services longer he must have a contract for another year, or he would quit respondent's service then and there. That he had been put off twice before and wanted an understanding or contract at once so that he could go ahead without worry. That McKittrick asked him how he was getting along in his department, and appellant said he was very busy, as they were in the height of the season getting men out—had about 110 salesmen on the line and others in preparation. That McKittrick then said: "Go ahead, you're all right. Get your men out, and don't let that worry you." That appellant took McKittrick at his word and worked until February 15th without any question in his mind. It was on February 15th that he was notified his services would be discontinued on March 1st. McKittrick denied this conversation as related by appellant, and said that, when accosted by the latter on December 23d, he (McKittrick) was working on his books in order to get out a report for a stockholders' meeting, and, when appellant said if he did not get a contract he would leave, that he (McKittrick) said: "Mr. Embry, I am just getting ready for the stockholders' meeting to-morrow. I have no time to take it up now. I have told you before I would not take it up until I had these matters out of the way. You will have to see me at a later time. I said: 'Go back upstairs and get your men out on the road.' I may have asked him one or two other questions relative to the department, I don't remember. The whole conversation did not take more than a minute."

. . .

It is assigned for error that the court required the jury, in order to return a verdict for appellant, not only to find the conversation occurred as appellant swore, but that both parties intended by such conversation to contract with each other for plaintiff's employment for the year from December, 1903, at a salary of $2,000. If it appeared from the record that there was a dispute between the parties as to the terms on which appellant wanted re-employment, there might have been sound reason for inserting this clause in the instruction; but no issue was made that they split on terms; the testimony of McKittrick tending to prove only that he refused to enter into a contract with appellant regarding another year's employment until the annual meeting of stockholders was out of the way. Indeed, as to the proposed terms McKittrick agrees with Embry, for the former swore as follows: "Mr. Embry said he wanted to know about the renewal of his contract. Said if he did not have the contract made he would leave." As the two witnesses coincided as to the terms of the proposed re-employment, there was no reason for inserting the above-mentioned clause in the instruction in order that it might be settled by the jury whether or not plaintiff, if employed for one year from December 23, 1903, was to be paid $2,000 a year. Therefore it remains to determine whether or not this part of the instruction was a correct statement of the law in regard to what was necessary to constitute a contract between the parties; that is to say, whether the formation of a contract by what, according to Embry, was said, depended on the intention of both Embry and McKittrick. Or, to put the question more precisely: Did what was said constitute a contract of re-employment on the previous terms irrespective of the intention or purpose of McKittrick?

rule

Judicial opinion and elementary treatises abound in statements of the rule that to constitute a contract there must be a meeting of the minds of the parties, and both must agree to the same thing in the same sense. Generally speaking, this may be true; but it is not literally or universally true. That is to say, the inner intention of parties to a conversation subsequently alleged to create a contract cannot either make a contract of what transpired, or prevent one from arising, if the words used were sufficient to constitute a contract. In so far as their intention is an influential element, it is only such intention as the words or acts of the parties indicate; not one secretly cherished which is inconsistent with those words or acts. . . . In Smith v. Hughes, 6 Queen's Bench (Law Reports)[,] 597, 607, it was said: "If, whatever a man's real intention may be, he so conducts himself that a reasonable man would believe that he was assenting to the terms proposed by the other party, and that other party upon that belief enters into the contract with him, the man thus conducting himself would be equally bound as if he had intended to agree to the other party's terms." And that doctrine was adopted in Phillip v. Gallant, 62 N.Y. 256. In 9 Cyc. 245, we find the following text: "The law imputes to a person an intention corresponding to the reasonable meaning of his words and acts. It judges his intention by his outward expressions and excludes all questions in regard to his unexpressed intention. If his words or acts, judged by a reasonable standard, manifest an intention to agree in regard to the matter in question, that agreement is established, and it is immaterial what may be the real, but unexpressed, state of his mind on the subject." . . . In view of those authorities, we hold that, though McKittrick may not have intended to employ Embry by what transpired between them according to the latter's testimony, yet if what McKittrick said would have been taken by a reasonable man to be an employment, and Embry so understood it, it constituted a valid contract of employment for the ensuing year.

holding

The next question is whether or not the language used was of that character, namely, was such that Embry, as a reasonable man, might consider he was re-employed for the ensuing year on the previous terms, and act accordingly. We do not say that in every instance it would be for the court to pronounce on this question, because, peradventure, instances might arise in which there would be such an ambiguity in the language relied on to show an assent by the obligor to the proposal of the obligee that it would be for the jury to say whether a reasonable mind would take it to signify acceptance of the proposal. . . . Embry was demanding a renewal of his contract, saying he had been put off from time to time, and that he had only a few days before the end of the year in which to seek employment from other houses, and that he would quit then and there unless he was reemployed. McKittrick inquired how he was getting along with the department, and Embry said they, i.e., the employees of the department, were very busy getting out salesmen. Whereupon McKittrick said: "Go ahead, you are all right. Get your men out, and do not let that worry you." We think no reasonable man would construe that answer to Embry's demand that he be employed for another year, otherwise than as an assent to the demand, and that Embry had the right to rely on it as an assent. The natural inference is, though we do not find it testified to, that Embry was at work getting samples ready for the salesmen to use during the ensuing season. Now, when he was complaining of the worry and mental distress he was under because of his

reasoning

uncertainty about the future, and his urgent need, either of an immediate contract with respondent, or a refusal by it to make one, leaving him free to seek employment elsewhere, McKittrick must have answered as he did for the purpose of assuring appellant that any apprehension was needless, as appellant's services would be retained by the respondent. The answer was unambiguous, and we rule that if the conversation was according to appellant's version, and he understood he was employed, it constituted in law a valid contract of re-employment, and the court erred in making the formation of a contract depend on a finding that both parties intended to make one. It was only necessary that Embry, as a reasonable man, had a right to and did so understand.

. . .

The judgment is reversed, and the cause remanded. All concur.

LUCY ~ P
v.
ZEHMER ~ D

Supreme Court of Appeals of Virginia
196 Va. 493
1954

BUCHANAN, J.

brothers

This suit was instituted by W.O. Lucy and J.C. Lucy, complainants, against A.H. Zehmer and Ida S. Zehmer, his wife, defendants, to have specific performance of a contract by which it was alleged the Zehmers had sold to W.O. Lucy a tract of land owned by A.H. Zehmer in Dinwiddie county containing 471.6 acres, more or less, known as the Ferguson farm, for $50,000. J.C. Lucy, the other complainant, is a brother of W.O. Lucy, to whom W.O. Lucy transferred a half interest in his alleged purchase.

The instrument sought to be enforced was written by A.H. Zehmer on December 20, 1952, in these words: "We hereby agree to sell to W.O. Lucy the Ferguson Farm complete for $50,000.00, title satisfactory to buyer," and signed by the defendants, A.H. Zehmer and Ida S. Zehmer.

The answer of A.H. Zehmer admitted that at the time mentioned W.O. Lucy offered him $50,000 cash for the farm, but that he, Zehmer, considered that the offer was made in jest; that so thinking, and both he and Lucy having had several drinks, he wrote out "the memorandum" quoted above and induced his wife to sign it; that he did not deliver the memorandum to Lucy, but that Lucy picked it up, read it, put it in his pocket, attempted to offer Zehmer $5 to bind the bargain, which Zehmer refused to accept, and realizing for the first time that Lucy was serious, Zehmer assured him that he had no intention of selling the farm and that the whole matter was a joke. Lucy left the premises insisting that he had purchased the farm.

P H

Depositions were taken and the decree appealed from was entered holding that the complainants had failed to establish their right to specific performance, and dismissing their bill. The assignment of error is to this action of the court.

W.O. Lucy, a lumberman and farmer, thus testified in substance: . . . Seven or eight years ago he had offered Zehmer $20,000 for the [Ferguson] farm which Zehmer had accepted, but the agreement was verbal and Zehmer backed out. On the night of December 20, 1952, . . . [h]e entered the restaurant [owned by Zehmer]. . . . He asked Zehmer if he had sold the Ferguson farm. Zehmer replied that he had not. Lucy said, "I bet you wouldn't take $50,000.00 for that place." Zehmer replied, "Yes, I would too; you wouldn't give fifty." Lucy said he would and told Zehmer to write up an agreement to that effect. Zehmer took a restaurant check and wrote on the back of it, "I do hereby agree to sell to W.O. Lucy the Ferguson Farm for $50,000 complete." Lucy told him he had better change it to "We" because Mrs. Zehmer would have to sign it too. Zehmer then tore up what he had written, wrote the agreement quoted above and asked Mrs. Zehmer, who was at the other end of the counter ten or twelve feet away, to sign it. Mrs. Zehmer said she would for $50,000 and signed it. Zehmer brought it back and gave it to Lucy, who offered him $5 which Zehmer refused, saying, "You don't need to give me any money, you got the agreement there signed by both of us."

The discussion leading to the signing of the agreement, said Lucy, lasted thirty or forty minutes, during which Zehmer seemed to doubt that Lucy could raise $50,000. . . .

Lucy took a partly filled bottle of whiskey into the restaurant with him for the purpose of giving Zehmer a drink if he wanted it. Zehmer did, and he and Lucy had one or two drinks together. Lucy said that while he felt the drinks he took he was not intoxicated, and from the way Zehmer handled the transaction he did not think he was either.

. . . Next day Lucy telephoned J.C. Lucy and arranged with the latter to take a half interest in the purchase and pay half of the consideration. On Monday he engaged an attorney to examine the title. The attorney reported favorably on December 31 and on January 2 Lucy wrote Zehmer . . . asking when Zehmer would be ready to close the deal. Zehmer replied by letter, mailed January 13, asserting that he had never agreed or intended to sell.

Mr. and Mrs. Zehmer were called by the complainants as adverse witnesses. [Mr.] Zehmer testified in substance as follows:

He bought this farm more than ten years ago for $11,000. He had had twenty-five offers, more or less, to buy it, including several from Lucy, who had never offered any specific sum of money. He had given them all the same answer, that he was not interested in selling it. . . . When he entered the restaurant around eight-thirty [on December 20] Lucy was there and he could see that he was "pretty high." He said to Lucy, "Boy, you got some good liquor, drinking, ain't you?" Lucy then offered him a drink. "I was already high as a Georgia pine, and didn't have any more better sense than to pour another great big slug out and gulp it down, and he took one too."

After they had talked a while Lucy asked whether he still had the Ferguson farm. He replied that he had not sold it and Lucy said, "I bet you wouldn't take $50,000.00

for it." Zehmer asked him if he would give $50,000 and Lucy said yes. Zehmer replied, "You haven't got $50,000 in cash." Lucy said he did and Zehmer replied that he did not believe it. . . .

Finally, said Zehmer, Lucy told him if he didn't believe he had $50,000, "you sign that piece of paper here and say you will take $50,000.00 for the farm. "He, Zehmer, "just grabbed the back off of a guest check there" and wrote on the back of it. At that point in his testimony Zehmer asked to see what he had written to "see if I recognize my own handwriting." He examined the paper and exclaimed, "Great balls of fire, I got 'Firgerson' for Ferguson, I have got satisfactory spelled wrong. I don't recognize that writing if I would see it, wouldn't know it was mine."

After Zehmer had, as he described it, "scribbled this thing off," Lucy said, "Get your wife to sign it." Zehmer walked over to where she was and she at first refused to sign but did so after he told her that he "was just needling him [Lucy], and didn't mean a thing in the world, that I was not selling the farm." Zehmer then "took it back over there. . . . [Lucy] reached and picked it up, and when I looked back again he had it in his pocket and he dropped a five dollar bill over there, and he said, 'Here is five dollars payment on it.' . . . I said, 'Hell no, that is beer and liquor talking. I am not going to sell you the farm. I have told you that too many times before.'"

Mrs. Zehmer testified that when Lucy came into the restaurant he looked as if he had had a drink. When Zehmer came in he took a drink out of a bottle that Lucy handed him. . . . Lucy and Zehmer were talking but she did not pay too much attention to what they were saying. She heard Lucy ask Zehmer if he had sold the Ferguson farm, and Zehmer replied that he had not and did not want to sell it. Lucy said, "I bet you wouldn't take $50,000 cash for that farm," and Zehmer replied, "You haven't got $50,000 cash." . . . Lucy asked him if he would put it in writing that he would sell him this farm. Zehmer then wrote on the back of a pad, "I agree to sell the Ferguson Place to W.O. Lucy for $50,000.00 cash." Lucy said, "All right, get your wife to sign it." Zehmer came back to where she was standing and said, "You want to put your name to this?" She said "No," but he said in an undertone, "It is nothing but a joke," and she signed it.

. . .

On examination by her own counsel she said that her husband laid this piece of paper down after it was signed; that Lucy said to let him see it, took it, folded it and put it in his wallet, then said to Zehmer, "Let me give you $5.00," but Zehmer said, "No, this is liquor talking. I don't want to sell the farm, I have told you that I want my son to have it. This is all a joke." Lucy then said at least twice, "Zehmer, you have sold your farm," wheeled around and started for the door. . . . She said you could tell definitely that he was drinking and she said to her husband, "You should have taken him home," but he said, "Well, I am just about as bad off as he is."

. . .

The defendants insist that the evidence was ample to support their contention that the writing sought to be enforced was prepared as a bluff or dare to force Lucy to admit that he did not have $50,000; that the whole matter was a joke; and no binding contract was ever made between the parties.

It is an unusual, if not bizarre, defense. When made to the writing admittedly prepared by one of the defendants and signed by both, clear evidence is required to sustain it.

In his testimony Zehmer claimed that he "was high as a Georgia pine," and that the transaction "was just a bunch of two doggoned drunks bluffing to see who could talk the biggest and say the most." That claim is inconsistent with his attempt to testify in great detail as to what was said and what was done. It is contradicted by other evidence as to the condition of both parties, and rendered of no weight by the testimony of his wife that when Lucy left the restaurant she suggested that Zehmer drive him home. The record is convincing that Zehmer was not intoxicated to the extent of being unable to comprehend the nature and consequences of the instrument he executed, and hence that instrument is not to be invalidated on that ground. . . . It was in fact conceded by defendants' counsel in oral argument that under the evidence Zehmer was not too drunk to make a valid contract.

The evidence is convincing also that Zehmer wrote two agreements, the first one beginning "I hereby agree to sell." Zehmer first said he could not remember about that, then that "I don't think I wrote but one out." Mrs. Zehmer said that what he wrote was "I hereby agree," but that the "I" was changed to "We" after that night. The agreement that was written and signed is in the record and indicates no such change. Neither are the mistakes in spelling that Zehmer sought to point out readily apparent.

The appearance of the contract, the fact that it was under discussion for forty minutes or more before it was signed; Lucy's objection to the first draft because it was written in the singular, and he wanted Mrs. Zehmer to sign it also; the rewriting to meet that objection and the signing by Mrs. Zehmer; the discussion of what was to be included in the sale, the provision for the examination of the title, the completeness of the instrument that was executed, the taking possession of it by Lucy with no request or suggestion by either of the defendants that he give it back, are facts which furnish persuasive evidence that the execution of the contract was a serious business transaction rather than a casual, jesting matter as defendants now contend.

. . .

If it be assumed, contrary to what we think the evidence shows, that Zehmer was jesting about selling his farm to Lucy and that the transaction was intended by him to be a joke, nevertheless the evidence shows that Lucy did not so understand it but considered it to be a serious business transaction and the contract to be binding on the Zehmers as well as on himself. The very next day he arranged with his brother to put up half the money and take a half interest in the land. The day after that he employed an attorney to examine the title. The next night, Tuesday, he was back at Zehmer's place and there Zehmer told him for the first time, Lucy said, that he wasn't going to sell and he told Zehmer, "You know you sold that place fair and square." After receiving the report from his attorney that the title was good he wrote to Zehmer that he was ready to close the deal.

Not only did Lucy actually believe, but the evidence shows he was warranted in believing, that the contract represented a serious business transaction and a good faith sale and purchase of the farm.

In the field of contracts, as generally elsewhere, "We must look to the outward expression of a person as manifesting his intention rather than to his secret and unexpressed intention. 'The law imputes to a person an intention corresponding to the reasonable meaning of his words and acts.'" First Nat'l Bank v. Roanoke Oil Co., 169 Va. 99.

At no time prior to the execution of the contract had Zehmer indicated to Lucy by word or act that he was not in earnest about selling the farm. They had argued about it and discussed its terms, as Zehmer admitted, for a long time. Lucy testified that if there was any jesting it was about paying $50,000 that night. The contract and the evidence show that he was not expected to pay the money that night. Zehmer said that after the writing was signed he laid it down on the counter in front of Lucy. Lucy said Zehmer handed it to him. In any event there had been what appeared to be a good faith offer and a good faith acceptance, followed by the execution and apparent delivery of a written contract. Both said that Lucy put the writing in his pocket and then offered Zehmer $5 to seal the bargain. Not until then, even under the defendants' evidence, was anything said or done to indicate that the matter was a joke. Both of the Zehmers testified that when Zehmer asked his wife to sign he whispered that it was a joke so Lucy wouldn't hear and that it was not intended that he should hear.

The mental assent of the parties is not requisite for the formation of a contract. If the words or other acts of one of the parties have but one reasonable meaning, his undisclosed intention is immaterial except when an unreasonable meaning which he attaches to his manifestations is known to the other party. Restatement of the Law of Contracts, §71. . . . An agreement or mutual assent is of course essential to a valid contract but the law imputes to a person an intention corresponding to the reasonable meaning of his words and acts. If his words and acts, judged by a reasonable standard, manifest an intention to agree, it is immaterial what may be the real but unexpressed state of his mind. . . .

So a person cannot set up that he was merely jesting when his conduct and words would warrant a reasonable person in believing that he intended a real agreement. . . .

Whether the writing signed by the defendants and now sought to be enforced by the complainants was the result of a serious offer by Lucy and a serious acceptance by the defendants, or was a serious offer by Lucy and an acceptance in secret jest by the defendants, in either event it constituted a binding contract of sale between the parties.

. . .

The complainants are entitled to have specific performance of the contracts sued on. . . .

Reversed and remanded.

EMPRO MANUFACTURING CO.
v.
BALL-CO MANUFACTURING, INC.

U.S. Court of Appeals, Seventh Circuit
870 F.2d 423
1989

EASTERBROOK, J.

custom

rule

We have a <u>pattern common</u> in commercial life. Two firms reach concord on the general terms of their transaction. They sign a document, captioned "agreement in principle" or "letter of intent," memorializing these terms but anticipating further negotiations and decisions—an appraisal of the assets, the clearing of a title, the list is endless. One of these terms proves divisive, and the deal collapses. The party that perceives itself the loser then claims that the preliminary document has legal force independent of the definitive contract. Ours is such a dispute.

Ball-Co Manufacturing, a maker of specialty valve components, floated its assets on the market. Empro Manufacturing showed interest. After some preliminary negotiations, Empro sent Ball-Co a three-page "letter of intent" to purchase the assets of Ball-Co and S.B. Leasing, a partnership holding title to the land under Ball-Co's plant. Empro proposed a price of $2.4 million, with $650,000 to be paid on closing and a 10-year promissory note for the remainder, the note to be secured by the "inventory and equipment of Ballco." The letter stated "[t]he general terms and conditions of such proposal (which will be subject to and incorporated in a formal, definitive Asset Purchase Agreement signed by both parties)." Just in case Ball-Co might suppose that Empro had committed itself to buy the assets, paragraph four of the letter stated that "Empro's purchase shall be subject to the satisfaction of certain conditions precedent to closing including, but not limited to" the definitive Asset Purchase Agreement and, among five other conditions, "[t]he approval of the shareholders and board of directors of Empro."

Although Empro left itself escape hatches, as things turned out Ball-Co was the one who balked. The parties signed the letter of intent in November 1987 and negotiated through March 1988 about many terms. Security for the note proved to be the sticking point. Ball-Co wanted a security interest in the land under the plant; Empro refused to yield.

When Empro learned that Ball-Co was negotiating with someone else, it filed this <u>diversity suit</u>. Contending that the letter of intent obliges Ball-Co to sell only to it, Empro asked for a temporary restraining order. The district judge . . . concluded that the statement, appearing twice in the letter, that the agreement is "subject to" the execution of a definitive contract meant that the letter has no independent force.

PH / issue

. . .

Because letters of intent are written without the care that will be lavished on the definitive agreement, it may be a bit much to put dispositive weight on "subject to" in every case. . . . [These terms] might have been used carelessly, and if the full agreement showed that the formal contract was to be nothing but a memorial of an agreement already reached, the letter of intent would be enforceable. *Borg-Warner Corp. v. Anchor Coupling Co.,* 16 Ill. 2d 234, 156 N.E.2d 513 (1958). . . . *Borg-Warner* is such a case. One party issued an option, which called itself "firm and binding"; the other party accepted; the court found this a binding contract even though some terms remained open. After all, an option to purchase is nothing if not binding in advance of the definitive contract. The parties to *Borg-Warner* conceded that the option and acceptance usually would bind; the only argument in the case concerned whether the open terms were so important that a contract could not arise even if the parties wished to be bound, a subject that divided the court. See 156 N.E.2d at 930-36 (Schaefer, J., dissenting).

A canvass of the terms of the letter Empro sent does not assist it, however. "Subject to" a definitive agreement appears twice. The letter also recites, twice, that it contains the "general terms and conditions," implying that each side retained the right to make (and stand on) additional demands. Empro insulated itself from binding effect by listing, among the conditions to which the deal was "subject," the "approval of the shareholders and board of directors of Empro." The board could veto a deal negotiated by the firm's agents for a reason such as the belief that Ball-Co had been offered too much (otherwise the officers, not the board, would be the firm's final decisionmakers, yet state law vests major decisions in the board). The shareholders could decline to give their assent for any reason (such as distrust of new business ventures) and could not even be required to look at the documents, let alone consider the merits of the deal. See Earl Sneed, *The Shareholder May Vote As He Pleases: Theory and Fact,* 22 U. Pittsburgh L. Rev. 23, 31-36, 40-42 (1960) (collecting cases). Empro even took care to require the return of its $5,000 in earnest money "without set off, in the event this transaction is not closed," although the seller usually gets to keep the earnest money if the buyer changes its mind. So Empro made clear that it was free to walk.

Neither the text nor the structure of the letter suggests that it was to be a one-sided commitment, an option in Empro's favor binding only Ball-Co. From the beginning Ball-Co assumed that it could negotiate terms in addition to, or different from, those in the letter of intent. The cover letter from Ball-Co's lawyer returning the signed letter of intent to Empro stated that the "terms and conditions are generally acceptable" but that "some clarifications are needed in Paragraph 3(c) (last sentence)," the provision concerning Ball-Co's security interest. "Some clarifications are needed" is an ominous noise in a negotiation, foreboding many a stalemate. Although we do not know what "clarifications" counsel had in mind, the specifics are not important. It is enough that even on signing the letter of intent Ball-Co proposed to change the bargain, conduct consistent with the purport of the letter's text and structure.

The shoals that wrecked this deal are common hazards in business negotiations. Letters of intent and agreements in principle often, and here, do no more than set the stage for negotiations on details. Sometimes the details can be ironed out; sometimes they can't. Illinois, as *Chicago Investment, Interway,* and *Feldman* show, allows parties to approach agreement in stages, without fear that by reaching a preliminary understanding they have bargained away their privilege to disagree on the specifics. . . .

AFFIRMED.

INTERNATIONAL CASINGS GROUP, INC.
v.
PREMIUM STANDARD FARMS, INC.

U.S. District Court, W.D. Mo.
358 F. Supp. 2d 863
2005

LAUGHREY, J.

Pending before the Court is Plaintiff International Casing Group's ("ICG") Motion for Preliminary Injunction. For the reasons set forth below, the Court grants ICG's Motion.

I. BACKGROUND

Defendant Premium Standard Farms ("PSF") is a pork producer that has sold its hog casings to ICG for over six years. The two PSF facilities that supply their hog casings to ICG are located in Milan, Missouri ("Milan facility"), and Clinton, North Carolina ("Clinton facility"). ICG has its own equipment and employees on site at the Clinton and Milan facilities to harvest and process the casings.

Prior to May 2002, PSF and ICG had long term output contracts for both facilities. In May 2002, PSF and ICG terminated these contracts. However, the parties continued performing under the terms of their contracts, and in June 2002, they resumed negotiations regarding new terms for both facilities. The parties negotiated a myriad of issues, including, but not limited to, an electrical room that needed re-wiring at the Clinton facility, pricing adjustments related to quality control issues (frequently referred to as the bloody guts issue) and a blower pipe at the Clinton facility. Many of these negotiations occurred via e-mail between the parties and both entities consistently relayed negotiation terms and positions to one another via electronic correspondence. The negotiations were protracted.

In early 2004, Kent Pummill ("Pummill") represented PSF in its negotiations with ICG and Tom Sanecki ("Sanecki") represented ICG. In a series of e-mails from March and April 2004, Pummill and Sanecki discussed several open issues. Because of the importance of these e-mails, the Court includes them verbatim. All of the following e-mails were sent in 2004. . . .

02/19	Sender: Kent Pummill	Recipient: Tom Sanecki

Here is where we are at. We agree that there is some blood in the casings as with all CO_2 systems. We don't agree it is an 8 cent discount. We would like to offer the following: 2 cent discount on the Clinton contract; we [PSF] will pay 100% of the electrical that was completed last year; you pay for putting in the stainless steel pipe going to your building. . . . Where are your sticking points, so we can get both plants under contract and behind us?

Thanks, Kent

02/26	Sender: Kent Pummill	Recipient: Tom Sanecki

Did you get my e-mail. What is your counter-offer? I agree, we have gone too long. Lets get this cleaned up.

Thanks, Kent

02/26	Sender: Tom Sanecki	Recipient: Kent Pummill

I am in LA this week, I will call you next week to discuss, or would you prefer Eric and I come to KC for a quick meeting next week. We would be available Tuesday-Thursday.

02/26	Sender: Kent Pummill	Recipient: Tom Sanecki

Bo is traveling. Shoot me your counter offer next week, and lets get this moving.

03/18	Sender: Tom Sanecki	Recipient: Kent Pummill

I will be out of the office thru 03/29/04.

I have the following questions and I think we should schedule a meeting in KC to get this resolved. . . . Electrical room and blow pipe—not to beat a dead horse but, I think getting the guts, undamaged, to the casing department should be PSF's responsibility. ICG paid for the blow system and it has worked for years. It has only been since it has been disassembled by your maintenance department for cleaning that we have been having problems with damaged guts.

The quote we have is for $25,000, I expect this to go up due to the increases in the cost of steel, my guess is an additional $8,000-$10,000. We also need to make sure that the finish is not going to cause damage. My suggestion is that ICG will pay for the pipe and turn the blower system over to PSF, if PSF will extend both contracts an additional two years.

The remaining issue is the compensation for the bloody guts. $0.02 is not enough to compensate for the additional processing required. I suggest that we schedule a meeting for either 04/06/04 or 04/07/04 in KC. Please let me know your thoughts.

03/23	Sender: Kent Pummill	Recipient: Tom Sanecki

We might as well schedule a meeting then, because if you want more than 2 cents, then our plan is to put it back out to bid. . . . We have paid for the electrical room. You pay for the pipe. Sounds like it just comes down to the discount #. We will do a 2 cent discount at Clinton and will go 5 years on a new contract for both plants. Your choice, this or us putting both plants back out to bid. Let me know, we would be glad to meet.

Thanks, Kent

04/19	Sender: Tom Sanecki	Recipient: Kent Pummill

I am not happy about the $0.02. . . . The pipe vs. the electrical room is ok, and the sooner we get this contract signed the better, we need to get this pipe replaced. It is effecting our yields. Do we agree that when ICG pays for the pipe replacement and we have the 5 year contract that PSF will take responsibility and ownership of the pipe?

Can we do something about the costs we have incurred with the bloody guts we have already processed? This started in January 15, 2003, so for 16+ months. Can we get an additional $0.02 for the next 16 months or an additional $0.005 off for the 5 year contract?

Please call me when you get a chance [phone number deleted].

04/20	Sender: Kent Pummill	Recipient: Tom Sanecki

Send the new contracts with a decrease of $0.025 for the next 5 years at Clinton. We will take ownership of the new pipe installed by ICG after it is installed.

Thanks, Kent

04/27	Sender: Tom Sanecki	Recipient: Kent Pummill

I have sent you 4 copies of each contract. I have initialed and signed each. Please have Bo sign and initial and return 2 copies to ICG.

I put the effective date of the $0.025 reduction at Clinton for 05/03/2004. ICG will get the blow pipe replaced ASAP after receiving the signed contracts. PSF will maintain the blow system and at the end of the new contract it will become PSF's property.

PSF will pay for the electrical room upgrades at Clinton. Thanks for your help.

04/27	Sender: Kent Pummill	Recipient: Tom Sanecki

Will do. Thank you. Kent

05/10	Sender: Tom Sanecki	Recipient: Kent Pummill

How are the contracts going? ? ? ? ?

05/10	**Sender: Kent Pummill**	**Recipient: Tom Sanecki**

Legal has them. I will double check this morning.

06/07	**Sender: Kent Pummill**	**Recipient: Tom Sanecki**

Finally got them back from Legal and Bo Manly.

Bo is adamant about not going 5 years. He turned 180 degrees on me. He wants just 3. If you can agree with me on 3 years, then I will mark through and initial the "2G" section and change and initial the term to 3 years, and get Bo to sign and send them on their way. I thought we were home free; we are real close. Will this work for you? I will take another penny off the price for Clinton to get this signed and off my desk. I think you and I are both tired and want this off our desks. Let me know.

Kent

06/21	**Sender: Tom Sanecki**	**Recipient: Kent Pummill**

OK, but as you can imagine I am surprised by this change. Do you want to mark-up your contract and mark the price schedule, then sign and send to me. We will get the blow pipe done ASAP. Thanks.

06/21	**Sender: Kent Pummill**	**Recipient: Tom Sanecki**

We will mark up the contract and send it to you. Thanks, Kent.

Send me a new pricing schedule, and I will attach the new one to Clinton's contracts.

06/21	**Sender: Tom Sanecki**	**Recipient: Kent Pummill**

Shall we make these prices effective 06/28/2004?

06/21	**Sender: Kent Pummill**	**Recipient: Tom Sanecki**

That is fine.

The "contracts"[1] referred to in Sanecki's April 27, 2004, e-mail outlined the payment mechanism for the casings and provided that the price of the casings would be based on a price benchmark contained in the Pratt Report, which is a trade publication used by the casings industry. The pricing schedule was attached to each "contract," incorporated by reference, signed by Sanecki and sent to PSF. The pricing schedule reflected that ICG was paying less for the casings from the Clinton facility than those from the Milan facility. These "contracts" were for five years.

In his June 7 e-mail to Sanecki, Pummill agrees to take off another penny for the Clinton casings in exchange for a three instead of a five year contract. After receiving Sanecki's agreement to the three year duration, Pummill marked up the contracts and gave them to Robert W. (Bo) Manly ("Manly") for Manly's signature. Manly is the

---

1. Sanecki referred to these documents as contracts. The Court does not believe a contract was reached as of April 27, 2004; hence, the use of quotation marks.

president of PSF. While awaiting Manly's signature on the contracts, ICG and PSF implemented the new pricing schedules as of June 28, 2004. In July 2004, Sanecki inquired a few times about obtaining the written contracts and Pummill responded that Manly still had them.

On August 2, 2004, Pummill e-mailed Sanecki to tell him that Calvin Held ("Held") was now supervising both the Milan and Clinton facilities and that Manly wanted Held to "approve" the contracts for the two facilities. Pummill also indicated that Held was inquiring about why ICG was paying less money for the casings from the Clinton facility than the casings from the Milan facility. In September 2004, Sanecki met with Held to discuss the price disparity between the two facilities. It appears that Held did not notify Sanecki at that meeting that PSF would not honor the pricing arrangement. The new prices continued to be paid even after the meeting.

On November 17, 2004, PSF sent ICG written notice of its intent to terminate the parties' business relationship. . . . On January 7, 2005, the Court held an evidentiary hearing regarding ICG's Motion for Preliminary Injunction. Pending resolution of that Motion, the parties are performing under the terms reached as of June 21, 2004. . . .

II. DISCUSSION

In determining whether to grant a preliminary injunction, courts weigh four factors: (1) the probability that the movant will succeed on the merits; (2) the threat of irreparable harm to the movant; (3) the balance between the harm to the movant and any harm that granting the injunction will cause to other parties to the litigation; and (4) the public interest. *Dataphase Sys., Inc. v. C L Sys., Inc.,* 640 F.2d 109 (8th Cir. 1981). [Only subpart 1 is included.—Eds.]

A. Success on the Merits

1. Meeting of the Minds

To be successful, ICG must establish that it has a contract with PSF. The parties agree that this transaction is controlled by the UCC which provides:

> (1) A contract for sale of goods may be made in any manner sufficient to show agreement, including conduct by both parties which recognizes the existence of such a contract.
>
> . . .
>
> (3) Even though one or more terms are left open, a contract for sale does not fail for indefiniteness if the parties have intended to make a contract and there is a reasonably certain basis for giving an appropriate remedy.

Mo. Rev. Stat. §400.2-204. PSF contends that it has no agreement with ICG because there was never a "meeting of the minds," particularly, with reference to price.

PSF is correct that ICG must establish that there was a "meeting of the minds" between ICG and PSF. . . . Whether a meeting of the minds exists, however, "is determined objectively by looking at the intent of the parties as expressed by their actual words or acts." *Paul's Rod & Bearing, Ltd. v. Kelly*, 847 S.W.2d 68 (Mo. Ct. App. 1991). A meeting of the minds cannot be "determined on the undisclosed assumption or secret surmise of either party." *Computer Network, Ltd. v. Purcell Tire & Rubber Co.*, 747 S.W.2d 669 (Mo. Ct. App. 1988). This is because Missouri follows the objective theory of contracts. "The objective theory lays stress on the outward manifestation of assent made to the other party in contrast to the older idea that a contract was a true 'meeting of the minds.'" *Id.* (quoting J. Calamari & J. Perillo, Contracts §2-13, at 23 (2d ed. 1977)).

There is substantial evidence to show that PSF and ICG did reach a meeting of the minds on June 21, 2004 for a new three year, hog casing, output contract for the Milan and Clinton facilities. The parties had been negotiating since 2002 and had resolved most of the issues in dispute by April of 2004. Price, the bloody guts issue and the defective pipe at the Clinton facility were still being discussed. On March 23, Kent Pummill, who had authority to negotiate on behalf of PSF, said: "We have paid for the electrical room. You pay for the [Clinton] pipe. Sounds like it just comes down to the discount #. We will do a 2 cent discount at Clinton and will go 5 years on a new contract for both plants. Your choice, this or us putting both plants back out to bid. Let me [k]now, we would be glad to meet."

Tom Sanecki, who had authority to negotiate for ICG, responded by accepting some of Pummill's proposal and raising additional issues. The following day, Pummill instructs Sanecki to send the new contracts with a decrease of $.025. Mr. Sanecki does so and there is no response from PSF until June 7, 2004 when Mr. Pummill writes: "Finally got them [contracts] back from legal and Bo Manly. . . . Bo is adamant about not going 5 years. He turned 180 degrees on me. He wants just 3. If you can agree with me on 3 years, then I will mark through and initial the '2G' section and change and initial the term to 3 years, and get Bo to sign and send them on their way. I thought we were home free; we are real close. Will this work for you? I will take another penny off the price for Clinton to get this signed and off my desk."

Mr. Sanecki responds OK. At that point, both parties had agreed on all the essential terms of the contract. While PSF now contends that the price issue was unresolved, that argument is inconsistent with its agreement to implement the new prices effective June 28, 2004 pursuant to an e-mail exchange between Sanecki and Pummill on June 21, 2004. That agreement occurred on the same day that both sides had resolved all outstanding issues under discussion and Pummill had offered a lower price for the Clinton facility and Sanecki had accepted it.

. . .

Sometime after June 21, 2004, and before August 2, 2004, PSF placed Calvin Held over both the Clinton and Milan facilities. August 2 is the first time that PSF notifies ICG that Held is "approving both contracts." An inquiry is made by PSF on that date as to why there is a difference between the price at Milan and the price at Clinton. A meeting is arranged with Held and at that meeting he is told by Sanecki the reason for the price differential. It does not appear that PSF told ICG at that meeting that the price being paid pursuant to the June 21 agreement was unacceptable or notified ICG that it would no longer pay that price. In fact, the price was paid by PSF through 2004. Indeed, the new prices remained in effect even after PSF notified ICG that it must vacate the Milan and Clinton facilities. While it is possible that a jury may conclude differently, it is more likely that a jury will believe that Held, the new PSF manager, didn't like the deal that had been struck for his facilities and PSF was back tracking on an agreement that had already been made.

Finally, PSF contends that there was no meeting of the minds on June 21, 2004, because the agreement was never reduced to writing and signed by both parties. However, merely because parties intend a written memorialization of the agreed upon terms does not demonstrate that they intend the writing to be a condition precedent to the formation of a contract. "Mutual manifestations of assent that are in themselves sufficient to make a contract will not be prevented from so operating by the mere fact that the parties also manifest an intention to prepare and adopt a written memorial thereof. . . ." 1 Restatement of the Law of Contracts, Ch. 3, §26. The real question is whether the parties intended a written document to be a condition precedent to the formation of a binding contract. . . .

Considering the evidence presented at the preliminary injunction hearing, the Court concludes that a jury is likely to find that the parties intended that their agreement be reduced to writing as a memorialization. They did not intend the writing to be a condition precedent to the formation of the contract. Pummill's e-mail on June 7, 2004, said that everything looked fine except two things. Sanecki then agreed to PSF's proposal concerning those two things. The parties then implemented the new pricing structure which was the major stumbling block to the formation of the contract. In his June 21 e-mail, Pummill says that "we" will mark up the contracts to conform to the agreement and PSF was then to send them to ICG. At no time does Pummill say "I" will mark them up and then give them to Manley for his approval, and if Manly approves them, we will send them to you. There is nothing in the communications or the actions of the parties that suggest that no contract was formed until the paper documents were formally signed by both Sanecki and Manly. . . .

Nor is there objective evidence to indicate that Pummill did not have the authority to enter into the agreement on behalf of PSF. The evidence strongly suggests that he had authority to bind PSF. While there is evidence that suggests that Sanecki did not want to make repairs required by the terms of the agreement until there was a writing, this does not mean that the parties intended the written documents be a condition precedent to the formation of a contract. Sanecki was obviously concerned about making the repairs on the defendant's property in the event that PSF attempted to backtrack on its agreement. It was also a minor issue in comparison to the implementation of the new pricing structure which was done as of June 28, 2004. It is probable that a jury will find that a written document with a formal signature was not a condition precedent to the formation of the contract. . . .

Because the parties' writings in April and June 2004 manifest a meeting of the minds regarding their intentions to enter into an agreement and because those writings are authenticated in a way that satisfies the Statute of Frauds, the Court finds that ICG is more likely to succeed on the merits of its claim. Although ICG's success is not guaranteed because some of the issues are factual in nature and reserved for juries, the Court finds that it is more likely than not based on the evidence before the Court at this juncture. Additionally, the Court finds that ICG cannot obtain cover goods that are of the same quality and degree as those produced by PSF and that ICG will suffer the greater harm if the Court does not grant ICG's pending Motion. Finally, the Court finds that the public interest weighs in favor of enforcing the parties' agreement. Therefore, the four factors outlined in *Dataphase*, 640 F.2d at 114, weigh in favor of granting ICG's Motion for Injunction.

III. CONCLUSION

Accordingly, it is hereby ORDERED that International Casing Group, Inc.'s Motion for Preliminary Injunction is GRANTED.

(u)

JOSEPH MARTIN, JR., DELICATESSEN appellee (p)
v.
SCHUMACHER appellant (D)
Court of Appeals of New York
52 N.Y.2d 105
1981

FUCHSBERG, J.

This case raises an issue fundamental to the law of contracts. It calls upon us to review a decision of the Appellate Division, which held that a realty lease's provision that the rent for a renewal period was "to be agreed upon" may be enforceable.   issue

. . . In 1973, the appellant, as landlord, leased a retail store to the respondent for a five-year term at a rent graduated upwards from $500 per month for the first year to $650 for the fifth. The renewal clause stated that "[t]he Tenant may renew this lease for an additional period of five years at annual rentals to be agreed upon; Tenant shall give Landlord thirty (30) days written notice, to be mailed certified mail, return receipt requested, of the intention to exercise such right." It is not disputed that the tenant gave timely notice of its desire to renew or that, once the landlord made it clear that he would do so only at a rental starting at $900 a month, the tenant engaged an appraiser who opined that a fair market rental value would be $545.41.

The tenant thereupon commenced an action for specific performance in Supreme Court, Suffolk County, to compel the landlord to extend the lease for the additional term at the appraiser's figure or such other sum as the court would decide was reasonable. For his part, the landlord in due course brought a holdover proceeding in the local District Court to evict the tenant. On the landlord's motion for summary judgment, the Supreme Court, holding that a bald agreement to agree on a   PH future rental was unenforceable for uncertainty as a matter of law, dismissed the tenant's complaint. . . .

It was on appeal by the tenant from these orders that the Appellate Division, expressly overruling an established line of cases in the process, reinstated the tenant's complaint and granted consolidation. In so doing, it reasoned that "a renewal clause in a lease providing for future agreement on the rent to be paid during the renewal term is enforceable if it is established that the parties' intent was not to terminate in the event of a failure to agree." It went on to provide that, if the tenant met that burden, the trial court could proceed to set a "reasonable rent." . . .

PH

We begin our analysis with the basic observation that, unless otherwise mandated by law (e.g., residential emergency rent control statutes), a contract is a private "ordering" in which a party binds himself to do, or not to do, a particular thing. . . . This liberty is no right at all if it is not accompanied by freedom not to contract. The corollary is that, before one may secure redress in our courts because another has failed to honor a promise, it must appear that the promisee assented to the obligation in question.

rule — protect autonomy

issue ?

It also follows that, before the power of law can be invoked to enforce a promise, it must be sufficiently certain and specific so that what was promised can be ascertained. Otherwise, a court, in intervening, would be imposing its own conception of what the parties should or might have undertaken, rather than confining itself to the implementation of a bargain to which they have mutually committed themselves. Thus, definiteness as to material matters is of the very essence in contract law. Impenetrable vagueness and uncertainty will not do. . . .

reasoning

Dictated by these principles, it is rightfully well settled in the common law of contracts in this State that a mere agreement to agree, in which a material term is left for future negotiations, is unenforceable. . . . This is especially true of the amount to be paid for the sale or lease of real property. . . . The rule applies all the more, and not the less, when, as here, the extraordinary remedy of specific performance is sought. . . .

holding

This is not to say that the requirement for definiteness in the case before us now could only have been met by explicit expression of the rent to be paid. The concern is with substance, not form. It certainly would have sufficed, for instance, if a methodology for determining the rent was to be found within the four corners of the lease, for a rent so arrived at would have been the end product of agreement between the parties themselves. Nor would the agreement have failed for indefiniteness because it invited recourse to an objective extrinsic event, condition or standard on which the amount was made to depend. All of these, *inter alia*, would have come within the embrace of the maxim that what can be made certain is certain (9 Coke 47a). . . .

But the renewal clause here in fact contains no such ingredients. Its unrevealing, unamplified language speaks to no more than "annual rentals to be agreed upon." Its simple words leave no room for legal construction or resolution of ambiguity. . . .

terms specifying intent must be reasonably clear

Finally, in this context, we note that the tenant's reliance on May Metropolitan Corp. v. May Oil Burner Corp. (290 NY 260) is misplaced. There the parties had executed a franchise agreement for the sale of oil burners. The contract provided for annual renewal, at which time each year's sales quota was "to be mutually agreed upon." In holding that the defendant's motion for summary judgment should have been denied, the court indicated that the plaintiff should be given an opportunity to establish that a series of annual renewals had ripened into a course of dealing from which it might be possible to give meaning to an otherwise uncertain term. This decision, in the more fluid sales setting in which it occurred, may be seen as a precursor to the subsequently enacted Uniform Commercial Code's treatment of open terms in contracts for the sale of goods (see Uniform Commercial Code, §1-205(1), §2-204(d)(3); see, also, Restatement, Contracts 2d, §249). As the tenant candidly concedes, the code, by its very terms, is limited to the sale of goods. The *May* case is therefore not applicable to real estate contracts. Stability is a hallmark of the law controlling such transactions. . . . *R F R*

. . .

For all these reasons, the order of the Appellate Division should be reversed, with costs, and the orders of the Supreme Court, Suffolk County, reinstated. . . . *disposition*

MEYER, J. (Concurring).

While I concur in the result because the facts of this case do not fit the rule of *May Metropolitan Corp. v. May Oil Burner Corp.* (290 NY 260), I cannot concur in the majority's rejection of that case as necessarily inapplicable to litigation concerning leases. That the setting of that case was commercial and that its principle is now incorporated in a statute (the Uniform Commercial Code) which by its terms is not applicable to real estate is irrelevant to the question whether the principle can be applied in real estate cases. . . .

To the extent that the majority opinion can be read as holding that no course of dealing between the parties to a lease could make a clause providing for renewal at a rental "to be agreed upon" enforceable I do not concur.

JASEN, J. (Dissenting in part).

While I recognize that the traditional rule is that a provision for renewal of a lease must be "certain" in order to render it binding and enforceable, in my view the better rule would be that if the tenant can establish its entitlement to renewal under the lease, the mere presence of a provision calling for renewal at "rentals to be agreed upon" should not prevent judicial intervention to fix rent at a reasonable rate in order to avoid a forfeiture. Therefore, I would affirm the order of the Appellate Division for the reasons stated in the opinion of Justice Leon D. Lazer at the Appellate Division.

Chief Judge COOKE and Judges GABRIELLI, JONES and WACHTLER concur with Judge FUCHSBERG; Judge MEYER concurs in a memorandum; Judge JASEN dissents in part and on defendant's appeal votes to affirm in a memorandum.

Problems

1. Infiniti and Beyond. D.P. McIllmoil owned a 1995 Infiniti G20 sedan that he wanted to sell in order to purchase a new Infiniti automobile. He went to Frawley Motor Company, which dealt in Infiniti automobiles of different models and prices. McIllmoil and Frawley both signed the following agreement: "McIll-moil agrees to purchase a new Infiniti car from Frawley. Frawley agrees to purchase McIllmoil's 1995 Infiniti G20, serial number 79293, for $1,000." Frawley paid McIllmoil $1,000 for his sedan, but McIllmoil refused to purchase a new Infiniti from Frawley. What result if Frawley sues?

2. A Ship Without Peer. Raffles agreed to sell to Wichelhaus cotton arriving in Liverpool, England, from Bombay, India, on the ship *Peerless*. There were two ships named *Peerless* bound from Bombay, but at materially different times; one was scheduled to leave in October, the other in December. The parties did not discuss time or the existence of more than one *Peerless*. Wichelhaus knew only of the first ship, and Raffles knew only of the second. When the second *Peerless* arrived in Liverpool, Wichelhaus refused to take possession of its cotton or pay the contract price, and Raffles brought suit for breach of contract. How should the court rule?

3. Facebook Friend Request. Cameron Winklevoss, Tyler Winklevoss, and Divya Narendra (the Winklevosses) sued Mark Zuckerberg and Facebook, Inc., claiming that Zuckerberg stole the idea for Facebook (the social networking web-site) from them. At the end of a day-long mediation with multiple attorneys present, the parties signed a handwritten, one-and-a-third-page "Term Sheet & Settlement Agreement." According to the document, the Winklevosses would sell their competing web site, ConnectU, to Facebook for a specified amount of cash and Facebook common stock, and "Facebook will determine the form & documentation of the acquisition of ConnectU's shares [] consistent with a stock and cash for stock acquisition." The document also claimed to be "binding" and purported to end all disputes between the parties. When the parties could not agree on the language in the 130 pages of the final deal documents, the Winkle-vosses claimed the Settlement Agreement was unenforceable because it lacked material terms, and Facebook sued to enforce it. How should the court rule?

4. The Employer E-mail. General Dynamics Government Systems Corpora-tion sent an e-mail announcement to its entire work force with the subject line "G. DeMuro—New Dispute Resolution Policy." The e-mail contained a page-long letter from General Dynamics President Gerard DeMuro informing employ-ees that the company had developed a new policy for resolving legal issues arising out of workplace disputes, and, that the policy now included arbitration. Two linked documents disclosed that the policy would take effect the next day for anyone who continued to work for General Dynamics and that arbitration would be the exclusive means of dispute resolution. The company's tracking system indicated that Roderick Campbell opened the e-mail two minutes after it was sent, but the system did not track whether Campbell opened the linked documents.

Campbell later sued General Dynamics in federal district court alleging disability discrimination, and General Dynamics moved to compel arbitration of Campbell's claim. Undisputed affidavits established the following facts: General Dynamics used e-mail regularly for company-wide communications; e-mail was the most widely used method of communication within the company; e-mails were sent to the work force under President DeMuro's signature only a few times a year and always concerned important matters; e-mail was not the usual method used by the company to handle personnel matters; and prior significant alterations to the employment relationship at the company were memorialized on paper and required a signature by the employee acknowledging notice. Does the arbitration provision constitute an element of Campbell's employment contract with General Dynamics?

5. The Bankruptcy Claim. Mesa Air Group held an unsecured claim for $35 million against Delta Airlines, then under bankruptcy protection. Steven Kleckner of APS Capital Corporation, which specialized in the purchase and resale of debts, spoke several times with Mesa's Chief Financial Officer about APS's buying Mesa's claim against Delta, and the two agreed that APS would purchase the claim for 58 percent of its $35 million face value. Kleckner immediately sent Mesa the following e-mail:

> Please allow this e-mail to serve as a preliminary confirmation of our Delta Airlines Inc. (the "Debtor") transaction with a trade date of April 20, 2007. You have verbally agreed to sell approximately $35,000,000.00 face amount ("Purchase Amount") general unsecured claims against the debtor at fifty eight cents on the dollar (or 58% of the Purchase Amount).
>
> Given the lateness of the hour here, I will follow-up on Monday with a formal written trade confirmation with customary terms that will memorialize the key terms of this transaction and provide for the negotiation and execution of a more extensive purchase-and-sale/assignment agreement.

On Monday, Kleckner sent Mesa a "draft formal transaction confirmation" that included, in addition to the stated price and description of the assets, a variety of other terms, including a condition of closure that APS identify a third-party buyer for the asset. Mesa objected to several of the terms and proposed its own set of terms. Eventually, APS indicated it would not continue with the transaction, and Mesa sued for breach of contract. Both sides filed motions for summary judgment. How should the court rule?

2. Offer

Mutual assent is sometimes indicated simultaneously, such as when two (or more) parties indicate their assent to the terms of a transaction by signing a detailed written agreement at the same moment. When communication is sequential, however, mutual assent usually takes the form of an "offer" made by one party paired with an "acceptance" provided by another. We begin by considering what communications satisfy the legal definition of an offer, and then we take up the complementary topic of acceptance.

According to the Restatement, an offer is "the manifestation of willingness to enter into a bargain, so made as to justify another person in understanding that his assent to that bargain is invited and will conclude it." Rest. (2d) Contracts §24. Viewed slightly differently, an offer is a promise to provide a specified performance, conditional on the offeree assenting to the terms proposed. Particular words or actions are not determinative of the existence of an offer. Instead, determining whether an offer has been made depends on a global analysis, not only of the words stated but also of their context, including the nature of the communication and any preexisting relationship between the parties.

In the following set of cases, courts grapple with whether common types of communication establish the manifestation of commitment necessary to constitute offers, or are instead merely invitations to negotiate. *Interstate Industries, Inc. v. Barclay Industries, Inc.* and *Nordyne, Inc. v. International Controls & Measurements Corporation* deal with price quotations; *Craft v. Elder & Johnston Company* and *Lefkowitz v. Great Minneapolis Surplus Store, Inc.* concern advertisements; and *Consolidated Freightways Corp. of Delaware v. Williams* addresses reward postings. The final two cases, *Leonard v. Pepsico, Inc.* and *Harris v. Time, Inc.,* bring together several of the issues considered in this section and the previous section. Pay careful attention to what features of the communications and the surrounding circumstances the courts consider relevant to the "offer" inquiry, and how much weight they appear to place on various facts.

INTERSTATE INDUSTRIES, INC.
v.
BARCLAY INDUSTRIES, INC.

U.S. Court of Appeals, Seventh Circuit
540 F.2d 868
1976

SPRECHER, J.

I

This diversity action was commenced by Interstate Industries, Inc. (Interstate), plaintiff-appellee, to recover damages from Barclay Industries, Inc. (Barclay), defendant-appellant, for breach of an alleged contract.

. . .

Over a five year period Interstate was involved in numerous business transactions with Barclay in which goods manufactured by Barclay were delivered in Interstate's facility in Michigan City, Indiana. On August 23, 1973, Barclay sent a letter from its offices in Lodi, New Jersey advising Interstate that it would be able to manufacture fiberglass panels in accordance with certain specified standards. The letter included the prices Barclay would charge for manufacturing the panels and expressly stated that the "price quotation is based on orders of 75,000 sq. ft. or more (truckload quantities) freight prepaid. Order less than 75,000 sq. ft. add $.01/sq. ft., F.O.B. Lodi." In November, Interstate mailed two purchase orders to

Barclay's New Jersey office with "F.O.B. Delvd." notations in the upper right hand corners. On January 16, 1974, Barclay sent a letter from its New Jersey office informing Interstate that it would be unable to provide the panels requested in the purchase orders.

In April 1975, Interstate filed a complaint against Barclay for breach of contract in the United States District Court for the Northern District of Indiana basing subject matter jurisdiction upon diversity of citizenship. Process was served on Barclay by certified mail at Lodi, New Jersey.

Barclay filed a motion to dismiss the complaint or in the alternative to quash the return of service on the ground that the court lacked personal jurisdiction over Barclay. On August 15, 1975, the motion was denied. Barclay then filed a motion requesting the district court to reconsider its August order or to grant Barclay permission to take an interlocutory appeal pursuant to 28 U.S.C. §1292(b). On October 3, 1975, the district court denied Barclay's motion to reconsider the August order but granted it permission to file an interlocutory appeal. Shortly thereafter, by order of this court, Barclay was permitted to appeal the October order of the district court.

[handwritten: appeal before all initial claims are settled]

II

We shall first review the order and memorandum of August 15, 1975 denying Barclay's motion to dismiss or in the alternative quash service of the summons. The district court utilized Indiana Trial Rule 4.4 to determine whether it had personal jurisdiction over Barclay. . . .

After reviewing the pleadings and affidavits, the district court found that Interstate's complaint alleged the existence of a contract "to supply . . . goods or materials to be furnished . . ." in Indiana. Thus, the court concluded that it had personal jurisdiction over Barclay pursuant to Trial Rule 4.4(A)(1). Furthermore, the court reasoned that since Barclay had sufficient minimum contacts with Indiana, exercising personal jurisdiction would not violate the due process clause of the Fourteenth Amendment. . . .

In order to decide whether the district court had personal jurisdiction over the defendant, we must consider whether the correspondence between the parties constituted an enforceable contract to deliver goods in Indiana. *[handwritten: issue]*

According to Section 2-204 of the Uniform Commercial Code:

> (1) A contract for sale of goods may be made in any manner sufficient *to show agreement*, including conduct by both parties which recognizes the existence of such a contract.
> (2) An agreement sufficient to constitute a contract for sale may be found even though the moment of its making is undetermined.
> (3) Even though one or more terms are left open a contract for sale does not fail for indefiniteness if *the parties have intended to make a contract* and there is a reasonably certain basis for giving an appropriate remedy. (Citations omitted, emphasis added.)

[handwritten: rule]

To form a contract then, it is necessary to show agreement or a meeting of the minds. Restatement of Contracts §20 (1932), in part provides: "A manifestation of mutual assent by the parties to an informal contract is essential to its formation and the acts by which such assent is manifested must be done with the intent to do those acts; . . ."

. . .

The first step toward mutual assent in the formation of a contract is an offer by one of the parties. As the Restatement of Contracts §22 (1932) states: "The manifestation of mutual assent almost invariably takes the form of an offer or proposal by one party accepted by the other party or parties." An offer is defined as "a promise which is in its terms conditional upon an act, forbearance or return promise being given in exchange for the promise or its performance." Restatement of Contracts §24 (1932).

In the instant case the district court characterized Barclay's August letter which informed Interstate of the cost of manufacturing the fiberglass panels as an offer. Because the Uniform Commercial Code provides no guidelines as to when a communication will constitute an offer, we must look to case law and other authorities for guidance. Specifically, we must decide whether the price quotation constituted an offer or an invitation to make an offer.

As Judge Sparks indicated in R.E. Crummer & Co. v. Nuveen, 147 F.2d 3, 5 (7th Cir. 1945), citing 12 Am. Jur. Contracts §§28, 29 (1938), the distinction between when a price quotation constitutes an offer rather than an invitation to make an offer is critical:

> . . . A general offer must be distinguished from a general invitation to make an offer. . . . A mere quotation of price must be distinguished from an offer. From the nature of the subject, the question whether certain acts or conduct constitute a definite proposal upon which a binding contract may be predicated without any further action on the part of the person from whom it proceeds or a mere preliminary step which is not susceptible, without further action by such party, of being converted into a binding contract depends upon the nature of the particular acts or conduct in question and the circumstances attending the transaction. It is impossible to formulate a general principle or criterion for its determination. Accordingly, whether a communication naming a price is a quotation or an offer depends upon the intention of the owner as it is manifested by the facts and circumstances of each particular case. . . .

[Other cited cases omitted.] These cases are closely aligned with the principals and comments enumerated in Restatement of Contracts §25 (1932): "If from a promise, or manifestation of intention, or from the circumstances existing at the time, the person to whom the promise or manifestation is addressed knows or has reason to know that the person making it does not intend it as an expression of his fixed purpose until he has given a further expression of assent, he has not made an offer."

> It is often difficult to draw an exact line between offers and negotiations preliminary thereto. It is common for one who wishes to make a bargain to try to induce the other party to the intended transaction to make the definite offer, he himself suggesting with more or less definiteness the nature of the contract he is willing to enter into. Besides any direct

language indicating an intent to defer the formation of a contract, the definiteness or indefiniteness of the words used in opening the negotiation must be considered, as well as the usages of business, and indeed all accompanying circumstances. (Comment a.)

. . .

With these principles in mind, we turn to Barclay's letter containing the price quotations. It is not disputed that the letter: (1) advised Interstate of the availability; (2) specifically referred to its contents as a "price quotation"; (3) contained no language which indicated that an offer was being made; and (4) failed to mention the quantity, the time of delivery or payment terms. Under these circumstances, we are compelled to find that Barclay's letter did not constitute an offer. Consequently, the contract to supply goods to be furnished in Indiana that was alleged in Interstate's complaint did not exist and there was no basis for personal jurisdiction over the defendant. Nor are we persuaded by plaintiff's assertion that the court had personal jurisdiction over the defendant because it was "doing business" in Indiana. Because the district court did not find in either of its orders or memoranda that jurisdiction over Barclay could be maintained pursuant to Trial Rule 4.4(A)(1), but rather focused on the provisions concerning "goods to be supplied in the state," that question is not before the court. Thus, we shall not give further consideration to this issue.

Finally, having decided that the court lacked jurisdiction over the defendant, the issue of due process has become moot.

Accordingly, the judgment of the district court is vacated and remanded to the district court for further proceedings consistent with this opinion.

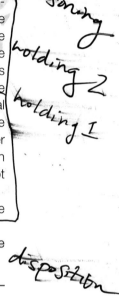

NORDYNE, INC.
v.
INTERNATIONAL CONTROLS & MEASUREMENTS CORP.

U.S. Court of Appeals, Eighth Circuit
262 F.3d 843
2001

ARNOLD, J.

. . .

Nordyne had purchased control boards from ICM for approximately ten years. . . . In 1997, ICM began marketing a new version of the control panel Nordyne had been purchasing. ICM sent the first quotation for this product to Nordyne on May 13, 1997. Upon Nordyne's determination that one of the new features was not necessary for its purposes, ICM modified the control panel, and on July 29, 1997, tendered a new quotation for the unit as modified. This quotation was for Nordyne's estimated annual usage of 40,000 units at $9.87 per unit. The quotation provided that it was valid until December 31, 1997, that "[b]lanket orders must be fully released within one year," that standard commercial packaging would apply, that shipment would be "net 30 days; FOB Syracuse, NY," and that all orders were non-cancelable and non-returnable.

. . .

Nordyne asked to see manufactured samples of the new control panel. On September 12, 1997, ICM sent five such samples to Nordyne with a letter from ICM's home office stating, "Full blown manufacturing of this device is awaiting your sign off of these check samples as approved for production. Please review the samples and 'sign off' this document and send it back by return fax so that we may fulfill your production requirements in a timely manner." On September 15, Nordyne signed [the document].

. . .

Nordyne argues that . . . the July 1997 quotation did not amount to an offer because (1) it was not for immediate acceptance, . . . was subject to . . . ICM's providing acceptable samples, and (2) it did not specify quantity and did not include a delivery schedule.

. . .

Under Missouri case law, an "offer is made when the offer leads the offeree to reasonably believe that an offer has been made." *Id.* The Restatement (Second) of Contracts §24 defines offer as "the manifestation of willingness to enter into a bargain, so made as to justify another person in understanding that his assent to that bargain is invited and will conclude it." The general rule is that a price quotation, such as one appearing in a catalogue or on a flyer, is not an offer, but is rather a suggestion to induce offers by others. However, a price quotation, "if detailed enough, can amount to an offer creating the power of acceptance; to do so it must reasonably appear from the price quote that assent to the quote is all that is needed to ripen the offer into a contract." *Id.;* see also *The Boese-Hilburn Co. v. Dean Machinery Co.,* 616 S.W.2d 520, 524 (Mo. App. 1981). Factors relevant in determining whether a price quotation is an offer include the extent of prior inquiry, the completeness of the terms of the suggested bargain, and the number of persons to whom the price quotation is communicated. Restatement (Second) of Contracts §26, comment *c.*

Here all factors weigh in ICM's favor. ICM and Nordyne had been communicating for several months regarding the contract at issue before the July 29, 1997, quotation was sent, this quotation was sent only to Nordyne, and the quotation included quantity, price, and time in which to accept, as well as packaging, shipping, and payment terms. We note that the quotation was for a product specifically designed for Nordyne. We find Nordyne's argument that the quotation was not an offer because it did not contain a delivery schedule to be without merit.

. . .

We also reject Nordyne's argument that the quotation could not be the offer because the quantity was not definite. The quoted price-per-unit was based on Nordyne's own estimated annual usage of 40,000 units. Once Nordyne signed the production approval, we believe it was bound to purchase approximately this many units, just as ICM was bound to provide them at the quoted price.

CRAFT — P
v.
ELDER & JOHNSTON CO. D

Court of Appeals of Ohio, Second District, Montgomery County
38 N.E.2d 416
1941

BARNES, J.

On or about January 31, 1940, the defendant, the Elder & Johnston Company, carried an advertisement in the Dayton Shopping News, an offer for sale of a certain all electric sewing machine for the sum of $26 as a "Thursday Only Special." Plaintiff in her petition, after certain formal allegations, sets out the substance of the above advertisement carried by defendant in the Dayton Shopping News. She further alleges that the above publication is an advertising paper distributed in Montgomery County and throughout the city of Dayton; that on Thursday, February 1, 1940, she tendered to the defendant company $26 in payment for one of the machines offered in the advertisement, but that defendant refused to fulfill the offer and has continued to so refuse. The petition further alleges that the value of the machine offered was $175 and she asks damages in the sum of $149 plus interest from February 1, 1940.

. . .

The particular advertisement set forth on page 9 of the publication can not be reproduced in this opinion, but may be described as containing a cut of the machine and other printed matter including the price of $26 and all conforming substantially to the allegations of the petition.

The trial court dismissed plaintiff's petition as evidenced by a journal entry, the pertinent portion of which reads as follows: "Upon consideration the court finds that said advertisement was not an offer which could be accepted by plaintiff to form a contract, and this case is therefore dismissed with prejudice to a new action, at costs of plaintiff."

. . .

From the cases cited in connection with our own independent investigation, we find that very generally courts hold against liability under offers made through advertisements. Very generally in these cases the courts base their findings upon theories quite different from our analysis. With all due respect to the pronouncements of able jurists, we are not impressed with these theories.

We will now briefly make reference to some of the authorities.

"It is clear that in the absence of special circumstances an ordinary newspaper advertisement is not an offer, but is an offer to negotiate—an offer to receive offers—or, as it is sometimes called, an offer to chaffer." Restatement of the Law of Contracts, Par. 25, Page 31.

Under the above paragraph the following illustration is given, "A, a clothing merchant, advertises overcoats of a certain kind for sale at $50. This is not an offer but an invitation to the public to come and purchase."

"Thus, if goods are advertised for sale at a certain price, it is not an offer and no contract is formed by the statement of an intending purchaser that he will take a specified quantity of the goods at that price. The construction is rather favored that such an advertisement is a mere invitation to enter into a bargain rather than an offer. So a published price list is not an offer to sell the goods listed at the published price." Williston on Contracts, Revised Edition, Vol. 1, Par. 27, Page 54.

"The commonest example of offers meant to open negotiations and to call forth offers in the technical sense are advertisements, circulars and trade letters sent out by business houses. While it is possible that the offers made by such means may be in such form as to become contracts, they are often merely expressions of a willingness to negotiate." Page on the Law Contracts, 2d Ed., Vol. 1, Page 112, Par. 84.

"Business advertisements published in newspapers and circulars sent out by mail or distributed by hand stating that the advertiser has a certain quantity or quality of goods which he wants to dispose of at certain prices, are not offers which become contracts as soon as any person to whose notice they may come signifies his acceptance by notifying the other that he will take a certain quantity of them. They are merely invitations to all persons who may read them that the advertiser is ready to receive offers for the goods at the price stated." 13 Corpus Juris 289, Par. 97.

"But generally a newspaper advertisement or circular couched in general language and proper to be sent to all persons interested in a particular trade or business, or a prospectus of a general and descriptive nature, will be construed as an invitation to make an offer." 17 Corpus Juris Secundum, Contracts, page 389, §46, Column 2.

. . .

We are constrained to the view that the trial court committed no prejudicial error in dismissing plaintiff's petition.

The judgment of the trial court will be affirmed and costs adjudged against the plaintiff-appellant.

LEFKOWITZ
v.
GREAT MINNEAPOLIS SURPLUS STORE, INC.
Supreme Court of Minnesota
251 Minn. 188
1957

Murphy, J.

This is an appeal from an order of the Municipal Court of Minneapolis denying the motion of the defendant for amended findings of fact, or, in the alternative, for a new trial. The order for judgment awarded the plaintiff the sum of $138.50 as damages for breach of contract.

This case grows out of the alleged refusal of the defendant, Great Minneapolis Surplus Store, to sell to the plaintiff, Morris Lefkowitz, a certain fur piece which it had offered for sale in a newspaper advertisement. It appears from the record that on April 6, 1956, the defendant published the following advertisement in a Minneapolis newspaper:

"Saturday 9 A.M.. Sharp 3 Brand New Fur Coats Worth to $100.00
First Come First Served $1 Each"

On April 13, the defendant again published an advertisement in the same newspaper as follows:

"Saturday 9 A.M.. 2 Brand New Pastel Mink 3-Skin Scarfs
Selling for $89.50
Out they go Saturday. Each . . . $1.00
1 Black Lapin Stole Beautiful, worth $139.50 . . . $1.00
First Come First Served"

The record supports the findings of the court that on each of the Saturdays following the publication of the above-described ads the plaintiff was the first to present himself at the appropriate counter in the defendant's store and on each occasion demanded the coat and the stole so advertised and indicated his readiness to pay the sale price of $1. On both occasions, the defendant refused to sell the merchandise to the plaintiff, stating on the first occasion that by a "house rule" the offer was intended for women only and sales would not be made to men, and on the second visit that plaintiff knew defendant's house rules.

The trial court properly disallowed plaintiff's claim for the value of the fur coats since the value of these articles was speculative and uncertain. The only evidence of value was the advertisement itself to the effect that the coats were "Worth to $100.00," how much less being speculative especially in view of the price for which they were offered for sale. With reference to the offer of the defendant on April 13, 1956, to sell the "1 Black Lapin Stole * * * worth $139.50 * * *" the trial court held that the value of this article was established and granted judgment in favor of the plaintiff for that amount less the $1 quoted purchase price.

1. The defendant contends that a newspaper advertisement offering items of mer-chandise for sale at a named price is a "unilateral offer" which may be withdrawn without notice. He relies upon authorities which hold that, where an advertiser pub-lishes in a newspaper that he has a certain quantity or quality of goods which he wants to dispose of at certain prices and on certain terms, such advertisements are not offers which become contracts as soon as any person to whose notice they may come signifies his acceptance by notifying the other that he will take a certain quantity of them. Such advertisements have been construed as an invitation for an offer of sale on the terms stated, which offer, when received, may be accepted or rejected and which therefore does not become a contract of sale until accepted by the seller; and until a contract has been so made, the seller may modify or revoke such prices or terms. . . .

The defendant relies principally on Craft v. Elder & Johnston Co. In that case, the court discussed the legal effect of an advertisement offering for sale, as a one-day special, an electric sewing machine at a named price. . . .

The test of whether a binding obligation may originate in advertisements addressed to the general public is "whether the facts show that some performance was promised in positive terms in return for something requested." 1 Williston, Contracts (Rev. ed.) §27.

The authorities emphasize that, where the offer is clear, definite, and explicit, and leaves nothing open for negotiation, it constitutes an offer, acceptance of which will complete the contract. The most recent case on the subject is Johnson v. Capital City Ford Co., La. App., 85 So. 2d 75, in which the court pointed out that a newspaper advertisement relating to the purchase and sale of automobiles may constitute an offer, acceptance of which will consummate a contract and create an obligation in the offeror to perform according to the terms of the published offer.

Whether in any individual instance a newspaper advertisement is an offer rather than an invitation to make an offer depends on the legal intention of the parties and the surrounding circumstances. . . . We are of the view on the facts before us that the offer by the defendant of the sale of the Lapin fur was clear, definite, and explicit, and left nothing open for negotiation. The plaintiff having successful managed to be the first one to appear at the seller's place of business to be served, as requested by the advertisement, and having offered the stated purchase price of the article, he was entitled to performance on the part of the defendant. We think the trial court was correct in holding that there was in the conduct of the parties a sufficient mutuality of obligation to constitute a contract of sale.

2. The defendant contends that the offer was modified by a "house rule" to the effect that only women were qualified to receive the bargains advertised. The advertisement contained no such restriction. This objection may be disposed of briefly by stating that, while an advertiser has the right at any time before acceptance to modify his offer, he does not have the right, after acceptance, to impose new or arbitrary conditions not contained in the published offer. . . .

Affirmed.

CONSOLIDATED FREIGHTWAYS CORP. OF DELAWARE
v.
WILLIAMS

Court of Appeals of Georgia, Division No. 1
139 Ga. App. 302
1976

STOLZ, J.

This is an action by an employee against his employer to recover a reward, offered by the employer, for having furnished information leading to the arrest and conviction of an individual found stealing property from the employer. The reward sign, posted at the defendant's terminal in Fulton County, read as follows: "Up to $5,000 reward is being offered by Consolidated Freightways for information leading to the arrest and conviction of any individual found stealing or concealing freight or other property from Consolidated Freightways. We feel that all employees should be trusted. However, a dishonorable act on the part of one individual can cast suspicion on the rest of us. It is our firm intention to quickly apprehend and prosecute any dishonorable person who may appear among us. All information will be held in strict confidence. Call Collect—CF Security Office—503-227-2561 Ext. 252 or contact your supervisor or terminal manager."

The defendant appeals from the verdict and Judgment for the plaintiff for $5,000.

1. The denials of the defendant's motions for a directed verdict were not error. Following are substantially the defendant-appellant's contentions and our rulings thereon.

That the reward was not offered to the plaintiff, who was a supervisor, as is illustrated by the fact that the sign indicated that the acceptor should contact his supervisor. "The construction which will uphold a contract in whole and in every part is to be preferred, and the whole contract should be looked to in arriving at the construction of any part." Code §20-704(4). The general wording of the reward offer indicates that it is directed to the employees generally, e.g., ". . . all employees should be trusted . . . a dishonorable act on the part of one individual can cast suspicion on the rest of us. It is our firm intention to quickly apprehend and prosecute any dishonorable person who may appear among us . . . contact your supervisor. . . ." The instruction to "contact your supervisor" did not necessarily exclude supervisors as offerees; the evidence showed that many of the defendant's supervisors also had supervisors over them, which would exclude a large part of the employees under that construction. Furthermore, the alternative instruction, "or terminal manager," might apply to supervisors who accept and act on the offer.

With all of the English language at its command, the employer-offeror did not explicitly limit the offer to any particular class of persons. "The intention of the parties may differ among themselves. In such case, the meaning placed on the contract by one party, and known to [b]e thus understood by the other party, at the time, shall be held as the true meaning." Code §20-704(3). Although the defendant introduced some evidence that it had never paid a reward to a supervisor, and evidence which might indicate that the plaintiff knew this, the jury was authorized to believe the plaintiff's testimony that he knew of no such policy or understanding.

"If the construction is doubtful, that which goes most strongly against the party executing the instrument, or undertaking the obligation, is generally to be preferred." Code §20-704 "This undertaking must be construed in light of the substantial purpose which influenced the parties to enter into the contract in the first place, . . . and the surrounding circumstances may be looked to in determining the intention of the parties to the contract, and where the terms of the contract will permit it should be given a construction which will advance its beneficial purpose." *Orkin Exterminating Co. v. Buchanan*, 108 Ga. App. 449.

Although some of the above is applicable to bilateral contracts, i[t] can also be applied in construing this unilateral contract offer. "General offers of a reward or money payment are frequently made by publication, requesting or inviting the doing of some non-promissory act such as the return of a lost article, the giving of information, the arrest of a fugitive, the use of a medicine, the winning of a contest, . . . the advance of goods or money to a third person. In these cases, the act is both the acceptance and the only subject of agreed exchange to be received by the offeror. Unless otherwise specified in the offer, no notice of acceptance by the offeree is necessary; his act is enough." Corbin on Contracts (One volume ed.), §70, at 114.

. . .

The surrounding circumstances here were that the employer offeror was losing thousands of dollars worth of property by theft. The beneficial purpose of the reward offer was to curb this theft. This purpose could be better served by broadening the offer to include all employees. While some employees, including those in supervisory positions, might report observed thefts out of a sense of loyalty to their employer, or civic or moral duty, the monetary offer added a stronger incentive for both supervisory and non-supervisory employees.

That the testimony showed that the plaintiff-employee did not rely on the offer at the time he performed the acts necessary to observe and detect the thief. Although the plaintiff testified that he was not thinking specifically about the reward while attempting to observe the theft, the evidence showed that he was well aware of the reward offer sign and had every reason to believe that he was eligible for it by his acts of acceptance.

> "Ordinarily the motive that induces one to offer a reward is his desire to procure the performance that he requests. Ordinarily, also, the motive that induces someone to render the requested performance is his desire for the reward that he knows has been offered. Even in the case of the offeror, however, his desire for the performance may not be his sole motive; and in the case of an acceptor, the requested service may be rendered from motives wholly other than a desire for the offered reward. . . . In any case, it is certain that in rendering a requested performance it is not necessary that the sole motive of the offeree shall be his desire for the offered reward. It need not even be his principal or prevailing motive. The motivating causes of human action are always complex and are frequently not clearly thought out or expressed by the actor himself. This being true, it is desirable that not much weight should be given to the motives of an offeree and that no dogmatic requirement should be embodied in a stated rule of law." Corbin, op. cit., §58, at 91, 93.

The defendant-employer, having received the benefit of the plaintiff's acceptance of its offer, cannot be heard to assert the technicality of a requirement that the offer be accepted with absolute and exclusive reliance thereon at the time.

That the reward "contract" or offer was too indefinite to be enforceable in that it offered merely "up to $5,000," and that there was no value of the acceptance shown on which to base a recovery under quantum meruit. Had the defendant-offeror tendered the plaintiff-acceptor any amount of reward, it might be heard to make this objection. Absent such a tender, however, the plaintiff was justified in seeking the maximum amount offered, and there was sufficient evidence of the amounts of the theft losses to authorize the award of this maximum amount.

That there was no consideration flowing to the defendant-employer since the plaintiff-employee's scope of employment allegedly included the duty of reporting thefts coming under his observation. The plaintiff testified that there was nothing in the defendant's manual that gives the duties of every employee "from terminal man on down." "Whether or not the servant was acting within the scope of his employment . . . is usually a jury question." A-1 Bonding Service v. Hunter, 125 Ga. App. 173. Furthermore, even if there was an explicit or implicit duty on the part of the plaintiff to report any observed thefts in his work area, and although his observations were made during his normal working hours, the plaintiff had someone temporarily assume his duties as dock foreman while he hid out of sight in a trailer, in order to observe unseen. This was above and beyond his routine duty of observing incidents of theft, and was his own idea, according to the plaintiff's testimony.

The evidence authorized the finding that the plaintiff was eligible to accept the defendant's reward offer and that he fully complied with all of its conditions. Enumerated errors . . . are without merit. . . .

The verdict and judgment were not error for any reason contended.

Judgment affirmed.

BELL, C.J., and CLARK, J., concur.

LEONARD
v.
PEPSICO, INC.
U.S. District Court, S.D.N.Y.
88 F. Supp. 2d 116
1999

K. WOOD, J.

Plaintiff brought this action seeking, among other things, specific performance of an alleged offer of a Harrier Jet, featured in a television advertisement for defendant's "Pepsi Stuff" promotion. Defendant has moved for summary judgment pursuant to Federal Rule of Civil Procedure 56. For the reasons stated below, defendant's motion is granted.

I. BACKGROUND

This case arises out of a promotional campaign conducted by defendant, the producer and distributor of the soft drinks Pepsi and Diet Pepsi. The promotion, entitled "Pepsi Stuff," encouraged consumers to collect "Pepsi Points" from specially marked packages of Pepsi or Diet Pepsi and redeem these points for merchandise featuring the Pepsi logo. Before introducing the promotion nationally, defendant conducted a test of the promotion in the Pacific Northwest from October 1995 to March 1996. A Pepsi Stuff catalog was distributed to consumers in the test market, including Washington State. Plaintiff is a resident of Seattle, Washington. While living in Seattle, plaintiff saw the Pepsi Stuff commercial that he contends constituted an offer of a Harrier Jet.

A. The Alleged Offer

Because whether the television commercial constituted an offer is the central question in this case, the Court will describe the commercial in detail. The commercial opens upon an idyllic, suburban morning, where the chirping of birds in sun-dappled trees welcomes a paperboy on his morning route. As the newspaper hits the stoop of a conventional two-story house, the tattoo of a military drum introduces the subtitle, "MONDAY 7:58 AM." The stirring strains of a martial air mark the appearance of a well-coiffed teenager preparing to leave for school, dressed in a shirt emblazoned with the Pepsi logo, a red-white-and-blue ball. While the teenager confidently preens, the military drumroll again sounds as the subtitle "T-SHIRT 75 PEPSI POINTS" scrolls across the screen. Bursting from his room, the teenager strides down the hallway wearing a leather jacket. The drumroll sounds again, as the subtitle "LEATHER JACKET 1450 PEPSI POINTS" appears. The teenager opens the door of his house and, unfazed by the glare of the early morning sunshine, puts on a pair of sunglasses. The drumroll then accompanies the subtitle "SHADES 175 PEPSI POINTS." A voiceover then intones, "Introducing the new Pepsi Stuff catalog," as the camera focuses on the cover of the catalog.

The scene then shifts to three young boys sitting in front of a high school building. The boy in the middle is intent on his Pepsi Stuff Catalog, while the boys on either side are each drinking Pepsi. The three boys gaze in awe at an object rushing overhead, as the military march builds to a crescendo. The Harrier Jet is not yet visible, but the observer senses the presence of a mighty plane as the extreme winds generated by its flight create a paper maelstrom in a classroom devoted to an otherwise dull physics lesson. Finally, the Harrier Jet swings into view and lands by the side of the school building, next to a bicycle rack. Several students run for cover, and the velocity of the wind strips one hapless faculty member down to his underwear. While the faculty member is being deprived of his dignity, the voiceover announces: "Now the more Pepsi you drink, the more great stuff you're gonna get."

The teenager opens the cockpit of the fighter and can be seen, helmetless, holding a Pepsi. "[L]ooking very pleased with himself," (Plaintiff's Memorandum at 3) the teenager exclaims, "Sure beats the bus," and chortles. The military drumroll sounds a final time, as the following words appear: "HARRIER FIGHTER 7,000,000 PEPSI POINTS." A few seconds later, the following appears in more stylized script: "Drink Pepsi—Get Stuff." With that message, the music and the commercial end with a triumphant flourish.

Inspired by this commercial, plaintiff set out to obtain a Harrier Jet. Plaintiff explains that he is "typical of the 'Pepsi Generation' . . . he is young, has an adventurous spirit, and the notion of obtaining a Harrier Jet appealed to him enormously." Plaintiff consulted the Pepsi Stuff Catalog. The Catalog specifies the number of Pepsi Points required to obtain promotional merchandise. The Catalog includes an Order Form which lists, on one side, fifty-three items of Pepsi Stuff merchandise redeemable for Pepsi Points. Conspicuously absent from the Order Form is any entry or description of a Harrier Jet. The amount of Pepsi Points required to obtain the listed merchandise ranges from 15 (for a "Jacket Tattoo" ("Sew 'em on your jacket, not your arm.")) to 3300 (for a "Fila Mountain Bike" ("Rugged. All-terrain. Exclusively for Pepsi.")). It should be noted that plaintiff objects to the implication that because an item was not shown in the Catalog, it was unavailable.

The rear foldout pages of the Catalog contain directions for redeeming Pepsi Points for merchandise. These directions note that merchandise may be ordered "only" with the original Order Form. The Catalog notes that in the event that a consumer lacks enough Pepsi Points to obtain a desired item, additional Pepsi Points may be purchased for ten cents each; however, at least fifteen original Pepsi Points must accompany each order

Although plaintiff initially set out to collect 7,000,000 Pepsi Points by consuming Pepsi products, it soon became clear to him that he "would not be able to buy (let alone drink) enough Pepsi to collect the necessary Pepsi Points fast enough." Reevaluating his strategy, plaintiff "focused for the first time on the packaging materials in the Pepsi Stuff promotion," and realized that buying Pepsi Points would be a more promising option. Through acquaintances, plaintiff ultimately raised about $700,000.

B. Plaintiff's Efforts to Redeem the Alleged Offer

On or about March 27, 1996, plaintiff submitted an Order Form, fifteen original Pepsi Points, and a check for $700,008.50. Plaintiff appears to have been represented by counsel at the time he mailed his check; the check is drawn on an account of plaintiff's first set of attorneys. At the bottom of the Order Form, plaintiff wrote in "1 Harrier Jet" in the "Item" column and "7,000,000" in the "Total Points" column. In a letter accompanying his submission, plaintiff stated that the check was to purchase additional Pepsi Points "expressly for obtaining a new Harrier jet as advertised in your Pepsi Stuff commercial."

. . .

This letter was apparently sent onward to the advertising company responsible for the actual commercial, BBDO. In a letter dated May 30, 1996, BBDO explained to plaintiff that: "I find it hard to believe that you are of the opinion that the Pepsi Stuff commercial ("Commercial") really offers a new Harrier Jet. The use of the Jet was clearly a joke that was meant to make the Commercial more humorous and entertaining. In my opinion, no reasonable person would agree with your analysis of the Commercial."

. . .

II. DISCUSSION

A. The Legal Framework

1. Standard for Summary Judgment

. . . To prevail on a motion for summary judgment, the moving party therefore must show that there are no such genuine issues of material fact to be tried, and that he or she is entitled to judgment as a matter of law. See Fed. R. Civ. P. 56(c); Celotex Corp. v. Catrett, 477 U.S. 317 (1986). . . .

. . . Although a court considering a motion for summary judgment must view all evidence in the light most favorable to the non-moving party, and must draw all reasonable inferences in that party's favor, . . . the nonmoving party "must do more than simply show that there is some metaphysical doubt as to the material facts." Matsushita Elec. Indus. Co. v. Zenith Radio Corp., 475 U.S. 574 (1986). If, based on the submissions to the court, no rational fact-finder could find in the non-movant's favor, there is no genuine issue of material fact, and summary judgment is appropriate. See Anderson [v. Liberty Lobby], 477 U.S. [242,] at 250 [(1986)].

The question of whether or not a contract was formed is appropriate for resolution on summary judgment. "Summary judgment is proper when the 'words and actions that allegedly formed a contract [are] so clear themselves that reasonable people could not differ over their meaning.'" . . .

. . .

B. Defendant's Advertisement Was Not an Offer

1. Advertisements as Offers

The general rule is that an advertisement does not constitute an offer. The Restatement (Second) of Contracts explains that:

> Advertisements of goods by display, sign, handbill, newspaper, radio or television are not ordinarily intended or understood as offers to sell. The same is true of catalogues, price lists and circulars, even though the terms of suggested bargains may be stated in some detail. It is of course possible to make an offer by an advertisement directed to the general public (see §29), but there must ordinarily be some language of commitment or some invitation to take action without further communication.

Restatement (Second) Contracts §26 cmt. b (1979). . . .

The exception to the rule that advertisements do not create any power of acceptance in potential offerees is where the advertisement is "clear, definite, and explicit, and leaves nothing open for negotiation," in that circumstance, "it constitutes an offer, acceptance of which will complete the contract." Lefkowitz v. Great Minneapolis Surplus Store. . . .

The present case is distinguishable from *Lefkowitz*. First, the commercial cannot be regarded in itself as sufficiently definite, because it specifically reserved the details of the offer to a separate writing, the Catalog. The commercial itself made no mention of the steps a potential offeree would be required to take to accept the alleged offer of a Harrier Jet. The advertisement in *Lefkowitz*, in contrast, "identified the person who could accept." Corbin, supra, §2.4, at 119. . . . Second, even if the Catalog had included a Harrier Jet among the items that could be obtained by redemption of Pepsi Points, the advertisement of a Harrier Jet by both television commercial and catalog would still not constitute an offer . . . [T]he absence of any words of limitation such as "first come, first served," renders the alleged offer sufficiently indefinite that no contract could be formed. . . . "A customer would not usually have reason to believe that the shopkeeper intended exposure to the risk of a multitude of acceptances resulting in a number of contracts exceeding the shopkeeper's inventory." Farnsworth, supra, at 242. There was no such danger in *Lefkowitz*, owing to the limitation "first come, first served."

The Court finds, in sum, that the Harrier Jet commercial was merely an advertisement.

2. Rewards as Offers

In opposing the present motion, plaintiff largely relies on a different species of unilateral offer, involving public offers of a reward for performance of a specified act. Because these cases generally involve public declarations regarding the efficacy or trustworthiness of specific products, one court has aptly characterized these authorities as "prove me wrong" cases. . . . The most venerable of these precedents is the case of Carlill v. Carbolic Smoke Ball Co. (Court of Appeal, 1892), a quote from which heads plaintiff's memorandum of law: "[I]f a person chooses to make extravagant promises . . . he probably does so because it pays him to make them, and, if he has made them, the extravagance of the promises is no reason in law why he should not be bound by them." *Carbolic Smoke Ball*, 1 Q.B. at 268 (Bowen, L.J.).

Long a staple of law school curricula, *Carbolic Smoke Ball* owes its fame not merely to "the comic and slightly mysterious object involved," A.W. Brian Simplson, Quackery and Contract Law; Carlill v. Carbolic Smoke Ball (1893), in Leading Cases in the Common Law 259, 281 (1995), but also to its role in developing the law of unilateral offers. The case arose during the London influenza epidemic of the 1890s. Among other advertisements of the time, for Clarke's World Famous Blood Mixture, Towle's Pennyroyal and Steel Pills for Females, Sequah's Prairie Flower, and Epp's Glycerine Jube-Jubes appeared solicitations for the Carbolic Smoke Ball.

The advertisement was construed as offering a reward because it sought to induce performance, unlike an invitation to negotiate, which seeks a reciprocal promise. As Lord Justice Lindley explained, "advertisements offering rewards . . . are offers to anybody who performs the conditions named in the advertisement, and anybody who does perform the condition accepts the offer." Because Mrs. Carlill had complied with the terms of the offer, yet contracted influenza, she was entitled to £100.

. . .

Other "reward" cases underscore the distinction between typical advertisements, in which the alleged offer is merely an invitation to negotiate for purchase of commercial goods, and promises of reward, in which the alleged offer is intended to induce a potential offeree to perform a specific action, often for noncommercial reasons. In Newman v. Schiff, 778 F.2d 460 (8th Cir. 1985), for example, the Fifth Circuit held that a tax protestor's assertion that, "If anybody calls this show . . . and cites any section of the code that says an individual is required to file a tax return, I'll pay them $100,000," would have been an enforceable offer had the plaintiff called the television show to claim the reward while the tax protestor was appearing. See id. at 466-68. . . . James v. Turilli, 473 S.W.2d 757 (Mo. Ct. App. 1971), arose from a boast by defendant that the "notorious Missouri desperado" Jesse James had not been killed in 1882, as portrayed in song and legend, but had lived under the alias "J. Frank Dalton" at the "Jesse James Museum" operated by none other than defendant. Defendant offered $10,000 "to anyone who could prove me wrong." See id. at 758-59. The widow of the outlaw's son demonstrated, at trial, that the outlaw had in fact been killed in 1882. On appeal, the court held that defendant should be liable to pay the amount offered. . . .

In the present case, the Harrier Jet commercial did not direct that anyone who appeared at Pepsi headquarters with 7,000,000 Pepsi Points on the Fourth of July would receive a Harrier Jet. Instead, the commercial urged consumers to accumulate Pepsi Points and to refer to the Catalog to determine how they could redeem their Pepsi Points. The commercial sought a reciprocal promise, expressed through acceptance of, and compliance with, the terms of the Order Form. As noted previously, the Catalog contains no mention of the Harrier Jet. Plaintiff states that he "noted that the Harrier Jet was not among the items described in the catalog, but this did not affect [his] understanding of the offer." It should have.[10]

. . . Because the alleged offer in this case was, at most, an advertisement to receive offers rather than an offer of reward, plaintiff cannot show that there was an offer made in the circumstances of this case.

C. An Objective, Reasonable Person Would Not Have Considered the Commercial an Offer

Plaintiff's understanding of the commercial as an offer must also be rejected because the Court finds that no objective person could reasonably have concluded that the commercial actually offered consumers a Harrier Jet.

---

10. In his affidavit, plaintiff places great emphasis on a press release written by defendant, which characterizes the Harrier Jet as "the ultimate Pepsi stuff award." Plaintiff simply ignores the remainder of the release, which makes no mention of the Harrier Jet even as it sets forth in detail the number of points needed to redeem other merchandise.

1. Objective Reasonable Person Standard

In evaluating the commercial, the Court must not consider defendant's subjective intent in making the commercial, or plaintiff's subjective view of what the commercial offered, but what an objective, reasonable person would have understood the commercial to convey. . . .

. . . An obvious joke, of course, would not give rise to a contract. . . . On the other hand, if there is no indication that the offer is "evidently in jest," and that an objective, reasonable person would find that the offer was serious, then there may be a valid offer. . . . [S]ee also Lucy v. Zehmer. . . .

2. Necessity of a Jury Determination

Plaintiff also contends that summary judgment is improper because the question of whether the commercial conveyed a sincere offer can be answered only by a jury. . . . [P]laintiff argues that a federal judge comes from a "narrow segment of the enormously broad American socio-economic spectrum," and, thus, that the question whether the commercial constituted a serious offer must be decided by a jury composed of, *inter alia,* members of the "Pepsi Generation," who are, as plaintiff puts it, "young, open to adventure, willing to do the unconventional." Plaintiff essentially argues that a federal judge would view his claim differently than fellow members of the "Pepsi Generation."

. . . This case . . . presents a question of whether there was an offer to enter into a contract, requiring the Court to determine how a reasonable, objective person would have understood defendant's commercial. Such an inquiry is commonly performed by courts on a motion for summary judgment. . . .

3. Whether the Commercial Was "Evidently Done in Jest"

Plaintiff's insistence that the commercial appears to be a serious offer requires the Court to explain why the commercial is funny. Explaining why a joke is funny is a daunting task; as the essayist E.B. White has remarked, "Humor can be dissected, as a frog can, but the thing dies in the process. . . ." The commercial is the embodiment of what defendant appropriately characterizes as "zany humor."

First, the commercial suggests, as commercials often do, that use of the advertised product will transform what, for most youth, can be a fairly routine and ordinary experience. The military tattoo and stirring martial music, as well as the use of subtitles in a Courier font that scroll terse messages across the screen, such as "MONDAY 7:58 AM," evoke military and espionage thrillers. The implication of the commercial is that Pepsi Stuff merchandise will inject drama and moment into hitherto unexceptional lives. The commercial in this case thus makes the exaggerated claims similar to those of many television advertisements: that by consuming the featured clothing, car, beer, or potato chips, one will become attractive, stylish, desirable, and admired by all. A reasonable viewer would understand such advertisements as mere puffery, not as statements of fact, . . . and refrain from interpreting the promises of the commercial as being literally true.

Second, the callow youth featured in the commercial is a highly improbable pilot, one who could barely be trusted with the keys to his parents' car, much less the prize aircraft of the United States Marine Corps. Rather than checking the fuel gauges on his aircraft, the teenager spends his precious preflight minutes preening. The youth's concern for his coiffure appears to extend to his flying without a helmet. Finally, the teenager's comment that flying a Harrier Jet to school "sure beats the bus" evinces an improbably insouciant attitude toward the relative difficulty and danger of piloting a fighter plane in a residential area, as opposed to taking public transportation.[12]

Third, the notion of traveling to school in a Harrier Jet is an exaggerated adolescent fantasy. In this commercial, the fantasy is underscored by how the teenager's schoolmates gape in admiration, ignoring their physics lesson. The force of the wind generated by the Harrier Jet blows off one teacher's clothes, literally defrocking an authority figure. As if to emphasize the fantastic quality of having a Harrier Jet arrive at school, the Jet lands next to a plebeian bike rack. This fantasy is, of course, extremely unrealistic. No school would provide landing space for a student's fighter jet, or condone the disruption the jet's use would cause.

Fourth, the primary mission of a Harrier Jet, according to the United States Marine Corps, is to "attack and destroy surface targets under day and night visual conditions." . . . The jet is designed to carry a considerable armament load, including Sidewinder and Maverick missiles. . . . In light of the Harrier Jet's well-documented function in attacking and destroying surface and air targets, armed reconnaissance and air interdiction, and offensive and defensive anti-aircraft warfare, depiction of such a jet as a way to get to school in the morning is clearly not serious even if, as plaintiff contends, the jet is capable of being acquired "in a form that eliminates [its] potential for military use."

Fifth, the number of Pepsi Points the commercial mentions as required to "purchase" the jet is 7,000,000. To amass that number of points, one would have to drink 7,000,000 Pepsis (or roughly 190 Pepsis a day for the next hundred years—an unlikely possibility), or one would have to purchase approximately $700,000 worth of Pepsi Points. The cost of a Harrier Jet is roughly $23 million dollars, a fact of which plaintiff was aware when he set out to gather the amount he believed necessary to accept the alleged offer. Even if an objective, reasonable person were not aware of this fact, he would conclude that purchasing a fighter plane for $700,000 is a deal too good to be true.[13]

Plaintiff argues that a reasonable, objective person would have understood the commercial to make a serious offer of a Harrier Jet because there was "absolutely

---

12. In this respect, the teenager of the advertisement contrasts with the distinguished figures who testified to the effectiveness of the Carbolic Smoke Ball. . . .

13. In contrast, the advertisers of the Carbolic Smoke Ball emphasized their earnestness, stating in the advertisement that "£1,000 is deposited with the Alliance Bank, shewing our sincerity in the matter."

no distinction in the manner" in which the items in the commercial were presented. Plaintiff also relies upon a press release highlighting the promotional campaign, issued by defendant, in which "[n]o mention is made by [defendant] of humor, or anything of the sort." These arguments suggest merely that the humor of the promotional campaign was tongue in cheek. . . . In light of the obvious absurdity of the commercial, the Court rejects plaintiff's argument that the commercial was not clearly in jest.

4. Plaintiff's Demands for Additional Discovery

. . .

Plaintiff argues that additional discovery is necessary as to how defendant reacted to his "acceptance," suggesting that it is significant that defendant twice changed the commercial, the first time to increase the number of Pepsi Points required to purchase a Harrier Jet to 700,000,000, and then again to amend the commercial to state the 700,000,000 amount and add "(Just Kidding)." Plaintiff concludes that, "Obviously, if PepsiCo truly believed that no one could take seriously the offer contained in the original ad that I saw, this change would have been totally unnecessary and superfluous." The record does not suggest that the change in the amount of points is probative of the seriousness of the offer. The increase in the number of points needed to acquire a Harrier Jet may have been prompted less by the fear that reasonable people would demand Harrier Jets and more by the concern that unreasonable people would threaten frivolous litigation. . . .

Finally, plaintiff's assertion that he should be afforded an opportunity to determine whether other individuals also tried to accumulate enough Pepsi Points to "purchase" a Harrier Jet is unavailing. The possibility that there were other people who interpreted the commercial as an "offer" of a Harrier Jet does not render that belief any more or less reasonable. The alleged offer must be evaluated on its own terms. Having made the evaluation, the Court concludes that summary judgment is appropriate on the ground that no reasonable, objective person would have understood the commercial to be an offer.

. . .

III. CONCLUSION

In sum, . . . plaintiff's demand cannot prevail as a matter of law. First, the commercial was merely an advertisement, not a unilateral offer. Second, the tongue-in-cheek attitude of the commercial would not cause a reasonable person to conclude that a soft drink company would be giving away fighter planes as part of a promotion. . . .

For the reasons stated above, the Court grants defendant's motion for summary judgment.

HARRIS
v.
TIME, INC.

Court of Appeal, First District, Division 5, California
191 Cal. App. 3d 449
1987

KING, J.

In this action where plaintiffs suffered no damage or loss other than having been enticed by the external wording of a piece of bulk rate mail to open the envelope, believing that doing so would result in the receipt of a free plastic calculator watch, we hold that the maxim "the law disregards trifles" applies and dismissal of the action was proper on this ground.

Mark Harris, Joshua Gnaizda and Richard Baker appeal from a judgment of dismissal of this class action lawsuit arising from their receipt of a direct mail advertisement from Time, Inc. They contend the court erred when it sustained Time's demurrer as to cause of action for breach of contract and granted summary judgment as to causes of action for unfair advertising. We affirm.

It all began one day when Joshua Gnaizda, the three-year-old son of a prominent Bay Area public interest attorney, received what he (or his mother) thought was a tantalizing offer in the mail from Time. The front of the envelope contained two see-through windows partially revealing the envelope's contents. One window showed Joshua's name and address. The other revealed the following statement: "JOSHUA A. GNAIZDA, I'LL GIVE YOU THIS VERSATILE NEW CALCULATOR WATCH FREE Just for, Opening this Envelope Before Feb. 15, 1985." Beneath the offer was a picture of the calculator watch itself. Joshua's mother opened the envelope and apparently realized she had been deceived by a ploy to get her to open a piece of junk mail. The see-through window had not revealed the full text of Time's offer. Printed below the picture of the calculator watch, and not viewable through the see-through window, were the following additional words: "AND MAILING THIS CERTIFICATE TODAY!" The certificate itself clearly required that Joshua purchase a subscription to Fortune magazine in order to receive the free calculator watch.

As is so often true in life situations these days, the certificate contained both good news and bad news. The good news was that Joshua could save up to 66 percent on the subscription, which might even be tax deductible. Even more important to the bargain hunter, prices might never be this low again. The bad news was that Time obviously had no intention of giving Joshua the versatile new calculator watch just for opening the envelope.

Although most of us, while murmuring an appropriate expletive, would have simply thrown away the mailer, and some might have stood on principle and filed an action in small claims court to obtain the calculator watch, Joshua's father did something a little different: he launched a $15 million lawsuit in San Francisco Superior Court.

The action was prosecuted by Joshua, through his father, and by Mark Harris and Richard Baker, who had also received the same mailer. We are not informed of the ages of Harris and Baker. The complaint alleged one cause of action for breach of contract, three causes of action for statutory unfair advertising, and four causes of action for promissory estoppel and fraud.

The complaint sought the following relief: (1) a declaration that all recipients of the mailer were entitled to receive the promised item or to rescind subscriptions they had purchased, (2) an injunction against future similar mailings, (3) compensatory damages in an amount equal to the value of the item, and (4) $15 million punitive damages to be awarded to a consumer fund "to be used for education and advocacy on behalf of consumer protection and enforcement of laws against unfair business practices."

The complaint also alleged that before commencing litigation, Joshua's father demanded that Time give Joshua a calculator watch without requiring a subscription. Time not only refused to give a watch, it did not even give Joshua or his father the time of day.

. . .

II. BREACH OF CONTRACT

In sustaining the demurrer as to the cause of action for breach of contract, the court stated no specific grounds for its ruling. Time had argued the complaint did not allege an offer, did not allege adequate consideration, and did not allege notice of performance by the plaintiffs. On appeal, plaintiffs challenge each of these points as a basis for dismissal.

A. Offer

On the first point, Time argues there was no contract because the text of the unopened mailer amounted to a mere advertisement rather than an offer.

It is true that advertisements are not typically treated as offers, but merely as invitations to bargain. (1 Corbin on Contracts (1963) §25, pp. 74-75; Rest. 2d, Contracts, §26, com[.] b, at p. 76.) There is, however, a fundamental exception to this rule: an advertisement can constitute an offer, and form the basis of a unilateral contract, if it calls for performance of a specific act without further communication and leaves nothing for further negotiation. (Lefkowitz v. Great Minneapolis Surplus Store (1957) 251 Minn. 188 [86 N.W.2d 689, 691]; 1 Corbin on Contracts (1963) §§25, 64, pp. 75-76, 264-270; Rest. 2d, Contracts, §26, com. b, at p. 76.) This is a basic rule of contract law, contained in the Restatement Second of Contracts and normally encountered within the first few weeks of law school in cases such as Lefkowitz (furs advertised for sale at specified date and time for "$1.00 First Come First Served") and Carlill v. Carbolic Smoke Ball Co. (1893) 1 Q.B. 256 (advertisement of reward to anyone who caught influenza after using seller's medicine). (See, e.g., Murphy & Speidel, Studies in Contract Law (3d ed. 1984) pp. 112, 154.)

The text of Time's unopened mailer was, technically, an offer to enter into a unilateral contract: the promisor made a promise to do something (give the recipient a calculator watch) in exchange for the performance of an act by the promise (opening the envelope). Time was not in the same position as a seller merely advertising price; the proper analogy is to a seller promising to give something to a customer in exchange for the customer's act of coming to the store at a specified time. (Lefkowitz v. Great Minneapolis Surplus Store, supra, 86 N.W.2d 689.)

B. Consideration

Time also argues that there was no contract because the mere act of opening the envelope was valueless and therefore did not constitute adequate consideration. Technically, this is incorrect. It is basic modern contract law that, with certain exceptions not applicable here (such as illegality or preexisting legal duty), any bargained-for act or forbearance will constitute adequate consideration for a unilateral contract. (Rest. 2d, Contracts, §71; see 1 Witkin, Summary of Cal. Law (8th ed. 1973) Contracts, §§162-169, pp. 153-162.) Courts will not require equivalence in the values exchanged or otherwise question the adequacy of the consideration. (Schumm v. Berg (1951) 37 Cal. 2d 174, 185 [231 P.2d 39, 21 A.L.R.2d 1051]; Rest. 2d, Contracts, §79.) If a performance is bargained for, there is no further requirement of benefit to the promisor or detriment to the promisee. (Rest. 2d, Contracts, §79, coms. *a* & *b* at pp. 200-201.)

Moreover, the act at issue here—the opening of the envelope, with consequent exposure to Time's sales pitch—may have been relatively insignificant to the plaintiffs, but it was of great value to Time. At a time when our homes are bombarded daily by direct mail advertisements and solicitations, the name of the game for the advertiser or solicitor is to *get the recipient to open the envelope*. Some advertisers, like Time in the present case, will resort to ruse or trick to achieve this goal. From Time's perspective, the opening of the envelope was "valuable consideration" in every sense of that phrase.

Thus, assuming (as we must at this juncture) that the allegations of the complaint are true, Time made an offer proposing a unilateral contract, and plaintiffs supplied adequate consideration for that contract when they performed the act of opening the envelope and exposing themselves to the sales pitch within.

. . .

III. CONCLUSION

As a final argument, Time claims the judgment of dismissal was correct based on the legal maxim "de minimis non curat lex," or "the law disregards trifles." (Civ. Code, §3533.) In this age of the consumer class action this maxim usually has little value. However, the present action is "de minimis" in the extreme. This lawsuit is an absurd waste of the resources of this court, the superior court, the public interest law firm handling the case and the citizens of California whose taxes fund our judicial system. It is not a use for which our legal system is designed.

As a practical matter, plaintiffs' real complaint is that they were tricked into opening a piece of junk mail, *not* that they were misled into buying anything or expending more than the effort necessary to open an envelope. If Joshua's mother lost the initial skirmish in the battle of direct mail advertising by opening the envelope, she could have won the war by simply throwing the thing away. If she were angry she might even have returned Time's business reply envelope empty, requiring Time to pay the return postage. If she felt particularly hostile, she might have inserted a nasty note or other evidence of her displeasure in the reply envelope. A $15 million lawsuit, filed in a superior court underfunded and already overburdened with serious felony prosecutions and complex civil litigation involving catastrophic injury from asbestos, prescription drugs and intrauterine devices, is a vast overreaction. The law may permit junk mail to be delivered for a lower cost than the individual citizen must pay. It does not require that the public subsidize junk litigation.

For many, an unpleasant aspect of contemporary American life is returning to the sanctity of one's home each day and emptying the mailbox, only to be inundated with advertisements and solicitations. Some days, among all of the junk mail, one is fortunate to be able to locate a bill, let alone a letter from a friend or loved one. Insult is added to injury when one realizes that individual citizens must pay first class postage rates to send their mail, while junk mail, for reasons apparent only to Congress and the United States Postal Service, is sent at less one-half of that rate. The irritation level soars to new heights when, succumbing to the cleverness or ruse of the sender of junk mail and believing one is being offered something for nothing, one actually opens an envelope and examines its contents, both of which would otherwise been deposited unopened in their rightful place, the garbage can. Snake oil salesmen have been replaced by bulk rate advertisers whose wares must be causing our postal carriers' backs to be nearing the breaking point under the weight of such mail.

As much as one might decry this intrusion into our lives and our homes and sympathize with Joshua's plight, eliminating it lies with Congress, not the courts. The courts cannot solve every complaint or right every technical wrong, particularly one which causes no actual damage beyond the loss of the few seconds it takes to open an envelope and examine its contents. Our courts are too heavily overburdened to be used as a vehicle to punish by one whose only real damage is feeling foolish for having opened what obviously was junk mail.

We therefore affirm, despite the partial technical validity of the action, because the judgment is correct based on the "de minimis" theory. A judgment that is correct on any theory will be affirmed even if the reasons stated by the trial court in support of the judgment were wrong. (Davey v. Southern Pacific Co., *supra*, 116 Cal. at p. 329.)

The judgment is affirmed. The parties shall bear their own costs on appeal.

Problems

1. The Bradley Block. W.H. Owen wrote to R.G. Tunison: "Will you sell me your store property which is located on Main St. in Bucksport, Me. Running from Montgomery's Drug Store on one corner to a Grocery Store on the other, for the sum of $6,000.00?" Tunison replied: "In reply to your letter of Oct. 23rd . . . in which you inquire about the Bradley Block, Bucksport, Me. Because of the improvements which have been added and an expenditure of several thousand dollars it would not be possible for me to sell it unless I was to receive $16,000.00 cash." Owen wrote back: "Accept your offer for Bradley block Bucksport terms sixteen thousand cash." Tunison refused to tender the property and Owen sued. Was there a contract?

2. Carloads of Mason Jars. How would you classify the following series of exchanges between two companies—buyer Crunden-Martin Woodenware Company and seller Fairmount Glass Works—regarding the purchase of glass canning jars (also known as fruit or Mason jars)? Was a contract formed?

> Buyer letter of April 20: "Please advise us the lowest price you can make us on our order for ten car loads of green Mason jars, complete, with caps, packed one dozen in a case. State terms and cash discount."

> Seller letter of April 23: "Replying to your letter, we quote you fruit jars, complete, in one-dozen boxes: Pints $4.50, quarts $5.00, half gallons $6.50, per gross, for immediate acceptance."

> Buyer telegram of April 24: "Your letter received. Enter order ten car loads per your quotation. Specifications mailed."

> Seller telegram of April 24: "Impossible to book your order. Output all sold."

3. An Offer Too Good to Be True? With new, 1955-model automobiles due to arrive soon, Capital City Ford of Baton Rouge, Louisiana, attempted to generate interest in its current inventory by publishing the following advertisement in local newspapers:

> TWO FOR ONE . . . For two weeks BUY A NEW '54 FORD NOW TRADE EVEN FOR A '55 FORD

> Don't Wait—Buy a 1954 Ford now, when the 1955 models come out we'll trade even for your '54. You pay only sales tax and license fee. Your '55 Ford will be the same model, same body style, accessory group, etc. A sure thing for you—a gamble for us, but we'll take it. Hurry, though, this offer good only for the remainder of September.

> The 1954 car must be returned with only normal wear and tear. Physical damage, such as dented fenders, torn upholstery, etc. must be charged to owner or repaired at owner's expense. No convertibles or Skyliners on this basis.

After seeing the advertisement, Leland Johnson purchased a 1954 Ford sedan from Capital City. When the new models arrived three months later, Johnson returned to the dealer and requested that the dealer exchange his (undamaged) car for a new model. Did Capital City's advertisement constitute an offer giving Johnson the ability to form a contract by accepting?

4. A Buyer's Remorse. Chris Esposito, an agent of Prestige Motors Sales, placed a BMW for sale "without reserve" on the Internet auction website eBay. eBay allows sellers to auction an item with or without a "reserve" price, the "lowest price that the seller is willing to accept for the item." Joseph Malcolm subsequently placed the winning bid for the vehicle on eBay. Malcolm later refused to pay for the BMW. If Prestige Motors sues for enforcement, what is the likely outcome? As part of your analysis, you should consider Rest. (2d) Contracts §28 and U.C.C. §2-328.

5. A Lawyer's Boast. Nelson Serrano was accused of killing his business partner in Orlando, Florida, in 1997. Following the trial, Serrano's attorney, James Mason, appeared on a television news program. Mason claimed that Serrano could not have committed the crime because he was photographed by a surveillance camera at a La Quinta hotel in Atlanta shortly after the crime was committed. To have been in both places, Serrano would have had to travel from a crowded airplane at the Atlanta airport, through the airport, and to the La Quinta hotel 5 miles away in less than 30 minutes, a feat Mason said was impossible. Mason then said, "I challenge anybody to show me. I'll pay them a million dollars if they can do it." The reporter asked, "If they can do it in the time allotted?" Mason responded, "Twenty-eight minutes. Can't happen. Didn't happen."

One year later, law student Dustin Kolodziej traced Serrano's alleged route. Kolodziej videotaped himself traveling from a jet at the Atlanta airport to the hotel in less than 28 minutes. He sent the videotape to Mason and requested the $1 million. When Mason refused to pay, Kolodziej filed suit. Should he recover?

3. Acceptance

Once an offer has been made, an acceptance of that offer is necessary to bind the parties. According to the Restatement, an acceptance is defined as "a manifestation of assent to the terms thereof made by the offeree in a manner invited or required by the offer." Rest. (2d) Contracts §50. This definition suggests that an utterance or an act must satisfy two requirements to operate as an acceptance. First, like an offer, an acceptance must manifest a willingness to be bound in a contractual relationship. Concerning this requirement, the analysis of whether a communication constitutes an acceptance is identical to the analysis of whether a communication constitutes an offer. Second, unlike an offer, which may propose any substantive terms and communicate them in any way, an acceptance must reflect the terms of the offer and be provided in the way in which the offer instructs. See also Rest. (2d) Contracts §58. A purported acceptance that is conditional on terms additional to or different from those proposed in the offer is not effective as an acceptance and instead constitutes a counteroffer. Rest. (2d) Contracts §59. (Note, however, that a purported acceptance that requests a change in terms but does not depend on acquiescence to that request can still operate as an acceptance. Rest. (2d) Contracts §61.) The requirement that the acceptance mirror the offer is known as the "mirror image rule," and it reinforces the fact that, as is commonly observed, the offeror is the master of the offer.

Offerors often do not specify precisely how the offer may be accepted. The law provides a number of default rules that govern in these circumstances:

1. The offer may either seek acceptance in the form of a promise to perform on the part of the offeree (called a "bilateral" contract because both parties make a promise) or in the performance itself (called a "unilateral" contract because only one promise is involved). In the absence of a specification, however, the offeree may accept by either promise or performance. Rest. (2d) Contracts §32.

2. An offer may prescribe the time, place, or manner of acceptance, but if it fails to do so, or only provides suggestions in this regard, the offeree may accept in any reasonable way. Rest. (2d) Contracts §60.

3. An offer may require that acceptance be indicated with particular words or a particular act, in the absence of such direction the offeree may indicate acceptance in any manner and by any medium reasonable under the circumstances. Rest. (2d) Contracts §30. The offeror may not, however, identify the offeree's silence or inaction in the face of the offer as the means of acceptance, as this would risk undermining the first requirement of an acceptance—that it demonstrate assent to be bound in a contractual relationship. Silence or inaction can indicate acceptance, however, if the context indicates the offeree's consent to such a manner of acceptance. Rest. (2d) Contracts §69.

4. If the offer fails to specify that the offeree must notify the offeror of the acceptance, an offeree who accepts by promise must provide notice unless the offeror otherwise receives seasonable notification. Rest. (2d) Contracts §56. An offeree who accepts by performance, however, need not provide notice unless she has reason to know the offeror is not likely to learn of the performance seasonably. Rest. (2d) Contracts §54.

With the effectiveness of a purported acceptance subject to such a variety of rules, the range of legal issues that can arise is myriad and, to some degree, defies categorization. *Carlill v. Carbolic Smoke Ball Company*, a famous case often used to illustrate what communications constitute an offer, also requires an analysis of what acts constitute an acceptance. *Glover v. Jewish War Veterans* considers whether an acceptance requires that the offeree have actual notice of an offer. *Corinthian Pharmaceutical Systems, Inc. v. Lederle Laboratories* considers a problem of performance that does not mirror that offer's specifications.

CARLILL
v.
CARBOLIC SMOKE BALL CO.

In the Court of Appeal, Queen's Bench
1 Q.B. 256
1892

Appeal from a decision of HAWKINS, J.

The defendants, who were the proprietors and vendors of a medical preparation called "The Carbolic Smoke Ball," inserted in the *Pall Mall Gazette* of November 13, 1891, and in other newspapers, the following advertisement:

> "100£. reward will be paid by the Carbolic Smoke Ball Company to any person who contracts the increasing epidemic influenza, colds, or any disease caused by taking cold, after having used the ball three times daily for two weeks according to the printed directions supplied with each ball. 1000£ is deposited with the Alliance Bank, Regent Street, shewing our sincerity in the matter.

> "During the last epidemic of influenza many thousand carbolic smoke balls were sold as preventives against this disease, and in no ascertained case was the disease contracted by those using the carbolic smoke ball.

> "One carbolic smoke ball will last a family several months, making it the cheapest remedy in the world at the price, 10s., post free. The ball can be refilled at a cost of 5s. Address, Carbolic Smoke Ball Company, 27, Princes Street, Hanover Square, London."

The plaintiff, a lady, on the faith of this advertisement, bought one of the balls at a chemist's, and used it as directed, three times a day, from November 20, 1891, to January 17, 1892, when she was attacked by influenza. Hawkins, J., held that she was entitled to recover the 100£. The defendants appealed.

Finlay, Q.C., and *T. Terrell,* for the defendants. The facts shew that there was no binding contract between the parties. . . . The advertisement is too vague to be the basis of a contract; there is no limit as to time, and no means of checking the use of the ball. Anyone who had influenza might come forward and depose that he had used the ball for a fortnight, and it would be impossible to disprove it. In order to make a contract by fulfilment of a condition, there must either be a communication of intention to accept the offer, or there must be the performance of some overt act.

Dickens, Q.C., and *W.B. Allen,* for the plaintiff. The advertisement clearly was an offer by the defendants; it was published that it might be read and acted on, and they cannot be heard to say that it was an empty boast, which they were under no obligation to fulfil. The offer was duly accepted. An advertisement was addressed to all the public—as soon as a person does the act mentioned, there is a contract with him. It never was intended that a person proposing to use the smoke ball should go to the office and obtain a repetition of the statements in the advertisement. The promise is to the person who does an act, not to the person who says he is going to do it and then does it. As to the want of restriction as to time, there are several possible constructions of the terms; they may mean that, after you have used it for a fortnight, you will be safe so long as you go on using it, or that you will be safe during the prevalence of the epidemic. Or the true view may be that a fortnight's use will make a person safe for a reasonable time.

Finlay, Q.C., in reply. There is no binding contract. There is no more consideration in using the ball than in contracting the influenza. Here no service to the defendants was requested, for it was no benefit to them that the balls should be used: their interest was only that they should be sold. Then as to the want of limitation as to time, it is conceded that the defendants cannot have meant to contract without some limit, and three limitations have been suggested. The limitation "during the prevalence of the epidemic" is inadmissible, for the advertisement applies to colds as well as influenza. The limitation "during use" is excluded by the language "after having used." The third is, "within a reasonable time," and that is probably what was intended; but it cannot be deduced from the words; so the fair result is that there was no legal contract at all.

LINDLEY, L.J.

We must first consider whether this was intended to be a promise at all, or whether it was a mere puff which meant nothing. Was it a mere puff? My answer to that question is No, and I base my answer upon this passage: "1000£. is deposited with the Alliance Bank, shewing our sincerity in the matter." Now, for what was that money deposited or that statement made except to negative the suggestion that this was a mere puff and meant nothing at all? The deposit is called in aid by the advertiser as proof of his sincerity in the matter—that is, the sincerity of his promise to pay this 100£ in the event which he has specified. Then it is contended that it is not binding. In the first place, it is said that it is not made with anybody in particular. Now that point is common to the words of this advertisement and to the words of all other advertisements offering rewards. They are offers to anybody who performs the conditions named in the advertisement, and anybody who does perform the condition accepts the offer.

But then it is said, "Supposing that the performance of the conditions is an acceptance of the offer, that acceptance ought to have been notified." Unquestionably, as a general proposition, when an offer is made, it is necessary in order to make a binding contract, not only that it should be accepted, but that the acceptance should be notified. I, however, think that the true view, in a case of this kind, is that the person who makes the offer shews by his language and from the nature of the transaction that he does not expect and does not require notice of the acceptance apart from notice of the performance.

We, therefore, find here all the elements which are necessary to form a binding contract enforceable in point of law, subject to two observations. First of all it is said that this advertisement is so vague that you cannot really construe it as a promise. When are the smoke balls to be used? No time is fixed, and, construing the offer most strongly against the person who has made it, one might infer that any time was meant. I do not think that business people or reasonable people would understand the words as meaning that if you took a smoke ball and used it three times daily for two weeks you were to be guaranteed against influenza for the rest of your life, and I think it would be pushing the language of the advertisement too far to construe it as meaning that. But if it does not mean that, what does it mean? It is for the defendants to shew what it does mean; and it strikes me that there are two, and possibly three, reasonable constructions to be put on this advertisement, any one of which will answer the purpose of the plaintiff. Possibly it may be limited to persons catching the "increasing epidemic" (that is, the then prevailing epidemic), or any colds or diseases caused by taking cold, during the prevalence of the increasing epidemic. That is one suggestion; but it does not commend itself to me. Another suggested meaning is that you are warranted free from catching this epidemic, or colds or other diseases caused by taking cold, whilst you are using this remedy after using it for two weeks. If that is the meaning, the plaintiff is right, for she used the remedy for two weeks and went on using it till she got the epidemic. Another meaning, and the one which I rather prefer, is that the reward is offered to any person who contracts the epidemic or other disease within a reasonable time after having used the smoke ball. Then it is asked, What is a reasonable time? It has been suggested that there is no standard of reasonableness; that it depends upon the reasonable time for a germ to develop! It strikes me that a reasonable time may be ascertained in a business sense and in a sense satisfactory to a lawyer, in this way; find out from a chemist what the ingredients are; find out from a skilled physician how long the effect of such ingredients on the system could be reasonably expected to endure so as to protect a person from an epidemic or cold, and in that way you will get a standard to be laid before a jury, or a judge without a jury, by which they might exercise their judgment as to what a reasonable time would be. It strikes me, I confess, that the true construction of this advertisement is that 100£ will be paid to anybody who uses this smoke ball three times daily for two weeks according to the printed directions, and who gets the influenza or cold or other diseases caused by taking cold within a reasonable time after so using it; and if that is the true construction, it is enough for the plaintiff.

It is quite obvious that in the view of the advertisers a use by the public of their remedy, if they can only get the public to have confidence enough to use it, will react and produce a sale which is directly beneficial to them. Therefore, the advertisers get out of the use an advantage which is enough to constitute a consideration.

Does not the person who acts upon this advertisement and accepts the offer put himself to some inconvenience at the request of the defendants? It appears to me that there is a distinct inconvenience, not to say a detriment, to any person who so uses the smoke ball. I am of opinion, therefore, that there is ample consideration for the promise.

It appears to me, therefore, that the defendants must perform their promise, and, if they have been so unwary as to expose themselves to a great many actions, so much the worse for them.

BOWEN, L.J. concur

I am of the same opinion. . . .

But it was said there was no check on the part of the persons who issued the advertisement, and that it would be an insensate thing to promise £100 to a person who used the smoke ball unless you could check or superintend his manner of using it. The answer to that argument seems to me to be that if a person chooses to make extravagant promises of this kind he probably does so because it pays him to make them, and, if he has made them, the extravagance of the promises is no reason in law why he should not be bound by them.

It was also said that the contract is made with all the world—that is, with everybody; and that you cannot contract with everybody. It is not a contract made with all the world. There is the fallacy of the argument. It is an offer made to all the world; and why should not an offer be made to all the world which is to ripen into a contract with anybody who comes forward and performs the condition? It is an offer to become liable to any one who, before it is retracted, performs the condition, and, although the offer is made to the world, the contract is made with that limited portion of the public who come forward and perform the condition on the faith of the advertisement. It is not like cases in which you offer to negotiate, or you issue advertisements that you have got a stock of books to sell, or houses to let, in which case there is no offer to be bound by any contract. Such advertisements are offers to negotiate—offers to receive offers—offers to chaffer, as, I think, some learned judge in one of the cases has said. If this is an offer to be bound, then it is a contract the moment the person fulfils the condition.

. . . Then it was said that there was no notification of the acceptance of the contract. One cannot doubt that, as an ordinary rule of law, an acceptance of an offer made ought to be notified to the person who makes the offer, in order that the two minds may come together. Unless this is done the two minds may be apart, and there is not that consensus which is necessary according to the English law—I say nothing about the laws of other countries—to make a contract. But there is this clear gloss to be made upon that doctrine, that as notification of acceptance is required for the benefit of the person who makes the offer, the person who makes the offer may dispense with notice to himself if he thinks it desirable to do so, and I suppose there can be no doubt that where a person in an offer made by him to another person, expressly or impliedly intimates a particular mode of acceptance as sufficient to make the bargain binding, it is only necessary for the other person to whom such offer is made to follow the indicated method of acceptance; and if the person making the offer, expressly or impliedly intimates in his offer that it will be sufficient to act on the proposal without communicating acceptance of it to himself, performance of the condition is a sufficient acceptance without notification.

. . .

Now, if that is the law, how are we to find out whether the person who makes the offer does intimate that notification of acceptance will not be necessary in order to constitute a binding bargain? In many cases you look to the offer itself. In many cases you extract from the character of the transaction that notification is not required, and in the advertisement cases it seems to me to follow as an inference to be drawn from the transaction itself that a person is not to notify his acceptance of the offer before he performs the condition, but that if he performs the condition notification is dispensed with. It seems to me that from the point of view of common sense no other idea could be entertained. If I advertise to the world that my dog is lost, and that anybody who brings the dog to a particular place will be paid some money, are all the police or other persons whose business it is to find lost dogs to be expected to sit down and write me a note saying that they have accepted my proposal? Why, of course, they at once look after the dog, and as soon as they find the dog they have performed the condition. The essence of the transaction is that the dog should be found, and it is not necessary under such circumstances, as it seems to me, that in order to make the contract binding there should be any notification of acceptance. It follows from the nature of the thing that the performance of the condition is sufficient acceptance without the notification of it, and a person who makes an offer in an advertisement of that kind makes an offer which must be read by the light of that common sense reflection. He does, therefore, in his offer impliedly indicate that he does not require notification of the acceptance of the offer.

5 A.L. SMITH, L.J.   concur

The first point in this case is, whether the defendants' advertisement which appeared in the Pall Mall Gazette was an offer which, when accepted and its conditions performed, constituted a promise to pay, assuming there was good consideration to uphold that promise, or whether it was only a puff from which no promise could be implied, or, as put by Mr. Finlay, a mere statement by the defendants of the confidence they entertained in the efficacy of their remedy. If I may paraphrase it, it means this: "If you"—that is one of the public as yet not ascertained, but who, as Lindley and Bowen, L.JJ., have pointed out, will be ascertained by the performing the condition—"will hereafter use my smoke ball three times daily for two weeks according to my printed directions, I will pay you 100£ if you contract the influenza within the period mentioned in the advertisement." Now, is there not a request there? It comes to this: "In consideration of your buying my smoke ball, and then using it as I prescribe, I promise that if you catch the influenza within a certain time I will pay you 100£."

In my judgment, therefore, this first point fails, and this was an offer intended to be acted upon, and, when acted upon and the conditions performed, constituted a promise to pay.

Appeal dismissed. (H.C.J.)

GLOVER

v.

JEWISH WAR VETERANS OF THE UNITED STATES OF AMERICA, POST NO. 58

Municipal Court of Appeals for the District of Columbia
68 A.2d 233
1949

CLAGETT, J.

The issue determinative of this appeal is whether a person giving information leading to the arrest of a murderer without any knowledge that a reward has been offered for such information by a non-governmental organization is entitled to collect the reward. The trial court decided the question in the negative and instructed the jury to return a verdict for defendant. Claimant appeals from the judgment on such instructed verdict.

The controversy grows out of the murder on June 5, 1946, of Maurice L. Bernstein, a local pharmacist. The following day, June 6, Post No. 58, Jewish War Veterans of the United States, communicated to the newspapers an offer of a reward of $500 "to the person or persons furnishing information resulting in the apprehension and conviction of the persons guilty of the murder of Maurice L. Bernstein." Notice of the reward was published in the newspaper June 7. A day or so later Jesse James Patton, one of the men suspected of the crime, was arrested and the police received information that the other murderer was Reginald Wheeler and that Wheeler was the "boy friend" of a daughter of Mary Glover, plaintiff and claimant in the present case. On the evening of June 11 the police visited Mary Glover, who in answer to questions informed them that her daughter and Wheeler had left the city on June 5. She told the officers she didn't know exactly where the couple had gone, whereupon the officers asked for names of relatives whom the daughter might be visiting. In response to such questions she gave the names and addresses of several relatives, including one at Ridge Spring, South Carolina, which was the first place visited by the officers and where Wheeler was arrested in company with plaintiff's daughter on June 13. Wheeler and Patton were subsequently convicted of the crime.

Claimant's most significant testimony was that she first learned that a reward had been offered on June 12, the day after she had given the police officers the information which enabled them to find Wheeler. Claimant's husband, who was present during the interview with the police officers, also testified that at the time of the interview he didn't know that any reward had been offered for Wheeler's arrest, that nothing was said by the police officers about a reward and that he didn't know about it "until we looked into the paper about two or three days after that."

Since it is clear that the question is one of contract law, it follows that, at least so far as private rewards are concerned, there can be no contract unless the claimant when giving the desired information knew of the offer of the reward and acted with the intention of accepting such offer; otherwise the claimant gives the information not in the expectation of receiving a reward but rather out of a sense of public duty or other motive unconnected with the reward. "In the nature of the case," according to Professor Williston, "it is impossible for an offeree actually to assent to an offer unless he knows of its existence."

The American Law Institute in its Restatement of the Law of Contracts follows the same rule, thus: "It is impossible that there should be an acceptance unless the offeree knows of the existence of the offer." The Restatement gives the following illustration of the rule just stated: "A offers a reward for information leading to the arrest and conviction of a criminal. B, in ignorance of the offer, gives information leading to his arrest and later, with knowledge of the offer and intent to accept it, gives other information necessary for conviction. There is no contract."

We have considered the reasoning in state decisions following the contrary rule. Mostly, they involve rewards offered by governmental bodies and in general are based upon the theory that the government is benefited equally whether or not the claimant gives the information with knowledge of the reward and that therefore the government should pay in any event. We believe that the rule adopted by Professor Williston and the Restatement and in the majority of the cases is the better reasoned rule and therefore we adopt it. We believe furthermore that this rule is particularly applicable in the present case since the claimant did not herself contact the authorities and volunteer information but gave the information only upon questioning by the police officers and did not claim any knowledge of the guilt or innocence of the criminal but only knew where he probably could be located.

Affirmed.

CORINTHIAN PHARMACEUTICAL SYSTEMS, INC. (P)
v.
LEDERLE LABORATORIES (D)
U.S. District Court, S.D. Ind.
724 F. Supp. 605
1989

McKINNEY, J.

This diversity action comes before the Court on the defendant's motion for summary judgment. Defendant Lederle Laboratories is a pharmaceutical manufacturer and distributor that makes a number of drugs, including the DTP vaccine. Plaintiff Corinthian Pharmaceutical is a distributor of drugs that purchases supplies from manufacturers such as Lederle Labs and then resells the product to physicians and other providers. One of the products that Corinthian buys and distributes with some regularity is the DTP vaccine. [Under the terms of a settlement agreement in a prior, unrelated dispute, Corinthian] "may order additional vials of [vaccine] from Lederle at the market price and under the terms and conditions of sale in effect as of the date of the order."

. . .

Lederle periodically issued a price list to its customers for all of its products. Each price list stated that all orders were subject to acceptance by Lederle at its home office, and indicated that the prices shown "were in effect at the time of publication but are submitted without offer and are subject to change without notice." The price list further stated that changes in price "take immediate effect and unfilled current orders and back orders will be invoiced at the price in effect at the time shipment is made."

From 1985 through early 1986, Corinthian made a number of purchases of the vaccine from Lederle Labs. During this period of time, the largest single order ever placed by Corinthian with Lederle was for 100 vials. When Lederle Labs filled an order it sent an invoice to Corinthian. The one page, double-sided invoice contained the specifics of the transaction on the front, along with form statement at the bottom that the transaction "is governed by seller's standard terms and conditions of sale set forth on back hereof, notwithstanding any provisions submitted by buyer."

"Acceptance of the order is expressly conditioned on buyer's assent to seller's terms and conditions."

On the back of the seller's form, the above language was repeated, with the addition that the "[s]eller specifically rejects any different or additional terms and conditions and neither seller's performance nor receipt of payment shall constitute an acceptance of them." The reverse side also stated that prices are subject to change without notice at any time prior to shipment, and that the seller would not be liable for failure to perform the contract if the materials reasonably available to the seller were less than the needs of the buyer. The President of Corinthian admits seeing such conditions before and having knowledge of their presence on the back of the invoices, and Corinthian stipulates that all Lederle's invoices have this same language.

During this period of time, product liability lawsuits concerning DTP increased, and insurance became more difficult to procure. As a result, Lederle decided in early 1986 to self-insure against such risks. In order to cover the costs of self-insurance, Lederle concluded that a substantial increase in the price of the vaccine would be necessary.

In order to communicate the price change to its own sales people, Lederle's Price Manager prepared "PRICE LETTER NO. E-48." This document was dated May 19, 1986, and indicated that effective May 20, 1986, the price of the DTP vaccine would be raised from $51.00 to $171.00 per vial. Price letters such as these were routinely sent to Lederle's sales force, but did not go to customers. Corinthian Pharmaceutical did not know of the existence of this internal price letter until a Lederle representative presented it to Corinthian several weeks after May 20, 1986.

Additionally, Lederle Labs also wrote a letter dated May 20, 1986, to its customers announcing the price increase and explaining the liability and insurance problems that brought about the change. Corinthian somehow gained knowledge of this letter on May 19, 1986, the date before the price increase was to take effect. In response to the knowledge of the impending price increase, Corinthian immediately ordered 1,000 vials of DTP vaccine from Lederle. Corinthian placed its order on May 19, 1986, by calling Lederle's "Telgo" system. The Telgo system is a telephone computer ordering system that allows customers to place orders over the phone by communicating with a computer. After Corinthian placed its order with the Telgo system, the computer gave Corinthian a tracking number for its order. On the same date, Corinthian sent Lederle two written confirmations of its order. On each form Corinthian stated that this "order is to receive the $64.32 per vial price."

On June 3, 1986, Lederle sent invoice 1771 to Corinthian for 50 vials of DTP vaccine priced at $64.32 per vial. The invoice contained the standard Lederle conditions noted above. The 50 vials were sent to Corinthian and were accepted. At the same time, Lederle sent its customers, including Corinthian, a letter regarding DTP vaccine pricing and orders. This letter stated that the "enclosed represents a partial shipment of the order for DTP vaccine, which you placed with Lederle on May 19, 1986." The letter stated that under Lederle's standard terms and conditions of sale the normal policy would be to invoice the order at the price when shipment was made. However, in light of the magnitude of the price increase, Lederle had decided to make an exception to its terms and conditions and ship a portion of the order at the lower price. The letter further stated that the balance would be priced at $171.00, and that shipment would be made during the week of June 16. The letter closed, "If for any reason you wish to cancel the balance of your order, please contact [us] . . . on or before June 13."

Based on these facts, Corinthian brings this action seeking specific performance for the 950 vials of DTP vaccine that Lederle Labs chose not to deliver. . . .

Under Rule 56(c) of the Federal Rules of Civil Procedure, summary judgment "shall be rendered forthwith if the pleadings, depositions, answers to interrogatories, and admissions on file, together with the affidavits, if any, show that there is no genuine issue as to any material fact and that the moving party is entitled to judgment as a matter of law." . . .

DISCUSSION

Despite the lengthy recitation of facts, this is a straightforward sale of goods problem resembling those found in a contracts or sales casebook. The fundamental question is whether Lederle Labs agreed to sell Corinthian 1,000 vials of DTP vaccine at $64.32 per vial. As shown below, the undisputed material facts mandate the conclusion as a matter of law that no such agreement was ever formed.

A. Lederle Labs Never Agreed to Sell 1,000 Vials at the Lower Price

Initially, it should be noted that this is a sale of goods covered by the Uniform Commercial Code, and that both parties are merchants under the Code. . . . The starting point in this analysis is where did the first offer originate. An offer is "the manifestation of willingness to enter into a bargain, so made as to justify another person in understanding that his assent to that bargain is invited and will conclude it." Restatement (Second), Contracts §4. The only possible conclusion in this case is that Corinthian's "order" of May 19, 1986, for 1,000 vials at $64.32 was the first offer. Nothing that the seller had done prior to this point can be interpreted as an offer.

First, the price lists distributed by Lederle to its customers did not constitute offers. It is well settled that quotations are mere invitations to make an offer, . . . *Corbin on Contracts* §§26, 28 (1982), particularly where, as here, the price lists specifically stated that prices were subject to change without notice and that all orders were subject to acceptance by Lederle.

Second, neither Lederle's internal price memorandum nor its letter to customers dated May 20, 1986, can be construed as an offer to sell 1,000 vials at the lower price. There is no evidence that Lederle intended Corinthian to receive the internal price memorandum, nor is there anything in the record to support the conclusion that the May 20, 1986, letter was an offer to sell 1,000 vials to Corinthian at the lower price. If anything, the evidence shows that Corinthian was not supposed to receive this letter until after the price increase had taken place. Moreover, the letter, just like the price lists, was a mere quotation (i.e., an invitation to submit an offer) sent to all customers. As such, it did not bestow on Corinthian nor other customers the power to form a binding contract for the sale of one thousand, or, for that matter, one million vials of vaccine.

Thus, as a matter of law, the first offer was made by Corinthian when it phoned in and subsequently confirmed its order for 1,000 vials at the lower price. The next question, then, is whether Lederle ever accepted that offer.

Under the Code, an acceptance need not be the mirror-image of the offer. U.C.C. §2-207. However, the offeree must still do some act that manifests the intention to accept the offer and make a contract. Under §2-206, an offer to make a contract shall be construed as inviting acceptance in any manner and by any medium reasonable in the circumstances. The first question regarding acceptance, therefore, is whether Lederle accepted the offer prior to sending the 50 vials of vaccine.

The record is clear that Lederle did not communicate or do any act prior to shipping the 50 vials that could support the finding of an acceptance. When Corinthian placed its order, it merely received a tracking number from the Telgo computer. Such an automated, ministerial act cannot constitute an acceptance. Thus, there was no acceptance of Corinthian's offer prior to the delivery of 50 vials.

The next question, then, is what is to be made of the shipment of 50 vials and the accompanying letter. Section 2-206(b) of the Code speaks to this issue:

> [A]n order or other offer to buy goods for prompt or current shipment shall be construed as inviting acceptance either by a prompt promise to ship or by the prompt or current shipment of conforming or non-conforming goods, *but such a shipment of non-conforming goods does not constitute an acceptance if the seller seasonably notifies the buyer that the shipment is offered only as an accommodation to the buyer.*

§2-206 (emphasis added). Thus, under the Code a seller accepts the offer by shipping goods, whether they are conforming or not, but if the seller ships non-conforming goods *and* seasonably notifies the buyer that the shipment is a mere accommodation, then the seller has not, in fact, accepted the buyer's offer. . . . The accommodation letter, which Corinthian is sure it received, clearly stated that the 50 vials were being sent at the lower price as an exception to Lederle's general policy, and that the balance of the offer would be invoiced at the higher price. The letter further indicated that Lederle's proposal to ship the balance of the order at the higher price could be rejected by the buyer. . . . Where, as here, the notification is properly made, the shipment of nonconforming goods is treated as a counteroffer just as at common law, and the buyer may accept or reject the counteroffer under normal contract rules.

Thus, the end result of this analysis is that Lederle Lab's price quotations were mere invitations to make an offer, that by placing its order Corinthian made an offer to buy 1,000 vials at the low price, that by shipping 50 vials at the low price Lederle's response was non-conforming, but the non-conforming response was a mere accommodation and thus constituted a counteroffer. Accordingly, there being no genuine issues of material fact on these issues and the law being in favor of the seller, summary judgment must be granted for Lederle Labs. . . . For all these reasons, the defendant's motion for summary judgment is granted.

Problems

1. **Assent in a Digital Age.** In 2004, Pe Young Chung and Suk Chung entered into a five-year lease with landlord Ron Choi to operate a restaurant on Choi's property. In 2006, the Chungs decided to sell their business. To make the sale possible, they sought to negotiate rental terms applicable to prospective purchasers. The italicized text is from their e-mail exchange.

On April 4, 2006, Choi sent the Chungs' lawyer the following e-mail:

hi jack,
below are the rental terms that are acceptable to us should tenant sell his business.

1. *oct 06 to oct 07: $2,300*
2. *oct 07 to oct 08: $2,500*
3. *oct 08 to oct 09: $2,700*
4. *tenant shall remain liable under the lease for at least 2 years after sale of business.*
   Afterward, new tenant shall be solely liable.
   please call me if you have questions jack.
   —ron

On April 20, 2006, the Chungs' lawyer responded with the following terms:

1. *1st 3 years of new lease $2,300.00;*
2. *Next 3 years $2,500.00;*
3. *Upon sale of business; seller will pay lump sum of $12,500.00 to landlord;*
4. *Current tenant shall remain liable on new lease for 1.5 years (no change).*

On April 29, 2006, Choi responded that *"all the terms look fine . . ."* but added:

let's look at new tenant's credit report before we accept the offer in it's [sic] entirety however. please email me your fax number so I can fax you the credit report consent form.

Also, we'd like both the husband and wife's (new tenant's) name to be on the lease, as well as any corporation they are using for the business.

Is there a contract between the Chungs and Choi? no, counteroffer negates prior offer + must be accepted separately by Chungs.

2. An Offer Too Good to Be True? (Reprise). Capital City Ford advertised an offer, good through the end of September, to allow purchasers of a 1954 model Ford to trade in that car for a 1955 version of the same model at no charge when the new vehicles arrived later in the year (see Section B.2, Problem 3 for the full text of the advertisement). Leland Johnson went to the Capital City showroom prior to the end of September and purchased a 1954 model sedan, using a combination of cash and a trade-in allowance that the dealership gave him for his old car. Johnson said nothing to the dealership about the advertisement or his desire to trade in the car at a later date, and none of the salesmen mentioned to Johnson the advertisement or the possibility of making a trade-in at a later date. In December 1954, when the new models arrived, Johnson returned to the dealership and asked to exchange his car for a 1955 model at no charge, as specified in the advertisement. The dealership refused his request. Had Johnson successfully accepted the offer made by Capital City in its advertisement, thus forming a contract?

3. Where's the Beef? Tweedy was a traveling salesman in Mississippi for Wilson & Company, a meat-packing business. R.L. Ammons, who ran a wholesale grocery business in Mississippi, ordered shortening on repeated occasions from Tweedy over a six-month period. The order form included this provision: "This order taken subject to acceptance by seller's authorized agent at point of shipment." In the past, Ammons's orders were accepted and shipped no later than one week after they were placed. On or about August 11, Ammons placed an order with Tweedy for 60,000 pounds of shortening at $7\frac{1}{2}$ cents per pound. On August 23 and 24, Ammons placed a second order for "prompt shipment" of 942 cases of shortening (43,916 pounds). By September 4, Ammons had received neither the shortening nor a communication from Wilson & Company or Tweedy. In response to Ammons's inquiry about the status of his order, Wilson & Company informed him that the orders had been declined. Between August 11 and September 4, the price of shortening had risen from $7\frac{1}{2}$ cents to 9 cents per pound. If Ammons sues Wilson & Company, what is the likely outcome?

4. Termination of Offers

Every offer that is made is destined for one of two fates. Either it is accepted by the offeree, in which case it ripens into a contract that binds both parties, or it is terminated, in which case it legally ceases to exist. Termination destroys the offeree's power of acceptance. The parties may still decide to contract, of course, and they may choose to do so on the same terms as those previously proposed, but a new offer must be made, and then accepted, before a contract can be formed. The law provides for four termination events: the revocation of an offer by the offeror; the rejection of an offer by the offeree; the lapse (or expiration) of the offer in accordance with its terms or, as a default, in a reasonable time; or the death or incapacity of the offeror or offeree. Rest. (2d) Contracts §36.

Because an offer cannot be terminated once accepted and cannot be accepted once terminated, difficult questions often arise when the success or timing of either an attempt to terminate or an attempt to accept is in doubt. The following trio of cases considers disputes concerning which legally significant act occurred first in time.

Ever-Tite Roofing Corporation v. Green considers whether a purported acceptance was made in a timely manner and before an attempted revocation was effective.

Dickinson v. Dodds turns on the question of what constitutes the revocation of an offer, but a full understanding of the dispute requires some background knowledge about option contracts. An option contract makes an offer irrevocable for a period of time. During this time, the offeree is unbound and may decide not to accept the offer and form a contract, but the offeror lacks her usual power to revoke the offer. For example, under an option contract for the purchase of a house, the buyer can seek mortgage financing or attempt to sell her current residence knowing that the seller is not free to sell the house to another suitor, while the buyer maintains her complete freedom to abandon the deal for any reason or no reason. The traditional view, reflected in *Dickinson*, is that a promise that provides one party with an option must be supported by consideration (independent of the consideration that would be provided if the option were to be exercised). See Rest. (2d) Contracts §25. In the prior example, for instance, the buyer might make a payment for the option (which might be described as a nonrefundable deposit) or promise to cease looking for other houses during the time of the option. Modern contract law has loosened the consideration requirement. The UCC creates an exception to the consideration requirement for so-called firm offers that are documented in a signed writing and cannot extend beyond three months. U.C.C. §2-205. The Restatement adopts a similar rule, allowing a writing plus nominal consideration to create an option contract. Rest. (2d) Contracts §87.

Morrison v. Thoelke addresses arguments for and against the "mailbox rule"—really a set of rules which fixes the time at which acceptances and revocations (and also rejections) are deemed effective when there is a lag between the time they are dispatched by one party and received by the other. See Rest. (2d) Contracts §§40, 63.

EVER-TITE ROOFING CORP. (P)
v.
GREEN (D)

Court of Appeal of Louisiana, Second Circuit
83 So. 2d 449
1955

AYRES, J.

This is an action for damages allegedly sustained by plaintiff as the result of the breach by the defendants of a written contract for the re-roofing of defendants' residence. Defendants denied that their written proposal or offer was ever accepted by plaintiff in the manner stipulated therein for its acceptance, and hence contended no contract was ever entered into. The trial court sustained defendants' defense and rejected plaintiff's demands and dismissed its suit at its costs. From the judgment thus rendered and signed, plaintiff appealed.

PH

Defendants executed and signed an instrument June 10, 1953, for the purpose of obtaining the services of plaintiff in re-roofing their residence situated in Webster Parish, Louisiana. The document set out in detail the work to be done and the price therefor to be paid in monthly installments. This instrument was likewise signed by plaintiff's sale representative, who, however, was without authority to accept the contract for and on behalf of the plaintiff. This alleged contract contained these provisions:

"This agreement shall become binding only upon written acceptance hereof, by the principal or authorized officer of the Contractor, or upon commencing performance of the work. This contract is Not Subject to Cancellation. It is understood and agreed that this contract is payable at office of Ever-Tite Roofing Corporation, 5203 Telephone, Houston, Texas. It is understood and agreed that this Contract provides for attorney's fees and in no case less than ten per cent attorney's fees in the event same is placed in the hands of an attorney for collecting or collected through any court, and further provides for accelerated maturity for failure to pay any installment of principal or interest thereon when due.

"This written agreement is the only and entire contract covering the subject matter hereof and no other representations have been made unto Owner except these herein contained. No guarantee on repair work, partial roof jobs, or paint jobs."

Inasmuch as this work was to be performed entirely on credit, it was necessary for plaintiff to obtain credit reports and approval from the lending institution which was to finance said contract. With this procedure defendants were more or less familiar and knew their credit rating would have to be checked and a report made. On receipt of the proposed contract in plaintiff's office on the day following its execution, plaintiff requested a credit report, which was made after investigation and which was received in due course and submitted by plaintiff to the lending agency. Additional information was requested by this institution, which was likewise in due course transmitted to the institution, which then gave its approval.

The day immediately following this approval, which was either June 18 or 19, 1953, plaintiff engaged its workmen and two trucks, loaded the trucks with the necessary roofing materials and proceeded from Shreveport to defendants' residence for the purpose of doing the work and performing the services allegedly contracted for the defendants. Upon their arrival at defendants' residence, the workmen found others in the performance of the work which plaintiff had contracted to do. Defendants notified plaintiff's workmen that the work had been contracted to other parties two days before and forbade them to do the work.

Formal acceptance of the contract was not made under the signature and approval of an agent of plaintiff. It was, however, the intention of plaintiff to accept the contract by commencing the work, which was one of the ways provided for in the instrument for its acceptance, as will be shown by reference to the extract from the contract quoted hereinabove.

The basis of the judgment appealed was that defendants had timely notified plaintiff before "commencing performance of work." The trial court held that notice to plaintiff's workmen upon their arrival with the materials that defendants did not desire them to commence the actual work was sufficient and timely to signify their intention to withdraw from the contract. With this conclusion we find ourselves unable to agree.

holding

Defendants at no time, from June 10, 1953, until plaintiff's workmen arrived for the purpose of commencing the work, notified or attempted to notify plaintiff of their intention to abrogate, terminate or cancel the contract.

Defendants evidently knew this work was to be processed through plaintiff's Shreveport office. The record discloses no unreasonable delay on plaintiff's part in receiving, processing or accepting the contract or in commencing the work contracted to be done. No time limit was specified in the contract within which it was to be accepted or within which the work was to be begun. It was nevertheless understood between the parties that some delay would ensue before the acceptance of the contract and the commencement of the work, due to the necessity of compliance with the requirements relative to financing the job through a lending agency. The evidence as referred to hereinabove shows that plaintiff proceeded with due diligence.

The general rule of law is that an offer proposed may be withdrawn before its acceptance and that no obligation is incurred thereby. This is, however, not without exceptions. For instance, Restatement of the Law of Contracts stated:

"(1) The power to create a contract by acceptance of an offer terminates at the time specified in the offer, or, if no time is specified, at the end of a reasonable time.

"What is a reasonable time is a question of fact depending on the nature of the contract proposed, the usages of business and other circumstances of the case which the offeree at the time of his acceptance either knows or has reason to know."

Therefore, since the contract did not specify the time within which it was to be accepted or within which the work was to have been commenced, a reasonable time must be allowed therefor in accordance with the facts and circumstances and the evident intention of the parties. A reasonable time is contemplated where no time is expressed. What is a reasonable time depends more or less upon the circumstances surrounding each particular case. The delays to process defendants' application were not unusual. The contract was accepted by plaintiff by the commencement of the performance of the work contracted to be done. This commencement began with the loading of the trucks with the necessary materials in Shreveport and transporting such materials and the workmen to defendants' residence. Actual commencement or performance of the work therefore began before any notice of dissent by defendants was given plaintiff. The proposition and its acceptance thus became a completed contract.

By their aforesaid acts defendants breached the contract. They employed others to do the work contracted to be done by plaintiff and forbade plaintiff's workmen to engage upon that undertaking. By this breach defendants are legally bound to respond to plaintiff in damages.

Plaintiff expended the sum of $85.37 in loading the trucks in Shreveport with materials and in transporting them to the site of defendants' residence in Webster Parish and in unloading them on their return, and for wages for the workmen for the time consumed. Plaintiff's Shreveport manager testified that the expected profit on this job was $226. None of this evidence is controverted or contradicted in any manner.

For the reasons assigned, the judgment appealed is annulled, avoided, reversed and set aside and there is now judgment in favor of plaintiff, Ever-Tite Roofing Corporation, against the defendants, G. T. Green and Mrs. Jessie Fay Green, for the full sum of $311.37, with 5 per cent per annum interest thereon from judicial demand until paid, and for all costs.

Reversed and rendered. *disposition*

DICKINSON (P)
v.
DODDS (D)

Court of Appeal, Queen's Bench—Chancery Division
2 Ch. D. (L.R.) 463
1876

On Wednesday, the 10th of June, 1874, the Defendant John Dodds signed and delivered to the Plaintiff, George Dickinson, a memorandum, of which the material part was as follows:

> "I hereby agree to sell to Mr. George Dickinson the whole of the dwelling-houses, garden ground, stabling, and outbuildings thereto belonging, situate at Croft, belonging to me, for the sum of £800. As witness my hand this tenth day of June, 1874.
> "£800. (Signed) John Dodds.";
> "P.S.—This offer to be left over until Friday, 9 o'clock, A.M. J.D. (the twelfth), 12th June, 1874.
> "(Signed) J. Dodds."

The bill alleged that Dodds understood and intended that the Plaintiff should have until Friday 9 A.M. within which to determine whether he would or would not purchase, and that he should absolutely have until that time the refusal of the property at the price of £800, and that the Plaintiff in fact determined to accept the offer on the morning of Thursday, the 11th of June, but did not at once signify his acceptance to Dodds, believing that he had the power to accept it until 9 A.M. on the Friday.

In the afternoon of the Thursday the Plaintiff was informed by a Mr. Berry that Dodds had been offering or agreeing to sell the property to Thomas Allan, the other Defendant. Thereupon the Plaintiff, at about half-past seven in the evening, went to the house of Mrs. Burgess, the mother-in-law of Dodds, where he was then staying, and left with her a formal acceptance in writing of the offer to sell the property. According to the evidence of Mrs. Burgess this document never in fact reached Dodds, she having forgotten to give it to him.

On the following (Friday) morning, at about seven o'clock, Berry, who was acting as agent for Dickinson, found Dodds at the Darlington railway station, and handed to him a duplicate of the acceptance by Dickinson, and explained to Dodds its purport. He replied that it was too late, as he had sold the property. A few minutes later Dickinson himself found Dodds entering a railway carriage, and handed him another duplicate of the notice of acceptance, but Dodds declined to receive it, saying, "You are too late. I have sold the property."

It appeared that on the day before, Thursday, the 11th of June, Dodds had signed a formal contract for the sale of the property to the Defendant Allan for £800, and had received from him a deposit of £40.

The bill in this suit prayed that the Defendant Dodds might be decreed specifically to perform the contract of the 10th of June, 1874; that he might be restrained from conveying the property to Allan; that Allan might be restrained from taking any such conveyance; that, if any such conveyance had been or should be made, Allan might be declared a trustee of the property for, and might be directed to convey the property to, the Plaintiff; and for damages.

JAMES, L.J.

The document, though beginning "I hereby agree to sell," was nothing but an offer, and was only intended to be an offer, for the Plaintiff himself tells us that he required time to consider whether he would enter into an agreement or not. Unless both parties had then agreed there was no concluded agreement then made; it was in effect and substance only an offer to sell. The Plaintiff, being minded not to complete the bargain at that time, added this memorandum—"This offer to be left over until Friday, 9 o'clock A.M., 12th June, 1874." That shews it was only an offer. There was no consideration given for the undertaking or promise, to whatever extent it may be considered binding, to keep the property unsold until 9 o'clock on Friday morning; but apparently Dickinson was of opinion, and probably Dodds was of the same opinion, that he (Dodds) was bound by that promise, and could not in any way withdraw from it, or retract it, until 9 o'clock on Friday morning, and this probably explains a good deal of what afterwards took place. But it is clear settled law, on one of the clearest principles of law, that this promise, being a mere nudum pactum, was not binding, and that at any moment before a complete acceptance by Dickinson of the offer, Dodds was as free as Dickinson himself. Well, that being the state of things, it is said that the only mode in which Dodds could assert that freedom was by actually and distinctly saying to Dickinson, "Now I withdraw my offer." It appears to me that there is neither principle nor authority for the proposition that there must be an express and actual withdrawal of the offer, or what is called a retractation. It must, to constitute a contract, appear that the two minds were at one, at the same moment of time, that is, that there was an offer continuing up to the time of the acceptance. If there was not such a continuing offer, then the acceptance comes to nothing. Of course it may well be that the one man is bound in some way or other to let the other man know that his mind with regard to the offer has been changed; but in this case, beyond all question, the Plaintiff knew that Dodds was no longer minded to sell the property to him as plainly and clearly as if Dodds had told him in so many words, "I withdraw the offer." This is evident from the Plaintiff's own statements in the bill.

The Plaintiff says in effect that, having heard and knowing that Dodds was no longer minded to sell to him, and that he was selling or had sold to some one else, thinking that he could not in point of law withdraw his offer, meaning to fix him to it, and endeavouring to bind him, "I went to the house where he was lodging, and saw his mother-in-law, and left with her an acceptance of the offer, knowing all the while that he had entirely changed his mind. I got an agent to watch for him at 7 o'clock the next morning, and I went to the train just before 9 o'clock, in order that I might catch him and give him my notice of acceptance just before 9 o'clock, and when that occurred he told my agent, and he told me, you are too late, and he then threw back the paper." It is to my mind quite clear that before there was any attempt at acceptance by the Plaintiff, he was perfectly well aware that Dodds had changed his mind, and that he had in fact agreed to sell the property to Allan. It is impossible, therefore, to say there was ever that existence of the same mind between the two parties which is essential in point of law to the making of an agreement. I am of opinion, therefore, that the Plaintiff has failed to prove that there was any binding contract between Dodds and himself.

MELLISH, L.J.:

If an offer has been made for the sale of property, and before that offer is accepted, the person who has made the offer enters into a binding agreement to sell the property to somebody else, and the person to whom the offer was first made receives notice in some way that the property has been sold to another person, can he after that make a binding contract by the acceptance of the offer? I am of opinion that he cannot. I am clearly of opinion that, just as when a man who has made an offer dies before it is accepted it is impossible that it can then be accepted, so when once the person to whom the offer was made knows that the property has been sold to some one else, it is too late for him to accept the offer, and on that ground I am clearly of opinion that there was no binding contract for the sale of this property by Dodds to Dickinson.

MORRISON

v.

THOELKE   *φ*

District Court of Appeal of Florida, Second District
155 So. 2d 889
1963

ALLEN, J.

A number of undisputed facts were established by the pleadings, including the facts that appellees are the owners of the subject property located in Orange County; that on November 26, 1957, appellants, as purchasers, executed a contract for the sale and purchase of the subject property and mailed the contract to appellees who were in Texas; and that on November 27, 1957, appellees executed the contract and placed it in the mails addressed to appellants' attorney in Florida. It is also undisputed that after mailing said contract, but prior to its receipt in Florida, appellees called appellants' attorney and cancelled and repudiated the execution and contract. Nonetheless, appellants, upon receipt of the contract caused the same to be recorded.

. . .

The rule that a contract is complete upon deposit of the acceptance in the mails, herein before referred to as "deposited acceptance rule" and also known as the "rule in Adams v. Lindsell," had its origin, insofar as the common law is concerned, in *Adams v. Lindsell*, 1 Barn. & Ald. 681, 106 Eng. Rep. 250 (K.B. 1818). In that case, the defendants had sent an offer to plaintiffs on September 2nd, indicating that they expected an answer "in course of post." The offer was misdirected and was not received and accepted until the 5th, the acceptance being mailed that day and received by defendant-offerors on the 9th. However, the defendants, who had expected to receive the acceptance on or before the 7th, sold the goods offered on the 8th of September. It was conceded that the delay had been occasioned by the fault of the defendants in initially misdirecting the offer.

. . .

[In the] American case, Tayloe v. Merchants' Fire Insurance Co. of Baltimore, 9 How. [50 U.S.] 390, 13 L. Ed. 187 (1850) the Supreme Court . . . closely followed the reasoning of Adams v. Lindsell. Holding an insurance contract complete upon posting of an acceptance, the Court wrote:

> The negotiation being carried on through the mail, the offer and acceptance cannot occur at the same moment of time; nor, for the same reason, can the meeting of the minds of the parties on the subject be known by each at the moment of concurrence; the acceptance must succeed the offer after the lapse of some interval of time; and, if the process is to be carried further in order to complete the bargain, and notice of the acceptance must be received, the only effect is to reverse the position of the parties, changing the knowledge of the completion from the one party to the other.

It is obviously impossible, therefore, under the circumstances stated, ever to perfect a contract by correspondence, if a knowledge of both parties at the moment they become bound is an essential element in making out the obligation. And as it must take effect, if effect is given at all to an endeavor to enter into a contract by correspondence, in the absence of the knowledge of one of the parties at the time of its consummation, it seems to us more consistent with the acts and declarations of the parties, to consider it complete on the transmission of the acceptance of the offer in the way they themselves contemplated; instead of postponing its completion till notice of such acceptance has been received and assented to by the company.

For why make the offer, unless intended that an assent to its terms should bind them? And why require any further assent on their part, after an unconditional acceptance by the party to whom it is addressed?

We have said that this view is in accordance with the usages and practices of these companies, as well as with the general principles of law governing contracts entered into by absent parties.

. . .

The problem raised by the impossibility of concurrent knowledge of manifest assent is discussed and a justification for the traditional rule is offered in Corbin, Contracts §78 (1950).

. . . When an offer is by mail and the acceptance also is by mail, the contract must date either from the mailing of the acceptance or from its receipt. In either case, one of the parties will be bound by the contract without being actually aware of that fact. If we hold the offeror bound on the mailing of the acceptance, he may change his position in ignorance of the acceptance; even though he waits a reasonable time before acting, he may still remain unaware that he is bound by contract because the letter of acceptance is delayed, or is actually lost or destroyed, in the mails. Therefore this rule is going to cause loss and inconvenience to the offeror in some cases. But if we adopt the alternative rule that the letter of acceptance is not operative until receipt, it is the offeree who is subjected to the danger of loss and inconvenience. He can not know that his letter has been received and that he is bound by contract until a new communication is received by him. His letter of acceptance may never have been received and so no letter of notification is sent to him; or it may have been received, and the letter of notification may be delayed or entirely lost in the mails. One of the parties must carry the risk of loss and inconvenience. We need a definite and uniform rule as to this. We can choose either rule; but we must choose one. We can put the risk on either party; but we must not leave it in doubt. The party not carrying the risk can then act promptly and with confidence in reliance on the contract; the party carrying the risk can insure against it if he so desires. The business community could no doubt adjust itself to either rule; but the rule throwing the risk on the offeror has the merit of closing the deal more quickly and enabling performance more promptly. It must be remembered that in the vast majority of cases the acceptance is neither lost nor delayed; and promptness of action is of importance in all of them. Also it is the offeror who has invited the acceptance.

. . .

Another justification offered for the rule . . . proposes that the making of an offer constitutes an expression of assent to the terms of the contract and that the "overt act" of depositing a written acceptance in the post represents the offeror's assent, whereupon the "concluding prerequisite" of a contract, mutual assent, is formed and the contract is complete. Critics of the rule respond by pointing out that the deposit of a letter in the mail is, in and of itself, a neutral factor, charged with legal significance only because the rule makes this particular "overt act" significant: signing a contract but then pocketing it could be, they argue, viewed as equally conclusive.

. . .

. . . Depreciating the alleged risk to the offeror, proponents argue that having made an offer by post the offeror is seldom injured by a slight delay in knowing it was accepted, whereas the offeree, under any other rule, would have to await both the transmission of the acceptance and notification of its receipt before being able to rely on the contract he unequivocally accepted. Finally, proponents point out that the offeror can always expressly condition the contract on his receipt of an acceptance and, should he fail to do so, the law should not afford him this advantage.

Opponents of the rule argue as forcefully that all of the disadvantages of delay or loss in communication which would potentially harm the offeree are equally harmful to the offeror. Why, they ask, should the offeror be bound by an acceptance of which he has no knowledge? Arguing specific cases, opponents of the rule point to the inequity of forbidding the offeror to withdraw his offer after the acceptance was posted but before he had any knowledge that the offer was accepted; they argue that to forbid the offeree to withdraw his acceptance, as in the instant case, scant hours after it was posted but days before the offeror knew of it, is unjust and indefensible. Too, the opponents argue, the offeree can always prevent the revocation of an offer by providing consideration, by buying an option.

In short, both advocates and critics muster persuasive argument. As Corbin indicated, there must be a choice made, and such choice may, by the nature of things, seem unjust in some cases. Weighing the arguments with reference not to specific cases but toward a rule of general application and recognizing the general and traditional acceptance of the rule as well as the modern changes in effective long-distance communication, it would seem that the balance tips, whether heavily or near imperceptively, to continued adherence to the "Rule in Adams v. Lindsell." This rule, although not entirely compatible with ordered, consistent and sometime artificial principles of contract advanced by some theorists, is, in our view, in accord with the practical considerations and essential concepts of contract law. See Llewellyn, Our Case Law of Contracts; Offer and Acceptance II, 48 Yale L.J. 779, 795 (1939). Outmoded precedents may, on occasion, be discarded and the function of justice should not be the perpetuation of error, but, by the same token, traditional rules and concepts should not be abandoned save on compelling ground.

. . .

In the instant case, an unqualified offer was accepted and the acceptance made manifest. Later, the offerees sought to repudiate their initial assent. Had there been a delay in their determination to repudiate permitting the letter to be delivered to appellant, no question as to the invalidity of the repudiation would have been entertained. As it were, the repudiation antedated receipt of the letter. However, adopting the view that the acceptance was effective when the letter of acceptance was deposited in the mails, the repudiation was equally invalid and cannot alone support the summary decree for appellees.

Problems

1. Negotiations Off Track. On December 5, Minneapolis & St. Louis Railway Company sent a letter to Columbus Rolling-Mill Company requesting prices for steel rails and iron rails. Columbus replied by letter on December 8, explaining that it did not make steel rails and offering to sell 2,000 to 5,000 tons of iron rails at specified prices. Railway responded by telegram on December 16 that it "accepted" the offer to sell 1,200 tons of iron rails, and it also sent a letter confirming the content of the telegram. On December 18, Columbus responded by telegram that it could not book the order at the "present price." Railway sent a December 19 telegram "accepting" the offer to sell 2,000 tons. Columbus refused to deliver, and Railway sued. What result?

2. A Well-Timed Acceptance. David and Elizabeth Kidd's dog bit a child, Mikaila Sherrod. Acting through a guardian ad litem, Sherrod submitted a claim to the Kidds for damages. On June 14, 2005, the Kidds offered $31,000 to settle the claim. On July 12, 2005, Sherrod filed suit. On July 20, 2005, the Kidds increased their offer to $32,000. The parties proceeded to mandatory arbitration on April 28, 2006. On May 5, 2006, the arbitrator awarded Sherrod just over $25,000. On May 9, 2006, Sherrod wrote to the Kidds, accepting their July 20, 2005 offer. Did the parties have a contract to settle the case for $32,000?

3. For ¼ of 1 percent. On December 30, John Hancock Mutual Life Insurance Company sent a letter to Houston Dairy agreeing to make the recipient an $800,000 loan at an interest rate of 9.25 percent provided that Houston Dairy returned written acceptance and a cashier's check for a $16,000 nonrefundable deposit within 7 days. On January 18, Houston Dairy's president dispatched the written confirmation and cashier's check. On January 23, John Hancock received the communication, deposited the check in its bank, and sent the information necessary to close the loan to its loan closing attorney. On January 28, the two parties' attorneys discussed how they would go about closing the loan. On January 30, Houston Dairy received a loan commitment from another lender at an interest rate of 9 percent and immediately asked John Hancock for a refund of the $16,000. John Hancock refused, and Houston Dairy sued. Did the parties have a contract?

4. The Deceased Offeree. Coronet Properties Company, a New York real estate development company, was converting a rent-controlled apartment building into a "co-op"—a form of apartment ownership in which owners purchase shares in a nonprofit corporation that owns the building. Coronet offered shares to the current tenants at a below-market price. Elisabeth De Kovessey was a tenant in the building at the time of the offer, but died before she could accept. After Coronet refused its proffered acceptance, De Kovessey's estate sued to enforce the contract. The trial court granted summary judgment in favor of the estate, and the appeals court affirmed. The New York Court of Appeals granted review. How should the court rule?

5. A Foreclosed Offer? James and Barbara Gibbs submitted an offer to purchase a house on which American Savings & Loan had recently foreclosed. American Savings sent a written counteroffer that included a signature line on which the Gibbses could indicate their acceptance. The Gibbses received the counteroffer on the morning of June 6, and both signed it immediately. That same morning, Barbara Gibbs placed the signed document in a typed envelope, handed that envelope to the mail clerk in her office, and instructed him to mail it, which she testified that he did immediately. Approximately one hour later, an employee of American Savings telephoned Barbara and told her the counteroffer was issued in error and was therefore revoked. The signed document arrived at American Savings two days later, bearing a postmark of June 7. American Savings claimed there was no contract of sale, and the Gibbses sued. Who should prevail?

Chapter 3

Affirmative Defenses to Contract Enforcement

If both parties assent to an agreement supported by consideration, they have formed a contract, and that contract is presumptively enforceable. Notwithstanding this presumption, however, one party can sometimes avoid enforcement by asserting an affirmative defense.

In the usual case, enforcement of contracts can be understood as being consistent with the principle of personal autonomy (i.e., enforcement supports the voluntary choice of the parties to be bound to an agreement) and the principle of efficiency (i.e., a voluntary contract makes parties better off than they would otherwise be, thus increasing total social welfare). Some circumstances, however, cast doubt on the accuracy of one or both of these assumptions. The doctrines considered in this chapter can be understood as providing courts with tools to step in and provide paternalistic protection when it is particularly likely that a contract does not, in fact, further these principles. As you study the following eight doctrines, consider whether they are well tailored to this general purpose. Consider also whether the benefits that the individual doctrines provide in terms of protection justify the implicit cost of reducing the predictability and certainty of enforcement, on which contracting parties rely.

The statute of frauds, where applicable, protects against the enforcement of alleged contracts that were never actually formed or, arguably, contracts that were formed but were ill considered by the parties. The doctrines of infancy and incapacity offer protection for groups that, due to their status, seem particularly likely to enter into contracts that do not serve their deeper interests. The duress and misrepresentation doctrines enable courts to police behavior by one contracting party that can lead the other to enter contracts that are either not truly voluntary or not sufficiently informed. Unconscionability, a modern innovation, can be understood as combining concerns about the status of one party and the behavior of the other. Finally, the public policy doctrine provides courts with a tool to protect the interests of individuals not party to a contract, and society generally, when contracts that are both voluntary and desirable for the contracting parties threaten to create unjustified external harms.

A. THE STATUTE OF FRAUDS

Reducing the terms of a contract to writing reduces the likelihood that contemporaneous misunderstandings or faulty memories will lead to later disputes between parties. Documentation can also increase predictability when litigation arises and reduce the likelihood of outright fraud. Notwithstanding these obvious benefits of written over oral communication, the American legal system generally does not require written evidence of a contract's terms as a prerequisite for enforcement, as cases like *Hawkins v. McGee* and *Hamer v. Sidway* demonstrate. The statute of frauds delineates the exceptions to this rule.

In 1677, the British Parliament enacted the original statute of frauds, entitled "An Act for the prevention of Frauds and Perjuries." Most American legislatures later adopted similar statutes, with some variations as to the specifics. Such statutes continue in force in most American jurisdictions today. The Restatement identifies five categories of contracts commonly subject to state statutes of frauds: contracts that call for an executor or administrator of an estate to answer for the debts of the decedent; contracts that call for one person to answer for the duties of another; contracts for which marriage provides consideration; contracts for the sale of interests in land; and contracts not to be performed within one year of the making of the contract. Rest. (2d) Contracts §110. To this list, the UCC adds contracts for the sale of goods that exceed $500 in value, U.C.C. §2-201, and leases of goods where total payments exceed $1,000. U.C.C. §2A-201. A contract that falls within the statute of frauds technically need not be a *written contract* in order to be enforced, so long as a written memorandum evidences the existence and essential terms of the contract and is signed by the party against whom the contract is being enforced (known as "the party to be charged"). Rest. (2d) Contracts §131.

An introductory contracts course cannot provide sufficient time for a thorough canvassing of the range of issues raised by the statute of frauds, but the following set of cases identifies and explores three types of questions that arise. The first two cases, *C.R. Klewin, Inc. v. Flagship Properties, Inc.* and *McInerney v. Charter Golf, Inc.*, concern the statute's scope: the specific issue in these cases is whether contracts of indefinite duration fall within the statute's "one-year" provision. The next two cases, *Bazak International Corporation v. Mast Industries, Inc.* and *Crabtree v. Elizabeth Arden Sales Corporation*, consider the parameters of the statute's writing and signature requirements. The final case, *Chomicky v. Buttolph*, examines whether a party's admission that an oral contract was formed or "part performance" by one of the parties serves as a substitute for satisfaction of the statute.

C.R. KLEWIN, INC.
v.
FLAGSHIP PROPERTIES, INC.
Supreme Court of Connecticut
220 Conn. 569
1991

PETERS, J.

The sole question before us in this certified appeal is whether the provision of the statute of frauds, General Statutes §52-550(a)(5), requiring a writing for an "agreement that is not to be performed within one year from the making thereof," renders unenforceable an oral contract that fails to specify explicitly the time for performance when performance of that contract within one year of its making is exceedingly unlikely. . . .

The plaintiff, C.R. Klewin, Inc. (Klewin), is a Connecticut based corporation that provides general construction contracting and construction management services. The defendants, Flagship Properties and DKM Properties (collectively Flagship), are engaged in the business of real estate development; although located outside Connecticut, they do business together in Connecticut under the trade name ConnTech.

Flagship became the developer of a major project (ConnTech Project) in Mansfield, near the University of Connecticut's main campus. The master plan for the project included the construction of twenty industrial buildings, a 280 room hotel and convention center, and housing for 592 graduate students and professors. The estimated total cost of the project was $120 million.

In March, 1986, Flagship representatives held a dinner meeting with Klewin representatives. Flagship was considering whether to engage Klewin to serve as construction manager on the ConnTech Project. During the discussions, Klewin advised that its fee would be 4 percent of the cost of construction plus 4 percent for its overhead and profit. This fee structure was, however, subject to change depending on when different phases of the project were to be constructed. The meeting ended with Flagship's representative shaking hands with Klewin's agent and saying, "You've got the job. We've got a deal." No other specific terms or conditions were conclusively established at trial. The parties publicized the fact that an agreement had been reached and held a press conference, which was videotaped. Additionally, they ceremoniously signed, without filling in any of the blanks, an American Institute of Architects Standard Form of Agreement between Owner and Construction Manager.

Construction began May 4, 1987, on the first phase of the ConnTech Project, called Celeron Square. The parties entered into a written agreement regarding the construction of this one part of the project. Construction was fully completed by the middle of October, 1987. By that time, because Flagship had become dissatisfied with Klewin's work, it began negotiating with other contractors for the job as construction manager on the next stage of the ConnTech Project. In March, 1988, Flagship contracted with another contractor to perform the sitework for Celeron Square II, the next phase of the project.

. . .

I

The Connecticut statute of frauds has its origins in a 1677 English statute entitled "An Act for the prevention of Fraud and Perjuries." See 6 W. Holdsworth, A History of English Law (1927) pp. 379-84. The statute appears to have been enacted in response to developments in the common law arising out of the advent of the writ of assumpsit, which changed the general rule precluding enforcement of oral promises in the King's courts. Thereafter, perjury and the subornation of perjury became a widespread and serious problem. Furthermore, because juries at that time decided cases on their own personal knowledge of the facts, rather than on the evidence introduced at trial, a requirement, in specified transactions, of "some memorandum or note . . . in writing, and signed by the party to be charged" placed a limitation on the uncontrolled discretion of the jury. See 2 A. Corbin, Contracts (1950) §275, pp. 2-3; 6 W. Holdsworth, supra, pp. 387-89; An Act for Prevention of Fraud and Perjuries, 29 Car. 2, c. 3, §4 (1677), quoted in J. Perillo, "The Statute of Frauds in the Light of the Functions and Dysfunctions of Form," 43 Fordham L. Rev. 39, 39 n.2 (1974). Although the British Parliament repealed most provisions of the statute, including the one-year provision, in 1954; see The Law Reform (Enforcement of Contracts) Act, 2 & 3 Eliz. 2, c. 34 (1954); the statute nonetheless remains the law virtually everywhere in the United States.

Modern scholarly commentary has found much to criticize about the continued viability of the statute of frauds. The statute has been found wanting because it serves none of its purported functions very well; see J. Perillo, supra; and because it permits or compels economically wasteful behavior; see M. Braunstein, "Remedy, Reason, and the Statute of Frauds: A Critical Economic Analysis," 1989 Utah L. Rev. 383. It is, however, the one-year provision that is at issue in this case that has caused the greatest puzzlement among commentators. As Professor Farnsworth observes, "of all the provisions of the statute, it is the most difficult to rationalize.

> "If the one-year provision is based on the tendency of memory to fail and of evidence to go stale with the passage of time, it is ill-contrived because the one-year period does not run from the making of the contract to the proof of the making, but from the making of the contract to the completion of performance. If an oral contract that cannot be performed within a year is broken the day after its making, the provision applies though the terms of the contract are fresh in the minds of the parties. But if an oral contract that can be performed within a year is broken and suit is not brought until nearly six years (the usual statute of limitations for contract actions) after the breach, the provision does not apply, even though the terms of the contract are no longer fresh in the minds of the parties.
>
> "If the one-year provision is an attempt to separate significant contracts of long duration, for which writings should be required, from less significant contracts of short duration, for which writings are unnecessary, it is equally ill-contrived because the one-year period does not run from the commencement of performance to the completion of performance, but from the making of the contract to the completion of performance. If an oral contract to work for one day, 13 months from now, is broken, the provision applies, even though the duration of performance is only one day. But if an oral contract to work for a year beginning today is broken, the provision does not apply, even though the duration of performance is a full year."

2 E. Farnsworth, Contracts (2d Ed. 1990) §6.4, pp. 110-11; see also Goldstick v. ICM Realty, 788 F.2d 456, 464 (7th Cir. 1986); D & N Boening, Inc. v. Kirsch Beverages, Inc., 63 N.Y.2d 449, 454, 472 N.E.2d 992, 483 N.Y.S.2d 164 (1984); 1 Restatement (Second), Contracts (1979) §130, comment a; J. Calamari & J. Perillo, Contracts (3d Ed. 1987) §19-18, p. 807.[6]

. . .

In any case, the one-year provision no longer seems to serve any purpose very well, and today its only remaining effect is arbitrarily to forestall the adjudication of possibly meritorious claims. For this reason, the courts have for many years looked on the provision with disfavor, and have sought constructions that limited its application. See, e.g., Landes Construction Co. v. Royal Bank of Canada, 833 F.2d 1365, 1370 (9th Cir. 1987) (noting policy of California courts "of restricting the application of the statute to those situations precisely covered by its language"); Cunningham v. Healthco, Inc., 824 F.2d 1448, 1455 (5th Cir. 1987) (one-year provision does not apply if the contract "conceivably" can be performed within one year); Hodge v. Evans Financial Corporation, 823 F.2d 559, 561 (D.C. Cir. 1987) (statute of frauds "has long been construed narrowly and literally"); Goldstick v. ICM Realty, supra, 464 ("Courts tend to take the concept of 'capable of full performance' quite literally . . . because they find the one-year limitation irksome.").

II

Our case law in Connecticut, like that in other jurisdictions, has taken a narrow view of the one-year provision of the statute of frauds now codified as §52-550(a)(5). In *Russell v. Slade*, 12 Conn. 455, 460 (1838), this court held that "it has been repeatedly adjudged, that unless it appear *from the agreement itself*, that it is *not* to be performed within a year, the statute does not apply. . . . The statute of frauds plainly means an agreement *not* to be performed within the space of a year, and *expressly* and *specifically* so agreed. A *contingency* is not within it; nor any case that *depends upon contingency*. It does *not* extend to cases where the thing only *may* be performed within the year." (Emphases in original; citation and internal quotation marks omitted.)

A few years later, in Clark v. Pendleton, 20 Conn. 495, 508 (1850), the statute was held not to apply to a contract that was to be performed following a voyage that both parties expected to take one and one-half years. "It is not alleged in any form, that it was made with reference to, or that its performance was to depend on the termination of a voyage which would necessarily occupy that time. It is only alleged, that it was expected by the parties, that the defendant would be absent for the period of eighteen months. But this expectation, which was only an opinion or belief of the parties, and the mental result of their private thoughts, *constituted no part of the agreement itself*; nor was it connected with it, so as to explain or give a

---

6. Even the statute's most notable defender chose not to mention the one-year provision when he contended that the statute is "in essence better adapted to our needs than when it was first passed." K. Llewellyn, "What Price Contract? An Essay in Perspective," 40 Yale L.J. 704, 747 (1931).

construction to it, although it naturally would, and probably did, form one of the motives which induced them to make the agreement. The thing thus anticipated did not enter into the contract, *as one of its terms*; and according to it, as stated, the defendant, whenever he should have returned, after having embarked on the voyage, whether before or after the time during which it was thus expected to continue, would be under an obligation to perform his contract with the plaintiff. As it does not therefore *appear, by its terms, as stated*, that it was not to be performed within a year from the time when it was made, it is not within the statute." (Emphases added.)

rule

In this century, in Appleby v. Noble, 101 Conn. 54 (1924), this court held that "'[a] contract is not within this clause of the statute unless *its terms are so drawn* that it cannot by any possibility be performed fully within one year.'" (Emphasis added.) In Burkle v. Superflow Mfg. Co., 137 Conn. 488 (1951), we delineated the line that separates contracts that are within the one-year provision from those that are excluded from it. "Where *the time for performance is definitely fixed at more than one year*, the contract is, of course, within the statute. . . . If no time is *definitely fixed* but full performance may occur within one year through the happening of a contingency upon which the contract depends, it is not within the statute." (Emphases added; citations omitted.)

More recently, in Finley v. Aetna Life & Casualty Co., 202 Conn. 190 (1987), we stated that "'[u]nder the prevailing interpretation, the enforceability of a contract under the one-year provision does not turn on the actual course of subsequent events, nor on the expectations of the parties as to the probabilities. Contracts of uncertain duration are simply excluded; the provision covers *only* those contracts whose performance *cannot possibly* be completed within a year.' (Emphasis added.) 1 Restatement (Second), Contracts, [§130, comment a]. . . ."

In light of this unbroken line of authority, the legislature's decision repeatedly to reenact the provision in language virtually identical to that of the 1677 statute suggests legislative approval of the restrictive interpretation that this court has given to the one-year provision. "[T]he action of the General Assembly in re-enacting the statute, including the clause in question . . . is presumed to have been done in the light of those decisions." Turner v. Scanlon, 146 Conn. 149 (1959); see also Ralston Purina Co. v. Board of Tax Review, 203 Conn. 425 (1987).

III

. . .

Most other jurisdictions follow a similar rule requiring an express contractual provision specifying that performance will extend for more than one year. Only "[a] few jurisdictions, contrary to the great weight of authority . . . hold that the intention of the parties may put their oral agreement within the operation of the Statute." 3 S. Williston, Contracts (3d Ed. W. Jaeger 1960) §495, pp. 584-85. In "the leading case on this section of the Statute"; id., p. 578; the Supreme Court of the United States undertook an extensive survey of the case law up to that time and concluded that "[i]t . . . appears to have been the settled construction of this clause of the statute in England, before the Declaration of Independence, that an oral agreement which, according to the intention of the parties, *as shown by the terms of the contract*, might be fully performed within a year from the time it was made, was not within the statute, although the time of its performance was uncertain, and might probably extend, and be expected by the parties to extend, and did in fact extend, beyond the year. The several States of the Union, in reenacting this provision of the statute of frauds in its original words, must be taken to have adopted the known and settled construction which it had received by judicial decisions in England." (Emphasis added.) Warner v. Texas & Pacific R. Co., 164 U.S. 418, 422-23, 17 S. Ct. 147, 41 L. Ed. 495 (1896). The agreement at issue was one in which a lumbermill agreed to provide grading and ties and the railway agreed to construct rails and a switch and maintain the switch as long as the lumbermill needed it for shipping purposes. Although the land adjoining the lumbermill contained enough lumber to run a mill for thirty years, and the lumbermill used the switch for thirteen years, the court held that the contract was not within the statute. "The parties may well have expected that the contract would continue in force for more than one year; it may have been very improbable that it would not do so; and it did in fact continue in force for a much longer time. But they made no stipulation which in terms, or by reasonable inference, required that result. The question is not what the probable, or expected, or actual performance of the contract was; but whether the contract, *according to the reasonable interpretation of its terms*, required that it should not be performed within the year." (Emphasis added.) Id., 434; see also Walker v. Johnson, 96 U.S. 424, 427, 24 L. Ed. 834 (1877); McPherson v. Cox, 96 U.S. 404, 416-17, 24 L. Ed. 746 (1877).

Because the one-year provision "is an anachronism in modern life . . . we are not disposed to expand its destructive force." Farmer v. Arabian American Oil Co., 277 F.2d 46, 51 (2d Cir. 1960). When a contract contains no express terms about the time for performance, no sound reason of policy commends judicial pursuit of a collateral inquiry into whether, at the time of the making of the contract, it was realistically possible that performance of the contract would be completed within a year. Such a collateral inquiry would not only expand the "destructive force" of the statute by extending it to contracts not plainly within its terms, but would also inevitably waste judicial resources on the resolution of an issue that has nothing to do with the merits of the case or the attainment of a just outcome. See 2 A. Corbin, supra, §275, p. 14 (the statute "has been in part the cause of an immense amount of litigation as to whether a promise is within the statute or can by any remote possibility be taken out of it. This latter fact is fully evidenced by the space necessary to be devoted to the subject in this volume and by the vast number of cases to be cited.").

We therefore hold that an oral contract that does not say, in express terms, that performance is to have a specific duration beyond one year is, as a matter of law, the functional equivalent of a contract of indefinite duration for the purposes of the statute of frauds. Like a contract of indefinite duration, such a contract is enforceable because it is outside the proscriptive force of the statute regardless of how long completion of performance will actually take.

The first certified question is answered "yes." The second certified question is answered "no." No costs will be taxed in this court to either party.

McINERNEY
v.
CHARTER GOLF, INC.

Supreme Court of Illinois
176 Ill. 2d 482
1997

HEIPLE, J.

Is an employee's promise to forgo another job opportunity in exchange for a guarantee of lifetime employment sufficient consideration to modify an existing employment-at-will relationship? If "yes," must such an agreement be in writing to satisfy the requirements of the statute of frauds? These questions, among others, must be answered in plaintiff Dennis McInerney's appeal from an order of the appellate court affirming a grant of summary judgment in favor of the defendant, Charter Golf, Inc. Although we conclude that a promise for a promise is sufficient consideration to modify a contract—even an employment contract—we further conclude that the statute of frauds requires that a contract for lifetime employment be in writing.

The facts are uncomplicated. This case comes to us on a grant of summary judgment, so our review is de novo (Barnett v. Zion Park District, 171 Ill. 2d 378, 385 (1996)), and we will consider "the pleadings, depositions, and admissions on file, together with the affidavits, if any," to determine whether a genuine issue of material fact exists (735 ILCS 5/2-1005(c) (West 1994)). From 1988 through 1992, Dennis McInerney worked as a sales representative for Charter Golf, Inc., a company which manufactures and sells golf apparel and supplies. Initially, McInerney's territory included Illinois but was later expanded to include Indiana and Wisconsin. In 1989, McInerney allegedly was offered a position as an exclusive sales representative for Hickey-Freeman, an elite clothier which manufactured a competing line of golf apparel. Hickey-Freeman purportedly offered McInerney an 8% commission.

Intending to inform Charter Golf of his decision to accept the Hickey-Freeman offer of employment, McInerney called Jerry Montiel, Charter Golf's president. Montiel wanted McInerney to continue to work for Charter Golf and urged McInerney to turn down the Hickey-Freeman offer. Montiel promised to guarantee McInerney a 10% commission on sales in Illinois and Wisconsin "for the remainder of his life," in a position where he would be subject to discharge only for dishonesty or disability. McInerney allegedly accepted Charter Golf's offer and, in exchange for the guarantee of lifetime employment, gave up the Hickey-Freeman offer. McInerney then continued to work for Charter Golf.

In 1992, the relationship between Charter Golf and McInerney soured: Charter Golf fired McInerney. McInerney then filed a complaint in the circuit court of Cook County, alleging breach of contract. The trial court granted Charter Golf's motion for summary judgment after concluding that the alleged oral contract was unenforceable under the statute of frauds because the contract amounted to an agreement which could not be performed within a year from its making. The appellate court affirmed, but on a wholly different ground. No. 1-94-1764 (unpublished order under Supreme Court Rule 23). The appellate court held that the putative contract between McInerney and Charter Golf suffered from a more fundamental flaw, namely, that no contract for lifetime employment even existed because a promise to forbear another job opportunity was insufficient consideration to convert an existing employment-at-will relationship into a contract for lifetime employment.

This court accepted McInerney's petition for leave to appeal (155 Ill. 2d R. 315), and for the reasons set forth below, we affirm on other grounds.

ANALYSIS

Employment contracts in Illinois are presumed to be at-will and are terminable by either party; this rule, of course, is one of construction which may be overcome by showing that the parties agreed otherwise. Duldulao v. St. Mary of Nazareth Hospital Center, 115 Ill. 2d 482, 489 (1987). As with any contract, the terms of an employment contract must be clear and definite (*Duldulao*, 115 Ill. 2d at 490) and the contract must be supported by consideration (Ladesic v. Servomation Corp., 140 Ill. App. 3d 489, 491 (1986); Martin v. Federal Life Insurance Co., 109 Ill. App. 3d 596, 602 (1982); Heuvelman v. Triplett Electrical Instrument Co., 23 Ill. App. 2d 231, 235 (1959)).

A. Consideration

Although the rules of contract law are well-established and straightforward, a conflict has emerged in the appellate court decisions on the subject of consideration in the context of a lifetime employment contract. Several decisions have held that a promise of lifetime employment, which by its terms purports to alter an employment-at-will contract, must be supported by "additional" consideration beyond the standard employment duties. *Heuvelman*, 23 Ill. App. 2d at 235-36; Koch v. Illinois Power Co., 175 Ill. App. 3d 248, 252 (1988); *Ladesic*, 140 Ill. App. 3d at 492-93. These cases have held that an employee's rejecting an outside job offer in exchange for a promised guarantee of lifetime employment is not sufficient consideration to alter an employment-at-will relationship. *Heuvelman*, 23 Ill. App. 2d at 236, 161 N.E.2d 875; *Koch*, 175 Ill. App. 3d at 252; *Ladesic*, 140 Ill. App. 3d at 492-93. The premise underlying these cases is that the employee simply weighs the benefits of the two positions, and by accepting one offer the employee necessarily rejects the other. As such, these cases have reasoned that the employee has not given up anything of value, and thus there is no consideration to support the promise of lifetime employment. *Koch*, 175 Ill. App. 3d at 252; *Ladesic*, 140 Ill. App. 3d at 492-93.

One case, however, has taken issue with this analysis. In Martin v. Federal Life Insurance Co., the appellate court held that an enforceable contract for lifetime employment was formed when an employee relinquished a job offer in exchange for a promise of permanent employment from his current employer. Martin v. Federal Life Insurance Co., 109 Ill. App. 3d 596, 601, 65 Ill. Dec. 143, 440 N.E.2d 998

(1982). The *Martin* court recognized that there was consideration in an exchange of promises: the employer promised to give up his right to terminate the employee at-will, and in exchange the employee agreed to continue working for his current employer and to forgo a lucrative opportunity with a competitor. *Martin*, 109 Ill. App. 3d at 601.

. . .

In the instant case, Charter Golf argues that an employee's promise to forgo another employment offer in exchange for an employer's promise of lifetime employment is not sufficient consideration. But why not? The defendant has failed to articulate any principled reason why this court should depart from traditional notions of contract law in deciding this case. While we recognize that some cases have indeed held that such an exchange is "inadequate" or "insufficient" consideration to modify an employment-at-will relationship, we believe that those cases have confused the conceptual element of consideration with more practical problems of proof. As we discussed above, this court has held that a promise for a promise constitutes consideration to support the existence of a contract. To hold otherwise in the instant case would ignore the economic realities underlying the case. Here McInerney gave up a lucrative job offer in exchange for a guarantee of lifetime employment; and in exchange for giving up its right to terminate McInerney at will, Charter Golf retained a valued employee. Clearly both parties exchanged bargained-for benefits in what appears to be a near textbook illustration of consideration.

Of course, not every relinquishment of a job offer will necessarily constitute consideration to support a contract. On the related issue of mutuality of obligation, Charter Golf complains that McInerney's promise to continue working was somehow illusory, because it alleges that McInerney had the power to terminate the employment relationship at his discretion while it lacked any corresponding right. The court's decision in Armstrong Paint & Varnish Works v. Continental Can Co., 301 Ill. 102, 108 (1922), teaches that "where there is any other consideration for the contract mutuality of obligation is not essential." Charter Golf's argument on this point fails because McInerney continued working for Charter Golf and relinquished his right to accept another job opportunity. When, as here, the employee relinquishes something of value in a bargained-for exchange for the employer's guarantee of permanent employment, a contract is formed.

B. Statute of Frauds

So there is a contract, but should we enforce it? Charter Golf argues that the oral contract at issue in this case violates the statute of frauds and is unenforceable because it is not capable of being performed within one year of its making. By statute in Illinois, "[n]o action shall be brought . . . upon any agreement that is not to be performed within the space of one year from the making thereof, unless . . . in writing and signed by the party to be charged." 740 ILCS 80/1 (West 1994). Our statute tracks the language of the original English Statute of Frauds and Perjuries. 29 Charles II ch. 3 (1676). The English statute enacted by Parliament had as its stated purpose the prohibition of those "many fraudulent practices, which are commonly endeavored to be upheld by perjury and subordination of perjury." 29 Charles II ch. 3, introductory clause (1676). Illinois' statute of frauds seeks to do the same by barring actions based upon nothing more than loose verbal statements.

The period of one year, although arbitrary, recognizes that with the passage of time evidence becomes stale and memories fade. The statute proceeds from the legislature's sound conclusion that while the technical elements of a contract may exist, certain contracts should not be enforced absent a writing. It functions more as an evidentiary safeguard than as a substantive rule of contract. As such, the statute exists to protect not just the parties to a contract, but also—perhaps more importantly—to protect the fact finder from charlatans, perjurers and the problems of proof accompanying oral contracts.

There are, of course, exceptions to the statute of frauds' writing requirement which permit the enforcement of certain oral contracts required by the statute to be in writing. One such exception is the judicially created exclusion for contracts of uncertain duration. In an effort to significantly narrow the application of the statute, many courts have construed the words "not to be performed" to mean "not capable of being performed" within one year. See Restatement (Second) of Contracts §130 (1981). These cases hold that if performance is possible by its terms within one year, the contract is not within the statute regardless of how unlikely it is that it will actually be performed within one year. Under this interpretation, the actual course of subsequent events and the expectations of the parties are entirely irrelevant. Restatement (Second) of Contracts §130, Comment a (1981). A contract for lifetime employment would then be excluded from the operation of the statute because the employee could, in theory, die within one year, and thus the contract would be "capable of being performed."[1]

We find such an interpretation hollow and unpersuasive. A "lifetime" employment contract is, in essence, a permanent employment contract. Inherently, it anticipates a relationship of long duration—certainly longer than one year. In the context of an employment-for-life contract, we believe that the better view is to treat the contract as one "not to be performed within the space of one year from the making thereof." To hold otherwise would eviscerate the policy underlying the statute of frauds and would invite confusion, uncertainty and outright fraud. Accordingly, we hold that a writing is required for the fair enforcement of lifetime employment contracts.

The plaintiff argues that the statute of frauds' writing requirement is nonetheless excused because he performed, either fully or partially, according to the terms of the oral contract. Illinois courts have held that a party who has fully performed an oral

---

1. In attempting to rein in this exception to the statute of frauds, some courts have made a distinction—at times quite attenuated—between death as full performance and death operating to terminate or excuse the contract. *See, e.g., Sinclair v. Sullivan Chevrolet Co.*, 45 Ill. App. 2d 10, 15 (1964); *Martin, supra; Gilliland v. Allstate Insurance Co.*, 69 Ill. App. 3d 630 (1979). Under this view, an oral contract for employment for a stated period longer than one year will not be enforced because, although the employee could die within one year of the making of the contract, these courts elect to treat that contingency as an excuse or termination of the contract and not as performance. This distinction, while perhaps logical in other contexts, is meaningless in our case where the complete performance contemplated by the parties, *i.e.,* employment for life, is identical to the event giving rise to termination or excuse. Under the terms of the oral contract alleged in this case, the employee's death would have resulted in full performance.

contract within the one-year provision may nonetheless have the contract enforced. American College of Surgeons v. Lumbermens Mutual Casualty Co., 142 Ill. App. 3d 680, 700 (1986); Meyer v. Logue, 100 Ill. App. 3d 1039, 1043 (1981); Noesges v. Servicemaster Co., 233 Ill. App. 3d 158, 163 (1992). Full or complete performance of the instant contract, by its terms, would have required the plaintiff to work until his death, but our plaintiff lives.

A party's partial performance generally does not bar application of the statute of frauds, unless it would otherwise be "impossible or impractical to place the parties in status quo or restore or compensate" the performing party for the value of his performance. Mapes v. Kalva Corp., 68 Ill. App. 3d 362, 368 (1979); see also Payne v. Mill Race Inn, 152 Ill. App. 3d 269, 278 (1987). This so-called exception resembles the doctrines of restitution, estoppel and fraud, and exists to avoid a "virtual fraud" from being perpetrated on the performing party. Barrett v. Geisinger, 148 Ill. 98 (1893); see also Restatement (Second) of Contracts §130, Comment e (1981). In any event, our plaintiff has been fully compensated for the work that he performed. Accordingly, part performance—on these facts—will not take the case out of the statute of frauds.

. . .

Appellate court judgment affirmed.

NICKELS, J. (dissenting).

I agree with the majority's conclusion that plaintiff's promise to forgo another job opportunity is sufficient consideration in return for defendant's promise of lifetime employment to plaintiff. However, I disagree with the majority's holding that the employment contract in the case at bar must be in writing because it falls within the requirements of the statute of frauds.

The writing requirement applies to "any agreement that is not to be performed within the space of one year from the making thereof." 740 ILCS 80/1 (West 1994). Commenting on this language, the Restatement (Second) of Contracts observes:

> "[T]he enforceability of a contract under the one-year provision does not turn on the actual course of subsequent events, nor on the expectations of the parties as to the probabilities. Contracts of uncertain duration are simply excluded; the provision covers only those contracts whose performance cannot possibly be completed within a year." Restatement (Second) of Contracts §130, Comment a, at 328 (1981).

A contract of employment for life is necessarily one of uncertain duration. Since the employee's life may end within one year, and, as the majority acknowledges, the contract would be fully performed upon the employee's death (176 Ill. 2d at 490 n. 1), the contract is not subject to the statute of frauds' one-year provision. See Restatement (Second) of Contracts §130, Illustration 2, at 328 (1981); see also 72 Am. Jur. 2d Statute of Frauds §14, at 578 (1974) ("The rule generally accepted by the authorities is that an agreement or promise the performance or duration of which is contingent on the duration of human life is not within the statute"); J. Calamari & J. Perillo, The Law of Contracts §19-20 (3d ed. 1987) ("if A promises . . . to employ X for life, the promise is not within the Statute because it is not for a fixed term and the contract by its terms is conditioned upon the continued life of X and the condition may cease to exist within a year because X may die within a year"). It is irrelevant whether the parties anticipate that the employee will live for more than a year or whether the employee actually does so.

The majority acknowledges that "many courts" subscribe to this view. More accurately, the Restatement rule represents "the prevailing interpretation" of the statute of frauds' one-year provision. Restatement (Second) of Contracts §130, Comment a, at 328 (1981). Only a "distinct minority" of cases have ascribed significance to whether the parties expected that a contract would take more than a year to perform. J. Calamari & J. Perillo, The Law of Contracts §19-18, at 808 (3d ed. 1987). . . .

BAZAK INTERNATIONAL CORP.
v.
MAST INDUSTRIES, INC.
Court of Appeals of New York
73 N.Y.2d 113
1989

KAYE, J.

This dispute between textile merchants concerning an alleged oral agreement to sell fabric centers on the "merchant's exception" to the Statute of Frauds (UCC 2-201[2]). We conclude that annotated purchase order forms signed by the buyer, sent to the seller and retained without objection, fall within the merchant's exception, satisfying the statutory requirement of a writing even without the seller's signature. It was therefore error to dismiss the buyer's breach of contract action on Statute of Frauds grounds, and deny it any opportunity to prove that the alleged agreement had indeed been made.

For purposes of this dismissal motion, we accept the facts as stated by plaintiff buyer (Bazak International). On April 22, 1987 Karen Fedorko, marketing director of defendant seller (Mast Industries), met with Tuvia Feldman, plaintiff's president, at Feldman's office. Fedorko offered to sell Feldman certain textiles that Mast was closing out, and the two negotiated all the terms of an oral agreement except price. At a meeting the following day, Fedorko and Feldman agreed on a price of $103,330. Fedorko told Feldman that Bazak would receive written invoices for the goods the next day and that the textiles would be delivered shortly. When no invoices arrived, Feldman contacted Fedorko, who assured him that everything was in order and that the invoices were on the way. However, on April 30, 1987, Fedorko had Feldman come to the New York City offices of Mast's parent company where, following Fedorko's instructions, Feldman sent five purchase orders by telecopier to Mast's Massachusetts office. That same day Feldman received written confirmation of Mast's receipt of the orders. Mast made no objection to the terms set forth in the telecopied purchase orders, but never delivered the textiles despite Bazak's demands.

Bazak then filed a complaint alleging breach of contract and fraud, which Mast moved to dismiss for failure to state a cause of action, based upon the lack of documentary evidence (CPLR 3211[a][7]). Mast contended that the only writings alleged in the complaint—the purchase orders sent by Bazak to Mast, and Mast's confirmation of receipt of the purchase orders—were insufficient under UCC 2-201 to satisfy the Statute of Frauds. In addition, Mast argued that the complaint did not make out a cause of action for fraud, but merely duplicated the contract allegations.

[The] Supreme Court denied the motion to dismiss, but the Appellate Division reversed, holding that the breach of contract claim was barred by the Statute of Frauds, and that the fraud claim merely disguised a flawed breach of contract claim. The focal issue before us on Bazak's appeal from that order is whether the disputed documents qualified as confirmatory writings within the "merchant's exception" to the Statute of Frauds (UCC 2-201[2]). We conclude that they did, and therefore reverse the Appellate Division order.

At the heart of the dispute are two issues involving the telecopied purchase orders. First, the parties disagree as to the standard for determining whether the purchase orders are confirmatory documents: Mast asserts that there is a presumption against application of UCC 2-201(2)—if the memorandum on its face is such that a reasonable merchant could reasonably conclude that it was not a confirmation, then the claim is barred as a matter of law by the Statute of Frauds. Bazak, on the other hand, argues for a less restrictive standard—that is, a requirement only that the writings afford a belief that the alleged oral contract rests on a real transaction, a requirement Bazak contends that it has met. Second, the parties disagree as to the application of the governing standard to this complaint. Bazak contends that the purchase orders were sent in confirmation of the agreement already reached, and that there is sufficient support for that interpretation in the documents themselves; Mast argues that on their face, the purchase orders are no more than offers to enter into an agreement, and thus inadequate to satisfy the Statute of Frauds.

As to both issues, we are essentially in agreement with Bazak, and therefore reverse the order dismissing its complaint.

. . .

DESCRIPTION OF THE WRITINGS

A total of five printed purchase order forms, all of them on Bazak's letterhead, were telecopied by Feldman to Mast from the offices of Mast's parent company. The first four are individual orders for various quantities of different types of fabric, while the fifth summarizes the orders and states the total price. All are dated April 23, 1987—the date of the alleged oral contract. On each form, are the handwritten words "As prisented [sic] by Karen Fedorko." At the bottom of each form are several lines of small type reading: "All claims must be made within 5 days after receipt of goods. No allowances or returns after goods are cut. This is only an offer and not a contract unless accepted in writing by the seller, and subject to prior sale." Each form concludes with two signature lines, one for "Bazak International Corp." and one for "customers acceptance." Each form is signed by Bazak, but the space for "customers acceptance" remains blank.

An interoffice memorandum confirms that the purchase orders were telecopied to Mast's Massachusetts office from the premises of Mast's parent company on April 30, 1987.

THE WRITINGS AS CONFIRMATIONS OF A CONTRACT

The Statute of Frauds remains a vital part of the law of this State. A contract for the sale of goods for the price of $500 or more is not enforceable "unless there is some writing sufficient to indicate that a contract for sale has been made between the parties and signed by the party against whom enforcement is sought or by his authorized agent or broker." (UCC 2-201[1].) That section further provides that the only indispensable term in such a writing is quantity.

Undisputedly, the alleged oral contract in this case was for the sale of more than $500 worth of goods, and the only writings were not signed by Mast, against whom enforcement is sought. Bazak claims, however, that the orders fall under the merchant's exception to the signature requirement contained in UCC 2-201(2): "Between merchants if within a reasonable time a writing in confirmation of the contract and sufficient against the sender is received and the party receiving it has reason to know its contents, it satisfies the requirements of subsection (1) against such party unless written notice of objection to its contents is given within 10 days after it is received." Bazak contends that the purchase orders are writings in confirmation of the oral agreement reached between Fedorko and Feldman, and that having failed to object to their contents Mast cannot now assert the Statute of Frauds defense.

At the outset, we are called upon to define the standard to be applied in determining whether a document can be construed as a confirmatory writing under UCC 2-201(2): are explicit words of confirmation necessary? Should there be a presumption against application of the section? Relying on a New Jersey case, Trilco Term. v. Prebilt Corp. (167 NJ Super 449, 400 A2d 1237, affd without opn 174 NJ Super 24, 415 A2d 356), and a subsequent Federal case applying Trilco, Norminjil Sportswear Corp. v. TG & Y Stores Co. (644 F Supp 1 [SDNY]), Mast argues that confirmatory language is necessary, and that an exacting standard should be imposed.

The cases cited by Mast do stand for the proposition that a writing offered as confirmatory in satisfaction of UCC 2-201(2) is insufficient unless it explicitly alerts the recipient to the fact that it is intended to confirm a previous agreement. In Trilco, the lower court stated its belief that as a policy matter, a more stringent test was appropriate under UCC 2-201(2) than that applied under UCC 2-201(1) to determine if a writing was "sufficient to indicate that a contract for sale has been made," because under the merchant's exception, a party could be bound by a writing it had not signed. The Federal District Court in *Norminjil* found this reasoning persuasive in what it perceived to be the absence of any New York case law on the point.

We disagree. . . .

But even writing on a clean slate, we reject the exacting standard proposed by *Trilco* and *Norminjil* as inconsistent with the letter and spirit of the relevant UCC sales provisions.

UCC 2-201(1) requires that the writing be "sufficient to indicate" a contract, while UCC 2-201(2) calls for a writing "in confirmation of the contract." We see no reason for importing a more stringent requirement of explicitness to the latter section, and holding merchants engaged in business dealings to a higher standard of precision in their word choices. The official comment describes UCC 2-201(1) as simply requiring "that the writing afford a basis for believing that the offered oral evidence rests on a real transaction." As Karl Llewellyn, a principal drafter of UCC 2-201, explained to the New York Law Revision Commission: "What the section does * * * is to require some objective guaranty, other than word of mouth, that there really has been some deal." (1954 Report of NY Law Rev Commn, at 119.) We hold that the same standard applies under UCC 2-201(1) and 2-201(2), noting that this conclusion accords with the majority of courts and commentators that have considered the issue (see, e.g., Rubin & Sons v. Consolidated Pipe Co., 396 Pa 506, 153 A2d 472, 476; Azevedo v. Minister, 86 Nev 576, 471 P2d 661, 666; M.K. Metals v. Container Recovery Corp., 645 F2d 583, 591 [8th Cir]; Dura-Wood Treating Co. v. Century Forest Indus., 675 F2d 745, 749 [5th Cir]; Perdue Farms v. Motts, Inc., 459 F Supp 7, 15-16 [ND Miss]; 2 Anderson, Uniform Commercial Code §2-201:133, at 79 [3d ed]; 6C Bender's UCC Service, Willier & Hart, UCC Reporter-Digest §2-201, at 2-182; 1 White & Summers, op. cit., §2-5, at 87-88).

Special merchant rules are sprinkled throughout article 2 of the Uniform Commercial Code, distinguishing the obligations of business people from other (see, UCC 2-103[1][b]; 2-205, 2-207[2]; 2-209[2]; 2-312[3]; 2-314[1]; 2-327[1][c]; 2-402[2]; 2-403[2]; 2-509[3]; 2-603[1]; 2-605[1][b]; and 2-609[2]). Among the suggested motivations was to state clear, sensible rules better adjusted to the reality of what commercial transactions were (or should be), thereby promoting predictable, dependable, decent business practices (see, Hillinger, The Article 2 Merchant Rules: Karl Llewellyn's Attempt to Achieve The Good, The True, The Beautiful in Commercial Law, 73 Geo LJ 1141 [1985]). Section 2-201(2) recognized the common practice among merchants, particularly small businesses, to enter into oral sales agreements later confirmed in writing by one of the parties. Absent such a provision, only the party receiving the confirmatory writing could invoke the Statute of Frauds, giving that party the option of enforcing the contract or not, depending on how advantageous the transaction proved to be. UCC 2-201(2) was intended to address that inequity; it encourages the sending of confirmatory writings by removing the unfairness to the sender. (See, 1954 Report of NY Law Rev Comm'n, at 115.)

In imposing a requirement that the writing explicitly state that it is sent in confirmation, the understandable concern of the New Jersey court in *Trilco* was that the effect of UCC 2-201(2) was "to bind a merchant to a writing that he did not sign"

(167 NJ Super, at 455), and thus to create a new potential unfairness: a merchant might unilaterally create a binding contract simply by dispatching unsolicited purchase orders, thus unfairly disadvantaging the recipient. Consequently, the court perceived it was necessary to require that the writing contain explicit language of confirmation or reference to the prior agreement, so the recipient could know that the sender was asserting the existence of a contract, and hence had a "meaningful opportunity" to exercise the right of objection found in UCC 2-201(2) (id., at 454, 400 A2d, at 1240). This argument is not without merit. However, in our view it overlooks other protections provided by UCC 2-201.

A confirmatory writing does not satisfy the requirements of UCC 2-201(2) unless it is "sufficient against the sender." This alone provides some protection against abuse, for the sending merchant itself runs the risk of being held to a contract. Moreover, while we hold that explicit words of confirmation are not required, the writing still must satisfy the test articulated in UCC 2-201(1) that it be "sufficient to indicate that a contract for sale has been made." A purchase order, standing alone, is unlikely to meet this test. On the other hand, if the writing contains additional evidence that it is based upon a prior agreement, then as a policy matter it is not unfair to require the recipient to make written objection where there is an intent to disavow it. True, a rule requiring explicit confirmatory language or an express reference to the prior agreement could be applied mechanically and would afford the broadest possible protection to recipients of unsolicited orders. But that rigidity and breadth also could work unnecessary injustice and be unresponsive to the realities of business practice, which was a likely motivation for the merchant's exception in the first instance. Indeed, such a rule would reintroduce the very unfairness addressed by the reform, for the sending merchant still would be bound by the writing while the recipient could ignore it or enforce it at will (see, Comment, The Merchant's Exception to the UCC's Statute of Frauds, 32 Villanova L Rev 133, [1987]).

Finally, as additional protection against abuse and inequity, we note that the consequence of a failure to give timely written notice of objection to a confirmatory writing is only to remove the bar of the Statute of Frauds. The burden of proving that a contract was indeed made remains with the plaintiff, as does the burden of proving the terms of the contract. By the same token, the defendant remains free to urge that no contract was made, or that it differed from the one claimed by plaintiff (UCC 2-201, official comment 3). Thus, UCC 2-201(2) neither binds the receiving merchant to an agreement it has not made nor delivers an undeserved triumph to the sending merchant. It does no more than permit the sender to proceed with an attempt to prove its allegations.

We therefore conclude that, in determining whether writings are confirmatory documents within UCC 2-201(2), neither explicit words of confirmation nor express references to the prior agreement are required, and the writings are sufficient so long as they afford a basis for believing that they reflect a real transaction between the parties.

It remains for us to apply this standard to the facts and determine whether the documents in issue satisfy the requirements of UCC 2-201(2).

Of the various requirements of UCC 2-201(2), four are not in controversy. There is no dispute that both parties are merchants, that the writing was sent within a reasonable time after the alleged agreement, that it was received by someone with reason to know of its contents, and that no written objection was made. If the writings can be construed as confirming the alleged oral agreement, they are sufficient under UCC 2-201(1) against Bazak—the sender—since Bazak signed them. Thus, the open question is whether, applying the governing standard, the documents here were sufficient to indicate the existence of a prior agreement.

Cases considering whether writings containing the words "order" or "purchase order" could satisfy the "confirmatory" requirement of UCC 2-201(2) fall into two categories. In some, the writings on their face contemplated only a future agreement, and they were held insufficient to overcome the Statute of Frauds defense (see, e.g., Arcuri v. Weiss, 198 Pa Super 506); in others, there was language clearly indicating that a contract had already been made, and the writings were deemed sufficient (see, e.g., Dura-Wood Treating Co. v. Century Forest Indus., 675 F2d 74; Perdue Farms v. Motts, Inc., 459 F Supp 7). The writings here do not fit neatly into either group. However, taken as a whole, there is sufficient evidence that the writings rest on a real transaction, and therefore satisfy the Statute of Frauds.

We first address Mast's contention—apparently decisive in the Appellate Division—that the small print at the foot of the forms to the effect that they are "only an offer and not a contract unless accepted in writing by the seller" must be given literal effect and precludes the possibility that the writings were confirmatory of an agreement. While an express disclaimer generally would suffice to disqualify a memorandum as confirmatory of an oral agreement (see, 1 White & Summers, op. cit., §2-4, at 85), it is plain from the face of these documents that the printed matter was entirely irrelevant to the dealings between these parties. The forms themselves bespeak their purpose: to record a sale by Bazak as seller, not a purchase by Bazak as buyer. The language regarding claims, allowances and returns are clearly all referable to a transaction in which Bazak was the seller, as is the signature line for Bazak. Read literally, these forms would not even have allowed for Mast's signature; the line for "customers acceptance" is obviously inapplicable—Bazak, not Mast, was the customer. In short, though Mast is free to argue at trial that different inferences should be drawn, the forms indicate that Bazak simply used its seller's documents to record its confirmation of the alleged contract, and that the small print at the bottom of the page was no part of that communication.

The handwritten notations on the purchase order forms provide a basis for believing that the documents were in furtherance of a previous agreement. The terms set forth are highly specific; precise quantities, descriptions, prices per unit and payment terms are stated. The documents refer to an earlier presentation by defendant's agent Karen Fedorko. The date April 23, 1987 is written on the forms and the date April 30 on the transmission, indicating reference to a transaction that took place a week before they were sent. Finally, Mast itself relayed Bazak's forms. The telecopier transmittal sheet shows that the forms were sent to Mast by defendant's own parent company in New York, using its facilities—obviously suggesting that the forms were not merely unsolicited purchase orders from Bazak, but that their content reflected an agreement that had been reached between the parties.

While no one of these factors would be sufficient under UCC 2-201(2), considered together they adequately indicate confirmation of a preexisting agreement so as to permit Bazak to go forward and prove its allegations.

Finally on this issue, addressing the dissent, it is apparent that a philosophical difference divides the court. The plain implication of the dissent is that express confirmatory language is needed because "ambiguous" confirmatory writings unfairly burden receiving merchants. The majority, by contrast, perceives that the Code intended to place such a burden on the receiving merchant because there is less unfairness in requiring it to disavow than in denying the sending merchant who has failed to use any magic words an opportunity to prove the existence of a contract. A merchant bent on fraud, of course, can easily send documents containing express confirmation of a nonexistent oral contract, so it is difficult to see how our reading of the statute "weakens" its protection against fraud (dissenting opn, at 131). The protection consists of requiring a writing that provides a basis for belief that it rests on a real transaction—no more, no less. If the writing is sufficient to indicate the existence of a contract, it is also sufficient at the pleading stage to support an inference that the receiving merchant knew full well what it was. . . .

ALEXANDER, J. (dissenting).

As alleged by Bazak International Corp. (Bazak), on April 22 and 23, 1987, Ms. Karen Fedorko, marketing director of defendant Mast Industries, Inc. (Mast), met with Bazak's corporate officer, Tuvia Feldman, and allegedly negotiated all the terms of an oral agreement, pursuant to which Bazak was to purchase certain knitted textiles from Mast at a price of $103,330.

Approximately one week later, on or about April 30, 1987, Bazak sent Mast five purchase orders prepared by Bazak and bearing Bazak's signature. These orders recite the description, quantity and price terms of the goods and four of the orders are also inscribed "As prisented [sic] by Karen Fedorko," presumably a reference to the meetings of April 22 and 23. None of the orders, however, refer to any "agreement," "contract," "sale," "purchase" or anything else to indicate that an agreement had been reached by the parties on that date or thereafter. Indeed, near the bottom of each order, a disclaimer states: "this in [sic] only an offer and not a contract unless accepted in writing by the seller." Further, the orders include two signature lines, one signed by Bazak, and the other, which is blank, labeled "CUSTOMERS ACCEPTANCE." It is undisputed that Mast received the orders but did not sign them or object to them within 10 days.

. . .

The majority concludes that the merchant's exception of UCC 2-201(2) does not require that writings contain express confirmatory language (compare, Trilco Term. v. Prebilt Corp., 167 NJ Super 449, 400 A2d 1237, 1239-1241, affd without opn 174 NJ Super 24, 415 A2d 356; Norminjil Sportswear Corp. v. T G & Y Stores Co., 644 F Supp 1, 3-4 [SDNY]; see generally, 1 White & Summers, Uniform Commercial Code §2-5, at 87-88 [3d ed—Practitioner's]; Comment, The Merchant's Exception to the Uniform Commercial Code's Statute of Frauds, 32 Villanova L Rev 133, 173-180) and that writings satisfy both UCC 2-201(1) and (2) when they are "sufficient to indicate that a contract for sale has been made between the parties" (UCC 2-201[1]) and are therefore "sufficient against the sender" (UCC 2-201[2]). In my view, however, it is unnecessary to reach the question of whether UCC 2-201(2) requires that writings "in confirmation of the contract" contain express confirmatory language because Bazak's purchase orders do not satisfy UCC 2-201(1). As the only proper inference to be drawn from the plain language of the purchase orders is that they are offers, the majority's determination that they evidence a completed contract is nothing more than speculation. These purchase orders expressly state that they are offers, and even if this plain language can be disregarded, the remaining language of the orders is ambiguous at best. By holding that the requirements of UCC 2-201 are satisfied by these writings, the majority undermines the very protections the statute was intended to afford.

UCC 2-201(1) and (2) provide:

> "(1) Except as otherwise provided in this section a contract for the sale of goods for the price of $500 or more is not enforceable by way of action or defense unless there is some writing sufficient to indicate that a contract for sale has been made between the parties and signed by the party against whom enforcement is sought or by his authorized agent or broker. A writing is not insufficient because it omits or incorrectly states a term agreed upon but the contract is not enforceable under this paragraph beyond the quantity of goods shown in such writing.
>
> "(2) Between merchants if within a reasonable time a writing in confirmation of the contract and sufficient against the sender is received and the party receiving it has reason to know of its contents, it satisfies the requirements of subsection (1) against such party unless written notice of objection to its contents is given within ten days after it is received."

UCC 2-201(1) bars actions to enforce alleged oral agreements for the sale of goods worth $500 or more unless the agreement is evidenced by a writing signed by the person against whom enforcement is sought. While UCC 2-201 was intended to eliminate some of the rigidity of the former Statute of Frauds, subdivision (1)'s requirement that the writing be "sufficient to indicate that a contract for sale has been made between the parties" is the statute's primary safeguard against fraudulent commercial practices (Howard Constr. Co. v. Jeff-Cole Quarries, 669 SW2d 221 [Mo]). The merchant's exception of UCC 2-201(2) does not in any way diminish this safeguard, rather, it permits a writing to satisfy the statute even though it is not signed by the merchant against whom it is to be enforced.

The official comment explains that a writing sufficiently "[indicates] that a contract for sale has been made" (UCC 2-201[1]) when it [affords] a basis for believing that the offered oral evidence rests on a real transaction" (UCC 2-201, official comment 1). While the majority correctly articulates this standard, it misapplies this standard by holding that these writings, which are at best ambiguous, satisfy the statute.

Even a most liberal construction of UCC 2-201(1) requires at least that the writing indicate that the existence of a contract is more probable than not (see, 1 White & Summers, op. cit., §2-4, at 84-85; see also, Comment, The Merchant's

Exception to the Uniform Commercial Code's Statute of Frauds, 32 Villanova L Rev 133, 173). This construction serves the statute's purpose of preventing fraud without unduly burdening commercial transactions (Comment, The Merchant's Exception to the Uniform Commercial Code's Statute of Frauds, op. cit., at 137-138; Dorman & Co. v. Noon Hour Food Prods., 501 F Supp 294, 296; Norminjil Sportswear Corp. v. TG & Y Stores Co., 644 F Supp 1, 3, supra; see also, Cohon & Co. v. Russell, 23 NY2d 569, 574) and comports with the operation of the merchant's exception of UCC 2-201(2). That subsection denies the Statute of Frauds defense to only those merchants who "unreasonably [fail] to reply to a letter of confirmation" (Hawkland, Sales and Bulk Sales Under the Uniform Commercial Code, at 28-29). Significantly, UCC 2-201(2) binds the receiving merchant only when it "has reason to know of [the] contents" of the writing, indicating that the contents of the writing must at least put the receiving merchant on notice that the sender believes that a contract was made. Thus, to satisfy UCC 2-201(1) and therefore be "sufficient against the sender" (UCC 2-201[2]), the writing must at least allow for the reasonable inference that a contract was made and therefore that the writing rests on a real transaction (see, Howard Constr. Co. v. Jeff-Cole Quarries, 669 SW2d 221, 227 [Mo], supra; Rubin & Sons v. Consolidated Pipe Co., 396 Pa 506, 153 A2d 472, 475-476).

. . .

Here, the majority's conclusion that there is sufficient evidence that Bazak's purchase orders evidence a completed contract is refuted by the writings themselves. As indicated earlier, the writings are at best ambiguous, allowing for equally probable inferences that the parties either engaged only in negotiations or entered a contract. They do not demonstrate that the existence of a contract is more probable than not (1 White & Summers §2-4) and therefore cannot satisfy the statute. Indeed, in view of this manifest ambiguity, a finding that these purchase orders "indicate that a contract for sale has been made" would require resort to the extraneous evidence of the practices and intentions of the parties offered by Bazak. Consideration of such evidence outside the terms of the documents themselves, however, is clearly precluded by the Statute of Frauds (UCC 2-201).

The purchase orders, by their own terms, are only offers. Each form states "this in [sic] only an offer and not a contract unless accepted in writing by the seller." The plain import of this language, in this action where defendant was a seller, was that defendant would not be bound unless it signed the form. The majority attempts to avoid the import of this plain language, urging that it should be disregarded because this printed statement is on a form plaintiff usually used when acting as a seller and thus is meaningless in this alleged transaction where plaintiff was acting as a buyer (majority opn, at 123-124). Significantly, plaintiff, who prepared the documents, never indicated on any of the forms that this disclaimer should be disregarded and, fully aware of the existence of the disclaimer, signed each form on the line provided beneath it. Moreover, the fact that plaintiff usually used these forms in its capacity as a seller is not properly considered in evaluating the sufficiency of the documents on their face (Scheck v. Francis, 26 NY2d 466, 472).

Even if the "offer" language properly could be disregarded, the purchase orders nevertheless are ambiguous and therefore insufficient to "indicate that a contract for sale has been made" (UCC 2-201[1]). Four of the purchase orders merely list quantities of goods and prices, with the additional notation "as prisented [sic] by Karen Fedorko." This reference to a presentation by defendant's employee is simply that—there is no indication that an agreement was reached at that presentation. Additionally, the list of goods and prices, as well as the totals contained in the fifth purchase order similarly provide no basis for inferring that a contract was made before the orders were drafted. They do not list delivery terms or other special requirements of the seller which might indicate that an agreement had been reached (cf., M.K. Metals v. Container Recovery Corp., 645 F2d 583, supra). The fact that the purchase orders were transmitted from defendant's home office, while possibly unusual, sheds no light on whether the parties had reached an agreement. Thus, nothing in the purchase orders reasonably leads to the conclusion that the existence of a completed contract is more probable than not.

Finally, the majority's holding that these purchase orders satisfy UCC 2-201(1) and (2) substantially weakens the statute's protection against fraud. To assert the Statute of Frauds defense, merchants will be required to promptly respond to writings which provide no notice that the sender believes that they have a contract and which may in fact indicate to the contrary: that the sender has submitted an offer. Such a rule unfairly burdens the receiving merchants and effectively negates the very purpose and intent of UCC 2-201(2): to put both the sending merchant and the receiving merchant on equal footing. . . .

CRABTREE
v.
ELIZABETH ARDEN SALES CORP.
Court of Appeals of New York
305 N.Y. 48
1953

FULD, J.

In September of 1947, Nate Crabtree entered into preliminary negotiations with Elizabeth Arden Sales Corporation, manufacturers and sellers of cosmetics, looking toward his employment as sales manager. Interviewed on September 26th, by Robert P. Johns, executive vice-president and general manager of the corporation, who had apprised him of the possible opening, Crabtree requested a three-year contract at $25,000 a year. Explaining that he would be giving up a secure well-paying job to take a position in an entirely new field of endeavor—which he believed would take him some years to master—he insisted upon an agreement for a definite term. And he repeated his desire for a contract for three years to Miss Elizabeth Arden, the corporation's president. When Miss Arden finally indicated that she was prepared to offer a two-year contract, based on an annual salary of $20,000 for the first six months, $25,000 for the second six months and $30,000 for the second year, plus expenses of $5,000 a year for each of those years, Crabtree replied that that offer was "interesting." Miss Arden thereupon had her personal secretary make this memorandum on a telephone order blank that happened to be at hand:

EMPLOYMENT AGREEMENT WITH
NATE CRABTREE Date Sept 26-1947
At 681 - 5th Ave 6: PM

. . . .

Begin 20000.
6 months 25000.
6 months 30000.
5000. - per year
Expense money
[2 years to make good]
Arrangement with
Mr Crabtree
By Miss Arden
Present Miss Arden
Mr John
Mr Crabtree
Miss OLeary

A few days later, Crabtree phoned Mr. Johns and telegraphed Miss Arden; he accepted the "invitation to join the Arden organization," and Miss Arden wired back her "welcome." When he reported for work, a "pay-roll change" card was made up and initialed by Mr. Johns, and then forwarded to the payroll department. Reciting that it was prepared on September 30, 1947, and was to be effective as of October 22d, it specified the names of the parties, Crabtree's "Job Classification" and, in addition, contained the notation that

This employee is to be paid as follows:
First six months of employment $20,000. per annum
Next six months of employment 25,000. per annum
After one year of employment 30,000. per annum
Approved by RPJ [initialed]

After six months of employment, Crabtree received the scheduled increase from $20,000 to $25,000, but the further specified increase at the end of the year was not paid. Both Mr. Johns and the comptroller of the corporation, Mr. Carstens, told Crabtree that they would attempt to straighten out the matter with Miss Arden, and, with that in mind, the comptroller prepared another "pay-roll change" card, to which his signature is appended, noting that there was to be a "Salary increase" from $25,000 to $30,000 a year, "per contractual arrangements with Miss Arden." The latter, however, refused to approve the increase and, after further fruitless discussion, plaintiff left defendant's employ and commenced this action for breach of contract.

At the ensuing trial, defendant denied the existence of any agreement to employ plaintiff for two years, and further contended that, even if one had been made, the statute of frauds barred its enforcement. The trial court found against defendant on both issues and awarded plaintiff damages of about $14,000, and the Appellate Division, two justices dissenting, affirmed. Since the contract relied upon was not to be performed within a year, the primary question for decision is whether there was a memorandum of its terms, subscribed by defendant, to satisfy the statute of frauds (Personal Property Law, §31).[3]

Each of the two payroll cards—the one initialed by defendant's general manager, the other signed by its comptroller—unquestionably constitutes a memorandum under the statute. That they were not prepared or signed with the intention of evidencing the contract, or that they came into existence subsequent to its execution, is of no consequence (see Marks v. Cowdin, 226 N.Y. 138, 145; Spiegel v. Lowenstein, 162 App. Div. 443, 448-449; see, also, Restatement, Contracts, §§209, 210, 214); it is enough, to meet the statute's demands, that they were signed with intent to authenticate the information contained therein and that such information does evidence the terms of the contract. (See Marks v. Cowdin, 226 N.Y. 138; Bayles v. Strong, 185 N.Y. 582, affg. 104 App. Div. 153; Spiegel v. Lowenstein, supra, 162 App. Div. 443, 448; see, also, 2 Corbin on Contracts [1951], pp. 732-733, 763-764; 2 Williston on Contracts [rev. ed. 1936], pp. 1682-1683.) Those two writings contain all of the essential terms of the contract—the parties to it, the position that plaintiff was to assume, the salary that he was to receive—except that relating to the duration of plaintiff's employment. Accordingly, we must consider whether that item, the length of the contract, may be supplied by reference to the earlier unsigned office memorandum, and, if so, whether its notation, "2 years to make good," sufficiently designates a period of employment.

The statute of frauds does not require the "memorandum * * * to be in one document. It may be pieced together out of separate writings, connected with one another either expressly or by the internal evidence of subject matter and occasion." (Marks v. Cowdin, 226 N.Y. 138, 145; see, also, 2 Williston, p. 1671; Restatement, Contracts, §208, subd. [a].) Where each of the separate writings has been subscribed by the party to be charged, little if any difficulty is encountered. (See, e.g., Marks v. Cowdin, supra, 226 N.Y. 138, 144-145.) Where, however, some writings have been signed, and others have not—as in the case before us—there is basic disagreement as to what constitutes a sufficient connection permitting the unsigned papers to be considered as part of the statutory memorandum. The courts of some jurisdictions insist that there be a reference, of varying degrees of specificity, in the signed writing to that unsigned, and, if there is no such reference, they refuse to permit consideration of the latter in determining whether the memorandum satisfies the statute. (See, e.g., Osborn v. Phelps, 19 Conn. 63; Hewitt Grain & Provision Co. v. Spear, 222 Mich. 608.) That conclusion is based upon a

---

3. While our opinion is limited to treatment of that question, we have, of course, considered the other points argued.

construction of the statute which requires that the connection between the writings and defendant's acknowledgment of the one not subscribed, appear from examination of the papers alone, without the aid of parol evidence. The other position—which has gained increasing support over the years—is that a sufficient connection between the papers is established simply by a reference in them to the same subject matter or transaction. (See, e.g., Frost v. Alward, 176 Cal. 691; Lerned v. Wannemacher, 91 Mass. 412.) The statute is not pressed "to the extreme of a literal and rigid logic" (Marks v. Cowdin, supra, 226 N.Y. 138, 144), and oral testimony is admitted to show the connection between the documents and to establish the acquiescence, of the party to be charged, to the contents of the one unsigned. (See Beckwith v. Talbot, 95 U.S. 289; Oliver v. Hunting, 44 Ch. D. 205, 208-209; see, also, 2 Corbin §§512-518; cf. Restatement, Contracts, §208, subd[b], par. [iii].)

The view last expressed impresses us as the more sound, and, indeed—although several of our cases appear to have gone the other way (see, e.g., Newbery v. Wall, 65 N.Y. 484; Wilson v. Lewiston Mill, 150 N.Y. 314)—this court has on a number of occasions approved the rule, and we now definitively adopt it, permitting the signed and unsigned writings to be read together, provided that they clearly refer to the same subject matter or transaction. (See, e.g., Peabody v. Speyers, 56 N.Y. 230; Raubitschek v. Blank, 80 N.Y. 478; Peck v. Vandemark, 99 N.Y. 29; Coe v. Tough, 116 N.Y. 273; Delaware Mills v. Carpenter Bros., 235 N.Y. 537, affg. 200 App. Div. 324.)

The language of the statute—"Every agreement . . . is void, unless . . . some note or memorandum thereof be in writing, and subscribed by the party to be charged" (Personal Property Law, §31)—does not impose the requirement that the signed acknowledgment of the contract must appear from the writings alone, unaided by oral testimony. The danger of fraud and perjury, generally attendant upon the admission of parol evidence, is at a minimum in a case such as this. None of the terms of the contract are supplied by parol. All of them must be set out in the various writings presented to the court, and at least one writing, the one establishing a contractual relationship between the parties, must bear the signature of the party to be charged, while the unsigned document must on its face refer to the same transaction as that set forth in the one that was signed. Parol evidence—to portray the circumstances surrounding the making of the memorandum—serves only to connect the separate documents and to show that there was assent, by the party to be charged, to the contents of the one unsigned. If that testimony does not convincingly connect the papers, or does not show assent to the unsigned paper, it is within the province of the judge to conclude, as a matter of law, that the statute has not been satisfied. True, the possibility still remains that, by fraud or perjury, an agreement never in fact made may occasionally be enforced under the subject matter or transaction test. It is better to run that risk, though, than to deny enforcement to all agreements, merely because the signed document made no specific mention of the unsigned writing. As the United States Supreme Court declared, in sanctioning the admission of parol evidence to establish the connection between the signed and unsigned writings. "There may be cases in which it would be a violation of reason and common sense to ignore a reference which derives its significance from such [parol] proof. If there is ground for any doubt in the matter, the general rule should be enforced.

But where there is no ground for doubt, its enforcement would aid, instead of discouraging, fraud." (Beckwith v. Talbot, supra, 95 U.S. 289, 292; see, also, Raubitschek v. Blank, supra, 80 N.Y. 478; Freeland v. Ritz, 154 Mass. 257, 259; Gall v. Brashier, 169 F.2d 704, 708-709; 2 Corbin, op. cit., §512, and cases cited.)

Turning to the writings in the case before us—the unsigned office memo, the payroll change form initialed by the general manager Johns, and the paper signed by the comptroller Carstens—it is apparent, and most patently, that all three refer on their face to the same transaction. The parties, the position to be filled by plaintiff, the salary to be paid him, are all identically set forth; it is hardly possible that such detailed information could refer to another or a different agreement. Even more, the card signed by Carstens notes that it was prepared for the purpose of a "Salary increase per contractual arrangements with Miss Arden." That certainly constitutes a reference of sorts to a more comprehensive "arrangement," and parol is permissible to furnish the explanation.

The corroborative evidence of defendant's assent to the contents of the unsigned office memorandum is also convincing. Prepared by defendant's agent, Miss Arden's personal secretary, there is little likelihood that that paper was fraudulently manufactured or that defendant had not assented to its contents. Furthermore, the evidence as to the conduct of the parties at the time it was prepared persuasively demonstrates defendant's assent to its terms. Under such circumstances, the courts below were fully justified in finding that the three papers constituted the "memorandum" of their agreement within the meaning of the statute.

Nor can there be any doubt that the memorandum contains all of the essential terms of the contract. (See N.E.D. Holding Co. v. McKinley, 246 N.Y. 40; Friedman & Co. v. Newman, 255 N.Y. 340.) Only one term, the length of the employment, is in dispute. The September 26th office memorandum contains the notation, "2 years to make good." What purpose, other than to denote the length of the contract term, such a notation could have, is hard to imagine. Without it, the employment would be at will (see Martin v. New York Life Ins. Co., 148 N.Y. 117, 121), and its inclusion may not be treated as meaningless or purposeless. Quite obviously, as the courts below decided, the phrase signifies that the parties agreed to a term, a certain and definite term, of two years, after which, if plaintiff did not "make good," he would be subject to discharge. And examination of other parts of the memorandum supports that construction. Throughout the writings, a scale of wages, increasing plaintiff's salary periodically, is set out; that type of arrangement is hardly consistent with the hypothesis that the employment was meant to be at will. The most that may be argued from defendant's standpoint is that "2 years to make good," is a cryptic and ambiguous statement. But, in such a case, parol evidence is admissible to explain its meaning. (See Martocci v. Greater New York Brewery, 301 N.Y. 57, 63; Marks v. Cowdin, supra, 226 N.Y. 138, 143-144; 2 Williston, op. cit., §576; 2 Corbin, op. cit., §527.) Having in mind the relations of the parties, the course of the negotiations and plaintiff's insistence upon security of employment, the purpose of the phrase—or so the trier of the facts was warranted in finding—was to grant plaintiff the tenure he desired.

CHOMICKY
v.
BUTTOLPH

𝒷

Supreme Court of Vermont
147 Vt. 128
1986

Hɪʟʟ, J

Defendants are landowners of lakeside property on Lake Dunmore. Their property is divided by a road. Intending to retain title to the undeveloped back lot together with a 50-foot strip leading to the lake, defendants offered the front lakeside lot and summer cottage for sale.

Plaintiffs inspected the property, and entered into negotiations with defendants. The parties eventually reached an understanding, and plaintiffs' attorney drew up a purchase and sale contract that reflected the terms of their agreement. Both parties signed the contract in August, 1985; the closing was to occur in mid-October. The contract, however, was made contingent on the defendants obtaining a subdivision permit from the Leicester Planning Commission.

While defendants' subdivision petition was pending, plaintiff Eugene Chomicky telephoned defendants to discuss an alternative that would allow them to proceed with the sale in the event that the permit was denied. Plaintiff proposed that defendants retain an easement granting them a 50-foot right-of-way in lieu of outright ownership. Mr. Buttolph told Mr. Chomicky that they had considered that option, but that his wife was opposed to it. He agreed to discuss it with her again.

On October 1, Mr. Buttolph called the plaintiffs, and indicated that the right-of-way arrangement previously discussed was acceptable in the event that the Leicester Planning Commission did not approve their subdivision permit.

The Commission met on October 12, 1985, and denied defendants' permit application. On October 13, defendants called plaintiffs and advised them that "the deal was off." They now wanted to sell the whole parcel or nothing. Plaintiffs sued for specific performance on the oral contract allegedly concluded over the phone.

A contract involving the sale of land or interests therein is controlled by the Statute of Frauds. See 12 V.S.A. §181(5). As a general rule, such contracts must be in writing to be enforceable. See Couture v. Lowery, 122 Vt. 239, 243 (1961). Moreover, any proposed changes or modifications "are subjected to the same requirements of form as the original provisions." Evarts v. Forte, 135 Vt. 306, 311 (1977).

According to plaintiffs, defendants have admitted to the existence of the oral contract in question, and are thus precluded from setting up the Statute of Frauds as a defense to this action. . . .

[W]hile the writing requirement is imposed primarily as a shield against possible fraud, see *Couture*, supra, 122 Vt. at 243, it also "promotes deliberation, seriousness, certainty, and shows that the act was a genuine act of volition." Rabel, The Statute of Frauds and Comparative Legal History, 63 L.Q. Rev. 174, 178 (1947). In short, it helps to ensure that contracts for the sale of land or interests therein are not entered into improvidently. Thus, in *Couture*, supra, 122 Vt. at 243, we expressly stated that "[one] may admit the sale of land by a verbal contract, and yet defend an action for specific performance by pleading the statute." See also Radke v. Brenon, 271 Minn. 35, 37-38 (1965) (fact that defendant admits parol contract sued upon does not preclude him from setting up and insisting upon the Statute of Frauds as a defense to the action).

A party can certainly waive the benefit of the statute, *Couture*, supra, 122 Vt. at 243, 168 A.2d at 298 (citations omitted); however, we have no occasion to address this issue here as defendants specifically pleaded the Statute of Frauds as an affirmative defense to plaintiffs' complaint.

. . .

"The validation of an oral contract to convey real estate in spite of the prohibition against enforcement of the Statute of Frauds depends on the doctrine of part performance." Jasmin v. Alberico, 135 Vt. 287, 289 (1977). The doctrine of part performance, as we have repeatedly stated, is invoked to give relief to those who substantially and irretrievably change their position in reliance on the oral agreement. Id. at 290 (citing Towsley v. Champlain Oil Co., 127 Vt. 541, 543 (1969)). Moreover, we have consistently held that the reliance must be something beyond injury compensable by money to warrant taking the contract outside the statute. Id. at 289-90 (citing *Troy*, supra, 132 Vt. at 82; Cooley v. Hatch, 91 Vt. 128, 133 (1917)).

Plaintiffs contend that the doctrine of part performance was properly invoked as they made financing arrangements, and conducted a title search in preparation for closing. "[Activities] in preparation for [a] proposed transfer of title . . . , though perhaps troublesome, belong to that class of responsibilities that fall into the lot of any prospective seller [or purchaser] of real estate, and are not . . . the kind of imposition supporting the equitable relief sought." *Towsley*, supra, 127 Vt. at 543-44.

Plaintiffs also claim that their $5,000 downpayment constitutes sufficient reliance to warrant the granting of specific performance. This claim merits little or no comment as we have repeatedly emphasized that "money payments on the purchase are not enough to give the oral agreement enforceable status, even coupled with possession, in the face of the Statute of Frauds." *Jasmin*, supra, 135 Vt. at 290; see also *Troy*, supra, 132 Vt. at 82 (simple possession coupled with fractional payment of total purchase price is not such part performance as would take the oral contract outside the statute). The equities are even less compelling in this case than in the two cases just cited as plaintiffs never entered into possession or made improvements on the property. . . .

Problems

1. The Timber Cutter. A.S. McClanahan received an oral offer from the Otto-Marmet Coal & Mining Company to pay him to cut down all the trees on two tracts of land in order to provide wooden stakes for Otto-Marmet's mine. McClanahan worked the land for over two years before the company told him they would not pay him anymore and proceeded to hire someone else to do the work.

McClanahan sued the mine for breach of contract, and the company argued that recovery was barred by the statute of frauds because the agreement was for greater than one year and not memorialized in writing. At trial, when McClanahan was asked how long he expected the job to take, he answered, "I don't hardly know. I did not expect it to take more than five or six years." The lawyer for the mine followed up, "And you calculated to take five or six years to cut it off?" To which McClanahan replied "Yes, at the way they used the posts." Should McClanahan be entitled to recover for breach of contract?

2. Dirt Cheap. Ray DePugh wanted to construct a lake, and the Mead Corporation wanted dirt and clay. On this basis, the two agreed that Mead would excavate a portion of DePugh's land and pay half the market value of the soil it collected. A written agreement was drafted, which provided that

> DePugh hereby grants to Mead the license and right to enter upon and use the Property (and any easements and access rights relating thereto) to excavate, remove and purchase Borrow and to restore, seed and mulch the Property as provided herein until such operations are completed.

Neither party signed the agreement, and after Mead had surveyed the land, DePugh decided that he did not want to follow through with the plans. Mead sued for breach of contract. DePugh raised the statute of frauds as a defense. Who should prevail?

3. An Expensive Typo. As a result of a proofreading error, Lexus of Westminster placed a newspaper advertisement offering a used Jaguar XJ6 automobile worth approximately $37,000 for sale for $25,995. Along with a physical description and the price, the advertisement included the car's unique vehicle identification number and the following text: "All cars plus tax, lic., doc., smog & bank fees. On approved credit. Ad expires 4/27/97." The ad prominently displayed the name "Lexus of Westminster" in three places and included a map showing directions to the dealership. When Brian Donovan came to the dealership and attempted to accept the offer, the dealership refused to tender the car. Donovan sued, and the dealer defended on the ground that the statute of frauds was not satisfied. Who should prevail?

4. A House Sale? Tom and Debbie Rosenfeld thought they had purchased their dream home. They met the owner, Michael Zerneck, and made him an all-cash offer. After a discussion, Zerneck sent this response via e-mail:

> Dear Tom & Debbie,
> This note is to confirm yesterday's telephone conversation in which I accepted your all cash offer of $3,525,000 for 18 PPW, with no contingencies for financing or sale of your present residence, to close no later than July 1, 2004.
>   As we discussed, please contact Liz early next week to schedule your inspection. My attorney will prepare a contract of sale, to be signed after your engineer's report. (What is the contact information for your attorney? Will you be making the purchase jointly? What is your present address?)

We look forward to continuing cordial relations regarding the sale of this very special home to you and your family.

With kind regards,

Michael

The inspection was satisfactory, but Zerneck subsequently refused to sell the house to the Rosenfelds at the agreed upon price. The Rosenfelds sued for breach of contract. Zerneck claimed that his e-mail did not satisfy the statute of frauds. Is he correct?

B. INFANCY

The law of infancy provides one of the clearest "bright-line" rules in contract law: contracts entered into by an individual under the age of majority are voidable at the election of the minor, or "infant," before or within a reasonable time after reaching the age of majority. Rest. (2d) Contracts §14. Although the basic rule is simple and applied consistently across the United States, the consequences of the minor's decision to avoid a contract and the breadth of exceptions to the rule provide ample room for dispute and subtle variations across jurisdictions.

One important question, explored in *Halbman v. Lemke* and *Dodson v. Schrader*, is whether a minor who disaffirms a contract must compensate the adult for depreciation of or damage to the assets provided by the adult prior to disaffirmance. Relatedly, should this question be resolved with a bright-line rule, or should the answer depend on whether the terms of the contract were unfair to the minor, whether the minor damaged the assets or merely subjected them to normal wear and tear, whether the minor deceived the adult about his age, or whether the minor is using the infancy doctrine as a defense to a breach of contract lawsuit or suing to rescind the agreement and obtain the return of his property?

Contracts that minors enter into for "necessaries" receive special treatment under the infancy doctrine, but what constitutes a "necessary" and what safeguards, if any, prevent an adult from exploiting an infant in such transactions? *Webster Street Partnership, Ltd. v. Sheridan* considers these issues.

HALBMAN
v.
LEMKE

Supreme Court of Wisconsin
298 N.W.2d 562
1980

CALLOW, J.

On this review we must decide whether a minor who disaffirms a contract for the purchase of a vehicle which is not a necessity must make restitution to the vendor for damage sustained by the vehicle prior to the time the contract was disaffirmed. . . .

issue

I.

This matter was before the trial court upon stipulated facts. On or about July 13, 1973, James Halbman, Jr. (Halbman), a minor, entered into an agreement with Michael Lemke (Lemke) whereby Lemke agreed to sell Halbman a 1968 Oldsmobile for the sum of $1,250. Lemke was the manager of L & M Standard Station in Greenfield, Wisconsin, and Halbman was an employee at L & M. At the time the agreement was made Halbman paid Lemke $1,000 cash and took possession of the car. Arrangements were made for Halbman to pay $25 per week until the balance was paid, at which time title would be transferred. About five weeks after the purchase agreement, and after Halbman had paid a total of $1,100 of the purchase price, a connecting rod on the vehicle's engine broke. . . .

. . . On October 15, 1973, Halbman returned the title to Lemke by letter which disaffirmed the purchase contract and demanded the return of all money theretofore paid by Halbman. Lemke did not return the money paid by Halbman.

. . .

II.

The sole issue before us is whether a minor, having disaffirmed a contract for the purchase of an item which is not a necessity and having tendered the property back to the vendor, must make restitution to the vendor for damage to the property prior to the disaffirmance. Lemke argues that he should be entitled to recover for the damage to the vehicle up to the time of disaffirmance. . . .

Neither party challenges the absolute right of a minor to disaffirm a contract for the purchase of items which are not necessities. That right, variously known as the doctrine of incapacity or the "infancy doctrine," is one of the oldest and most venerable of our common law traditions. See: Grauman, Marx & Cline Co. v. Krienitz, 142 Wis. 556, 560, 126 N.W. 50 (1910); 2 Williston, Contracts sec. 226 (3d ed. 1959); 42 Am. Jur. 2d Infants sec. 84 (1969). Although the origins of the doctrine are somewhat obscure, it is generally recognized that its purpose is the protection of minors from foolishly squandering their wealth through improvident contracts with crafty adults who would take advantage of them in the marketplace. Kiefer v. Fred Howe Motors, Inc., 39 Wis. 2d 20, 24, 158 N.W.2d 288 (1968). Thus it is settled law in this state that a contract of a minor for items which are not necessities is void or voidable at the minor's option. Id. at 23, 158 N.W.2d 288; Schoenung v. Gallet, 206 Wis. 52, 55, 238 N.W. 852 (1931); Grauman, Marx & Cline v. Krienitz, supra, 142 Wis. at 560-61, 126 N.W. 50; Thormaehlen v. Kaeppel, 86 Wis. 378, 380, 56 N.W. 1089 (1893).

Once there has been a disaffirmance, however, as in this case between a minor vendee and an adult vendor, unresolved problems arise regarding the rights and responsibilities of the parties relative to the disposition of the consideration exchanged on the contract. As a general rule a minor who disaffirms a contract is entitled to recover all consideration he has conferred incident to the transaction. Schoenung v. Gallet, supra. In return the minor is expected to restore as much of the consideration as, at the time of disaffirmance, remains in the minor's possession. Thormaehlen v. Kaeppel, supra, 86 Wis. at 380, 56 N.W. 1089; Grauman, Marx & Cline v. Krienitz, supra, 142 Wis. at 560-61, 126 N.W. 50. See also: Restatement of Restitution, sec. 62, comment b, (1937); Restatement (Second) of Contracts, sec. 18B, comment c (Tent. Draft No. 1, 1964). The minor's right to disaffirm is not contingent upon the return of the property, however, as disaffirmance is permitted even where such return cannot be made. Olson v. Veum, 197 Wis. 342, 345, 222 N.W. 233 (1928). See also: Nelson v. Browning, 391 S.W.2d 873, 875-76 (Mo. 1965); Boudreaux v. State Farm Mutual Auto. Ins. Co., 385 So. 2d 480, 483 (La. App. 1980); Williston, supra, sec. 238, 39-41.

The return of property remaining in the hands of the minor is not the issue presented here. In this case we have a situation where the property cannot be returned to the vendor in its entirety because it has been damaged and therefore diminished in value, and the vendor seeks to recover the depreciation. Although this court has been cognizant of this issue on previous occasions, we have not heretofore resolved it. See: Schoenung v. Gallet, supra, 206 Wis. at 57-58, 238 N.W. 852; Wallace v. Newdale Furniture Co., 188 Wis. 205, 207-08, 205 N.W. 819 (1925).

The law regarding the rights and responsibilities of the parties relative to the consideration exchanged on a disaffirmed contract is characterized by confusion, inconsistency, and a general lack of uniformity as jurisdictions attempt to reach a fair application of the infancy doctrine in today's marketplace. See: Robert G. Edge, Voidability of Minors' Contracts: A Feudal Doctrine in a Modern Economy, 1 Ga. L. Rev. 205 (1967); Walter D. Navin, Jr., The Contracts of Minors Viewed from the Perspective of Fair Exchange, 50 N.C. L. Rev. 517 (1972); Note, Restitution in Minors' Contracts in California, 19 Hastings L. Rev. 1199 (1968); 52 Marq. L. Rev. 437 (1969). See also: John D. McCamus, Restitution of Benefits Conferred Under Minors' Contracts, 28 U.N.B.L.J. 89 (1979); Annot., Infant's Liability for Use or Depreciation of Subject Matter, in Action to Recover Purchase Price Upon His Disaffirmance of Contract to Purchase Goods, 12 A.L.R.3d 1174 (1967). That both parties rely on this court's decision in Olson v. Veum, supra, is symptomatic of the problem.

In *Olson* a minor, with his brother, an adult, purchased farm implements and materials, paying by signing notes payable at a future date. Prior to the maturity of the first note, the brothers ceased their joint farming business, and the minor abandoned his interest in the material purchased by leaving it with his brother. The vendor initiated an action against the minor to recover on the note, and the minor (who had by then reached majority) disaffirmed. The trial court ordered judgment for the plaintiff on the note, finding there had been insufficient disaffirmance to sustain the plea of infancy. This court reversed, holding that the contract of a minor for the purchase of items which are not necessities may be disaffirmed even when the minor cannot make restitution. Lemke calls our attention to the following language in that decision:

> "To sustain the judgment below is to overlook the substantial distinction between a mere denial by an infant of contract liability where the other party is seeking to enforce it and those cases where he who was the minor not only disaffirms such contract but seeks the

aid of the court to restore to him that with which he has parted at the making of the contract. In the one case he is using his infancy merely as a shield, in the other also as a sword."197 Wis. at 344, 222 N.W. 233.

From this Lemke infers that when a minor, as a plaintiff, seeks to disaffirm a contract and recover his consideration, different rules should apply than if the minor is defending against an action on the contract by the other party. This theory is not without some support among scholars. See: Calamari and Perillo, The Law of Contracts, sec. 126, 207-09 (Hornbook Series 1970), treating separately the obligations of the infant as a plaintiff and the infant as a defendant.

Additionally, Lemke advances the thesis in the dissenting opinion by court of appeals Judge Cannon, arguing that a disaffirming minor's obligation to make restitution turns upon his ability to do so. For this proposition, the following language in Olson v. Veum, supra, 197 Wis. at 345, 222 N.W. 233, is cited:

> The authorities are clear that when it is shown, as it is here, that the infant cannot make restitution, then his absolute right to disaffirm is not to be questioned.

In this case Lemke argues that the *Olson* language excuses the minor only when restitution is not possible. Here Lemke holds Halbman's $1,100, and accordingly there is no question as to Halbman's ability to make restitution.

Halbman argues in response that, while the "sword-shield" dichotomy may apply where the minor has misrepresented his age to induce the contract, that did not occur here and he may avoid the contract without making restitution notwithstanding his ability to do so.

The principal problem is the use of the word "restitution" in *Olson*. A minor, as we have stated, is under an enforceable duty to return to the vendor, upon disaffirmance, as much of the consideration as remains in his possession. When the contract is disaffirmed, title to that part of the purchased property which is retained by the minor revests in the vendor; it no longer belongs to the minor. See, e.g., Restatement (Second) of Contracts, §18B, comment c (Tent. Draft No. 1, 1964). The rationale for the rule is plain: a minor who disaffirms a purchase and recovers his purchase price should not also be permitted to profit by retaining the property purchased. The infancy doctrine is designed to protect the minor, sometimes at the expense of an innocent vendor, but it is not to be used to bilk merchants out of property as well as proceeds of the sale. Consequently, it is clear that, when the minor no longer possesses the property which was the subject matter of the contract, the rule requiring the return of property does not apply.[1] The minor will not be

---

1. Although we are not presented with the question here, we recognize there is considerable disagreement among the authorities on whether a minor who disposes of the property should be made to restore the vendor with something in its stead. The general rule appears to limit the minor's responsibility for restoration to specie only. Terrace Company v. Calhoun, 37 Ill. App. 3d 757 (1976); Adamowski v. Curtiss-Wright Flying Service, 300 Mass. 281 (1938); Quality Motors v. Hays, 216 Ark. 264 (1949). But see: Boyce v. Doyle, 113 N.J. Super. 240 (1971), adopting a "status quo" theory which requires the minor to restore the precontract status quo, even if it means returning proceeds or other value; Fisher v. Taylor Motor Co., 249 N.C. 617 (1959), requiring the minor to restore

required to give up what he does not have. We conclude that *Olson* does no more than set forth the foregoing rationale and that the word "restitution" as it is used in that opinion is limited to the return of the property to the vendor. We do not agree with Lemke and the court of appeals' dissent that Olson requires a minor to make restitution for loss or damage to the property if he is capable of doing so.

Here Lemke seeks restitution of the value of the depreciation by virtue of the damage to the vehicle prior to disaffirmance. Such a recovery would require Halbman to return more than that remaining in his possession. It seeks compensatory value for that which he cannot return. Where there is misrepresentation by a minor or willful destruction of property, the vendor may be able to recover damages in tort. See, e.g., Kiefer v. Fred Howe Motors, Inc., supra; 42 Am. Jur. 2d Infants §105 (1969). But absent these factors, as in the present case, we believe that to require a disaffirming minor to make restitution for diminished value is, in effect, to bind the minor to a part of the obligation which by law he is privileged to avoid. See: Nelson v. Browning, supra at 875-76; Williston, supra, §§238, 39-41.

The cases upon which the petitioner relies for the proposition that a disaffirming minor must make restitution for loss and depreciation serve to illustrate some of the ways other jurisdictions have approached this problem of balancing the needs of minors against the rights of innocent merchants. In Barber v. Gross, 74 S.D. 254 (1952), the South Dakota Supreme Court held that a minor could disaffirm a contract as a defense to an action by the merchant to enforce the contract but that the minor was obligated by a South Dakota statute, upon sufficient proof of loss by the plaintiff, to make restitution for depreciation. Cain v. Coleman, 396 S.W.2d 251 (Tex. Civ. App. 1965), involved a minor seeking to disaffirm a contract for the purchase of a used car where the dealer claimed the minor had misrepresented his age. In reversing summary judgment granted in favor of the minor, the court recognized the minor's obligation to make restitution for the depreciation of the vehicle. The Texas court has also ruled, in a case where there was no issue of misrepresentation, that upon disaffirmance and tender by a minor the vendor is obligated to take the property "as is." Rutherford v. Hughes, 228 S.W.2d 909, 912 (Tex. Civ. App. 1950). Scalone v. Talley Motors, Inc., 158 N.Y.S.2d 615 (1957), and Rose v. Sheehan Buick, Inc., 204 So. 2d 903 (Fla. App. 1967), represent the proposition that a disaffirming minor must do equity in the form of restitution for loss or depreciation of the property returned. Because these cases would at some point force the minor to bear the cost of the very improvidence from which the infancy doctrine is supposed to protect him, we cannot follow them.

As we noted in *Kiefer*, modifications of the rules governing the capacity of infants to contract are best left to the legislature. Until such changes are forthcoming, however, we hold that, absent misrepresentation or tortious damage to the property,

---

only the property remaining in the hands of the minor, "'or account for so much of its value as may have been invested in other property which he has in hand or owns and controls.'" Id. at 97. Finally, some attention is given to the "New Hampshire Rule" or benefits theory which requires the disaffirming minor to pay for the contract to the extent he benefited from it. Hall v. Butterfield, 59 N.H. 354 (1879); Porter v. Wilson, 106 N.H. 270 (1965). See also: 19 Hastings L.J. 1199, 1205-08 (1968); 52 Marq. L. Rev. 437 (1969); Calamari and Perillo, The Law of Contracts, secs. 129, 215-16 (Hornbook Series 1970).

a minor who disaffirms a contract for the purchase of an item which is not a necessity may recover his purchase price without liability for use, depreciation, damage, or other diminution in value.

Recently the Illinois Court of Appeals came to the same conclusion. In Weisbrook v. Clyde C. Netzley, Inc., 58 Ill. App. 3d 862 (1978), a minor sought to disaffirm a contract for the purchase of a vehicle which developed engine trouble after its purchase. In the minor's action the dealer counterclaimed for restitution for use and depreciation. The court affirmed judgment for the minor and, with respect to the dealer's claim for restitution, stated:

> In the present case, of course, the minor plaintiff never misrepresented his age and, in fact, informed defendant that he was 17 years old. Nor did plaintiff represent to defendant that his father was to be the owner or have any interest in the automobile. There is no evidence in the present case that plaintiff at the time of entering the contract with defendant intended anything more than to enjoy his new automobile. He borrowed the total purchase price and paid it to defendant carrying out the transaction fully at the time of taking delivery of the vehicle. Plaintiff sought to disaffirm the contract and the return of the purchase price only when defendant declined to make repairs to it. In these circumstances we believe the weight of authority would permit the minor plaintiff to disaffirm the voidable contract and that defendant-vendor would not be entitled to recoup any damages which he believes he suffered as a result thereof.

Id. at 1107. See also: Johnson Motors, Inc. v. Coleman, 232 So. 2d 716 (Miss. 1970); Rutherford v. Hughes, supra; Fisher v. Taylor Motor Co., 249 N.C. 617 (1959). We believe this result is consistent with the purpose of the infancy doctrine.

The decision of the court of appeals is affirmed.

DODSON
v.
SHRADER

Supreme Court of Tennessee
824 S.W.2d 545
1992

O'BRIEN, J.

This is an action to disaffirm the contract of a minor for the purchase of a pick-up truck and for a refund of the purchase price. The issue is whether the minor is entitled to a full refund of the money he paid or whether the seller is entitled to a setoff for the decrease in value of the pick-up truck while it was in the possession of the minor.

In early April of 1987, Joseph Eugene Dodson, then 16 years of age, purchased a used 1984 pick-up truck from Burns and Mary Shrader. The Shraders owned and operated Shrader's Auto Sales in Columbia, Tennessee. Dodson paid $4,900 in cash for the truck, using money he borrowed from his girlfriend's grandmother. At the time of the purchase there was no inquiry by the Shraders, and no misrepresentation by Mr. Dodson, concerning his minority. However, Mr. Shrader did testify that at the time he believed Mr. Dodson to be 18 or 19 years of age.

In December 1987, nine (9) months after the date of purchase, the truck began to develop mechanical problems. A mechanic diagnosed the problem as a burnt valve, but could not be certain without inspecting the valves inside the engine. Mr. Dodson did not want, or did not have the money, to effect these repairs. He continued to drive the truck despite the mechanical problems. One month later, in January, the truck's engine "blew up" and the truck became inoperable.

Mr. Dodson parked the vehicle in the front yard at his parents' home where he lived. He contacted the Shraders to rescind the purchase of the truck and requested a full refund. The Shraders refused to accept the tender of the truck or to give Mr. Dodson the refund requested.

Mr. Dodson then filed an action in general sessions court seeking to rescind the contract and recover the amount paid for the truck. The general sessions court dismissed the warrant and Mr. Dodson perfected a de novo appeal to the circuit court. At the time the appeal was filed in the circuit court Mr. Shrader, through counsel, declined to accept the tender of the truck without compensation for its depreciation. Before the circuit court could hear the case, the truck, while parked in Dodson's front yard, was struck on the left front fender by a hit-and-run driver. At the time of the circuit court trial, according to Shrader, the truck was worth only $500 due to the damage to the engine and the left front fender.

The case was heard in the circuit court in November 1988. The trial judge, based on previous common-law decisions and, under the doctrine of stare decisis reluctantly granted the rescission. The Shraders were ordered, upon tender and delivery of the truck, to reimburse the $4,900 purchase price to Mr. Dodson. The Shraders appealed. The Court of Appeals, per Todd, J., affirmed; Cantrell, J., concurring separately, Koch, J., dissenting.

. . .

As noted by the Court of Appeals, the rule in Tennessee, as modified, is in accord with the majority rule on the issue among our sister states. This rule is based upon the underlying purpose of the "infancy doctrine" which is to protect minors from their lack of judgment and "from squandering their wealth through improvident contracts with crafty adults who would take advantage of them in the market-place." Halbman v. Lemke, 99 Wis. 2d at 245 (1980).

There is, however, a modern trend among the states, either by judicial action or by statute, in the approach to the problem of balancing the rights of minors against those of innocent merchants. As a result, two (2) minority rules have developed which allow the other party to a contract with a minor to refund less than the full consideration paid in the event of rescission.

The first of these minority rules is called the "Benefit Rule." E.g., Hall v. Butterfield, 59 N.H. 354 (1879); Johnson v. Northwestern Mut. Life Insurance Co., 56 Minn. 365 (1894); Berglund v. American Multigraph Sales Co., 135 Minn. 67 (1916); Porter v. Wilson, 106 N.H. 270 (1965); Valencia v. White, 134 Ariz. 139 (Ariz. App. 1982). The rule holds that, upon rescission, recovery of the full purchase price is subject to a deduction for the minor's use of the merchandise. This rule recognizes that the traditional rule in regard to necessaries has been extended so far as to hold an infant bound by his contracts, where he failed to restore what he has received under them to the extent of the benefit actually derived by him from what he has received from the other party to the transaction. See Porter v. Wilson, 106 N.H. 270 (1965); Valencia v. White, supra, 2 Williston on Contracts, §238, p. 43 (3rd Ed. Jaeger 1959).

The other minority rule holds that the minor's recovery of the full purchase price is subject to a deduction for the minor's "use" of the consideration he or she received under the contract, or for the "depreciation" or "deterioration" of the consideration in his or her possession. See Carter v. Jays Motors, 3 N.J. Super. 82 (N.J. S. Ct., App. Div. 1949); Creer v. Active Automobile Exch., 99 Conn. 266 (Conn. 1923); Rodriguez v. Northern Auto Auction, 35 Misc. 2d 395 (N.Y. App. Div. 1962); Pettit v. Liston, 97 Ore. 464 (Ore. 1920).

. . .

We state the rule to be followed hereafter, in reference to a contract of a minor, to be where the minor has not been overreached in any way, and there has been no undue influence, and the contract is a fair and reasonable one, and the minor has actually paid money on the purchase price, and taken and used the article purchased, that he ought not to be permitted to recover the amount actually paid, without allowing the vender of the goods reasonable compensation for the use of, depreciation, and willful or negligent damage to the article purchased, while in his hands. If there has been any fraud or imposition on the part of the seller or if the contract is unfair, or any unfair advantage has been taken of the minor inducing him to make the purchase, then the rule does not apply. Whether there has been such an overreaching on the part of the seller, and the fair market value of the property returned, would always, in any case, be a question for the trier of fact. This rule will fully and fairly protect the minor against injustice or imposition, and at the same time it will be fair to a business person who has dealt with such minor in good faith.

This rule is best adapted to modern conditions under which minors are permitted to, and do in fact, transact a great deal of business for themselves, long before they have reached the age of legal majority. Many young people work and earn money and collect it and spend it often times without any oversight or restriction. The law does not question their right to buy if they have the money to pay for their purchases. It seems intolerably burdensome for everyone concerned if merchants and business people cannot deal with them safely, in a fair and reasonable way. Further, it does not appear consistent with practice of proper moral influence upon young people, tend to encourage honesty and integrity, or lead them to a good and useful business future, if they are taught that they can make purchases with their own money, for their own benefit, and after paying for them, and using them until they are worn out and destroyed, go back and compel the vendor to return to them what they have paid upon the purchase price. Such a doctrine can only lead to the corruption of principles and encourage young people in habits of trickery and dishonesty.

. . .

We note that in this case, some nine (9) months after the date of purchase, the truck purchased by the plaintiff began to develop mechanical problems. Plaintiff was informed of the probable nature of the difficulty which apparently involved internal problems in the engine. He continued to drive the vehicle until the engine "blew up" and the truck became inoperable. Whether or not this involved gross negligence or intentional conduct on his part is a matter for determination at the trial level. It is not possible to determine from this record whether a counterclaim for tortious damage to the vehicle was asserted. After the first tender of the vehicle was made by plaintiff, and refused by the defendant, the truck was damaged by a hit-and-run driver while parked on plaintiff's property. The amount of that damage and the liability for that amount between the purchaser and the vendor, as well as the fair market value of the vehicle at the time of tender, is also an issue for the trier of fact.

The case is remanded to the trial court for further proceedings in accordance with this judgment. The costs on appellate review are assessed equally between the parties.

WEBSTER STREET PARTNERSHIP, LTD.
v.
SHERIDAN

Supreme Court of Nebraska
220 Neb. 9
1985

KRIVOSHA, C.J.

. . . Webster Street is a partnership owning real estate in Omaha, Nebraska. On September 18, 1982, Webster Street, through one of its agents, Norman Sargent, entered into a written lease with Sheridan and Wilwerding for a second floor apartment at 3007 Webster Street. The lease provided that Sheridan and Wilwerding would pay to Webster Street by way of monthly rental the sum of $250 due on the first day of each month until August 15, 1983. The lease also required the payment of a security deposit in the amount of $150 and a payment of $20 per month for utilities during the months of December, January, February, and March. Liquidated damages in the amount of $5 per day for each day the rent was late were also provided for by the lease.

The evidence conclusively establishes that at the time the lease was executed both tenants were minors and, further, that Webster Street knew that fact. At the time the lease was entered into, Sheridan was 18 and did not become 19 until November 5, 1982. Wilwerding was 17 at the time the lease was executed and never gained his majority during any time relevant to this case.

The tenants paid the $150 security deposit, $100 rent for the remaining portion of September 1982, and $250 rent for October 1982. They did not pay the rent for the month of November 1982, and on November 5 Sargent advised Wilwerding that unless the rent was paid immediately, both boys would be required to vacate the premises. The tenants both testified that, being unable to pay the rent, they moved from the premises on November 12. In fact, a dispute exists as to when the two tenants relinquished possession of the premises, but in view of our decision that dispute is not of any relevance.

In a letter dated January 7, 1983, Webster Street's attorney made written demand upon the tenants for damages in the amount of $630.94. On January 12, 1983, the tenants' attorney denied any liability, refused to pay any portion of the amount demanded, stated that neither tenant was of legal age at the time the lease was executed, and demanded return of $150 security deposit.

Plt

. . .

As a general rule, an infant does not have the capacity to bind himself absolutely by contract. See Smith v. Wade, 169 Neb. 710 (1960); 43 C.J.S. Infants §166 (1978). The right of the infant to avoid his contract is one conferred by law for his protection against his own improvidence and the designs of others. See Burnand v. Irigoyen, 30 Cal. 2d 861 (1947). The policy of the law is to discourage adults from contracting with an infant; they cannot complain if, as a consequence of violating that rule, they are unable to enforce their contracts. As stated in Curtice Co. v. Kent, 89 Neb. 496, 500 (1911): "The result seems hardly just to the [adult], but persons dealing with infants do so at their peril. The law is plain as to their disability to contract, and safety lies in refusing to transact business with them."

rule

RPR

However, the privilege of infancy will not enable an infant to escape liability in all cases and under all circumstances. For example, it is well established that an infant is liable for the value of necessaries furnished him. 42 Am. Jur. 2d Infants §65 (1969). See, also, Burnand v. Irigoyen, supra; Merrick v. Stephens, 337 S.W.2d 713 (Mo. App. 1960); Englebert v. Troxell, 40 Neb. 195 (1894). An infant's liability for necessaries is based not upon his actual contract to pay for them but upon a contract implied by law, or, in other words, a quasi-contract. 42 Am. Jur. 2d, supra.

Just what are necessaries, however, has no exact definition. The term is flexible and varies according to the facts of each individual case. In Cobbey v. Buchanan, 48 Neb. 391, 397 (1896), we said: "'The meaning of the term "necessaries" cannot be defined by a general rule applicable to all cases; the question is a mixed one of law and fact, to be determined in each case from the particular facts and circumstances in such case.'" A number of factors must be considered before a court can conclude whether a particular product or service is a necessary. As stated in Schoenung v. Gallet, 206 Wis. 52, 54 (1931):

> The term "necessaries," as used in the law relating to the liability of infants therefor, is a relative term, somewhat flexible, except when applied to such things as are obviously requisite for the maintenance of existence, and depends on the social position and situation in life of the infant, as well as upon his own fortune and that of his parents. The particular infant must have an actual need for the articles furnished; not for mere ornament or pleasure. The articles must be useful and suitable, but they are not necessaries merely because useful or beneficial. Concerning the general character of the things furnished, to be necessaries the articles must supply the infant's personal needs, either those of his body or those of his mind. However, the term "necessaries" is not confined to merely such things as are required for a bare subsistence. There is no positive rule by means of which it may be determined what are or what are not necessaries, for what may be considered

necessary for one infant may not be necessaries for another infant whose state is different as to rank, social position, fortune, health, or other circumstances, the question being one to be determined from the particular facts and circumstances of each case. (Citation omitted.)

This appears to be the law as it is generally followed throughout the country.

In Ballinger v. Craig, 95 Ohio App. 545 (1953), the defendants were husband and wife and were 19 years of age at the time they purchased a house trailer. Both were employed. However, prior to the purchase of the trailer, the defendants were living with the parents of the husband. The Court of Appeals for the State of Ohio held that under the facts presented the trailer was not a necessary. The court stated:

> To enable an infant to contract for articles as necessaries, he must have been in actual need of them, and obliged to procure them for himself. They are not necessaries as to him, however necessary they may be in their nature, if he was already supplied with sufficient articles of the kind, or if he had a parent or guardian who was able and willing to supply them. The burden of proof is on the plaintiff to show that the infant was destitute of the articles, and had no way of procuring them except by his own contract. (Citation omitted) Id. at 547.

Under Ohio law the marriage of the parties did not result in their obtaining majority. In 42 Am. Jur. 2d Infants §67 at 68-69 (1969), the author notes:

> Thus, articles are not necessaries for an infant if he has a parent or guardian who is able and willing to supply them, and an infant residing with and being supported by his parent according to his station in life is not absolutely liable for things which under other circumstances would be considered necessaries.

The undisputed testimony is that both tenants were living away from home, apparently with the understanding that they could return home at any time. Sheridan testified:

Q: During the time that you were living at 3007 Webster, did you at any time, feel free to go home or anything like that?
A: Well, I had a feeling I could, but I just wanted to see if I could make it on my own.
Q: Had you been driven from your home?
A: No.
Q: You didn't have to go?
A: No.
Q: You went freely?
A: Yes.
Q: Then, after you moved out and went to 3417 for a week or so, you were again to return home, is that correct?
A: Yes, sir.

It would therefore appear that in the present case neither Sheridan nor Wilwerding was in need of shelter but, rather, had chosen to voluntarily leave home, with the understanding that they could return whenever they desired. One may at first blush believe that such a rule is unfair. Yet, on further consideration, the wisdom of the rule is apparent. If, indeed, landlords may not contract with minors, except at their peril, they may refuse to do so. In that event, minors who voluntarily leave home but who are free to return will be compelled to return to their parents' home—a result which is desirable. We therefore find that both the municipal court and the district court erred in finding that the apartment, under the facts in this case, was a necessary.

. . .

Because the rental of the apartment was not a necessary, the minors had the right to avoid the contract, either during their minority or within a reasonable time after reaching their majority. See Smith v. Wade, 169 Neb. 710, 100 N.W.2d 770 (1960). Disaffirmance by an infant completely puts an end to the contract's existence, both as to him and as to the adult with whom he contracted. Curtice Co. v. Kent, 89 Neb. 496, 131 N.W. 944 (1911). Because the parties then stand as if no contract had ever existed, the infant can recover payments made to the adult, and the adult is entitled to the return of whatever was received by the infant. Id.

The record shows that Pat Wilwerding clearly disaffirmed the contract during his minority. Moreover, the record supports the view that when the agent for Webster Street ordered the minors out for failure to pay rent and they vacated the premises, Sheridan likewise disaffirmed the contract. The record indicates that Sheridan reached majority on November 5. To suggest that a lapse of 7 days was not disaffirmance within a reasonable time would be foolish. Once disaffirmed, the contract became void; therefore, no contract existed between the parties, and the minors were entitled to recover all of the moneys which they paid and to be relieved of any further obligation under the contract. The judgment of the district court for Douglas County, Nebraska, is therefore reversed and the cause remanded with directions to vacate the judgment in favor of Webster Street and to enter a judgment in favor of Matthew Sheridan and Pat Wilwerding in the amount of $500, representing September rent in the amount of $100, October rent in the amount of $250, and the security deposit in the amount of $150.

REVERSED AND REMANDED WITH DIRECTIONS.

Problems

1. The 17-Year-Old Race Car Driver. Alexander Del Santo paid a registration fee to participate in a "novice" automobile race at Bristol County Stadium. In order to participate, entrants were required to sign several documents, including a broad waiver that released the race organizer and Bristol from liability for any loss or injury that might be sustained on the track. Del Santo concealed the fact that he was a minor by falsifying his date of birth on the race application.

During the race, the steeply banked track was slick with rain and Del Santo lost control of his vehicle, flipped over, and came to rest in the middle of the track. While he was attempting to remove his seatbelt, another driver struck Del Santo's car, causing him serious injury.

Del Santo never explicitly attempted to disaffirm the waiver agreement but, five months after turning 18, he sued the stadium's owner, alleging that its negligence caused his injuries. The trial court granted summary judgment to the stadium owner on the strength of the signed liability release. Del Santo appealed the judgment, citing the infancy doctrine. How should the appellate court rule?

2. Employment Assistance. At the age of 19, Bobby Rogers was a married, high school graduate only 22 hours away from earning a college degree in civil engineering, but he was an infant under North Carolina law. With his wife pregnant and in need of money, Rogers dropped out of school and entered into a contract with an employment agency, Gastonia Personnel Corporation, that required him to pay the agency a fee if it provided a lead that led to a job. Rogers accepted a job offer following an interview arranged by the agency but subsequently refused to pay the agency's fee of $295. The agency sued for breach of contract. Should it be permitted to recover?

C. INCAPACITY

If paternalistic motives cause the law to protect minors from the consequences of improvidently taking on contractual duties, the same concerns counsel in favor of providing similar protection to individuals who lack mental capacity by virtue of mental illness or intoxication. There are two significant differences, however, between minors on one hand and adults deserving of extra protection on the other.

 First, while minors can be identified by their chronological age, it is less clear what signs of mental impairment justify paternalistic legal protection. According to the Restatement, parties are potentially entitled to avoid or rescind contractual obligations if they are either unable to understand the nature and consequences of a transaction (often called the "cognitive" test) *or* if they are unable to act reasonably in relation to the transaction (often called the "affective" or "volitional" test). Rest. (2d) Contracts §15(1). Not all jurisdictions, however, recognize both of these standards.

 Second, because minority is usually easier to identify than mental incompetence, the concern that protecting an infirm party can interfere with the legitimate expectations of a contracting partner who has no reason to know of the infirmity is arguably more significant in the case of incapacity than in the case of infancy. The Restatement approach to incapacity deals with this problem by placing some limits on the right to avoid where a contracting partner lacks reason to know of the party's condition and by allowing judges the flexibility to limit relief when providing restitution cannot prevent unjust results. Rest. (2d) Contracts §§15(1)(b), 15(2).

In the trio of cases that follows, *In re Marriage of Davis*, *Hauer v. Union State Bank of Wautoma*, and *Farnum v. Silvano*, courts in three jurisdictions grapple with the choice of mental incompetency standards, the difficulty of applying those standards, and the extent to which the consequences of incapacity depend on the extent to which the infirm party's counterpart had reason to know of the condition. *First State Bank of Sinai v. Hyland* considers whether and to what extent intoxication should be treated like mental illness and support a claim of incapacity. See also Rest. (2d) Contracts §16.

y

IN RE MARRIAGE OF DAVIS
Court of Appeals of Oregon
193 Or. App. 279
2004

PER CURIAM.

Wife appeals from a judgment denying her request to set aside a stipulated dissolution judgment. Wife argues that she was not mentally competent at the time that she stipulated to the judgment and that the trial court erred in finding otherwise; in particular, she asserts that the trial court applied the wrong legal test in determining her competency. We review the trial court's choice of legal standard for errors of law and affirm.

In denying wife's motion, the trial court noted that courts have applied two tests to determine mental competency in similar circumstances: the "cognitive test" and the "affective test." Under the cognitive test, a person is competent if he or she has the capacity "to understand the nature of the act and to apprehend its consequences." Gore v. Gadd, 268 Or. 527, 528, 522 P.2d 212 (1974) (internal quotation marks omitted). The cognitive test is the test that Oregon courts appear to follow. Wife argues, however, that we should adopt the broader affective test. Under the affective test, a person is incompetent if the person is "unable to act in a reasonable manner in relation to the transaction and the other party has reason to know of his condition." Restatement (Second) of Contracts §15(1)(b) (1979).

rule

As noted in the concurrence, in some cases, Oregon courts may have applied certain aspects of the affective test in determining competency. Nevertheless, the cognitive test appears to be the law of this state, and we are bound to follow it. Accordingly, we hold that the trial court did not err in applying the cognitive test. The record supports the trial court's conclusion that, under the cognitive test, wife was competent to enter into the stipulated judgment. We affirm on wife's other assignments of error without discussion.

Affirmed.

DEITS, C.J., concurring:

I agree with the majority that the trial court did not err in applying the cognitive test or in concluding that, under the cognitive test, wife was mentally competent to enter into the stipulated judgment. However, I write separately to note that it may be appropriate to reexamine and clarify the law of mental competency to enter into contracts in light of recent developments in this area of the law.

Husband and wife were married for approximately 17 years. The parties have two minor children, who were 8 and 10 years old at the time that the stipulated judgment was entered. The marriage apparently involved numerous instances of domestic violence. Husband was arrested on one occasion for domestic abuse while the parties were living in Arizona. Wife obtained two restraining orders against husband in Oregon, and he was arrested for violating a restraining order on one occasion. Husband ultimately moved out of the parties' residence in April 2000 and filed for dissolution the following September.

Wife began seeing a clinical social worker in May 2000, shortly after the parties separated. The social worker testified that wife "loved [husband] enormously and she feared him enormously." Wife was diagnosed as suffering from depression, post-traumatic stress disorder, and battered woman's syndrome. Wife's social worker indicated that wife's great fear of husband was triggered by seeing husband and that, when one is in a significant amount of fear, "you can't think straight. I mean you can't think at all literally in terms of the hemispheres of the brain. The hemisphere that's thinking is disabled by the stress brought on by the feared person." The social worker also stated that wife was deeply grieving and working 60 hours a week in a job in which she was sustaining "vicarious trauma" because she was translating for the Department of Human Services, a job that had the potential of recalling her own incidents of domestic violence. Wife's first lawyer described wife as "very emotionally distraught and that's putting it mildly. She was sort of [on] a roller coaster in terms of emotional states. One day she would be * * * fine and another day, she would be sobbing and she was very fragile emotionally * * *." Wife's second lawyer described wife's emotional state during the course of the dissolution proceedings in a similar fashion, stating that she would go from being in a calm state to "crying in a hysterical kind of spells."

On March 13, 2001, the parties attended a settlement conference in an attempt to work out a property division and custody arrangement. At issue in part were the parties' stock options in Intel and their interest in a computer software company.[4] Wife testified that, during that meeting, she was not thinking about the property division but rather that "the next day was going to be the last that I was going to be married to [husband]." The conference was adjourned at one point because emotions elevated to what the parties felt was an unproductive level. During the adjournment, husband and wife were left alone. Wife expressed her desire to reconcile with husband, and, as the trial court found, husband "left the door ajar on that issue." When the settlement conference reconvened, the parties arrived at a tentative agreement to split the Intel stock options. The parties' interest in the computer software company was not discussed. Wife left the conference that day "in hopes that she was somehow going to pull the marriage back together." The parties shared a phone call later that night, but they did not discuss negotiations about the settlement.

---

4. Although there was some question about the exact value of the interest in the software company, three years before the dissolution hearing, husband had received a buyout offer of $1,214,000 and refused it because he thought that the value was higher. At the hearing on wife's motion to set aside the judgment, an expert testified that the interest could be worth as much as $2,905,000.

The settlement conference continued the next day. On her way to the conference, wife told her children that she was "going to go and get my marriage back." Wife's attorney thought that wife seemed "pretty upbeat" that morning and that wife told him that she believed that she and husband were reconciling. When wife saw husband that morning, she was "happy to see him. I saw him dressing very nice, and I just felt like maybe we were going to get married." Husband, however, stated that he wanted to proceed with the dissolution. From that point, wife "sort of lost it." Her attorney would attempt to explain something to her and "tears would just be rolling down her eyes. She was shaking * * *. Then it would seem like all of a sudden she would come back and she'd take a deep breath and then it seemed like she was tracking and then I'd look over again and she would be crying again. So, it was sort of like this roller coaster."

Husband's attorney had arrived on that day with a proposed stipulated judgment, which, according to wife's attorney, gave all the Intel stock and all of the interest in the software company to husband. Wife's attorney believed that the parties had agreed to split the stock and had assumed that they would reach a similar agreement about the interest in the software company. Wife's attorney advised her not to take less than half of the stock and half of their interest in the company. At that point, wife looked "[s]ort of like a zombie." She asked to speak to her husband in private, and according to wife, husband verbally assaulted her.

. . .

When the attorneys returned, wife told her attorney that "I want this over, let's go." Her attorney attempted to dissuade her, but wife was adamant that she wanted the proceedings to be over. Wife told her attorney to "[g]ive [husband] what he wants" and that she did not want anything. In the end, against the advice of her attorney, wife signed an agreement under which husband received all of the Intel stock options and all of the interest in the software company. Wife later recalled that she had heard the voices of the judge and lawyers talking but "not really understanding what was going on." Her only goal at that time was to "go-go far-go away. * * * I say my only want * * * was to go away from this place, run and go, and go to sleep[.]"

Approximately a week after the settlement conference, wife was admitted to a hospital psychiatric unit for several days. A psychologist who examined wife on March 29 and 30 concluded that wife was not capable of engaging in rational decision making on the day that she entered into the stipulated judgment. He concluded that "all of her decision-making processes were going to be compromised," reflected in wife's "floating" and "emotional over-control" behavior. He diagnosed wife as suffering from a severe degree of emotional disturbance and stated that people, like wife, who are in a dissociative state are "going to be doing whatever they can do to extricate themselves from that spot as rapidly as possible. Basically they're going to give in." In addition, wife's social worker also concluded that wife may not have understood anything that happened on March 14.

Wife moved to set aside the stipulated judgment a month after she entered into it. Wife claimed, in part, that she was not competent at the time that she signed the stipulated judgment and she was therefore incapable of giving her consent to the agreement. After hearing significant testimony, the trial court discussed the two tests for determining competency: the traditional cognitive test and the more modern affective test. The trial court determined that it was obligated under the law to apply the cognitive test and that, under that test, wife had been mentally competent to enter into the stipulated judgment. Accordingly, although the trial court found that the stipulated judgment was "grossly inequitable in its substance," the court refused to set it aside.

. . . Oregon case law is not entirely clear. Generally, the cognitive test appears to be the rule of law in Oregon. A few cases, however, contain language suggesting that our courts have been receptive to adopting elements of the affective test. Nonetheless, I must agree with the trial court that the cognitive test is the test most recently adopted and employed in our case law and was, accordingly, the proper test to apply in this case.

Oregon courts have traditionally stated and employed the "cognitive test" for mental competency to enter a contract. Under that test, a person is competent if he or she has "the capacity to understand the nature of the act and to apprehend its consequences." *Gore v. Gadd*, 268 Or. 527, 528, 522 P.2d 212 (1974) (internal quotation marks omitted). . . .

The "affective test," also termed the "modern test" or the "volitional test," has been adopted by some other jurisdictions. Under the affective test, a person may be aware of the nature and consequences of his or her conduct, but is considered incompetent because mental illness has rendered him or her "incapable of making a rational judgment in the execution of the transaction * * *." *Gore*, 268 Or. at 528, 522 P.2d 212.

. . .

The commentary to the Restatement notes that

> "[i]t is now recognized that there is a wide variety of types and degrees of mental incompetency. Among them are congenital deficiencies in intelligence, the mental deterioration of old age, the effects of brain damage caused by accident or organic disease, and mental illnesses evidenced by such symptoms as delusions, hallucinations, delirium, confusion and depression. * * * [A] person may be able to understand almost nothing, or only simple or routine transactions, or he may be incompetent only with respect to a particular type of transaction. Even though understanding is complete, he may lack the ability to control his acts in the way that the normal individual can and does control them * * *. Where a person has some understanding of a particular transaction which is affected by mental illness or defect, the controlling consideration is whether the transaction in its result is one which a reasonably competent person might have made."

Restatement §15 comment b.

. . . [T]he Oregon Supreme Court, in its most recent direct statement on this issue, has indicated that the cognitive test continues to be the law in Oregon. In *Gore*, the plaintiff urged the Supreme Court to adopt the affective test, arguing that the cognitive test is too restrictive. 268 Or. at 528-29, 522 P.2d 212. The plaintiff relied on *Ortelere;* another New York case, *Faber v. Sweet Style Mfg. Co.*, 40 Misc. 2d 212, 242 N.Y.S.2d 763 (Sup. Ct. Nassau County 1963); and the *Restatement*.

The Supreme Court observed that "the test for competency heretofore applied in Oregon * * * [is] the 'cognitive test.'" *Id.* at 528, 522 P.2d 212. In response to the plaintiff's argument that the court should adopt the affective test, the court stated:

"Th[e New York] cases, responding to advances in psychiatric knowledge, [held] that competence can be lost through 'affective' as well as 'cognitive' disorders. Psychiatry teaches that one who is afflicted with an affective disorder, such as a manic-depressive psychotic, may be impelled to act irrationally although fully conscious of what he is doing."

Id. at 529, 522 P.2d 212. The court declined, however, to adopt the affective test— not because the court considered the cognitive test to be better, but because the plaintiff was competent under either test: "As we have already explained, the evidence conclusively shows that plaintiff was competent under the cognitive test. *Assuming, without deciding, that the test of competency should be extended to include affective disorders*, we find the evidence to be insufficient to establish that plaintiff was incompetent." *Id.* at 530, 522 P.2d 212 (emphasis added). Since *Gore*, Oregon courts have, consistently with *Gore*'s implied retention of the cognitive test, continued to use the cognitive test only. . . .

In my view, the affective test reflects a more up-to-date understanding of human behavior and is more consistent with modern psychological theories of mental health. It appears that courts in other jurisdictions that have recently considered the question have agreed with my view. *See* Gregory E. Maggs, *Ipse Dixit: The Restatement (Second) of Contracts and the Modern Development of Contract Law*, 66 Geo. Wash. L. Rev. 508, 518-19 (1998) (nearly all courts considering the issue have adopted the affective test). Although the majority correctly holds that we are bound to follow precedent, which requires us to employ the cognitive test, it would seem appropriate to reevaluate this test and adopt a test incorporating all or part of the affective test, such as that included in the *Restatement.* The application of the affective test, as incorporated in the *Restatement,* to this case would likely lead to a different and more equitable result.

For the reasons stated above, I concur.

5

HAUER
v.
UNION STATE BANK OF WAUTOMA
Court of Appeals of Wisconsin
192 Wis. 2d 576
1995

SNYDER, Judge.

The issues in this case arise out of a loan made by Union State Bank of Wautoma to Kathy Hauer. The Bank appeals from a judgment which (1) voided the loan on the grounds that Hauer lacked the mental capacity to enter into the loan, (2) required the Bank to return Hauer's collateral and (3) dismissed the Bank's counterclaim which sought to recover the proceeds of the loan from Hauer. Because we conclude that there is evidence in the record to support the jury's findings that Hauer was mentally incompetent at the time of the loan and that the Bank failed to act in good faith in granting the loan, we affirm.

I. FACTS

In order to place the loan in context, we must first set forth the relevant events giving rise to the loan. The following facts are taken from court documents and undisputed testimony at trial.

In 1987, Hauer suffered a brain injury in a motorcycle accident. She was subsequently adjudicated to be incompetent, resulting in a guardian being appointed by the court. On September 20, 1988, Hauer's guardianship was terminated based upon a letter from her treating physician, Kenneth Viste. Viste opined that Hauer had recovered to the point where she had ongoing memory, showed good judgment, was reasonable in her goals and plans and could manage her own affairs. Her monthly income after the accident was $900, which consisted of social security disability and interest income from a mutual fund worth approximately $80,000.

On October 18, 1988, the Bank loaned Ben Eilbes $7600 to start a small business. In December, Eilbes requested but was denied an additional $2000 loan from the Bank. By June of 1989, Eilbes was in default on the loan. Around this time, Eilbes met Hauer through her daughter, who told Eilbes about the existence of Hauer's mutual fund. Eilbes subsequently discussed his business with Hauer on several occasions and Hauer expressed an interest in becoming an investor in the business. Because Hauer could only sell her stocks at certain times, Eilbes suggested that she take out a short-term loan using the stocks as collateral. Eilbes told Hauer that if she loaned him money, he would give her a job, pay her interest on the loan and pay the loan when it came due. Hauer agreed.

Eilbes then contacted Richard Schroeder, assistant vice president of the Bank, and told Schroeder that Hauer wanted to invest in his business but that she needed short-term financing and could provide adequate collateral. Eilbes told Schroeder that he would use the money invested by Hauer in part to either bring the payments current on his defaulted loan or pay the loan off in full. Schroeder then called Hauer's stockbroker and financial consultant, Stephen Landolt, in an effort to verify the existence of Hauer's fund. Landolt told Schroeder that Hauer needed the interest income to live on and that he wished the Bank would not use it as collateral for a loan. Schroeder also conceded that it was possible that Landolt told him that Hauer was suffering from brain damage, but did not specifically recall that part of their conversation.

At some later date Eilbes met personally with Schroeder in order to further discuss the potential loan to Hauer, after which Schroeder indicated that the Bank would be willing to loan Hauer $30,000. Schroeder gave Eilbes a loan application to give to Hauer to fill out. On October 26, 1989, Hauer and Eilbes went to the Bank to meet with Schroeder and sign the necessary paperwork. Prior to this date, Schroeder had not spoken to or met with Hauer. During this meeting Schroeder explained the terms of the loan to Hauer—that she would sign a consumer single-payment note due in six months and give the Bank a security interest in her mutual fund as collateral. Schroeder did not notice anything that would cause him to believe that Hauer did not understand the loan transaction.

On April 26, 1990, the date the loan matured, Hauer filed suit against the Bank and Eilbes. Hauer subsequently amended her complaint three times. The Bank filed a counterclaim for judgment on the defaulted loan after Hauer's first amended complaint. In Hauer's third amended complaint, she alleged the following specific cause[] of action: (1) the Bank knew or should have known that she lacked the mental capacity to understand the loan. . . .

Prior to trial and over the Bank's objection, Hauer dismissed Eilbes because he appeared to be judgment proof and was filing bankruptcy. A twelve-person jury subsequently found that Hauer lacked the mental capacity to enter into the loan and that the Bank failed to act in good faith toward Hauer in the loan transaction. The trial court denied the Bank's motions after verdict and entered judgment voiding the loan contract, dismissing the Bank's counterclaim and ordering the Bank to return Hauer's collateral. The Bank appeals.

. . .

II. MENTAL CAPACITY TO CONTRACT

Over the Bank's objection, the jury was presented with the following special verdict question: Did the plaintiff, Kathy Hauer, lack the mental capacity to enter into the loan transaction at the time of that transaction? The jury answered this question, "Yes." In denying the Bank's motions after verdict, the trial court held that based on this finding, the note and security agreement were "void or voidable." Further, the court ruled that Hauer was not liable for repayment of the $30,000 loan because she no longer possessed the funds.

The Bank in its motions after verdict and on appeal argues that the jury's verdict as to mental incompetency is invalid. The Bank contends that Hauer failed to state a claim upon which relief can be granted or, in the alternative, that the evidence does not support the jury's verdict.

A. Mental Incompetence-Cause of Action

We first address the Bank's argument that Hauer's claim of mental incompetence fails to state a claim for which relief can be granted. This presents a question of law which we review independently. . . . The Bank contends that a claim of mental incompetence is an affirmative defense to an action to enforce a contract only and that Hauer cannot avail herself of such a defense because she failed to plead any affirmative defenses. We disagree.

We have previously recognized that the vast majority of courts have held that an incompetent person's transactions are voidable—the incompetent has the power to avoid the contract entirely. *See Production Credit Ass'n v. Kehl*, 148 Wis. 2d 225, 229-30, 434 N.W.2d 816, 818 (Ct. App. 1988); *see also* 5 Samuel Williston, Williston on Contracts §10:3 (4th ed. 1993). Further, Wisconsin has long recognized a cause of action to rescind a contract or conveyance based upon the lack of mental competency at the time of the transaction. . . . Accordingly, we conclude that Hauer properly stated a cause of action to void the loan contract.

B. Sufficiency of the Evidence

The Bank argues that even if Hauer has a cause of action to void the contract based upon the lack of mental capacity, the record is devoid of credible evidence to sustain the jury's verdict. In reviewing a jury's verdict, we will sustain the verdict if there is any credible evidence to support it. . . . The weight and credibility of the evidence are left to the province of the jury. When the evidence permits more than one inference, this court must accept the inference that favors the jury's verdict.

The law presumes that every adult person is fully competent until satisfactory proof to the contrary is presented. *First Nat'l Bank*, 92 Wis. 2d [518,] 529-30, 285 N.W.2d [614,] 620 [(1979)]. The burden of proof is on the person seeking to void the act. *Nyka v. State*, 268 Wis. 644, 646, 68 N.W.2d 458, 460 (1955). The test for determining competency is whether the person involved had sufficient mental ability to know what he or she was doing and the nature and consequences of the transaction. *First Nat'l Bank*, 92 Wis. 2d at 530, 285 N.W.2d at 620; *see also* Restatement (Second) of Contracts §15(1)(a) (1979). Almost any conduct may be relevant, as may lay opinions, expert opinions and prior and subsequent adjudications of incompetency. Restatement, *supra*, at §15 cmt. c.

Our review of the record reveals that there is credible evidence which the jury could have relied on in reaching its verdict. First, it is undisputed that Hauer was under court-appointed guardianship approximately one year before the loan transaction. Second, Hauer's testimony indicates a complete lack of understanding of the nature and consequences of the transaction.[2] Third, Hauer's psychological expert, Charles Barnes, testified that when he treated her in 1987, Hauer was "very deficient in her cognitive abilities, her abilities to remember and to read, write and spell . . . she was very malleable, gullible, people could convince her of almost anything." Barnes further testified that because Hauer's condition had not changed in any significant way by 1990 when he next evaluated her, she was "incompetent and . . . unable to make reasoned decisions" on the date she made the loan.

The Bank argues that Barnes's testimony was irrelevant and erroneously admitted because Viste, Hauer's treating neurologist, informed the court that in his opinion Hauer was no longer in need of a guardian and could manage her own affairs a year prior to the loan. The Bank contends that Hauer should be judicially estopped from asserting incompetence at the time of the loan after convincing the court the

---

2. For example, Hauer testified that she believed that she was merely cosigning a loan for Eilbes and that he was responsible for paying it back.

previous year that she was competent. However, competency must be determined on the date the instrument was executed.

The Bank further points out that both Eilbes and Schroeder testified that Hauer was much different at trial than she was on the day the loan was executed. Nevertheless, the weight and credibility of the evidence are for the jury to decide, not this court. The jury apparently gave more credence to Hauer's and Barnes's testimony than Schroeder's testimony and Viste's 1988 opinion. In sum, while we agree that there is evidence which the jury could have relied on to find that Hauer was competent, we must accept the inference that favors the jury's verdict when the evidence permits more than one inference. *Fehring*, 118 Wis. 2d at 305-06, 347 N.W.2d at 598.

III. EFFECT OF INCOMPETENCE

Having concluded that Hauer stated a claim for relief and that sufficient credible evidence was presented to sustain the jury's verdict, we now turn to the unresolved problem regarding the rights and responsibilities of the parties relative to the disposition of the consideration exchanged in the loan transaction. We must decide the legal question of whether Hauer may recover her collateral without liability for the loan proceeds. We review questions of law independently of the trial court.

Postverdict, the trial court ruled that Hauer's action to void the contract required the Bank to return her collateral and Hauer to return any loan proceeds in her possession. However, it is undisputed that Hauer loaned the entire $30,000 to Eilbes and that the money had long since disappeared. On appeal, the Bank contends that equity dictates that the proper remedy upon voiding the loan transaction is to return the parties to their preloan status—the Bank must return Hauer's stocks and Hauer must be held liable to the Bank for $30,000.

The trial court offered two explanations for voiding the contract but not holding Hauer liable for repayment of the loan: (1) the law and policy of the "infancy doctrine" set forth in *Halbman v. Lemke*, 99 Wis. 2d 241, 298 N.W.2d 562 (1980), and (2) the jury's finding that the Bank failed to act in good faith. We will address each in turn.

A. Infancy Doctrine

In *Halbman*, our supreme court held that a minor who disaffirms a contract may recover the purchase price without liability for use, depreciation or other diminution in value. As a general rule, a minor who disaffirms a contract is expected to return as much of the consideration as remains in the minor's possession. However, the minor's right to disaffirm is permitted even where the minor cannot return the property. The trial court ruled that the infancy doctrine was analogous and applies when the voidness arises from mental incapacity to contract. We disagree.

The purpose of the infancy doctrine is to protect "minors from foolishly squandering their wealth through improvident contracts with crafty adults who would take advantage of them in the marketplace." *Id.* at 245, 298 N.W.2d at 564. The common law has long recognized this policy to protect minors. *Id.* However, "[a] contract made by a person who is mentally incompetent requires the reconciliation of two conflicting policies: the protection of justifiable expectations and of the security of transactions, and the protection of persons unable to protect themselves against imposition." Restatement, *supra*, §15 cmt. a.

The trial court's analogy fails given the fact that the two types of incapacity are essentially dissimilar. Williston, *supra*, §10:3. "An infant is often mentally competent in fact to understand the force of his bargain, but it is the policy of the law to protect the minor. By contrast, the adult mental incompetent may be subject to varying degrees of infirmity or mental illness, not all equally incapacitating." *Id.* This difference in part accounts for the majority of jurisdictions holding that absent fraud or knowledge of the incapacity by the other contracting party, the contractual act of an incompetent is voidable by the incompetent only if avoidance accords with equitable principles. Accordingly, we conclude that the infancy doctrine does not apply to cases of mental incompetence.

B. Good Faith

The jury was presented with the following special verdict question: "Did the defendant, Union State Bank of Wautoma, fail to act in good faith toward [Hauer] in the loan transaction?" The jury answered that question, "Yes." In denying the Bank's motions after verdict, the court concluded that even if the infancy doctrine did not apply, the jury's finding that the Bank failed to act in good faith in the loan transaction distinguished this case from the "general rule" providing that the person seeking relief from a contract must return the consideration paid. We agree.

. . .

3. Mental Incompetency and Common Law Duty of Good Faith

. . .

Wisconsin common law, like other states, reads the duty of good faith into every contract. *See Market Street Assocs. Ltd. Partnership v. Frey*, 941 F.2d 588, 592 (7th Cir. 1991) (citing Wisconsin law). The great weight of authority from other jurisdictions provides that the unadjudicated mental incompetence of one of the parties is not a sufficient reason for setting aside an executed contract if the parties cannot be restored to their original positions, provided that the contract was made in good faith, for a fair consideration and without knowledge of the incompetence. Williston, *supra*, §10:3.

Stated differently, if the contract is made on fair terms and the other party has no reason to know of the incompetency, the contract ceases to be voidable where performance in whole or in part changes the situation such that the parties cannot be restored to their previous positions. Restatement, *supra*, §15 cmt. f. If, on the other hand, the other party knew of the incompetency or took unfair advantage of the incompetent, consideration dissipated without benefit to the incompetent need not be restored. *Id.* at cmt. e.

. . .

We conclude that the finding that the Bank knew or had reason to know that Hauer was mentally incompetent to understand the nature of the loan at the time it was entered into is inherent and intertwined in the jury's finding that the Bank failed to act in good faith. This is necessarily true because the Bank could not have been found to have lacked good faith as a matter of law absent knowledge of the incompetency. The two findings are inseparable.

4. Sufficiency of the Evidence

The last question we must address is whether there was any credible evidence to sustain the jury's verdict that the Bank failed to act in good faith. If there is, we are bound to sustain the jury's verdict.

The Bank contends that "[t]he record is devoid of any evidence that the Bank had knowledge of any facts which created a suspicion that it should not enter the loan." We agree with the trial court's summary that there is evidence in the record "that there were flags up that would prompt a reasonable banker to move more slowly and more carefully in the transaction."

For example, the Bank knew that Eilbes was in default of his loan at the Bank. Eilbes approached the Bank and laid all the groundwork for a loan to be given to a third-party investor, Hauer, whom the Bank did not know. Eilbes told Schroeder that he would make his defaulted loan current or pay it off entirely with Hauer's investment. Schroeder testified that upon investigating the matter initially, Hauer's stockbroker told him not to use Hauer's fund as collateral because she needed the fund to live on and Hauer could not afford to lose the fund. He further testified that it was possible that the stockbroker told him that Hauer suffered a brain injury. In addition, Hauer's banking expert opined that the Bank should not have made the loan. Accordingly, we conclude that the evidence and reasonable inferences that can be drawn from the evidence support the jury's conclusion that the Bank failed to act in good faith.

. . .

Judgment affirmed.

FARNUM
v.
SILVANO

Appeals Court of Massachusetts, Barnstable
27 Mass. App. Ct. 536
1989

KASS, J.

On the basis of a finding that Viola Farnum enjoyed a lucid interval when she conveyed her house to Joseph Silvano, III, for approximately half its market value, a Probate Court judge decided that Farnum had capacity to execute the deed.

A different test measures competence to enter into a contract and we, therefore, reverse the judgment.

We take the facts from the trial judge's findings, which have support in the record and are not clearly erroneous. Mass. R. Civ. P. 52(a), 365 Mass. 816 (1974). When she sold her real estate in South Yarmouth on July 14, 1986, Farnum was ninety years of age. The sale price was $64,900. At that time, the fair market value of the property was $115,000. Indeed, at the closing, the buyer, Silvano, obtained a mortgage loan from a bank of $65,000. Silvano, age twenty-four, knew Farnum from mowing her lawn and doing other landscape work. Farnum trusted him and had confidence in him. Before entering into the transaction, Silvano had been put on notice of the inadequacy of the price he was going to pay. He had been warned not to proceed by Farnum's nephew, Harry Gove, who is now Farnum's guardian and is pressing this action for rescission on her behalf.

Farnum's mental competence had begun to fail seriously in 1983, three years before she delivered a deed to the South Yarmouth real estate. That failure manifested itself in aberrant conduct. She would lament not hearing from sisters who were dead. She would wonder where the people upstairs in her house had gone, but there was no upstairs to her house. She offered to sell the house to a neighbor for $35,000. (He declined, recognizing the property was worth much more.) She became abnormally forgetful. Frequently she locked herself out of her house and broke into it, rather than calling on a neighbor with whom she had left a key (on one occasion, she broke and entered through a basement window). She hid her cat to protect it from "the cops . . . looking for my cat." She would express a desire to return to Cape Cod although she was on Cape Cod. She easily became lost. Payment of her bills required the assistance of her sister and her nephew, who also balanced her check book.

There were several hospitalizations during the three-year period preceding the conveyance in 1986. On May 2, 1985, a brain scan examination disclosed organic brain disease. By January, 1987, some six months after the conveyance, Farnum was admitted to Cape Cod Hospital for treatment of dementia and seizure disorder. She was discharged to a nursing home.

In connection with drawing the deed and effecting the transfer of real estate, Farnum was represented by a lawyer selected and paid by Silvano. That lawyer, and a lawyer for the bank which was making a loan to Silvano, attended the closing at Farnum's house. At the closing Farnum was, as the trial judge expressed it, "aware of what was going on." She was cheerful, engaged in pleasantries, and made instant coffee for those present. After the transaction, however, Farnum insisted to others—her sister and nephew, for example—that she still owned the property. That may have been consistent with Farnum's ambivalence about giving up her home and going to a nursing home.

It was not unusual, the judge concluded, for Farnum to be perfectly coherent and "two minutes later" be confused. When she signed the deed, "she was coherent or in a lucid interval."

. . .

Competence to enter into a contract presupposes something more than a transient surge of lucidity. It involves not merely comprehension of what is "going on," but an ability to comprehend the nature and quality of the transaction, together with an understanding of its significance and consequences. *Sutcliffe v. Heatley*, 232 Mass. 231, 232-233, 122 N.E. 317 (1919). . . . In the act of entering into a contract there are reciprocal obligations, and it is appropriate, when mental incapacity, as here, is manifest, to require a baseline of reasonableness.

In *Krasner v. Berk*, [366 Mass. 464, 468,] 319 N.E.2d 897 [(1974)], the court cited with approval the synthesis of those principles now appearing in the Restatement (Second) of Contracts §15(1) (1981), which regards as voidable a transaction entered into with a person who, "by reason of mental illness or defect (a) . . . is unable to understand in a reasonable manner the nature and consequences of the transaction, or (b) . . . is unable to act in a reasonable manner in relation to the transaction and the other party has reason to know of [the] condition."

Applied to the case at hand, Farnum could be aware that she was selling her house to Silvano for much less than it was worth, while failing to understand the unreasonableness of doing so at a time when she faced serious cash demands for rent, home care, or nursing home charges. . . .

On the basis of the trial judge's findings, we think Farnum did not possess the requisite contextual understanding. She suffered mental disease which had manifested itself in erratic and irrational conduct and was confirmed by diagnostic test. Her physician did not think she was competent to live alone. Relatively soon after the transaction, Farnum's mental deficits grew so grave that it became necessary to hospitalize her. The man to whom she sold her property for less than its value was not a member of her family or someone who had cared for her for long duration. Silvano's explanation that he gave Farnum the additional consideration of agreeing to let her stay in the house for some time after the closing is unpersuasive, as the purchase and sale agreement and the deed are silent about any such agreement. Farnum was not represented by a lawyer who knew her and considered her over-all interests as a primary concern. The mission of the lawyer secured by Silvano, and paid by him, was to effect the transaction. As we have observed, Farnum faced growing cash demands for her maintenance, and, in her circumstances, it was not rational to part with a major asset for a cut-rate price.

The decisive factor which we think makes Farnum's delivery of her deed to Silvano voidable was his awareness of Farnum's inability to act in a reasonable manner. See Restatement (Second) of Contracts §15(1)(b). Silvano knew or had reason to know of Farnum's impaired condition from her conduct, which at the times material caused concern to her relatives, her neighbors, and her physician. See *Ortelere v. Teachers' Retirement Bd.*, 25 N.Y.2d at 205, 303 N.Y.S.2d 362, 250 N.E.2d 460. Silvano was aware that he was buying the house for about half its value.[1] He had been specifically warned by Farnum's nephew about the unfairness of the transaction and Farnum's mental disability.

. . .

---

1. The judge's finding of a fair market value of $115,000 was based on an appraisal of the real estate received in evidence. Under the purchase and sale agreement, Silvano was to receive the furniture and furnishings as well for his purchase price.

Farnum is entitled to rescission of the conveyance. Silvano shall deliver a deed to the real estate in question to Farnum's guardian in his capacity as such, in return for the consideration paid by Silvano. The object of rescission is to arrive so far as possible at full restoration of the status quo before the transaction which is being cancelled. . . . The judgment is vacated, and the case is remanded to the Probate Court for the entry of a judgment of rescission consistent with this opinion.

So ordered.

FIRST STATE BANK OF SINAI
v.
HYLAND

Supreme Court of South Dakota
399 N.W.2d 894
1987

HENDERSON, J.

PROCEDURAL HISTORY/ISSUES

Plaintiff-appellant First State Bank of Sinai (Bank) sued defendant-appellee Mervin Hyland (Mervin) seeking to hold him responsible for payment on a promissory note which he cosigned. Upon trial to the court, the circuit court entered findings of fact, conclusions of law, and judgment holding Mervin not liable for the note's payment. . . . We reverse and remand.

FACTS

On March 10, 1981, Randy Hyland (Randy) and William Buck (Buck), acting for Bank, executed two promissory notes. One note was for $6,800 and the other note was for $3,000. Both notes became due on September 19, 1981.

The notes remained unpaid on their due date and Bank sent notice to Randy informing him of the delinquencies. . . . Randy requested an extension. Buck agreed, but on the condition that Randy's father, Mervin, act as cosigner. One $9,800 promissory note dated October 20, 1981 (the two notes of $6,800 and $3,000 were combined) was created. Randy was given the note for the purpose of obtaining his father's signature. According to Randy, Mervin signed the note on October 20 or 21, 1981.

Mervin had transacted business with Bank since 1974. Previously, he executed approximately 60 promissory notes with Bank. Mervin was apparently a good customer and paid all of his notes on time. Buck testified that he knew Mervin drank, but that he was unaware of any alcohol-related problems.

Randy returned to the Bank about one week later. Mervin had properly signed the note. In Buck's presence, Randy signed the note, which had an April 20, 1982 due date.

On April 20, 1982, the note was unpaid. Buck notified Randy of the overdue note. On May 5, 1982, Randy appeared at the Bank. He brought a blank check signed by Mervin with which the interest on the note was to be paid. Randy filled in the check amount at the Bank for $899.18 (the amount of interest owing). Randy also requested that the note be extended. Buck agreed, but required Mervin's signature as a prerequisite to any extension. A two-month note for $9,800 with a due date of July 2, 1982, was prepared and given to Randy.

Randy did not secure his father's signature on the two-month note, and Mervin testified that he refused to sign that note. On June 22, 1982, Randy filed for bankruptcy which later resulted in the total discharge of his obligation on the note.

On July 14, 1982, Buck sent a letter to Randy and Mervin informing them of Bank's intention to look to Mervin for the note's payment. On December 19, 1982, Bank filed suit against Mervin, requesting $9,800 principal and interest at the rate of 17% until judgment was entered. Mervin answered on January 14, 1983. His defense hinged upon the assertion that he was incapacitated through the use of liquor when he signed the note. He claimed he had no recollection of the note, did not remember seeing it, discussing it with his son, or signing it.

Randy testified that when he brought the note home to his father, the latter was drunk and in bed. Mervin then rose from his bed, walked into the kitchen, and signed the note. Later, Randy returned to the Bank with the signed note.

The record reveals that Mervin was drinking heavily from late summer through early winter of 1981. During this period, Mervin's wife and son accepted responsibility for managing the farm. Mervin's family testified that his bouts with liquor left him weak, unconcerned with regard to family and business matters, uncooperative, and uncommunicative. When Mervin was drinking, he spent most of his time at home, in bed.

Mervin's problems with alcohol have five times resulted in his involuntary commitment to hospitals. Two of those commitments occurred near the period of the October 1981 note. On September 10, 1981, Mervin was involuntarily committed to the Human Services Center at Yankton. He was released on September 19, 1981. On November 20, 1981, he was involuntarily committed to River Park at Pierre.

Between the periods of his commitments, September 19, 1981 until November 20, 1981, Mervin did transact some business himself. On October 3, Mervin and Buck (Bank) executed a two-month promissory note enabling the former to borrow $5,000 for the purchase of livestock. Mervin also paid for farm goods and services with his personal check on September 29, October 1 (purchased cattle at Madison Livestock Auction), October 2, and October 5, 1981. Mervin testified that during October 1981, he had personally hauled his grain to storage elevators and made decisions concerning when grain was sold. Additionally, Mervin continued to operate his automobile, often making trips to purchase liquor.

A trial was held on October 4, 1985. Mervin was found to be entirely without understanding (as a result of alcohol consumption) when he signed the October 20, 1981 promissory note. The court pointed to Mervin's lack of personal care and nonparticipation in family life and farming business as support for finding the contractual relationship between the parties void at its inception. It was further held that Bank had failed to show Mervin's subsequent ratification of the contract. Bank appeals.

DECISION

. . . Historically, the void contract concept has been applied to nullify agreements made by mental incompetents who have contracted either entirely without understanding or after a judicial determination of incapacity had been entered. *See Dexter v. Hall*, 82 U.S. (15 Wall.) 9, 21 L. Ed. 73 (1873); Restatement (Second) of Contracts §12 (1981). Incapacitated intoxicated persons have been treated similarly to mental incompetents in that their contracts will either be void or voidable depending upon the extent of their mental unfitness at the time they contracted. 2 S. Williston, *supra*, at §260; Restatement (Second) of Contracts §16. A void contract is without legal effect in that the law neither gives remedy for its breach nor recognizes any duty of performance by a promisor. Restatement (Second) of Contracts §7, comment a. Therefore, the term "void contract" is a misnomer because if an agreement is void, at its genesis, no contract (void or otherwise) was ever created. *See* J. Calamari & J. Perillo, *The Law of Contracts* §1-11 (2d ed. 1977).

Mervin had numerous and prolonged problems stemming from his inability to handle alcohol. However, he was not judicially declared incompetent during the note's signing. Therefore, a void contract could only exist if Mervin was "entirely without understanding" (incompetent) when he signed the note.

The phrase "entirely without understanding" has been a subject of this Court's scrutiny from at least 1902. *Mach v. Blanchard*, 15 S.D. 432, 90 N.W. 1042 (1902). It has evolved in the law to apply in those situations where the person contracting did not possess the mental dexterity required to comprehend the nature and ultimate effect of the transaction in which he was involved. *See Fischer v. Gorman*, 65 S.D. 453, 458-60, 274 N.W. 866, 870 (1937). A party attempting to avoid his contract must carry the burden of proving that he was entirely without understanding when he contracted. *Christensen v. Larson*, 77 N.W.2d 441, 446-47 (N.D. 1956). Lapse of memory, carelessness of person and property, and unreasonableness are not determinative of one's ability to presently enter into an agreement. *Hochgraber v. Balzer*, 66 S.D. 630, 634, 287 N.W. 585, 587 (1939). Neither should a contract be found void because of previous or subsequent incompetence. *Heward v. Sutton*, 75 Nev. 452, 345 P.2d 772 (1959); 41 Am. Jur. 2d *Incompetent Persons* §69 (1968). Our inquiry must always focus on the person's mental acuity and understanding of the transaction at the time contracting occurred.

To show that he was entirely without understanding when he signed the note, Mervin points to his family's testimony that he was unconcerned with family and business, uncooperative, antisocial, and unkempt. He also notes his involuntary commitments in the Fall of 1981.

Yet, Mervin engaged in farm operations, drove his truck, executed a promissory note (on October 3, 1981, for cattle he bought, which note was paid approximately two months thereafter), and paid for personal items by check drawn on his bank circa the period that he signed the note. Obviously, Mervin had an understanding to transact business; the corollary is that he was not entirely without understanding. In addition, only Randy was present when his father signed the note, and Randy's testimony (during his deposition and at trial) was vague and inconsistent on the crucial points of Mervin's demeanor when he signed the note and the general circumstances surrounding the event. Randy did, however, testify at his December 9, 1982 bankruptcy hearing that his dad knew he was signing a note. Thirdly, Mervin was not judicially committed during the note's signing and the presumption via SDCL 27A-14-2[1] must be that his discharge from Yankton on September 19, 1981, was an indication of his improved well-being. We therefore hold that Mervin failed to carry the burden of proving his incompetence (entirely without understanding) when he signed the note and we consequently rule that his obligation to Bank was not void. In so holding, we determine that the findings of fact and conclusions of law are clearly erroneous as we are, based on the entire evidence, left with a definite and firm conviction that a mistake has been committed.

. . .

Contractual obligations incurred by intoxicated persons may be voidable. *See* 2 S. Williston, *supra*, at §260. Voidable contracts (contracts other than those entered into following a judicial determination of incapacity, or entirely without understanding) may be rescinded by the previously disabled party. However, disaffirmance must be prompt, upon the recovery of the intoxicated party's mental abilities, and upon his notice of the agreement, if he had forgotten it. 2 S. Williston, *supra*, at §260; Restatement (Second) of Contracts §16, comment c. SDCL 53-11-4 provides that "[t]he party rescinding a contract must rescind promptly, upon discovering the facts which entitle him to rescind. . . ." *See also Kane v. Schnitzler*, 376 N.W.2d 337 (S.D. 1985). This Court in *Kane* noted that a delay in rescission which causes prejudice to the other party will extinguish the first party's right to disaffirm. *Id.*, 376 N.W.2d at 340.

A voidable contract may also be ratified by the party who had contracted while disabled. Upon ratification, the contract becomes a fully valid legal obligation. Ratification can either be express or implied by conduct. *Bank of Hoven v. Rausch*, 382 N.W.2d 39, 41 (S.D. 1986). In addition, failure of a party to disaffirm a contract over a period of time may, by itself, ripen into a ratification, especially if rescission will result in prejudice to the other party. *See Kane*, 376 N.W.2d 337; 2 S. Williston, *supra* at §260.

Mervin received both verbal notice from Randy and written notice from Bank on or about April 27, 1982, that the note was overdue. On May 5, 1982, Mervin paid the interest owing with a check which Randy delivered to Bank. This by itself could amount to ratification through conduct. If Mervin wished to avoid the contract, he should have then exercised his right of rescission. We find it impossible to believe that Mervin paid almost $900 in interest without, in his own mind, accepting

---

1. SDCL 27A-14-2 provides:

   A patient involuntarily committed may be discharged or provisionally discharged when, in the opinion of the administrator of the community mental health center or the center, *the patient's behavior is no longer that which precipitated or caused his admission.* The patient may agree to continue treatment voluntarily. (Emphasis added.)

responsibility for the note. His assertion that paying interest on the note relieved his obligation is equally untenable in light of his numerous past experiences with promissory notes.

In addition, Mervin's failure to rescind, coupled with his apparent ratification, could have jeopardized the Bank's chances of ever receiving payment on the note. As we know, Mervin unquestionably was aware of his obligation in late April 1982. If he had disaffirmed then, Bank could have actively pursued Randy and possibly collected some part of the debt. By delaying his rescission, and by paying the note's back interest, Mervin lulled Bank into a false sense of security that may have hurt it when on June 22, 1982, Randy filed for bankruptcy and was later fully discharged of his obligation on the note.

We conclude that Mervin's obligation to Bank [i]s not void because he did not show that he was entirely without understanding when he signed the note. Mervin's obligation on the note was voidable and his subsequent failure to disaffirm (lack of rescission) and his payment of interest (ratification) then transformed the voidable contract into one that is fully binding upon him.

We reverse and remand.

Problems

1. Change in Retirement Plan. Participants in a New York schoolteacher's pension plan could choose between a retirement benefits package that provides them with a higher monthly annuity that continues until they die, or a lower monthly payment that continues until both they and their spouse die. Grace Ortelere registered for the lower monthly benefit in order to provide a benefit to her husband if she were to die first. At age 60, she suffered from a "nervous breakdown," took a leave of absence from her job, and received treatment for cerebral arteriosclerosis. When her leave expired, she was still too ill to work, and she applied for retirement benefits. At that time, she provided notice to the pension plan that she wished to change her retirement election to the larger monthly payment without survivorship benefits—which the pension plan accepted—even though her husband had had to quit his job to care for her and, at that point, his life expectancy exceeded hers. Her intention was clearly communicated, in writing, and met the pension plan's formal requirements for a change of election.

Two months after retiring, Mrs. Ortelere died. Her husband sued the Teachers' Retirement Board to rescind the change of election on the grounds of mental incapacity. Mrs. Ortelere's psychiatrist testified that at the time she had suffered from "involutional psychosis," and that people with her condition "can't think rationally," and even say things like "I don't know whether I should get up or whether I should stay in bed." How should the court rule?

2. The Cadillac Lease. Rhonda Proctor received state disability benefits based on her diagnosis of bipolar disorder and physical ailments. One day, after searching the Internet for cars, she visited the showroom of Classic Automotive, looking disheveled with no make-up and unfixed hair, and emerged with a lease on a Cadillac that required monthly payments almost as large as her disability check. She did not test drive the car, used the term "buying" rather than "leasing" when discussing the transaction at the dealership, and noticeably had difficulty removing the keys from her key ring that belonged to a used Pontiac that she traded in at the same time. Proctor later admitted that she knew at the time that she was signing a lease agreement. She also claimed to have gone on a "shopping spree" in the next several days, during which she maxed out her credit card, become increasingly upset, and contemplated suicide.

Proctor subsequently sought rescission of the transaction on grounds of mental incapacity. Classic Automotive moved for summary judgment. How should the court rule?

3. The Whirlwind Wedding. One day, Nellie Malley and two of her friends drove Q.C. Guidici 45 miles from his home in Loyalton, California, to Reno, Nevada, with two purposes in mind: to transfer title of Guidici's farm to Malley and to arrange a marriage between the two. The group lacked certain information about the farm necessary to arrange for its legal transfer, however, forcing them to return to Loyalton for the necessary information and then retrace their path to Reno. A lawyer was then able to transfer title to the property, and Guidici and Malley were married by a justice of the peace later in the evening.

Shortly thereafter, Guidici sued for rescission of the property transaction, claiming that he had been drinking excessively for two weeks prior to the events in question, and that he had no memory of transferring the deed or getting married. Several witnesses confirmed seeing Guidici in a drunken state in the days leading up to the wedding, and a neighbor testified that she had seen the pair in Reno on the day in question, with Guidici staggering and Malley attempting to put him in the car. The notary who recorded the deed testified that Guidici had looked "dazed and kind of stupid" at the time of the transfer of the property deed, but that the notary assumed this "was because he was a foreigner and could not understand English very well." The attorney who prepared the deed did not testify that he noticed anything unusual in Guidici's behavior.

Is Guidici entitled to rescission of the transaction?

D. DURESS

The doctrine of duress allows courts to protect parties from the consequences of agreements that satisfy the technical requirements of contract but were not entered into voluntarily. Although the underlying goal of protecting party autonomy is clear, courts have struggled to distinguish between negotiating behavior that constitutes impermissible coercion and ordinary hard bargaining on the part of a party upon whom circumstances have endowed superior bargaining power. It is commonplace for one party to reluctantly accept a disagreeable proposal made by another because her alternative possible courses of action are even more disagreeable. A rule that were to render all contracts meeting this description potentially voidable would threaten to undermine confidence in the certainty of contractual obligations and create a disincentive for parties with bargaining power to enter into mutually beneficial transactions.

In the language of the Restatement, the balance between acceptable leverage and unacceptable coercion is struck by permitting parties to avoid enforcement of contracts coerced by an "improper threat" on the part of the offeror that the offeree has "no reasonable alternative" but to accept. Rest. (2d) Contracts §§175, 176. This two-part test provides a structure for analysis, but it obviously begs the dual questions of what type of threat is "improper" and what alternatives to acquiescence are "reasonable."

The first case below, *Duncan v. Hensley,* exemplifies the extreme case of physical duress, in which the offeror "persuades" the offeree to accept a proposal by threat of death or bodily injury should the offeree decline. Allowing the offeree to avoid enforcement of such agreements presents little risk of chilling desirable commercial activity, so the outcome is uncontroversial. More difficult questions arise, however, when plaintiffs seek to avoid contracts they entered in response to threats made to their economic interests. The remaining cases explore variations on a theme: one party threatens to breach an existing contract—by withholding payment or refusing to perform a service—unless her counterpart will agree to modify the terms of the original agreement. The second party acquiesces and then, after obtaining the desirable payment or service, challenges the enforceability of the modification (and seeks enforcement of the original bargain). *Levine v. Blumenthal* and *Alaska Packers' Association v. Domenico* approach the issue raised in those cases as one of consideration. *Austin Instrument, Inc. v. Loral Corporation* and *The Centech Group, Inc. v. Getronicswang Company* represent the modern trend of addressing the problem under the rubric of "economic duress."

DUNCAN
v.
HENSLEY

Supreme Court of Arkansas
248 Ark. 1083
1970

MATTHEWS, J.

. . .

Appellee and Appellant Graddy S. Duncan (who will hereinafter be referred to as Appellant) were married September 16, 1964. . . .

On June 26, 1968, the Appellee and Appellant entered into a property settlement agreement, in contemplation of divorce, under the terms of which Appellee was to receive the 440-acre farm located in Newton County, Arkansas, together with the household furniture located in Newton County, Arkansas, cattle and horses upon the Newton County farm and a 1968 Volkswagen automobile. The agreement recited that a 1961 Volkswagen registered in the name of Appellant would be transferred to Larry B. Hensley and further recited that any other automobiles, trucks or equipment registered in the name of the husband should be his sole and exclusive property. On the same date, Appellant executed a quitclaim deed to Appellee covering the Newton County lands.

Thereafter, on August 1, 1968, Appellee was granted a decree of divorce from the Appellant in which decree it was recited that the property settlement agreement filed therein should be approved and incorporated as a part of such decree. On February 4, 1969, Appellee, Joyce Hensley, executed and delivered to the Appellant a quitclaim deed conveying to him the Newton County lands and a bill of sale covering certain cattle, quarter horses, farm machinery, implements and tools situated on the Newton County lands and the house trailer, also situated thereon. The deed recited a consideration of Ten ($10.00) Dollars and other valuable consideration paid, and the bill of sale a consideration of Ten ($10.00) Dollars and other legal considerations paid. Both instruments were recorded on February 4, 1969.

On May 28, 1969, Appellee filed her suit to cancel these instruments and the decree from which this appeal comes was entered on September 4, 1969.

. . .

In Burr v. Burton, 18 Ark. 214, at page 233, this Court said:

> A contract made by a party, under compulsion, is void; because consent is of the essence of a contract, and where there is compulsion, there is no consent, for this must be voluntary. Such a contract is void for another reason. It is founded in wrong or fraud. It is not, however, all compulsion which has this effect; it must amount to duress. But this duress may be either actual violence, or threat. 1 Parsons on Cont. 319.
>
> The bill alleges, that Philip P. Burton threatened complainant, and the apprehension of personal violence was one of the inducements to the execution of the notes.
>
> Duress, by threats, says Mr. Parsons (Id. 320), exists not where-ever a party has entered into a contract under the influence of a threat, but only where such a threat excites a fear of some grievous wrong, as of death, or great bodily injury, or unlawful imprisonment.

In National Life & Accident Insurance Co. v. Blanton, 192 Ark. 1165, the rule in the Burton case was re-affirmed and was somewhat enlarged in the case of Perkins Oil Company of Delaware v. Fitzgerald, 197 Ark. 14, where it is said:

> To the same effect were numerous cases cited and discussed, all of which we have examined and determined that they arrive at, or reach the same uniform conclusions as those wherein such contracts were fairly and openly entered into without fraud, mistake,

deception or any form of duress. They were ordinarily held to be good. But in those cases in which these contracts were induced by some form of fraud, by over-reaching, by deceptive promises, relied upon, or by some form of duress, sufficient under all the prevailing facts and circumstances to impair the deliberate judgment to the extent that it might be determined that although the contract had been signed, it had not been agreed to, such contracts have uniformly been held voidable at the instance of the injured party.

At the conclusion of the testimony, the trial Court made findings and in part said:

> The Court finds and holds that the evidence is clear and convincing that this defendant (Appellant) Graddy Duncan, came from Louisiana and approached this plaintiff (Appellee), on February 4, 1969 with the intention of depriving her of most of the rest of the assets that she had and more particularly this farm and most of the horses and such other items as she still owned, and that he went to her place of business and later threatened her life and finally by use of such threats, which the Court finds were direct and real and of such a nature as to place her in fear of grievous bodily wrong or even death, prevailed upon her to go with him to the office of a realtor and have these papers prepared conveying over to him all of the farm, and she was the sole owner at the time of this four hundred forty (440) acres of land and improvements on it, and these animals mentioned in the bill of sale or agreement that she executed on that date. The Court finds that since the instruments were executed under those circumstances and involuntarily and against her will that they should both be cancelled in their entirety, and the Court so decrees.

With these conclusions of the Chancellor, we agree.

. . .

Appellee testified that prior to February 4, 1969, she had seen the Appellant only on two occasions subsequent to August 1, 1968, the date of the divorce decree, these being times when he returned to Newton County to pick up items belonging to him, the last time being in November of 1968; that on the morning of February 4, 1969, the Appellant came to the office of the Boone County Veterinarian Clinic in Harrison, Arkansas, where she was employed and prevailed upon her to enter his truck for the purpose of talking with him and after accompanying her to the Post Office, drove toward Newton County and onto a dirt road where he stated that Appellee was going to sign everything over to him or she was going to be dead; that Appellant also made threats against the life of one Bill Hardin and his daughter who had accompanied her to work that day. She testified that in reaction to these statements she was very scared because she believed Appellant and as a consequence, agreed to sign the papers transferring the farm and the items described in the bill of sale over to Appellant. They then went to the real estate office of Al Hochberger, in Jasper, Arkansas, the real estate man who had sold them the 440-acre ranch, and he prepared the deed and bill of sale which were executed and acknowledged in his presence, and thereafter by the parties taken on the same day to the

Newton County Court House and made of record. Appellee further testified that while they were at the real estate office she made a list of the horses on the ranch to be used by Mr. Hochberger in preparing the deed and thereafter while the papers were being recorded Appellant wrote on this piece of paper the words "midnight, March 9, 1969" and told her that unless she was off the ranch by that date that she would be dead. She testified that when she returned to the veterinary office that she was very upset, hysterical and did not have very good control of herself.

Appellee testified she believed Appellant because she had seen him in violent rages specifically referring to an instance when he had beaten a horse in her presence and another time when he had threatened to kill the owner of a bull that had been permitted to get in with the cows on the Louisiana ranch; that this violence was demonstrated in a family argument that arose over the use of a television set; that prior to their marriage Appellant had told Appellee that if she didn't marry him no one else would and she considered this to be a threat. . . .

Appellants argue that even if the Court should determine that Appellee discharged the burden of proof as to establishing duress, and we have held she did, then she is estopped by reason of her failure to make known to any of the persons the parties contacted on February 4, 1969, that she was acting under duress of Appellant and by her further delay in asserting such duress until the filing of her complaint on May 28, 1969. Appellee testified that she continued under the burden of Appellant's threats until she left Newton County about March 8, 1969 and we do not find an unreasonable period of delay in filing the suit to set aside the instruments. . . .

She did not have to make it known to anyone at the time. Unreasonable

LEVINE
v.
BLUMENTHAL
Supreme Court of New Jersey
186 A. 457
1936

Heher, J.

By an indenture dated April 16, 1931, plaintiff leased to defendants, for the retail merchandising of women's wearing apparel, store premises situate in the principal business district of the city of Paterson. The term was two years, to commence on May 1 next ensuing, with an option of renewal for the further period of three years; and the rent reserved was $2,100 for the first year, and $2,400 for the second year, payable in equal monthly installments in advance.

The state of the case settled by the district court judge sets forth that defendants adduced evidence tending to show that, in the month of April, 1932, before the expiration of the first year of the term, they advised plaintiff that "it was absolutely impossible for them to pay any increase in rent; that their business had so fallen down that they had great difficulty in meeting the present rent of $175 per month; that if the plaintiff insisted upon the increase called for in the lease, they would be forced to remove from the premises or perhaps go out of business altogether"; and that plaintiff agreed to allow them to remain under the same rental "until business improved." For eleven months of the second year of the term rent was paid by defendants, and accepted by plaintiff, at the rate of $175 per month. The option of renewal was not exercised; and defendants surrendered the premises at the expiration of the term, leaving the last month's rent unpaid. This action was brought to recover the unpaid balance of the rent reserved by the lease for the second year—$25 per month for eleven months, and $200 for the last month.

The insistence is that the current trade depression had disabled the lessees in respect of the payment of the full rent reserved, and a consideration sufficient to support the secondary agreement arose out of these special circumstances.

It is elementary that the subsequent agreement, to impose the obligation of a contract, must rest upon a new and independent consideration. The principle is firmly imbedded in our jurisprudence that a promise to do what the promisor is already legally bound to do is an unreal consideration. It has been criticized, at least in some of its special applications, as "mediaeval" and wholly artificial—one that operates to defeat the "reasonable bargains of business men." But these strictures are not well grounded. It is a principle, almost universally accepted, that an act or forebearance required by a legal duty owing to the promisor that is neither doubtful nor the subject of honest and reasonable dispute is not a sufficient consideration. Williston on Contracts.

Yet any consideration for the new undertaking, however insignificant, satisfies this rule. For instance, an undertaking to pay part of the debt before maturity, or at a place other than where the obligor was legally bound to pay, or to pay in property, regardless of its value, or to effect a composition with creditors by the payment of less than the sum due, has been held to constitute a consideration sufficient in law. The test is whether there is an additional consideration adequate to support an ordinary contract, and consists of something which the debtor was not legally bound to do or give.

And there is authority for the view that, where there is no illegal preference, a payment of part of a debt, "accompanied by an agreement of the debtor to refrain from voluntary bankruptcy," is a sufficient consideration for the creditor's promise to remit the balance of the debt. But the mere fact that the creditor "fears that the debtor will go into bankruptcy, and that the debtor contemplates bankruptcy proceedings," is not enough; that alone does not prove that the creditor requested the debtor to refrain from such proceedings.

The cases to the contrary either create arbitrary exceptions to the rule, or profess to find a consideration in the form of a new undertaking which in essence was not a tangible new obligation or a duty not imposed by the lease, or, in any event, was not the price "bargained for as the exchange for the promise" and therefore do violence to the fundamental principle. They exhibit the modern tendency, especially in the matter of rent reductions, to depart from the strictness of the basic common-law rule and give effect to what has been termed a "reasonable" modification of the primary contract.

So tested, the secondary agreement at issue is not supported by a valid consideration; and it therefore created no legal obligation. General economic adversity, however disastrous it may be in its individual consequences, is never a warrant for judicial abrogation of this primary principle of the law of contracts. Judgment affirmed.

ALASKA PACKERS' ASS'N
v.
DOMENICO

Circuit Court of Appeals, Ninth Circuit
117 F. 99
1902

Ross, J.

The libel in this case was based upon a contract alleged to have been entered into between the libelants and the appellant corporation on the 22d day of May, 1900, at Pyramid Harbor, Alaska, by which it is claimed the appellant promised to pay each of the libelants, among other things, the sum of $100 for services rendered and to be rendered. In its answer the respondent denied the execution, on its part, of the contract sued upon, averred that it was without consideration.

The evidence shows without conflict that on March 26, 1900, at San Francisco, the libelants entered into a written contract with the appellants, whereby they agreed to go from San Francisco to Pyramid Harbor, Alaska, and return, on board such vessel as might be designated by the appellant, and to work for the appellant during the fishing season of 1900, at Pyramid Harbor, as sailors and fishermen, agreeing to do "regular ship's duty, both up and down, discharging and loading; and to do any other work whatsoever when requested to do so by the captain or agent of the Alaska Packers' Association." By the terms of this agreement, the appellant was to pay each of the libelants $50 for the season, and two cents for each red salmon in the catching of which he took part.

On the 15th day of April, 1900 the libelants sailed for Pyramid Harbor, where the appellants had about $150,000 invested in a salmon cannery. The libelants arrived there early in April [likely May—Eds.] of the year mentioned, and began to unload the vessel and fit up the cannery. A few days thereafter, to wit, May 19th, they stopped work in a body, and demanded of the company's superintendent there in charge $100 for services in operating the vessel to and from Pyramid Harbor, instead of the sums stipulated for in and by the contracts; stating that unless they were paid this additional wage they would stop work entirely, and return to San Francisco. The evidence showed, and the court below found, that it was impossible for the appellant to get other men to take the places of the libelants, the place being remote, the season short and just opening; so that, after endeavoring for several days without success to induce the libelants to proceed with their work in accordance with their contracts, the company's superintendent, on the 22d day of May, so far yielded to their demands as to instruct his clerk to copy the contract executed in San Francisco, including the words "Alaska Packers' Association" at the end, substituting, for the $50 and $60 payments, respectively, of those contracts, the sum of $100. Upon the return of the libelants to San Francisco at the close of the fishing season, they demanded pay in accordance with the terms of the alleged contract of May 22d, when the company denied its validity, and refused to pay other than as provided for by the contract of March 26th.

On the trial in the court below, the libelants undertook to show that the fishing nets provided by the respondent were defective, and that it was on that account that they demanded increased wages. On that point, the evidence was substantially conflicting, and the finding of the court was against the libelants.

The evidence being sharply conflicting in respect to these facts, the conclusions of the court, who heard and saw the witnesses, will not be disturbed.

The real questions in the case as brought here are questions of law, and, in the view that we take of the case, it will be necessary to consider but one of those. Assuming that the appellant's superintendent at Pyramid Harbor was authorized to make the alleged contract of May 22d, and that he executed it on behalf of the appellant, was it supported by a sufficient consideration? From the foregoing statement of the case, it will have been seen that the libelants agreed in writing, for certain stated compensation, to render their services to the appellant in remote waters where the season for conducting fishing operations is extremely short, and in which enterprise the appellant had a large amount of money invested; and, after having entered upon the discharge of their contract, and at a time when it was impossible for the appellant to secure other men in their places, the libelants, without any valid cause, absolutely refused to continue the services they were under contract to perform unless the appellant would consent to pay them more money. Consent to such a demand, under such circumstances, if given, was, in our opinion, without consideration, for the reason that it was based solely upon the libelants' agreement to render the exact services, and none other, that they were already under contract to render. The case shows that they willfully and arbitrarily broke that obligation. As a matter of course, they were liable to the appellant in damages, and it is quite probable, as suggested by the court below in its opinion, that they may have been unable to respond in damages. But we are unable to agree with the conclusions there drawn, from these facts, in these words:

> Under such circumstances, it would be strange, indeed, if the law would not permit the defendant to waive the damages caused by the libelants' breach, and enter into the contract sued upon,—a contract mutually beneficial to all the parties thereto, in that it gave to the libelants reasonable compensation for their labor, and enabled the defendant to employ to advantage the large capital it had invested in its canning and fishing plant.

Certainly, it cannot be justly held, upon the record in this case, that there was any voluntary waiver on the part of the appellant of the breach of the original contract. The circumstances of the present case bring it, we think, directly within the sound and just observations of the supreme court of Minnesota.

> No astute reasoning can change the plain fact that the party who refuses to perform, and thereby coerces a promise from the other party to the contract to pay him an increased compensation for doing that which he is legally bound to do, takes an unjustifiable advantage of the necessities of the other party. Surely it would be a travesty on justice to hold that the party so making the promise for extra pay was estopped from asserting that the promise was without consideration. A party cannot lay the foundation of an estoppel by his own wrong, where the promise is simply a repetition of a subsisting legal promise. There can be no consideration for the promise of the other party, and there is no warrant for inferring that the parties have voluntarily rescinded or modified their contract. The promise cannot be legally enforced, although the other party has completed his contract in reliance upon it.

In Lingenfelder v. Brewing Co., the court, in holding void a contract by which the owner of a building agreed to pay its architect an additional sum because of his refusal to otherwise proceed with the contract, said:

> It is urged upon us by respondents that this was a new contract. New in what? Jungenfeld was bound by his contract to design and supervise this building. Under the new promise, he was not to do anything more or anything different. What benefit was to accrue to Wainwright? He was to receive the same service from Jungenfeld under the new, that Jungenfeld was bound to tender under the original, contract. What loss, trouble, or inconvenience could result to Jungenfeld that he had not already assumed? To permit plaintiff to recover under such circumstances would be to offer a premium upon bad faith, and invite men to violate their most sacred contracts that they may profit by their own wrong. That a promise to pay a man for doing that which he is already under contract to do is without consideration is conceded by respondents. The learned counsel for respondents do not controvert the general proposition. The contention is that, when Jungenfeld declined to go further on his contract, the defendant then had the right to sue for damages, and not having elected to sue Jungenfeld, but having acceded to his demand for the additional compensation defendant cannot now be heard to say his promise is without consideration. While it is true Jungenfeld became liable in damages for the obvious breach of his contract, we do not think it follows that defendant is estopped from showing its promise was made without consideration. What we hold is that, when a party merely does what he has already obligated himself to do, he cannot demand an additional compensation therefor; and although, by taking advantage of the necessities of his adversary, he obtains a promise for more, the law will regard it as nudum pactum, and will not lend its process to aid in the wrong.

It results from the views above expressed that the judgment must be reversed, and the cause remanded, with directions to the court below to enter judgment for the respondent, with costs. It is so ordered.

AUSTIN INSTRUMENT, INC.
v.
LORAL CORP.

Court of Appeals of New York
29 N.Y.2d 124
1971

FULD, C.J.

The defendant, Loral Corporation, seeks to recover payment for goods delivered under a contract which it had with plaintiff Austin Instrument, Inc., on the ground that the evidence establishes, as a matter of law, that it was forced to agree to an increase in price on the items in question under circumstances amounting to economic duress.

In July of 1965, Loral was awarded a $6,000,000 contract by the Navy for the production of radar sets. The contract contained a schedule of deliveries, a liquidated damages clause applying to late deliveries and a cancellation clause in case of default by Loral. The latter thereupon solicited bids for some 40 precision gear components needed to produce the radar sets, and awarded Austin a subcontract to supply 23 such parts. That party commenced delivery in early 1966.

In May, 1966, Loral was awarded a second Navy contract for the production of more radar sets and again went about soliciting bids. Austin bid on all 40 gear components but, on July 15, a representative from Loral informed Austin's president, Mr. Krauss, that his company would be awarded the subcontract only for those items on which it was low bidder. The Austin officer refused to accept an order for less than all 40 of the gear parts and on the next day he told Loral that Austin would cease deliveries of the parts due under the existing subcontract unless Loral consented to substantial increases in the prices provided for by that agreement—both retroactively for parts already delivered and prospectively on those not yet shipped—and placed with Austin the order for all 40 parts needed under Loral's second Navy contract. Shortly thereafter, Austin did, indeed, stop delivery. After contacting 10 manufacturers of precision gears and finding none who could produce the parts in time to meet its commitments to the Navy,[1] Loral acceded to Austin's demands; in a letter dated July 22, Loral wrote to Austin that "We have feverishly surveyed other sources of supply and find that because of the prevailing military exigencies, were they to start from scratch as would have to be the case, they could not even remotely begin to deliver on time to meet the delivery requirements

---

1. The best reply Loral received was from a vendor who stated he could commence deliveries sometime in October.

established by the Government. Accordingly, we are left with no choice or alternative but to meet your conditions."

Loral thereupon consented to the price increases insisted upon by Austin under the first subcontract and the latter was awarded a second subcontract making it the supplier of all 40 gear parts for Loral's second contract with the Navy,[2] Although Austin was granted until September to resume deliveries, Loral did, in fact, receive parts in August and was able to produce the radar sets in time to meet its commitments to the Navy on both contracts. After Austin's last delivery under the second subcontract in July, 1967, Loral notified it of its intention to seek recovery of the price increases.

On September 15, 1967, Austin instituted this action against Loral to recover an amount in excess of $17,750 which was still due on the second subcontract. On the same day, Loral commenced an action against Austin claiming damages of some $22,250—the aggregate of the price increases under the first subcontract—on the ground of economic duress. The two actions were consolidated and, following a trial, Austin was awarded the sum it requested and Loral's complaint against Austin was dismissed on the ground that it was not shown that "it could not have obtained the items in question from other sources in time to meet its commitment to the Navy under the first contract." A closely divided Appellate Division affirmed (35 AD2d 387). There was no material disagreement concerning the facts; as Justice Steuer stated in the course of his dissent below, "[t]he facts are virtually undisputed, nor is there any serious question of law. The difficulty lies in the application of the law to these facts." (35 AD2d 392.)

The applicable law is clear and, indeed, is not disputed by the parties. A contract is voidable on the ground of duress when it is established that the party making the claim was forced to agree to it by means of a wrongful threat precluding the exercise of his free will. (See Allstate Med. Labs. v. Blaivas, 20 NY2d 654; Kazaras v. Manufacturers Trust Co., 4 NY2d 930; Adams v. Irving Nat. Bank, 116 N.Y. 606, 611; see, also, 13 Williston, Contracts [3d ed. 1970], §1603, p. 658.) The existence of economic duress or business compulsion is demonstrated by proof that "immediate possession of needful goods is threatened" (Mercury Mach. Importing Corp. v. City of New York, 3 NY2d 418, 425) or, more particularly, in cases such as the one before us, by proof that one party to a contract has threatened to breach the agreement by withholding goods unless the other party agrees to some further demand. (See, e.g., du Pont de Nemours & Co. v. Hass Co., 303 N.Y. 785; Gallagher Switchboard Corp. v. Heckler Elec. Co., 36 Misc 2d 225; see, also, 13 Williston, Contracts [3d ed. 1970], §1617, p. 705.) However, a mere threat by one party to breach the contract by not delivering the required items, though wrongful, does not in itself constitute economic duress. It must also appear that the threatened party could not obtain the goods from another source of supply and that the ordinary remedy of an action for breach of contract would not be adequate. We find without any support in the record the conclusion reached by the courts below that Loral failed to establish that it was the victim of economic duress. On the contrary, the evidence makes out a classic case, as a matter of law, of such duress.

---

2. Loral makes no claim in this action on the second subcontract.

It is manifest that Austin's threat—to stop deliveries unless the prices were increased deprived Loral of its free will. As bearing on this, Loral's relationship with the Government is most significant. As mentioned above, its contract called for staggered monthly deliveries of the radar sets, with clauses calling for liquidated damages and possible cancellation on default. Because of its production schedule, Loral was, in July, 1966, concerned with meeting its delivery requirements in September, October and November, and it was for the sets to be delivered in those months that the withheld gears were needed. Loral had to plan ahead, and the substantial liquidated damages for which it would be liable, plus the threat of default, were genuine possibilities. Moreover, Loral did a substantial portion of its business with the Government, and it feared that a failure to deliver as agreed upon would jeopardize its chances for future contracts. These genuine concerns do not merit the label "'self-imposed, undisclosed and subjective'" which the Appellate Division majority placed upon them. It was perfectly reasonable for Loral, or any other party similarly placed, to consider itself in an emergency, duress situation.

. . .

We find unconvincing Austin's contention that Loral, in order to meet its burden, should have contacted the Government and asked for an extension of its delivery dates so as to enable it to purchase the parts from another vendor. Aside from the consideration that Loral was anxious to perform well in the Government's eyes, it could not be sure when it would obtain enough parts from a substitute vendor to meet its commitments. The only promise which it received from the companies it contacted was for commencement of deliveries, not full supply, and, with vendor delay common in this field, it would have been nearly impossible to know the length of the extension it should request. It must be remembered that Loral was producing a needed item of military hardware. Moreover, there is authority for Loral's position that nonperformance by a subcontractor is not an excuse for default in the main contract. (See, e.g., McBride & Wachtel, Government Contracts, §35.10.) In light of all this, Loral's claim should not be held insufficiently supported because it did not request an extension from the Government.

Loral, as indicated above, also had the burden of demonstrating that it could not obtain the parts elsewhere within a reasonable time, and there can be no doubt that it met this burden. The 10 manufacturers whom Loral contacted comprised its entire list of "approved vendors" for precision gears, and none was able to commence delivery soon enough.[6] As Loral was producing a highly sophisticated item of military machinery requiring parts made to the strictest engineering standards, it would be unreasonable to hold that Loral should have gone to other vendors, with whom it was either unfamiliar or dissatisfied, to procure the needed parts. As Justice Steuer noted in his dissent, Loral "contacted all the manufacturers whom it believed capable of making these parts" (35 AD2d, at p. 393), and this was all the law requires.

It is hardly necessary to add that Loral's normal legal remedy of accepting Austin's breach of the contract and then suing for damages would have been inadequate

---

6. Loral as do many manufacturers, maintains a list of "approved vendors," that is, vendors whose products, facilities, techniques and performance have been inspected and found satisfactory.

under the circumstances, as Loral would still have had to obtain the gears elsewhere with all the concomitant consequences mentioned above. In other words, Loral actually had no choice, when the prices were raised by Austin, except to take the gears at the "coerced" prices and then sue to get the excess back.

Austin's final argument is that Loral, even if it did enter into the contract under duress, lost any rights it had to a refund of money by waiting until July, 1967, long after the termination date of the contract, to disaffirm it. It is true that one who would recover moneys allegedly paid under duress must act promptly to make his claim known. (See Oregon Pacific R. R. Co. v. Forrest, 128 N.Y. 83, 93; Port Chester Elec. Constr. Corp. v. Hastings Terraces, 284 App. Div. 966, 967.) In this case, Loral delayed making its demand for a refund until three days after Austin's last delivery on the second subcontract. Loral's reason—for waiting until that time—is that it feared another stoppage of deliveries which would again put it in an untenable situation. Considering Austin's conduct in the past, this was perfectly reasonable, as the possibility of an application by Austin of further business compulsion still existed until all of the parts were delivered.

In sum, the record before us demonstrates that Loral agreed to the price increases in consequence of the economic duress employed by Austin. Accordingly, the matter should be remanded to the trial court for a computation of its damages.

The order appealed from should be modified, with costs, by reversing so much thereof as affirms the dismissal of defendant Loral Corporation's claim and, except as so modified, affirmed.

BERGAN, J.

Whether acts charged as constituting economic duress produce or do not produce the damaging effect attributed to them is normally a routine type of factual issue.

Here the fact question was resolved against Loral both by the Special Term and by the affirmance at the Appellate Division. It should not be open for different resolution here.

In summarizing the Special Term's decision and its own, the Appellate Division decided that "the conclusion that Loral acted deliberately and voluntarily, without being under immediate pressure of incurring severe business reverses, precludes a recovery on the theory of economic duress" (35 AD2d 387, 391).

When the testimony of the witnesses who actually took part in the negotiations for the two disputing parties is examined, sharp conflicts of fact emerge. Under Austin's version the request for a renegotiation of the existing contract was based on Austin's contention that Loral had failed to carry out an understanding as to the items to be furnished under that contract and this was the source of dissatisfaction which led both to a revision of the existing agreement and to entering into a new one.

This is not necessarily and as a matter of law to be held economic duress. On this appeal it is needful to look at the facts resolved in favor of Austin most favorably to that party. Austin's version of events was that a threat was not made but rather a request to accommodate the closing of its plant for a customary vacation period in accordance with the general understanding of the parties.

Moreover, critical to the issue of economic duress was the availability of alternative suppliers to the purchaser Loral. The demonstration is replete in the direct testimony of Austin's witnesses and on cross-examination of Loral's principal and purchasing agent that the availability of practical alternatives was a highly controverted issue of fact. On that issue of fact the explicit findings made by the Special Referee were affirmed by the Appellate Division. Nor is the issue of fact made the less so by assertion that the facts are undisputed and that only the application of equally undisputed rules of law is involved.

Austin asserted and Loral admitted on cross-examination that there were many suppliers listed in a trade registry but that Loral chose to rely only on those who had in the past come to them for orders and with whom they were familiar. It was, therefore, at least a fair issue of fact whether under the circumstances such conduct was reasonable and made what might otherwise have been a commercially understandable renegotiation an exercise of duress.

The order should be affirmed.

Judges Burke, Scileppi and Gibson concur with Chief Judge Fuld; Judge Bergan dissents and votes to affirm in a separate opinion in which Judges Breitel and Jasen concur.

Ordered accordingly.

CENTECH GROUP, INC.
v.
GETRONICSWANG CO.

U.S. Court of Appeals, Fourth Circuit
2002 WL 479767
2002

Per Curiam.

Appellant Centech entered into a contract with the Navy that required Centech to convert 55 million microfiche personnel records into digital form by June 30, 1997. Centech then awarded I-NET a subcontract to design and develop a data conversion system.

Centech became delinquent in its performance of the prime contract with the Navy. On February 29, 1996, Centech and I-NET agreed to a memorandum of understanding ("Original MOU"), which stated, in part:

> I-NET agrees to assume liability for performance of the prime contract from CENTECH . . . *by either of the following methods*:
>
> **a.** Novation of the Contract from CENTECH to I-NET. . . .
>
> **b.** Substantial Restructuring of the Subcontract Agreement to Allow I-NET to Perform the Majority of the Remaining Work in Compliance with Applicable Government Regulations. . . .

c. If a. or b. above are not possible, the parties agree to work in good faith to restructure the current prime/subcontract arrangement to achieve essentially the same objectives with the Government's approval.

J.A. 38 (emphasis added). I-NET also agreed, in the original MOU, to award $9.25 million in subcontracts to Centech over a three-year period, and to provide Centech with $20 million in bid/teaming opportunities over a two-year period. J.A. 38-39.

The parties were unable to agree to a novation or a substantial restructuring. On May 31, 1996, they entered into a new "memorandum of understanding" ("Revised MOU"), which expressly stated that it *"supersedes all other previous agreements* between [Centech] and [I-NET] made pursuant to the [Navy] contract." J.A. 182 (emphasis added). It also provided that I-NET

agrees to assume full liability for the timely, and satisfactory performance and delivery of the services described in the prime contract and to indemnify Centech Group against all contractual claims and losses arising from any failure to perform such services in a timely or satisfactory manner.

J.A. 182 (emphasis added). The Revised MOU further stated that the parties have agreed with the Navy that the Navy/Centech prime contract would be terminated and I-NET would enter into a new contract with the Navy. J.A. 182. Under the Revised MOU, I-NET agreed to "use commercially reasonable efforts to identify and pursue bid/teaming opportunities offering projected total contract revenue of $10 million to Centech Group." J.A. 183.

Centech now sues I-NET, claiming that I-NET breached the Original MOU. . . . The district court rejected Centech's claim that the Revised MOU was not a valid contract. Centech appeals.

. . .

Centech . . . asserts that the Revised MOU is invalid because it was procured by duress. Centech claims that I-NET "threatened" to discontinue its performance under its subcontract with Centech, which induced Centech to sign the Revised MOU. I-NET's alleged "threat" hardly constitutes the coercive circumstances necessary for a claim of economic duress. For duress to exist under Virginia law, "not only must a threat be improper, but it must leave the aggrieved party *without any reasonable alternative other than to assent to the contract.*" King v. Donnkenny, Inc., 84 F. Supp. 2d 736, 739 (W.D. Va. 2000) (emphasis added). Centech had many "reasonable alternatives" other than to sign the Revised MOU in response to I-NET's alleged threat. It could have filed a declaratory judgment or an anticipatory lawsuit against I-NET, or it could have sought to renegotiate its prime contract with the Navy, to name just a few.

The record shows that the Revised MOU was the result of arms-length discussions between sophisticated corporate parties, and Centech even consulted with its in-house counsel, Grant Moy, before signing the Revised MOU. We find Centech's claim of duress to be without merit.

Problems

1. A Hard Hops Bargain. Because of business disruptions caused by World War II, the Kips Bay Brewing Company found that it could obtain hops, a necessary ingredient in beer, only from one supplier: Hugo V. Lowei. When Lowei refused to sell to Kips Bay except under a three-year contract, the latter reluctantly agreed. When the hops shortage later eased, Kips Bay refused to honor the remainder of the agreement, and it defended against Lowei's breach of contract lawsuit by alleging duress. Which party should prevail?

2. The Cash-Strapped Barge Operator. Totem Marine Tug & Barge contracted with Alyeska Pipeline Services Company to transport pipeline construction materials from Houston, Texas, to southern Alaska. Difficulties plagued the relationship, and Alyeska ultimately terminated the contract. Totem then billed Alyeska approximately $300,000 for services already performed and alleged that Alyeska acknowledged the validity of the charges but nonetheless told Totem that invoices might not be paid for six or eight months. Totem was in urgent need of cash as its debts had come due. Totem's attorney advised Alyeska that Totem faced bankruptcy if the payments were not forthcoming and, after negotiations, Alyeska agreed to pay Totem $97,500 in return for Totem releasing Alyeska from all further claims. Totem subsequently filed a lawsuit against Alyeska to rescind the settlement agreement and to recover the balance allegedly due on the original contract. The trial court granted summary judgment for Alyeska, and Totem appealed. Was Alyeska entitled to summary judgment, or did Totem allege sufficient facts to obtain a trial?

3. The Embarrassed Lover. Following a date with Louis Fiege, Hilda Boehm became pregnant. She claimed that Fiege was the child's father and threatened to bring a legal action for paternity unless he agreed to make child support payments, which Fiege then promised to do. Two years later, Fiege learned from the results of a blood test that he could not have been the father of Boehm's child, and he stopped making the child support payments. Boehm then sued Fiege for breach of contract. Fiege claimed that he had never had sexual intercourse with Boehm, but that he had paid her child support because "he did not want his mother to know" about Boehm's allegations, which a legal proceeding would have made public. Is Boehm entitled to judgment, or does Fiege have a valid defense? Should it matter whether the trier of fact believes Boehm's claim that the couple had sexual intercourse or Fiege's claim that they did not?

E. MISREPRESENTATION

Like duress, the misrepresentation doctrine enables parties to avoid enforcement of contracts that are inconsistent with their autonomous preferences. In the case of duress, the problem is that the manifested assent to the contract is involuntary in an important respect. In case of misrepresentation, the assent itself is not coerced, but instead the complaining party lacked information at the time of contracting that, if known, would have caused that party to withhold consent. Whether a party convinced his counterpart to agree to purchase a vehicle for $100,000 by holding a gun to her head or by telling her that the car was a Ferrari when it was actually a Honda, nonenforcement can be justified by the observation that the first party's behavior violated accepted social norms of fair dealing, that the agreement did not reflect the counterpart's autonomous choice, or that the transaction would likely violate the principle of Pareto efficiency (i.e., that at least one party is made subjectively better off by the result and that neither is made subjectively worse off).

As is also true of the duress doctrine, the difficult cases concerning misrepresentation arise from a lack of clarity over whether the party seeking avoidance was in fact mistreated and whether he should have taken self-protective steps to avoid entering into a contract that he would later regret. And, again, the law inevitably must balance one party's claim to protection from exploitation against the other's claim to the protection of his reliance on the other's manifestation of assent. According to the Restatement, this balance is struck by allowing a party to avoid enforcement if his assent was induced by (a) an assertion not in accordance with the facts, that was (b) material or fraudulent, and upon which (c) he was justified in relying. Rest. (2d) Contracts §§159, 162, 164.

Read together, the first four cases in this section—*Swinton v. Whitinsville Savings Bank, Weintraub v. Krobatsch, Stambovsky v. Ackley,* and *Stroup v. Conant*—demonstrate the judicial struggle with the most fundamental problem of the misrepresentation doctrine: whether a party's failure to disclose a material fact in the bargaining process should be treated the same as an affirmative assertion not in accordance with the facts. In the final case, *Vokes v. Arthur Murray, Inc.,* the act in question is unquestionably an "assertion," but it is less clear whether the assertion was false, whether it was material, or whether the listener was justified in relying upon it.

SWINTON
v.
WHITINSVILLE SAVINGS BANK
Supreme Judicial Court of Massachusetts
311 Mass. 677
1942

QUA, J.

The declaration alleges that on or about September 12, 1938, the defendant sold the plaintiff a house in Newton to be occupied by the plaintiff and his family as a dwelling; that at the time of the sale the house "was infested with termites, an insect that is most dangerous and destructive to buildings"; that the defendant knew the house was so infested; that the plaintiff could not readily observe this condition upon inspection; that "knowing the internal destruction that these insects were creating in said house," the defendant falsely and fraudulently concealed from the plaintiff its true condition; that the plaintiff at the time of his purchase had no knowledge of the termites, exercised due care thereafter, and learned of them about August 30, 1940; and that, because of the destruction that was being done and the dangerous condition that was being created by the termites, the plaintiff was put to great expense for repairs and for the installation of termite control in order to prevent the loss and destruction of said house.

There is no allegation of any false statement or representation, or of the uttering of a half truth which may be tantamount to a falsehood. There is no intimation that the defendant by any means prevented the plaintiff from acquiring information as to the condition of the house. There is nothing to show any fiduciary relation between the parties, or that the plaintiff stood in a position of confidence toward or dependence upon the defendant. So far as appears the parties made a business deal at arm's length. The charge is concealment and nothing more; and it is concealment in the simple sense of mere failure to reveal, with nothing to show any peculiar duty to speak. The characterization of the concealment as false and fraudulent of course adds nothing in the absence of further allegations of fact. Province Securities Corp. v. Maryland Casualty Co., 269 Mass. 75, 92, 168 S.E. 252.

If this defendant is liable on this declaration every seller is liable who fails to disclose any nonapparent defect known to him in the subject of the sale which materially reduces its value and which the buyer fails to discover. Similarly it would seem that every buyer would be liable who fails to disclose any nonapparent virtue known to him in the subject of the purchase which materially enhances its value and of which the seller is ignorant. See Goodwin v. Agassiz, 283 Mass. 358. The law has not yet, we believe, reached the point of imposing upon the frailties of human nature a standard so idealistic as this. That the particular case here stated by the plaintiff possesses a certain appeal to the moral sense is scarcely to be denied. Probably the reason is to be found in the facts that the infestation of buildings by termites has not been common in Massachusetts and constitutes a concealed risk against which buyers are off their guard. But the law cannot provide special rules for termites and can hardly attempt to determine liability according to the varying probabilities of the existence and discovery of different possible defects in the subjects of trade. The rule of nonliability for bare nondisclosure has been stated and followed by this court in Matthews v. Bliss, 22 Pick. 48, 52, 53; Potts v. Chapin, 133 Mass. 276; Van Houten v. Morse, 162 Mass. 414; Phinney v. Friedman, 224 Mass. 531, 533; Windram Mfg. Co. v. Boston Blacking Co., 239 Mass. 123, 126; Wellington v. Rugg, 243 Mass. 30, 35, 36; and Brockton Olympia Realty Co. v. Lee, 266 Mass. 550, 561. It is adopted in the American Law Institute's Restatement of Torts, §551. See Williston on Contracts, Rev. Ed., §§1497, 1498, 1499.

The order sustaining the demurrer is affirmed, and judgment is to be entered for the defendant. Keljikian v. Star Brewing Co., 303 Mass. 53, 55-63.

So ordered.

WEINTRAUB
v.
KROBATSCH

8

Supreme Court of New Jersey
64 N.J. 445
1974

JACOBS, J.

. . . Mrs. Weintraub owned and occupied a six-year-old Englishtown home which she placed in the hands of a real estate broker (The Serafin Agency, Inc.) for sale. The Krobatsches were interested in purchasing the home, examined it while it was illuminated and found it suitable. On June 30, 1971 Mrs. Weintraub, as seller, and the Krobatsches, as purchasers, entered into a contract for the sale of the property for $42,500. The contract provided that the purchasers had inspected the property and were fully satisfied with its physical condition, that no representations had been made and that no responsibility was assumed by the seller as to the present or future condition of the premises. A deposit of $4,250 was sent by the purchasers to the broker to be held in escrow pending the closing of the transaction. The purchasers requested that the seller have the house fumigated and that was done. A fire after the signing of the contract caused damage but the purchasers indicated readiness that there be adjustment at closing.

During the evening of August 25, 1971, prior to closing, the purchasers entered the house, then unoccupied, and as they turned the lights on they were, as described in their petition for certification, "astonished to see roaches literally running in all directions, up the walls, drapes, etc." On the following day their attorney wrote a letter to Mrs. Weintraub, care of her New York law firm, advising that on the previous day "it was discovered that the house is infested with vermin despite the fact that an exterminator has only recently serviced the house" and asserting that "the presence of vermin in such great quantities, particularly after the exterminator was done, rendered the house as unfit for human habitation at this time and therefore, the contract is rescinded." On September 2, 1971 an exterminator wrote to Mr. Krobatsch advising that he had examined the premises and that "cockroaches were found to have infested the entire house." He said he could eliminate them for a relatively modest charge by two treatments with a twenty-one day interval but that it would be necessary to remove the carpeting "to properly treat all the infested areas."

Mrs. Weintraub rejected the rescission by the purchasers and filed an action in the Law Division joining them and the broker as defendants. . . . At the argument on the motions it was evident that the purchasers were claiming fraudulent concealment or nondisclosure by the seller as the basis for their rescission. Thus at one point their attorney said: "Your honor, I would point out, and it is in my clients' affidavit, every time that they inspected this house prior to this time every light in the place was illuminated. Now, these insects are nocturnal by nature and that is not a point I think I have to prove through someone. I think Webster's dictionary is sufficient.

By keeping the lights on it keeps them out of sight. These sellers had to know they had this problem. You could not live in a house this infested without knowing about it."

The Law Division denied the motion by the purchasers for summary judgment but granted Mrs. Weintraub's motion and directed that the purchasers pay her the sum of $4,250. . . .

Before us the purchasers contend that they were entitled to a trial on the issue of whether there was fraudulent concealment or nondisclosure entitling them to rescind; if there was, then clearly they were under no liability to either the seller or the broker and would be entitled to the return of their deposit held by the broker in escrow. See Keen v. James, 39 N.J. Eq. 527, 540 (E. & A. 1885) where Justice Dixon, speaking for the then Court of last resort, pointed out that "silence may be fraudulent" and that relief may be granted to one contractual party where the other suppresses facts which he, "under the circumstances, is bound in conscience and duty to disclose to the other party, and in respect to which he cannot, innocently, be silent." 39 N.J. Eq. at 540-541. See also Grossman Furniture Co. v. Pierre, 119 N.J. Super. 411, 420, 291 A.2d 858 (Essex Co. Ct.1972); Heuter v. Coastal Air Lines, Inc., Supra, 12 N.J. Super. at 495-497, 79 A.2d 880; 12 Williston, Contracts §1498 (3d ed. 1970); Prosser, Torts 695-99 (4th ed. 1971); Keeton, "Fraud-Concealment and Non-Disclosure," 15 Tex. L. Rev. 1 (1936); Goldfarb, "Fraud and Nondisclosure in the Vendor-Purchaser Relation," 8 Wes. Res. L. Rev. 5 (1956).

Mrs. Weintraub asserts that she was unaware of the infestation and the Krobatsches acknowledge that, if that was so, then there was no fraudulent concealment or nondisclosure on her part and their claim must fall. But the purchasers allege that she was in fact aware of the infestation and at this stage of the proceedings we must assume that to be true. She contends, however, that even if she were fully aware she would have been under no duty to speak and that consequently no complaint by the purchasers may legally be grounded on her silence. She relies primarily on cases such as Swinton v. Whitinsville Sav. Bank, 311 Mass. 677, 42 N.E.2d 808, 141 A.L.R. 965 (1942). . . . Swinton is pertinent but, as Dean Prosser has noted (Prosser, Supra at 696), it is one of a line of "singularly unappetizing cases" which are surely out of tune with our times.

In Swinton the plaintiff purchased a house from the defendant and after he occupied it he found it to be infested with termites. The defendant had made no verbal or written representations but the plaintiff, asserting that the defendant knew of the termites and was under a duty to speak, filed a complaint for damages grounded on fraudulent concealment. The Supreme Judicial Court of Massachusetts sustained a demurrer to the complaint and entered judgment for the defendant. In the course of its opinion the court acknowledged that "the plaintiff possesses a certain appeal to the moral sense" but concluded that the law has not "reached the point of imposing upon the frailties of human nature a standard so idealistic as this." 42 N.E.2d at 808-809. That was written several decades ago and we are far from certain that it represents views held by the current members of the Massachusetts court. See Kannavos v. Annino, 356 Mass. 42 (1969). In any event we are certain that it does not represent our sense of justice or fair dealing and it has understandably been rejected in persuasive opinions elsewhere. See Obde v. Schlemeyer, 56 Wash. 2d 449 (1960); Loghry v. Capel, 257 Iowa 285 (1965); Williams v. Benson, 3 Mich. App. 9 (1966); Sorrell v. Young, 6 Wash. App. 220, *451 (1971); Lawson v. Citizens & Southern National Bank of S.C., 259 S.C. 477 (1972); Cf. Clauser v. Taylor, 44 Cal. App. 2d 453 (1941); Simmons v. Evans, Tenn. 282, 206 S.W.2d 295 (1947); Piazzini v. Jessup, 153 Cal. App. 2d 58 (1957); Rich v. Rankl, 6 Conn. Cir. 185, 269 A.2d 84, 88 (1969); Ford v. Broussard, 248 So. 2d 629 (La. App. 1971). See also Restatement 2d, Torts §551 (Tent. Draft No. 12 (1966)); Keeton, "Rights of Disappointed Purchasers," 32 Tex. L. Rev. 1 (1953); Cf. Bixby, "Let the Seller Beware: Remedies for the Purchase of a Defective Home," 49 J. Urban Law 533 (1971); Haskell, "The Case for an Implied Warranty of Quality in Sales of Real Property," 53 Geo. L.J. 633 (1965); Note, "Implied Warranties in Sales of Real Estate—The Trend to Abolish Caveat Emptor," 22 DePaul L. Rev. 510 (1972).

In Obde v. Schlemeyer, Supra, 56 Wash. 2d 449, 353 P.2d 672, the defendants sold an apartment house to the plaintiff. The house was termite infested but that fact was not disclosed by the sellers to the purchasers who later sued for damages alleging fraudulent concealment. The sellers contended that they were under no obligation whatever to speak out and they relied heavily on the decision of the Massachusetts court in *Swinton* (311 Mass. 677). The Supreme Court of Washington flatly rejected their contention, holding that though the parties had dealt at arms' length the sellers were under "a duty to inform the plaintiffs of the termite condition" of which they were fully aware. 353 P.2d at 674; Cf. Hughes v. Stusser, 68 Wash. 2d 707 (1966). In the course of its opinion the court quoted approvingly from Dean Keeton's article Supra, in 15 Tex. L. Rev. 1. There the author first expressed his thought that when Lord Cairns suggested in Peek v. Gurney, L.R. 6 H.L. 377 (1873), that there was no duty to disclose facts, no matter how "morally censurable" (at 403), he was expressing nineteenth century law as shaped by an individualistic philosophy based on freedom of contracts and unconcerned with morals. He then made the following comments which fairly embody a currently acceptable principle on which the holding in *Obde* may be said to be grounded:

> In the present stage of the law, the decisions show a drawing away from this idea, and there can be seen an attempt by many courts to reach a just result in so far as possible, but yet maintaining the degree of certainty which the law must have. The statement may often be found that if either party to a contract of sale conceals or suppresses a material fact which he is in good faith bound to disclose then his silence is fraudulent.

The attitude of the courts toward nondisclosure is undergoing a change and contrary to Lord Cairns' famous remark it would seem that the object of the law in these cases should be to impose on parties to the transaction a duty to speak whenever justice, equity, and fair dealing demand it. This statement is made only with reference to instances where the party to be charged is an actor in the transaction. This duty to speak does not result from an implied representation by silence, but exists because a refusal to speak constitutes unfair conduct. 15 Tex. L. Rev. at 31.

. . .

In Loghry v. Capel, Supra, the plaintiffs purchased a duplex from the defendants. They examined the house briefly on two occasions and signed a document stating that they accepted the property in its "present condition." 132 N.W.2d at 419. They made no inquiry about the subsoil and were not told that the house had been constructed on filled ground. They filed an action for damages charging that the sellers had fraudulently failed to disclose that the duplex was constructed on improperly compacted filled ground. The jury found in their favor and the verdict was sustained on appeal in an opinion which pointed out that "fraud may consist of concealment of a material fact." 132 N.W.2d at 419. The purchasers' stipulation that they accepted the property in its present condition could not be invoked to bar their claim. See Wolford v. Freeman, 150 Neb. 537, 35 N.W.2d 98 (1948), where the court pointed out that the purchase of property "as is" does not bar rescission grounded on fraudulent conduct of the seller. 35 N.W.2d at 103.

In Simmons v. Evans, Supra, the defendants owned a home which was serviced by a local water company. The company supplied water during the daytime but not at night. The defendants sold their home to the plaintiffs but made no mention of the limitation on the water service. The plaintiffs filed an action to rescind their purchase but the lower court dismissed it on the ground that the defendants had not made any written or verbal representations and the plaintiffs had "inspected the property, knew the source of the water supply, and could have made specific inquiry of these defendants or ascertained from other sources the true situation and, therefore, are estopped." 206 S.W.2d at 296. The dismissal was reversed on appeal in an opinion which took note of the general rule that "one may be guilty of fraud by his silence, as where it is expressly incumbent upon him to speak concerning material matters that are entirely within his own knowledge." 206 S.W.2d at 296. With respect to the plaintiffs' failure to ascertain the water situation before their purchase the court stated that the plaintiffs were surely not required "to make a night inspection in order to ascertain whether the water situation with reference to this residence was different from what it was during the day." 206 S.W.2d at 297.

. . . [T]he purchasers here were entitled to withstand the seller's motion for summary judgment. They should have been permitted to proceed with their efforts to establish by testimony that they were equitably entitled to rescind because the house was extensively infested in the manner described by them, the seller was well aware of the infestation, and the seller deliberately concealed or failed to disclose the condition because of the likelihood that it would defeat the transaction. The seller may of course defend factually as well as legally and since the matter is primarily equitable in nature the factual as well as legal disputes will be for the trial judge alone. See Hubbard v. International Mercantile Agency, 68 N.J. Eq. 434, 436, 59 A. 24 (Ch. 1904); Kueper v. Pyramid Bond & Mortgage Corp., 117 N.J. Eq. 110, 114-115, 174 A. 723 (E. & A. 1934); Cf. Steiner v. Stein, 2 N.J. 367, 66 A.2d 719 (1949); Bilotti v. Accurate Forming Corp., 39 N.J. 184, 198-199, 188 A.2d 24 (1963).

If the trial judge finds such deliberate concealment or nondisclosure of the latent infestation not observable by the purchasers on their inspection, he will still be called upon to determine whether, in the light of the full presentation before him, the concealment or nondisclosure was of such significant nature as to justify rescission. Minor conditions which ordinary sellers and purchasers would reasonably disregard as of little or no materiality in the transaction would clearly not call for judicial intervention. While the described condition may not have been quite as major as in the termite cases which were concerned with structural impairments, to the purchasers here it apparently was of such magnitude and was so repulsive as to cause them to rescind immediately though they had earlier indicated readiness that there be adjustment at closing for damage resulting from a fire which occurred after the contract was signed. We are not prepared at this time to say that on their showing they acted either unreasonably or without equitable justification.

Our courts have come a long way since the days when the judicial emphasis was on formal rules and ancient precedents rather than on modern concepts of justice and fair dealing. . . . [T]he judgment entered in the Appellate Division is:

Reversed and Remanded.

STAMBOVSKY
v.
ACKLEY

Supreme Court, Appellate Division, First Department, New York
572 N.Y.S.2d 672
1991

Rubin, J.

Plaintiff, to his horror, discovered that the house he had recently contracted to purchase was widely reputed to be possessed by poltergeists, reportedly seen by defendant seller and members of her family on numerous occasions over the last nine years. Plaintiff promptly commenced this action seeking rescission of the contract of sale. Supreme Court reluctantly dismissed the complaint, holding that plaintiff has no remedy at law in this jurisdiction.

The unusual facts of this case, as disclosed by the record, clearly warrant a grant of equitable relief to the buyer who, as a resident of New York City, cannot be expected to have any familiarity with the folklore of the Village of Nyack. Not being a "local," plaintiff could not readily learn that the home he had contracted to purchase is haunted. Whether the source of the spectral apparitions seen by defendant seller are parapsychic or psychogenic, having reported their presence in both a national publication ("Readers' Digest") and the local press (in 1977 and 1982, respectively), defendant is estopped to deny their existence and, as a matter of law, the house is haunted. More to the point, however, no divination is required to conclude that it is defendant's promotional efforts in publicizing her close encounters with these spirits which fostered the home's reputation in the community. In 1989, the house was included in a five-home walking tour of Nyack and described in a November 27th newspaper article as "a riverfront Victorian (with ghost)." The impact of the reputation thus created goes to the very essence of the bargain between the parties, greatly impairing both the value of the property and its potential for resale. The extent of this impairment may be presumed for the purpose of reviewing the disposition of this motion to dismiss the cause of action for rescission (*Harris v. City of New York*, 147 A.D.2d 186, 188-189, 542 N.Y.S.2d 550) and represents merely an issue of fact for resolution at trial.

While I agree with Supreme Court that the real estate broker, as agent for the seller, is under no duty to disclose to a potential buyer the phantasmal reputation of the premises and that, in his pursuit of a legal remedy for fraudulent misrepresentation against the seller, plaintiff hasn't a ghost of a chance, I am nevertheless moved by the spirit of equity to allow the buyer to seek rescission of the contract of sale and recovery of his down payment. New York law fails to recognize any remedy for damages incurred as a result of the seller's mere silence, applying instead the strict rule of caveat emptor. Therefore, the theoretical basis for granting relief, even under the extraordinary facts of this case, is elusive if not ephemeral.

"Pity me not but lend thy serious hearing to what I shall unfold" (William Shakespeare, Hamlet, Act I, Scene V [Ghost]).

From the perspective of a person in the position of plaintiff herein, a very practical problem arises with respect to the discovery of a paranormal phenomenon: "Who you gonna' call?" as the title song to the movie "Ghostbusters" asks. Applying the strict rule of caveat emptor to a contract involving a house possessed by poltergeists conjures up visions of a psychic or medium routinely accompanying the structural engineer and Terminix man on an inspection of every home subject to a contract of sale. It portends that the prudent attorney will establish an escrow account lest the subject of the transaction come back to haunt him and his client—or pray that his malpractice insurance coverage extends to supernatural disasters. In the interest of avoiding such untenable consequences, the notion that a haunting is a condition which can and should be ascertained upon reasonable inspection of the premises is a hobgoblin which should be exorcised from the body of legal precedent and laid quietly to rest.

It has been suggested by a leading authority that the ancient rule which holds that mere non-disclosure does not constitute actionable misrepresentation "finds proper application in cases where the fact undisclosed is patent, or the plaintiff has equal opportunities for obtaining information which he may be expected to utilize, or the defendant has no reason to think that he is acting under any misapprehension" (Prosser, Law of Torts §106, at 696 [4th ed. 1971]). However, with respect to transactions in real estate, New York adheres to the doctrine of caveat emptor and imposes no duty upon the vendor to disclose any information concerning the premises unless there is a confidential or fiduciary relationship between the parties or some conduct on the part of the seller which constitutes "active concealment." Normally, some affirmative misrepresentation or partial disclosure is required to impose upon the seller a duty to communicate undisclosed conditions affecting the premises.

. . .

The doctrine of caveat emptor requires that a buyer act prudently to assess the fitness and value of his purchase and operates to bar the purchaser who fails to exercise due care from seeking the equitable remedy of rescission (*see, e.g., Rodas v. Manitaras*, 159 A.D.2d 341, 552 N.Y.S.2d 618). For the purposes of the instant motion to dismiss the action pursuant to CPLR 3211(a)(7), plaintiff is entitled to every favorable inference which may reasonably be drawn from the pleadings (*Arrington v. New York Times Co.*, 55 N.Y.2d 433, 442, 449 N.Y.S.2d 941, 434 N.E.2d 1319; *Rovello v. Orofino Realty Co.*, 40 N.Y.2d 633, 634, 389 N.Y.S.2d 314, 357 N.E.2d 970), specifically, in this instance, that he met his obligation to conduct an inspection of the premises and a search of available public records with respect to title. It should be apparent, however, that the most meticulous inspection and the search would not reveal the presence of poltergeists at the premises or unearth the property's ghoulish reputation in the community. Therefore, there is no sound policy reason to deny plaintiff relief for failing to discover a state of affairs which the most prudent purchaser would not be expected to even contemplate (*see, Da Silva v. Musso*, 53 N.Y.2d 543, 551, 444 N.Y.S.2d 50, 428 N.E.2d 382).

The case law in this jurisdiction dealing with the duty of a vendor of real property to disclose information to the buyer is distinguishable from the matter under review. The most salient distinction is that existing cases invariably deal with the physical condition of the premises (*e.g., London v. Courduff, supra* [use as a landfill]; *Perin v. Mardine Realty Co.*, 5 A.D.2d 685, 168 N.Y.S.2d 647 *affd.* 6 N.Y.2d 920, 190 N.Y.S.2d 995, 161 N.E.2d 210 [sewer line crossing adjoining property without owner's consent]), defects in title (*e.g., Sands v. Kissane*, 282 App. Div. 140, 121 N.Y.S.2d 634 [remainderman]), liens against the property (*e.g., Noved Realty Corp. v. A.A.P. Co., supra*), expenses or income (*e.g., Rodas v. Manitaras, supra* [gross receipts]) and other factors affecting its operation. No case has been brought to this court's attention in which the property value was impaired as the result of the reputation created by information disseminated to the public by the seller (or, for that matter, as a result of possession by poltergeists).

Where a condition which has been created by the seller materially impairs the value of the contract and is peculiarly within the knowledge of the seller or unlikely to be discovered by a prudent purchaser exercising due care with respect to the subject transaction, nondisclosure constitutes a basis for rescission as a matter of equity. Any other outcome places upon the buyer not merely the obligation to exercise care in his purchase but rather to be omniscient with respect to any fact which may affect the bargain. No practical purpose is served by imposing such a burden upon a purchaser. To the contrary, it encourages predatory business practice and offends the principle that equity will suffer no wrong to be without a remedy.

. . .

To the extent New York law may be said to require something more than "mere concealment" to apply even the equitable remedy of rescission, the case of *Junius Construction Corporation v. Cohen*, 257 N.Y. 393, 178 N.E. 672, *supra*, while not precisely on point, provides some guidance. In that case, the seller disclosed that an official map indicated two as yet unopened streets which were planned for construction at the edges of the parcel. What was not disclosed was that the same map indicated a third street which, if opened, would divide the plot in half. The court held that, while the seller was under no duty to mention the planned streets at all, having undertaken to disclose two of them, he was obliged to reveal the third (*see also, Rosenschein v. McNally*, 17 A.D.2d 834, 233 N.Y.S.2d 254).

In the case at bar, defendant seller deliberately fostered the public belief that her home was possessed. Having undertaken to inform the public at large, to whom she has no legal relationship, about the supernatural occurrences on her property, she may be said to owe no less a duty to her contract vendee. It has been remarked that the occasional modern cases which permit a seller to take unfair advantage of a buyer's ignorance so long as he is not actively misled are "singularly unappetizing" (Prosser, Law of Torts §106, at 696 [4th ed. 1971]). Where, as here, the seller not only takes unfair advantage of the buyer's ignorance but has created and perpetuated a condition about which he is unlikely to even inquire, enforcement of the contract (in whole or in part) is offensive to the court's sense of equity. Application of the remedy of rescission, within the bounds of the narrow exception to the doctrine of caveat emptor set forth herein, is entirely appropriate to relieve the unwitting purchaser from the consequences of a most unnatural bargain.

Accordingly, the judgment of the Supreme Court, New York County (Edward H. Lehner, J.), entered April 9, 1990, which dismissed the complaint pursuant to CPLR 3211(a)(7), should be modified, on the law and the facts and in the exercise of discretion, and the first cause of action seeking rescission of the contract reinstated, without costs.

SMITH, J. (dissenting).

I would affirm the dismissal of the complaint by the motion court.

Plaintiff seeks to rescind his contract to purchase defendant Ackley's residential property and recover his down payment. Plaintiff alleges that Ackley and her real estate broker, defendant Ellis Realty, made material misrepresentations of the property in that they failed to disclose that Ackley believed that the house was haunted by poltergeists. Moreover, Ackley shared this belief with her community and the general public through articles published in *Reader's Digest* (1977) and the local newspaper (1982). In November 1989, approximately two months after the parties entered into the contract of sale but subsequent to the scheduled October 2, 1989 closing, the house was included in a five-house walking tour and again described in the local newspaper as being haunted.

Prior to closing, plaintiff learned of this reputation and unsuccessfully sought to rescind the $650,000 contract of sale and obtain return of his $32,500 down payment without resort to litigation. The plaintiff then commenced this action for that relief and alleged that he would not have entered into the contract had he been so advised and that as a result of the alleged poltergeist activity, the market value and resaleability of the property was greatly diminished. Defendant Ackley has counterclaimed for specific performance.

"It is settled law in New York that the seller of real property is under no duty to speak when the parties deal at arm's length. The mere silence of the seller, without some act or conduct which deceived the purchaser, does not amount to a concealment that is actionable as a fraud. The buyer has the duty to satisfy himself as to the quality of his bargain pursuant to the doctrine of caveat emptor, which in New York State still applies to real estate transactions." *London v. Courduff*, 141 A.D.2d 803,

804, 529 N.Y.S.2d 874, *app. dism'd.*, 73 N.Y.2d 809, 537 N.Y.S.2d 494, 534 N.E.2d 332 (1988).

The parties herein were represented by counsel and dealt at arm's length. This is evidenced by the contract of sale which, *inter alia*, contained various riders and a specific provision that all prior understandings and agreements between the parties were merged into the contract, that the contract completely expressed their full agreement and that neither had relied upon any statement by anyone else not set forth in the contract. There is no allegation that defendants, by some specific act, other than the failure to speak, deceived the plaintiff. Nevertheless, a cause of action may be sufficiently stated where there is a confidential or fiduciary relationship creating a duty to disclose and there was a failure to disclose a material fact, calculated to induce a false belief. *County of Westchester v. Welton Becket Assoc.*, 102 A.D.2d 34, 50-51, 478 N.Y.S.2d 305, *aff'd.*, 66 N.Y.2d 642, 495 N.Y.S.2d 364, 485 N.E.2d 1029 (1985). However, plaintiff herein has not alleged and there is no basis for concluding that a confidential or fiduciary relationship existed between these parties to an arm's length transaction such as to give rise to a duty to disclose. In addition, there is no allegation that defendants thwarted plaintiff's efforts to fulfill his responsibilities fixed by the doctrine of caveat emptor. *See London v. Courduff, supra*, 141 A.D.2d at 804, 529 N.Y.S.2d 874.

Finally, if the doctrine of caveat emptor is to be discarded, it should be for a reason more substantive than a poltergeist. The existence of a poltergeist is no more binding upon the defendants than it is upon this court.

Based upon the foregoing, the motion court properly dismissed the complaint.

STROUP
v.
CONANT
Supreme Court of Oregon
520 P.2d 337
1974

Tongue, J.

This is a suit to rescind a lease of space in a building in which the tenant undertook to operate the "Birds & Bees Adult Book Store." Plaintiff's complaint alleged that she was induced to enter into the lease in reliance upon the false representation by defendant that he intended to use the leased premises for the sale of watches, wallets, chains, novelties and a few books and magazines and imported items. Defendant appeals from a decree rescinding the lease. We affirm.

Defendant contends that there was no evidence of misrepresentation, reliance or damage. It thus becomes necessary to summarize the evidence, although not in completely unexpurgated form.

Defendant states in his brief that he informed plaintiff of his intent to sell "a variety of items," including magazines, "for adults only." Plaintiff, however, denies any such conversation. Plaintiff's son, who represented her in negotiating the lease, testified that defendant called him by telephone in response to a newspaper advertisement for lease of the premises, located on S.E. Division Street in Portland; that he asked defendant what his business was and was told that defendant intended to conduct "a variety type operation" and to sell watches, wallets, chains, trinkets and a few books and novelties, but did not say that he intended to operate an "adult book store" or to sell pornographic material.

Plaintiff's attorney then prepared a one year lease, with an option to renew for one additional year. The lease provided, among other things, that the premises were to be used "for the sale of gifts, novelties, etc." . . .

On April 6, 1973, plaintiff's son received a telephone call from another tenant who operated a gun shop in the same building complaining that "you've ruined me" and informing him of the adult book store in the adjacent premises. Plaintiff testified that her son had reported to her that the premises had been rented for a variety and gift store and that she would not have signed the lease if she had known of defendant's intent to operate an adult book store on the premises. Upon visiting the premises, plaintiff's son found large signs in the store windows, and upon going inside he saw no watches, wallets, chains or novelties for sale, but only racks of pornographic magazines and books. He then called plaintiff's lawyer.

During the next few days one of the residents in the neighborhood, after going into the store and purchasing three magazines whose titles had best be left unstated, circulated a petition of "protest" upon which he secured 300 signatures in the neighborhood, which he described as "predominantly residential." The two other tenants in the building, the operators of a meat market and a paint store, also complained to plaintiff that the adjacent adult book store "spoils their business," and plaintiff was "deluged" with telephone calls.

On April 10, 1973, plaintiff's attorney wrote a letter to defendant charging him with violating the terms of the lease and demanding that he vacate the premises immediately. At that time, however, plaintiff did not tender the return of the first and last months' rent, as previously paid by defendant, claiming that she was entitled to that money.

On May 4, 1973, after defendant had apparently refused to move out, plaintiff filed a complaint seeking to rescind the lease and offering to "do complete equity and restore the status quo." Defendant filed a general denial and awaited trial, which was held on August 8, 1973.

Plaintiff then offered testimony of the foregoing facts. Defendant, in addition to testifying that he informed plaintiff by telephone of his intent to operate an adult book store (which she denied), stated that it "would be pretty hard to describe over a phone." He also testified that he didn't "have anything pornographic," and that although his literature was "devoted to various states or types of sexual activity * * * there is a lot of reading that is written by doctors." Defendant agreed, however, with the observation by the learned trial judge, that in talking about adult books he was "not talking about Charles Dickens or Thomas Wolfe." Upon examination of the pictorial "literature" offered in evidence it appears that this may well have been the understatement of this permissive age. Defendant also said that he exhibited moving pictures, presumably in "living color."

Based upon this record we have no hesitation in holding that there was ample basis to support the decision by this trial court in its decree rescinding this lease, dated September 17, 1973.

Even assuming that one who seeks to rent premises for the operation of such an "adult book store" and who does not disclose the nature of his intended operation may, by remaining silent, be able to acquire a binding lease from either an unsuspecting or a willing landlord, regardless of neighborhood protests, this is not such a case.

In Heise et ux. v. Pilot Rock Lbr. Co., 222 Or. 78, 89-90, 352 P.2d 1072, 1077 (1960), this court stated the following rule:

> * * * Not only (are) affirmative misrepresentations * * * a basis for an action based upon fraud * * * half-truths and concealment of special knowledge (may also provide such a basis) when there is a duty to speak, and (one) undertaking to speak fails to tell or conceals the truth. When the purchaser undertakes to answer inquiries, he must tell the truth, and concealment under such circumstances is fraudulent. * * *

There was ample evidence of misrepresentation by "half-truths and concealment of special knowledge" in this case, as well as reliance thereon by plaintiff, despite defendant's testimony to the contrary.

VOKES
v.
ARTHUR MURRAY, INC.

District Court of Appeal of Florida, Second District
212 So. 2d 906
1968

PIERCE, J.

This is an appeal by Audrey E. Vokes, plaintiff below, from a final order dismissing with prejudice, for failure to state a cause of action, her fourth amended complaint, hereinafter referred to as plaintiff's complaint.

Defendant Arthur Murray, Inc., a corporation, authorizes the operation throughout the nation of dancing schools under the name of "Arthur Murray School of Dancing" through local franchised operators, one of whom was defendant J. P. Davenport whose dancing establishment was in Clearwater.

Plaintiff Mrs. Audrey E. Vokes, a widow of 51 years and without family, had a yen to be "an accomplished dancer" with the hopes of finding "new interest in life." So, on February 10, 1961, a dubious fate, with the assist of a motivated acquaintance, procured her to attend a "dance party" at Davenport's "School of Dancing" where she whiled away the pleasant hours, sometimes in a private room, absorbing his accomplished sales technique, during which her grace and poise were elaborated upon and her rosy future as "an excellent dancer" was painted for her in vivid and glowing colors. As an incident to this interlude, he sold her eight 1/2-hour dance lessons to be utilized within one calendar month therefrom, for the sum of $14.50 cash in hand paid, obviously a baited "come on."

Thus she embarked upon an almost endless pursuit of the terpsichorean art during which, over a period of less than sixteen months, she was sold fourteen "dance courses" totalling in the aggregate 2302 hours of dancing lessons for a total cash outlay of $31,090.45, all at Davenport's dance emporium. All of these fourteen courses were evidenced by execution of a written "Enrollment Agreement—Arthur Murray's School of Dancing" with the addendum in heavy black print, "No one will be informed that you are taking dancing lessons. Your relations with us are held in strict confidence," setting forth the number of "dancing lessons" and the "lessons in rhythm sessions" currently sold to her from time to time, and always of course accompanied by payment of cash of the realm.

These dance lesson contracts and the monetary consideration therefor of over $31,000 were procured from her by means and methods of Davenport and his associates which went beyond the unsavory, yet legally permissible, perimeter of "sales puffing" and intruded well into the forbidden area of undue influence, the suggestion of falsehood, the suppression of truth, and the free exercise of rational judgment, if what plaintiff alleged in her complaint was true. From the time of her first contact with the dancing school in February, 1961, she was influenced unwittingly by a constant and continuous barrage of flattery, false praise, excessive compliments, and panegyric encomiums, to such extent that it would be not only inequitable, but unconscionable, for a Court exercising inherent chancery power to allow such contracts to stand.

She was incessantly subjected to overreaching blandishment and cajolery. She was assured she had "grace and poise"; that she was "rapidly improving and developing in her dancing skill"; that the additional lessons would "make her a beautiful dancer, capable of dancing with the most accomplished dancers"; that she was "rapidly progressing in the development of her dancing skill and gracefulness", etc., etc. She was given "dance aptitude tests" for the ostensible purpose of "determining" the number of remaining hours instructions needed by her from time to time.

At one point she was sold 545 additional hours of dancing lessons to be entitled to award of the "Bronze Medal" signifying that she had reached "the Bronze Standard," a supposed designation of dance achievement by students of Arthur Murray, Inc. Later she was sold an additional 926 hours in order to gain the "Silver Medal," indicating she had reached "the Silver Standard," at a cost of $12,501.35. At one point, while she still had to her credit about 900 unused hours of instructions, she was induced to purchase an additional 24 hours of lessons to participate in a trip to Miami at her own expense, where she would be "given the opportunity to dance with members of the Miami Studio." She was induced at another point to purchase an additional 123 hours of lessons in order to be not only eligible for the Miami trip but also to become "a life member of the Arthur Murray Studio," carrying with it certain dubious emoluments, at a further cost of $1,752.30. . . . Also, when she still had 1100 unused hours to her credit, she was prevailed upon to purchase an additional 347 hours at a cost of $4,235.74, to qualify her to receive a "Gold Medal" for achievement, indicating she had advanced to "the Gold Standard." . . .

All the foregoing sales promotions, illustrative of the entire fourteen separate contracts, were procured by defendant Davenport and Arthur Murray, Inc., by false representations to her that she was improving in her dancing ability, that she had excellent potential, that she was responding to instructions in dancing grace, and that they were developing her into a beautiful dancer, whereas in truth and in fact she did not develop in her dancing ability, she had no "dance aptitude," and in fact had difficulty in "hearing that musical beat." The complaint alleged that such representations to her "were in fact false and known by the defendant to be false and contrary to the plaintiff's true ability, the truth of plaintiff's ability being fully known to the defendants, but withheld from the plaintiff for the sole and specific intent to deceive and defraud the plaintiff and to induce her in the purchasing of additional hours of dance lessons." It was averred that the lessons were sold to her "in total disregard to the true physical, rhythm, and mental ability of the plaintiff." In other words, while she first exulted that she was entering the "spring of her life," she finally was awakened to the fact there was "spring" neither in her life nor in her feet.

The complaint prayed that the Court decree the dance contracts to be null and void and to be cancelled, that an accounting be had, and judgment entered against, the defendants "for that portion of the $31,090.45 not charged against specific hours of instruction given to the plaintiff." The Court held the complaint not to state a cause of action and dismissed it with prejudice. We disagree and reverse.

The material allegations of the complaint must, of course, be accepted as true for the purpose of testing its legal sufficiency. Defendants contend that contracts can only be rescinded for fraud or misrepresentation when the alleged misrepresentation is as to a material fact, rather than an opinion, prediction or expectation, and that the statements and representations set forth at length in the complaint were in the category of "trade puffing," within its legal orbit.

It is true that "generally a misrepresentation, to be actionable, must be one of fact rather than of opinion." Tonkovich v. South Florida Citrus Industries, Inc., Fla. App. 1966, 185 So. 2d 710. But this rule has significant qualifications, applicable here. It does not apply where there is a fiduciary relationship between the parties, or where there has been some artifice or trick employed by the representor, or where the parties do not in general deal at "arm's length" as we understand the phrase, or where the representee does not have equal opportunity to become apprised of the truth or falsity of the fact represented. As stated by Judge Allen of this Court in *Ramel v. Chasebrook Construction Company*, Fla. App. 1961, 135 So. 2d 876: "A statement of a party having . . . superior knowledge may be regarded as a statement of fact although it would be considered as opinion if the parties were dealing on equal terms."

It could be reasonably supposed here that defendants had "superior knowledge" as to whether plaintiff had "dance potential" and as to whether she was noticeably improving in the art of terpsichore. And it would be a reasonable inference from the undenied averments of the complaint that the flowery eulogiums heaped upon her by defendants as a prelude to her contracting for 1944 additional hours of instruction in order to attain the rank of the Bronze Standard, thence to the bracket of the Silver Standard, thence to the class of the Gold Bar Standard, and finally to the crowning plateau of a Life Member of the Studio, proceeded as much or more from the urge to "ring the cash register" as from any honest or realistic appraisal of her dancing prowess or a factual representation of her progress.

Even in contractual situations where a party to a transaction owes no duty to disclose facts within his knowledge or to answer inquiries respecting such facts, the law is if he undertakes to do so he must disclose the whole truth. From the face of the complaint, it should have been reasonably apparent to defendants that her vast outlay of cash for the many hundreds of additional hours of instruction was not justified by her slow and awkward progress, which she would have been made well aware of if they had spoken the "whole truth."

In Hirschman v. Hodges, etc., 1910, 59 Fla. 517, 51 So. 550, it was said that ". . . what is plainly injurious to good faith ought to be considered as a fraud sufficient to impeach a contract," and that an improvident agreement may be avoided ". . . because of surprise, or mistake, [w]ant of freedom, undue influence, the suggestion of falsehood, or the suppression of truth."

We repeat that where parties are dealing on a contractual basis at arm's length with no inequities or inherently unfair practices employed, the Courts will in general "leave the parties where they find themselves." But in the case sub judice, from the allegations of the unanswered complaint, we cannot say that enough of the accompanying ingredients, as mentioned in the foregoing authorities, were not present which otherwise would have barred the equitable arm of the Court to her. In our view, from the showing made in her complaint, plaintiff is entitled to her day in Court.

It accordingly follows that the order dismissing plaintiff's last amended complaint with prejudice should be and is reversed.

Reversed.

Problems

1. A Machine That Will Not Last a Lifetime. Lorraine Corporation purchased 128 copy machines from Royal Business Machines, whose salesman represented that the machines were of "good quality" and "would last a lifetime." When the machines began to experience problems soon after, Lorraine brought suit, alleging misrepresentation. Does it have a valid cause of action?

2. The Oil Leak. V.S.H. Realty was considering purchasing an oil storage facility from Texaco. During negotiations, Texaco provided a written statement that Texaco had not received "any notice, demand, or communication from any local, county, state, or federal department or agency regarding modifications or improvements to the facility or any part thereof" and a disclosure that oil had "migrated under [Texaco's] garage building across Marginal Street from the terminal [and that] the fuel oil underground as a result of heavy rains or high tides, seeps into the boiler room of the garage building." V.S.H. claimed later that it had also made "repeated inquiries" about oil leaks on the facility property, to which Texaco never specifically responded. V.S.H. ultimately agreed to pay $2.8 million for the storage facility, and the agreement stated that V.S.H. had inspected the facility and accepted it "as is" without warranties by Texaco concerning its condition.

One month after signing the agreement, V.S.H. discovered oil seeping from the ground on the storage facility property, and learned that the U.S. Coast Guard was investigating the property for possible oil leaks. V.S.H. sued to rescind the agreement on grounds of misrepresentation, and Texaco moved to dismiss the complaint. How should the court rule?

3. The Treaty of Ghent. On February 18, 1815, Hector Organ entered into an agreement to purchase 111 hogsheads of tobacco from the trading firm Laidlaw & Company in the city of New Orleans, at the prevailing market price. Organ had just learned that the Treaty of Ghent had been signed, ending the War of 1812 and signaling the end of the British blockade of American ports, but this information would not become widely available until published in a handbill the following morning.

News of the peace treaty caused an immediate 50 percent increase in the price of tobacco, and Laidlaw refused to turn over the contracted quantity to Organ. Organ sued. What result?

4. Ignore Facebook Friend Request. Following extensive discovery and a mediation session, the content of which the parties agreed would be privileged and inadmissible in any judicial proceeding, the Winklevosses agreed to settle their claims against Facebook for, among other things, a specified number of shares of Facebook stock (see Chapter 2.B.1, Problem 3 "Facebook Friend Request"). After the parties signed the agreement, Facebook informed the Winklevosses that an internal valuation completed for tax purposes valued the company's shares at $8.88/share. The Winklevosses alleged that during the mediation Facebook led them to believe that the shares were worth four times as much, and that they would not have signed the agreement had they not been misled. The Winklevosses sought to avoid enforcement of the settlement agreement on the grounds that it was procured by fraud. Should the Winklevosses prevail if they can prove Facebook provided them with false or misleading information concerning the value of the shares?

F. UNCONSCIONABILITY

In the usual case, judicial enforcement of contracts is consistent with the principles of both autonomy and efficiency. The presence of infancy, incapacity, duress, or misrepresentation raise questions as to whether enforcement would serve one or both of these core principles. The unconscionability doctrine reflects a somewhat uneasy suspicion that some contracts might fail to reflect true party autonomy or fail to make both parties better off than they otherwise would be notwithstanding the inapplicability of these other doctrines.

The black letter law of unconscionability provides little guidance as to the doctrine's boundaries, however. Both the Restatement and the UCC include relevant provisions, but neither defines the term "unconscionable" itself. See Rest. (2d) Contracts §208; U.C.C. §2-302. Most courts require evidence of one or more procedural defects in the bargaining process ("procedural unconscionability") *and* substantive unfairness in the resulting agreement ("substantive unconscionability") before they will invoke the doctrine, but what facts are necessary to satisfy these dual requirements remain obscure. The following trio of cases—*Williams v. Walker-Thomas Furniture Company*, *Frostifresh Corporation v. Reynoso*, and *Zapatha v. Dairy Mart, Inc.*—is indicative of the ongoing struggle on the part of courts to apply both prongs of the test.

Claims of infancy, incapacity, duress, or misrepresentation generally reflect the plaintiff's desire to avoid the entire contract, so the remedy in successful cases is usually rescission. In unconscionability cases, however, plaintiffs often challenge the validity of specific terms rather than of the entire agreement, which raises questions as to the appropriate remedial action subsequent to a finding of unconscionability. Again, the black letter law offers little assistance. The Restatement provides that courts may refuse to enforce the entire contract, refuse to enforce the offending term while leaving the remainder of the contract intact, or reform the offending term, but it provides no guidance as to how courts should choose among these options. Rest. (2d) Contracts §208.

WILLIAMS
V.
WALKER-THOMAS FURNITURE CO.
District of Columbia Court of Appeals
198 A.2d 914
1964

QUINN, J.

Appellant, a person of limited education separated from her husband, is maintaining herself and her seven children by means of public assistance. During the period 1957-1962 she had a continuous course of dealings with appellee from which she purchased many household articles on the installment plan. These included sheets, curtains, rugs, chairs, a chest of drawers, beds, mattresses, a washing machine, and a stereo set. In 1963 appellee filed a complaint in replevin for possession of all the items purchased by appellant, alleging that her payments were in default and that it retained title to the goods according to the sales contracts. By the writ of replevin appellee obtained a bed, chest of drawers, washing machine, and the stereo set. After hearing testimony and examining the contracts, the trial court entered judgment for appellee.

Appellant's principal contentions on appeal are (1) there was a lack of meeting of the minds, and (2) the contracts were against public policy.

Appellant signed fourteen contracts in all. They were approximately six inches in length and each contained a long paragraph in extremely fine print. One of the sentences in this paragraph provided that payments, after the first purchase, were to be prorated on all purchases then outstanding. Mathematically, this had the effect of keeping a balance due on all items until the time balance was completely eliminated. It meant that title to the first purchase, remained in appellee until the fourteenth purchase, made some five years later, was fully paid.

At trial appellant testified that she understood the agreements to mean that when payments on the running account were sufficient to balance the amount due on an individual item, the item became hers. She testified that most of the purchases were made at her home; that the contracts were signed in blank; that she did not read the instruments; and that she was not provided with a copy. She admitted, however, that she did not ask anyone to read or explain the contracts to her.

We have stated that "one who refrains from reading a contract and in conscious ignorance of its terms voluntarily assents thereto will not be relieved from his bad bargain." Bob Wilson, Inc. v. Swann, Inc., D.C. Mun. App., 168 A.2d 198 (1961) "One who signs a contract has a duty to read it and is obligated according to its terms." Hollywood Credit Clothing Co. v. Gibson, D.C. App., 188 A.2d 348, 349 (1963). "It is as much the duty of a person who cannot read the language in which a contract is written to have someone read it to him before he signs it, as it is the duty of one who can read to peruse it himself before signing it." Stern v. Moneyweight Scale, 42 App. D.C. 162, 165 (1914).

A careful review of the record shows that appellant's assent was not obtained "by fraud or even misrepresentation falling short of fraud." Hollywood Credit Clothing Co. v. Gibson, supra. This is not a case of mutual misunderstanding but a unilateral mistake. Under these circumstances, appellant's first contention is without merit.

Appellant's second argument presents a more serious question. The record reveals that prior to the last purchase appellant had reduced the balance in her account to $164. The last purchase, a stereo set, raised the balance due to $678. Significantly, at the time of this and the preceding purchases, appellee was aware of appellant's financial position. The reverse side of the stereo contract listed the name of appellant's social worker and her $218 monthly stipend from the government. Nevertheless, with full knowledge that appellant had to feed, clothe and support both herself and seven children on this amount, appellee sold her a $514 stereo set.

We cannot condemn too strongly appellee's conduct. It raises serious questions of sharp practice and irresponsible business dealings. A review of the legislation in the District of Columbia affecting retail sales and the pertinent decisions of the highest court in this jurisdiction disclose, however, no ground upon which this court can declare the contracts in question contrary to public policy. We note that were the Maryland Retail Installment Sales Act, Art. 83 §§128-153, or its equivalent, in force in the District of Columbia, we could grant appellant appropriate relief. We think Congress should consider corrective legislation to protect the public from such exploitive contracts as were utilized in the case at bar.

Affirmed.

WILLIAMS
v.
∿ WALKER-THOMAS FURNITURE CO.
U.S. Court of Appeals, D.C. Circuit
350 F.2d 445
1965

J. SKELLY WRIGHT, J.

Appellee, Walker-Thomas Furniture Company, operates a retail furniture store in the District of Columbia. During the period from 1957 to 1962 each appellant in these cases purchased a number of household items from Walker-Thomas, for which payment was to be made in installments. The terms of each purchase were contained in a printed form contract which set forth the value of the purchased item and purported to lease the item to appellant for a stipulated monthly rent payment. The contract then provided, in substance, that title would remain in Walker-Thomas until the total of all the monthly payments made equaled the stated value of the item, at which time appellants could take title. In the event of a default in the payment of any monthly installment, Walker-Thomas could repossess the item.

The contract further provided that "the amount of each periodical installment payment to be made by (purchaser) to the Company under this present lease shall be inclusive of and not in addition to the amount of each installment payment to be made by (purchaser) under such prior leases, bills or accounts; and all payments now and hereafter made by (purchaser) shall be credited pro rata on all outstanding leases, bills and accounts due the Company by (purchaser) at the time each such payment is made." The effect of this rather obscure provision was to keep a balance due on every item purchased until the balance due on all items, whenever purchased, was liquidated. As a result, the debt incurred at the time of purchase of each item was secured by the right to repossess all the items previously purchased by the same purchaser, and each new item purchased automatically became subject to a security interest arising out of the previous dealings.

On May 12, 1962, appellant Thorne purchased an item described as a Daveno, three tables, and two lamps, having total stated value of $391.10. Shortly thereafter, he defaulted on his monthly payments and appellee sought to replevy all the items purchased since the first transaction in 1958. Similarly, on April 17, 1962, appellant

Williams bought a stereo set of stated value of $514.95.[1] She too defaulted shortly thereafter, and appellee sought to replevy all the items purchased since December, 1957. The Court of General Sessions granted judgment for appellee. The District of Columbia Court of Appeals affirmed, and we granted appellants' motion for leave to appeal to this court.

Appellants' principal contention, rejected by both the trial and the appellate courts below, is that these contracts, or at least some of them, are unconscionable and, hence, not enforceable. . . . We do not agree that the court lacked the power to refuse enforcement to contracts found to be unconscionable. In other jurisdictions, it has been held as a matter of common law that unconscionable contracts are not enforceable. While no decision of this court so holding has been found, the notion that an unconscionable bargain should not be given full enforcement is by no means novel. In Scott v. United States, 79 U.S. (12 Wall.) 443 (1870), the Supreme Court stated: "If a contract be unreasonable and unconscionable, but not void for fraud, a court of law will give to the party who sues for its breach damages, not according to its letter, but only such as he is equitably entitled to."[2] Since we have never adopted or rejected such a rule, the question here presented is actually one of first impression.

Congress has recently enacted the Uniform Commercial Code, which specifically provides that the court may refuse to enforce a contract which it finds to be unconscionable at the time it was made. 28 D.C. Code §2-302 (Supp. IV 1965). The enactment of this section, which occurred subsequent to the contracts here in suit, does not mean that the common law of the District of Columbia was otherwise at the time of enactment, nor does it preclude the court from adopting a similar rule in the exercise of its powers to develop the common law for the District of Columbia. In fact, in view of the absence of prior authority on the point, we consider the congressional adoption of §2-302 persuasive authority for following the rationale of the cases from which the section is explicitly derived. Comment, §2-302, Uniform Commercial Code (1962). Accordingly, we hold that where the element of unconscionability is present at the time a contract is made, the contract should not be enforced.

Unconscionability has generally been recognized to include an absence of meaningful choice on the part of one of the parties together with contract terms which are unreasonably favorable to the other party. Whether a meaningful choice is present in a particular case can only be determined by consideration of all the circumstances surrounding the transaction. In many cases the meaningfulness of the choice is negated by a gross inequality of bargaining power. The manner in which the contract was entered is also relevant to this consideration. Did each party to the contract, considering his obvious education or lack of it, have a reasonable opportunity to understand the terms of the contract, or were the important terms hidden in a maze of fine print and minimized by deceptive sales practices? Ordinarily, one who signs an agreement without full knowledge of its terms might be held to assume the risk that he has entered a one-sided bargain. See Restatement,

---

1. At the time of this purchase her account showed a balance of $164 still owing from her prior purchases. The total of all the purchases made over the years in question came to $1,800. The total payments amounted to $1,400.
2. Campbell Soup Co. v. Wentz, 3 Cir., 172 F.2d 80 (1948); Indianapolis Morris Plan Corporation v. Sparks, 132 Ind. App. 145 (1961); Henningsen v. Bloomfield Motors, Inc., 32 N.J. 358 (1960).

Contracts §70 (1932). But when a party of little bargaining power, and hence little real choice, signs a commercially unreasonable contract with little or no knowledge of its terms, it is hardly likely that his consent, or even an objective manifestation of his consent, was ever given to all the terms. In such a case the usual rule that the terms of the agreement are not to be questioned should be abandoned and the court should consider whether the terms of the contract are so unfair that enforcement should be withheld.

In determining reasonableness or fairness, the primary concern must be with the terms of the contract considered in light of the circumstances existing when the contract was made. The test is not simple, nor can it be mechanically applied. The terms are to be considered "in the light of the general commercial background and the commercial needs of the particular trade or case." Corbin suggests the test as being whether the terms are "so extreme as to appear unconscionable according to the mores and business practices of the time and place." 1 Corbin, Contracts §128 (1963)[.] We think this formulation correctly states the test to be applied in those cases where no meaningful choice was exercised upon entering the contract.

Because the trial court and the appellate court did not feel that enforcement could be refused, no findings were made on the possible unconscionability of the contracts in these cases. Since the record is not sufficient for our deciding the issue as a matter of law, the cases must be remanded to the trial court for further proceedings.

So ordered.

DANAHER, J. (dissenting).

The District of Columbia Court of Appeals obviously was as unhappy about the situation here presented as any of us can possibly be. Its opinion in the *Williams* case, quoted in the majority text, concludes: "We think Congress should consider corrective legislation to protect the public from such exploitive contracts as were utilized in the case at bar."

My view is thus summed up by an able court which made no finding that there had actually been sharp practice. Rather the appellant seems to have known precisely where she stood.

There are many aspects of public policy here involved. What is a luxury to some may seem an outright necessity to others. Is public oversight to be required of the expenditures of relief funds? A washing machine, e.g., in the hands of a relief client might become a fruitful source of income. Many relief clients may well need credit, and certain business establishments will take long chances on the sale of items, expecting their pricing policies will afford a degree of protection commensurate with the risk. . . .

I mention such matters only to emphasize the desirability of a cautious approach to any such problem, particularly since the law for so long has allowed parties such great latitude in making their own contracts. I dare say there must annually be thousands upon thousands of installment credit transactions in this jurisdiction, and one can only speculate as to the effect the decision in these cases will have.

I join the District of Columbia Court of Appeals in its disposition of the issues.

FROSTIFRESH CORP.
v.
REYNOSO

District Court, Nassau County, Second District, New York
274 N.Y.S.2d 757
1966

DONOVAN, J.

Plaintiff brings this action for $1364.10, alleging that the latter amount is owed by the defendants to the plaintiff on account of the purchase of a combination-refrigerator-freezer for which they agreed to pay the sum of $1145.88. The balance of the amount consists of a claim for attorney fees in the amount of $227.35 and a late charge of $22.87. The only payment made on account of the original indebtedness is the sum of $32.00.

The contract for the refrigerator-freezer was negotiated orally in Spanish between the defendants and a Spanish speaking salesman representing the plaintiff. In that conversation the defendant husband told the salesman that he had but one week left on his job and he could not afford to buy the appliance. The salesman distracted and deluded the defendants by advising them that the appliance would cost them nothing because they would be paid bonuses or commissions of $25.00 each on the numerous sales that would be made to their neighbors and friends. Thereafter there was submitted to and signed by the defendants a retail installment contract entirely in English. The retail contract was neither translated nor explained to the defendants. In that contract there was a cash sales price set forth of $900.00. To this was added a credit charge of $245.88, making a total of $1145.88 to be paid for the appliance.

The plaintiff admitted that cost to the plaintiff corporation for the appliance was $348.00. No defense of fraud was set forth in the pleadings and accordingly such defense is not available.

However, in the course of the trial, it did appear to the court that the contract might be unconscionable. This court therefore continued the trial at an adjourned date to afford a reasonable opportunity to the parties to present evidence as to the commercial setting, purpose and effect of the contract.

The court finds that the sale of the appliance at the price and terms indicated in this contract is shocking to the conscience. The service charge, which almost equals the price of the appliance is in and of itself indicative of the oppression which was practiced on these defendants. Defendants were handicapped by a lack of knowledge, both as to the commercial situation and the nature and terms of the contract which was submitted in a language foreign to them.

The question presented in this case is simply this: Does the court have the power under section 2-302 of the Uniform Commercial Code to refuse to enforce the price and credit provisions of the contract in order to prevent an unconscionable result.

It is normally stated that the parties are free to make whatever contracts they please so long as there is no fraud or illegality (Allegheny College v. National Chautauqua County Bank, 246 N.Y. 369, 159 N.E. 173, 57 L.R.A. 980).

However, it is the apparent intent of the Uniform Commercial Code to modify this general rule by giving the courts power "to police explicitly against the contracts or clauses which they find to be unconscionable. . . . The principle is one of the prevention of oppression and unfair surprise." (See the official comment appended to the statute in the note on page 193, McKinney's Uniform Commercial Code, volume 62 1/2 Part I.)

The comment cites Campbell Soup Company v. Wentz, 3 Cir., 172 F.2d 80, to illustrate the principle. It is interesting to note that the *Wentz* case involved oppression with respect to the price Campbell Company agreed to pay for carrots, the price specified in the contract being $23.00 to $33.00 a ton. In the particular case Wentz, the farmer, refused to deliver carrots at the contract price, since the market price at such time had increased to $90.00 a ton. The Court of Appeals said "We think it too hard a bargain and too one-sided an agreement to entitle the plaintiff to relief in a court of conscience" (p. 83).

In the instant case the court finds that here, too, it was "too hard a bargain" and the conscience of the court will not permit the enforcement of the contract as written. Therefore the plaintiff will not be permitted to recover on the basis of the price set forth in the retail installment contract, namely $900.00 plus $245.85 as a service charge.

However, since the defendants have not returned the refrigerator-freezer, they will be required to reimburse the plaintiff for the cost to the plaintiff, namely $348.00. No allowance is made on account of any commissions the plaintiff may have paid to salesmen or for legal fees service charges or any other matters of overhead.

Accordingly the plaintiff may have judgment against both defendants in the amount of $348.00 with interest, less the $32.00 paid on account, leaving a net balance of $316.00 with interest from December 26, 1964.

FROSTIFRESH CORP.
v.
REYNOSO

Supreme Court, Appellate Term, Second Department, New York
281 N.Y.S. 2d 964
1967

PER CURIAM.

Judgment unanimously reversed, without costs, and a new trial ordered limited to an assessment of plaintiff's damages and entry of judgment thereon.

While the evidence clearly warrants a finding that the contract was unconscionable (Uniform Commercial Code, §2-302), we are of the opinion that plaintiff should recover its net cost for the refrigerator-freezer, plus a reasonable profit, in addition to trucking and service charges necessarily incurred and reasonable finance charges.

ZAPATHA
v.
DAIRY MART, INC.

Supreme Judicial Court of Massachusetts
408 N.E.2d 1370
1980

WILKINS, J.

We are concerned here with the question whether Dairy Mart, Inc. (Dairy Mart), lawfully undertook to terminate a franchise agreement under which the Zapathas operated a Dairy Mart store on Wilbraham Road in Springfield. The Zapathas brought this action seeking to enjoin the termination of the agreement, alleging that the contract provision purporting to authorize the termination of the franchise agreement without cause was unconscionable and that Dairy Mart's conduct was an unfair and deceptive act or practice in violation of G.L. c. 93A. The judge ruled that Dairy Mart did not act in good faith, that the termination provision was unconscionable, and that Dairy Mart's termination of the agreement without cause was an unfair and deceptive act. We granted Dairy Mart's application for direct appellate review of a judgment that stated that Dairy Mart could terminate the agreement only for good cause and that the attempted termination was null and void. We reverse the judgments.

Mr. Zapatha is a high school graduate who had attended college for one year and had also taken college evening courses in business administration and business law. From 1952 to May, 1973, he was employed by a company engaged in the business of electroplating. He rose through the ranks to foreman and then to the position of operations manager, at one time being in charge of all metal finishing in the plant with 150 people working under him. In May, 1973, he was discharged and began looking for other opportunities, in particular a business of his own. Several months later he met with a representative of Dairy Mart. Dairy Mart operates a chain of franchised "convenience" stores. The Dairy Mart representative told Mr. Zapatha that working for Dairy Mart was being in business for one's self and that such a business was very stable and secure. Mr. Zapatha signed an application to be considered for a franchise. In addition, he was presented with a brochure entitled "Here's a Chance," which made certain representations concerning the status of a franchise holder.

Dairy Mart approved Mr. Zapatha's application and offered him a store in Agawam. On November 8, 1973, a representative of Dairy Mart showed him a form of franchise agreement, entitled Limited Franchise and License Agreement, asked him to read it, and explained that his wife would have to sign the agreement as well.

. . . . The termination provision . . . allowed either party, after twelve months, to terminate the agreement without cause on ninety days' written notice. In the event of termination initiated by it without cause, Dairy Mart agreed to repurchase the saleable merchandise inventory at retail prices, less 20%.

The Dairy Mart representative read and explained the termination provision to Mr. Zapatha. Mr. Zapatha later testified that, while he understood every word in the provision, he had interpreted it to mean that Dairy Mart could terminate the agreement only for cause. The Dairy Mart representative advised Mr. Zapatha to take the agreement to an attorney and said "I would prefer that you did." However, he also told Mr. Zapatha that the terms of the contract were not negotiable. The Zapathas signed the agreement without consulting an attorney. When the Zapathas took charge of the Agawam store, a representative of Dairy Mart worked with them to train them in Dairy Mart's methods of operation.

In 1974, another store became available on Wilbraham Road in Springfield, and the Zapathas elected to surrender the Agawam store. They executed a new franchise agreement, on an identical printed form, relating to the new location.

In November, 1977, Dairy Mart presented a new and more detailed form of "Independent Operator's Agreement" to the Zapathas for execution. Some of the terms were less favorable to the store operator than those of the earlier form of agreement. Mr. Zapatha told representatives of Dairy Mart that he was content with the existing contract and had decided not to sign the new agreement. On January 20, 1978, Dairy Mart gave written notice to the Zapathas that their contract was being terminated effective in ninety days. The termination notice stated that Dairy Mart "remains available to enter into discussions with you with respect to entering into a new Independent Operator's Agreement; however, there is no assurance that Dairy Mart will enter into a new Agreement with you, or even if entered into, what terms such Agreement will contain." The notice also indicated that Dairy Mart was prepared to purchase the Zapathas' saleable inventory.

. . .

We consider first the plaintiffs' argument that the termination clause of the franchise agreement, authorizing Dairy Mart to terminate the agreement without cause, on ninety days' notice, was unconscionable by the standards expressed in G.L. c. 106, §2-302. The same standards are set forth in Restatement (Second) of Contracts §234 (Tent. Drafts Nos. 1-7, 1973). The issue is one of law for the court, and the test is to be made as of the time the contract was made. G.L. c. 106, §2-302(1), and comment 3 of the Official Comments. See W.L. May Co. v. Philco-Ford Corp., 273 Or. 701, 707, 543 P.2d 283 (1975). In measuring the unconscionability of the termination provision, the fact that the law imposes an obligation of good faith on Dairy Mart in its performance under the agreement should be weighed. See W.L. May Co. v. Philco-Ford Corp., supra at 709, 543 P.2d 283.

The official comment to §2-302 states that "(t)he basic test is whether, in the light of the general commercial background and the commercial needs of the particular trade or case, the clauses involved are so one-sided as to be unconscionable under the circumstances existing at the time of the making of the contract. . . . The principle is one of prevention of oppression and unfair surprise . . . and not of disturbance of allocation of risks because of superior bargaining power." Official Comment 1 to U.C.C. §2-302. Unconscionability is not defined in the Code, nor do the views expressed in the official comment provide a precise definition. The annotation prepared by the Massachusetts Advisory Committee on the Code states that "(t)he section appears to be intended to carry equity practice into the sales field." See 1 R. Anderson, Uniform Commercial Code §2-302:7 (1970) to the same effect. This court has not had occasion to consider in any detail the meaning of the word "unconscionable" in §2-302. Because there is no clear, all-purpose definition of "unconscionable," nor could there be, unconscionability must be determined on a case by case basis (see Commonwealth v. Gustafsson, 370 Mass. 181, 187, 346 N.E.2d 706 (1976)), giving particular attention to whether, at the time of the execution of the agreement, the contract provision could result in unfair surprise and was oppressive to the allegedly disadvantaged party.

. . .

We find no potential for unfair surprise to the Zapathas in the provision allowing termination without cause. We view the question of unfair surprise as focused on the circumstances under which the agreement was entered into.[13] The termination provision was neither obscurely worded, nor buried in fine print in the contract. Contrast Williams v. Walker-Thomas Furniture Co., 350 F.2d 445, 449 (D.C. Cir. 1965). The provision was specifically pointed out to Mr. Zapatha before it was signed; Mr. Zapatha testified that he thought the provision was "straightforward," and he declined the opportunity to take the agreement to a lawyer for advice. The Zapathas had ample opportunity to consider the agreement before they signed it. . . . We conclude that a person of Mr. Zapatha's business experience and education should not have been surprised by the termination provision and, if in fact he was, there was no element of unfairness in the inclusion of that provision in the agreement. See Fleischmann Distilling Corp. v. Distillers Co., 395 F. Supp. 221, 233 ("(i)t is the exceptional commercial setting where a claim of unconscionability will be allowed"). Contrast Johnson v. Mobil Oil Corp., 415 F. Supp. 264, 268-269 (illiterate service station operator incapable of reading dealer contract).

We further conclude that there was no oppression in the inclusion of a termination clause in the franchise agreement. We view the question of oppression as directed to the substantive fairness to the parties of permitting the termination provisions to operate as written. The Zapathas took over a going business on premises provided by Dairy Mart, using equipment furnished by Dairy Mart. As an investment, the Zapathas had only to purchase the inventory of goods to be sold but, as Dairy Mart concedes, on termination by it without cause Dairy Mart was obliged to repurchase all the Zapathas' saleable merchandise inventory, including items not purchased from Dairy Mart, at 80% of its retail value. There was no potential for forfeiture or loss of investment. There is no question here of a need for a reasonable time to recoup the franchisees' initial investment. See McGinnis Piano & Organ Co. v. Yamaha Int'l Corp., 480 F.2d 474, 480 (8th Cir. 1973); Gellhorn, Limitations on Contract Termination Rights Franchise Cancellations, 1967 Duke L.J. 465, 479-481.

13. As we shall note subsequently, the concept of oppression deals with the substantive unfairness of the contract term. This two-part test for unconscionability involves determining whether there was "an absence of meaningful choice on the part of one of the parties, together with contract terms which are unreasonably favorable to the other party." Williams v. Walker-Thomas Furniture Co., 350 F.2d 445, 449 (D.C. Cir. 1965). See Corenswet, Inc. v. Amana Refrigeration, Inc., 594 F.2d 129, 139 (5th Cir. 1979). The inquiry involves a search for components of "procedural" and "substantive" unconscionability. See generally Leff, *Unconscionability and the Code—The Emperor's New Clause*, 115 Pa. L. Rev. 485 (1967). See also Johnson v. Mobil Oil Corp., 415 F. Supp. 264, 268 (E.D. Mich. 1976); Fleischmann Distilling Corp. v. Distillers Co., 395 F. Supp. 221, 232-233 (S.D.N.Y. 1975).

The Zapathas were entitled to their net profits through the entire term of the agreement. They failed to sustain their burden of showing that the agreement allocated the risks and benefits connected with termination in an unreasonably disproportionate way and that the termination provision was not reasonably related to legitimate commercial needs of Dairy Mart. See Gellhorn, supra at 512. See also Central Ohio Co-op Milk Producers, Inc. v. Rowland, 29 Ohio App. 2d 236, 281 N.E.2d 42, 58 Ohio Op. 2d 421, 423 (1972); W.L. May Co. v. Philco-Ford Corp., 273 Or. 701, 708, 543 P.2d 283 (1975). To find the termination clause oppressive merely because it did not require cause for termination would be to establish an unwarranted barrier to the use of termination at will clauses in contracts in this Commonwealth, where each party received the anticipated and bargained for consideration during the full term of the agreement.

Problems

1. A Steep Price for New Siding. At the urging of a door-to-door salesman, 83-year-old Pearl Maxwell refinanced her home in order to raise cash for a variety of home repairs, including the replacement of siding and windows. Before refinancing, Maxwell owed $100,000 on her mortgage. Under the terms of the new, 16 percent interest rate, negative amortization mortgage loan (monthly payments were less than the interest due, so the balance owed would increase each month)—which allowed Maxwell to pay $23,000 in cash for home repairs—Maxwell was obligated to pay the lender $2,000 per month for five years followed by a balloon payment of $150,000, which included over $12,000 in finance charges. Maxwell's total annual household income (including that of the granddaughter who lived with her) at the time of the refinance was just over $24,000, meaning that the monthly payments would equal 98.5 percent of household income.

At some point, Maxwell stopped making the monthly payments, and the mortgage was then purchased from the original lender by Fairbanks Capital Corporation, which specialized in purchasing and servicing subprime and nonperforming loans. Fairbanks initiated foreclosure proceedings, and Maxwell filed for Chapter 13 bankruptcy protection. Fairbanks could provide no evidence that, at the time of the refinancing agreement, the original lender had provided Maxwell with various disclosure statements required by federal and state real estate law, such as statements of the percentage rate of interest, finance charges, number of payments, and total payments, that the loan included negative amortization, and that Maxwell had been given the statutorily provided number of days to rescind the agreement after entering it. Maxwell's granddaughter testified that they were given no documents at the time of closing.

In the bankruptcy litigation, Maxwell alleged that the mortgage contract that she entered into to refinance her home was unconscionable, and she sought rescission of that agreement. Should she prevail?

2. Fire Damage. On the evening of August 23, Wanda Gary's house suffered significant damage in a fire. That same night, she hired Repair Masters Construction to board up the house until it could be repaired. While the contractor was completing the work, one of his salesmen convinced Gary to sign a contract with Repair Masters for completion of all repairs, the scope (and price) of which Repair Masters would specify to Gary's insurance company. The contract included a term stating that, should Gary cancel the contract for any reason before repairs began, she would be obligated to pay Repair Masters 15 percent of the yet-to-be-determined cost of repairs.

When Gary's insurance company would not accept Repair Masters's bid on the repairs, Gary notified Repair Masters that she wanted to cancel the agreement. Repair Masters then billed Gary for 15 percent of its estimate. Gary refused to pay, alleging that the agreement was unconscionable. Repair Masters brought a lawsuit for breach of contract. Who should prevail?

3. Employment Arbitration. After Jacquelin Davis began working as a paralegal for the law firm of O'Melveny & Meyers, the firm adopted, as a condition of employment, a new dispute resolution program (DRP). A memo detailing the DRP was distributed via interoffice mail and was also made available electronically. Employees were directed to pose any questions they might have to the human resources department. The DRP required arbitration of most legal claims arising out of the employment relationship or termination of employment, required the aggrieved party to institute proceedings within one year of the date the claim arose, and forbade employees from talking about any claims. The policy did not cover employee claims for workers' compensation or unemployment benefits, claims concerning Employee Retirement Income Security Act (ERISA) benefits, or claims by the firm for injunctive relief arising from alleged breaches of attorney-client privilege or the disclosure of other confidential information.

After Lee Caley began working for the Gulfstream Aerospace Corporation, the company adopted, as a condition of employment, a new DRP. Caley was mailed a copy of the procedures, which were also distributed electronically and posted on company bulletin boards. The DRP required arbitration of employment-related legal disputes between an employee and Gulfstream with certain categorical exceptions (such as ERISA benefit claims and workers' compensation claims), and also provided that no claims covered under the agreement could be raised as class action claims in arbitration.

Both Davis and Caley later filed lawsuits against their employers alleging various violations of federal labor and employment statutes. Both defendants moved for dismissal and an order for the plaintiffs to arbitrate their claims. The United States District Court for the Central District of California granted O'Melveny's motion, and the United States District Court for the Northern District of Georgia granted Gulfstream's motion. Both plaintiffs appealed, alleging that the arbitration requirements were unconscionable. Who should prevail? Are the cases distinguishable?

4. The Broken Water Heater. In December 1984, Elizabeth and Charles Maxwell purchased a solar water heater from a door-to-door salesman for the now-defunct National Solar Corporation. The purchase price was $6,512, which the Maxwells, with National's assistance, financed through a ten-year loan at 19.5 percent interest from Fidelity Financial Services, making the total cost of the water heater nearly $15,000. At the time, Elizabeth earned $400 per month working part time as a hotel maid and Charles earned approximately $1,800 per month working for the local paper. They lived in a modest neighborhood, and their home had a market value of approximately $40,000. In connection with the financing transaction, Elizabeth and Charles signed numerous documents, including documents that clearly stated that a lien would be placed on the Maxwell's home as security for payment on the water heater. Despite the fact that the water heater was installed imcorrectly and did not work properly, the Maxwells made payments on it for approximately three and one-half years, reducing the loan balance to $5,733. They brought a declaratory judgment action seeking, *inter alia*, a declaration that the 1984 contract was unenforceable on the grounds that it was unconscionable. The trial court granted Fidelity's motion for summary judgment. Should the appellate court uphold this ruling?

G. PUBLIC POLICY

Courts will refuse to enforce an otherwise valid contract if the agreement contravenes "public policy." Rest. (2d) Contracts §§178, 179. How, though, is a judge to determine the relevant "public policy" without rendering the law a reflection of the judge's personal policy preferences? The answer is that identifying public policy requires courts to analyze the statutory pronouncements of legislatures and, in some cases, the well-established judicial pronouncements resolving disputes in common law cases.

When the legislature has either clearly prohibited a type of conduct altogether or prohibited the exchange of consideration for that conduct, judicial invocation of the public policy doctrine to refuse to enforce contracts for that conduct is uncontroversial. Contracts for murder or for prostitution, for example, are clearly unenforceable under the doctrine. Difficult cases arise when a contract's subject matter does not fall squarely into a prohibited category but the legislative branch has cast disapproval on a related course of conduct, either out of paternalistic motives (i.e., the protection of a particular class of actors who might choose to engage in the conduct) or concern about negative externalities that arise from the conduct (i.e., negative effects of the conduct on specific third parties or society generally). In such cases, judges struggle to determine whether or not it is possible to infer legislative disapproval of the contract before them. In some circumstances, different statutes might provide contradictory implications, with one suggesting disapproval of a particular type of contract and another implying approval.

The public policy doctrine is invoked across a range of circumstances, but some of the most contentious issues have arisen in the context of agreements concerning intimate relationships. In the first pair of cases below, *In the Matter of Baby M.* and *Johnson v. Calvert*, the courts struggle with whether to enforce contracts between would-be parents and surrogate mothers. In the second pair of cases, *Marvin v. Marvin* and *Hewitt v. Hewitt*, the courts similarly struggle with the enforceability of contracts for domestic living arrangements.

IN THE MATTER OF BABY M.
Supreme Court of New Jersey
109 N.J. 396
1988

WILENTZ, C.J.

In this matter the Court is asked to determine the validity of a contract that purports to provide a new way of bringing children into a family. For a fee of $10,000, a woman agrees to be artificially inseminated with the semen of another woman's husband; she is to conceive a child, carry it to term, and after its birth surrender it to the natural father and his wife. The intent of the contract is that the child's natural mother will thereafter be forever separated from her child. The wife is to adopt the child, and she and the natural father are to be regarded as its parents for all purposes. The contract providing for this is called a "surrogacy contract," the natural mother inappropriately called the "surrogate mother."

We invalidate the surrogacy contract because it conflicts with the law and public policy of this State. While we recognize the depth of the yearning of infertile couples to have their own children, we find the payment of money to a "surrogate" mother illegal, perhaps criminal, and potentially degrading to women. Although in this case we grant custody to the natural father, the evidence having clearly proved such custody to be in the best interests of the infant, we void both the termination of the surrogate mother's parental rights and the adoption of the child by the wife/stepparent. We thus restore the "surrogate" as the mother of the child. We remand the issue of the natural mother's visitation rights to the trial court, since that issue was not reached below and the record before us is not sufficient to permit us to decide it *de novo*.

We find no offense to our present laws where a woman voluntarily and without payment agrees to act as a "surrogate" mother, provided that she is not subject to a binding agreement to surrender her child. Moreover, our holding today does not preclude the Legislature from altering the current statutory scheme, within constitutional limits, so as to permit surrogacy contracts. Under current law, however, the surrogacy agreement before us is illegal and invalid.

I. FACTS

In February 1985, William Stern and Mary Beth Whitehead entered into a surrogacy contract. It recited that Stern's wife, Elizabeth, was infertile, that they wanted a child, and that Mrs. Whitehead was willing to provide that child as the mother with Mr. Stern as the father.

The contract provided that through artificial insemination using Mr. Stern's sperm, Mrs. Whitehead would become pregnant, carry the child to term, bear it, deliver it to the Sterns, and thereafter do whatever was necessary to terminate her maternal rights so that Mrs. Stern could thereafter adopt the child. Mrs. Whitehead's husband, Richard, was also a party to the contract; Mrs. Stern was not. Mr. Whitehead promised to do all acts necessary to rebut the presumption of paternity under the Parentage Act. N.J.S.A. 9:17-43a(1),-44a. Although Mrs. Stern was not a party to the surrogacy agreement, the contract gave her sole custody of the child in the event of Mr. Stern's death. Mrs. Stern's status as a nonparty to the surrogate parenting agreement presumably was to avoid the application of the baby—selling statute to this arrangement. N.J.S.A. 9:3-54.

Mr. Stern, on his part, agreed to attempt the artificial insemination and to pay Mrs. Whitehead $10,000 after the child's birth, on its delivery to him. In a separate contract, Mr. Stern agreed to pay $7,500 to the Infertility Center of New York ("ICNY"). The Center's advertising campaigns solicit surrogate mothers and encourage infertile couples to consider surrogacy. ICNY arranged for the surrogacy contract by bringing the parties together, explaining the process to them, furnishing the contractual form, and providing legal counsel.

The history of the parties' involvement in this arrangement suggests their good faith. William and Elizabeth Stern were married in July 1974, having met at the University of Michigan, where both were Ph.D. candidates. Due to financial considerations and Mrs. Stern's pursuit of a medical degree and residency, they decided to defer starting a family until 1981. Before then, however, Mrs. Stern learned that she might have multiple sclerosis and that the disease in some cases renders pregnancy a serious health risk. Her anxiety appears to have exceeded the actual risk, which current medical authorities assess as minimal. Nonetheless that anxiety was evidently quite real, Mrs. Stern fearing that pregnancy might precipitate blindness, paraplegia, or other forms of debilitation. Based on the perceived risk, the Sterns decided to forego having their own children. The decision had special significance for Mr. Stern. Most of his family had been destroyed in the Holocaust. As the family's only survivor, he very much wanted to continue his bloodline.

Initially the Sterns considered adoption, but were discouraged by the substantial delay apparently involved and by the potential problem they saw arising from their age and their differing religious backgrounds. They were most eager for some other means to start a family.

The paths of Mrs. Whitehead and the Sterns to surrogacy were similar. Both responded to advertising by ICNY. The Sterns' response, following their inquiries into adoption, was the result of their long-standing decision to have a child. Mrs. Whitehead's response apparently resulted from her sympathy with family members and others who could have no children (she stated that she wanted to give another couple the "gift of life"); she also wanted the $10,000 to help her family.

Both parties, undoubtedly because of their own self-interest, were less sensitive to the implications of the transaction than they might otherwise have been. Mrs. Whitehead, for instance, appears not to have been concerned about whether the Sterns would make good parents for her child; the Sterns, on their part, while conscious of the obvious possibility that surrendering the child might cause grief to Mrs. Whitehead, overcame their qualms because of their desire for a child. At any rate, both the Sterns and Mrs. Whitehead were committed to the arrangement; both thought it right and constructive.

. . .

Mrs. Whitehead realized, almost from the moment of birth, that she could not part with this child. She had felt a bond with it even during pregnancy. Some indication of the attachment was conveyed to the Sterns at the hospital when they told Mrs. Whitehead what they were going to name the baby. She apparently broke into tears and indicated that she did not know if she could give up the child. She talked about how the baby looked like her other daughter, and made it clear that she was experiencing great difficulty with the decision.

Nonetheless, Mrs. Whitehead was, for the moment, true to her word. Despite powerful inclinations to the contrary, she turned her child over to the Sterns on March 30 at the Whiteheads' home.

The Sterns were thrilled with their new child. They had planned extensively for its arrival, far beyond the practical furnishing of a room for her. It was a time of joyful celebration—not just for them but for their friends as well. The Sterns looked forward to raising their daughter, whom they named Melissa. While aware by then that Mrs. Whitehead was undergoing an emotional crisis, they were as yet not cognizant of the depth of that crisis and its implications for their newly-enlarged family.

Later in the evening of March 30, Mrs. Whitehead became deeply disturbed, disconsolate, stricken with unbearable sadness. She had to have her child. She could not eat, sleep, or concentrate on anything other than her need for her baby. The next day she went to the Sterns' home and told them how much she was suffering.

The depth of Mrs. Whitehead's despair surprised and frightened the Sterns. She told them that she could not live without her baby, that she must have her, even if only for one week, that thereafter she would surrender her child. The Sterns, concerned that Mrs. Whitehead might indeed commit suicide, not wanting under any circumstances to risk that, and in any event believing that Mrs. Whitehead would keep her word, turned the child over to her. It was not until four months later, after a series of attempts to regain possession of the child, that Melissa was returned to the Sterns, having been forcibly removed from the home where she was then living with Mr. and Mrs. Whitehead, the home in Florida owned by Mary Beth Whitehead's parents.

The struggle over Baby M began when it became apparent that Mrs. Whitehead could not return the child to Mr. Stern. Due to Mrs. Whitehead's refusal to relinquish the baby, Mr. Stern filed a complaint seeking enforcement of the surrogacy contract. He alleged, accurately, that Mrs. Whitehead had not only refused to comply with the surrogacy contract but had threatened to flee from New Jersey with the child in order to avoid even the possibility of his obtaining custody. The court papers asserted that if Mrs. Whitehead were to be given notice of the application for an order requiring her to relinquish custody, she would, prior to the hearing, leave the state with the baby. And that is precisely what she did. After the order was entered, *ex parte*, the process server, aided by the police, in the presence of the Sterns, entered Mrs. Whitehead's home to execute the order. Mr. Whitehead fled with the child, who had been handed to him through a window while those who came to enforce the order were thrown off balance by a dispute over the child's current name.

The Whiteheads immediately fled to Florida with Baby M. They stayed initially with Mrs. Whitehead's parents, where one of Mrs. Whitehead's children had been living. For the next three months, the Whiteheads and Melissa lived at roughly twenty different hotels, motels, and homes in order to avoid apprehension. From time to time Mrs. Whitehead would call Mr. Stern to discuss the matter; the conversations, recorded by Mr. Stern on advice of counsel, show an escalating dispute about rights, morality, and power, accompanied by threats of Mrs. Whitehead to kill herself, to kill the child, and falsely to accuse Mr. Stern of sexually molesting Mrs. Whitehead's other daughter.

Eventually the Sterns discovered where the Whiteheads were staying, commenced supplementary proceedings in Florida, and obtained an order requiring the Whiteheads to turn over the child. Police in Florida enforced the order, forcibly removing the child from her grandparents' home. She was soon thereafter brought to New Jersey and turned over to the Sterns. The prior order of the court, issued *ex parte*, awarding custody of the child to the Sterns *pendente lite*, was reaffirmed by the trial court after consideration of the certified representations of the parties (both represented by counsel) concerning the unusual sequence of events that had unfolded. Pending final judgment, Mrs. Whitehead was awarded limited visitation with Baby M.

The Sterns' complaint, in addition to seeking possession and ultimately custody of the child, sought enforcement of the surrogacy contract. Pursuant to the contract, it asked that the child be permanently placed in their custody, that Mrs. Whitehead's parental rights be terminated, and that Mrs. Stern be allowed to adopt the child, *i.e.*, that, for all purposes, Melissa become the Sterns' child.

. . .

Although clearly expressing its view that the surrogacy contract was valid, the trial court devoted the major portion of its opinion to the question of the baby's best interests. The inconsistency is apparent. The surrogacy contract calls for the surrender of the child to the Sterns, permanent and sole custody in the Sterns, and termination of Mrs. Whitehead's parental rights, all without qualification, all regardless of any evaluation of the best interests of the child. As a matter of fact the contract recites (even before the child was conceived) that it is in the best interests of the child to be placed with Mr. Stern. In effect, the trial court awarded custody to Mr. Stern, the natural father, based on the same kind of evidence and analysis as might be expected had no surrogacy contract existed. Its rationalization, however, was that while the surrogacy contract was valid, specific performance would not be granted unless that remedy was in the best interests of the child. The factual issues confronted and decided by the trial court were the same as if Mr. Stern and Mrs. Whitehead had had the child out of wedlock, intended or unintended, and then disagreed about custody. The trial court's awareness of the irrelevance of the contract in the court's determination of custody is suggested by its remark that beyond the question of the child's best interests, "[a]ll other concerns raised by counsel constitute commentary." 217 N.J. Super. at 323, 525 A.2d 1128.

. . .

II. INVALIDITY AND UNENFORCEABILITY OF SURROGACY CONTRACT

We have concluded that this surrogacy contract is invalid. Our conclusion has two bases: direct conflict with existing statutes and conflict with the public policies of this State, as expressed in its statutory and decisional law.

. . .

A. Conflict with Statutory Provisions

The surrogacy contract conflicts with: (1) laws prohibiting the use of money in connection with adoptions; (2) laws requiring proof of parental unfitness or abandonment before termination of parental rights is ordered or an adoption is granted.

(1) Our law prohibits paying or accepting money in connection with any placement of a child for adoption. N.J.S.A. 9:3-54a. Violation is a high misdemeanor. N.J.S.A. 9:3-54c. Excepted are fees of an approved agency (which must be a non-profit entity, N.J.S.A. 9:3-38a) and certain expenses in connection with childbirth. N.J.S.A. 9:3-54b.[4]

Considerable care was taken in this case to structure the surrogacy arrangement so as not to violate this prohibition. The arrangement was structured as follows: the adopting parent, Mrs. Stern, was not a party to the surrogacy contract; the money paid to Mrs. Whitehead was stated to be for her services—not for the adoption; the sole purpose of the contract was stated as being that "of giving a child to William Stern, its natural and biological father"; the money was purported to be "compensation for services and expenses and in no way . . . a fee for termination of parental rights or a payment in exchange for consent to surrender a child for adoption"; the fee to the Infertility Center ($7,500) was stated to be for legal representation, advice, administrative work, and other "services." Nevertheless, it seems clear that the money was paid and accepted in connection with an adoption.

---

4. N.J.S.A. 9:3-54 reads as follows:

  a. No person, firm, partnership, corporation, association or agency shall make, offer to make or assist or participate in any placement for adoption and in connection therewith
     (1) Pay, give or agree to give any money or any valuable consideration, or assume or discharge any financial obligation; or
     (2) Take, receive, accept or agree to accept any money or any valuable consideration.
  b. The prohibition of subsection a. shall not apply to the fees or services of any approved agency in connection with a placement for adoption, nor shall such prohibition apply to the payment or reimbursement of medical, hospital or other similar expenses incurred in connection with the birth or any illness of the child, or to the acceptance of such reimbursement by a parent of the child.
  c. Any person, firm, partnership, corporation, association or agency violating this section shall be guilty of a high misdemeanor.

The Infertility Center's major role was first as a "finder" of the surrogate mother whose child was to be adopted, and second as the arranger of all proceedings that led to the adoption. Its role as adoption finder is demonstrated by the provision requiring Mr. Stern to pay another $7,500 if he uses Mary Beth Whitehead again as a surrogate, and by ICNY's agreement to "coordinate arrangements for the adoption of the child by the wife." The surrogacy agreement requires Mrs. Whitehead to surrender Baby M for the purposes of adoption. The agreement notes that Mr. *and Mrs.* Stern wanted to have a child, and provides that the child be "placed" with Mrs. Stern in the event Mr. Stern dies before the child is born. The payment of the $10,000 occurs only on surrender of custody of the child and "completion of the duties and obligations" of Mrs. Whitehead, including termination of her parental rights to facilitate adoption by Mrs. Stern. As for the contention that the Sterns are paying only for services and not for an adoption, we need note only that they would pay nothing in the event the child died before the fourth month of pregnancy, and only $1,000 if the child were stillborn, even though the "services" had been fully rendered. Additionally, one of Mrs. Whitehead's estimated costs, to be assumed by Mr. Stern, was an "Adoption Fee," presumably for Mrs. Whitehead's incidental costs in connection with the adoption.

Mr. Stern knew he was paying for the adoption of a child; Mrs. Whitehead knew she was accepting money so that a child might be adopted; the Infertility Center knew that it was being paid for assisting in the adoption of a child. The actions of all three worked to frustrate the goals of the statute. It strains credulity to claim that these arrangements, touted by those in the surrogacy business as an attractive alternative to the usual route leading to an adoption, really amount to something other than a private placement adoption for money.

The prohibition of our statute is strong. Violation constitutes a high misdemeanor, N.J.S.A. 9:3-54c, a third-degree crime, N.J.S.A. 2C:43-1b, carrying a penalty of three to five years imprisonment. N.J.S.A. 2C:43-6a(3). The evils inherent in baby-bartering are loathsome for a myriad of reasons. The child is sold without regard for whether the purchasers will be suitable parents. N. Baker, *Baby Selling: The Scandal of Black Market Adoption* 7 (1978). The natural mother does not receive the benefit of counseling and guidance to assist her in making a decision that may affect her for a lifetime. In fact, the monetary incentive to sell her child may, depending on her financial circumstances, make her decision less voluntary. Furthermore, the adoptive parents may not be fully informed of the natural parents' medical history.

Baby-selling potentially results in the exploitation of all parties involved. Conversely, adoption statutes seek to further humanitarian goals, foremost among them the best interests of the child. H. Witmer, E. Herzog, E. Weinstein, & M. Sullivan, *Independent Adoptions: A Follow-Up Study* 32 (1967). The negative consequences of baby-buying are potentially present in the surrogacy context, especially the potential for placing and adopting a child without regard to the interest of the child or the natural mother.

(2) The termination of Mrs. Whitehead's parental rights, called for by the surrogacy contract and actually ordered by the court, 217 N.J. Super. at 399-400, 525

A.2d 1128, fails to comply with the stringent requirements of New Jersey law. Our law, recognizing the finality of any termination of parental rights, provides for such termination only where there has been a voluntary surrender of a child to an approved agency or to the Division of Youth and Family Services ("DYFS"), accompanied by a formal document acknowledging termination of parental rights, N.J.S.A. 9:2-16,-17; N.J.S.A. 9:3-41; N.J.S.A. 30:4C-23, or where there has been a showing of parental abandonment or unfitness. A termination may ordinarily take one of three forms: an action by an approved agency, an action by DYFS, or an action in connection with a private placement adoption. The three are governed by separate statutes, but the standards for termination are substantially the same, except that whereas a written surrender is effective when made to an approved agency or to DYFS, there is no provision for it in the private placement context. *See* N.J.S.A. 9:2-14; N.J.S.A. 30:4C-23.

. . .

In order to terminate parental rights under the private placement adoption statute, there must be a finding of "intentional abandonment or a very substantial neglect of parental duties without a reasonable expectation of a reversal of that conduct in the future." N.J.S.A. 9:3-48c(1). This requirement is similar to that of the prior law (*i.e.*, "forsaken parental obligations," L.1953, c. 264, §2(d) (codified at N.J.S.A. 9:3-18(d) (repealed))), and to that of the law providing for termination through actions by approved agencies, N.J.S.A. 9:2-13(d). *See also In re Adoption by J.J.P.*, 175 N.J. Super. 420, 427, 419 A.2d 1135 (App. Div. 1980) (noting that the language of the termination provision in the present statute, N.J.S.A. 9:3-48c(1), derives from this Court's construction of the prior statute in *In re Adoption of Children by D.*, 61 N.J. 89, 94-95, 293 A.2d 171 (1972)).

In *Sees v. Baber*, 74 N.J. 201, 377 A.2d 628 (1977) we distinguished the requirements for terminating parental rights in a private placement adoption from those required in an approved agency adoption. We stated that in an unregulated private placement, "neither consent nor voluntary surrender is singled out as a statutory factor in terminating parental rights." *Id.* at 213, 377 A.2d 628. *Sees* established that without proof that parental obligations had been forsaken, there would be no termination in a private placement setting.

. . .

In this case a termination of parental rights was obtained not by proving the statutory prerequisites but by claiming the benefit of contractual provisions. From all that has been stated above, it is clear that a contractual agreement to abandon one's parental rights, or not to contest a termination action, will not be enforced in our courts. The Legislature would not have so carefully, so consistently, and so substantially restricted termination of parental rights if it had intended to allow termination to be achieved by one short sentence in a contract.

Since the termination was invalid, it follows, as noted above, that adoption of Melissa by Mrs. Stern could not properly be granted.

. . .

B. Public Policy Considerations

The surrogacy contract's invalidity, resulting from its direct conflict with the above statutory provisions, is further underlined when its goals and means are measured against New Jersey's public policy. The contract's basic premise, that the natural parents can decide in advance of birth which one is to have custody of the child, bears no relationship to the settled law that the child's best interests shall determine custody. *See Fantony v. Fantony*, 21 N.J. 525, 536-37, 122 A.2d 593 (1956); *see also Sheehan v. Sheehan*, 38 N.J. Super. 120, 125, 118 A.2d 89 (App. Div. 1955) ("WHATEVER THE AGREEMENT OF THE PARENTS, The Ultimate determination of custody lies with the court in the exercise of its supervisory jurisdiction as *parens patriae*."). The fact that the trial court remedied that aspect of the contract through the "best interests" phase does not make the contractual provision any less offensive to the public policy of this State.

The surrogacy contract guarantees permanent separation of the child from one of its natural parents. Our policy, however, has long been that to the extent possible, children should remain with and be brought up by both of their natural parents. That was the first stated purpose of the previous adoption act, L.1953, c. 264, §1, codified at N.J.S.A. 9:3-17 (repealed): "it is necessary and desirable (a) to protect the child from unnecessary separation from his natural parents. . . ." While not so stated in the present adoption law, this purpose remains part of the public policy of this State. *See, e.g., Wilke v. Culp*, 196 N.J. Super. 487, 496, 483 A.2d 420 (App. Div. 1984), certif. den., 99 N.J. 243, 491 A.2d 728 (1985); *In re Adoption by J.J.P., supra*, 175 N.J. Super. at 426, 419 A.2d 1135. This is not simply some theoretical ideal that in practice has no meaning. The impact of failure to follow that policy is nowhere better shown than in the results of this surrogacy contract. A child, instead of starting off its life with as much peace and security as possible, finds itself immediately in a tug-of-war between contending mother and father.

The surrogacy contract violates the policy of this State that the rights of natural parents are equal concerning their child, the father's right no greater than the mother's. "The parent and child relationship extends equally to every child and to every parent, regardless of the marital status of the parents." N.J.S.A. 9:17-40. As the Assembly Judiciary Committee noted in its statement to the bill, this section establishes "the principle that regardless of the marital status of the parents, all children *and all parents* have equal rights with respect to each other." *Statement to Senate No. 888*, Assembly Judiciary, Law, Public Safety and Defense Committee (1983) (emphasis supplied). The whole purpose and effect of the surrogacy contract was to give the father the exclusive right to the child by destroying the rights of the mother.

The policies expressed in our comprehensive laws governing consent to the surrender of a child, discussed *supra* at 1244-1246, stand in stark contrast to the surrogacy contract and what it implies. Here there is no counseling, independent or otherwise, of the natural mother, no evaluation, no warning.

The only legal advice Mary Beth Whitehead received regarding the surrogacy contract was provided in connection with the contract that she previously entered into with another couple. Mrs. Whitehead's lawyer was referred to her by the Infertility

Center, with which he had an agreement to act as counsel for surrogate candidates. His services consisted of spending one hour going through the contract with the Whiteheads, section by section, and answering their questions. Mrs. Whitehead received no further legal advice prior to signing the contract with the Sterns.

Mrs. Whitehead was examined and psychologically evaluated, but if it was for her benefit, the record does not disclose that fact. The Sterns regarded the evaluation as important, particularly in connection with the question of whether she would change her mind. Yet they never asked to see it, and were content with the assumption that the Infertility Center had made an evaluation and had concluded that there was no danger that the surrogate mother would change her mind. From Mrs. Whitehead's point of view, all that she learned from the evaluation was that "she had passed." It is apparent that the profit motive got the better of the Infertility Center. Although the evaluation was made, it was not put to any use, and understandably so, for the psychologist warned that Mrs. Whitehead demonstrated certain traits that might make surrender of the child difficult and that there should be further inquiry into this issue in connection with her surrogacy. To inquire further, however, might have jeopardized the Infertility Center's fee. The record indicates that neither Mrs. Whitehead nor the Sterns were ever told of this fact, a fact that might have ended their surrogacy arrangement.

Under the contract, the natural mother is irrevocably committed before she knows the strength of her bond with her child. She never makes a totally voluntary, informed decision, for quite clearly any decision prior to the baby's birth is, in the most important sense, uninformed, and any decision after that, compelled by a pre-existing contractual commitment, the threat of a lawsuit, and the inducement of a $10,000 payment, is less than totally voluntary. Her interests are of little concern to those who controlled this transaction.

Although the interest of the natural father and adoptive mother is certainly the predominant interest, realistically the *only* interest served, even they are left with less than what public policy requires. They know little about the natural mother, her genetic makeup, and her psychological and medical history. Moreover, not even a superficial attempt is made to determine their awareness of their responsibilities as parents.

Worst of all, however, is the contract's total disregard of the best interests of the child. There is not the slightest suggestion that any inquiry will be made at any time to determine the fitness of the Sterns as custodial parents, of Mrs. Stern as an adoptive parent, their superiority to Mrs. Whitehead, or the effect on the child of not living with her natural mother.

This is the sale of a child, or, at the very least, the sale of a mother's right to her child, the only mitigating factor being that one of the purchasers is the father. Almost every evil that prompted the prohibition on the payment of money in connection with adoptions exists here.

The differences between an adoption and a surrogacy contract should be noted, since it is asserted that the use of money in connection with surrogacy does not pose the risks found where money buys an adoption. Katz, "Surrogate Motherhood and the Baby-Selling Laws," 20 Colum. J.L. & Soc. Probs. 1 (1986).

First, and perhaps most important, all parties concede that it is unlikely that surrogacy will survive without money. Despite the alleged selfless motivation of surrogate mothers, if there is no payment, there will be no surrogates, or very few. That conclusion contrasts with adoption; for obvious reasons, there remains a steady supply, albeit insufficient, despite the prohibitions against payment. The adoption itself, relieving the natural mother of the financial burden of supporting an infant, is in some sense the equivalent of payment.

Second, the use of money in adoptions does not *produce* the problem—conception occurs, and usually the birth itself, before illicit funds are offered. With surrogacy, the "problem," if one views it as such, consisting of the purchase of a woman's procreative capacity, at the risk of her life, is caused by and originates with the offer of money.

Third, with the law prohibiting the use of money in connection with adoptions, the built-in financial pressure of the unwanted pregnancy and the consequent support obligation do not lead the mother to the highest paying, ill-suited, adoptive parents. She is just as well-off surrendering the child to an approved agency. In surrogacy, the highest bidders will presumably become the adoptive parents regardless of suitability, so long as payment of money is permitted.

Fourth, the mother's consent to surrender her child in adoptions is revocable, even after surrender of the child, unless it be to an approved agency, where by regulation there are protections against an ill-advised surrender. In surrogacy, consent occurs so early that no amount of advice would satisfy the potential mother's need, yet the consent is irrevocable.

The main difference, that the unwanted pregnancy is unintended while the situation of the surrogate mother is voluntary and intended, is really not significant. Initially, it produces stronger reactions of sympathy for the mother whose pregnancy was unwanted than for the surrogate mother, who "went into this with her eyes wide open." On reflection, however, it appears that the essential evil is the same, taking advantage of a woman's circumstances (the unwanted pregnancy or the need for money) in order to take away her child, the difference being one of degree.

In the scheme contemplated by the surrogacy contract in this case, a middle man, propelled by profit, promotes the sale. Whatever idealism may have motivated any of the participants, the profit motive predominates, permeates, and ultimately governs the transaction. The demand for children is great and the supply small. The availability of contraception, abortion, and the greater willingness of single mothers to bring up their children has led to a shortage of babies offered for adoption. *See* N. Baker, *Baby Selling: The Scandal of Black Market Adoption, supra; Adoption and Foster Care, 1975: Hearings on Baby Selling Before the Subcomm. on Children and Youth of the Senate Comm. on Labor and Public Welfare*, 94th Cong. 1st Sess. 6 (1975) (Statement of Joseph H. Reid, Executive Director, Child Welfare League of America, Inc.). The situation is ripe for the entry of the middleman who will bring some equilibrium into the market by increasing the supply through the use of money.

Intimated, but disputed, is the assertion that surrogacy will be used for the benefit of the rich at the expense of the poor. *See, e.g.*, Radin, "Market Inalienability," 100 Harv. L. Rev. 1849, 1930 (1987). In response it is noted that the Sterns are not rich and the Whiteheads not poor. Nevertheless, it is clear to us that it is unlikely that surrogate mothers will be as proportionately numerous among those women in the top twenty percent income bracket as among those in the bottom twenty percent. Put differently, we doubt that infertile couples in the low-income bracket will find upper income surrogates.

In any event, even in this case one should not pretend that disparate wealth does not play a part simply because the contrast is not the dramatic "rich versus poor." At the time of trial, the Whiteheads' net assets were probably negative-Mrs. Whitehead's own sister was foreclosing on a second mortgage. Their income derived from Mr. Whitehead's labors. Mrs. Whitehead is a homemaker, having previously held part-time jobs. The Sterns are both professionals, she a medical doctor, he a bio-chemist. Their combined income when both were working was about $89,500 a year and their assets sufficient to pay for the surrogacy contract arrangements.

The point is made that Mrs. Whitehead *agreed* to the surrogacy arrangement, supposedly fully understanding the consequences. Putting aside the issue of how compelling her need for money may have been, and how significant her understanding of the consequences, we suggest that her consent is irrelevant. There are, in a civilized society, some things that money cannot buy.

. . .

JOHNSON
v.
CALVERT
Supreme Court of California
5 Cal. 4th 84
1993

Panelli, J.

. . .

In this case we address several of the legal questions raised by recent advances in reproductive technology.

Mark and Crispina Calvert are a married couple who desired to have a child. Crispina was forced to undergo a hysterectomy in 1984. Her ovaries remained capable of producing eggs, however, and the couple eventually considered surrogacy. In 1989 Anna Johnson heard about Crispina's plight from a coworker and offered to serve as a surrogate for the Calverts.

On January 15, 1990, Mark, Crispina, and Anna signed a contract providing that an embryo created by the sperm of Mark and the egg of Crispina would be implanted in Anna and the child born would be taken into Mark and Crispina's home "as their child." Anna agreed she would relinquish "all parental rights" to the child in favor of Mark and Crispina. In return, Mark and Crispina would pay Anna $10,000 in a series of installments, the last to be paid six weeks after the child's birth. Mark and Crispina were also to pay for a $200,000 life insurance policy on Anna's life.

The zygote was implanted on January 19, 1990. Less than a month later, an ultrasound test confirmed Anna was pregnant.

Unfortunately, relations deteriorated between the two sides. Mark learned that Anna had not disclosed she had suffered several stillbirths and miscarriages. Anna felt Mark and Crispina did not do enough to obtain the required insurance policy. She also felt abandoned during an onset of premature labor in June.

In July 1990, Anna sent Mark and Crispina a letter demanding the balance of the payments due her or else she would refuse to give up the child. The following month, Mark and Crispina responded with a lawsuit, seeking a declaration they were the legal parents of the unborn child. Anna filed her own action to be declared the mother of the child, and the two cases were eventually consolidated. The parties agreed to an independent guardian ad litem for the purposes of the suit.

The child was born on September 19, 1990, and blood samples were obtained from both Anna and the child for analysis. The blood test results excluded Anna as the genetic mother. The parties agreed to a court order providing that the child would remain with Mark and Crispina on a temporary basis with visits by Anna.

At trial in October 1990, the parties stipulated that Mark and Crispina were the child's genetic parents. After hearing evidence and arguments, the trial court ruled that Mark and Crispina were the child's "genetic, biological and natural" father and mother, that Anna had no "parental" rights to the child, and that the surrogacy contract was legal and enforceable against Anna's claims. The court also terminated the order allowing visitation. Anna appealed from the trial court's judgment. The Court of Appeal for the Fourth District, Division Three, affirmed. We granted review.

. . .

Disregarding the presumptions of paternity that have no application to this case, then, we are left with the undisputed evidence that Anna, not Crispina, gave birth to the child and that Crispina, not Anna, is genetically related to him. Both women thus have adduced evidence of a mother and child relationship as contemplated by the Act. (Civ. Code, §§7003, subd. (1), 7004, subd. (a), 7015; Evid. Code, §§621, 892.)

Because two women each have presented acceptable proof of maternity, we do not believe this case can be decided without enquiring into the parties' intentions as manifested in the surrogacy agreement. Mark and Crispina are a couple who desired to have a child of their own genetic stock but are physically unable to do so without the help of reproductive technology. They affirmatively intended the birth of the child, and took the steps necessary to effect in vitro fertilization. But for their acted-on intention, the child would not exist. Anna agreed to facilitate the procreation of Mark's and Crispina's child. The parties' aim was to bring Mark's and Crispina's child into the world, not for Mark and Crispina to donate a zygote to Anna. Crispina from the outset intended to be the child's mother. Although the gestative function Anna performed was necessary to bring about the child's birth, it is safe to say that Anna would not have been given the opportunity to gestate or deliver the child had she, prior to implantation of the zygote, manifested her own intent to be the child's mother. No reason appears why Anna's later change of heart should vitiate the determination that Crispina is the child's natural mother.

. . .

Anna urges that surrogacy contracts violate several social policies. Relying on her contention that she is the child's legal, natural mother, she cites the public policy embodied in Penal Code section 273,[11] prohibiting the payment for consent to adoption of a child. She argues further that the policies underlying the adoption laws of this state are violated by the surrogacy contract because it in effect constitutes a prebirth waiver of her parental rights.

. . .

We disagree. Gestational surrogacy differs in crucial respects from adoption and so is not subject to the adoption statutes. The parties voluntarily agreed to participate in in vitro fertilization and related medical procedures before the child was conceived; at the time when Anna entered into the contract, therefore, she was not vulnerable to financial inducements to part with her own expected offspring. As discussed above, Anna was not the genetic mother of the child. The payments to Anna under the contract were meant to compensate her for her services in gestating the fetus and undergoing labor, rather than for giving up "parental" rights to the child. Payments were due both during the pregnancy and after the child's birth. We are, accordingly, unpersuaded that the contract used in this case violates the public policies embodied in Penal Code section 273 and the adoption statutes. For the same reasons, we conclude these contracts do not implicate the policies underlying the statutes governing termination of parental rights. (See Welf. & Inst. Code, §202.)

. . .

Finally, Anna and some commentators have expressed concern that surrogacy contracts tend to exploit or dehumanize women, especially women of lower economic status. Anna's objections center around the psychological harm she asserts may result from the gestator's relinquishing the child to whom she has given birth. Some have also cautioned that the practice of surrogacy may encourage society to view children as commodities, subject to trade at their parents' will.

We are all too aware that the proper forum for resolution of this issue is the Legislature, where empirical data, largely lacking from this record, can be studied and rules of general applicability developed. However, in light of our responsibility to decide this case, we have considered as best we can its possible consequences.

We are unpersuaded that gestational surrogacy arrangements are so likely to cause the untoward results Anna cites as to demand their invalidation on public

---

11. Penal Code section 273 provides, in pertinent part, as follows: "(a) It is a misdemeanor for any person or agency to offer to pay money or anything of value, or to pay money or anything of value, to a parent for the placement for adoption, for the consent to an adoption, or for cooperation in the completion of an adoption of his or her child. [¶] (b) This section does not make it unlawful to pay the maternity-connected medical or hospital and necessary living expenses of the mother preceding and during confinement as an act of charity, as long as the payment is not contingent upon placement of the child for adoption, consent to the adoption, or cooperation in the completion of the adoption."

See also Penal Code section 181, which provides: "Every person who holds, or attempts to hold, any person in involuntary servitude, or assumes, or attempts to assume, rights of ownership over any person, or who sells, or attempts to sell, any person to another, or receives money or anything of value, in consideration of placing any person in the custody, or under the power or control of another, or who buys, or attempts to buy, any person, or pays money, or delivers anything of value, to another, in consideration of having any person placed in his custody, or under his power or control, or who knowingly aids or assists in any manner any one thus offending, is punishable by imprisonment in the state prison for two, three, or four years."

policy grounds. Although common sense suggests that women of lesser means serve as surrogate mothers more often than do wealthy women, there has been no proof that surrogacy contracts exploit poor women to any greater degree than economic necessity in general exploits them by inducing them to accept lower-paid or otherwise undesirable employment. We are likewise unpersuaded by the claim that surrogacy will foster the attitude that children are mere commodities; no evidence is offered to support it. The limited data available seem to reflect an absence of significant adverse effects of surrogacy on all participants.

The argument that a woman cannot knowingly and intelligently agree to gestate and deliver a baby for intending parents carries overtones of the reasoning that for centuries prevented women from attaining equal economic rights and professional status under the law. To resurrect this view is both to foreclose a personal and economic choice on the part of the surrogate mother, and to deny intending parents what may be their only means of procreating a child of their own genetic stock. Certainly in the present case it cannot seriously be argued that Anna, a licensed vocational nurse who had done well in school and who had previously borne a child, lacked the intellectual wherewithal or life experience necessary to make an informed decision to enter into the surrogacy contract.

. . .

KENNARD, J.

When a woman who wants to have a child provides her fertilized ovum to another woman who carries it through pregnancy and gives birth to a child, who is the child's legal mother? Unlike the majority, I do not agree that the determinative consideration should be the intent to have the child that originated with the woman who contributed the ovum. In my view, the woman who provided the fertilized ovum and the woman who gave birth to the child both have substantial claims to legal motherhood. Pregnancy entails a unique commitment, both psychological and emotional, to an unborn child. No less substantial, however, is the contribution of the woman from whose egg the child developed and without whose desire the child would not exist.

For each child, California law accords the legal rights and responsibilities of parenthood to only one "natural mother." When, as here, the female reproductive role is divided between two women, California law requires courts to make a decision as to which woman is the child's natural mother, but provides no standards by which to make that decision. The majority's resort to "intent" to break the "tie" between the genetic and gestational mothers is unsupported by statute, and, in the absence of appropriate protections in the law to guard against abuse of surrogacy arrangements, it is ill-advised. To determine who is the legal mother of a child born of a gestational surrogacy arrangement, I would apply the standard most protective of child welfare-the best interests of the child.

. . .

The ethical, moral and legal implications of using gestational surrogacy for human reproduction have engendered substantial debate. A review of the scholarly literature that addresses gestational surrogacy reveals little consensus on the desirability of surrogacy arrangements, particularly those involving paid surrogacy, or on how best to decide questions of the parentage of children born of such arrangements.

Surrogacy proponents generally contend that gestational surrogacy, like the other reproductive technologies that extend the ability to procreate to persons who might not otherwise be able to have children, enhances "individual freedom, fulfillment and responsibility." (Shultz, *Reproductive Technology, supra,* 1990 Wis. L. Rev. 297, 303.) Under this view, women capable of bearing children should be allowed to freely agree to be paid to do so by infertile couples desiring to form a family.

Surrogacy critics, however, maintain that the payment of money for the gestation and relinquishment of a child threatens the economic exploitation of poor women who may be induced to engage in commercial surrogacy arrangements out of financial need. (Capron & Radin, *Choosing Family Law Over Contract Law as a Paradigm for Surrogate Motherhood,* in Surrogate Motherhood, *supra,* p. 62.) Some fear the development of a "breeder" class of poor women who will be regularly employed to bear children for the economically advantaged. (See *Women and Children Used in Systems of Surrogacy: Position Statement of the Institute on Women and Technology,* in Surrogate Motherhood, *supra,* at p. 322; and Corea, *Junk Liberty,* testimony before Cal. Assem. Judiciary Com., April 5, 1988, in Surrogate Motherhood, *supra,* at pp. 325, 335.) Others suggest that women who enter into surrogacy arrangements may underestimate the psychological impact of relinquishing a child they have nurtured in their bodies for nine months. (See Macklin, *Artificial Means of Reproduction and Our Understanding of the Family, supra,* 21 Hastings Center Rep. 5, 10.)

Gestational surrogacy is also said to be "dehumanizing" (Capron & Radin, *Choosing Family Law Over Contract Law as a Paradigm for Surrogate Motherhood,* in Surrogate Motherhood, *supra,* at p. 62) and to "commodify" women and children by treating the female reproductive capacity and the children born of gestational surrogacy arrangements as products that can be bought and sold (Radin, *Market-Inalienability* (1987) 100 Harv. L. Rev. 1849, 1930-1932). The commodification of women and children, it is feared, will reinforce oppressive gender stereotypes and threaten the well-being of all children. (*Medical Technology, supra,* 103 Harv. L. Rev. 1519, 1550; Annas, *Fairy Tales Surrogate Mothers Tell,* in Surrogate Motherhood, *supra,* p. 50.) Some critics foresee promotion of an ever-expanding "business of surrogacy brokerage." (E.g., Goodwin, *Determination of Legal Parentage, supra,* 26 Fam. L.Q. at p. 283.)

Whether surrogacy contracts are viewed as personal service agreements or agreements for the sale of the child born as the result of the agreement, commentators critical of contractual surrogacy view these contracts as contrary to public policy and thus not enforceable.

Proponents and critics of gestational surrogacy propose widely differing approaches for deciding who should be the legal mother of a child born of a gestational surrogacy arrangement. Surrogacy advocates propose to enforce preconception contracts in which gestational mothers have agreed to relinquish parental rights, and, thus, would make "bargained-for intentions determinative of legal parenthood." (Shultz, *Reproductive Technology, supra,* 1990 Wis. L. Rev. at p. 323.)

Professor Robertson, for instance, contends that "The right to noncoital, collaborative reproduction also includes the right of the parties to agree how they should allocate their obligations and entitlements with respect to the child. Legal presumptions of paternity and maternity would be overridden by this agreement of the parties." (Robertson, *Procreative Liberty and the Control of Conception, Pregnancy, and Childbirth, supra*, 69 Va. L. Rev. 405, 436; see also Shalev, Birth Power: The Case for Surrogacy, *supra*, at p. 141 [arguing for enforcing the parties' legal expectations].)

Surrogacy critics, on the other hand, consider the unique female role in human reproduction as the determinative factor in questions of legal parentage. They reason that although males and females both contribute genetic material for the child, the act of gestating the fetus falls only on the female. (See Radin, *Market-Inalienability, supra*, 100 Harv. L. Rev. 1849, 1932, fn. 285 [pointing out the "asymmetrical" interests of males and females in human reproduction].) Accordingly, in their view, a woman who, as the result of gestational surrogacy, is not genetically related to the child she bears is like any other woman who gives birth to a child. In either situation the woman giving birth is the child's mother. (See Capron & Radin, *Choosing Family Law Over Contract Law as a Paradigm for Surrogate Motherhood*, in Surrogate Motherhood, *supra*, at pp. 64-65.) Under this approach, the laws governing adoption should govern the parental rights to a child born of gestational surrogacy. Upon the birth of the child, the gestational mother can decide whether or not to relinquish her parental rights in favor of the genetic mother.

In making the intent of the genetic mother who wants to have a child the dispositive factor, the majority renders a certain result preordained and inflexible in every such case: as between an intending genetic mother and a gestational mother, the genetic mother will, under the majority's analysis, always prevail. The majority recognizes no meaningful contribution by a woman who agrees to carry a fetus to term for the genetic mother beyond that of mere employment to perform a specified biological function.

The majority's approach entirely devalues the substantial claims of motherhood by a gestational mother such as Anna. True, a woman who enters into a surrogacy arrangement intending to raise the child has by her intent manifested an assumption of parental responsibility in addition to her biological contribution of providing the genetic material. (See *Adoption of Kelsey S., supra*, 1 Cal. 4th at pp. 838, 849, 4 Cal. Rptr. 2d 615, 823 P.2d 1216.) But the gestational mother's biological contribution of carrying a child for nine months and giving birth is likewise an assumption of parental responsibility. (See Dolgin, *Just a Gene: Judicial Assumptions About Parenthood* (1993) 40 UCLA L. Rev. 637, 659.) A pregnant woman's commitment to the unborn child she carries is not just physical; it is psychological and emotional as well.

. . .

In the absence of legislation that is designed to address the unique problems of gestational surrogacy, this court should look not to tort, property or contract law, but to family law, as the governing paradigm and source of a rule of decision.

The allocation of parental rights and responsibilities necessarily impacts the welfare of a minor child. And in issues of child welfare, the standard that courts frequently apply is the best interests of the child. (See §§222.20, 222.36, 224.64

[matters relating to adoption and temporary placement], 4600 [child custody], 4601 [visitation].) Indeed, it is highly significant that the UPA itself looks to a child's best interests in deciding another question of parental rights. (§7017, subd. (d)(2).) This "best interests" standard serves to assure that in the judicial resolution of disputes affecting a child's well-being, protection of the minor child is the foremost consideration. Consequently, I would apply "the best interests of the child" standard to determine who can best assume the social and legal responsibilities of motherhood for a child born of a gestational surrogacy arrangement.

MARVIN
v.
3   # MARVIN

Supreme Court of California
18 Cal. 3d 660
1976

TOBRINER, J.

. . . In the instant case plaintiff and defendant lived together for seven years without marrying; all property acquired during this period was taken in defendant's name. When plaintiff sued to enforce a contract under which she was entitled to half the property and to support payments, the trial court granted judgment on the pleadings for defendant, thus leaving him with all property accumulated by the couple during their relationship. . . .

Since the trial court rendered judgment for defendant on the pleadings, we must accept the allegations of plaintiff's complaint as true, determining whether such allegations state, or can be amended to state, a cause of action. (*Sullivan v. County of Los Angeles* (1974) 12 Cal. 3d 710, 714-715, fn. 3 [117 Cal. Rptr. 241, 527 P.2d 865]; 4 Witkin, Cal. Procedure (2d ed. 1971) pp. 2817-2818.) We turn therefore to the specific allegations of the complaint.

Plaintiff avers that in October of 1964 she and defendant "entered into an oral agreement" that while "the parties lived together they would combine their efforts and earnings and would share equally any and all property accumulated as a result of their efforts whether individual or combined." Furthermore, they agreed to "hold themselves out to the general public as husband and wife" and that "plaintiff would further render her services as a companion, homemaker, housekeeper and cook to . . . defendant."

Shortly thereafter plaintiff agreed to "give up her lucrative career as an entertainer [and] singer" in order to "devote her full time to defendant . . . as a companion, homemaker, housekeeper and cook"; in return defendant agreed to "provide for all of plaintiff's financial support and needs for the rest of her life."

Plaintiff alleges that she lived with defendant from October of 1964 through May of 1970 and fulfilled her obligations under the agreement. During this period the parties as a result of their efforts and earnings acquired in defendant's name substantial real and personal property, including motion picture rights worth over $1 million. In May of 1970, however, defendant compelled plaintiff to leave his household. He continued to support plaintiff until November of 1971, but thereafter refused to provide further support.

. . .

Defendant first and principally relies on the contention that the alleged contract is so closely related to the supposed "immoral" character of the relationship between plaintiff and himself that the enforcement of the contract would violate public policy. He points to cases asserting that a contract between nonmarital partners is unenforceable if it is "involved in" an illicit relationship or made in "contemplation" of such a relationship. A review of the numerous California decisions concerning contracts between nonmarital partners, however, reveals that the courts have not employed such broad and uncertain standards to strike down contracts. The decisions instead disclose a narrower and more precise standard: a contract between nonmarital partners is unenforceable only *to the extent* that it *explicitly* rests upon the immoral and illicit consideration of meretricious sexual services.

. . .

Although the past decisions hover over the issue in the somewhat wispy form of the figures of a Chagall painting, we can abstract from those decisions a clear and simple rule. The fact that a man and woman live together without marriage, and engage in a sexual relationship, does not in itself invalidate agreements between them relating to their earnings, property, or expenses. Neither is such an agreement invalid merely because the parties may have contemplated the creation or continuation of a nonmarital relationship when they entered into it. Agreements between nonmarital partners fail only to the extent that they rest upon a consideration of meretricious sexual services. Thus the rule asserted by defendant, that a contract fails if it is "involved in" or made "in contemplation" of a nonmarital relationship, cannot be reconciled with the decisions.

The three cases cited by defendant which have *declined* to enforce contracts between nonmarital partners involved consideration that *was* expressly founded upon an illicit sexual services. In *Hill v. Estate of Westbrook, supra*, 95 Cal. App. 2d 599, the woman promised to keep house for the man, to live with him as man and wife, and to bear his children; the man promised to provide for her in his will, but died without doing so. Reversing a judgment for the woman based on the reasonable value of her services, the Court of Appeal stated that "the action is predicated upon a claim which seeks, among other things, the reasonable value of living with decedent in meretricious relationship and bearing him two children. . . . The law does not award compensation for living with a man as a concubine and bearing him children. . . . As the judgment is at least in part, for the value of the claimed services for which recovery cannot be had, it must be reversed." (95 Cal. App. 2d at p. 603.) Upon retrial, the trial court found that it could not sever the contract and place an independent value upon the legitimate services performed by claimant. We therefore affirmed a judgment for the estate. (*Hill v. Estate of Westbrook* (1952) 39 Cal. 2d 458 [247 P.2d 19].)

In the only other cited decision refusing to enforce a contract, *Updeck v. Samuel* (1954) 123 Cal. App. 2d 264 [266 P.2d 822], the contract "was based on the consideration that the parties live together as husband and wife." (123 Cal. App. 2d at p. 267.) Viewing the contract as calling for adultery, the court held it illegal.

The decision in the *Hill* and *Updeck* cases thus demonstrate that a contract between nonmarital partners, even if expressly made in contemplation of a common living arrangement, is invalid only if sexual acts form an inseparable part of the consideration for the agreement. In sum, a court will not enforce a contract for the pooling of property and earnings if it is explicitly and inseparably based upon services as a paramour. The Court of Appeal opinion in *Hill*, however, indicates that even if sexual services are part of the contractual consideration, any *severable* portion of the contract supported by independent consideration will still be enforced.

. . .

Similarly, in the present case a standard which inquires whether an agreement is "involved" in or "contemplates" a nonmarital relationship is vague and unworkable. Virtually all agreements between nonmarital partners can be said to be "involved" in some sense in the fact of their mutual sexual relationship, or to "contemplate" the existence of that relationship. Thus defendant's proposed standards, if taken literally, might invalidate all agreements between nonmarital partners, a result no one favors. Moreover, those standards offer no basis to distinguish between valid and invalid agreements. By looking not to such uncertain tests, but only to the consideration underlying the agreement, we provide the parties and the courts with a practical guide to determine when an agreement between nonmarital partners should be enforced.

. . .

We are aware that many young couples live together without the solemnization of marriage, in order to make sure that they can successfully later undertake marriage. This trial period, preliminary to marriage, serves as some assurance that the marriage will not subsequently end in dissolution to the harm of both parties. We are aware, as we have stated, of the pervasiveness of nonmarital relationships in other situations.

The mores of the society have indeed changed so radically in regard to cohabitation that we cannot impose a standard based on alleged moral considerations that have apparently been so widely abandoned by so many. Lest we be misunderstood, however, we take this occasion to point out that the structure of society itself largely depends upon the institution of marriage, and nothing we have said in this opinion should be taken to derogate from that institution. The joining of the man and woman in marriage is at once the most socially productive and individually fulfilling relationship that one can enjoy in the course of a lifetime.

We conclude that the judicial barriers that may stand in the way of a policy based upon the fulfillment of the reasonable expectations of the parties to a nonmarital relationship should be removed. As we have explained, the courts now hold that express agreements will be enforced unless they rest on an unlawful meretricious consideration. . . .

Since we have determined that plaintiff's complaint states a cause of action for breach of an express contract, and, as we have explained, can be amended to state a cause of action independent of allegations of express contract, we must conclude that the trial court erred in granting defendant a judgment on the pleadings.

The judgment is reversed and the cause remanded for further proceedings consistent with the views expressed herein.

HEWITT
v.
HEWITT
Supreme Court of Illinois
77 Ill. 2d 49
1979

UNDERWOOD, J.

The issue in this case is whether plaintiff Victoria Hewitt, whose complaint alleges she lived with defendant Robert Hewitt from 1960 to 1975 in an unmarried, family-like relationship to which three children have been born, may recover from him "an equal share of the profits and properties accumulated by the parties" during that period.

. . .

The factual background alleged or testified to is that in June 1960, when she and defendant were students at Grinnell College in Iowa, plaintiff became pregnant; that defendant thereafter told her that they were husband and wife and would live as such, no formal ceremony being necessary, and that he would "share his life, his future, his earnings and his property" with her; that the parties immediately announced to their respective parents that they were married and thereafter held themselves out as husband and wife; that in reliance on defendant's promises she devoted her efforts to his professional education and his establishment in the practice of pedodontia, obtaining financial assistance from her parents for this purpose; that she assisted defendant in his career with her own special skills and although she was given payroll checks for these services she placed them in a common fund; that defendant, who was without funds at the time of the marriage, as a result of her efforts now earns over $80,000 a year and has accumulated large amounts of property, owned either jointly with her or separately; that she has given him every assistance a wife and mother could give, including social activities designed to enhance his social and professional reputation.

The amended complaint was also dismissed, the trial court finding that Illinois law and public policy require such claims to be based on a valid marriage. The appellate court reversed, stating that because the parties had outwardly lived a conventional married life, plaintiff's conduct had not "so affronted public policy that she should be denied any and all relief" (62 Ill. App. 3d 861, 869, 20 Ill. Dec. 476, 482, 380 N.E.2d 454, 460), and that plaintiff's complaint stated a cause of action on an express oral contract. We granted leave to appeal. Defendant apparently does not contest his obligation to support the children, and that question is not before us.

. . .

In finding that plaintiff's complaint stated a cause of action on an express oral contract, the appellate court adopted the reasoning of the California Supreme Court in the widely publicized case of Marvin v. Marvin (1976), 18 Cal. 3d 660, 134 Cal. Rptr. 815, 557 P.2d 106, quoting extensively therefrom. . . .

It is apparent that the *Marvin* court adopted a pure contract theory, under which, if the intent of the parties and the terms of their agreement are proved, the pseudo-conventional family relationship which impressed the appellate court here is irrelevant; recovery may be had unless the implicit sexual relationship is made the explicit consideration for the agreement. . . .

. . . We are aware, of course, of the increasing judicial attention given the individual claims of unmarried cohabitants to jointly accumulated property, and the fact that the majority of courts considering the question have recognized an equitable or contractual basis for implementing the reasonable expectations of the parties unless sexual services were the explicit consideration. (See cases collected in Annot., 31 A.L.R.2d 1255 (1953) and A.L.R.2d Later Case Service supplementing vols. 25 to 31.) The issue of unmarried cohabitants' mutual property rights, however, as we earlier noted, cannot appropriately be characterized solely in terms of contract law, nor is it limited to considerations of equity or fairness as between the parties to such relationships. There are major public policy questions involved in determining whether, under what circumstances, and to what extent it is desirable to accord some type of legal status to claims arising from such relationships. Of substantially greater importance than the rights of the immediate parties is the impact of such recognition upon our society and the institution of marriage. Will the fact that legal rights closely resembling those arising from conventional marriages can be acquired by those who deliberately choose to enter into what have heretofore been commonly referred to as "illicit" or "meretricious" relationships encourage formation of such relationships and weaken marriage as the foundation of our family-based society? In the event of death shall the survivor have the status of a surviving spouse for purposes of inheritance, wrongful death actions, workmen's compensation, etc.? And still more importantly: what of the children born of such relationships? What are their support and inheritance rights and by what standards are custody questions resolved? What of the sociological and psychological effects upon them of that type of environment? Does not the recognition of legally enforceable property and custody rights emanating from nonmarital cohabitation in practical effect equate with the legalization of common law marriage at least in the circumstances of this case? And, in summary, have the increasing numbers of unmarried cohabitants and changing mores of our society (Bruch, Property Rights of De Facto Spouses Including Thoughts on the Value of Homemakers' Services, 10 Fam. L.Q. 101, 102-03 (1976); Nielson, In re Cary: A Judicial Recognition of Illicit Cohabitation, 25 Hastings L.J. 1226 (1974)) reached the point at which the general welfare of the citizens of this State is best served by a return to something resembling the judicially created common law marriage our legislature outlawed in 1905?

Illinois' public policy regarding agreements such as the one alleged here was implemented long ago in Wallace v. Rappleye (1882), 103 Ill. 229, 249, where this court said: "An agreement in consideration of future illicit cohabitation between the plaintiffs is void." This is the traditional rule, in force until recent years in all jurisdictions. (See, e. g., Gauthier v. Laing (1950), 96 N.H. 80, 70 A.2d 207; Grant v. Butt (1941), 198 S.C. 298, 17 S.E.2d 689.) Section 589 of the Restatement of Contracts (1932) states, "A bargain in whole or in part for or in consideration of illicit sexual intercourse or of a promise thereof is illegal." See also 6A Corbin, Contracts sec. 1476 (1962), and cases cited therein.

It is true, of course, that cohabitation by the parties may not prevent them from forming valid contracts about independent matters, for which it is said the sexual relations do not form part of the consideration. (Restatement of Contracts secs. 589, 597 (1932); 6A Corbin, Contracts sec. 1476 (1962).) Those courts which allow recovery generally have relied on this principle to reduce the scope of the rule of illegality. Thus, California courts long prior to *Marvin* held that an express agreement to pool earnings is supported by independent consideration and is not invalidated by cohabitation of the parties, the agreements being regarded as simultaneous but separate. (See, e. g., Trutalli v. Meraviglia (1932), 215 Cal. 698, 12 P.2d 430; see also Annot., 31 A.L.R.2d 1255 (1953), and cases cited therein.) More recently, several courts have reasoned that the rendition of housekeeping and homemaking services such as plaintiff alleges here could be regarded as the consideration for a separate contract between the parties, severable from the illegal contract founded on sexual relations. In Latham v. Latham (1976), 274 Or. 421, 547 P.2d 144, and Carlson v. Olson (Minn. 1977), 256 N.W.2d 249, on allegations similar to those in this case, the Minnesota Supreme Court adopted *Marvin* and the Oregon court expressly held that agreements in consideration of cohabitation were not void, stating:

> "We are not validating an agreement in which the only or primary consideration is sexual intercourse. The agreement here contemplated all the burdens and amenities of married life." 274 Or. 421, 427, 547 P.2d 144, 147.

The real thrust of plaintiff's argument here is that we should abandon the rule of illegality because of certain changes in societal norms and attitudes. It is urged that social mores have changed radically in recent years, rendering this principle of law archaic. It is said that because there are so many unmarried cohabitants today the courts must confer a legal status on such relationships. This, of course, is the rationale underlying some of the decisions and commentaries. If this is to be the result, however, it would seem more candid to acknowledge the return of varying forms of common law marriage than to continue displaying the naivete we believe involved in the assertion that there are involved in these relationships contracts separate and independent from the sexual activity, and the assumption that those contracts would have been entered into or would continue without that activity.

Even if we were to assume some modification of the rule of illegality is appropriate, we return to the fundamental question earlier alluded to: If resolution of this issue rests ultimately on grounds of public policy, by what body should that policy be determined? *Marvin*, viewing the issue as governed solely by contract law, found judicial policy-making appropriate. Its decision was facilitated by California precedent and that State's no-fault divorce law. In our view, however, the situation alleged here was not the kind of arm's length bargain envisioned by traditional contract principles, but an intimate arrangement of a fundamentally different kind. The issue, realistically, is whether it is appropriate for this court to grant a legal status to a private arrangement substituting for the institution of marriage sanctioned by the State. The question whether change is needed in the law governing the rights of parties in this delicate area of marriage-like relationships involves evaluations of sociological data and alternatives we believe best suited to the superior investigative and fact-finding facilities of the legislative branch in the exercise of its traditional authority to declare public policy in the domestic relations field. (Strukoff v. Strukoff (1979), 76 Ill. 2d 53, 27 Ill. Dec. 762, 389 N.E.2d 1170; Siegall v. Solomon (1960), 19 Ill. 2d 145, 166 N.E.2d 5.) That belief is reinforced by the fact that judicial recognition of mutual property rights between unmarried cohabitants would, in our opinion, clearly violate the policy of our recently enacted Illinois Marriage and Dissolution of Marriage Act. Although the Act does not specifically address the subject of nonmarital cohabitation, we think the legislative policy quite evident from the statutory scheme.

The Act provides:

"This Act shall be liberally construed and applied to promote its underlying purposes, which are to:

(1) provide adequate procedures for the solemnization and registration of marriage;

(2) strengthen and preserve the integrity of marriage and safeguard family relationships." (Ill. Rev. Stat.1977, ch. 40, par. 102.)

We cannot confidently say that judicial recognition of property rights between unmarried cohabitants will not make that alternative to marriage more attractive by allowing the parties to engage in such relationships with greater security. As one commentator has noted, it may make this alternative especially attractive to persons who seek a property arrangement that the law does not permit to marital partners. (Comment, 90 Harv. L. Rev. 1708, 1713 (1977).) This court, for example, has held void agreements releasing husbands from their obligation to support their wives. In thus potentially enhancing the attractiveness of a private arrangement over marriage, we believe that the appellate court decision in this case contravenes the Act's policy of strengthening and preserving the integrity of marriage.

The Act also provides: "Common law marriages contracted in this State after June 30, 1905 are invalid." (Ill. Rev. Stat. 1977, ch. 40, par. 214.) The doctrine of common law marriage was a judicially sanctioned alternative to formal marriage designed to apply to cases like the one before us. In Port v. Port (1873), 70 Ill. 484, this court reasoned that because the statute governing marriage did not "prohibit or declare void a marriage not solemnized in accordance with its provisions, a marriage without observing the statutory regulations, if made according to the common law, will still be a valid marriage." (70 Ill. 484, 486.) This court held that if the parties declared their present intent to take each other as husband and wife and thereafter did so a valid common law marriage existed. (Cartwright v. McGown (1887), 121 Ill. 388, 398, 12 N.E. 737.) Such marriages were legislatively abolished in 1905, presumably because of the problems earlier noted, and the above-quoted language expressly reaffirms that policy.

While the appellate court denied that its decision here served to rehabilitate the doctrine of common law marriage, we are not persuaded. Plaintiff's allegations disclose a relationship that clearly would have constituted a valid common law marriage in this State prior to 1905. The parties expressly manifested their present intent to be husband and wife; immediately thereafter they assumed the marital status; and for many years they consistently held themselves out to their relatives and the public at large as husband and wife. Revealingly, the appellate court relied on the fact that the parties were, to the public, husband and wife in determining that the parties' living arrangement did not flout Illinois public policy. It is of course true, as plaintiff argues, that unlike a common law spouse she would not have full marital rights in that she could not, for example, claim her statutory one-third share of defendant's property on his death. The distinction appears unimpressive, however, if she can claim one-half of his property on a theory of express or implied contract.

Further, in enacting the Illinois Marriage and Dissolution of Marriage Act, our legislature considered and rejected the "no-fault" divorce concept that has been adopted in many other jurisdictions, including California. (See Uniform Marriage and Divorce Act secs. 302, 305.) Illinois appears to be one of three States retaining fault grounds for dissolution of marriage. (Ill. Rev. Stat. 1977, ch. 40, par. 401; Comment, Hewitt v. Hewitt, Contract Cohabitation and Equitable Expectations Relief for Meretricious Spouses, 12 J. Mar. J. Prac. & Proc. 435, 452-53 (1979).) Certainly a significantly stronger promarriage policy is manifest in that action, which appears to us to reaffirm the traditional doctrine that marriage is a civil contract between three parties[:] the husband, the wife and the State. (Johnson v. Johnson (1942), 381 Ill. 362, 45 N.E.2d 625; VanKoten v. VanKoten (1926), 323 Ill. 323, 154 N.E. 146.) The policy of the Act gives the State a strong continuing interest in the institution of marriage and prevents the marriage relation from becoming in effect a private contract terminable at will. This seems to us another indication that public policy disfavors private contractual alternatives to marriage.

Lastly, in enacting the Illinois Marriage and Dissolution of Marriage Act, the legislature adopted for the first time the civil law concept of the putative spouse. The Act provides that an unmarried person may acquire the rights of a legal spouse only if he goes through a marriage ceremony and cohabits with another in the good-faith belief that he is validly married. When he learns that the marriage is not valid his status as a putative spouse terminates; common law marriages are expressly excluded. (Ill. Rev. Stat. 1977, ch. 40, par. 305.) The legislature thus extended legal recognition to a class of nonmarital relationships, but only to the extent of a party's good-faith belief in the existence of a valid marriage. Moreover, during the legislature's deliberations on the Act *Marvin* was decided and received wide publicity. (See Note, 12 J. Mar. J. Prac. & Proc. 435, 450 (1979).) These circumstances in our opinion constitute a recent and unmistakable legislative judgment disfavoring the grant of mutual property rights to knowingly unmarried cohabitants. We have found no case in which recovery has been allowed in the face of a legislative declaration as recently and clearly enacted as ours. Even if we disagreed with the wisdom of that judgment, it is not for us to overturn or erode it. Davis v. Commonwealth Edison Co. (1975), 61 Ill. 2d 494, 496-97, 336 N.E.2d 881.

Actually, however, the legislature judgment is in accord with the history of common law marriage in this country. "Despite its judicial acceptance in many states, the doctrine of common-law marriage is generally frowned on in this country, even in some of the states that have accepted it." (52 Am. Jur. 2d 902 Marriage sec. 46 (1970).) Its origins, early history and problems are detailed in In re Estate of Ooeder (1966), 7 Ohio App. 2d 271, 220 N.E.2d 547, where that court noted that some 30 States did not authorize common law marriage. Judicial criticism has been widespread even in States recognizing the relationship. (See, e. g., Baker v. Mitchell (1941), 143 Pa. Super. 50, 54, 17 A.2d 738, 741, "a fruitful source of perjury and fraud . . ."; Sorensen v. Sorensen (1904), 68 Neb. 500, 100 N.W. 930.) "It tends to weaken the public estimate of the sanctity of the marriage relation. It puts in doubt the certainty of the rights of inheritance. It opens the door to false pretenses of marriage and the imposition on estates of suppositious heirs." 7 Ohio App. 2d 271, 290, 220 N.E.2d 547, 561.

. . .

We accordingly hold that plaintiff's claims are unenforceable for the reason that they contravene the public policy, implicit in the statutory scheme of the Illinois Marriage and Dissolution of Marriage Act, disfavoring the grant of mutually enforceable property rights to knowingly unmarried cohabitants. The judgment of the appellate court is reversed and the judgment of the circuit court of Champaign County is affirmed.

Appellate court reversed; circuit court affirmed.

Problems

1. The Effective Lobbyist. Lobbyist Alfred Arcidi entered into a consulting contract with the National Association of Government Employees, a union made up of state, federal, and municipal workers, that called for Arcidi to be paid $250,000 if the Massachusetts Turnpike Authority (MTA) awarded a contract to a subsidiary of the union that managed real estate development projects. Massachusetts law provides that "[n]o person shall make any agreement whereby any compensation or thing of value is to be paid to any person contingent upon a decision [by a Massachusetts officer or 'authority,' including the MTA]."

The contract was awarded, and the union paid Arcidi $200,000. Arcidi sued the union for the $50,000 unpaid balance on the contract, and the union counterclaimed for the return of the $200,000 already paid. Which side is entitled to recover?

2. The Unlicensed Subcontractor. Pacific West Construction (Pac-West) won a public works bid to build a hospital in Idaho and subcontracted a portion of the work to Quality Interiors. Quality did not possess the public works license required for it to work as a subcontractor on the job, so the two companies agreed that Quality would perform its work under the pretense that its laborers were actually Pac-West employees.

After working on the job for more than a month, Quality had a dispute with Pac-West over the scope of its responsibilities under the subcontract. Pac-West ultimately ordered the Quality workers off the jobsite and subsequently refused to make any payments on the subcontract. Bill Barry, Quality's owner, sued Pac-West for breach of contract. Should public policy concerns affect the court's enforcement of the contract terms?

3. Skipping Bail. As part of the purchase of bail bonds from Colorado bondsman Robert Thorpe, Gerald Lee consented to be apprehended and returned by any agent hired by the bondsman should Lee depart from the jurisdiction. Shortly thereafter, Lee fled to Utah, where he was pursued and captured by Miles Langley, a bail bond recovery agent working for Thorpe. Utah law provides legal protections for actions taken by bail bond recovery agents to apprehend fugitives when the agents are licensed by the state. The law also establishes requirements for qualifying for a license, including necessary training and a minimum number of hours worked in law enforcement. Langley was a licensed bail bond recovery agent in Colorado, but not in Utah.

Lee brought a civil lawsuit against Langley alleging, among other things, false imprisonment, and Langley moved for summary judgment on the ground that Lee consented to his apprehension as part of the bail contract. Assume (a) that the facts would support Lee's false imprisonment claim were it not for the bail contract, and (b) that Utah's bail bond statute would protect Langley if Langley were a licensed bail bond recovery agent in Utah. How, if at all, should Utah public policy affect the court's ruling as to whether the bail contract is enforceable to defeat Lee's lawsuit?

4. Father or Sperm Donor? Unable to conceive a child due to a tubal ligation, Ivonne Ferguson asked Joel McKiernan, her former boyfriend, to provide her with sperm so that she could have a child by *in vitro* fertilization. Ferguson agreed to release McKiernan from any claims of financial responsibility for the child, and McKiernan agreed not to seek parental rights. McKiernan provided a sperm sample at the office of Ferguson's physician, which was used to fertilize McKiernan's eggs *in vitro*. Resulting embryos were then implanted into Ferguson's womb, and she subsequently gave birth to twins. Several years later, Ferguson sued McKiernan for parental support.

Pennsylvania law provides that "in every case where children are born out of wedlock, they shall enjoy all the rights and privileges as if they had been born during the wedlock of their parents. . . ." The Uniform Parentage Act, a uniform law proposed by the American Bar Association and adopted by 19 states, but not Pennsylvania, provides that "[a] [sperm] donor is not a parent of a child conceived by means of assisted reproduction."

Who should prevail in the litigation?

Chapter 4

Contract Interpretation

What we think of as "contract law" consists of both the rules for determining whether two or more parties have a legally enforceable agreement and the rules for determining the substance of those agreements. Chapters 1-3 concern the first set of rules. Chapter 4 begins our exploration of the second set of rules. Formation and enforceability doctrines form the critical foundation of contract law. Contract interpretation doctrines, however, are arguably even more important due to the simple fact that parties are more likely to disagree over the content of their obligations than over whether they have entered into an enforceable agreement.

The issues considered in this chapter can be roughly divided into two categories. First, when a contract exists, *which* statements of rights and duties establish performance obligations or limitations? Section A begins by considering the extent to which terms included in standard form contracts are enforceable against the party that did not draft those terms, even though the non-drafting party often will not have read the terms or had any opportunity to bargain over them. Section B expands the inquiry to consider the UCC's attempts to determine rights and duties when parties use a form that conflicts with prior communications or competing forms that disagree. Section C concerns the parol evidence rule, which applies to conflicts that arise when the obligations memorialized in a final, written document are different from those on which the parties agreed at an earlier time.

Second, once it has been decided which terms form the substance of a contract, how is *meaning* inferred from or assigned to those terms? Section D considers the interpretive tools that courts use to identify the substantive requirements of contracts when parties agreed on certain language at the time of formation but later disagree about its meaning. Section E surveys the way courts interpret, in the context of individualized agreements, the requirement of "good faith and fair dealing" that the law imposes on all contractual relationships.

A. STANDARD FORM CONTRACTS

The principal doctrines of contract law evolved in centuries past, when parties usually created a new agreement for each new transaction. Such individualized contracting is no longer the norm, at least not for a large percentage of economic activity. Contracts today frequently are drafted by one party for use in multiple, similar transactions and then presented as "standard forms" to the other party for his or her assent. You have, no doubt, been a party to countless standardized forms in your life, ranging from minor transactions, such as updating software, to significant ones, like renting an apartment. Most standard form contracts are presented as contracts of adhesion, meaning that the drafting party offers the terms as a single, nonnegotiable, take-it-or-leave-it proposition.

Most merchants who sell goods or services to a large number of buyers and many commercial buyers who purchase from a variety of different vendors create standard form contracts to simplify deals, reduce transaction costs, and control their agents. Virtually all commentators agree that modern commerce depends upon this type of mechanism. Notwithstanding their obvious utility, standard form contracts are also notable for the well-known fact that very few non-drafting parties read their terms carefully, if at all. Non-drafting parties have challenged the enforceability of particular terms on the grounds that the non-drafting party lacked notice of those terms, that she had no meaningful choice but to accept those terms, or that the terms were substantively unfair.

Courts generally respond to such challenges to standard form contracts by observing that contracting parties have a "duty to read," and as a result, a lack of actual, specific notice of the content of a particular term in an agreed-upon contract is not sufficient grounds for contesting the enforceability of that term. (Many legislatures, however, have passed statutes that require certain types of terms be individually signed or initialed, in order to guarantee that non-drafting parties have actual notice of the terms.) The rationale behind a duty to read is intuitive: if enforceability depended on whether a non-drafting party actually read a particular term, there would be a powerful incentive for willful ignorance. Most courts have also determined that the adhesive nature of a term is not sufficiently problematic to justify non-enforcement, because non-drafting parties usually have the ability to shop for more desirable terms or to decline to enter into a particular type of transaction altogether if they are unhappy with the terms on offer.

Although enforceable as a general rule, standard form contracts coexist uneasily with classical contract law doctrine, which implicitly assumes that every term embodied in a contract reflects an autonomous choice by both parties to accept that term as part of the deal. The assumption of informed choice consequently ensures that every contract is economically efficient as between the parties, because parties will enter into agreements only if they believe that they will be made better off as a result. If this assumption is unjustified, as a factual matter, the conceptual edifice of contract law appears less solid. For this reason, courts often apply greater scrutiny to a term embodied in a standard form than they would apply to the same term had it been individually negotiated, and judges have refused to enforce such terms in some circumstances. The rules concerning when standard form terms are unenforceable remain contested and in flux.

The following set of cases illustrates how courts have struggled to identify consistent and meaningful criteria for evaluating concerns raised by standard forms. In the initial trio of cases—*Healy v. New York Central & Hudson River Railroad Company*, *Hill v. Gateway 2000, Inc.*, and *Specht v. Netscape Communications Corporation*—the courts are most concerned with whether the non-drafting party can be fairly said to have assented to the terms at issue. The next pair of cases—*O'Callaghan v. Walker & Beckwith Realty Company* and *Tunkl v. The Regents of the University of California*—primarily concerns the use of the public policy doctrine to police terms encased in standard forms. The final two cases—*Carnival Cruise Lines, Inc. v. Shute* and *Armendariz v. Foundation Health Psychcare Services, Inc.*—illustrate a judicial evolution from an inchoate concern with procedural and substantive fairness of standard form terms to the use of the unconscionability doctrine to evaluate whether such terms should be enforced as part of the parties' contract.

HEALY
v.
N.Y. CENTRAL & HUDSON RIVER R.R. CO.
Supreme Court, Appellate Division, Third Department, New York
138 N.Y.S. 287
1912

Lyon, J.

This action was brought to recover the value of a handbag and contents, which the plaintiff on the afternoon of November 4, 1911, checked at the parcel room of the defendant at its station in the city of Albany, receiving therefor a duplicate cardboard coupon, two by three inches in size, upon the face of which was printed:

> New York Central Lines
> New York Central & Hudson River Railroad Company.
> Duplicate Coupon.
> N. B.—See conditions on back.
> Albany.
> Received .. . .
> Delivered .. . .
> 73815
> Series A
> 251

Upon the back of the coupon was printed:

> New York Central & Hud. Riv. R.R. Co
> Duplicate Coupon.

> To claim parcel, this coupon must be presented at parcel room, Albany between the hours during which the room is open for business.
>
> Charges 10 cents for first 24 hours, and 5 cents for each additional 24 hours, or fraction thereof, on each piece of handbag, parcel, etc. Glass, china, etc., taken only at owner's risk of breakage. The depositor in accepting this duplicate coupon expressly agrees that the company shall not be liable to him or her for any loss or damage of any piece to an amount exceeding TEN DOLLARS.
>
> W. M. Skinner, General Baggage Agent.

The words assuming to limit the liability of the defendant were in fine print, with the exception of the words "ten dollars." The plaintiff, upon receiving the coupon, put it in his pocket without reading it, and without his attention having been called to the limitation of liability printed thereon. About 10 o'clock in the evening of that day the plaintiff presented the coupon at the parcel room and demanded his handbag. An investigation showed that, through the mistake of the person in charge of the parcel room, coupons had been mismatched, and the plaintiff's handbag had been delivered to another person. It has never been recovered, and its value, with the contents, was $70.10, for which sum, with costs, the lower court rendered judgment against the defendant. Liability for the loss is conceded, but the defendant claims that the liability is limited to $10, and that is the sole question involved upon this appeal.

. . .

. . . [U]nder the circumstances disclosed by the record the unreasonable condition printed upon the coupon, attempting to limit the liability of the defendant to not exceeding $10, was void. Had notice been given by the bailee to the bailor of the condition limiting the liability of the former, and the latter then seen fit to enter into the bailment, a different question would be presented. But in the case at bar no notice whatever was given to the bailor of the existence of this condition; neither was there anything connected with the transaction, which was for the mutual benefit of both parties, which would tend in any way to suggest to a reasonably prudent man, or lead him to suspect, the existence of such a special contract, or tend to put him on guard or on inquiry relative thereto.

The coupon was presumptively intended as between the parties to serve the special purpose of affording a means of identifying the parcel left by the bailor. In the mind of the bailor the little piece of cardboard, which was undoubtedly hurriedly handed to him, and which he doubtless as hurriedly slipped into his pocket, without any reasonable opportunity to read it, and hastened away without any suggestion having been made upon the part of the parcel room clerk as to the statements in fine print thereon, did not arise to the dignity of a contract by which he agreed that in the event of the loss of the parcel, even through the negligence of the bailee itself, he would accept therefor a sum which, perhaps, would be but a small fraction of its actual value.

The plaintiff having had no knowledge of the existence of the special contract limiting the liability of the defendant to an amount not exceeding $10, and not being chargeable with such knowledge, the minds of the parties never met thereon, and the plaintiff cannot be deemed to have assented thereto, and is not bound thereby.

The judgment entered upon the decision of the County Court, awarding to the plaintiff the full value of the handbag and contents, together with the costs of the action, should be affirmed, with costs of this appeal to the respondent.

All concur; HOUGHTON, J., in memorandum.

. . . The business of checking hand baggage at railway stations has become a large and important one. It seems to me that anyone in the ordinary course of business, checking his baggage at such a place, would regard the check received as a mere token to enable him to identify his baggage when called for, and that in no sense would he have any reason to believe that it embodied a contract exempting the bailee from liability or limiting the amount thereof. If the plaintiff knew that the defendant had limited its liability to $10, either by his attention being called to it or otherwise, then, of course, the law would deem him to have assented to it, so that a binding contract would be affected. If he did not know it, I think the law imposed no duty upon him to read his check to find whether or not there was a contract printed thereon, or that he was guilty of neglect in not so reading it, because he had no reason to apprehend that a contract was printed thereon.

On this ground I think the plaintiff was entitled to recover the full value of his bag and its contents. . . .

HILL
v.
GATEWAY 2000, INC.

U.S. Court of Appeals, Seventh Circuit
105 F.3d 1147
1997

EASTERBROOK, J.

A customer picks up the phone, orders a computer, and gives a credit card number. Presently a box arrives, containing the computer and a list of terms, said to govern unless the customer returns the computer within 30 days. Are these terms effective as the parties' contract, or is the contract term-free because the order-taker did not read any terms over the phone and elicit the customer's assent?

One of the terms in the box containing a Gateway 2000 system was an arbitration clause. Rich and Enza Hill, the customers, kept the computer more than 30 days before complaining about its components and performance. They filed suit in federal court arguing, among other things, that the product's shortcomings make Gateway a racketeer (mail and wire fraud are said to be the predicate offenses), leading to treble damages under RICO for the Hills and a class of all other purchasers. Gateway asked the district court to enforce the arbitration clause; the judge refused, writing that "[t]he present record is insufficient to support a finding of a valid arbitration agreement between the parties or that the plaintiffs were given adequate notice of the arbitration clause." Gateway took an immediate appeal, as is its right. 9 U.S.C. §16(a)(1)(A).

The Hills say that the arbitration clause did not stand out: they concede noticing the statement of terms but deny reading it closely enough to discover the agreement to arbitrate, and they ask us to conclude that they therefore may go to court. Yet an agreement to arbitrate must be enforced "save upon such grounds as exist at law or in equity for the revocation of any contract." 9 U.S.C. §2. *Doctor's Associates, Inc. v. Casarotto,* 517 U.S. 681 (1996), holds that this provision of the Federal Arbitration Act is inconsistent with any requirement that an arbitration clause be prominent. A contract need not be read to be effective; people who accept take the risk that the unread terms may in retrospect prove unwelcome. *Carr v. CIGNA Securities, Inc.,* 95 F.3d 544, 547 (7th Cir. 1996); *Chicago Pacific Corp. v. Canada Life Assurance Co.,* 850 F.2d 334 (7th Cir. 1988). Terms inside Gateway's box stand or fall together. If they constitute the parties' contract because the Hills had an opportunity to return the computer after reading them, then all must be enforced.

ProCD, Inc. v. Zeidenberg, 86 F.3d 1447 (7th Cir. 1996), holds that terms inside a box of software bind consumers who use the software after an opportunity to read the terms and to reject them by returning the product. Likewise, *Carnival Cruise Lines, Inc. v. Shute,* 499 U.S. 585 (1991), enforces a forum-selection clause that was included among three pages of terms attached to a cruise ship ticket. *ProCD* and *Carnival Cruise Lines* exemplify the many commercial transactions in which people pay for products with terms to follow; *ProCD* discusses others. 86 F.3d at 1451-52. The district court concluded in *ProCD* that the contract is formed when the consumer pays for the software; as a result, the court held, only terms known to the consumer at that moment are part of the contract, and provisos inside the box do not count. Although this is one way a contract could be formed, it is not the only way: "A vendor, as master of the offer, may invite acceptance by conduct, and may propose limitations on the kind of conduct that constitutes acceptance. A buyer may accept by performing the acts the vendor proposes to treat as acceptance." *Id.* at 1452. Gateway shipped computers with the same sort of accept-or-return offer ProCD made to users of its software. *ProCD* relied on the Uniform Commercial Code rather than any peculiarities of Wisconsin law; both Illinois and South Dakota, the two states whose law might govern relations between Gateway and the Hills, have adopted the UCC; neither side has pointed us to any atypical doctrines in those states that might be pertinent; *ProCD* therefore applies to this dispute.

Plaintiffs ask us to limit *ProCD* to software, but where's the sense in that? *ProCD* is about the law of contract, not the law of software. Payment preceding the revelation of full terms is common for air transportation, insurance, and many other endeavors. Practical considerations support allowing vendors to enclose the full legal terms with their products. Cashiers cannot be expected to read legal documents to customers before ringing up sales. If the staff at the other end of the phone for direct-sales operations such as Gateway's had to read the four-page statement of terms before taking the buyer's credit card number, the droning voice would anesthetize rather than enlighten many potential buyers. Others would hang up in a rage over the waste of their time. And oral recitation would not avoid customers' assertions (whether true or feigned) that the clerk did not read term X to them, or that they did not remember or understand it. Writing provides benefits for both sides of commercial transactions. Customers as a group are better off when vendors skip costly and ineffectual steps such as telephonic recitation, and use instead a simple approve-or-return device. Competent adults are bound by such documents, read or unread. For what little it is worth, we add that the box from Gateway was crammed with software. The computer came with an operating system, without which it was useful only as a boat anchor. See *Digital Equipment Corp. v. Uniq Digital Technologies, Inc.,* 73 F.3d 756, 761 (7th Cir. 1996). Gateway also included many application programs. So the Hills' effort to limit *ProCD* to software would not avail them factually, even if it were sound legally—which it is not.

For their second sally, the Hills contend that *ProCD* should be limited to executory contracts (to licenses in particular), and therefore does not apply because both parties' performance of this contract was complete when the box arrived at their home. This is legally and factually wrong: legally because the question at hand concerns the *formation* of the contract rather than its *performance*, and factually because both contracts were incompletely performed. *ProCD* did not depend on the fact that the seller characterized the transaction as a license rather than as a contract; we treated it as a contract for the sale of goods and reserved the question whether for other purposes a "license" characterization might be preferable. 86 F.3d at 1450. All debates about characterization to one side, the transaction in *ProCD* was no more executory than the one here: Zeidenberg paid for the software and walked out of the store with a box under his arm, so if arrival of the box with the product ends the time for revelation of contractual terms, then the time ended in *ProCD* before Zeidenberg opened the box. But of course ProCD had not completed performance with delivery of the box, and neither had Gateway. One element of the transaction was the warranty, which obliges sellers to fix defects in their products. The Hills have invoked Gateway's warranty and are not satisfied with its response, so they are not well positioned to say that Gateway's obligations were fulfilled when the motor carrier unloaded the box. What is more, both ProCD and Gateway promised to help customers to use their products. Long-term service and information obligations are common in the computer business, on both hardware and software sides. Gateway offers "lifetime service" and has a round-the-clock telephone hotline to fulfill this promise. Some vendors spend more money helping customers use their products than on developing and manufacturing them. The document in Gateway's box includes promises of future performance that some consumers value highly; these promises bind Gateway just as the arbitration clause binds the Hills.

. . .

At oral argument the Hills propounded still another distinction: the box containing ProCD's software displayed a notice that additional terms were within, while the box containing Gateway's computer did not. The difference is functional, not legal. Consumers browsing the aisles of a store can look at the box, and if they are unwilling to deal with the prospect of additional terms can leave the box alone, avoiding the transactions costs of returning the package after reviewing its contents. Gateway's box, by contrast, is just a shipping carton; it is not on display anywhere. Its function is to protect the product during transit, and the information on its sides is for the use of handlers rather than would-be purchasers.

Perhaps the Hills would have had a better argument if they were first alerted to the bundling of hardware and legal-ware after opening the box and wanted to return the computer in order to avoid disagreeable terms, but were dissuaded by the expense of shipping. What the remedy would be in such a case—could it exceed the shipping charges?—is an interesting question, but one that need not detain us because the Hills knew before they ordered the computer that the carton would include *some* important terms, and they did not seek to discover these in advance. Gateway's ads state that their products come with limited warranties and lifetime support. How limited was the warranty—30 days, with service contingent on shipping the computer back, or five years, with free onsite service? What sort of support was offered? Shoppers have three principal ways to discover these things. First, they can ask the vendor to send a copy before deciding whether to buy. The Magnuson-Moss Warranty Act requires firms to distribute their warranty terms on request, 15 U.S.C. §2302(b)(1)(A); the Hills do not contend that Gateway would have refused to enclose the remaining terms too. Concealment would be bad for business, scaring some customers away and leading to excess returns from others. Second, shoppers can consult public sources (computer magazines, the Web sites of vendors) that may contain this information. Third, they may inspect the documents after the product's delivery. Like Zeidenberg, the Hills took the third option. By keeping the computer beyond 30 days, the Hills accepted Gateway's offer, including the arbitration clause.

. . . The decision of the district court is vacated, and this case is remanded with instructions to compel the Hills to submit their dispute to arbitration.

SPECHT
v.
NETSCAPE COMMUNICATIONS CORP.
U.S. Court of Appeals, Second Circuit
306 F.3d 17
2002

SOTOMAYOR, J.

. . . Principally, we are asked to determine whether plaintiffs-appellees ("plaintiffs"), by acting upon defendants' invitation to download free software made available on defendants' webpage, agreed to be bound by the software's license terms (which included the arbitration clause at issue), even though plaintiffs could not have learned of the existence of those terms unless, prior to executing the download, they had scrolled down the webpage to a screen located below the download button. We agree with the district court that a reasonably prudent Internet user in circumstances such as these would not have known or learned of the existence of the license terms before responding to defendants' invitation to download the free software, and that defendants therefore did not provide reasonable notice of the license terms. In consequence, plaintiffs' bare act of downloading the software did not unambiguously manifest assent to the arbitration provision contained in the license terms.

. . .

. . . [P]laintiffs alleged that when they first used Netscape's Communicator—a software program that permits Internet browsing—the program created and stored on each of their computer hard drives a small text file known as a "cookie" that functioned "as a kind of electronic identification tag for future communications" between their computers and Netscape. . . . These processes, plaintiffs claim, constituted unlawful "eavesdropping" on users of Netscape's software products. . . .

. . . [P]laintiffs acknowledge that when they proceeded to initiate installation of Communicator, they were automatically shown a scrollable text of that program's license agreement and were not permitted to complete the installation until they had clicked on a "Yes" button to indicate that they accepted all the license terms. If a user attempted to install Communicator without clicking "Yes," the installation would be aborted. All five named user plaintiffs expressly agreed to Communicator's license terms by clicking "Yes." The Communicator license agreement that these plaintiffs saw made no mention of SmartDownload or other plug-in programs, and stated that "[t]hese terms apply to Netscape Communicator and Netscape Navigator" and that "all disputes relating to this Agreement (excepting any dispute relating to intellectual property rights)" are subject to "binding arbitration in Santa Clara County, California."

Although Communicator could be obtained independently of SmartDownload, all the named user plaintiffs, except Fagan, downloaded and installed Communicator in connection with downloading SmartDownload. Each of these plaintiffs allegedly arrived at a Netscape webpage captioned "SmartDownload Communicator" that urged them to "Download With Confidence Using SmartDownload!" At or near the bottom of the screen facing plaintiffs was the prompt "Start Download" and a tinted button labeled "Download." By clicking on the button, plaintiffs initiated the download of SmartDownload. . . .

The signal difference between downloading Communicator and downloading SmartDownload was that no clickwrap presentation accompanied the latter operation. Instead, once plaintiffs Gibson, Gruber, Kelly, and Weindorf had clicked on the "Download" button located at or near the bottom of their screen, and the downloading of SmartDownload was complete, these plaintiffs encountered no further information about the plug-in program or the existence of license terms governing its use. The sole reference to SmartDownload's license terms on the "SmartDownload Communicator" webpage was located in text that would have become visible to plaintiffs only if they had scrolled down to the next screen.

Had plaintiffs scrolled down instead of acting on defendants' invitation to click on the "Download" button, they would have encountered the following invitation: "Please review and agree to the terms of the *Netscape SmartDownload software license agreement* before downloading and using the software." Plaintiffs Gibson, Gruber, Kelly, and Weindorf averred in their affidavits that they never saw this reference to the SmartDownload license agreement when they clicked on the

"Download" button. They also testified during depositions that they saw no reference to license terms when they clicked to download SmartDownload, although under questioning by defendants' counsel, some plaintiffs added that they could not "remember" or be "sure" whether the screen shots of the SmartDownload page attached to their affidavits reflected precisely what they had seen on their computer screens when they downloaded SmartDownload.

In sum, plaintiffs Gibson, Gruber, Kelly, and Weindorf allege that the process of obtaining SmartDownload contrasted sharply with that of obtaining Communicator. Having selected SmartDownload, they were required neither to express unambiguous assent to that program's license agreement nor even to view the license terms or become aware of their existence before proceeding with the invited download of the free plug-in program. Moreover, once these plaintiffs had initiated the download, the existence of SmartDownload's license terms was not mentioned while the software was running or at any later point in plaintiffs' experience of the product.

Even for a user who, unlike plaintiffs, did happen to scroll down past the download button, SmartDownload's license terms would not have been immediately displayed in the manner of Communicator's clickwrapped terms. Instead, if such a user had seen the notice of SmartDownload's terms and then clicked on the underlined invitation to review and agree to the terms, a hypertext link would have taken the user to a separate webpage entitled "License & Support Agreements." The first paragraph on this page read, in pertinent part:

> The use of each Netscape software product is governed by a license agreement. You must read and agree to the license agreement terms BEFORE acquiring a product. Please click on the appropriate link below to review the current license agreement for the product of interest to you before acquisition. For products available for download, you must read and agree to the license agreement terms BEFORE you install the software. If you do not agree to the license terms, do not download, install or use the software.

Below this paragraph appeared a list of license agreements, the first of which was "*License Agreement for Netscape Navigator and Netscape Communicator Product Family* (Netscape Navigator, Netscape Communicator and Netscape SmartDownload)." If the user clicked on that link, he or she would be taken to yet another webpage that contained the full text of a license agreement that was identical in every respect to the Communicator license agreement except that it stated that its "terms apply to Netscape Communicator, Netscape Navigator, and Netscape SmartDownload." The license agreement granted the user a nonexclusive license to use and reproduce the software, subject to certain terms:

> BY CLICKING THE ACCEPTANCE BUTTON OR INSTALLING OR USING NETSCAPE COMMUNICATOR, NETSCAPE NAVIGATOR, OR NETSCAPE SMARTDOWNLOAD SOFTWARE (THE "PRODUCT"), THE INDIVIDUAL OR ENTITY LICENSING THE PRODUCT ("LICENSEE") IS CONSENTING TO BE BOUND BY AND IS BECOMING A PARTY TO THIS AGREEMENT. IF LICENSEE DOES NOT AGREE TO ALL OF THE

TERMS OF THIS AGREEMENT, THE BUTTON INDICATING NON-ACCEPTANCE MUST BE SELECTED, AND LICENSEE MUST NOT INSTALL OR USE THE SOFTWARE.

Among the license terms was a provision requiring virtually all disputes relating to the agreement to be submitted to arbitration:

> Unless otherwise agreed in writing, all disputes relating to this Agreement (excepting any dispute relating to intellectual property rights) shall be subject to final and binding arbitration in Santa Clara County, California, under the auspices of JAMS/EndDispute, with the losing party paying all costs of arbitration.

III. WHETHER THE USER PLAINTIFFS HAD REASONABLE NOTICE OF AND MANIFESTED ASSENT TO THE SMARTDOWNLOAD LICENSE AGREEMENT

Whether governed by the common law or by Article 2 of the Uniform Commercial Code ("UCC"), a transaction, in order to be a contract, requires a manifestation of agreement between the parties. *See Windsor Mills, Inc. v. Collins & Aikman Corp.,* 25 Cal. App. 3d 987, 991, 101 Cal. Rptr. 347, 350 (1972) ("[C]onsent to, or acceptance of, the arbitration provision [is] necessary to create an agreement to arbitrate."); *see also* Cal. Com. Code §2204(1) ("A contract for sale of goods may be made in any manner sufficient to show agreement, including conduct by both parties which recognizes the existence of such a contract."). Mutual manifestation of assent, whether by written or spoken word or by conduct, is the touchstone of contract. *Binder v. Aetna Life Ins. Co.,* 75 Cal. App. 4th 832, 848, 89 Cal. Rptr. 2d 540, 551 (1999); *cf.* Restatement (Second) of Contracts §19(2) (1981) ("The conduct of a party is not effective as a manifestation of his assent unless he intends to engage in the conduct and knows or has reason to know that the other party may infer from his conduct that he assents."). Although an onlooker observing the disputed transactions in this case would have seen each of the user plaintiffs click on the SmartDownload "Download" button, *see Cedars Sinai Med. Ctr. v. Mid-West Nat'l Life Ins. Co.,* 118 F. Supp. 2d 1002, 1008 (C.D. Cal. 2000) ("In California, a party's intent to contract is judged objectively, by the party's outward manifestation of consent."), a consumer's clicking on a download button does not communicate assent to contractual terms if the offer did not make clear to the consumer that clicking on the download button would signify assent to those terms, *see Windsor Mills,* 25 Cal. App. 3d at 992, 101 Cal. Rptr. at 351 ("[W]hen the offeree does not know that a proposal has been made to him this objective standard does not apply."). California's common law is clear that "an offeree, regardless of apparent manifestation of his consent, is not bound by inconspicuous contractual provisions of which he is unaware, contained in a document whose contractual nature is not obvious." *Id.; see also Marin Storage & Trucking, Inc. v. Benco Contracting & Eng'g, Inc.,* 89 Cal. App. 4th 1042, 1049, 107 Cal. Rptr. 2d 645, 651 (2001) (same).

. . .

Defendants argue that plaintiffs must be held to a standard of reasonable prudence and that, because notice of the existence of SmartDownload license terms was on the next scrollable screen, plaintiffs were on "inquiry notice" of those terms. We disagree with the proposition that a reasonably prudent offeree in plaintiffs' position would necessarily have known or learned of the existence of the Smart-Download license agreement prior to acting, so that plaintiffs may be held to have assented to that agreement with constructive notice of its terms. *See* Cal. Civ. Code §1589 ("A voluntary acceptance of the benefit of a transaction is equivalent to a consent to all the obligations arising from it, so far as the facts are known, or ought to be known, to the person accepting."). It is true that "[a] party cannot avoid the terms of a contract on the ground that he or she failed to read it before signing." *Marin Storage & Trucking,* 89 Cal. App. 4th at 1049, 107 Cal. Rptr. 2d at 651. But courts are quick to add: "An exception to this general rule exists when the writing does not appear to be a contract and the terms are not called to the attention of the recipient. In such a case, no contract is formed with respect to the undisclosed term." *Id.; cf. Cory v. Golden State Bank,* 95 Cal. App. 3d 360, 364, 157 Cal. Rptr. 538, 541 (1979) ("[T]he provision in question is effectively hidden from the view of money order purchasers until after the transactions are completed. . . . Under these circumstances, it must be concluded that the Bank's money order purchasers are not chargeable with either actual or constructive notice of the service charge provision, and therefore cannot be deemed to have consented to the provision as part of their transaction with the Bank.").

. . .

We are not persuaded that a reasonably prudent offeree in these circumstances would have known of the existence of license terms. Plaintiffs were responding to an offer that did not carry an immediately visible notice of the existence of license terms or require unambiguous manifestation of assent to those terms. Thus, plaintiffs' "apparent manifestation of . . . consent" was to terms "contained in a document whose contractual nature [was] not obvious." *Windsor Mills,* 25 Cal. App. 3d at 992, 101 Cal. Rptr. at 351. Moreover, the fact that, given the position of the scroll bar on their computer screens, plaintiffs may have been aware that an unexplored portion of the Netscape webpage remained below the download button does not mean that they reasonably should have concluded that this portion contained a notice of license terms. In their deposition testimony, plaintiffs variously stated that they used the scroll bar "[o]nly if there is something that I feel I need to see that is on—that is off the page," or that the elevated position of the scroll bar suggested the presence of "mere[ ] formalities, standard lower banner links" or "that the page is bigger than what I can see." Plaintiffs testified, and defendants did not refute, that plaintiffs were in fact unaware that defendants intended to attach license terms to the use of SmartDownload.

We conclude that in circumstances such as these, where consumers are urged to download free software at the immediate click of a button, a reference to the existence of license terms on a submerged screen is not sufficient to place consumers on inquiry or constructive notice of those terms.

ᴎ

O'CALLAGHAN
v.
WALLER & BECKWITH REALTY CO.
Supreme Court of Illinois
15 Ill. 2d 436
1959

SCHAEFER, J.

This is an action to recover for injuries allegedly caused by the defendant's negli-gence in maintaining and operating a large apartment building. Mrs. Ella O'Calla-ghan, a tenant in the building, was injured when she fell while crossing the paved courtyard on her way from the garage to her apartment. She instituted this action to recover for her injuries, alleging that they were caused by defective pavement in the courtyard. Before the case was tried Mrs. O'Callaghan died and her administrator was substituted as plaintiff. The jury returned a verdict for the plaintiff in the sum of $14,000, and judgment was entered on the verdict. Defendant appealed. The Appel-late Court held that the action was barred by an exculpatory clause in the lease that Mrs. O'Callaghan had signed, and that a verdict should have been directed for the defendant. 15 Ill. App. 2d 349, 146 N.E.2d 198. It therefore reversed the judgment and remanded the case with directions to enter judgment for the defendant. We granted leave to appeal.

In reaching its conclusion the Appellate Court relied upon our recent decision in Jackson v. First National Bank, 415 Ill. 453, 114 N.E.2d 721. There we considered the validity of such an exculpatory clause in a lease of property for business pur-poses. We pointed out that contracts by which one seeks to relieve himself from the consequences of his own negligence are generally enforced "unless (1) it would be against the settled public policy of the State to do so, or (2) there is something in the social relationship of the parties militating against upholding the agreement." 415 Ill. at page 460, 114 N.E.2d at page 725. And we held that there was nothing in the public policy of the State or in the social relationship of the parties to forbid enforce-ment of the exculpatory clause there involved.

The exculpatory clause in the lease now before us clearly purports to relieve the lessor and its agents from any liability to the lessee for personal injuries or property damage caused by any act or neglect of the lessor or its agents. It does not appear to be amenable to the strict construction to which such clauses are frequently sub-jected. See 175 A.L.R. 8, 89. The plaintiff does not question its applicability, and she concedes that if it is valid it bars her recovery. She argues vigorously, however, that such a clause is contrary to public policy, and so invalid, in a lease of residential property.

Freedom of contract is basic to our law. But when that freedom expresses itself in a provision designed to absolve one of the parties from the consequences of his own negligence, there is danger that the standards of conduct which the law has developed for the protection of others may be diluted. These competing considera-tions have produced results that are not completely consistent. This court has refused to enforce contracts exculpating or limiting liability for negligence between common carriers and shippers of freight or paying passengers (Chicago and Northwestern Railway Co. v. Chapman, 133 Ill. 96, 24 N.E. 417, 8 L.R.A. 508), between telegraph companies and those sending messages (Tyler, Ullman & Co. v. Western Union Telegraph Co., 60 Ill. 421), and between masters and servants (Campbell v. Chicago, Rock Island and Pacific Railway Co., 243 Ill. 620, 90 N.E. 1106). The obvious public interest in these relationships, coupled with the dominant position of those seeking exculpation, were compelling considerations in these decisions, which are in accord with similar results in other jurisdictions. See 175 A.L.R. 8.

On the other hand, as pointed out in the *Jackson* case, the relation of lessor and lessee has been considered a matter of private concern. Clauses that exculpate the landlord from the consequences of his negligence have been sustained in residential as well as commercial leases. Manaster v. Gopin, 1953, 330 Mass. 569, 116 N.E.2d 134; Mackenzie v. Ryan, 1950, 230 Minn. 378, 41 N.W.2d 878; Kirshenbaum v. General Outdoor Advertising Co., 1932, 258 N.Y. 489, 180 N.E. 245, 84 A.L.R. 645; King v. Smith, 1933, 47 Ga. App. 360, 170 S.E. 546; Wright v. Sterling Land Co., 1945, 157 Pa. Super. 625, 43 A.2d 614; 6 Williston on Contracts, sec. 1715D; 6 Corbin on Contracts, sec. 1472. There are intimations in other jurisdictions that run counter to the current authority. See Kuzmiak v. Brookchester, Inc., 1955, 33 N.J. Super. 575, 111 A.2d 425; Kay v. Cain, 1946, 81 U.S. App. D.C. 24, 154 F.2d 305. The New Hampshire court applies to exculpatory clauses in all leases its uniform rule that any attempt to contract against liability for negligence is contrary to public policy. Papakalos v. Shaka, 1941, 91 N.H. 265, 18 A.2d 377. But apart from the *Papakalos* case we know of no court of last resort that has held such clauses invalid in the absence of a statute so requiring.

A contract shifting the risk of liability for negligence may benefit a tenant as well as a landlord. See Cerny-Pickas & Co. v. C.R. Jahn Co., 7 Ill. 2d 393, 131 N.E.2d 100. Such an agreement transfers the risk of a possible financial burden and so lessens the impact of the sanctions that induce adherence to the required standard of care. But this consideration is applicable as well to contracts for insurance that indemnify against liability for one's own negligence. Such contracts are accepted, and even encouraged. See Ill. Rev. Stat.1957, chap. 95 1/2, pars. 7-202(1) and 7-315.

The plaintiff contends that due to a shortage of housing there is a disparity of bargaining power between lessors of residential property and their lessees that gives landlords an unconscionable advantage over tenants. And upon this ground it is said that exculpatory clauses in residential leases must be held to be contrary to public policy. No attempt was made upon the trial to show that Mrs. O'Callaghan was at all concerned about the exculpatory clause, that she tried to negotiate with the defendant about its modification or elimination, or that she made any effort to rent an apartment elsewhere. To establish the existence of a widespread housing shortage the plaintiff points to numerous statutes designed to alleviate the shortage (see Ill. Rev. Stat.1957, chap. 67 1/2, passim) and to the existence of rent control during the period of the lease. 65 Stat. 145 (1947), 50 U.S.C.A. Appendix, §1894.

Unquestionably there has been a housing shortage. That shortage has produced an active and varied legislative response. Since legislative attention has been so sharply focused upon housing problems in recent years, it might be assumed that the legislature has taken all of the remedial action that it thought necessary or desirable. One of the major legislative responses was the adoption of rent controls which placed ceilings upon the amount of rent that landlords could charge. But the very existence of that control made it impossible for a lessor to negotiate for an increased rental in exchange for the elimination of an exculpatory clause. We are asked to assume, however, that the legislative response to the housing shortage has been inadequate and incomplete, and to augment it judicially.

The relationship of landlord and tenant does not have the monopolistic characteristics that have characterized some other relations with respect to which exculpatory clauses have been held invalid. There are literally thousands of landlords who are in competition with one another. The rental market affords a variety of competing types of housing accommodations, from simple farm house to luxurious apartment. The use of a form contract does not of itself establish disparity of bargaining power. That there is a shortage of housing at one particular time or place does not indicate that such shortages have always and everywhere existed, or that there will be shortages in the future. Judicial determinations of public policy cannot readily take account of sporadic and transitory circumstances. They should rather, we think, rest upon a durable moral basis. Other jurisdictions have dealt with this problem by legislation. McKinney's Consol. Laws of N.Y. Ann., Real Property Laws, sec. 234, Vol. 49, Part I; Ann. Laws of Mass., Vol. 6, c. 186, sec. 15. On our opinion the subject is one that is appropriate for legislative rather than judicial action.

The judgment of the Appellate Court is affirmed.

BRISTOW, J. and DAILY, C.J. (dissenting).

We cannot accept the conclusions and analysis of the majority opinion, which in our judgment not only arbitrarily eliminates the concept of negligence in the landlord and tenant relationship, but creates anomalies in the law, and will produce grievous social consequences for hundreds of thousands of persons in this State.

According to the undisputed facts in the instant case, this form lease with its exculpatory clause, was executed in a metropolitan area in 1947, when housing shortages were so acute that "waiting lists" were the order of the day, and gratuities to landlords to procure shelter were common. (U.S. Sen. Rep. 1780, Committee on Banking & Currency, vol. II, 81st Cong., 2nd Sess. (1950), p. 2565 et seq.; Cremer v. Peoria Housing Authority, 399 Ill. 579, 589, 78 N.E.2d 276.) While plaintiff admittedly did not negotiate about the exculpatory clause, as the majority opinion notes, the record shows unequivocally that the apartment would not have been rented to her if she had quibbled about any clause in the form lease. According to the uncontroverted testimony, "If a person refused to sign a (form) lease in the form it was in, the apartment would not be rented to him."

Apparently, the majority opinion has chosen to ignore those facts and prevailing circumstances, and finds instead that there were thousands of landlords competing with each other with a variety of rental units. Not only was the element of competition purely theoretical—and judges need not be more naive than other men—but there wasn't even theoretical competition, as far as the exculpatory clauses were concerned, since these clauses were included in all form leases used by practically all landlords in urban areas. Simmons v. Columbus Venetian Stevens Building, Inc., Ill. App., 155 N.E.2d 372; 1952 Ill. L. Forum, 321, 328. This meant that even if a prospective tenant were to "take his business elsewhere," he would still be confronted by the same exculpatory clause in a form lease offered by another landlord.

Thus, we are not construing merely an isolated provision of a contract specifically bargained for by one landlord and one tenant, "a matter of private concern," as the majority opinion myopically views the issue in order to sustain its conclusion. We are construing, instead, a provision affecting thousands of tenants now bound by such provisions, which were foisted upon them at a time when it would be pure fiction to state that they had anything but a Hobson's choice in the matter. Can landlords, by that technique, immunize themselves from liability for negligence, and have the blessings of this court as they destroy the concept of negligence and standards of law painstakingly evolved in the case law? That is the issue in this case, and the majority opinion at no time realistically faces it.

In resolving this issue, it is evident that despite the assertion in the majority opinion, there is no such thing as absolute "freedom of contract" in the law. West Coast Hotel Co. v. Parrish, 300 U.S. 379, 392. As Mr. Justice Holmes stated, "pretty much all law consists in forbidding men to do some things that they want to do, and contract is no more exempt from law than other acts." Dissent, Adkins v. Children's Hospital of District of Columbia, 261 U.S. 525, 568. Thus, there is no freedom to contract to commit a crime; or to contract to give a reward for the commission of a crime; or to contract to violate essential morality; or to contract to accomplish an unlawful purpose, or to contract in violation of public policy. 12 I.L.P. Contracts §§151, 154.

In the instant case we must determine whether the exculpatory clause in the lease offends the public policy of this State. We realize that there is no precise definition of "public policy" or rule to test whether a contract is contrary to public policy, so that each case must be judged according to its own peculiar circumstances. First Trust & Savings Bank of Kankakee v. Powers, 393 Ill. 97, 102, 65 N.E.2d 377. None would dispute, however, that there is a recognized policy of discouraging negligence and protecting those in need of goods or services from being overreached by those with power to drive unconscionable bargains.

Even the majority opinion recognizes this policy as a possible limitation on the concept of "freedom of contract" in its statement, "when that freedom expresses itself in a provision designed to absolve one of the parties from the consequences of his own negligence, there is danger that the standards of conduct which the law has developed for the protection of others may be diluted." Diluted? As applied in the instant case, the word is "destroyed." When landlords are no longer liable for failure to observe standards of care, or for conduct amounting to negligence by virtue of an exculpatory clause in a lease, then such standards cease to exist. They are not merely "diluted." Negligence cannot exist in abstraction. The exculpatory clause destroys the concept of negligence in the landlord-tenant relationship, and the majority opinion, in sustaining the validity of that clause, has given the concept of negligence in this relationship a "judicial burial."

This court, however, has refused to countenance such a destruction of standards of conduct and of the concept of negligence in other relationships. We have invalidated such exculpatory clauses as contrary to our public policy in contracts between common carriers and shippers or paying passengers (Checkley v. Illinois Central Railroad Co., 257 Ill. 491, 100 N.E. 942, 44 L.R.A., N.S., 1127; Chicago and Northwestern Railway Co. v. Chapman, 133 Ill. 96, 24 N.E. 417,8 L.R.A. 508); between telegraph companies and those sending messages (Tyler, Ullman & Co. v. Western Union Telegraph Co., 60 Ill. 421), and between employers and employees (Campbell v. Chicago, Rock Island and Pacific Railway Co., 243 Ill, 620, 90 N.E. 1106; Devine v. Delano, 272 Ill. 166, 111 N.E. 742; Consolidated Coal Co. of St. Louis v. Lundak, 196 Ill. 594, 63 N.E. 1079; Himrod Coal Co. v. Clark, 197 Ill. 514, 64 N.E. 282.)

By what logic and reasoning can you hold that such clauses are void and contrary to public policy in an employer-employee contract, but valid in contracts between landlords and tenants, as the majority opinion does? If the criterion for invalidating exculpatory clauses is the presence of "monopolistic characteristics" in the relationship, as the majority opinion suggests, then do employers have a greater monopoly on the labor market than landlords have on the tenant market? Is there less competition among employers for employees than among landlords for tenants? The facts defy any such reasoning. Nor are there any other cogent grounds for distinguishing between these categories.

---

5   TUNKL
v.
REGENTS OF THE UNIVERSITY OF CALIFORNIA
Supreme Court of California
383 P.2d 441
1963

Tobriner, J.

This case concerns the validity of a release from liability for future negligence imposed as a condition for admission to a charitable research hospital. For the reasons we hereinafter specify, we have concluded that an agreement between a hospital and an entering patient affects the public interest and that, in consequence, the exculpatory provision included within it must be invalid under Civil Code section 1668.

Hugo Tunkl brought this action to recover damages for personal injuries alleged to have resulted from the negligence of two physicians in the employ of the University of California Los Angeles Medical Center, a hospital operated and maintained by the Regents of the University of California as a nonprofit charitable institution. Mr. Tunkl died after suit was brought, and his surviving wife, as executrix, was substituted as plaintiff.

The University of California at Los Angeles Medical Center admitted Tunkl as a patient on June 11, 1956. The Regents maintain the hospital for the primary purpose of aiding and developing a program of research and education in the field of medicine; patients are selected and admitted if the study and treatment of their condition would tend to achieve these purposes. Upon his entry to the hospital, Tunkl signed a document setting forth certain "Conditions of Admission." The crucial condition number six reads as follows: "RELEASE: The hospital is a nonprofit, charitable institution. In consideration of the hospital and allied services to be rendered and the rates charged therefor, the patient or his legal representative agrees to and hereby releases The Regents of the University of California, and the hospital from any and all liability for the negligent or wrongful acts or omissions of its employees, if the hospital has used due care in selecting its employees."

. . .

We begin with the dictate of the relevant Civil Code section 1668. The section states: "All contracts which have for their object, directly or indirectly, to exempt anyone from responsibility for his own fraud, or willful injury to the person or property of another, or violation of law, whether willful or negligent, are against the policy of the law."

In one respect . . . the decisions are uniform. The cases have consistently held that the exculpatory provision may stand only if it does not involve "the public interest."[6] Interestingly enough, this theory found its first expression in a decision which did not expressly refer to section 1668. In Stephens v. Southern Pacific Co. (1895) 109 Cal. 86, 41 P. 783, a railroad company had leased land, which adjoined its depot, to a lessee who had constructed a warehouse upon it. The lessee covenanted that the railroad company would not be responsible for damage from fire "caused by any . . . means." (109 Cal. p. 87, 41 P. p. 783.) This exemption, under the court ruling[,] applied to the lessee's damage resulting from the railroad company's carelessly burning dry grass and rubbish. Declaring the contract not "violative of sound public policy" (109 Cal. p. 89, 41 P. p. 784), the court pointed out ". . . As far as this transaction was concerned, the parties, when contracting, stood upon common ground, and dealt with each other as A. and B. might deal with each other with reference to any private business undertaking. . . ." (109 Cal. p. 88, 41 P. p. 784.) The court concluded "that the *interests of the public* in the contract are more sentimental than real" (109 Cal. p. 95, 41 P. p. 786; emphasis added) and that the exculpatory provision was therefore enforceable.

In applying this approach and in manifesting their reaction as to the effect of the exemptive clause upon the public interest, some later courts enforced, and others invalidated such provisions under section 1668. Thus in Nichols v. Hitchcock Motor

---

6. The view that the exculpatory contract is valid only if the public interest is not involved represents the majority holding in the United States. Only New Hampshire, in definite opposition to "public interest" test, categorically refuses to enforce exculpatory provisions. The cases are collected in an extensive annotation in 175 A.L.R. 8 (1948). In addition to the California cases cited in the text and note 7 infra, the public interest doctrine is recognized in dictum in Sproul v. Cuddy (1955) 131 Cal. App. 2d 85, 95, 280 P.2d 158; Basin Oil Co. v. Baash-Ross Tool Co. (1954) 125 Cal. App. 2d 578, 594, 271 P.2d 122; Hubbard v. Matson Navigation Co. (1939) 34 Cal. App. 2d 475, 477, 93 P.2d 846. Each of these cases involved exculpatory clauses which were construed by the court as not applicable to the conduct of the defendant in question.

Co. (1937) 22 Cal. App. 2d 151, 159, 70 P.2d 654, 658, the court enforced an exculpatory clause on the ground that "the public neither had nor could have any interest whatsoever in the subject-matter of the contract, considered either as a whole or as to the incidental covenant in question. The agreement between the parties concerned 'their private affairs' only."

In Barkett v. Brucato (1953) 122 Cal. App. 2d 264, 276, 264 P. 2d 978, 987, which involved a waiver clause in a private lease, Justice Peters summarizes the previous decisions in this language: "These cases hold that the matter is simply one of interpreting a contract; that both parties are free to contract; that the relationship of landlord and tenant *does not affect the public interest*; that such a provision *affects only the private affairs of the parties. . . .*" (Emphasis added.)

On the other hand, courts struck down exculpatory clauses as contrary to public policy in the case of a contract to transmit a telegraph message (Union Constr. Co. v. Western Union Tel. Co. (1912) 163 Cal. 298, 125 P. 242) and in the instance of a contract of bailment (England v. Lyon Fireproof Storage Co. (1928) 94 Cal. App. 562, 271 P. 532). In Hiroshima v. Bank of Italy (1926) 78 Cal. App. 362, 248 P. 947, the court invalidated an exemption provision in the form used by a payee in directing a bank to stop payment on a check. The court relied in part upon the fact that "the banking public, as well as the particular individual who may be concerned in the giving of any stop notice, is interested in seeing that the bank is held accountable for the ordinary and regular performance of its duties, and also in seeing that directions in relation to the disposition of funds deposited in the bank are not heedlessly, negligently, and carelessly disobeyed, and money paid out contrary to directions given." (78 Cal. App. p. 377, 248 P. p. 953.) The opinion in *Hiroshima* was approved and followed in Grisinger v. Golden State Bank (1928) 92 Cal. App. 443, 268 P. 425.

If, then, the exculpatory clause which affects the public interest cannot stand, we must ascertain those factors or characteristics which constitute the public interest. The social forces that have led to such characterization are volatile and dynamic. No definition of the concept of public interest can be contained within the four corners of a formula. The concept, always the subject of great debate, has ranged over the whole course of the common law; rather than attempt to prescribe its nature, we can only designate the situations in which it has been applied. We can determine whether the instant contract does or does not manifest the characteristics which have been held to stamp a contract as one affected with a public interest.

In placing particular contracts within or without the category of those affected with a public interest, the courts have revealed a rough outline of that type of transaction in which exculpatory provisions will be held invalid. Thus the attempted but invalid exemption involves a transaction which exhibits some or all of the following characteristics. It concerns a business of a type generally thought suitable for public regulation. The party seeking exculpation is engaged in performing a service of great importance to the public, which is often a matter of practical necessity for some members of the public. The party holds himself out as willing to perform this service for any member of the public who seeks it, or at least for any member coming within certain established standards. As a result of the essential nature of the service, in the economic setting of the transaction, the party invoking exculpation possesses a decisive advantage of bargaining strength against any member of the public who seeks his services. In exercising a superior bargaining power the party confronts the public with a standardized adhesion contract of exculpation, and makes no provision whereby a purchaser may pay additional reasonable fees and obtain protection against negligence. Finally, as a result of the transaction, the person or property of the purchaser is placed under the control of the seller, subject to the risk of carelessness by the seller or his agents.

While obviously no public policy opposes private, voluntary transactions in which one party, for a consideration, agrees to shoulder a risk which the law would otherwise have placed upon the other party, the above circumstances pose a different situation. In this situation the releasing party does not really acquiesce voluntarily in the contractual shifting of the risk, nor can we be reasonably certain that he receives an adequate consideration for the transfer. Since the service is one which each member of the public, presently or potentially, may find essential to him, he faces, despite his economic inability to do so, the prospect of a compulsory assumption of the risk of another's negligence. The public policy of this state has been, in substance, to posit the risk of negligence upon the actor; in instances in which this policy has been abandoned, it has generally been to allow or require that the risk shift to another party better or equally able to bear it, not to shift the risk to the weak bargainer.

In the light of the decisions, we think that the hospital-patient contract clearly falls within the category of agreements affecting the public interest. To meet that test, the agreement need only fulfill some of the characteristics above outlined; here, the relationship fulfills all of them. Thus the contract of exculpation involves an institution suitable for, and a subject of, public regulation. (See Health & Saf. Code, §§1400-1421, 32000-32508.) That the services of the hospital to those members of the public who are in special need of the particular skill of its staff and facilities constitute a practical and crucial necessity is hardly open to question.

The hospital, likewise, holds itself out as willing to perform its services for those members of the public who qualify for its research and training facilities. While it is true that the hospital is selective as to the patients it will accept, such selectivity does not negate its public aspect or the public interest in it. The hospital is selective only in the sense that it accepts from the public at large certain types of cases which qualify for the research and training in which it specializes. But the hospital does hold itself out to the public as an institution which performs such services for those members of the public who can qualify for them.

In insisting that the patient accept the provision of waiver in the contract, the hospital certainly exercises a decisive advantage in bargaining. The would-be patient is in no position to reject the proffered agreement, to bargain with the hospital, or in lieu of agreement to find another hospital. The admission room of a hospital contains no bargaining table where, as in a private business transaction, the parties can debate the terms of their contract. As a result, we cannot but conclude that the instant agreement manifested the characteristics of the so-called adhesion contract. Finally, when the patient signed the contract, he completely placed himself in the control of the hospital; he subjected himself to the risk of its carelessness.

In brief, the patient here sought the services which the hospital offered to a selective portion of the public; the patient, as the price of admission and as a result of his inferior bargaining position, accepted a clause in a contract of adhesion waiving the hospital's negligence; the patient thereby subjected himself to control of the hospital and the possible infliction of the negligence which he had thus been compelled to waive. The hospital, under such circumstances, occupied a status different than a mere private party; its contract with the patient affected the public interest. We see no cogent current reason for according to the patron of the inn a greater protection than the patient of the hospital; we cannot hold the innkeeper's performance affords a greater public service than that of the hospital.

The judgment is reversed.

CARNIVAL CRUISE LINES, INC.
v.
SHUTE
Supreme Court of the United States
499 U.S. 585
1991

BLACKMUN, J.

In this admiralty case we primarily consider whether the United States Court of Appeals for the Ninth Circuit correctly refused to enforce a forum-selection clause contained in tickets issued by petitioner Carnival Cruise Lines, Inc., to respondents Eulala and Russel Shute.

I

The Shutes, through an Arlington, Wash., travel agent, purchased passage for a 7-day cruise on petitioner's ship, the *Tropicale*. Respondents paid the fare to the agent who forwarded the payment to petitioner's headquarters in Miami, Fla. Petitioner then prepared the tickets and sent them to respondents in the State of Washington. The face of each ticket, at its left-hand lower corner, contained this admonition:

"SUBJECT TO CONDITIONS OF CONTRACT ON LAST PAGES **IMPORTANT!** PLEASE READ CONTRACT—ON LAST PAGES 1, 2, 3" App. 15.

The following appeared on "contract page 1" of each ticket:

"TERMS AND CONDITIONS OF PASSAGE CONTRACT TICKET

. . .

"3. (a) The acceptance of this ticket by the person or persons named hereon as passengers shall be deemed to be an acceptance and agreement by each of them of all of the terms and conditions of this Passage Contract Ticket.

. . .

"8. It is agreed by and between the passenger and the Carrier that all disputes and matters whatsoever arising under, in connection with or incident to this Contract shall be litigated, if at all, in and before a Court located in the State of Florida, U.S.A., to the exclusion of the Courts of any other state or country."

The last quoted paragraph is the forum-selection clause at issue.

II

Respondents boarded the *Tropicale* in Los Angeles, Cal. The ship sailed to Puerto Vallarta, Mexico, and then returned to Los Angeles. While the ship was in international waters off the Mexican coast, respondent Eulala Shute was injured when she slipped on a deck mat during a guided tour of the ship's galley. Respondents filed suit against petitioner in the United States District Court for the Western District of Washington, claiming that Mrs. Shute's injuries had been caused by the negligence of Carnival Cruise Lines and its employees.

Petitioner moved for summary judgment, contending that the forum clause in respondents' tickets required the Shutes to bring their suit against petitioner in a court in the State of Florida. . . .

. . .

III

We begin by noting the boundaries of our inquiry. First, this is a case in admiralty, and federal law governs the enforceability of the forum-selection clause we scrutinize. See *Archawski v. Hanioti,* 350 U.S. 532, 533, 76 S. Ct. 617, 619, 100 L. Ed. 676 (1956); *The Moses Taylor,* 4 Wall. 411, 427, 18 L. Ed. 397 (1867); Tr. of Oral Arg. 36-37, 12, 47-48. Cf. *Stewart Organization, Inc. v. Ricoh Corp.,* 487 U.S. 22, 28-29, 108 S. Ct. 2239, 2243-2244, 101 L. Ed. 2d 22 (1988). Second, we do not address the question whether respondents had sufficient notice of the forum clause before entering the contract for passage. Respondents essentially have conceded that they had notice of the forum-selection provision. Brief for Respondents 26 ("The respondents do not contest the incorporation of the provisions nor [*sic*] that the forum selection clause was reasonably communicated to the respondents, as much as three pages of fine print can be communicated"). Additionally, the Court of Appeals evaluated the enforceability of the forum clause under the assumption, although "doubtful," that respondents could be deemed to have had knowledge of the clause. See 897 F.2d, at 389, and n. 11.

Within this context, respondents urge that the forum clause should not be enforced because, contrary to this Court's teachings in *The Bremen,* the clause was not the product of negotiation, and enforcement effectively would deprive respondents of their day in court. . . .

IV

A

Both petitioner and respondents argue vigorously that the Court's opinion in *The Bremen* governs this case, and each side purports to find ample support for its position in that opinion's broad-ranging language. This seeming paradox derives in large part from key factual differences between this case and *The Bremen,* differences that preclude an automatic and simple application of *The Bremen*'s general principles to the facts here.

In *The Bremen,* this Court addressed the enforceability of a forum-selection clause in a contract between two business corporations. An American corporation, Zapata, made a contract with Unterweser, a German corporation, for the towage of Zapata's oceangoing drilling rig from Louisiana to a point in the Adriatic Sea off the coast of Italy. The agreement provided that any dispute arising under the contract was to be resolved in the London Court of Justice. After a storm in the Gulf of Mexico seriously damaged the rig, Zapata ordered Unterweser's ship to tow the rig to Tampa, Fla., the nearest point of refuge. Thereafter, Zapata sued Unterweser in admiralty in federal court at Tampa. Citing the forum clause, Unterweser moved to dismiss. The District Court denied Unterweser's motion, and the Court of Appeals for the Fifth Circuit, sitting en banc on rehearing, and by a sharply divided vote, affirmed. *In re Complaint of Unterweser Reederei GmbH,* 446 F.2d 907 (1971).

This Court vacated and remanded, stating that, in general, "a freely negotiated private international agreement, unaffected by fraud, undue influence, or overweening bargaining power, such as that involved here, should be given full effect." 407 U.S., at 12-13, 92 S. Ct. at 1914-1915 (footnote omitted). The Court further generalized that "in the light of present-day commercial realities and expanding international trade we conclude that the forum clause should control absent a strong showing that it should be set aside." *Id.,* at 15, 92 S. Ct., at 1916. The Court did not define precisely the circumstances that would make it unreasonable for a court to enforce a forum clause. Instead, the Court discussed a number of factors that made it reasonable to enforce the clause at issue in *The Bremen* and that, presumably, would be pertinent in any determination whether to enforce a similar clause.

In this respect, the Court noted that there was "strong evidence that the forum clause was a vital part of the agreement, and [that] it would be unrealistic to think that the parties did not conduct their negotiations, including fixing the monetary terms, with the consequences of the forum clause figuring prominently in their calculations." *Id.,* at 14, 92 S. Ct., 1915 (footnote omitted). Further, the Court observed that it was not "dealing with an agreement between two Americans to resolve their essentially local disputes in a remote alien forum," and that in such a case, "the serious inconvenience of the contractual forum to one or both of the parties might carry greater weight in determining the reasonableness of the forum clause." *Id.,* at

17, 92 S. Ct., at 1917. The Court stated that even where the forum clause establishes a remote forum for resolution of conflicts, "the party claiming [unfairness] should bear a heavy burden of proof." *Ibid.*

In applying *The Bremen,* the Court of Appeals in the present litigation . . . rather automatically decided that the forum-selection clause was unenforceable because, unlike the parties in *The Bremen,* respondents are not business persons and did not negotiate the terms of the clause with petitioner. Alternatively, the Court of Appeals ruled that the clause should not be enforced because enforcement effectively would deprive respondents of an opportunity to litigate their claim against petitioner.

The Bremen concerned a "far from routine transaction between companies of two different nations contemplating the tow of an extremely costly piece of equipment from Louisiana across the Gulf of Mexico and the Atlantic Ocean, through the Mediterranean Sea to its final destination in the Adriatic Sea." These facts suggest that, even apart from the evidence of negotiation regarding the forum clause, it was entirely reasonable for the Court in *The Bremen* to have expected Unterweser and Zapata to have negotiated with care in selecting a forum for the resolution of disputes arising from their special towing contract.

In contrast, respondents' passage contract was purely routine and doubtless nearly identical to every commercial passage contract issued by petitioner and most other cruise lines. See, *e.g., Hodes v. S.N.C. Achille Lauro ed Altri-Gestione,* 858 F.2d 905, 910 (CA3 1988), cert. dism'd, 490 U.S. 1001, 109 S. Ct. 1633, 104 L. Ed. 2d 149 (1989). In this context, it would be entirely unreasonable for us to assume that respondents—or any other cruise passenger—would negotiate with petitioner the terms of a forum-selection clause in an ordinary commercial cruise ticket. Common sense dictates that a ticket of this kind will be a form contract the terms of which are not subject to negotiation, and that an individual purchasing the ticket will not have bargaining parity with the cruise line. But by ignoring the crucial differences in the business contexts in which the respective contracts were executed, the Court of Appeals' analysis seems to us to have distorted somewhat this Court's holding in *The Bremen.*

In evaluating the reasonableness of the forum clause at issue in this case, we must refine the analysis of *The Bremen* to account for the realities of form passage contracts. As an initial matter, we do not adopt the Court of Appeals' determination that a nonnegotiated forum-selection clause in a form ticket contract is never enforceable simply because it is not the subject of bargaining. Including a reasonable forum clause in a form contract of this kind well may be permissible for several reasons: First, a cruise line has a special interest in limiting the fora in which it potentially could be subject to suit. Because a cruise ship typically carries passengers from many locales, it is not unlikely that a mishap on a cruise could subject the cruise line to litigation in several different fora. See *The Bremen,* 407 U.S., at 13, and n.15, 92 S. Ct., at 1915, and n.15; *Hodes,* 858 F.2d, at 913. Additionally, a clause establishing *ex ante* the forum for dispute resolution has the salutary effect of dispelling any confusion about where suits arising from the contract must be brought and defended, sparing litigants the time and expense of pretrial motions to determine the correct forum and conserving judicial resources that otherwise would be devoted to deciding those motions. See *Stewart Organization,* 487 U.S., at 33, 108 S. Ct., at

2246 (concurring opinion). Finally, it stands to reason that passengers who purchase tickets containing a forum clause like that at issue in this case benefit in the form of reduced fares reflecting the savings that the cruise line enjoys by limiting the fora in which it may be sued. Cf. *Northwestern Nat. Ins. Co. v. Donovan,* 916 F.2d 372, 378 (CA7 1990).

. . .

It bears emphasis that forum-selection clauses contained in form passage contracts are subject to judicial scrutiny for fundamental fairness. In this case, there is no indication that petitioner set Florida as the forum in which disputes were to be resolved as a means of discouraging cruise passengers from pursuing legitimate claims. Any suggestion of such a bad-faith motive is belied by two facts: Petitioner has its principal place of business in Florida, and many of its cruises depart from and return to Florida ports. Similarly, there is no evidence that petitioner obtained respondents' accession to the forum clause by fraud or overreaching. Finally, respondents have conceded that they were given notice of the forum provision and, therefore, presumably retained the option of rejecting the contract with impunity. In the case before us, therefore, we conclude that the Court of Appeals erred in refusing to enforce the forum-selection clause.

. . .

V

The judgment of the Court of Appeals is reversed.
It is so ordered.

STEVENS, J., with whom MARSHALL, J., joins, dissenting.

The Court prefaces its legal analysis with a factual statement that implies that a purchaser of a Carnival Cruise Lines passenger ticket is fully and fairly notified about the existence of the choice of forum clause in the fine print on the back of the ticket. See *ante* [quoted in Blackmun's opinion—EDS.]. Even if this implication were accurate, I would disagree with the Court's analysis. But, given the Court's preface, I begin my dissent by noting that only the most meticulous passenger is likely to become aware of the forum-selection provision. I have therefore appended to this opinion a facsimile of the relevant text, using the type size that actually appears in the ticket itself. A careful reader will find the forum-selection clause in the 8th of the 25 numbered paragraphs.

Of course, many passengers, like the respondents in this case, see *ante*, will not have an opportunity to read paragraph 8 until they have actually purchased their tickets. By this point, the passengers will already have accepted the condition set forth in paragraph 16(a), which provides that "[t]he Carrier shall not be liable to make any refund to passengers in respect of . . . tickets wholly or partly not used by a passenger." Not knowing whether or not that provision is legally enforceable, I assume that the average passenger would accept the risk of having to file suit in Florida in the event of an injury, rather than canceling—without a refund—a planned vacation at the last minute. The fact that the cruise line can reduce its litigation costs, and therefore its liability insurance premiums, by forcing this choice on its passengers does not, in my opinion, suffice to render the provision reasonable. Cf. *Steven v. Fidelity & Casualty Co. of New York,* 58 Cal. 2d 862, 883, 27 Cal. Rptr. 172, 186, 377 P.2d 284, 298 (1962) (refusing to enforce limitation on liability in insurance policy because insured "must purchase the policy before he even knows its provisions").

. . .

Forum-selection clauses in passenger tickets involve the intersection of two strands of traditional contract law that qualify the general rule that courts will enforce the terms of a contract as written. Pursuant to the first strand, courts traditionally have reviewed with heightened scrutiny the terms of contracts of adhesion, form contracts offered on a take-or-leave basis by a party with stronger bargaining power to a party with weaker power. Some commentators have questioned whether contracts of adhesion can justifiably be enforced at all under traditional contract theory because the adhering party generally enters into them without manifesting knowing and voluntary consent to all their terms. See, *e.g.,* Rakoff, Contracts of Adhesion: An Essay in Reconstruction, 96 Harv. L. Rev. 1173, 1179-1180 (1983); Slawson, Mass Contracts: Lawful Fraud in California, 48 S. Cal. L. Rev. 1, 12-13 (1974); K. Llewellyn, The Common Law Tradition 370-371 (1960).

The common law, recognizing that standardized form contracts account for a significant portion of all commercial agreements, has taken a less extreme position and instead subjects terms in contracts of adhesion to scrutiny for reasonableness. Judge J. Skelly Wright set out the state of the law succinctly in *Williams v. Walker-Thomas Furniture Co.,* 121 U.S. App. D.C. 315, 319-320, 350 F.2d 445, 449-450 (1965) (footnotes omitted):

> Ordinarily, one who signs an agreement without full knowledge of its terms might be held to assume the risk that he has entered a one-sided bargain. But when a party of little bargaining power, and hence little real choice, signs a commercially unreasonable contract with little or no knowledge of its terms, it is hardly likely that his consent, or even an objective manifestation of his consent, was ever given to all of the terms. In such a case the usual rule that the terms of the agreement are not to be questioned should be abandoned and the court should consider whether the terms of the contract are so unfair that enforcement should be withheld.

See also *Steven,* 58 Cal. 2d, at 879-883, 27 Cal. Rptr., at 183-185, 377 P.2d, at 295-297; *Henningsen v. Bloomfield Motors, Inc.,* 32 N.J. 358, 161 A.2d 69 (1960).

The second doctrinal principle implicated by forum-selection clauses is the traditional rule that "contractual provisions, which seek to limit the place or court in which an action may . . . be brought, are invalid as contrary to public policy." See Dougherty, Validity of Contractual Provision Limiting Place or Court in Which Action May Be Brought, 31 A.L.R.4th 404, 409, §3 (1984). See also *Home Insurance Co. v. Morse,* 20 Wall. 445, 451, 22 L. Ed. 365 (1874). Although adherence to this general rule has declined in recent years, particularly following our decision in *The Bremen v. Zapata Off-Shore Co.,* 407 U.S. 1, 92 S. Ct. 1907, 32 L. Ed. 2d 513

(1972), the prevailing rule is still that forum-selection clauses are not enforceable if they were not freely bargained for, create additional expense for one party, or deny one party a remedy. See 31 A.L.R.4th, at 409-438 (citing cases). A forum-selection clause in a standardized passenger ticket would clearly have been unenforceable under the common law before our decision in *The Bremen,* see 407 U.S., at 9, and n. 10, 92 S. Ct., at 1912-13, and n. 10, and, in my opinion, remains unenforceable under the prevailing rule today.

The Bremen, which the Court effectively treats as controlling this case, had nothing to say about stipulations printed on the back of passenger tickets. That case involved the enforceability of a forum-selection clause in a freely negotiated international agreement between two large corporations providing for the towage of a vessel from the Gulf of Mexico to the Adriatic Sea. The Court recognized that such towage agreements had generally been held unenforceable in American courts,[5] but held that the doctrine of those cases did not extend to commercial arrangements between parties with equal bargaining power.

The federal statute that should control the disposition of the case before us today was enacted in 1936 when the general rule denying enforcement of forum-selection clauses was indisputably widely accepted. The principal subject of the statute concerned the limitation of shipowner liability, but as the following excerpt from the House Report explains, the section that is relevant to this case was added as a direct response to shipowners' ticketing practices.

> "During the course of the hearings on the bill (H.R. 9969) there was also brought to the attention of the committee a practice of providing on the reverse side of steamship tickets that in the event of damage or injury caused by the negligence or fault of the owner or his servants, the liability of the owner shall be limited to a stipulated amount, in some cases $5,000, and in others substantially lower amounts, or that in such event the question of liability and the measure of damages *shall be determined by arbitration.* The amendment to chapter 6 of title 48 of the Revised Statutes proposed to be made by section 2 of the committee amendment is intended to, and in the opinion of the committee will, *put a stop to all such practices and practices of a like character.*" H.R. Rep. No. 2517, 74th Cong., 2d Sess., 6-7 (1936) (emphasis added); see also S. Rep. No. 2061, 74th Cong., 2d Sess., 6-7 (1936).

The intent to "put a stop to all such practices and practices of a like character" was effectuated in the second clause of the statute. It reads:

> "It shall be unlawful for the manager, agent, master, or owner of any vessel transporting passengers between ports of the United States or between any such port

---

5. "In [*Carbon Black Export, Inc. v. The Monrosa,* 254 F.2d 297 (5th Cir. 1958), cert. dismissed, 359 U.S. 180, 79 S. Ct. 710, 3 L. Ed. 2d 723 (1959),] the Court of Appeals had held a forum-selection clause unenforceable, reiterating the traditional view of many American courts that 'agreements in advance of controversy whose object is to oust the jurisdiction of the courts are contrary to public policy and will not be enforced.'" 254 F.2d, at 300-301. *The Bremen v. Zapata Off-Shore Co.,* 407 U.S. 1, 6, 92 S. Ct. 1907, 1911, 32 L. Ed. 2d 513 (1972).

and a foreign port to insert in any rule, regulation, contract, or agreement any provision or limitation (1) purporting, in the event of loss of life or bodily injury arising from the negligence or fault of such owner or his servants, to relieve such owner, master, or agent from liability, or from liability beyond any stipulated amount, for such loss or injury, or (2) *purporting in such event to lessen, weaken, or avoid the right of any claimant to a trial by court of competent jurisdiction on the question of liability for such loss or injury, or the measure of damages therefor.* All such provisions or limitations contained in any such rule, regulation, contract, or agreement are declared to be against public policy and shall be null and void and of no effect." 46 U.S.C. App. §183c (emphasis added).

. . .

A liberal reading of the 1936 statute is supported by both its remedial purpose and by the legislative history's general condemnation of "all such practices." Although the statute does not specifically mention forum-selection clauses, its language is broad enough to encompass them. The absence of a specific reference is adequately explained by the fact that such clauses were already unenforceable under common law and would not often have been used by carriers, which were relying on stipulations that purported to exonerate them from liability entirely. Cf. *Moskal v. United States,* 498 U.S. 103, 110-113, 111 S. Ct. 461, 466-468, 112 L. Ed. 2d 449 (1990).

. . .

I respectfully dissent.

ARMENDARIZ
v.
FOUNDATION HEALTH PSYCHCARE SERVICES, INC.

Supreme Court of California
24 Cal. 4th 83
2000

Mosk, J.

In this case, we consider a number of issues related to the validity of a mandatory employment arbitration agreement, i.e., an agreement by an employee to arbitrate wrongful termination or employment discrimination claims rather than filing suit in court, which an employer imposes on a prospective or current employee as a condition of employment.

. . .

Marybeth Armendariz and Dolores Olague-Rodgers (hereafter the employees) . . . had filled out and signed employment application forms, which included an arbitration clause pertaining to any future claim of wrongful termination.

Later, they executed a separate employment arbitration agreement, containing the same arbitration clause. The clause states in full:

> "I agree as a condition of my employment, that in the event my employment is terminated, and I contend that such termination was wrongful or otherwise in violation of the conditions of employment or was in violation of any express or implied condition, term or covenant of employment, whether founded in fact or in law, including but not limited to the covenant of good faith and fair dealing, or otherwise in violation of any of my rights, I and Employer agree to submit any such matter to binding arbitration pursuant to the provisions of title 9 of Part III of the California Code of Civil Procedure, commencing at section 1280 et seq. or any successor or replacement statutes. I and Employer further expressly agree that in any such arbitration, my exclusive remedies for violation of the terms, conditions or covenants of employment shall be limited to a sum equal to the wages I would have earned from the date of any discharge until the date of the arbitration award. I understand that I shall not be entitled to any other remedy, at law or in equity, including but not limited to reinstatement and/or injunctive relief."
>
> . . .

D. UNCONSCIONABILITY OF THE ARBITRATION AGREEMENT

. . . In 1979, the Legislature enacted Civil Code section 1670.5, which codified the principle that a court can refuse to enforce an unconscionable provision in a contract. (*Perdue v. Crocker National Bank* (1985) 38 Cal. 3d 913, 925, 216 Cal. Rptr. 345, 702 P.2d 503.) As section 1670.5, subdivision (a) states: "If the court as a matter of law finds the contract or any clause of the contract to have been unconscionable at the time it was made the court may refuse to enforce the contract, or it may enforce the remainder of the contract without the unconscionable clause, or it may so limit the application of any unconscionable clause as to avoid any unconscionable result." Because unconscionability is a reason for refusing to enforce contracts generally, it is also a valid reason for refusing to enforce an arbitration agreement under Code of Civil Procedure section 1281, which, as noted, provides that arbitration agreements are "valid, enforceable and irrevocable, save upon such grounds as exist [at law or in equity] for the revocation of any contract." The United States Supreme Court, in interpreting the same language found in section 2 of the FAA (19 U.S.C. §2), recognized that "generally applicable contract defenses, such as fraud, duress, or *unconscionability,* may be applied to invalidate arbitration agreements. . . ." (*Doctor's Associates, Inc. v. Casarotto, supra,* 517 U.S. 681, 687, 116 S. Ct. 1652, 134 L. Ed. 2d 902, italics added.)

As explained in *A & M Produce Co.,* 135 Cal. App. 3d 473, 186 Cal. Rptr. 114, "unconscionability has both a 'procedural' and a 'substantive' element," the former focusing on "oppression" or "surprise" due to unequal bargaining power, the latter on "overly harsh" or "one-sided" results. (*Id.* at pp. 486-487, 186 Cal. Rptr. 114.) "The prevailing view is that [procedural and substantive unconscionability] must both be present in order for a court to exercise its discretion to refuse to enforce a contract or clause under the doctrine of unconscionability." (*Stirlen v. Supercuts, Inc.,* 51 Cal. App. 4th at p. 1533, 60 Cal. Rptr. 2d 138 (*Stirlen*).) But they need not be present in the same degree. "Essentially a sliding scale is invoked which disregards the regularity of the procedural process of the contract formation, that creates the terms, in proportion to the greater harshness or unreasonableness of the substantive terms themselves." (15 Williston on Contracts (3d ed. 1972) §1763A, pp. 226-227; see also *A & M Produce Co., supra,* 135 Cal. App. 3d at p. 487, 186 Cal. Rptr. 114.) In other words, the more substantively oppressive the contract term, the less evidence of procedural unconscionability is required to come to the conclusion that the term is unenforceable, and vice versa.

Applying the above principles to this case, we first determine whether the arbitration agreement is adhesive. There is little dispute that it is. It was imposed on employees as a condition of employment and there was no opportunity to negotiate.

Moreover, in the case of preemployment arbitration contracts, the economic pressure exerted by employers on all but the most sought-after employees may be particularly acute, for the arbitration agreement stands between the employee and necessary employment, and few employees are in a position to refuse a job because of an arbitration requirement. While arbitration may have its advantages in terms of greater expedition, informality, and lower cost, it also has, from the employee's point of view, potential disadvantages: waiver of a right to a jury trial, limited discovery, and limited judicial review. Various studies show that arbitration is advantageous to employers not only because it reduces the costs of litigation, but also because it reduces the size of the award that an employee is likely to get, particularly if the employer is a "repeat player" in the arbitration system. (Bingham, *Employment Arbitration: The Repeat Player Effect* (1997) 1 Employee Rts. & Employment Policy J. 189; Schwartz, *supra,* 1997 Wis. L. Rev. at pp. 60-61.) It is perhaps for this reason that it is almost invariably the employer who seeks to compel arbitration. (See Schwartz, *supra,* 1997 Wis. L. Rev. at pp. 60-63.)

Arbitration is favored in this state as a voluntary means of resolving disputes, and this voluntariness has been its bedrock justification. As we stated recently: "[P]olicies favoring the efficiency of private arbitration as a means of dispute resolution must sometimes yield to its fundamentally contractual nature, and to the attendant requirement that arbitration shall proceed as the parties themselves have agreed." (*Vandenberg v. Superior Court, supra,* 21 Cal. 4th at p. 831, 88 Cal. Rptr. 2d 366, 982 P.2d 229, italics omitted.) Given the lack of choice and the potential disadvantages that even a fair arbitration system can harbor for employees, we must be particularly attuned to claims that employers with superior bargaining power have imposed one-sided, substantively unconscionable terms as part of an arbitration agreement. "Private arbitration may resolve disputes faster and cheaper than judicial proceedings. Private arbitration, however, may also become an instrument of injustice imposed on a 'take it or leave it' basis. The courts must distinguish the former from the latter, to ensure that private arbitration systems resolve disputes not only with speed and economy but also with fairness." (*Engalla, supra,* 15 Cal. 4th at p. 989, 64 Cal. Rptr. 2d 843, 938 P.2d 903 (conc. opn. of Kennard, J.).) With this in mind, we turn to the employees' specific unconscionability claims.

. . . [T]he employees contend that the agreement is substantively unconscionable because it requires only employees to arbitrate their wrongful termination claims
against the employer, but does not require the employer to arbitrate claims it may
have against the employees. In asserting that this lack of mutuality is unconscionable, they rely primarily on the opinion of the Court of Appeal in *Stirlen, supra,* 51 Cal.
App. 4th 1519, 60 Cal. Rptr. 2d 138. The employee in that case was hired as a vice-
president and chief financial officer; his employment contract provided for arbitration
"'in the event there is any dispute arising out of [the employee's] employment with
the Company,'" including "the termination of that employment." (*Stirlen, supra,* 51
Cal. App. 4th at p. 1528, 60 Cal. Rptr. 2d 100.) The agreement specifically excluded
certain types of disputes from the scope of arbitration, including those relating to the
protection of the employer's intellectual and other property and the enforcement of a
postemployment covenant not to compete, which were to be litigated in state or
federal court. (*Ibid.*) The employee was to waive the right to challenge the jurisdiction
of such a court. (*Ibid.*) The arbitration agreement further provided that the damages
available would be limited to "'the amount of actual damages for breach of contract,
less any proper offset for mitigation of such damages.'" (*Id.* at p. 1529, 60 Cal. Rptr.
2d 138.) When an arbitration claim was filed, payments of any salary or benefits were
to cease "'without penalty to the Company,'" pending the outcome of the arbitration. (*Id.* at p. 1528, 60 Cal. Rptr. 2d 138.)

The *Stirlen* court concluded that the agreement was one of adhesion, even
though the employee in question was a high-level executive, because of the lack
of opportunity to negotiate. (*Stirlen, supra,* 51 Cal. App. 4th at pp. 1533-1534, 60
Cal. Rptr. 2d 138.) The court then concluded that the arbitration agreement was
substantively unconscionable. (*Id.* at p. 1541, 60 Cal. Rptr. 2d 138.) The court relied
in part on *Saika v. Gold* (1996) 49 Cal. App. 4th 1074, 56 Cal. Rptr. 2d 922 (*Saika*), in
which the court had refused to enforce a provision in an arbitration agreement
between a doctor and a patient that would allow a "trial de novo" if the arbitrator's
award was $25,000 or greater. The *Saika* court reasoned that such a clause was
tantamount to making arbitration binding when the patient lost the arbitration but not
binding if the patient won a significant money judgment. (*Saika, supra,* 49 Cal. App.
4th at pp. 1079-1080, 56 Cal. Rptr. 2d 922.) *Stirlen* concluded that the Supercuts
agreement lacked even the "modicum of bilaterality" that was present in *Saika*.
(*Stirlen, supra,* 51 Cal. App. 4th at p. 1541, 60 Cal. Rptr. 2d 138.) The employee
pursuing claims against the employer had to bear not only with the inherent shortcomings of arbitration—limited discovery, limited judicial review, limited procedural
protections—but also significant damage limitations imposed by the arbitration
agreement. (*Id.* at pp. 1537-1540, 60 Cal. Rptr. 2d 138.) The employer, on the
other hand, in pursuing its claims, was not subject to these disadvantageous limitations and had written into the agreement special advantages, such as a waiver of
jurisdictional objections by the employee if sued by the employer. (*Id.* at pp. 1541-
1542, 60 Cal. Rptr. 2d 138.)

The *Stirlen* court did not hold that all lack of mutuality in a contract of adhesion
was invalid. "We agree a contract can provide a 'margin of safety' that provides the
party with superior bargaining strength a type of extra protection for which it has a
legitimate commercial need without being unconscionable. However, unless the

'business realities' that create the special need for such an advantage are explained in the contract itself, which is not the case here, it must be factually established." (*Stirlen, supra,* 51 Cal. App. 4th at p. 1536, 60 Cal. Rptr. 2d 138.) The *Stirlen* court found no "business reality" to justify the lack of mutuality, concluding that the terms of the arbitration clause were "'so extreme as to appear unconscionable according to the mores and business practices of the time and place.'" (*Id.* at p. 1542, 60 Cal. Rptr. 2d 138.)

The court in *Kinney v. United HealthCare Services, Inc.* (1999) 70 Cal. App. 4th 1322, 83 Cal. Rptr. 2d 348 (*Kinney*), came to the same conclusion with respect to an arbitration agreement to compel the employee, but not the employer, to submit claims to arbitration. As the *Kinney* court stated: "Faced with the issue of whether a unilateral obligation to arbitrate is unconscionable, we conclude that it is. The party who is required to submit his or her claims to arbitration [forgoes] the right, otherwise guaranteed by the federal and state Constitutions, to have those claims tried before a jury. (U.S. Const., Amend. VII; Cal. Const., art. I, §16.) Further, except in extraordinary circumstances, that party has no avenue of review for an adverse decision, even if that decision is based on an error of fact or law that appears on the face of the ruling and results in substantial injustice to that party. [Citation.] By contrast, the party requiring the other to waive these rights retains all of the benefits and protections the right to a judicial forum provides. Given the basic and substantial nature of the rights at issue, we find that the unilateral obligation to arbitrate is itself so one-sided as to be substantively unconscionable." (*Kinney, supra,* 70 Cal. App. 4th at p. 1332, 83 Cal. Rptr. 2d 348.) The court also found that certain terms of the arbitration agreement—limits to discovery and caps on compensatory and punitive damages—"heightened" its unconscionability. (*Ibid.*)

We conclude that *Stirlen* and *Kinney* are correct in requiring this "modicum of bilaterality" in an arbitration agreement. Given the disadvantages that may exist for plaintiffs arbitrating disputes, it is unfairly one-sided for an employer with superior bargaining power to impose arbitration on the employee as plaintiff but not to accept such limitations when it seeks to prosecute a claim against the employee, without at least some reasonable justification for such one-sidedness based on "business realities." As has been recognized "'unconscionability turns not only on a "one-sided" result, but also on an absence of "justification" for it.'" (*A & M Produce Co., supra,* 135 Cal. App. 3d at p. 487, 186 Cal. Rptr. 114.) If the arbitration system established by the employer is indeed fair, then the employer as well as the employee should be willing to submit claims to arbitration. Without reasonable justification for this lack of mutuality, arbitration appears less as a forum for neutral dispute resolution and more as a means of maximizing employer advantage. Arbitration was not intended for this purpose. (See *Engalla, supra,* 15 Cal. 4th at p. 976, 64 Cal. Rptr. 2d 843, 938 P.2d 903.)

The employer cites a number of cases that have held that a lack of mutuality in an arbitration agreement does not render the contract illusory as long as the employer agrees to be bound by the arbitration of employment disputes. (*Michalski v. Circuit City Stores* (7th Cir. 1999) 177 F.3d 634; *Johnson v. Circuit City Stores* (4th Cir. 1998) 148 F.3d 373, 378.) We agree that such lack of mutuality does not render the contract illusory, i.e., lacking in mutual consideration. We conclude, rather, that in the context of an arbitration agreement imposed by the employer on the employee, such a one-sided term is unconscionable. Although parties are free to contract for asymmetrical remedies and arbitration clauses of varying scope, *Stirlen* and *Kinney* are correct that the doctrine of unconscionability limits the extent to which a stronger party may, through a contract of adhesion, impose the arbitration forum on the weaker party without accepting that forum for itself.

. . .

Applying these principles to the present case, we note the arbitration agreement was limited in scope to employee claims regarding wrongful termination. Although it did not expressly authorize litigation of the employer's claims against the employee, as was the case in *Stirlen* and *Kinney,* such was the clear implication of the agreement. Obviously, the lack of mutuality can be manifested as much by what the agreement does not provide as by what it does. (Cf. *24 Hour Fitness, Inc. v. Superior Court* (1998) 66 Cal. App. 4th 1199, 1205, 1212-1213, 78 Cal. Rptr. 2d 533 [employee arbitration clause in personnel handbook found not to be unconscionable where it pertains to "'any dispute aris[ing] from your employment'"].)

This is not to say that an arbitration clause must mandate the arbitration of all claims between employer and employee in order to avoid invalidation on grounds of unconscionability. Indeed, as the employer points out, the present arbitration agreement does not require arbitration of all conceivable claims that an employee might have against an employer, only wrongful termination claims. But an arbitration agreement imposed in an adhesive context lacks basic fairness and mutuality if it requires one contracting party, but not the other, to arbitrate all claims arising out of the same transaction or occurrence or series of transactions or occurrences. The arbitration agreement in this case lacks mutuality in this sense because it requires the arbitration of employee—but not employer—claims arising out of a wrongful termination. An employee terminated for stealing trade secrets, for example, must arbitrate his or her wrongful termination claim under the agreement while the employer has no corresponding obligation to arbitrate its trade secrets claim against the employee.

The unconscionable one-sidedness of the arbitration agreement is compounded in this case by the fact that it does not permit the full recovery of damages for employees, while placing no such restriction on the employer. Even if the limitation on FEHA damages is severed as contrary to public policy, the arbitration clause in the present case still does not permit full recovery of ordinary contract damages. The arbitration agreement specifies that damages are to be limited to the amount of backpay lost up until the time of arbitration. This provision excludes damages for prospective future earnings, so-called "front pay," a common and often substantial component of contractual damages in a wrongful termination case. (See 4 Wilcox, Cal. Employment Law (2000) §60.08[3][b], p. 60-102 and [2][b][iii], p. 60-97.) The employer, on the other hand, is bound by no comparable limitation should it pursue a claim against its employees.

The employer in this case, as well as the Court of Appeal, claim the lack of mutuality was based on the realities of the employees' place in the organizational hierarchy. As the Court of Appeal stated: "We . . . observe that the wording of the agreement most likely resulted from the employees' position within the organization and may reflect the fact that the parties did not foresee the possibility of any dispute arising from employment that was not initiated by the employee. Plaintiffs were lower-level supervisory employees, without the sort of access to proprietary information or control over corporate finances that might lead to an employer suit against them."

The fact that it is unlikely an employer will bring claims against a particular type of employee is not, ultimately, a justification for a unilateral arbitration agreement. It provides no reason for categorically exempting employer claims, however rare, from mandatory arbitration. Although an employer may be able, in a future case, to justify a unilateral arbitration agreement, the employer in the present case has not done so.

E. SEVERABILITY OF UNCONSCIONABLE PROVISIONS

The employees contend that the presence of various unconscionable provisions or provisions contrary to public policy leads to the conclusion that the arbitration agreement as a whole cannot be enforced. The employer contends that, insofar as there are unconscionable provisions, they should be severed and the rest of the agreement enforced.

As noted, Civil Code section 1670.5, subdivision (a) provides that "[i]f the court as a matter of law finds the contract or any clause of the contract to have been unconscionable at the time it was made the court may refuse to enforce the contract, or it may enforce the remainder of the contract without the unconscionable clause, or it may so limit the application of any unconscionable clause as to avoid any unconscionable result." Comment 2 of the Legislative Committee comment on section 1670.5, incorporating the comments from the Uniform Commercial Code, states: "Under this section the court, in its discretion, may refuse to enforce the contract as a whole if it is permeated by the unconscionability, or it may strike any single clause or group of clauses which are so tainted or which are contrary to the essential purpose of the agreement, or it may simply limit unconscionable clauses so as to avoid unconscionable results." (Legis. Com. com., at 9 West's Ann. Civ. Code (1985 ed.) p. 494 (Legislative Committee comment).)

Thus, the statute appears to give a trial court some discretion as to whether to sever or restrict the unconscionable provision or whether to refuse to enforce the entire agreement. But it also appears to contemplate the latter course only when an agreement is "permeated" by unconscionability. We could discover no published cases in California that address directly the question of when a trial court abuses its discretion by refusing to enforce an entire agreement, as the trial court did in this case, nor precisely what it means for an agreement to be "permeated" by unconscionability. But there is a good deal of statutory and case law discussing the related question of when it is proper to sever *illegal* contract terms—a subject to which we will now turn.

Civil Code section 1598 states that "[w]here a contract has but a single object, and such object is unlawful, whether in whole or in part, or wholly impossible of performance, or so vaguely expressed as to be wholly unascertainable, the entire contract is void." Section 1599 states that "[w]here a contract has several distinct objects, of which one at least is lawful, and one at least is unlawful, in whole or in part, the contract is void as to the latter and valid as to the rest." In *Keene v. Harling* (1964) 61 Cal. 2d 318, 320-321, 38 Cal. Rptr. 513, 392 P.2d 273 (*Keene*), we elaborated on those provisions: "'Whether a contract is entire or separable depends upon its language and subject matter, and this question is one of construction to be determined by the court according to the intention of the parties. If the contract is divisible, the first part may stand, although the latter is illegal. [Citation.]' [Citations.] It has long been the rule in this state that 'When the transaction is of such a nature that the good part of the consideration can be separated from that which is bad, the Courts will make the distinction, for the . . . law . . . [divides] according to common reason; and having made that void that is against law, lets the rest stand.'" (Fn. omitted; see also *Birbrower, Montalbano, Condon & Frank v. Superior Court* (1998) 17 Cal. 4th 119, 137-139, 70 Cal. Rptr. 2d 304, 949 P.2d 1 (*Birbrower*) [holding severable legal from illegal portions of attorney fee agreement].)

. . .

Two reasons for severing or restricting illegal terms rather than voiding the entire contract appear implicit in case law. The first is to prevent parties from gaining undeserved benefit or suffering undeserved detriment as a result of voiding the entire agreement—particularly when there has been full or partial performance of the contract. (See *Keene, supra,* 61 Cal. 2d at pp. 320-321, 38 Cal. Rptr. 513, 392 P.2d 273; *Birbrower, supra,* 17 Cal. 4th at pp. 137-139, 70 Cal. Rptr. 2d 304, 949 P.2d 1; *Saika, supra,* 49 Cal. App. 4th at p. 1082, 56 Cal. Rptr. 2d 922 [enforcing arbitration agreement already performed, while severing illegal trial de novo clause].) Second, more generally, the doctrine of severance attempts to conserve a contractual relationship if to do so would not be condoning an illegal scheme. (See e.g., *Werner v. Knoll, supra,* 89 Cal. App. 2d at pp. 476-477, 201 P.2d 45; *General Paint Corp. v. Seymour, supra,* 124 Cal. App. at pp. 614-615, 12 P.2d 990.) The overarching inquiry is whether "'the interests of justice . . . would be furthered'" by severance. (*Beynon v. Garden Grove Medical Group* (1980) 100 Cal. App. 3d 698, 713, 161 Cal. Rptr. 146.) Moreover, courts must have the *capacity* to cure the unlawful contract through severance or restriction of the offending clause, which, as discussed below, is not invariably the case.

The basic principles of severability that emerge from Civil Code section 1599 and the case law of illegal contracts appear fully applicable to the doctrine of unconscionability. Courts are to look to the various purposes of the contract. If the central purpose of the contract is tainted with illegality, then the contract as a whole cannot be enforced. If the illegality is collateral to the main purpose of the contract, and the illegal provision can be extirpated from the contract by means of severance or restriction, then such severance and restriction are appropriate. That Civil Code section 1670.5 follows this basic model is suggested by the Legislative Committee comment quoted above, which talks in terms of contracts not being enforced if "permeated" by unconscionability, and of clauses being severed if "so tainted or . . . contrary to the essential purpose of the agreement." (Leg. Com. com., *supra,* at p. 494.)

In this case, two factors weigh against severance of the unlawful provisions. First, the arbitration agreement contains more than one unlawful provision; it has both an unlawful damages provision and an unconscionably unilateral arbitration clause. Such multiple defects indicate a systematic effort to impose arbitration on an employee not simply as an alternative to litigation, but as an inferior forum that works to the employer's advantage. In other words, given the multiple unlawful provisions, the trial court did not abuse its discretion in concluding that the arbitration agreement is permeated by an unlawful purpose. (See *Graham Oil, supra,* 43 F.3d at pp. 1248-1249.)

Second, in the case of the agreement's lack of mutuality, such permeation is indicated by the fact that there is no single provision a court can strike or restrict in order to remove the unconscionable taint from the agreement. Rather, the court would have to, in effect, reform the contract, not through severance or restriction, but by augmenting it with additional terms. Civil Code section 1670.5 does not authorize such reformation by augmentation, nor does the arbitration statute. Code of Civil Procedure section 1281.2 authorizes the court to refuse arbitration if grounds for revocation exist, not to reform the agreement to make it lawful. Nor do courts have any such power under their inherent, limited authority to reform contracts. (See *Kolani v. Gluska* (1998) 64 Cal. App. 4th 402, 407-408, 75 Cal. Rptr. 2d 257 [power to reform limited to instances in which parties make mistakes, not to correct illegal provisions]; see also *Getty v. Getty* (1986) 187 Cal. App. 3d 1159, 1178-1179, 232 Cal. Rptr. 603.) Because a court is unable to cure this unconscionability through severance or restriction, and is not permitted to cure it through reformation and augmentation, it must void the entire agreement. (See *Stirlen, supra,* 51 Cal. App. 4th at p. 1552, 60 Cal. Rptr. 2d 138.)

Moreover, whether an employer is willing, now that the employment relationship has ended, to allow the arbitration provision to be mutually applicable, or to encompass the full range of remedies, does not change the fact that the arbitration agreement as written is unconscionable and contrary to public policy. Such a willingness "can be seen, at most, as an offer to modify the contract; an offer that was never accepted. No existing rule of contract law permits a party to resuscitate a legally defective contract merely by offering to change it." (*Stirlen, supra,* 51 Cal. App. 4th at pp. 1535-1536, 60 Cal. Rptr. 2d 138, fn. omitted.)

The approach described above is consistent with our holding in *Scissor-Tail, supra,* 28 Cal. 3d at page 831, 171 Cal. Rptr. 604, 623 P.2d 165. In that case, we found an arbitration agreement to be unconscionable because the agreement provided for an arbitrator likely to be biased in favor of the party imposing the agreement. (*Ibid.*) We nonetheless recognized that "[t]he parties have indeed agreed to arbitrate" and that there is a "strong public policy of this state in favor of resolving disputes by arbitration." (*Ibid.*) The court found a way out of this dilemma through the CAA, specifically Code of Civil Procedure section 1281.6, which provides in part: "If the arbitration agreement does not provide a method for appointing an arbitrator, the parties to the agreement who seek arbitration and against whom arbitration is sought may agree on a method of appointing an arbitrator and that method shall be followed. In the absence of an agreed method, or if the agreed method fails or for any reason cannot be followed, or when an arbitrator appointed fails to act and his or her successor has not been appointed, the court, on petition of a party to the arbitration agreement, shall appoint the arbitrator." Citing this provision, the court stated: "We therefore conclude that upon remand the trial court should afford the parties a reasonable opportunity to agree on a suitable arbitrator and, failing such agreement, the court should on petition of either party appoint the arbitrator." (*Scissor-Tail, supra,* 28 Cal. 3d at p. 831, 171 Cal. Rptr. 604, 623 P.2d 165.) Other cases, both before and after *Scissor-Tail,* have also held that the part of an arbitration clause providing for a less-than-neutral arbitration forum is severable from the rest of the clause. (See *Lewis v. Merrill Lynch, Pierce, Fenner & Smith* (1986) 183 Cal. App. 3d 1097, 1107, 228 Cal. Rptr. 345; *Richards v. Merrill Lynch, Pierce, Fenner & Smith* (1976) 64 Cal. App. 3d 899, 906, 135 Cal. Rptr. 26.)

Thus, in *Scissor-Tail* and the other cases cited above, the arbitration statute itself gave the court the power to reform an arbitration agreement with respect to the method of selecting arbitrators. There is no comparable provision in the arbitration statute that permits courts to reform an unconscionably one-sided agreement. . . .

Problems

1. Process for Slow Processors. DeWayne Hubbert purchased a computer online from Dell Corporation. To make a purchase on the Dell website, Hubbert had to fill out information on five separate web pages. Each page included a blue hyperlink to the "Terms and Conditions of Sale," which, in turn, provided, in all capital letters, that any dispute related to the purchase "SHALL BE RESOLVED EXCLUSIVELY AND FINALLY BY BINDING ARBITRATION ADMINISTERED BY THE NATIONAL ARBITRATION FORUM." The last three web pages also stated that "All sales are subject to Dell's Terms and Conditions of Sale." Dell did not require customers to acknowledge or assent to its terms and conditions. Dell did include a copy of the terms in the box sent to purchasers, along with notice of its "total satisfaction" policy—that is, purchasers could obtain a full refund if they returned their computers within 30 days. Hubbert did not return his computer and later sued Dell in state court, alleging that the company deceived him, and other customers, about the processing speed of the computer. Dell moved to enforce the arbitration clause. Who should prevail?

2. Death on the High Seas. When Bobbi Jo and Joel Wallis booked their Mediterranean cruise with Princess Cruises, Inc., they received a packet containing ticket coupons and a "Passage Contract." At the bottom of "Coupon 01" of the ticket packet was the warning headline "IMPORTANT NOTICE" in 1/8-inch type, followed by this statement in 1/16-inch type:

THIS TICKET INCLUDES THE PASSAGE CONTRACT TERMS SET FORTH AT THE END OF THIS PACKET WHICH ARE BINDING ON YOU. PLEASE READ ALL SECTIONS CAREFULLY AS THEY AFFECT YOUR LEGAL RIGHTS, PARTICULARLY SECTION 14 GOVERNING THE PROVISION

OF MEDICAL AND OTHER PERSONAL SERVICES AND SECTIONS 15
THROUGH 18 LIMITING THE CARRIER'S LIABILITY AND YOUR RIGHTS
TO SUE.

The warning headline and text was repeated four more times at the bottom of
"Coupon 04," "Coupon 07," "Coupon 08," and "Coupon 09." Text of similar
wording appeared across the top of the first page of the Passage Contract, located
behind the ticket coupons. On pages six and seven of the Passage Contract was a
paragraph headed "16. LIMITATIONS ON CARRIER'S LIABILITY; INDEM-
NIFICATION." The sixth and seventh sentences of the paragraph read:

> Carrier shall be entitled to any and all liability limitations, immunities and rights
> applicable to it under the "Convention Relating to the Carriage of Passengers and
> Their Luggage by Sea" of 1976 ("Athens Convention") which limits the Carrier's
> liability for death of or personal injury to a Passenger to no more than the applicable
> amount of Special Drawing Rights as defined therein, and all other limits for damage
> or loss of personal property. . . .

The 1976 Amendments to the Athens Convention (to which the United States is
not a signatory), in turn, define "Special Drawing Rights" as 46,666 international
units of account.

In the course of the cruise, Joel Wallis disappeared overboard; his decomposed
body later washed up on the Greek shore. Bobbi Jo Wallis sued Princess under a
number of legal theories, and Princess moved for partial summary judgment that
its liability was limited by its contract with the Wallises to $60,000. Should Prin-
cess prevail?

3. Old West. The Cody Country Chamber of Commerce sponsored mock gunfight performances on the streets of Cody, Wyoming, through a group called the
Cody Country Gunfighters Club, for the purpose of promoting local tourism.
To join the Club and perform in the gunfights, David Boehm was required to
sign an application with the following exculpatory clause:

> . . . I shall perform as a Gunfighter entirely at my own risk and shall hold harmless and
> release the Cody Chamber of Commerce . . . from any and all claims and damages
> which said participant may incur from participation in any and all activities sanc-
> tioned by the . . . Club.

While playing the role of a bandit gunned down by sheriff deputies in a mock
gunfight, Boehm suffered an injury to his eye. He sued the Chamber of Commerce
alleging negligence, and the Chamber sought summary judgment based on the
exculpatory clause. Should the contract language preclude Boehm's tort suit?

4. Cell Phones with No Class. Vincent and Liza Concepcion entered into a
contract with AT&T Mobility LLC for the sale and servicing of cellular telephones. The fine print in the AT&T-drafted agreement required that most disputes must be settled through arbitration, although it provided that AT&T will

pay all arbitration costs for non-frivolous claims and allowed customers to arbitrate small claims (under $10,000) via telephone or bring them in small claims court. It further specified that customers must bring any claims in their "individual capacity, and not . . . in any purported class or representative proceeding," and it similarly prohibited arbitrators from consolidating any suits into class action proceedings. When the Concepcions were charged $30.22 in sales tax for a supposedly "free" phone, they filed a class action claim against AT&T in federal court alleging fraud. AT&T argued that, under the contract, the Concepcions must arbitrate, and could bring only their individual claim rather than a class action.

California law provides that "contracts which . . . exempt anyone from responsibility for his own fraud . . . are against the policy of the law." Cal. Civ. Code §1668. The Federal Arbitration Act (FAA) provides that contractual arbitration provisions "shall be valid . . . and enforceable, save upon such grounds as exist at law or in equity for the revocation of any contract." The Supreme Court has interpreted the FAA to prohibit states from discriminating against arbitration clauses in contracts as such but to permit litigants to raise any general state law defenses to contract enforcement that they might have even when that means an arbitration clause would be invalidated.

Is the AT&T arbitration clause, which, if effective, would make it impossible for the Concepcions to bring any class action claim, enforceable?

B. THE BATTLE OF THE FORMS

What happens when both contracting parties simultaneously attempt to impose standard form contracts, and the terms embodied in the two forms are inconsistent? As you will recall from Chapter 2, the common law grants the offeror control over the terms of the offer. Under the mirror image rule, a purported acceptance that does not precisely mirror the terms of the offer is treated as a counteroffer—a rejection of the original offer coupled with a new offer by the original offeree.

Imagine that a buyer sends a purchase order form (the offer) calling for future delivery, and the seller responds with a standard acknowledgment form that does not precisely mirror the offer. Under the common law, the seller's response is a counteroffer. If the buyer does not read the form but merely notes that it agrees on key terms, then the buyer might never respond to this counteroffer. Silence, as you will also recall, usually does not amount to an acceptance. Thus, in the absence of a buyer response no contract has been formed. The seller is free to walk away from the transaction if some event, such as an increase in market prices, makes the deal unattractive. If the seller does deliver the goods, the buyer's acceptance of the goods amounts to an acceptance of the seller's counteroffer. (The same dynamic plays out to the buyer's benefit if the seller sends the first form.) The mirror image rule, then, acts as a "last shot" rule: the party that sends the last form controls the terms of the agreement.

As the first case in this section—*Leonard Pevar Company v. Evans Products Company*—illustrates, UCC Article 2 takes a different approach, replacing the common law regime with a more complicated formula for identifying which terms become part of the parties' contract. U.C.C. §2-207. The authors of the Restatement have recommended that courts apply this set of principles in non-UCC cases, Rest. (2d) Contracts §59, but courts have not uniformly heeded this guidance. *Klocek v. Gateway, Inc.*, examines the applicability of U.C.C. §2-207 to contracts involving only one form.

LEONARD PEVAR CO.
v.
EVANS PRODUCTS CO.

— builder
manufacture

U.S. District Court, District of Delaware
524 F. Supp. 546
1981

LATCHUM, C.J.

This is a diversity action by the Leonard Pevar Company ("Pevar") against the Evans Products Company ("Evans") for an alleged breach of express and implied warranties in Evans' sale to Pevar of medium density overlay plywood. Defendant denies liability, claiming that it expressly disclaims warranties and limited its liability in its contract with Pevar. The parties agree that their respective rights and liabilities in this action are governed by the Uniform Commercial Code. The parties have filed cross motions for summary judgment pursuant to Rule 56, F.R. Civ. P. This Court will deny both motions because it finds material facts that are in genuine dispute.

I. FACTS

In the fall of 1977, Pevar began obtaining price quotations for the purchase of medium density overlay plywood to be used in the construction of certain buildings for the State of Pennsylvania. As part of this process, Pevar's contract administrator, Marc Pevar, contacted various manufacturers of this product. Evans was one of the manufacturers contacted and was the supplier that quoted the lowest price for this material.

On October 12, 1977, Marc Pevar had a telephone conversation with Kenneth Kruger of Evans to obtain this price quotation. It is at this juncture that a material fact appears in dispute that precludes this Court from granting summary judgment. Pevar claims that on October 14 it again called Evans, ordered plywood, and entered into an oral contract of sale. Evans admits that Pevar called Evans, but denies that Evans accepted that order.

After the October 14th telephone conversation, Pevar sent a written purchase order to Evans for the plywood. In the purchase order, Pevar did not make any reference to warranties or remedies, but simply ordered the lumber specifying the price, quantity and shipping instructions. On October 19, 1979, Evans sent an acknowledgment to Pevar stating, on the reverse side of the acknowledgment and in boilerplate fashion, that the contract of sale would be expressly contingent upon Pevar's acceptance of all terms contained in the document.[12] One of these terms disclaim most warranties and another limited the "buyer's remedy" by restricting liability if the plywood proved to be defective. [A deleted footnote reprints the terms and states that "[b]oth of these terms were in boldface type[.]"—EDS.]

II. STATUTE OF FRAUDS

Evans contends that if Pevar and Evans entered into an oral contract, it would be unenforceable because it would be in violation of the statute of frauds. Section 2-201 generally provides that an oral contract for the sale of goods in excess of $500 is unenforceable. Section 2-201(2), however, provides an exception. If a written confirmation is sent to the receiving party, and the receiving party does not object to the confirmation within ten days, then the oral agreement may be enforceable. The Court finds that Pevar's written purchase order constituted a <u>confirmatory memorandum</u> and Evans' acknowledgment failed to provide sufficient notice of objection to Pevar's confirmation. The acknowledgment did not deny expressly the existence of the purported contract; rather, it merely asserted additional terms. Thus, the statute of frauds will not bar Pevar from proving the existence and terms of the contract[.]

III. BATTLE OF THE FORMS

Turning now to Section 2-207, it provides:

  (1) A definite and seasonable expression of acceptance or a written confirmation which is sent within a reasonable time operates as an acceptance even though it states terms additional to or different from those offered or agreed upon, unless acceptance is expressly made conditional on assent to the additional or different terms.[17]
  (2) The additional terms are to be construed as proposals for addition to the contract. Between merchants such terms become part of the contract unless:
    (a) the offer expressly limits acceptance to the terms of the offer;
    (b) they materially alter it; or
    (c) notification of objection to them has already been given or is given within a reasonable time after notice of them is received.
  (3) Conduct by both parties which recognizes the existence of a contract is sufficient to establish a contract for sale although the writings of the parties do not otherwise

---

12. Paragraph 1 of the Acknowledgment provided:

   Any acceptance by Seller contained herein is expressly made conditional on Buyer's assent to the additional or different terms contained herein. Any acceptance by Buyer contained herein is expressly limited to the terms herein.

17. The "unless" proviso in §2-207(1) does not apply to confirmatory memoranda because the parties have already entered into an agreement and one party does not have the power pursuant to §2-207 to terminate it unilaterally. . . .

establish a contract. In such case the terms of the particular contract consists of those terms on which the writings of the parties agree, together with any supplementary terms incorporated under any other provisions of this Act.

Section 2-207 was intended to eliminate the "ribbon matching" or "mirror" rule of common law, under which the terms of an acceptance or confirmation were required to be identical to the terms of the offer or oral agreement, respectively. The drafters of the Code intended to preserve an agreement, as it was originally conceived by the parties, in the face of additional material terms included in standard forms exchanged by merchants in the normal course of dealings. Section 2-207 recognizes that a buyer and seller can enter into a contract by one of three methods. First, the parties may agree orally and thereafter send confirmatory memoranda. §2-207(1). Second, the parties, without oral agreement, may exchange writings which do not contain identical terms, but nevertheless constitute a seasonable acceptance. §2-207(1). Third, the conduct of the parties may recognize the existence of a contract, despite the previous failure to agree orally or in writing. §2-207(3).

A. Oral Agreement Followed by Confirmation

Confirmation connotes that the parties reached an agreement before exchange of the forms in question. The purpose of the Code drafters here must have been to make clear that confirmations need not mirror each other in order to find contract. Simply stated, then, under this first clause of §2-207(1) it is reasonable to assume that the parties have a deal, that there is a contract even though terms of the writing exchanged do not match. All of the language following the comma in subsection (1) simply preserves for the offeree his right to make a counter-offer if he does so expressly. This phrase cannot possibly affect the deal between parties that have reached an agreement and then exchanged confirmations. In that situation it is too late for a counter-offer and subsection (2) must be applied to determine what becomes of the non-matching terms of the confirmations.

In the present case, paragraphs 9 and 12 of Evans' acknowledgment, which disclaimed warranties and limited liability, may include terms not in the original agreement. Generally, these types of clauses "materially alter" the agreement. Uniform Commercial Code, Comment 4 to §2-207. Nevertheless, the question of a material alteration rests upon the facts of each case. If the trier of fact determines that the acknowledgment includes additional terms which do not materially alter the oral agreement, then the terms will be incorporated into the agreement. If they materially alter it, however, the terms will not be included in the agreement, and the standardized "gap filler" provisions of Article Two will provide the terms of the contract. If the facts reveal that no oral agreement was created, then §2-207(1) may still apply, but in a different manner.

B. Written Documents Not Containing Identical Terms

The second situation in which §2-207(1) may apply is where the parties have not entered into an oral agreement but have exchanged writings which do not contain identical terms. If the Court determines that Pevar and Evans did not orally agree prior to the exchange of documents, then this second situation may apply. In such a case, both Pevar and Evans agree that Pevar's purchase order constituted an offer to purchase. The parties, however, disagree with the characterization of Evans' acknowledgment and Pevar's acceptance of and payment for the shipped goods. Evans contends that the terms disclaiming warranties and limiting liability in the acknowledgment should control because the acknowledgment constituted a counteroffer which Pevar accepted by receiving and paying for the goods. Evans argues that by inserting the "unless" proviso in the terms and conditions of acceptance of the acknowledgment, it effectively rejected and terminated Pevar's offer, and initiated a counteroffer; and when Pevar received and paid for the goods, it accepted the terms of the counteroffer.

Evans relies upon *Roto-Lith, Ltd. v. F.P. Bartlett & Co.,* 297 F.2d 497 (C.A.1, 1962) for the proposition that a buyer accepts the terms of the seller's counteroffer merely by receiving and paying for shipped goods. In *Roto-Lith*, the buyer of goods sent a written purchase order to the seller. The seller thereafter sent an acknowledgment, accepting the purchase order in part, but also added terms which disclaimed warranties and limited liabilities. The buyer received the goods but did not object to the seller's terms. The court found that the seller's acceptance (acknowledgment) was expressly conditional on assent to the additional terms and, therefore, a counteroffer. It held that the buyer accepted the terms of the counteroffer when it received and paid for the goods.

Roto-Lith has been widely criticized because it does not reflect the underlying principles of the Code. Rather, it reflects the orthodox common law reasoning—that the terms of the counteroffer control if the goods are accepted unless the counterofferee specifically objects to those terms. The drafters of the Code, however, intended to change the common law in an attempt to conform contract law to modern day business transactions. They believed that businessmen rarely read the terms on the back of standardized forms and that the common law, therefore, unduly rewarded the party who sent the last form prior to the shipping of the goods. The Code disfavors any attempt by one party to unilaterally impose conditions that would create hardship on another party. Thus, before a counteroffer is accepted, the counterofferee must expressly assent to the new terms.

This Court joins those courts that have rejected the *Roto-Lith* analysis. C. Itoh & Co. (America) Inc. v. Jordan International Co., 552 F.2d 1228 (C.A.7, 1977); Dorton v. Collins & Aikman Corp., 453 F.2d 1161 (C.A.6, 1972). . . . "It finds that (t)he consequence of a clause conditioning acceptance on assent to the additional or different terms is that as of the exchanged writings there is no contract. Either party may at this point in their dealing walk away from the transaction" or reach an express assent. *Itoh, supra.* Without the express assent by the parties no contract is created pursuant to §2-207(1).[21] Nevertheless, the parties' conduct may create a contract pursuant to §2-207(3).

C. Conduct Establishing the Existence of a Contract

③ Section 2-207(3) is the third method by which parties may enter into a contract. This section applies when the parties have not entered into an oral or written contract. Section 2-207(3) provides that "(c)onduct by both parties which recognizes the existence of a contract is sufficient to establish a contract for sale although the writing of the parties do not otherwise establish a contract." As *Dorton, supra,* noted:

> When no contract is recognized under Subsection 2-207(1) . . . the entire transaction aborts at this point. If, however, the subsequent conduct of the parties—particularly, performance by both parties under what they apparently believe to be a contract—recognizes the existence of a contract, under Subsection 2-207(3), such conduct by both parties is sufficient to establish a contract, notwithstanding the fact that no contract would have been recognized on the basis of their writings alone.

Section 2-207(3) also provides that where a contract has been consummated by the conduct of the parties, "the terms of the particular contract consist of those terms in which the writings of the parties agree, together with any supplementary terms incorporated under any other provisions of this Act."

An Order will be entered in accordance with this Memorandum Opinion.

KLOCEK
v.
GATEWAY, INC.

U.S. District Court, District of Kansas
104 F. Supp. 2d 1332
2000

Vratil, J.

. . .

Plaintiff brings individual and class action claims against Gateway, alleging that it induced him and other consumers to purchase computers and special support

---

21. Pevar and Evans had conversations subsequent to the shipping of the goods where Pevar did not object to the terms of Evans' acknowledgment. Evans, relying upon *Construction Aggregates Corp. v. Hewitt-Robbins Corp.,* 404 F.2d 505 (C.A.7), contends that Pevar's failure to object to the acknowledgment during these subsequent conversations constitutes an implicit acceptance of those terms. The facts in *Construction Aggregates* are readily distinguishable from the facts in this case. In that case, the buyer specifically objected to some terms of the acknowledgment, while remaining silent on the others. The court found that the purchaser thereby agreed to those terms in which it remained silent. Contrasting *Construction Aggregates,* Pevar and Evans did not specifically discuss Evans' acknowledgment. Thus, there is no basis to hold that Pevar consented to those terms.

packages by making false promises of technical support. *Complaint,* ¶¶3 and 4. Individually, plaintiff also claims breach of contract and breach of warranty, in that Gateway breached certain warranties that its computer would be compatible with standard peripherals and standard internet services. *Complaint,* ¶¶2, 5, and 6.

Gateway asserts that plaintiff must arbitrate his claims under Gateway's Standard Terms and Conditions Agreement ("Standard Terms"). Whenever it sells a computer, Gateway includes a copy of the Standard Terms in the box which contains the computer battery power cables and instruction manuals. At the top of the first page, the Standard Terms include the following notice:

> NOTE TO THE CUSTOMER:
> This document contains Gateway 2000's Standard Terms and Conditions. By keeping your Gateway 2000 computer system beyond five (5) days after the date of delivery, you accept these Terms and Conditions.

The notice is in emphasized type and is located inside a printed box which sets it apart from other provisions of the document. The Standard Terms are four pages long and contain 16 numbered paragraphs. Paragraph 10 provides the following arbitration clause:

> DISPUTE RESOLUTION. Any dispute or controversy arising out of or relating to this Agreement or its interpretation shall be settled exclusively and finally by arbitration. The arbitration shall be conducted in accordance with the Rules of Conciliation and Arbitration of the International Chamber of Commerce. The arbitration shall be conducted in Chicago, Illinois, U.S.A. before a sole arbitrator. Any award rendered in any such arbitration proceeding shall be final and binding on each of the parties, and judgment may be entered thereon in a court of competent jurisdiction.

. . .

The Uniform Commercial Code ("UCC") governs the parties' transaction under both Kansas and Missouri law. . . . Thus the issue is whether the contract of sale includes the Standard Terms as part of the agreement.

. . .

Gateway urges the Court to follow the Seventh Circuit decision in *Hill.* That case involved the shipment of a Gateway computer with terms similar to the Standard Terms in this case, except that Gateway gave the customer 30 days—instead of 5 days—to return the computer. In enforcing the arbitration clause, the Seventh Circuit relied on its decision in *ProCD,* where it enforced a software license which was contained inside a product box. *See Hill,* 105 F.3d at 1148-50. In *ProCD,* the Seventh Circuit noted that the exchange of money frequently precedes the communication of detailed terms in a commercial transaction. *See ProCD,* 86 F.3d at 1451. Citing UCC §2-204, the court reasoned that by including the license with the software, the vendor proposed a contract that the buyer could accept by using the software after having an opportunity to read the license.[8] *ProCD,* 86 F.3d at 1452. Specifically, the court stated:

> A vendor, as master of the offer, may invite acceptance by conduct, and may propose limitations on the kind of conduct that constitutes acceptance. A buyer may accept by performing the acts the vendor proposes to treat as acceptance.

ProCD, 86 F.3d at 1452. The *Hill* court followed the *ProCD* analysis, noting that "[p]ractical considerations support allowing vendors to enclose the full legal terms with their products." *Hill,* 105 F.3d at 1149.

The Court is not persuaded that Kansas or Missouri courts would follow the Seventh Circuit reasoning in *Hill* and *ProCD.* In each case the Seventh Circuit concluded without support that UCC §2-207 was irrelevant because the cases involved only one written form. *See ProCD,* 86 F.3d at 1452 (citing no authority); *Hill,* 105 F.3d at 1150 (citing *ProCD*). This conclusion is not supported by the statute or by Kansas or Missouri law. Disputes under §2-207 often arise in the context of a "battle of forms," *see, e.g., Diatom, Inc. v. Pennwalt Corp.,* 741 F.2d 1569, 1574 (10th Cir. 1984), but nothing in its language precludes application in a case which involves only one form. The statute provides:

> Additional terms in acceptance or confirmation.
>   (1) A definite and seasonable expression of acceptance or a written confirmation which is sent within a reasonable time operates as an acceptance even though it states terms additional to or different from those offered or agreed upon, unless acceptance is expressly made conditional on assent to the additional or different terms.
>   (2) The additional terms are to be construed as proposals for addition to the contract [if the contract is not between merchants]. . . .

K.S.A. §84-2-207; V.A.M.S. §400.2-207. By its terms, §2-207 applies to an acceptance or written confirmation. It states nothing which requires another form before the provision becomes effective. In fact, the official comment to the section specifically provides that §§2-207(1) and (2) apply "where an agreement has been reached orally . . . and is followed by one or both of the parties sending formal memoranda embodying the terms so far agreed and adding terms not discussed." Official Comment 1 of UCC §2-207. Kansas and Missouri courts have followed this analysis. *See Southwest Engineering Co. v. Martin Tractor Co.,* 205 Kan. 684, 695, 473 P.2d 18, 26 (1970) (stating in dicta that §2-207 applies where open offer is accepted by expression of acceptance in writing or where oral agreement is later confirmed in writing); *Central Bag Co. v. W. Scott and Co.,* 647 S.W.2d 828, 830 (Mo. App. 1983) (§§2-207(1) and (2) govern cases where one or both parties send written confirmation after oral contract). Thus, the Court concludes that Kansas and Missouri courts would apply §2-207 to the facts in this case. *Accord Avedon,* 126 F.3d at 1283 (parties agree that §2-207 controls whether arbitration clause in sales confirmation is part of contract).

---

8. Section 2-204 provides: "A contract for sale of goods may be made in any manner sufficient to show agreement, including conduct by both parties which recognizes the existence of such contract." K.S.A. §84-2-204; V.A.M.S. §400.2-204.

In addition, the Seventh Circuit provided no explanation for its conclusion that "the vendor is the master of the offer." *See ProCD,* 86 F.3d at 1452 (citing nothing in support of proposition); *Hill,* 105 F.3d at 1149 (citing *ProCD*). In typical consumer transactions, the purchaser is the offeror, and the vendor is the offeree. *See Brown Mach., Div. of John Brown, Inc. v. Hercules, Inc.,* 770 S.W.2d 416, 419 (Mo. App. 1989) (as general rule orders are considered offers to purchase); *Rich Prods. Corp. v. Kemutec Inc.,* 66 F. Supp. 2d 937, 956 (E.D. Wis. 1999) (generally price quotation is invitation to make offer and purchase order is offer). While it is possible for the vendor to be the offeror, *see Brown Machine,* 770 S.W.2d at 419 (price quote can amount to offer if it reasonably appears from quote that assent to quote is all that is needed to ripen offer into contract), Gateway provides no factual evidence which would support such a finding in this case. The Court therefore assumes for purposes of the motion to dismiss that plaintiff offered to purchase the computer (either in person or through catalog order) and that Gateway accepted plaintiff's offer (either by completing the sales transaction in person or by agreeing to ship and/or shipping the computer to plaintiff). *Accord Arizona Retail,* 831 F. Supp. at 765 (vendor entered into contract by agreeing to ship goods, or at latest, by shipping goods).

Under §2-207, the Standard Terms constitute either an expression of acceptance or written confirmation. As an expression of acceptance, the Standard Terms would constitute a counter-offer only if Gateway expressly made its acceptance conditional on plaintiff's assent to the additional or different terms. K.S.A. §84-2-207(1); V.A.M.S. §400.2-207(1). "[T]he conditional nature of the acceptance must be clearly expressed in a manner sufficient to notify the offeror that the offeree is unwilling to proceed with the transaction unless the additional or different terms are included in the contract." *Brown Machine,* 770 S.W.2d at 420. Gateway provides no evidence that at the time of the sales transaction, it informed plaintiff that the transaction was conditioned on plaintiff's acceptance of the Standard Terms. Moreover, the mere fact that Gateway shipped the goods with the terms attached did not communicate to plaintiff any unwillingness to proceed without plaintiff's agreement to the Standard Terms. *See, e.g., Arizona Retail,* 831 F. Supp. at 765 (conditional acceptance analysis rarely appropriate where contract formed by performance but goods arrive with conditions attached); *Leighton Indus., Inc. v. Callier Steel Pipe & Tube, Inc.,* 1991 WL 18413, *6, Case No. 89-C-8235 (N.D. Ill. Feb. 6, 1991) (applying Missouri law) (preprinted forms insufficient to notify offeror of conditional nature of acceptance, particularly where form arrives after delivery of goods).

Because plaintiff is not a merchant, additional or different terms contained in the Standard Terms did not become part of the parties' agreement unless plaintiff expressly agreed to them. *See* K.S.A. §84-2-207, Kansas Comment 2 (if either party is not a merchant, additional terms are proposals for addition to the contract that do not become part of the contract unless the original offeror expressly agrees). Gateway argues that plaintiff demonstrated acceptance of the arbitration provision by keeping the computer more than five days after the date of delivery. Although the Standard Terms purport to work that result, Gateway has not presented evidence that plaintiff expressly agreed to those Standard Terms. Gateway states only that it enclosed the Standard Terms inside the computer box for plaintiff to read afterwards. It provides no evidence that it informed plaintiff of the five-day review-and-return period as a condition of the sales transaction, or that the parties contemplated additional terms to the agreement. *See Step-Saver,* 939 F.2d at 99 (during negotiations leading to purchase, vendor never mentioned box-top license or obtained buyer's express assent thereto). The Court finds that the act of keeping the computer past five days was not sufficient to demonstrate that plaintiff expressly agreed to the Standard Terms. *Accord Brown Machine,* 770 S.W.2d at 421 (express assent cannot be presumed by silence or mere failure to object). Thus, because Gateway has not provided evidence sufficient to support a finding under Kansas or Missouri law that plaintiff agreed to the arbitration provision contained in Gateway's Standard Terms, the Court overrules Gateway's motion to dismiss.

. . .

IT IS THEREFORE ORDERED that the *Motion to Dismiss* (Doc. # 6) which defendant Gateway filed November 22, 1999 be and hereby is OVERRULED.

Problems

1. I Wish I Were an Oscar Mayer Weiner. Oscar Mayer Foods regularly purchased from Union Carbide plastic casings used in manufacturing sausages. Oscar Mayer would submit a purchase order for a specific quantity of casings, and Union Carbide would send an invoice. The following clause appeared on the back of the invoices and also in a price book that Union Carbide sent to customers from time to time:

> In addition to the purchase price, Buyer shall pay Seller the amount of all governmental taxes . . . that Seller may be required to pay with respect to the production, sale or transportation of any materials delivered hereunder.

In 1980, Oscar Mayer threatened to buy from another seller that would not have to charge Chicago sales tax because the seller took orders at an office outside Chicago. Union Carbide responded by directing Oscar Mayer to submit orders to Union Carbide's office outside of Chicago, and stopped charging sales taxes on Oscar Mayer's orders. The Illinois Tax Authority decided that Union Carbide should have been charging taxes and assessed Union Carbide for back taxes (as well as interest thereon) for its transactions with Oscar Mayer. Union Carbide sought reimbursement from Oscar Mayer, citing the indemnification clause included in the invoice. Is Oscar Mayer liable?

2. Combustible Thermostats. In 2008, East Kentucky Power Cooperative (EKPC) submitted a purchase order to Comverge for 2,500 programmable thermostats. The purchase order contained basic terms of the sale, including item description, quantity, unit price, and total price, and also included these provisions:

- These terms and conditions as set forth on this order are the only terms and conditions that govern this transaction.

- Any action to enforce this purchase order shall be brought in the Eastern District of Kentucky.

In response, Comverge sent its sales order acceptance form, which accepted EKPC's offer, but also stated:

- Our acceptance of Purchaser's order is conditioned upon Purchaser's agreement with these terms and conditions. With the exception of price, product type, and quantity, we reject any terms and conditions in Purchaser's order which are different from or additional to these terms and conditions.
- The parties agree that the appropriate courts sitting in Northern District of Georgia shall have sole and exclusive authority to hear and adjudicate any dispute arising out of this agreement.

Comverge subsequently shipped to EKPC 2,500 thermostats, which were installed in homes in Kentucky. After several Comverge thermostats burst into flames, EKPC removed all of the thermostats and filed a breach of warranty suit against Comverge in the Eastern District of Kentucky. Comverge filed a motion to dismiss or transfer the suit to the Northern District of Georgia. How should the court rule on the motion?

3. Lost Negatives. Newsweek Magazine contacted photographer Daniel Miller to express an interest in buying Miller's photos of the subject of a possible profile. During a phone conversation with Newsweek's photo editor, Miller agreed to send 72 negatives to Newsweek the same day by courier, and Newsweek agreed to pay Miller a standard rate of $100-$200 for any photo used in the article. Newsweek ultimately did not run the story, and Miller's photos were not used. Newsweek never returned the negatives, which were presumed lost. Miller brought suit against Newsweek for compensation based on the following provisions, which were in a delivery memo accompanying the negatives:

- Negatives may be held for 14 days' approval. A late fee of $5 per week per negative will be charged after such 14-day period.
- Recipient agrees that the reasonable minimum value of any lost or damaged negative shall be no less than $1500.

If the court concludes that UCC Article 2 governs this transaction, must Newsweek pay damages consistent with these provisions?

C. THE PAROL EVIDENCE RULE

Under certain circumstances, the parol evidence rule renders unenforceable agreements that were entered into prior to or simultaneously with the adoption of a written contract. The complexities of the doctrine begin with its misleading name. The parol evidence rule applies not only to parol (or oral) evidence but also to written evidence, such as communication by letter between parties prior to the drafting and signing of a written contract. This fact demonstrates that while in some cases the rule might work to prohibit the introduction of intentionally fraud-ulent, self-serving testimony concerning an alleged oral agreement, its primary purpose is to protect parties' reasonable expectation that a final written agreement supersedes earlier agreements and preliminary discussions that otherwise might be understood as promises. The parol evidence rule is technically a rule of substantive law rather than a rule of evidence, because it circumscribes what facts are relevant to the interpretation of a contract and not just the method by which parties may prove facts in court.

The first step in assessing the applicability of the parol evidence rule is to deter-mine the purpose for which the party seeking to introduce evidence of an agreement not reflected in the signed writing wishes to offer that evidence. If the evidence is being offered to challenge the validity of the signed writing or to prove the existence of a contract between the same parties but concerning a separate subject from that of the signed writing, the parol evidence rule does not apply and the evidence is admissible (subject to any limitations that arise from the law of evidence). If the evidence is offered for the purpose of proving the meaning of a term that appears in the signed writing, the parol evidence rule also does not apply, although whether the court gives weight to that evidence might depend on the rule of construction it applies, as discussed in Section D below. If the evidence is being offered in an attempt to prove that a term that does not appear in the signed writing constitutes a part of that agreement, the parol evidence rule does apply. Rest. (2d) Contracts §214.

When the parol evidence rule applies, this does not automatically render the proffered evidence inadmissible. If the term that the evidence seeks to prove is inconsistent with the contents of the signed writing, the evidence is, in fact, inad-missible. On the other hand, if the term is consistent with the signed writing, the evidence is admissible. Whether the term is consistent or inconsistent with the signed writing in turn depends on the level of completeness, or "integration," of the signed writing. If the signed writing is meant to be the entire statement of the parties' rights and responsibilities (a "completely integrated" agreement), any additional terms would be inconsistent with the writing, rendering evidence offered to prove any additional term inadmissible. But if the parties intended the signed writing to be an authoritative statement of the parties' rights and respon-sibilities concerning only certain issues (a "partially integrated" agreement), parol evidence is prohibited if offered to prove a term that contradicts the writing but not if offered to prove the existence of an additional term that is not inconsistent with the writing. Rest. (2d) Contracts §§213, 215, 216; see also U.C.C. §2-202.

This description of the contours of the parol evidence rule raises several difficult interpretive questions that have perplexed courts and led to inconsistencies across jur-isdictions. How should courts determine the scope of the written contract such that they can determine whether a term proven by parol evidence concerns the same con-tract as the one established by the signed writing or a separate contract? What evidence should courts look to in order to determine whether a signed writing is completely integrated or only partially integrated? What line differentiates a term that contradicts the signed writing from one that is additional to but consistent with that writing?

The first case in this section, *Gianni v. R. Russell & Company*, introduces the parol evidence rule, illustrating its basic operation. *Masterson v. Sine* and *Nelson v.*

Elway concern how courts should go about determining whether a writing is completely or partially integrated and, if it is only partially integrated, whether the proffered term is consistent or inconsistent with the writing. *Davis v. G.N. Mortgage Corporation* considers the complicated relationship of the parol evidence rule to challenges to a contract's enforceability when the evidence on which the challenge is based is inconsistent with terms in an integrated writing.

GIANNI
v.
R. RUSSELL & CO.

Supreme Court of Pennsylvania
281 Pa. 320
1924

SCHAFFER, J.

Plaintiff had been a tenant of a room in an office building in Pittsburgh wherein he conducted a store, selling tobacco, fruit, candy and soft drinks. Defendant acquired the entire property in which the storeroom was located, and its agent negotiated with plaintiff for a further leasing of the room. A lease for three years was signed. It contained a provision that the lessee should "use the premises only for the sale of fruit, candy, soda water," etc., with the further stipulation that "it is expressly understood that the tenant is not allowed to sell tobacco in any form, under penalty of instant forfeiture of this lease." The document was prepared following a discussion about renting the room between the parties and after an agreement to lease had been reached. It was signed after it had been left in plaintiff's hands and admittedly had been read over to him by two persons, one of whom was his daughter.

Plaintiff sets up that in the course of his dealings with defendant's agent it was agreed that, in consideration of his promises not to sell tobacco and to pay an increased rent, and for entering into the agreement as a whole, he should have the exclusive right to sell soft drinks in the building. No such stipulation is contained in the written lease. Shortly after it was signed defendant demised the adjoining room in the building to a drug company without restricting the latter's right to sell soda water and soft drinks. Alleging that this was in violation of the contract which defendant had made with him, and that the sale of these beverages by the drug company had greatly reduced his receipts and profits, plaintiff brought this action for damages for breach of the alleged oral contract, and was permitted to recover. Defendant has appealed.

Plaintiff's evidence was to the effect that the oral agreement had been made at least two days, possibly longer, before the signing of the instrument, and that it was repeated at the time he signed; that, relying upon it, he executed the lease. Plaintiff called one witness who said he heard defendant's agent say to plaintiff at a time admittedly several days before the execution of the lease that he would have the exclusive right to sell soda water and soft drinks, to which the latter replied if that was the case he accepted the tenancy. Plaintiff produced no witness who was present when the contract was executed to corroborate his statement as to what then occurred. Defendant's agent denied that any such agreement was made, either preliminary to or at the time of the execution of the lease.

Appellee's counsel argues this is not a case in which an endeavor is being made to reform a written instrument because of something omitted as a result of fraud, accident, or mistake, but is one involving the breach of an independent oral agreement which does not belong in the writing at all and is not germane to its provisions. We are unable to reach this conclusion.

"Where parties, without any fraud or mistake, have deliberately put their engagements in writing, the law declares the writing to be not only the best, but the only evidence of their agreement." Martin v. Berens, 67 Pa. 459, 463; Irvin v. Irvin, 142 Pa. 271, 287, 21 A. 816

"All preliminary negotiations, conversations and verbal agreements are merged in and superseded by the subsequent written contract, * * * and 'unless fraud, accident, or mistake be averred, the writing constitutes the agreement between the parties, and its terms cannot be added to nor subtracted from by parol evidence.'" Union Storage Co. v. Speck, 194 Pa. 126, 133, 45 A. 48, 49; Vito v. Birkel, 209 Pa. 206, 208, 58 A. 127.

The writing must be the entire contract between the parties if parol evidence is to be excluded, and to determine whether it is or not the writing will be looked at, and if it appears to be a contract complete within itself, "couched in such terms as import a complete legal obligation without any uncertainty as to the object or extent of the engagement, it is conclusively presumed that the whole engagement of the parties, and the extent and manner of their undertaking, were reduced to writing." Seitz v. Brewers' Refrigerating Machine Co., 141 U.S. 510, 517, 12 S. Ct. 46, 48 (35 L. Ed. 837).

When does the oral agreement come within the field embraced by the written one? This can be answered by comparing the two, and determining whether parties, situated as were the ones to the contract, would naturally and normally include the one in the other if it were made. If they relate to the same subject-matter, and are so interrelated that both would be executed at the same time and in the same contract, the scope of the subsidiary agreement must be taken to be covered by the writing. This question must be determined by the court.

In the case at bar the written contract stipulated for the very sort of thing which plaintiff claims has no place in it. It covers the use to which the storeroom was to be put by plaintiff and what he was and what he was not to sell therein. He was "to use the premises only for the sale of fruit, candy, soda water," etc., and was not "allowed to sell tobacco in any form." Plaintiff claims his agreement not to sell tobacco was part of the consideration for the exclusive right to sell soft drinks. Since his promise to refrain was included in the writing, it would be the natural thing to have included the promise of exclusive rights. Nothing can be imagined more pertinent to these provisions which were included than the one appellee avers.

In cases of this kind, where the cause of action rests entirely on an alleged oral understanding concerning a subject which is dealt with in a written contract it is presumed that the writing was intended to set forth the entire agreement as to that particular subject.

"In deciding upon this intent [as to whether a certain subject was intended to be embodied by the writing], the chief and most satisfactory index * * * is found in the circumstance whether or not the particular element of the alleged extrinsic negotiation is dealt with at all in the writing. If it is mentioned, covered, or dealt with in the writing, then presumably the writing was meant to represent all of the transaction on that element, if it is not, then probably the writing was not intended to embody that element of the negotiation." Wigmore on Evidence (2d Ed.) vol. 5, p. 309.

As the written lease is the complete contract of the parties, and since it embraces the field of the alleged oral contract, evidence of the latter is inadmissible under the parol evidence rule.

"The [parol evidence] rule also denies validity to a subsidiary agreement within [the] scope [of the written contract] if sued on as a separate contract, although except for [that rule], the agreement fulfills all the requisites of valid contract." 2 Williston, Contracts, 1222; Penn Iron Co. v. Diller, 1 Sad. 82, 1 A. 924; Krueger v. Nicola, 205 Pa. 38, 54 A. 494; Wodock v. Robinson, 148 Pa. 503, 24 A. 73.

There are, of course, certain exceptions to the parol evidence rule, but this case does not fall within any of them. Plaintiff expressly rejects any idea of fraud, accident, or mistake, and they are the foundation upon which any basis for admitting parol evidence to set up an entirely separate agreement within the scope of a written contract must be built. The evidence must be such as would cause a chancellor to reform the instrument, and that would be done only for these reasons (Pioso v. Bitzer, 209 Pa. 503, 58 A. 891) and this holds true where this essentially equitable relief is being given, in our Pennsylvania fashion, through common law forms.

We have stated on several occasions recently that we propose to stand for the integrity of written contracts. Wolverine Glass Co. v. Miller, 279 Pa. 138, 146, 123 A. 672; Evans v. Edelstein, 276 Pa. 516, 120 A. 473; Neville v. Kretzschmar, 271 Pa. 222, 114 A. 625. We reiterate our position in this regard.

The judgment of the court below is reversed, and is here entered for defendant.

MASTERSON
v.
SINE

Supreme Court of California
68 Cal. 2d 222
1968

Traynor, C.J.

Dallas Masterson and his wife Rebecca owned a ranch as tenants in common. On February 25, 1958, they conveyed it to Medora and Lu Sine by a grant deed "Reserving unto the Grantors herein an option to purchase the above described property on or before February 25, 1968" for the "same consideration as being paid heretofore plus their depreciation value of any improvements Grantees may add to the property from and after two and a half years from this date." Medora is Dallas' sister and Lu's wife. Since the conveyance Dallas has been adjudged bankrupt. His trustee in bankruptcy and Rebecca brought this declaratory relief action to establish their right to enforce the option.

The case was tried without a jury. Over defendants' objection the trial court admitted extrinsic evidence that by "the same consideration as being paid heretofore" both the grantors and the grantees meant the sum of $50,000 and by "depreciation value of any improvements" they meant the depreciation value of improvements to be computed by deducting from the total amount of any capital expenditures made by defendants grantees the amount of depreciation allowable to them under United States income tax regulations as of the time of the exercise of the option.

The court also determined that the parol evidence rule precluded admission of extrinsic evidence offered by defendants to show that the parties wanted the property kept in the Masterson family and that the option was therefore personal to the grantors and could not be exercised by the trustee in bankruptcy.

Defendants appeal. They contend that the option provision is too uncertain to be enforced and that extrinsic evidence as to its meaning should not have been admitted. The trial court properly refused to frustrate the obviously declared intention of the grantors to reserve an option to repurchase by an overly meticulous insistence on completeness and clarity of written expression. It properly admitted extrinsic evidence to explain the language of the deed to the end that the consideration for the option would appear with sufficient certainty to permit specific enforcement. The trial court erred, however, in excluding the extrinsic evidence that the option was personal to the grantors and therefore non-assignable.

When the parties to a written contract have agreed to it as an "integration"—a complete and final embodiment of the terms of an agreement—parol evidence cannot be used to add to or vary its terms. When only part of the agreement is integrated, the same rule applies to that part, but parol evidence may be used to prove elements of the agreement not reduced to writing.

The crucial issue in determining whether there has been an integration is whether the parties intended their writing to serve as the exclusive embodiment of their agreement. The instrument itself may help to resolve that issue. It may state, for example, that "there are no previous understandings or agreements not contained in the writing," and thus express the parties' "intention to nullify antecedent understandings or agreements." Any such collateral agreement itself must be examined, however, to determine whether the parties intended the subjects of negotiation it deals with to be included in, excluded from, or otherwise affected by the writing. Circumstances at the time of the writing may also aid in the determination of such integration.

California cases have stated that whether there was an integration is to be determined solely from the face of the instrument and that the question for the court is whether it "appears to be a complete . . . agreement. . . ." Neither of these strict formulations of the rule, however, has been consistently applied. The requirement that the writing must appear incomplete on its face has been repudiated in many cases where parol evidence was admitted "to prove the existence of a separate oral agreement as to any matter on which the document is silent and which is not inconsistent with its terms"—even though the instrument appeared to state a complete agreement. Even under the rule that the writing alone is to be consulted, it was found necessary to examine the alleged collateral agreement before concluding that proof of it was precluded by the writing alone.

In formulating the rule governing parol evidence, several policies must be accommodated. One policy is based on the assumption that written evidence is more accurate than human memory. This policy, however, can be adequately served by excluding parol evidence of agreements that directly contradict the writing. Another policy is based on the fear that fraud or unintentional invention by witnesses interested in the outcome of the litigation will mislead the finder of facts. McCormick has suggested that the party urging the spoken as against the written word is most often the economic underdog, threatened by severe hardship if the writing is enforced. In his view the parol evidence rule arose to allow the court to control the tendency of the jury to find through sympathy and without a dispassionate assessment of the probability of fraud or faulty memory that the parties made an oral agreement collateral to the written contract, or that preliminary tentative agreements were not abandoned when omitted from the writing. (See McCormick, Evidence.) He recognizes, however, that if this theory were adopted in disregard of all other considerations, it would lead to the exclusion of testimony concerning oral agreements whenever there is a writing and thereby often defeat the true intent of the parties.

Evidence of oral collateral agreements should be excluded only when the fact finder is likely to be misled. The rule must therefore be based on the credibility of the evidence. One such standard, adopted by section 240(1)(b) of the Restatement of Contracts, permits proof of a collateral agreement if it "is such an agreement as might *naturally* be made as a separate agreement by parties situated as were the parties to the written contract." The draftsmen of the Uniform Commercial Code would exclude the evidence in still fewer instances: "If the additional terms are such that, if agreed upon, they would *certainly* have been included in the document in the view of the court, then evidence of their alleged making must be kept from the trier of fact." (Com. 3, §2-202.)

The option clause in the deed in the present case does not explicitly provide that it contains the complete agreement, and the deed is silent on the question of assignability. Moreover, the difficulty of accommodating the formalized structure of a deed to the insertion of collateral agreements makes it less likely that all the terms of such an agreement were included. The statement of the reservation of the option might well have been placed in the recorded deed solely to preserve the grantors' rights against any possible future purchasers, and this function could well be served without any mention of the parties' agreement that the option was personal. There is nothing in the record to indicate that the parties to this family transaction, through experience in land transactions or otherwise, had any warning of the disadvantages of failing to put the whole agreement in the deed. This case is one, therefore, in which it can be said that a collateral agreement such as that alleged "might naturally be made as a separate agreement." *A fortiori,* the case is not one in which the parties "would certainly" have included the collateral agreement in the deed.

It is contended, however, that an option agreement is ordinarily presumed to be assignable if it contains no provisions forbidding its transfer or indicating that its performance involves elements personal to the parties. The fact that there is a written memorandum, however, does not necessarily preclude parol evidence rebutting a term that the law would otherwise presume. Of course a statute may preclude parol evidence to rebut a statutory presumption. Here, however, there is no such statute. In the absence of a controlling statute the parties may provide that a contract right or duty is nontransferable.

In the present case defendants offered evidence that the parties agreed that the option was not assignable in order to keep the property in the Masterson family. The trial court erred in excluding that evidence.

The judgment is reversed.

PETERS, J., TOBRINER, J., MOSK, J., and SULLIVAN, J., concurred.

BURKE, J.

I dissent. The majority opinion undermines the parol evidence rule as we have known it in this state since at least 1872 by declaring that parol evidence should have been admitted by the trial court to show that a written option, absolute and unrestricted in form, was intended to be limited and nonassignable. . . .

This new rule, not hitherto recognized in California, provides that proof of a claimed collateral oral agreement is admissible if it is such an agreement as might *naturally* have been made a separate agreement by the parties under the particular circumstances. I submit that this approach opens the door to uncertainty and confusion. Who can know what its limits are? Certainly I do not.

. . .

I would hold that the trial court ruled correctly on the proffered parol evidence, and would affirm the judgment.

McCOMB, J., concurred.

NELSON
v.
ELWAY

Supreme Court of Colorado (En Banc)
908 P.2d 102
1995

VOLLACK, C.J.:

. . .

In early 1991, [John J.] Pico, acting on behalf of [Mel T.] Nelson and Metro Toyota, began negotiations with John A. Elway, Jr. (Elway) and Rodney L. Buscher (Buscher) regarding the sale of Metro Toyota and the property upon which it was situated. On

March 14, 1991, pursuant to those negotiations, Elway and Buscher signed a "Buy–Sell Agreement" and a separate real estate contract to purchase Metro Toyota. The closing was scheduled for April 15, 1991.

Soon after the signing of these documents, Pico asked Nelson if he would be willing to sell both Metro Auto and Metro Toyota to Elway. Nelson stated that he would be willing to sell both dealerships along with the land upon which they were located if he received sufficient personal remuneration. Pico then began negotiating with Elway and Buscher regarding the sale of both dealerships. Through these negotiations it became apparent that Elway and Buscher were unwilling or unable to pay the full purchase price for the dealerships and the land upon which they were located.

In order to consummate the transaction, Pico suggested to Nelson that Elway and Buscher reimburse Nelson for his interest in Metro Toyota by paying Nelson $50 per vehicle sold by both dealerships for a period of seven years commencing on May 1, 1991. In exchange for this compensation arrangement, Elway and Buscher would purchase Metro Auto from Nelson at a greatly reduced purchase price. These terms, referred to by the parties as the "Service Agreement," were reduced to writing but never signed by the parties. Subsequently, on March 16, 1991, the parties signed a "Buy–Sell Agreement" and a separate real estate contract for the purchase of Metro Auto. This written, signed agreement did not incorporate the terms of the Service Agreement.

By early 1991, the dealerships owed GMAC over $3 million. In order to protect its security interests, on April 3, 1991, GMAC required Nelson to execute agreements referred to as "keeper letters," allowing GMAC significant control over the dealerships. GMAC imposed this requirement as consideration for its agreement to pay in excess of $890,000 in debt owed by Metro Auto and Metro Toyota at the closing of the sale of the dealerships to Elway and Buscher. Nelson knew that execution of these letters would preclude his ability to file for bankruptcy protection and proceed through re-organization. He alleges that he thus sought and received assurances from Elway and Buscher that the orally agreed upon, but as yet unsigned, Service Agreement would be honored.

. . . After closing, Nelson demanded that the respondents honor the Service Agreement. When the respondents refused, Nelson filed the instant action.

In his complaint, Nelson sought damages from Elway and Buscher for breach of contract. . . . The respondents then moved the trial court for summary judgment, which the court granted as to all counts. . . .

The first issue with regard to the breach of contract claim is whether the merger clauses in the Buy–Sell Agreements precluded the consideration of evidence that the parties intended the Service Agreement to be part of the overall agreement to sell the dealerships.[1] The petitioners argue that the court of appeals erred by ruling that

---

1. Paragraph 14 of both of the Buy–Sell Agreements (the "Merger Clauses") for Metro Toyota and Metro Auto, both signed on March 16, 1991, by Nelson, Elway, and Buscher, states:

> This Agreement constitutes the entire Agreement between the parties pertaining to the subject matter contained herein, and supersedes all prior agreements, representations and understandings of the parties. No modification or amendment of this Agreement shall be binding unless in writing and signed by the parties. . . .

the merger clauses precluded the consideration of the intent of the contracting parties. The respondents assert that the merger clauses wholly manifest the intention of the parties that only those terms of the transaction reduced to writing and signed at the closing would be enforceable terms of the agreement.

We agree with the court of appeals that the merger clauses preclude consideration of extrinsic evidence to ascertain the intent of the parties. Integration clauses generally allow contracting parties to limit future contractual disputes to issues relating to the express provisions of the contract. *Keller v. A.O. Smith Harvestore Prods.,* 819 P.2d 69, 72 (Colo. 1991). Therefore, the terms of a contract intended to represent a final and complete integration of the agreement between the parties are enforceable, and extrinsic evidence offered to prove the existence of prior agreements is inadmissible. *Id.; Sentinel Acceptance Corp. v. Colgate,* 162 Colo. 64, 66, 424 P.2d 380, 382 (1967). Even when extrinsic evidence is admissible to ascertain the intent of the parties, such evidence may not be used to demonstrate an intent that contradicts or adds to the intent expressed in the writing. *KN Energy, Inc. v. Great Western Sugar Co.,* 698 P.2d 769, 777 n. 9 (Colo. 1985).

. . .

The petitioners and respondents signed the March 16, 1991 Buy–Sell Agreements after extensive negotiation and numerous drafts of documents. By doing so, all parties expressly agreed, pursuant to the merger clauses, that the terms of those Buy–Sell Agreements would control the transaction and that all other agreements, oral or written, would be void. We will not step into a commercial transaction after the fact and attempt to ascertain the intent of the parties when that intent is clearly manifested by an express term in a written document. We thus conclude that the merger clauses in the March 16, 1991, Buy–Sell Agreements are dispositive as to the intent of the parties in this case. As there is no dispute as to any material fact with regard to this issue, the court of appeals correctly affirmed the trial court's order of summary judgment in favor of the respondents on this issue.

Lohr, J., dissenting.

. . .

. . . [According to Nelson's allegations, on] March 15, 1991, Elway and Nelson agreed that if Nelson made the up-front concessions envisioned by Elway regarding the sale price for the real estate and dealership assets [for Metro Auto], Nelson would receive deferred personal compensation through a side agreement ("service agreement") providing that Nelson was to receive $50.00 for every new or used vehicle sold by the dealerships for the next seven years. Both buy-sell agreements noted that sale of the dealerships was contingent on GMAC approval. The parties subsequently signed buy-sell and real estate contracts for Metro Auto on March 16, 1991.

Anticipating the pending sale of the dealerships, GMAC insisted that Nelson relinquish control over the dealerships on April 3, 1991. Since Nelson and Elway had yet to sign the service agreement, Nelson contacted Rodney L. Buscher and received assurances that the service agreement would be honored before relinquishing control to GMAC.

On April 8 or 9, 1991, Pico and Elway met at the Landmark Hotel to discuss the sale of Nelson's dealerships. During the meeting, GMAC called Pico and told Elway that they would not finance the deal if Elway signed a side agreement with Nelson. Despite Nelson's understanding that Elway would honor the service agreement, Elway informed Nelson on April 8 or 9, 1991, that the service agreement would not be signed. . . . Nevertheless, Nelson proceeded with the sale of the dealerships because he already had turned control over to GMAC and thereby eliminated a bankruptcy reorganization alternative that was previously under consideration.

. . .

Nelson . . . contends that Elway is liable for breach of contract in failing to honor the service agreement. The majority affirms the dismissal of Nelson's breach of contract claim on summary judgment, holding [] that the merger clauses in the buy-sell agreements preclude consideration of the alleged service agreement. . . . I disagree with the majority. . . .

First, merger clauses preclude consideration of extrinsic evidence only where the parties intend that the document containing the merger is exclusive. *ARB, Inc. v. E–Systems, Inc.,* 663 F.2d 189, 199 (D.C. Cir. 1980); *Darner Motor Sales v. Universal Underwriters,* 140 Ariz. 383, 393, 682 P.2d 388, 398 (1984); *Anderson & Nafziger v. G.T. Newcomb, Inc.,* 100 Idaho 175, 180, 595 P.2d 709, 714 (1979); *Sutton v. Stacey's Fuel Mart, Inc.,* 431 A.2d 1319, 1323 n.3 (Me. 1981). The very essence of this case is a dispute regarding whether the parties intended the service agreement to be part and parcel of the overall deal. Because Nelson's position is adequately supported in the record, the intention of the parties regarding the exclusivity of the document containing the merger agreement is a disputed issue of material fact. As a result, this case is inappropriate for summary judgment disposition. *See e.g., Jafay,* 848 P.2d at 900.

. . .

Nelson and Elway disagree regarding their intent to honor the alleged service agreement. The majority contends that the merger clauses in the buy-sell agreements affirmatively preclude consideration of extrinsic evidence such as the alleged oral service agreement, and refuses to look at "evidence outside the four corners of the contract to determine the intent of the parties." Maj. op. at 107. However, the "four corners" approach to contract interpretation is in decline. John D. Calamari & Joseph M. Perillo, *Contracts* §3-4, at 145-46 (3d ed. 1987); *cf.* II E. Allan Farnsworth, *Farnsworth on Contracts* §7.3, at 206 (1990); 3 Lawrence A. Cunningham & Arthur A. Jacobson, *Corbin on Contracts* §579, at 558 (1994 Supp.) ("Confining judges to the 'four corners' of the contract and 'objective' definitions of words led to very haphazard and unjust results, so that an entire body of exceptions, corollaries, practices, and fictions sprung up to work some flexibility into the process."). The "modern trend," *Darner,* 140 Ariz. at 393, 682 P.2d at 398, is that merger and integration clauses are to be afforded varying weight depending on the circumstances of the case. *Franklin v. White,* 493 N.E.2d 161, 166 (Ind. 1986); *see also ARB,* 663 F.2d at 199 (court must consider "the circumstances surrounding the making of the contract" to ascertain whether an integration clause serves to "express the genuine intention of the parties to make the written contract the complete and exclusive statement of their agreement"); *Darner,* 140 Ariz. at 393, 682 P.2d at 398 ("Evidence on surrounding circumstances, including negotiation, prior understandings, subsequent conduct and the like, is taken to determine the parties' intent with regard to integration of the agreement. . . . This method obtains even though the parties have bargained for and written the actual words found in the instrument."); *Anderson,* 100 Idaho at 180, 595 P.2d at 714 (courts "should consider not only the language of the agreement but all extrinsic evidence relevant to the issue of whether the parties intended the written agreement to be a complete integration"); Restatement (Second) of Contracts §209(2) (1979) ("Whether there is an integrated agreement is to be determined by the court as a question preliminary to determination of a question of interpretation or to application of the parol evidence rule."); Restatement (Second) of Contracts §210 cmt. b (1979) (for purposes of proving a complete integration, "a writing cannot of itself prove its own completeness, and wide latitude must be allowed for inquiry into circumstances bearing on the intention of the parties"); *cf. Whitney v. Halibut, Inc.,* 235 Md. 517, 202 A.2d 629, 634 (1964) ("an integration clause is not necessarily conclusive"); *Sutton,* 431 A.2d at 1323 n.3 ("A merger clause does not control the question of whether a writing was intended to be a completely integrated agreement."); *Neville v. Scott,* 182 Pa. Super. 448, 127 A.2d 755, 757 (1956) ("integration clause is not controlling"); 3 Arthur Linton Corbin, *Corbin on Contracts* §578, at 405-06, 406 n.43 (1960 & 1994 Supp.). As the United States Supreme Court describes, "even a written contractual provision declaring that the contract contains the complete agreement of the parties, and that no antecedent or extrinsic representations exist, does not conclusively bar subsequent proof that such additional agreements exist and should be given force." *Blackledge v. Allison,* 431 U.S. 63, 75 n.6, 97 S. Ct. 1621, 1630 n.6, 52 L. Ed. 2d 136 (1977).

Although I believe that merger and integration clauses are presumptively valid, in keeping with the honored tenets of contract law there is an exception such that "[w]here giving effect to the merger clause would frustrate and distort the parties' true intentions and understanding regarding the contract, the clause will not be enforced." *Zinn v. Walker,* 87 N.C. App. 325, 361 S.E.2d 314, 319 (1987). In particular, where the parties intend that both a written contract and an alleged oral agreement constitute components of an overall agreement, a merger clause does not preclude consideration of extrinsic evidence. . . . As we noted in *Keller v. A.O. Smith Harvestore Prods.,* "'a seller should not be allowed to hide behind an integration clause to avoid the consequences of a misrepresentation.'" 819 P.2d 69, 73 (Colo. 1991) (quoting *Formento v. Encanto Bus. Park,* 154 Ariz. 495, 499, 744 P.2d 22, 26 (Ct. App. 1987)).

The parties' intention that the buy-sell agreements constituted entire contracts, allegedly evidenced by the merger clauses within, was by no means clearly manifested. *See Sierra Diesel Injection Serv. v. Burroughs Corp.,* 874 F.2d 653, 657 (9th Cir. 1989) ("the presence of a merger clause while often taken as a strong sign of the parties' intent is not conclusive in all cases"). In this case, despite the disclaimer in both merger clauses that each buy-sell agreement constituted the entire agreement, the overall deal involved two buy-sell agreements and two real estate contracts. Furthermore, each buy-sell agreement made reference to the real estate contracts despite the exclusivity disclaimer. Regardless of the standard merger and integration language in the buy-sell agreements, it is clear that the parties intended their ultimate bargain to encompass other agreements, although the substantive weight of the alleged service agreement remains unclear. *See Gem Corrugated Box Corp. v. National Kraft Container Corp.,* 427 F.2d 499, 502-03 (2d Cir. 1970) ("The contract price was not attractive; consummation of the stock purchase agreement was the real inducement to enter into the requirements contract. . . . [I]t was the vital element of the overall transaction. Viewed in this proper perspective, it is plain that the provision in the requirements contract that it contains the entire agreement of the parties means that the writing contains the entire agreement as to its limited subject matter alone . . .").

. . .

At base, the parties are embroiled in a dispute regarding whether they intended the buy-sell agreements to be fully integrated and whether they intended the service agreement to be enforced. Nelson again supported his factual construction in the record, and as a result the parties' disagreement over the factual issues of integration, inducement and part performance cannot properly be resolved by summary judgment.

KIRSHBAUM and SCOTT, JJ., join in this dissent.

DAVIS
v.
G.N. MORTGAGE CORP.

U.S. Court of Appeals, Seventh Circuit
396 F.3d 869
2005

COFFEY, J.

On September 9, 1999, Thomas and Cathy Davis (the "Davises"), husband and wife and citizens of the State of Illinois, closed on a $288,000 adjustable rate mortgage loan (the "loan") with an initial interest rate of 10.9% from the GN Mortgage Corporation in order to refinance personal debt. Aside from the Davises, the only other party present at the loan closing was Patricia Bogdanovich ("Bogdanovich"), the closing agent for TICOR Title Insurance Company, which was the title company authorized by GN to conclude the transaction.

At the closing, which took place at TICOR's offices in Joliet, Illinois, Bogdanovich presented the Davises with two stacks of paper, each purportedly consisting of 24 documents and totaling 43 pages. Included in the stacks were duplicate copies of the proposed adjustable rate note, mortgage, adjustable rate rider to the mortgage, and accompanying documents entitled "Prepayment Penalty Note Addendum," "Alternative Mortgage Transaction Parity Act Disclosure," and "Notice of Right to Cancel." Although the Davises admit that they failed to read or compare the two sets of documents thoroughly at the time of the closing, they allege that Bogdanovich told them that the stacks were identical in content and accurately represented the agreement between themselves and GN, including a provision setting forth a *two-year* prepayment penalty period. The Davises signed all of the documents in one of the stacks and Bogdanovich delivered the signed stack to GN while the Davises retained the unsigned stack for their records.

Early in 2000, GN sold the Davises' mortgage, including all its rights and obligations emanating from the loan agreement, to Countrywide Home Loans, Inc. Thereafter, in the summer of 2001, the Davises requested that Countrywide apprise them of the amount required to satisfy the remaining balance on their loan as of its two-year anniversary, September 9, 2001. Countrywide responded by informing the Davises that a prepayment penalty of approximately $12,000 (six months' worth of interest on the loan) would apply if the loan was paid off prior to the expiration of the *five-year* prepayment penalty period, according to the signed prepayment penalty addendum in their loan file. This came as a surprise to the Davises, who had no knowledge that they had agreed to a five-year prepayment penalty rider and instead believed that they had signed, and were only subject to, a two-year prepayment penalty clause based on alleged representations by Bogdanovich as well as their own broker.

. . .

[T]he Davises chose to refinance their loan at a lower, fixed interest rate with another mortgage company paying Countrywide the contested $12,781.76 prepayment penalty in the process. . . . [They filed a complaint against G.N. Mortgage and Countrywide] alleging . . . that Countrywide breached the parties' contract by imposing a five-year prepayment penalty period; [and] that GN through their agent Bogdanovich intentionally committed common law fraud when they misrepresented the terms of the Davises' mortgage loan. . . . The district court granted the defendants summary judgment on all of the Davises' claims. We affirm.

. . .

The Davises claim Countrywide breached the September 9, 1999, loan contract by enforcing a five-year prepayment penalty rather than honoring an allegedly agreed-upon two-year prepayment penalty. However, the only evidence of any agreement to a two-year prepayment penalty period, beyond the statements the Davises claim Bogdanovich made at the closing, is an unsigned copy of a two-year prepayment penalty addendum that they (the Davises) received and retained from the closing for their records.

Illinois adheres to a "four corners rule" of contract interpretation, which provides that "'[a]n agreement, when reduced to writing, must be presumed to speak the intention of the parties who signed it. It speaks for itself, and the intention with which it was executed must be determined from the language used. It is not to be changed by extrinsic evidence.'" *Air Safety, Inc. v. Teachers Realty Corp.,* 185 Ill. 2d 457, 236 Ill. Dec. 8, 706 N.E.2d 882, 884 (1999) (quoting *Western Ill. Oil Co. v.*

Thompson, 26 Ill. 2d 287, 186 N.E.2d 285, 287 (1962)). This approach is consonant with the general rule under Illinois contract law that "if the contract imports on its face to be a complete expression of the whole agreement, it is presumed that the parties introduced into it every material item, and parol evidence cannot be admitted to add another item to the agreement. . . ."

Accordingly, our task is to determine whether the loan agreement is fully integrated, clear and unambiguous, *Krautsack v. Anderson,* 329 Ill. App. 3d 666, 263 Ill. Dec. 373, 768 N.E.2d 133, 146 (2002). The threshold question for us to examine is whether the contract in question, here the mortgage loan note, is a fully integrated document, despite the lack of a specific integration clause. *See J & B Steel Contractors, Inc.,* 205 Ill. Dec. 98, 642 N.E.2d at 1217. The determination of whether a contract is integrated is a question of law for the trial judge to decide. An integrated writing is one "intended by the parties to be a final and complete expression of the entire agreement," *Krautsack,* 263 Ill. Dec. 373, 768 N.E.2d at 146 (internal quotation marks omitted), which means it "'contains such language as imports a complete legal obligation,'" *Eichengreen v. Rollins, Inc.,* 325 Ill. App. 3d 517, 259 Ill. Dec. 89, 757 N.E.2d 952, 958 (2001) (quoting *Armstrong Paint & Varnish Works v. Continental Can Co.,* 301 Ill. 102, 133 N.E. 711, 713 (1921)). Importantly, "only the subject writing may be considered to determine the integration question." *Id.* at 957; *see also J & B Steel,* 205 Ill. Dec. 98, 642 N.E.2d at 1218-20 (affirming the vitality of this rule, which was first established in Illinois in *Armstrong,* 301 Ill. 102, 133 N.E. 711 (1921)).

The loan agreement entered into between GN and the Davises is fully integrated, final in nature, and creates a completed legal obligation between the parties. When viewing the loan agreement in its entirety, we find an uncomplicated set of documents that, when read together, clearly and specifically state that the loan is subject to a prepayment penalty period of five years duration, as provided for in a separately executed addendum. . . .

. . .

The Davises, in a separate count of their complaint, go on to allege that GN perpetrated a common law fraud during the execution of the contract, which occurs "where there is a surreptitious substitution of one paper for another, or where by some other trick or device a party is made to sign an instrument which he did not intend to execute." *Belleville Nat'l Bank v. Rose,* 119 Ill. App. 3d 56, 74 Ill. Dec. 779, 456 N.E.2d 281, 283 (1983) (citing *Turzynski v. Libert,* 122 Ill. App. 2d 352, 259 N.E.2d 295, 298 (1970)). The Davises claim that GN, along with its purported agent (Bogdanovich), mislead them by misrepresenting the terms of the mortgage loan at the closing. The Davises allege GN did so by presenting them with . . . versions of the prepayment penalty addendum . . . different from what they bargained for and expected.

Under applicable Illinois law, an allegation of fraud must be established by clear and convincing evidence. *Cwikla v. Sheir,* 345 Ill. App. 3d 23, 280 Ill. Dec. 158, 801 N.E.2d 1103, 1110 (2003). However, unlike the plaintiffs' breach of contract claim,

Illinois substantive law instructs that we are free to consider parol evidence to assist us in determining the true intent of the parties when a common law fraud has been alleged. *See O'Brien v. Cacciatore,* 227 Ill. App. 3d 836, 169 Ill. Dec. 506, 591 N.E.2d 1384, 1390 (1992); *McMahon Food Corp. v. Burger Dairy Co.,* 103 F.3d 1307, 1314 (7th Cir. 1996). Under Illinois law, the elements the plaintiffs need to satisfy in order to establish common law fraud are: "(1) a false statement of a material fact; (2) defendant's knowledge that the statement was false; (3) defendant's intent that the statement induce plaintiff to act; (4) plaintiff's reliance upon the truth of the statement; and (5) plaintiff's damages resulting from reliance on the statement." *Capiccioni v. Brennan Naperville, Inc.,* 339 Ill. App. 3d 927, 274 Ill. Dec. 461, 791 N.E.2d 553, 558 (2003).

In order to satisfy the reliance element of their claim, the Davises must demonstrate not only that they relied on the GN's representations regarding a two-year prepayment rider, but that they were justified in doing so. *See Soules v. Gen. Motors Corp.,* 79 Ill. 2d 282, 37 Ill. Dec. 597, 402 N.E.2d 599, 601 (1980). When addressing the issue of justified reliance, Illinois courts have long recognized that "a party is not justified in relying on representations made when he has ample opportunity to ascertain the truth of the representations before he acts. When he is afforded the opportunity of knowing the truth . . . he cannot be heard to say he was deceived by misrepresentations." *Elipas Enterprises, Inc. v. Silverstein,* 243 Ill. App. 3d 230, 183 Ill. Dec. 752, 612 N.E.2d 9, 13 (1993) (quoting *Schmidt v. Landfield,* 20 Ill. 2d 89, 169 N.E.2d 229, 232 (1960)); *see also Leon v. Max E. Miller & Son, Inc.,* 23 Ill. App. 3d 694, 320 N.E.2d 256, 260 (1974); *Miller v. William Chevrolet/GEO, Inc.,* 326 Ill. App. 3d 642, 260 Ill. Dec. 735, 762 N.E.2d 1, 9 (2001). This rule applies with equal force in instances where fraud is alleged with respect to the execution of a written contract. *See Belleville,* 74 Ill. Dec. 779, 456 N.E.2d at 284; *see also N. Trust Co. v. VIII S. Mich. Assoc.,* 276 Ill. App. 3d 355, 212 Ill. Dec. 750, 657 N.E.2d 1095, 1103 (1995) ("A party cannot close his eyes to the contents of a document and then claim that the other party committed fraud merely because it followed this contract."). This is the so-called "due diligence rule," *Kolson v. Vembu,* 869 F. Supp. 1315, 1322 (N.D. Ill. 1994), which defeats the Davises' common law fraud claim.

. . . [N]otwithstanding the alleged statements by Bogdanovich, the Davises had an opportunity and obvious obligation to read the documents before they signed them (as well as up to three days after signing to review and cancel the contract under federal law if they believed the agreement to be flawed). Due to the significance of the mortgage transaction (a $288,000 loan) and the Davises' preoccupation with the prepayment penalty agreement in particular, they were not justified in relying on the alleged verbal statements alone. The fact is that the Davises certainly had an incentive to independently read and understand the contract in order to confirm that the terms they were agreeing to, *especially the addendum regarding the prepayment penalty period,* were correctly set forth in the final version of the contract. . . . Thus, on the facts set forth here and in the record, we hold that the reliance element of the Davises' common law fraud claim cannot be met as a matter of law.

. . .

[T]he district court's order granting the defendants' motions for summary judgment is affirmed.

Problems

1. The Unfunded Escrow Account. John and Betty Jo Belzel hired Fountain Hill Millwork Building Supply Company to construct their home. The Belzels' bank agreed to finance the construction and to provide scheduled payments to Fountain Hill based on costs incurred. The bank required the Belzels to place $40,000 in escrow in case there were unanticipated costs in excess of the loan amount. The Belzels did not have the cash on hand to make the escrow deposit. In lieu of the escrow payment, the Belzels executed a written promissory note for $40,000 payable to Fountain Hill in 90 days. At the time of execution of the note, the Belzels and Fountain Hill orally agreed that the Belzels would not be liable for the $40,000 if the mortgage and any direct payments by the Belzels covered the total cost of construction. The written promissory note did not mention this oral agreement. The Belzels paid Fountain Hill $8,000 directly for an unanticipated expense. The mortgage was sufficient to cover all other costs of construction, and Fountain Hill was paid in full. Despite these payments, Fountain Hill sued the Belzels on the unpaid note. Does the parol evidence rule bar the Belzels from introducing evidence of their oral agreement?

2. Two Yards Short. The Pittsburgh Steelers professional football team planned to build a new stadium and started selling stadium builder licenses (SBLs) that would grant the licensee the right and obligation to purchase season tickets for their assigned seats. In October 1998, Ronald Yocca received a brochure (SBL Brochure) from the Steelers. It included a diagram of the general locations of the sections in the stadium and showed that the "Club I Section" would be located between the field's 20-yard lines. The brochure explained that any person interested in purchasing an SBL would be required to submit an application ranking their preferred sections, along with a nonrefundable deposit equaling one-third of the purchase price of the desired seats. The brochure also stated that no SBL applicant was assured the right to purchase an SBL and that the applicant's first seating preference was not guaranteed. SBL applicants would be given their actual seat assignments in the spring of 2001 when the seats had been installed in the stadium.

Yocca submitted an SBL application with the required deposit and was assigned a seat in the Club I Section. In September 1999, the Steelers sent

Yocca a "Stadium Builder License and Club Seat Agreement" (SBL Agreement), an "Additional Terms and Conditions of Stadium Builder License and Club Seat Agreement," and a set of diagrams that now showed the Club I Section included seats located between the field's 10-yard lines. The SBL Agreement contained an integration clause:

> *Entire Agreement; Modification.* This Agreement contains the entire agreement of the parties with respect to the matters provided for herein and shall supersede any representations or agreements previously made or entered into by the parties hereto. No modification hereto shall be enforceable unless in writing, signed by both parties.

Yocca signed the agreement and paid the balance due for the SBL. When he was assigned seats located adjacent to the 18-yard line (i.e, outside the original Club I boundaries), he sued. Does the parol evidence rule preclude him from introducing the SBL Brochure as evidence in support of his claim?

3. The Separate Arbitration Agreement. Jennifer Ritter bought a car from Grady Automotive Group. The purchase contract contained a merger clause stating that "[n]o oral representations are binding unless written on this form and all terms of the agreement are printed or written herein." Ritter simultaneously executed a separate document stating that all disputes arising out of the sale and related transactions, such as negotiations and financing, would be arbitrated. Several months later, Ritter was involved in an accident and sued Grady Automotive in court for defects in the car. Grady Automotive moved to compel arbitration, citing the arbitration agreement. Ritter argued that the merger clause in the purchase contract rendered the arbitration clause invalid. Does the parol evidence rule bar Grady Automotive from introducing the arbitration agreement as evidence of the contract?

4. The Topless Tennis Player. Anastasia Myskina, a Russian professional tennis player, agreed to model for a photo shoot for the cover of Conde Nast Publication's *Gentleman's Quarterly* (GQ) magazine. On the day of the photo shoot and before any photographs were taken, Myskina signed a release stating that she "hereby irrevocably consent[ed] to the use of [her] name and the pictures taken of [her] on [that date] by [Conde Nast] . . . and others it may authorize." The photographer, Mark Seliger, first took photographs for the GQ cover, in which she was depicted as Lady Godiva—nude on horseback, except for her hair and nude-colored underwear, which covered key places (the "Lady Godiva" photographs). Then, Seliger asked if he could take more photographs "for himself" of Myskina topless in blue jeans (the "topless" photographs). According to Myskina, she agreed on condition that the topless photographs would not be published anywhere. Conde Nast used the Lady Godiva photographs for GQ. Pursuant to authorization by Conde Nast, Seliger subsequently licensed the use of both the Lady Godiva photographs and the topless photographs, which then appeared in a Russian magazine. May Myskina introduce evidence of her oral agreement with Seliger in support of her lawsuit for breach of contract?

D. INTERPRETATION

Given the inherent malleability of language, it is unsurprising that, even when parties agree on what set of words comprise their contract obligations, they often disagree about the precise substance of those obligations, or "duties." Such disagreements no doubt comprise the majority of contract disputes. Courts have three basic methods of ascribing substantive meaning to the language found in contracts. If the parties share the same intent as to the meaning of contractual terms, that meaning governs. If the parties intend different meanings, but one party understands the other's meaning (and the opposite is not true), the meaning that is intended by one and understood by the other governs. When parties have different intentions and neither knows the meaning intended by the other, courts will search for the most objectively reasonable meaning. See Rest. (2d) Contracts §201.

The first analytic step is to determine whether the disputed term is susceptible to more than one meaning. Under the traditional textualist view, courts should first determine whether the term in question has a "plain meaning." If it does, that plain meaning governs, and no evidence beyond the four corners of the contract is admissible to suggest otherwise. Based on this view, extrinsic evidence is admissible to prove the meaning of the term only if the court first determines that the contractual language itself is ambiguous. The modern contextualist view, supported by the Restatement, is that words have no fixed, intrinsic meaning; they are symbols ascribed meaning by particular communities under particular circumstances. As Justice Holmes put the point, "A word is not a crystal, transparent and unchanged; it is the skin of a living thought and may vary greatly in color and content according to the circumstances and the time in which it is used." *Towne v. Eisner*, 245 U.S. 418, 425 (1918). It follows that terms lack a plain meaning, and the context in which the language is situated is always relevant in determining whether the term could have had either of the competing interpretations. The first trio of cases in this section, *W.W.W. Associates, Inc. v. Giancontieri, Pacific Gas & Electric Company v. G.W. Thomas Drayage & Rigging Company*, and *In re Soper's Estate*, illustrates the stakes in the doctrinal debate between the textualist and contextualist modes of interpretation.

The second analytic step is to determine the relevance and relative probativeness of evidence offered to support competing interpretations of the ambiguous text. *Frigaliment Importing Company v. B.N.S. International Sales Corporation* describes a palette of contextual tools, and *Atmel Corporation v. Vitesse Semiconductor Corporation, Beanstalk Group, Inc. v. AM General Corporation*, and *Oswald v. Allen* provide case studies of the use of various interpretative sources.

A final complexity of contract interpretation concerns the allocation of authority between the judge and the jury, a subject about which courts themselves are often confused. In general, the legal significance of a contract term is a matter of law for the judge to determine. If the proper meaning turns on extrinsic evidence that is reasonably subject to alternative interpretations, however, the court should defer to the trier of fact. Rest. (2d) Contracts §212.

W.W.W. ASSOCIATES, INC.
v.
GIANCONTIERI

Court of Appeals of New York
77 N.Y.2d 157
1990

KAYE, J.

In this action for specific performance of a contract to sell real property, the issue is whether an unambiguous reciprocal cancellation provision should be read in light of extrinsic evidence, as a contingency clause for the sole benefit of plaintiff purchaser, subject to its unilateral waiver. Applying the principle that clear, complete writings should generally be enforced according to their terms, we reject plaintiff's reading of the contract and dismiss its complaint.

Defendants, owners of a two-acre parcel in Suffolk County, on October 16, 1986 contracted for the sale of the property to plaintiff, a real estate investor and developer. The purchase price was fixed at $750,000—$25,000 payable on contract execution, $225,000 to be paid in cash on closing (to take place "on or about December 1, 1986"), and the $500,000 balance secured by a purchase-money mortgage payable two years later.

The parties signed a printed form Contract of Sale, supplemented by several of their own paragraphs. Two provisions of the contract have particular relevance to the present dispute—a reciprocal cancellation provision (para. 31) and a merger clause (para. 19). Paragraph 31, one of the provisions the parties added to the contract form, reads: "The parties acknowledge that Sellers have been served with process instituting an action concerned with the real property which is the subject of this agreement. In the event the closing of title is delayed by reason of such litigation it is agreed that closing of title will in a like manner be adjourned until after the conclusion of such litigation provided, *in the event such litigation is not concluded, by or before 6-1-87 either party shall have the right to cancel this contract whereupon the down payment shall be returned and there shall be no further rights hereunder.*" (Emphasis supplied.) Paragraph 19 is the form merger provision, reading: "All prior understandings and agreements between *seller* and *purchaser* are merged in this contract [and it] completely expresses their full agreement. It has been entered into after full investigation, neither party relying upon any statements made by anyone else that are not set forth in this contract."

The Contract of Sale, in other paragraphs the parties added to the printed form, provided that the purchaser alone had the unconditional right to cancel the contract within 10 days of signing (para. 32), and that the purchaser alone had the option to cancel if, at closing, the seller was unable to deliver building permits for 50 senior citizen housing units (para. 29).

The contract in fact did not close on December 1, 1986, as originally contemplated. As June 1, 1987 neared, with the litigation still unresolved, plaintiff on May 13 wrote defendants that it was prepared to close and would appear for closing on

May 28; plaintiff also instituted the present action for specific performance. On June 2, 1987, defendants canceled the contract and returned the down payment, which plaintiff refused. Defendants thereafter sought summary judgment dismissing the specific performance action, on the ground that the contract gave them the absolute right to cancel.

Plaintiff's claim to specific performance rests upon its recitation of how paragraph 31 originated. Those facts are set forth in the affidavit of plaintiff's vice-president, submitted in opposition to defendants' summary judgment motion.

As plaintiff explains, during contract negotiations it learned that, as a result of unrelated litigation against defendants, a lis pendens had been filed against the property. Although assured by defendants that the suit was meritless, plaintiff anticipated difficulty obtaining a construction loan (including title insurance for the loan) needed to implement its plans to build senior citizen housing units. According to the affidavit, it was therefore agreed that paragraph 31 would be added for plaintiff's sole benefit, as contract vendee. As it developed, plaintiff's fears proved groundless—the lis pendens did not impede its ability to secure construction financing. However, around March 1987, plaintiff claims it learned from the broker on the transaction that one of the defendants had told him they were doing nothing to defend the litigation, awaiting June 2, 1987 to cancel the contract and suggesting the broker might get a higher price.

Defendants made no response to these factual assertions. Rather, its summary judgment motion rested entirely on the language of the Contract of Sale, which it argued was, under the law, determinative of its right to cancel.

The trial court granted defendants' motion and dismissed the complaint, holding that the agreement unambiguously conferred the right to cancel on defendants as well as plaintiff. The Appellate Division, however, reversed and, after searching the record and adopting the facts alleged by plaintiff in its affidavit, granted summary judgment to plaintiff directing specific performance of the contract. We now reverse and dismiss the complaint.

agree w/ trial Court

Critical to the success of plaintiff's position is consideration of the extrinsic evidence that paragraph 31 was added to the contract solely for its benefit. The Appellate Division made clear that this evidence was at the heart of its decision: "review of the record reveals that under the circumstances of this case the language of clause 31 was intended to protect the plaintiff from having to purchase the property burdened by a notice of pendency filed as a result of the underlying action which could prevent the plaintiff from obtaining clear title and would impair its ability to obtain subsequent construction financing." . . .

We conclude, however, that the extrinsic evidence tendered by plaintiff is not material. In its reliance on extrinsic evidence to bring itself within the "party benefited" cases, plaintiff ignores a vital first step in the analysis: before looking to evidence of what was in the parties' minds, a court must give due weight to what was in their contract.

A familiar and eminently sensible proposition of law is that, when parties set down their agreement in a clear, complete document, their writing should as a rule be enforced according to its terms. Evidence outside the four corners of the document as to what was really intended but unstated or misstated is generally

holding

inadmissible to add to or vary the writing (*see, e.g., Mercury Bay Boating Club v. San Diego Yacht Club,* 76 N.Y.2d 256, 269-270, 557 N.Y.S.2d 851, 557 N.E.2d 87; *Judnick Realty Corp. v. 32 W. 32nd St. Corp.,* 61 N.Y.2d 819, 822, 473 N.Y.S.2d 954, 462 N.E.2d 131; *Long Is. R.R. Co. v. Northville Indus. Corp.,* 41 N.Y.2d 455, 393 N.Y.S.2d 925, 362 N.E.2d 558; *Oxford Commercial Corp. v. Landau,* 12 N.Y.2d 362, 365, 239 N.Y.S.2d 865, 190 N.E.2d 230). That rule imparts "stability to commercial transactions by safeguarding against fraudulent claims, perjury, death of witnesses * * * infirmity of memory * * * [and] the fear that the jury will improperly evaluate the extrinsic evidence." (Fisch, New York Evidence §42, at 22 [2d ed].) Such considerations are all the more compelling in the context of real property transactions, where commercial certainty is a paramount concern.

Whether or not a writing is ambiguous is a question of law to be resolved by the courts (*Van Wagner Adv. Corp. v. S & M Enters.,* 67 N.Y.2d 186, 191, 501 N.Y.S.2d 628, 492 N.E.2d 756). In the present case, the contract, read as a whole to determine its purpose and intent (*see, e.g., Rentways, Inc. v. O'Neill Milk & Cream Co.,* 308 N.Y. 342, 347, 126 N.E.2d 271), plainly manifests the intention that defendants, as well as plaintiff, should have the right to cancel after June 1, 1987 if the litigation had not concluded by that date; and it further plainly manifests the intention that all prior understandings be merged into the contract, which expresses the parties' full agreement (*see,* 3 Corbin, Contracts §578, at 402-403). Moreover, the face of the contract reveals a "logical reason" (152 A.D.2d, at 341, 548 N.Y.S.2d 580) for the explicit provision that the cancellation right contained in paragraph 31 should run to the seller as well as the purchaser. A seller taking back a purchase-money mortgage for two thirds of the purchase price might well wish to reserve its option to sell the property for cash on an "as is" basis if third-party litigation affecting the property remained unresolved past a certain date.

Thus, we conclude there is no ambiguity as to the cancellation clause in issue, read in the context of the entire agreement, and that it confers a reciprocal right on both parties to the contract.

The question next raised is whether extrinsic evidence should be considered in order to *create* an ambiguity in the agreement. That question must be answered in the negative. It is well settled that "extrinsic and parol evidence is not admissible to create an ambiguity in a written agreement which is complete and clear and unambiguous upon its face." (*Intercontinental Planning v. Daystrom, Inc.,* 24 N.Y.2d 372, 379, 300 N.Y.S.2d 817, 248 N.E.2d 576; *see also, Chimart Assocs. v. Paul,* 66 N.Y.2d 570, 573, 498 N.Y.S.2d 344, 489 N.E.2d 231.)

Plaintiff's rejoinder—that defendants indeed had the specified absolute right to cancel the contract, but it was subject to plaintiff's absolute prior right of waiver—suffers from a logical inconsistency that is evidence[d] in a mere statement of the argument. But there is an even greater problem. Here, sophisticated businessmen reduced their negotiations to a clear, complete writing. In the paragraphs immediately surrounding paragraph 31, they expressly bestowed certain options on the purchaser alone, but in paragraph 31 they chose otherwise, explicitly allowing both buyer and seller to cancel in the event the litigation was unresolved by June 1, 1987. By ignoring the plain language of the contract, plaintiff effectively rewrites the bargain that was struck. An analysis that begins with consideration of extrinsic evidence of what the parties meant, instead of looking first to what they said and reaching extrinsic evidence only when required to do so because of some identified ambiguity, unnecessarily denigrates the contract and unsettles the law.

. . .

Accordingly, the Appellate Division order should be reversed, with costs, defendants' motion for summary judgment granted, and the complaint dismissed.

PACIFIC GAS & ELECTRIC CO.
v.
G.W. THOMAS DRAYAGE & RIGGING CO.

Supreme Court of California
69 Cal. 2d 33
1968

TRAYNOR, C.J.

Defendant appeals from a judgment for plaintiff in an action for damages for injury to property under an indemnity clause of a contract.

In 1960 defendant entered into a contract with plaintiff to furnish the labor and equipment necessary to remove and replace the upper metal cover of plaintiff's steam turbine. Defendant agreed to perform the work "at [its] own risk and expense" and to "indemnify" plaintiff "against all loss, damage, expense and liability resulting from . . . injury to property, arising out of or in any way connected with the performance of this contract." Defendant also agreed to procure not less than $50,000 insurance to cover liability for injury to property. Plaintiff was to be an additional named insured, but the policy was to contain a cross-liability clause extending the coverage to plaintiff's property.

During the work the cover fell and injured the exposed rotor of the turbine. Plaintiff brought this action to recover $25,144.51, the amount it subsequently spent on repairs. During the trial it dismissed a count based on negligence and thereafter secured judgment on the theory that the indemnity provision covered injury to all property regardless of ownership.

Defendant offered to prove by admissions of plaintiff's agents, by defendant's conduct under similar contracts entered into with plaintiff, and by other proof that in the indemnity clause the parties meant to cover injury to property of third parties only and not to plaintiff's property. Although the trial court observed that the language used was "the classic language for a third party indemnity provision" and that "one could very easily conclude that . . . its whole intendment is to indemnify third parties," it nevertheless held that the "plain language" of the agreement also required defendant to indemnify plaintiff for injuries to plaintiff's property. Having determined that the contract had a plain meaning, the court refused to admit any extrinsic evidence that would contradict its interpretation.

When the court interprets a contract on this basis, it determines the meaning of the instrument in accordance with the ". . . extrinsic evidence of the judge's own linguistic education and experience." (Corbin on Contracts (1960 ed.)) The exclusion of testimony that might contradict the linguistic background of the judge reflects a judicial belief in the possibility of perfect verbal expression. (Wigmore on Evidence (3d ed. 1940).) This belief is a remnant of a primitive faith in the inherent potency and inherent meaning of words.

The test of admissibility of extrinsic evidence to explain the meaning of a written instrument is not whether it appears to the court to be plain and unambiguous on its face, but whether the offered evidence is relevant to prove a meaning to which the language of the instrument is reasonably susceptible. (*Continental Baking Co. v. Katz* (1968) 68 Cal. 2d 512. . . .)

A rule that would limit the determination of the meaning of a written instrument to its four-corners merely because it seems to the court to be clear and unambiguous, would either deny the relevance of the intention of the parties or presuppose a degree of verbal precision and stability our language has not attained.

Some courts have expressed the opinion that contractual obligations are created by the mere use of certain words, whether or not there was any intention to incur such obligations. Under this view, contractual obligations flow, not from the intention of the parties but from the fact that they used certain magic words. Evidence of the parties' intention therefore becomes irrelevant.

In this state, however, the intention of the parties as expressed in the contract is the source of contractual rights and duties.[5] A court must ascertain and give effect to this intention by determining what the parties meant by the words they used. Accordingly, the exclusion of relevant, extrinsic, evidence to explain the meaning of a written instrument could be justified only if it were feasible to determine the meaning the parties gave to the words from the instrument alone.

If words had absolute and constant referents, it might be possible to discover contractual intention in the words themselves and in the manner in which they were arranged. Words, however, do not have absolute and constant referents. "A word is a symbol of thought but has no arbitrary and fixed meaning like a symbol of algebra or chemistry, . . ." (*Pearson v. State Social Welfare Board* (1960) 54 Cal. 2d 184, 195.) The meaning of particular words or groups of words varies with the ". . . verbal context and surrounding circumstances and purposes in view of the linguistic education and experience of their users and their hearers or readers (not excluding judges). . . . A word has no meaning apart from these factors; much less does it have an objective meaning, one true meaning." (Corbin, *The Interpretation of Words and the Parol Evidence Rule* (1965) 50 Cornell L.Q. 161, 187.) Accordingly, the meaning of a writing ". . . can only be found by interpretation in the light of all the circumstances that reveal the sense in which the writer used the words. The exclusion of parol evidence regarding such circumstances merely because the words do not appear ambiguous to the reader can easily lead to the attribution to a written

---

5. "A contract must be so interpreted as to give effect to the mutual intention of the parties as it existed at the time of contracting, so far as the same is ascertainable and lawful." (Civ. Code, §1636; . . . *Universal Sales Corp. v. California Press Mfg. Co.* (1942) 20 Cal. 2d 751, 760 . . .).

instrument of a meaning that was never intended." (*Universal Sales Corp. v. California Press Mfg. Co., supra*, 20 Cal. 2d 751, 776 (concurring opinion). . . .)

Although extrinsic evidence is not admissible to add to, detract from, or vary the terms of a written contract, these terms must first be determined before it can be decided whether or not extrinsic evidence is being offered for a prohibited purpose. The fact that the terms of an instrument appear clear to a judge does not preclude the possibility that the parties chose the language of the instrument to express different terms. That possibility is not limited to contracts whose terms have acquired a particular meaning by trade usage, but exists whenever the parties' understanding of the words used may have differed from the judge's understanding.

Accordingly, rational interpretation requires at least a preliminary consideration of all credible evidence offered to prove the intention of the parties. (Civ. Code, §1647. . . .) Such evidence includes testimony as to the "circumstances surrounding the making of the agreement . . . including the object, nature and subject matter of the writing . . ." so that the court can "place itself in the same situation in which the parties found themselves at the time of contracting." (*Universal Sales Corp. v. California Press Mfg. Co., supra*, 20 Cal. 2d 751, 761. . . .) If the court decides, after considering this evidence, that the language of a contract, in the light of all the circumstances, "is fairly susceptible of either one of the two interpretations contended for . . ." (*Balfour v. Fresno C. & I. Co.* (1895) 109 Cal. 221, 225 . . .) extrinsic evidence relevant to prove either of such meanings is admissible.

In the present case the court erroneously refused to consider extrinsic evidence offered to show that the indemnity clause in the contract was not intended to cover injuries to plaintiff's property. Although that evidence was not necessary to show that the indemnity clause was reasonably susceptible of the meaning contended for by defendant, it was nevertheless relevant and admissible on that issue. Moreover, since that clause was reasonably susceptible of that meaning, the offered evidence was also admissible to prove that the clause had that meaning and did not cover injuries to plaintiff's property. Accordingly, the judgment must be reversed.

The judgment is reversed.

PETERS, J., MOSK, J., BURKE, J., SULLIVAN, J., and PEEK, J., concurred.

McCOMB, J., dissented.

IN RE SOPER'S ESTATE   7
Supreme Court of Minnesota
196 Minn. 60
1935

JULIUS OLSON, J.

Plaintiff appeals from an order denying her motion for new trial after the cause had been heard and decision rendered for defendant. The facts are not in substantial conflict. But solution of the legal problems presented thereby is decidedly contro-versial, at least so counsel for the parties seem to think.

Ira Collins Soper, a native of Kentucky, was the central figure in the drama now to be depicted. In October, 1911, he and plaintiff Adeline Johnson Westphal were united in marriage. In August, 1921, he suddenly disappeared.

He studiously and almost fiendishly made his disappearance take on the aspect of suicide. He wrote several suicide notes to his wife. His car was found at the bank of a nearby canal and so were his hat and portions of his clothing. Pinned to his business card and left in his car was a note reading: "This belongs to Mrs. Soper."

He managed to leave Louisville, that being his home, without clue or trace. He went to Minneapolis. There he assumed the name of John W. Young. By that name, and that name only, he was known to his business and social acquaintances from the time he came to Minneapolis until his death in 1932. In Minneapolis he became well acquainted and established both in a business and social way. He entered the fuel business and with one Karstens formed a corporation known as the Young Fuel Company. In 1922 he married a widow and they lived together as husband and wife and were so known until she died in 1925. In May, 1927, he married defendant Gertrude Whitby, another Minneapolis widow, with whom he had been acquainted and had kept company for some six or eight months prior to their marriage. They lived together as husband and wife from the time of this marriage until his death in 1932, when he actually did commit suicide. Gertrude in good faith believed him to be a widower, he having informed her and many others that his first wife died of pneumonia many years prior thereto.

Some time after Young's marriage to Gertrude, he and Karstens were inter-viewed by one Smith, an insurance agent, who devised a stock insurance plan whereby provision was to be made for the surviving partner of the fuel company to acquire the entire business in event of death of one of them, the surviving wife of such deceased partner to be compensated by life insurance to be taken out by each partner upon his life, premiums to be paid by the fuel company and charged as an item of operating expense. The purpose was to keep the corporate enterprise from becoming split up as to stock ownership in event of death of either owner. Each owner was to take out a policy of life insurance in the amount of $5,000 payable to First Minneapolis Trust Company, as trustee. The resulting agreement provides:

> Upon the decease of either John W. Young or Ferdinand J. Karstens, the Trust Company shall proceed to collect the proceeds of the Insurance Policies upon the life of such deceased Depositor, and shall handle and dispose of such proceeds as follows:
>
> The Trust Company shall deliver the stock certificate of the deceased Depositor to the surviving Depositor and it shall deliver the proceeds of the insurance on the life of the deceased Depositor to the wife of the deceased Depositor.

Shortly after Young's death the trustee collected the insurance money upon the policy issued upon his life and paid the proceeds over to defendant Gertrude as his surviving wife, and at the same time delivered to Karstens decedent's 200 shares in the fuel company. No one except Young knew anything about the first wife. She was to all intents and purposes, as to all arrangements and engagements heretofore related, entirely out of the picture.

Several months elapsed after these matters had been properly closed by the parties, as they in good faith thought, when Mrs. Soper, the true wife of Young, put in her appearance. . . . Mrs. Soper brought this suit against defendants to recover the insurance money.

. . .

We conclude that Gertrude neither did nor could take anything as the "wife" of Young. As a matter of law, she never became such. But this conclusion does not solve our problem because she does not lay claim to the insurance merely as his lawful wife, but as the person intended to be the beneficiary under the escrow agreement as fully as if her name had been written into that contract instead of the word "wife." So the real question presented is whether under the escrow agreement designating the "wife" of depositor Young as the beneficiary parol proof is admissible that Gertrude was so intended and not Mrs. Soper, the true wife. Plaintiffs claim that the written instrument is free from ambiguity, latent or otherwise, and that as such it was improper for the trial court to permit oral evidence to show who was intended thereby to be such beneficiary. They strenuously assert that the agreement is not subject to construction, that it is perfectly plain in its language, and that the only thing for the court to determine is whether Mrs. Soper was the lawful wife of the deceased husband, or if Gertrude was such.

From the facts and circumstances hereinbefore related, the conclusion seems inescapable that Gertrude was intended. She was the only one known or considered by the contracting parties. True, Young knew otherwise, but that he did not intend his real wife to take anything as beneficiary seems obvious. From the time he left Louisville and came to Minneapolis, and until some time after his death, no one amongst his business or social acquaintances knew anything of or concerning his true wife. Gertrude alone answered the descriptive designation of "wife." Public records disclosed her and her alone to be such. There was no one else.

The question of identification of the individual intended by the written instrument very often involves and requires oral proof. That is the situation here. The right to the money here involved is claimed by both Adeline Soper and Gertrude Young. In what manner may either establish relationship to the decedent as his "wife" except by means of oral testimony? Ira Collins Soper and John W. Young, in the absence of proof contra, would likely lead an inquirer to the view that two different men were involved. Adeline, to establish her relationship, was necessarily required to and did furnish proof, principally oral, that her husband, Ira Collins Soper, was in fact the same individual as John W. Young. Gertrude by similar means sought to establish her claim. Of course the proof was such as to require a finding sustaining Adeline's claim. No one questions that result. But until such proof was adduced, it is equally clear, both from public records in Hennepin county and general repute, that Gertrude had been duly married to John W. Young. All friends and acquaintances knew and recognized her as his wife. There was nothing in Minneapolis or in this state indicating otherwise. Were we to award the insurance fund to plaintiff Adeline, it is obvious that we would thereby be doing violence to the contract entered into by the decedent Young with his associate, Karstens. That agreement points to no one else than Gertrude as Young's "wife." To hold otherwise is to give the word "wife" "a fixed symbol," as "something inherent and objective, not subjective and personal." Dean Wigmore, in his excellent work on Evidence, has this to say: "The ordinary standard, or 'plain meaning,' is simply the meaning of the people who did not write the document. The fallacy consists in assuming that there is or ever can be some one real or absolute meaning. In truth, there can be only some person's meaning; and that person, whose meaning the law is seeking, is the writer of the document.'" . . .

. . .

After all, as we said in City of Marshall v. Gregoire, 193 Minn. 188, 198, 199, 259 N.W. 377, 381, 382, 98 A.L.R. 711: "A written contract is little more than a scrap of writing save as it operates with legal effect on matters extraneous to itself. Construction deals with the dynamic rather than the static phase of the instrument. The question is not just what words mean literally, but how they are intended to operate practically on the subject-matter. Thus, seemingly plain language becomes susceptible of construction, and frequently requires it, if ambiguity appears when attempt is made to operate the contract." That is the situation here. The trust agreement has become "susceptible of construction" because "ambiguity appears when attempt is made to operate the contract."

The order is affirmed.

I.M. OLSEN, J. (dissenting).

. . . A man can have only one wife. . . . The contract in this case designates the "wife" as the one to whom the money was to be paid. I am unable to construe this word to mean any one else than the only wife of Soper then living. . . .

FRIGALIMENT IMPORTING CO.
v.
B.N.S. INTERNATIONAL SALES CORP.

U.S. District Court, Southern District of New York
190 F. Supp. 116
1960

FRIENDLY, J.

The issue is, what is chicken? Plaintiff says "chicken" means a young chicken, suitable for broiling and frying. Defendant says "chicken" means any bird of that genus that meets contract specifications on weight and quality, including what it calls "stewing chicken" and plaintiff pejoratively terms "fowl." Dictionaries give both meanings, as well as some others not relevant here. To support its, plaintiff sends a number of volleys over the net; defendant essays to return them and adds a few serves of its own. Assuming that both parties were acting in good faith, the case nicely illustrates Holmes' remark "that the making of a contract depends not on the agreement of two minds in one intention, but on the agreement of two sets of external signs—not on the parties' having meant the same thing but on their having said the same thing." The Path of the Law. I have concluded that plaintiff has not sustained its burden of persuasion that the contract used "chicken" in the narrower sense.

The action is for breach of the warranty that goods sold shall correspond to the description. Two contracts are in suit. In the first, dated May 2, 1957, defendant, a New York sales corporation, confirmed the sale to plaintiff, a Swiss corporation, of

"US Fresh Frozen Chicken, Grade A, Government Inspected, Eviscerated 2 1/2-3 lbs. and 1 1/2-2 lbs. each all chicken individually wrapped in cryovac, packed in secured fiber cartons or wooden boxes, suitable for export

75,000 lbs. 2 1/2-3 lbs.............................@ $33.00
25,000 lbs. 1 1/2-2 lbs.............................@ $36.50
per 100 lbs. FAS New York

scheduled May 10, 1957 pursuant to instructions from Penson & Co., New York."[1]

The second contract, also dated May 2, 1957, was identical save that only 50,000 lbs. of the heavier "chicken" were called for, the price of the smaller birds was $37 per 100 lbs., and shipment was scheduled for May 30. The initial shipment under the first contract was short but the balance was shipped on May 17. When the initial shipment arrived in Switzerland, plaintiff found, on May 28, that the 2 1/2-3 lbs. birds were not young chicken suitable for broiling and frying but stewing chicken or "fowl"; indeed, many of the cartons and bags plainly so indicated. Protests ensued. Nevertheless, shipment under the second contract was made on May 29, the 2 1/2-3 lbs. birds again being stewing chicken. Defendant stopped the transportation of these at Rotterdam.

This action followed. Plaintiff says that, notwithstanding that its acceptance was in Switzerland, New York law controls; defendant does not dispute this, and relies on New York decisions. I shall follow the apparent agreement of the parties as to the applicable law.

Since the word "chicken" standing alone is ambiguous, I turn first to see whether the contract itself offers any aid to its interpretation. Plaintiff says the 1 1/2-2 lbs. birds necessarily had to be young chicken since the older birds do not come in that size, hence the 2 1/2-3 lbs. birds must likewise be young. This is unpersuasive—a contract for "apples" of two different sizes could be filled with different kinds of apples even though only one species came in both sizes. Defendant notes that the contract called not simply for chicken but for "US Fresh Frozen Chicken, Grade A, Government Inspected." It says the contract thereby

---

1. The Court notes the contract provision whereby any disputes are to be settled by arbitration by the New York Produce Exchange; it treats the parties' failure to avail themselves of this remedy as an agreement eliminating that clause of the contract.

incorporated by reference the Department of Agriculture's regulations, which favor its interpretation; I shall return to this after reviewing plaintiff's other contentions.

The first hinges on an exchange of cablegrams which preceded execution of the formal contracts. The negotiations leading up to the contracts were conducted in New York between defendant's secretary, Ernest R. Bauer, and a Mr. Stovicek, who was in New York for the Czechoslovak government at the World Trade Fair. A few days after meeting Bauer at the fair, Stovicek telephoned and inquired whether defendant would be interested in exporting poultry to Switzerland. Bauer then met with Stovicek, who showed him a cable from plaintiff dated April 26, 1957, announcing that they "are buyer" of 25,000 lbs. of chicken 2 1/2-3 lbs. weight, Cryovac packed, grade A Government inspected, at a price up to 33¢ per pound, for shipment on May 10, to be confirmed by the following morning, and were interested in further offerings. After testing the market for price, Bauer accepted, and Stovicek sent a confirmation that evening. Plaintiff stresses that, although these and subsequent cables between plaintiff and defendant, which laid the basis for the additional quantities under the first and for all of the second contract, were predominantly in German, they used the English word "chicken"; it claims this was done because it understood "chicken" meant young chicken whereas the German word, "Huhn," included both "Brathuhn" (broilers) and "Suppenhuhn" (stewing chicken), and that defendant, whose officers were thoroughly conversant with German, should have realized this. Whatever force this argument might otherwise have is largely drained away by Bauer's testimony that he asked Stovicek what kind of chickens were wanted, received the answer "any kind of chickens," and then, in German, asked whether the cable meant "Huhn" and received an affirmative response. . . .

Plaintiff's next contention is that there was a definite trade usage that "chicken" meant "young chicken." Defendant showed that it was only beginning in the poultry trade in 1957, thereby bringing itself within the principle that "when one of the parties is not a member of the trade or other circle, his acceptance of the standard must be made to appear" by proving either that he had actual knowledge of the usage or that the usage is "so generally known in the community that his actual individual knowledge of it may be inferred." (Wigmore, Evidence) Here there was no proof of actual knowledge of the alleged usage; indeed, it is quite plain that defendant's belief was to the contrary. In order to meet the alternative requirement, the law of New York demands a showing that "the usage is of so long continuance, so well established, so notorious, so universal and so reasonable in itself, as that the presumption is violent that the parties contracted with reference to it, and made it a part of their agreement.

Plaintiff endeavored to establish such a usage by the testimony of three witnesses and certain other evidence. Strasser, resident buyer in New York for a large chain of Swiss cooperatives, testified that "on chicken I would definitely understand a broiler." However, the force of this testimony was considerably weakened by the fact that in his own transactions the witness, a careful businessman, protected himself by using "broiler" when that was what he wanted and "fowl" when he wished older birds. Indeed, there are some indications, dating back to a remark of Lord Mansfield, Edie v. East India Co (1761), that no credit should be given "witnesses to usage, who could not adduce instances in verification." (Wigmore, Evidence) While Wigmore thinks this goes too far, a witness' consistent failure to rely on the alleged usage deprives his opinion testimony of much of its effect. Niesielowski, an officer of one of the companies that had furnished the stewing chicken to defendant, testified that "chicken" meant "the male species of the poultry industry. That could be a broiler, a fryer or a roaster," but not a stewing chicken; however, he also testified that upon receiving defendant's inquiry for "chickens," he asked whether the desire was for "fowl or frying chickens" and, in fact, supplied fowl, although taking the precaution of asking defendant, a day or two after plaintiff's acceptance of the contracts in suit, to change its confirmation of its order from "chickens," as defendant had originally prepared it, to "stewing chickens." Dates, an employee of Urner-Barry Company, which publishes a daily market report on the poultry trade, gave it as his view that the trade meaning of "chicken" was "broilers and fryers." In addition to this opinion testimony, plaintiff relied on the fact that the Urner-Barry service, the Journal of Commerce, and Weinberg Bros. & Co. of Chicago, a large supplier of poultry, published quotations in a manner which, in one way or another, distinguish between "chicken," comprising broilers, fryers and certain other categories, and "fowl," which, Bauer acknowledged, included stewing chickens. This material would be impressive if there were nothing to the contrary. However, there was, as will now be seen.

Defendant's witness Weininger, who operates a chicken eviscerating plant in New Jersey, testified "Chicken is everything except a goose, a duck, and a turkey. Everything is a chicken, but then you have to say, you have to specify which category you want or that you are talking about." Its witness Fox said that in the trade "chicken" would encompass all the various classifications. Sadina, who conducts a food inspection service, testified that he would consider any bird coming within the classes of "chicken" in the Department of Agriculture's regulations to be a chicken. The specifications approved by the General Services Administration include fowl as well as broilers and fryers under the classification "chickens." Statistics of the Institute of American Poultry Industries use the phrases "Young chickens" and "Mature chickens," under the general heading "Total chickens[,]" and the Department of Agriculture's daily and weekly price reports avoid use of the word "chicken" without specification.

Defendant advances several other points which it claims affirmatively support its construction. Primary among these is the regulation of the Department of Agriculture, 2 C.F.R. §70.300-70.370, entitled, "Grading and Inspection of Poultry and Edible Products Thereof." and in particular §70.301 which recited:

"*Chickens*. The following are the various classes of chickens:

   a) Broiler or fryer

   b) Roaster

   c) Capon

   d) Stag

e) Hen or stewing chicken or fowl

f) Cock or old rooster"

Defendant argues, as previously noted, that the contract incorporated these regulations by reference. Plaintiff answers that the contract provision related simply to grade and Government inspection and did not incorporate the Government definition of "chicken," and also that the definition in the Regulations is ignored in the trade. However, the latter contention was contradicted by Weininger and Sadina; and there is force in defendant's argument that the contract made the regulations a dictionary, particularly since the reference to Government grading was already in plaintiff's initial cable to Stovicek.

Defendant makes a further argument based on the impossibility of its obtaining broilers and fryers at the 33¢ price offered by plaintiff for the 2 1/2-3 lbs. birds. There is no substantial dispute that, in late April, 1957, the price for 2 1/2-3 lbs. broilers was between 35 and 37¢ per pound, and that when defendant entered into the contracts, it was well aware of this and intended to fill them by supplying fowl in these weights. It claims that plaintiff must likewise have known the market since plaintiff had reserved shipping space on April 23, three days before plaintiff's cable to Stovicek, or, at least, that Stovicek was chargeable with such knowledge. It is scarcely an answer to say, as plaintiff does in its brief, that the 33¢ price offered by the 2 1/2-3 lbs. "chickens" was closer to the prevailing 35¢ price for broilers than to the 30¢ at which defendant procured fowl. Plaintiff must have expected defendant to make some profit—certainly it could not have expected defendant deliberately to incur a loss.

Finally, defendant relies on conduct by the plaintiff after the first shipment had been received. On May 28 plaintiff sent two cables complaining that the larger birds in the first shipment constituted "fowl." Defendant answered with a cable refusing to recognize plaintiff's objection and announcing "We have today ready for shipment 50,000 lbs. chicken 2 1/2-3 lbs. 25,000 lbs. broilers 1 1/2-2 lbs.," these being the goods procured for shipment under the second contract, and asked immediate answer "whether we are to ship this merchandise to you and whether you will accept the merchandise." After several other cable exchanges, plaintiff replied on May 29 "Confirm again that merchandise is to be shipped since resold by us if not enough pursuant to contract chickens are shipped the missing quantity is to be shipped within ten days stop we resold to our customers pursuant to your contract chickens grade A you have to deliver us said merchandise we again state that we shall make you fully responsible for all resulting costs."[2] Defendant argues that if plaintiff was sincere in thinking it was entitled to young chickens, plaintiff would not have allowed the shipment under the second contract to go forward, since the distinction between broilers and chickens drawn in defendant's cablegram must have made it clear that the larger birds would not be broilers. However, plaintiff answers that the cables show plaintiff was insisting on delivery of young chickens and that defendant shipped old ones at its peril. Defendant's point would be highly relevant on another disputed

---

2. These cables were in German; "chicken," "broilers," and, on some occasions, "fowl," were in English.

issue—whether if liability were established, the measure of damages should be the difference in market value of broilers and stewing chicken in New York or the larger difference in Europe, but I cannot give it weight on the issue of interpretation. Defendant points out also that plaintiff proceeded to deliver some of the larger birds in Europe, describing them as "poulets"; defendant argues that it was only when plaintiff's customers complained about this that plaintiff developed the idea that "chicken" meant "young chicken." There is little force in this in view of plaintiff's immediate and consistent protests.

When all the evidence is reviewed, it is clear that defendant believed it could comply with the contracts by delivering stewing chicken in the 2 1/2-3 lbs. size. Defendant's subjective intent would not be significant if this did not coincide with an objective meaning of "chicken." Here it did coincide with one of the dictionary meanings, with the definition in the Department of Agriculture Regulations to which the contract made at least oblique reference, with at least some usage in the trade, with the realities of the market, and with what plaintiff's spokesman had said. Plaintiff asserts it to be equally plain that plaintiff's own subjective intent was to obtain broilers and fryers; the only evidence against this is the material as to market prices and this may not have been sufficiently brought home. In any event it is unnecessary to determine that issue. For plaintiff has the burden of showing that "chicken" was used in the narrower rather than in the broader sense, and this it has not sustained.

This opinion constitutes the Court's findings of fact and conclusions of law. Judgment shall be entered dismissing the complaint with costs.

ATMEL CORP.
v.
VITESSE SEMICONDUCTOR CORP.
Colorado Court of Appeals, Division I
30 P.3d 789
2001

METZGER, J.

Defendants, Vitesse Semiconductor Corporation, Robert L. West, Patrick H. Jenkins, and Lattie Alejo, appeal the preliminary injunction entered in favor of plaintiff, Atmel Corporation. They also appeal the order denying arbitration. We affirm the order, reverse the preliminary injunction to the extent it prohibits the individual defendants from participating in defendant Vitesse's hiring process involving Atmel employees who initiate contact, and to the extent it covers a period longer than the contract term, reverse the order setting Atmel's bond amount, and remand the cause for further proceedings.

Atmel is an established semiconductor company with a manufacturing facility in Colorado Springs that employs over 2,200 persons, constituting over two-thirds of the semiconductor labor force in that area. Vitesse, also a semiconductor company, recently built a manufacturing facility and began to hire employees. Many of its new employees had previously worked at Atmel, including defendants West, Jenkins, and Alejo. Although these companies do not compete in terms of their products or customer base, they do compete for employees in an extremely tight labor market.

When defendants West, Jenkins, and Alejo were hired at Atmel, they were required to sign an employment agreement that contained a "non-solicitation clause" pertaining to Atmel employees. After these defendants left Atmel's employment to work for defendant Vitesse as managers, they assisted in defendant Vitesse's efforts to hire qualified employees.

Contending defendants were "raiding" its work force, on November 24, 1997, Atmel filed this action and sought a temporary restraining order (TRO). Two weeks later, the trial court entered a TRO that prohibited the individual defendants from using Atmel's "confidential information" and from soliciting, recruiting, or attempting to persuade Atmel's current employees to leave their employment.

Later, after a four-day hearing, the trial court granted Atmel a preliminary injunction that was to remain in effect until March 5, 1999. That injunction forbade the individual defendants from soliciting Atmel's employees to apply for employment at Vitesse, screening resumes, conducting interviews, participating in hiring decisions, or making employment offers. These activities were prohibited even if employees of Atmel first initiated contact.

I.

Defendants contend the trial court erred in broadly interpreting the non-solicitation clauses so as to preclude the individual defendants' participation in any aspect of Vitesse's hiring process involving Atmel employees. We agree.

A contract must be interpreted in accordance with the plain meaning of its terms, *Wota v. Blue Cross & Blue Shield,* 831 P.2d 1307 (Colo. 1992), considering the circumstances that render it intelligible. *Lorenzen v. Mustard's Last Stand, Inc.,* 196 Colo. 265, 586 P.2d 12 (1978). A contract must always be interpreted in light of the intentions of the contracting parties. *Cache National Bank v. Lusher,* 882 P.2d 952 (Colo. 1994).

If a contract term is susceptible of more than one meaning, it is ambiguous. *Browder v. United States Fidelity & Guaranty Co.,* 893 P.2d 132 (Colo. 1995).

To clarify ambiguity in a contract, the court may look to extrinsic evidence, including evidence of industry custom. *See USI Properties East, Inc. v. Simpson,* 938 P.2d 168 (Colo. 1997). Even if a contract term is not ambiguous, evidence of industry standards may be used to demonstrate the parties' intent. *Benham v. Pryke,* 744 P.2d 67 (Colo. 1987). The determination whether a contract is ambiguous is a question of law; thus, our review is *de novo. Fibreglas Fabricators, Inc. v. Kylberg,* 799 P.2d 371 (Colo. 1990).

Here, the non-solicitation clauses in the individual defendants' contracts with Atmel provided: "Solicitation of Employees. I agree that I shall not for a period of one year following the termination of my relationship with the Company . . . either directly or indirectly . . . solicit, recruit or attempt to persuade any person to termi-nate such person's employment with the Company. . . ."

We hold the trial court's interpretation of the non-solicitation clauses was erro-neous and, thus, cannot stand.

First, the uncontroverted evidence established that the custom in the semicon-ductor industry is to interpret non-solicitation covenants to prohibit only solicitation. Two witnesses with extensive experience in the high technology industry (18 and 25 years, respectively) testified that they knew of no instance in that industry in which such a clause had been interpreted to preclude a former employee from having any involvement at all in his or her new employer's hiring process.

Second, recitals and titles may have material influence on the construction of the contract and the determination of the parties' intent. *Las Animas Consolidated Canal Co. v. Hinderlider,* 100 Colo. 508 (1937). Here, the titles of the clauses lend support to a restrictive interpretation. The clause in defendant Jenkins' contract is entitled "Non-Solicitation of Company Employees," and those in West's and Alejo's con-tracts are entitled "Solicitation of Employees." This choice of words supports a narrow construction, especially in light of the principle that, if any uncertainty exists in a contract prepared exclusively by an employer, as here, the contract should be construed against the employer. *Kuta v. Joint District No. 50(J),* 799 P.2d 379 (Colo. 1990); *Hamilton v. Stockton Unified School District,* 245 Cal. App. 2d 944 (5th Dist. 1966).

The selection of the sole term "solicitation" for all the contracts at issue estab-lishes the framework of and context for the clauses. Thus, use of the other disputed terms, "directly or indirectly . . . solicit, recruit or attempt to persuade," must be read in light of the titles of the clauses and in favor of the employees. *See Kuta v. Joint District No. 50(J), supra.*

"Solicit" means to approach with a request or plea. *Webster's Third New International Dictionary* 2169 (1986). "Recruit" means to "hire or otherwise obtain to provide services . . . secure the services of." *Webster's Third New International Dictionary* 1899 (1986). "Persuade" means to induce by argument, entreaty, or expostulation into some mental position. *Webster's Third New International Dictio-nary* 1687 (1986).

These definitions all imply actively initiated contact. Yet the terms of the preliminary injunction, which prohibit the individual defendants from any participation in the hiring process, are much more expansive.

Atmel argues that, because the non-solicitation clauses prohibited the individual defendants from engaging in the listed activities "directly or indirectly," the preliminary injunction is not overbroad. We disagree.

In the first place, because Atmel, as employer, drafted the non-solicitation clauses, construction and application of the term "indirectly" must be narrow. *See Kuta v. Joint District No. 50(J), supra.* To that extent, the preclusion of any and all participation in the hiring process is too expansive a remedy.

Moreover, a contract should never be interpreted to yield an absurd result. *See Sunshine v. M.R. Mansfield Realty, Inc.,* 195 Colo. 95, 575 P.2d 847 (1978). Prohibiting any indirect participation in hiring precludes the individual defendants from making any favorable comment about their employment at Vitesse to anyone who might convey that remark to an Atmel employee. As the trial court itself recognized, this could transform an innocent statement to a relative who is an Atmel employee, that work at Vitesse is enjoyable, into a violation of the preliminary injunction.

Consequently, because the well-established principles of contract interpretation, considered in light of the industry's custom and practices, the language used by the drafter, and the necessity for a sensible result require that the non-solicitation clause be interpreted narrowly, the trial court's broad interpretation in its preliminary injunction cannot stand.

This conclusion is bolstered by the fact that, if the non-solicitation clauses were interpreted as broadly as the preliminary injunction provides, they would be void as violative of the Colorado and California statutes that prohibit agreements in restraint of trade.

. . .

Consequently, to the extent the preliminary injunction prohibited the individual defendants from participating in defendant Vitesse's hiring practices concerning Atmel employees who initiated contact, it is overbroad and cannot stand. Thus, the first criterion for issuance of a preliminary injunction, a reasonable probability of success on the merits, has not been met.

Accordingly, since all the necessary criteria were not established, entry of the preliminary injunction to that extent was error, *see Rathke v. MacFarlane, supra,* and defendant Vitesse is entitled to damages and attorney fees. *See State v. Zahourek,* 935 P.2d 74 (Colo. App. 1996); *see also Lazy Dog Ranch v. Telluray Ranch Corp.,* 948 P.2d 74 (Colo. App. 1997), *rev'd on other grounds,* 965 P.2d 1229 (Colo. 1998).

. . .

BEANSTALK GROUP, INC.
v.
AM GENERAL CORP.
U.S. Court of Appeals, Seventh Circuit
283 F.3d 856
2002

POSNER, J.

Beanstalk, which serves owners of intellectual property by negotiating licenses of their property, brought this diversity suit for breach of its contract with AM General; the substantive issues are governed by the law of Indiana. The contract, called a "representation agreement," appointed Beanstalk an agent of AM General to obtain licenses to use the latter's "HUMMER" trademark. When the contract was made in 1997, AM General was the manufacturer of the Humvee, a military vehicle that is the successor to the jeep and like the jeep is also sold in a version intended for the civilian market, under the name "Hummer." Beanstalk named General Motors as an additional defendant for reasons that will appear in a moment. The district judge granted the defendants' motion to dismiss the complaint (to which Beanstalk had attached the representation agreement) for failure to state a claim. Fed. R. Civ. P. 12(b)(6). Since the representation agreement was part of a pleading rather than submitted separately, the judge could consider it without converting the defendants' motion to one for summary judgment. Fed. R. Civ. P. 12(c); *Berthold Types Ltd. v. Adobe Systems Inc.,* 242 F.3d 772, 775 (7th Cir. 2001).

The agreement made Beanstalk AM General's "sole and exclusive nonemployee representative" for the purpose of licensing the Hummer trademark and entitled Beanstalk to 35 percent of the "gross receipts . . . received on Owner's [AM General's] behalf . . . under any License Agreements" made while the representation agreement was in force. Each license agreement "shall provide for all payments thereunder to be made to Beanstalk on Owner's behalf," and Beanstalk is required to account quarterly to AM General for "all gross receipts actually received during the preceding calendar quarter under any License Agreements." AM General is given "the absolute right to veto, without cause and at its sole discretion," any proposed license, including renewals. "License agreement" is defined as "any agreement or arrangement, whether in the form of a license or otherwise, granting merchandising or other rights in the Property," which in turn is defined to mean trademarks and related rights. The contract, which is assignable (though by Beanstalk only with AM's consent) and contains an integration clause, was to continue until the end of 2000.

The agreement was drafted by Beanstalk, but this fact has little interpretive significance since AM General is a commercially sophisticated party represented by counsel. Most courts now agree with this exception to the principle that contracts are to be construed against the party that drafted it. *Western Sling & Cable Co. v. Hamilton,* 545 So. 2d 29, 31-32 (Ala. 1989); *Wood River Pipeline Co. v. Willbros Energy Services Co.,* 241 Kan. 580, 738 P.2d 866, 872 (1987); *Kinney v. Capitol-Strauss, Inc.,* 207 N.W.2d 574, 577 (Iowa 1973); *Dawn Equipment Co. v. Micro-Trak Systems, Inc.,* 186 F.3d 981, 989 n. 3 (7th Cir. 1999); *Northbrook Excess & Surplus Ins. Co. v. Procter & Gamble Co.,* 924 F.2d 633, 638-39 and n. 6 (7th Cir. 1991); *Missouri Pacific R.R. v. Kansas Gas & Electric Co.,* 862 F.2d 796, 799-800 (10th Cir. 1988); *First State Underwriters Agency of New England Reinsurance Corp. v. Travelers Ins. Co.,* 803 F.2d 1308, 1311-12 (3d Cir. 1986); *Eagle Leasing Corp. v. Hartford Fire Ins. Co.,* 540 F.2d 1257, 1261 (5th Cir. 1976). There are holdouts, illustrated by *Eastern Bus Lines, Inc. v. Board of Education,* 7 Conn. App. 581, 509 A.2d 1071, 1073-74 (1986), where the court, quoting an earlier opinion, said that "the party who actually does the writing of an instrument will presumably be guided by his own interests and goals in the transaction. He may choose shadings of expression, words more specific or more imprecise, according to the dictates of these interests." No doubt; but the other party, if commercially sophisticated and represented by counsel, will insist on clarification. Indiana has yet to take a stand on the exception, though the only case from Indiana that we can find which bears on it, *Nationwide Mutual Ins. Co. v. Neville,* 434 N.E.2d 585, 599 (Ind. App. 1982), leans in favor of rejecting it. No matter; AM does not need the rule in order to prevail. We add that the rule is in practice a makeweight rather than a tie breaker.

Beanstalk set about obtaining agreements for the licensing of the Hummer trademark. In 1999, however, two years into the representation agreement with Beanstalk, AM General entered into a joint-venture agreement with General Motors under which GM would design and engineer a new version of the Hummer, would make an interest-free loan of $235 million to AM General for the construction of a factory to manufacture the new version, would promise to buy a minimum number of the new vehicles, would obtain an option to buy up to 40 percent of AM General's common stock—and would acquire the Hummer trademark. . . .

Beanstalk argues that the agreement between AM General and GM, although of course not labeled a license agreement, was one because it transferred the Hummer trademark to GM and thus was an "agreement or arrangement, whether in the form of a license or otherwise, granting merchandising or other rights in the Property"; for the transfer gave GM the right, indeed the exclusive right, to merchandise the Hummer trademark, that is, the "Property." The contract thus is clear, Beanstalk argues—the joint venture was an "agreement" that "grant[ed]" GM "merchandising . . . rights" in the Hummer trademark and it did not have to be "in the form of a license" because the representation agreement says "in the form of a license *or otherwise*"—and under accepted principles of contract law we should look no further. Beanstalk wants 35 percent of so much of the consideration running from GM to AM General as represents the value of the Hummer trademark. We do not know what the consideration was, or what that value is, because no evidence has been taken—in fact, the joint-venture agreement is not even in the record, though the sketch we have just given of its terms is not contested.

Beanstalk is correct that written contracts are usually enforced in accordance with the ordinary meaning of the language used in them and without recourse to evidence, beyond the contract itself, as to what the parties meant. This presumption simplifies the litigation of contract disputes and, more important, protects contracting parties against being blindsided by evidence intended to contradict the deal that they thought they had graven in stone by using clear language. It is a strong presumption, motivated by an understandable distrust in the accuracy of litigation to reconstruct contracting parties' intentions, but it is rebuttable—here by two principles of contract interpretation that are closely related in the setting of this suit. The first is that a contract will not be interpreted literally if doing so would produce absurd results, in the sense of results that the parties, presumed to be rational persons pursuing rational ends, are very unlikely to have agreed to seek. *USA Life One Ins. Co. of Indiana v. Nuckolls,* 682 N.E.2d 534, 539 (Ind. 1997); *Haworth v. Hubbard,* 220 Ind. 611, 44 N.E.2d 967, 970 (1942); *Merheb v. Illinois State Toll Highway Authority,* 267 F.3d 710, 713 (7th Cir. 2001); *Funeral Financial Systems v. United States,* 234 F.3d 1015, 1018 (7th Cir. 2000); *Grun v. Pneumo Abex Corp.,* 163 F.3d 411, 420 (7th Cir. 1998); *Catalina Enterprises, Inc. Pension Trust v. Hartford Fire Ins. Co.,* 67 F.3d 63, 66 (4th Cir. 1995).

This is an interpretive principle, not a species of paternalism. "The letters between plaintiff and defendant were from one merchant to another. They are to be read as businessmen would read them, and only as a last resort are to be thrown out altogether as meaningless futilities. . . . If literalness is sheer absurdity, we are to seek some other meaning whereby reason will be instilled and absurdity avoided."

Outlet Embroidery Co. v. Derwent Mills, 254 N.Y. 179, 172 N.E. 462, 463 (1930) (Cardozo, C.J.). "There is a long tradition in contract law of reading contracts sensibly; contracts—certainly business contracts of the kind involved here—are not parlor games but the means of getting the world's work done. . . . True, parties *can* contract for preposterous terms. If contract language is crystal clear or there is independent extrinsic evidence that something silly was actually intended, a party may be held to its bargain, absent some specialized defense." *Rhode Island Charities Trust v. Engelhard Corp.,* 267 F.3d 3, 7 (1st Cir. 2001); see also *Dispatch Automation, Inc. v. Richards,* 280 F.3d 1116, 1118-19 (7th Cir. 2002). The second principle is that a contract must be interpreted as a whole. *Freigy v. Gargaro Co.,* 223 Ind. 342, 60 N.E.2d 288, 291 (1945); *Harseim v. Booth,* 134 Ind. 281, 33 N.E. 1016, 1017 (1893); *Allstate Ins. Co. v. Hammond,* 759 N.E.2d 1162, 1168 (Ind. App. 2001); *United States v. Schilling,* 142 F.3d 388, 395 (7th Cir. 1998); *LaSalle National Trust, N.A. v. ECM Motor Co.,* 76 F.3d 140, 144 (7th Cir. 1996); *A.D.E. Inc. v. Louis Joliet Bank & Trust Co.,* 742 F.2d 395, 396 (7th Cir. 1984); *Catalina Enterprises, Inc. Pension Trust v. Hartford Fire Ins. Co., supra,* 67 F.3d at 66. Sentences are not isolated units of meaning, but take meaning from other sentences in the same document.

The second principle thus is linguistic; the first reflects the fact that interpretation is a cultural as well as a linguistic undertaking. To interpret a contract or other document, it is not enough to have a command of the grammar, syntax, and vocabulary of the language in which the document is written. One must know something about the practical as well as the purely verbal context of the language to be interpreted. In the case of a commercial contract, one must have a general acquaintance with commercial practices. This doesn't mean that judges should have an M.B.A. or have practiced corporate or commercial law, but merely that they be alert citizens of a market-oriented society so that they can recognize absurdity in a business context. A blinkered literalism, a closing of one's eyes to the obvious, can produce nonsensical results, as this case illustrates. Beanstalk is in the business of merchandising trademarks. If, while the representation agreement was in effect, a toy company wanted to make a toy Hummer, Beanstalk was authorized to grant the toy company a license in exchange for a fee that it would split 35/65 with AM General. The joint-venture agreement was not that kind of arrangement. It was not an arrangement for the promotion of AM General's trademark. By the agreement creating the joint venture, AM General essentially transferred the Hummer business to General Motors, retaining a role limited to manufacturing, in a factory built with GM's money, a vehicle designed by, engineered by, and to be marketed by (that is the significance of the transfer of the trademark) GM. Quite apart from the option that GM also received to buy a large, doubtless controlling interest in AM General, it's as if AM General had sold its entire business, including its manufacturing assets and all its trademarks, to GM.

Beanstalk is not a business broker. It had nothing to do with the joint venture and indeed didn't even know about it until after it took place. The parties could hardly have intended that Beanstalk should get a commission if AM General decided, as in effect it did, to get out of the Hummer business. A business would not contract to pay an agent for work that the agent did not do but that the business did itself. Beanstalk and AM General must have known when they signed the representation agreement that if AM General ever sold its Hummer business, the trademark would go with it, as the purchaser would need it in order to identify the product, while AM General would no longer have any need or use for it. Indeed, AM General would have nothing to attach the trademark to. . . . The parties would hardly have intended Beanstalk to obtain a commission on the sale of the business merely because the sale would *inevitably* include the trademark. And they would not have wanted to burden the sale with the added cost of allocating the purchase price between the trademark and the other assets involved in the sale, as Beanstalk claims they must do in order to compute the commission to which it is entitled on the joint venture. . . .

The unreasonableness of Beanstalk's position can be seen most clearly by imagining that the joint venture had taken place the day after the representation agreement between Beanstalk and AM General went into effect. Then on Beanstalk's interpretation it would be entitled to 35 percent of the entire value of the Hummer trademark even though it had made absolutely no contribution to that value. That makes no sense. . . .

Beanstalk ignores relevant provisions of the contract, one of which engages Beanstalk to be AM General's "sole and exclusive *non-employee* representative," implying that AM General's employees can negotiate license agreements without going through Beanstalk. Beanstalk agrees with this interpretation, as it must (there is no possible ambiguity), but claims that even when an employee of AM General negotiates such an agreement with no involvement by Beanstalk, Beanstalk is entitled to 35 percent of the revenues that AM General obtains under the agreement. No reason is given why AM General would compensate Beanstalk for services rendered wholly by AM General's own employees, whom it must compensate. That would be paying double for the same service.

Further ignored are the provisions keying Beanstalk's commissions to gross receipts "received"—obviously by Beanstalk—"on Owner's [that is, AM General's] behalf" and requiring Beanstalk to account to AM General periodically for the gross receipts of the license agreements. This implies that Beanstalk would receive receipts only for license agreements that it negotiated. The implication is reinforced by the fact that the representation agreement contains no provision for compensating Beanstalk out of receipts received directly by AM General, for example under a license agreement negotiated by an employee of AM General.

Beanstalk goes so far as to argue that, whoever negotiates the license agreement, the receipts generated by it must be paid in the first instance to Beanstalk to enable it to take its 35 percent cut off the top. Beanstalk thus is arguing that not 35 percent but 100 percent of the consideration that GM paid AM General for the joint-venture agreement that represented the value of the Hummer trademark had to be paid to Beanstalk. Beanstalk's argument amounts to saying that if Chrysler hired it to license the Chrysler trademarks and then sold its entire automobile business to Daimler for $10 billion, Beanstalk would be entitled to an immediate cash receipt of $10 billion, from which it would deduct 35 percent of the value of the Chrysler trademarks and then remit the balance to Chrysler. Absurd.

Against all this it might be argued that to disregard a contractual term, whether on the basis that interpreting it literally would yield absurd results or that other terms in the contract alter the disputed term's apparent meaning, requires evidence and thus cannot be done on a motion to dismiss. Not so. For when we said earlier that the interpretation of a contract is a cultural as well as a linguistic undertaking, we did not add that the materials of interpretation are limited to literal meanings on the one hand and trial-type evidence on the other. The cultural background that a judge brings to the decision of a contract case includes as we said a general knowledge of how the world operates, including the commercial world, and this knowledge, precisely because it is general rather than being knowledge of the specific facts of the case ("adjudicative facts"), can show that the literal interpretation of a particular contractual term would be unsound, in which event no evidence need be taken. *Unelko Corp. v. Prestone Products Corp.*, 116 F.3d 237, 240 (7th Cir. 1997).

It would be different if Beanstalk, instead of standing on the literal terms of the representation agreement—on quicksand, in other words—wanted to present evidence to show that the agreement means what it says it means. The only evidence it wants to present is that before selling the Hummer business to GM, AM General approached Beanstalk and asked for an express exclusion from the representation agreement of any agreement "for the purpose of producing motor vehicles" even if such an agreement included a transfer of trademark rights. But of course. It was simple prudence for AM General to try to head off this lawsuit. It doesn't follow that the lawsuit has any merit. Indeed, to penalize AM General for attempting an amicable resolution of a potential dispute in advance would violate the spirit of the rule that makes settlement offers inadmissible in an adjudication on the merits. See Fed. R. Evid. 408.

. . .

AFFIRMED.

Rovner, J., dissenting in part.

I believe the majority has strayed beyond the bounds of Rule 12(b)(6) in affirming the dismissal of Beanstalk's breach of contract claim, and I therefore respectfully dissent. At this stage of the proceedings, we must accept all factual allegations in the complaint and draw all reasonable inferences from those facts in favor of the plaintiff. . . .

We all seem to agree that, when read literally, the contract clause defining "License Agreement" would include AM General's sale of its Hummer business, including the "Hummer" and "Humvee" trademarks, to General Motors. The majority holds that we may disregard the literal interpretation of a single clause whenever (1) this literal reading would produce absurd results, or (2) when the isolated clause takes on a different meaning when viewing the contract as a whole. I have no quarrel with either proposition as a correct statement of the law of contracts in Indiana, the relevant jurisdiction here. However, I do not agree that a literal interpretation of the defined term "License Agreement" would necessarily lead to absurd results. Moreover, when the contract is read as a whole, that term is at worst ambiguous. Under these circumstances, dismissal for failure to state a claim is inappropriate because there may be some set of facts that Beanstalk could prove which would entitle it to relief.

. . .

... [I]n the absence of discovery, the majority substitutes its own "cultural understanding," its own "cultural background," and its own general knowledge of the commercial world for a defined term in the contract, a dubious proposition at best. Judges are trained in law, not business, and however cosmopolitan we may be about the world of commerce, I think it an unwise practice to substitute our general knowledge of the business world for the express terms of a contract, especially in the absence of any discovery that might elucidate the parties' true intent. Beanstalk's affidavits reveal not only that AM General sought to change the terms of the contract to exclude the sale at issue here, but also that in early negotiations, Beanstalk explained to AM General that it expected a share of any license agreements that internal employees of AM General negotiated. *See* R. 24, at ¶4. The majority dismisses Beanstalk's interpretation of this term, arguing that this would be paying double for the same services. On this 12(b)(6) motion, however, we have no idea what the parties bargained for. Beanstalk could well have accepted a smaller commission than it normally obtains in order to get a cut of the in-house business. Beanstalk has argued on appeal that, because it was generally increasing the value of the trademarks, it was entitled to a share of any transfer of rights in the trademarks, whether or not it was directly involved in negotiating the deal. This explanation is not so absurd that Beanstalk should lose its claim as a matter of law, before we even allow discovery. Indeed, it is not absurd at all. Remember that at this stage of the proceedings, we must sustain the complaint unless it appears beyond doubt that the plaintiff can prove no set of facts in support of its claim which would entitle it to relief.

Finally, even when reading the contract as a whole, I believe the language is at worst ambiguous. The majority deftly points out various terms in the contract that render Beanstalk's interpretation suspect. I agree that when reading the contract as a whole, Beanstalk's claim is weak, and indeed might not survive summary judgment. But Rule 12(b)(6) is not a substitute for summary judgment, and we must avoid the temptation to weed out weak claims by bending the Federal Rules of Civil Procedure past the breaking point. . . . I believe we should . . . require discovery on the intentions of the contracting parties rather than substituting our own cultural understanding for ambiguous contract terms. . . .

OSWALD
v.
ALLEN

U.S. Court of Appeals, Second Circuit
417 F.2d 43
1969

MOORE, J.

Dr. Oswald, a coin collector from Switzerland, was interested in Mrs. Allen's collection of Swiss coins. In April of 1964 Dr. Oswald was in the United States and arranged to see Mrs. Allen's coins. The parties drove to the Newburgh Savings Bank of Newburgh, New York, where two of her collections referred to as the Swiss Coin Collection and the Rarity Coin Collection were located in separate vault boxes. After examining and taking notes on the coins in the Swiss Coin Collection, Dr. Oswald was shown several valuable Swiss coins from the Rarity Coin Collection. He also took notes on these coins and later testified that he did not know that they were in a separate "collection." The evidence showed that each collection had a different key number and was housed in labeled cigar boxes.

On the return to New York City, Dr. Oswald sat in the front seat of the car while Mrs. Allen sat in the back with Dr. Oswald's brother, Mr. Victor Oswald, and Mr. Cantarella of the Chase Manhattan Bank's Money Museum, who had helped arrange the meeting and served as Dr. Oswald's agent. Dr. Oswald could speak practically no English and so depended on his brother to conduct the transaction. After some negotiation a price of $50,000 was agreed upon. Apparently the parties never realized that the references to "Swiss coins" and the "Swiss Coin Collection" were ambiguous. The trial judge found that Dr. Oswald thought the offer he had authorized his brother to make was for all of the Swiss coins, while Mrs. Allen thought she was selling only the Swiss Coin Collection and not the Swiss coins in the Rarity Coin Collection.

On April 8, 1964, Dr. Oswald wrote to Mrs. Allen to "confirm my purchase of all your Swiss coins (gold, silver and copper) at the price of $50,000.00." The letter mentioned delivery arrangements through Mr. Cantarella. In response Mrs. Allen wrote on April 15, 1964, that "Mr. Cantarella and I have arranged to go to Newburgh Friday April 24." This letter does not otherwise mention the alleged contract of sale or the quantity of coins sold. . . . Dr. Oswald cabled from Switzerland to Mr. Alfred Barth of the Chase Manhattan Bank, giving instruction to proceed with the transaction. Upon receiving the cable, Barth wrote a letter to Mrs. Allen stating Dr. Oswald's understanding of the agreement and requesting her signature on a copy of the letter as a "mere formality." Mrs. Allen did not sign and return this letter. On April 24, Mrs. Allen's husband told Barth that his wife did not wish to proceed with the sale because her children did not wish her to do so.

Appellant attacks the conclusion of the Court below that a contract did not exist since the minds of the parties had not met. The opinion below states:

> ". . . plaintiff believed that he had offered to buy all Swiss coins owned by the defendant while defendant reasonably understood the offer which she accepted to relate to those of her Swiss coins as had been segregated in the particular collection denominated by her as the 'Swiss Coin Collection' . . ."

285 F. Supp. 488, 492 (S.D.N.Y. 1968). The trial judge based his decision upon his evaluation of the credibility of the witnesses, the records of the defendant, the values of the coins involved, the circumstances of the transaction and the reasonable probabilities. Such findings of fact are not to be set aside unless "clearly erroneous." Fed. R. Civ. P. 52(a). There was ample evidence upon which the trial judge could rely in reaching this decision.

In such a factual situation the law is settled that no contract exists. The Restatement of Contracts in section 71(a) adopts the rule of Raffles v. Wichelhaus, 2 Hurl. & C. 906, 159 Eng. Rep. 375 (Ex. 1864). Professor Young states that rule as follows:

> "when any of the terms used to express an agreement is ambivalent, and the parties understand it in different ways, there cannot be a contract unless one of them should have been aware of the other's understanding."

Young, Equivocation in Agreements, 64 Colum. L. Rev. 619, 621 (1964). Even though the mental assent of the parties is not requisite for the formation of a contract (see Comment to Restatement of Contracts 71 (1932)), the facts found by the trial judge clearly place this case within the small group of exceptional cases in which there is "no sensible basis for choosing between conflicting understandings." *Young*, at 647. The rule of Raffles v. Wichelhaus is applicable here.

Problems

1. The Prepayment Penalty. Trident Center (Trident) obtained a loan from Connecticut General Life Insurance Company (Connecticut General) to finance construction of an office building complex. The terms of the contract stated an interest rate of 12.25 percent for a term of 15 years and provided that Trident "shall not have the right to prepay the principal amount hereof in whole or in part" for the first 12 years. The contract also gave Connecticut General the option of demanding prepayment of the loan, along with a 10 percent prepayment fee, if Trident were to default on the loan within the first 12 years. Four years into the loan period, interest rates declined sharply, and Trident wished to prepay the loan and obtain cheaper financing elsewhere. It filed a lawsuit against Connecticut General seeking a declaratory judgment that it was entitled to prepay the loan if it added a 10 percent prepayment fee. Connecticut General filed a motion to dismiss Trident's lawsuit, and Trident objected on the ground that it was entitled to present evidence supporting its interpretation of the contract. The trial court granted Connecticut General's motion, and Trident appealed. How should the appellate court rule?

2. Not Such a Bon Voyage. Debbi Krenkel and her husband George, of Neptune, New Jersey, booked a stay at Atlantis Bahamas Resort, owned by Kerzner International Hotels. At check-in, the resort's agent asked them to sign a one-page form, identical in substance to one the Krenkels had signed when they visited the resort three years earlier, before he would hand them their room keys. Entitled

"Acknowledgment, Agreement and Release," the eight-paragraph document stated that the Krenkels would be liable for a specified daily room rate for the dates of their stay, allowed them to select a newspaper to be delivered to their room, and provided that:

> I agree that any claims I may have against the Resort Parties resulting from any events occurring in The Bahamas shall be governed by and constructed in accordance with the laws of the Commonwealth of The Bahamas, and further, irrevocably agree to the Supreme Court of The Bahamas as the exclusive venue for any such proceedings whatsoever.

The Krenkels asked the agent if the agreement only applied to water sports activities, and he said yes. They then signed the agreement below bold, capitalized letters stating "READ BEFORE SIGNING." The next day, Debbi was seriously injured when she slipped and fell on an outdoor path on the resort grounds. Is she limited to filing suit in the Bahamas?

3. A Snow Job. Polaris Industries, Inc., a snowmobile manufacturer, shipped its vehicles in disposable containers but was considering using returnable containers instead. ConFold Pacific, Inc., wanted to produce these returnable containers, and it conducted a reverse logistics analysis of Polaris's shipping needs to determine the most efficient way for Polaris to handle customer returns. The analysis was governed by a "Mutual Non-Disclosure Agreement—Logistics Consulting Version," a contract that was prepared by ConFold and executed by Polaris. The preamble of the agreement stated that "ConFold and Polaris [were] desirous of exchanging information for purposes of both companies developing future business with each other." The agreement protected "information relating to [ConFold's] proprietary software systems, documentation, and related consulting services," and contained an integration clause stating that it was the "entire Agreement between the two parties concerning the exchange and protection of proprietary information relating to the program."

Two months after the agreement was signed, Polaris requested proposals for designs of returnable containers from several firms, including ConFold, and ConFold submitted a design. ConFold had a confidentiality agreement specifically tailored to designs but did not ask Polaris to sign it. Polaris did not accept any of the design proposals it received at that time, but, several years later, it designed a returnable container and hired another manufacturer to produce it. ConFold alleged that Polaris used its design and breached the non-disclosure agreement by disclosing that design to another firm. Did the Mutual Non-Disclosure Agreement extend to ConFold's design?

4. The Los Angeles Angels of Anaheim. City of Anaheim (Anaheim) and Disney Baseball Enterprises (Disney) entered into a stadium lease agreement in connection with Disney's purchase of the California Angels Major League Baseball team. Section 11(f) of the agreement required Disney to change the team name "to include the name 'Anaheim' therein." Shortly after executing the lease, Disney renamed the team the "Anaheim Angels." Seven years later, Disney sold the team to defendant Angels Baseball. In early 2005, Angels Baseball changed the team's name to the "Los Angeles Angels of Anaheim." Anaheim sued, alleging the name change and Angel Baseball's systematic removal of the name "Anaheim" from the team's road jerseys, tickets, merchandise, and souvenirs breached section 11(f).

Trial testimony revealed that, during negotiations, Disney had rejected Anaheim's request to specify the team name as "Anaheim Angels." According to Anaheim, section 11(f) was intended to provide Disney with the flexibility to change the team mascot or to reverse the ordering of the city name and the mascot name (i.e., to make possible the moniker "Angels of Anaheim"), but that no one on either side had considered the possibility that the team name might be changed to have two geographical identifiers. Disney's negotiators did not directly contradict this recollection, but they testified that they sought maximum flexibility in naming rights in order to maximize the potential market value of the team should Disney decide to sell it, as it ultimately did. Which side should prevail?

5. Eminem Now for Sale on iTunes. Prior to the invention of digital music "downloads," record company Aftermath acquired exclusive rights to the works of recording artist Marshal Mathers, better known as "Eminem." The contract contained a "Records Sold" provision, which provided that the artist would receive between 12 and 20 percent of the adjusted retail price of all "full price records sold in the United States . . . through normal retail channels." The contract also contained a "Masters Licensed" provision, which provided that "[n]otwithstanding the foregoing," the artist would receive 50 percent of revenues earned "on masters licensed by [Aftermath] to others for their manufacture and sale of records or for any other uses." When the industry invented digital downloads as a way of distributing music, Aftermath entered into a "licensing" agreement with Apple Computer, Inc. that permitted Apple to use the master recordings ("masters") of Eminem's songs to sell digital downloads to consumers through its iTunes online store. Aftermath paid Eminem royalties according to the "Records Sold" provision. Eminem's assignee brought suit for breach of contract, claiming that the "Masters Licensed" provision entitled it to half of the revenues Aftermath received from Apple. The parties agreed that neither side had contemplated the invention of digital download technology at the time of contracting.

A federal district court judge found the contract ambiguous and reasonably susceptible to either interpretation and denied both parties' motions for summary judgment. At trial, Aftermath's expert witness testified that, according to music industry custom, the "Masters Licensed" provision concerned the use of recordings only in third-party products, such as multiple-artist compilation albums, movies, and television commercials. The jury returned a verdict for Aftermath, and Eminem's assignees appealed. How should the appellate court rule?

E. THE IMPLIED DUTY OF GOOD FAITH AND FAIR DEALING

"Every contract imposes upon each party a duty of good faith and fair dealing in its performance and its enforcement." Rest. (2d) Contracts §205; see also U.C.C. §1-304. The duty itself is immutable—that is, parties are not free to disclaim it as part of their contract—but parties do have some control over how it is applied in particular circumstances, as a result of the interpretive convention that the duty cannot trump explicit contractual entitlements.

Because the duty as stated is a broad standard rather than a bright-line rule, it is difficult to predict when and how a court will invoke it in particular cases. The following set of cases reflects, however, that the duty is invoked most often (a) when one party acts in a way that appears to deprive the other of its legitimate expectations under the contract or (b) when one party exercises discretion that is allocated to it by the contract in an arbitrary or exploitative way. This description of the law suggests that the good faith doctrine presents plentiful opportunities for disagreement in particular cases: what one party considers its *legitimate* expectation is often considered illegitimate by the other party, who contends that there is no express prohibition of the actions in question. And actions considered arbitrary or exploitative by one party are often viewed by the other party as an appropriate pursuit of its self-interest permitted by the contract's express allocation of discretion.

DALTON
v.
EDUCATIONAL TESTING SERVICE
Court of Appeals of New York
87 N.Y.2d 384
1995

KAYE, J.

. . .

In May 1991, Brian Dalton took the SAT, which was administered by ETS, at Holy Cross High School in Queens where Dalton was a junior. Six months later, in November, he took the examination a second time, as a senior, this time at John Bowne High School in Queens, and his combined score increased 410 points.

Because Dalton's score increased by more than 350 points, his test results fell within the ETS category of "Large Score Differences" or "discrepant scores." In accordance with ETS policy, members of the ETS Test Security Office therefore reviewed his May and November answer sheets. Upon a finding of disparate handwriting, the answer sheets were submitted to a document examiner, who opined that they were completed by separate individuals. Dalton's case was then forwarded to the Board of Review, which preliminarily decided that substantial evidence supported cancelling Dalton's November score.

Upon registering for the November SAT, Dalton had signed a statement agreeing to the conditions in the New York State edition of the Registration Bulletin, which reserved to ETS "the right to cancel any test score . . . if ETS believes that there is reason to question the score's validity." The Registration Bulletin further provided that, if "the validity of a test score is questioned because it may have been obtained unfairly, ETS [will] notif[y] the test taker of the reasons for questioning the score" and offer the test-taker the following five options: (1) the opportunity to provide additional information, (2) confirmation of the score by taking a free retest, (3) authorization for ETS to cancel the score and refund all fees, (4) third-party review by any institution receiving the test score or (5) arbitration.

As specified in the Registration Bulletin, ETS apprised Dalton of its preliminary decision to cancel his November SAT score in a letter from Test Security Specialist Celeste M. Eppinger. Noting the handwriting disparity and the substantial difference between his May and November test results, Eppinger informed Dalton that "[t]he evidence suggests that someone else may have completed your answer sheet and that the questioned scores may be invalid." She advised him that he could supply "any additional information that will help explain" this or, alternatively, elect one of the other options.

. . .

Dalton opted to present additional information to the Board of Review, including the following: verification that he was suffering from mononucleosis during the May examination; diagnostic test results from a preparatory course he took prior to the November examination (he had taken no similar course prior to the May SAT) that were consistent with his performance on that test; a statement from an ETS proctor who remembered Dalton's presence during the November examination; and statements from two students—one previously unacquainted with Dalton—that he had been in the classroom during that test. Dalton further provided ETS with a report from a document examiner obtained by his family who concluded that Dalton was the author of both sets of answer sheets.

ETS, after several Board of Review meetings, submitted the various handwriting exemplars to a second document examiner who, like its first, opined that the May and November tests were not completed by the same individual. As a result, ETS continued to question the validity of Dalton's November score.

. . .

II

By accepting ETS' standardized form agreement when he registered for the November SAT, Dalton entered into a contract with ETS. *See, AEB & Assocs. Design Group v. Tonka Corp.,* 853 F Supp 724, 732. Implicit in all contracts is a covenant of good faith and fair dealing in the course of contract performance. *See, Van Valkenburgh, Nooger & Neville v. Hayden Publ. Co.,* 30 NY2d 34, 45, *cert denied* 409 US 875).

Encompassed within the implied obligation of each promisor to exercise good *Rule* faith are "'any promises which a reasonable person in the position of the promisee would be justified in understanding were included.'" *Rowe v. Great Atl. & Pac. Tea Co.,* 46 NY2d 62, 69, quoting 5 Williston, Contracts §1293, at 3682 [rev. ed. 1937]. This embraces a pledge that "neither party shall do anything which will have the *RFR* effect of destroying or injuring the right of the other party to receive the fruits of the contract." *Kirke La Shelle Co. v. Armstrong Co.,* 263 NY 79, 87. Where the contract contemplates the exercise of discretion, this pledge includes a promise not to act arbitrarily or irrationally in exercising that discretion. *See, Tedeschi v. Wagner Coll.,* 49 NY2d 652, 659. The duty of good faith and fair dealing, however, is not without limits, and no obligation can be implied that "would be inconsistent with other terms of the contractual relationship." *Murphy v. American Home Prods. Corp.,* 58 NY2d 293, 304.

The parties here agreed to the provisions in the Registration Bulletin, which expressly permit cancellation of a test score so long as ETS found "reason to question" its validity after offering the test-taker the five specified options. Nothing in the contract compelled ETS to prove that the test-taker cheated. Nor did the invitation to the test-taker to furnish ETS with relevant information reasonably and realistically translate into any requirement that ETS conduct a field investigation or gather evidence to verify or counter the test-taker's documentation. Indeed, such an obligation would be inconsistent with the contractual language placing the burden squarely on the test-taker to overcome the ETS finding of score invalidity. ETS, therefore, was under no duty, express or implied, to initiate an external investigation into a questioned score.

The contract, however, did require that ETS consider any relevant material that *good* Dalton supplied to the Board of Review. The Registration Bulletin explicitly afforded *faith* Dalton the option to provide ETS with relevant information upon notification that ETS *duty* questioned the legitimacy of his test score. Having elected to offer this option, it was certainly reasonable to expect that ETS would, at the very least, consider any relevant material submitted in reaching its final decision.

. . .

To be sure, the Procedures for Questioned Scores warned Dalton "to provide only additional information that is relevant to the questions being raised." The Eppinger letter to Dalton, however, informed him that his November score was possibly invalid precisely because ETS believed "that someone else may have completed [his] answer sheet." Thus, ETS expressly framed the dispositive question as one of suspected impersonation. Because the statements from the classroom proctor and November test-takers corroborated Dalton's contention that he was present at and in fact took the November examination, they were relevant to this issue.

Likewise, inasmuch as the medical documentation concerning Dalton's health at the time of the May SAT provided an explanation for his poor performance on that examination, and the consistent diagnostic test results demonstrated his ability to achieve such a dramatic score increase, these items were also germane to the question whether it was Dalton or an imposter who completed the November examination. Indeed, in its manual, Policies and Procedures Concerning Scores of Questionable Validity—which details internal ETS procedure regarding questioned scores—ETS offers several examples of "relevant information" that a test-taker might provide, including "a doctor's report that the candidate was under the influence of medication at the time the low score was earned." Regarding "a case of possible impersonation" in particular, the manual suggests that "other test results might demonstrate that the questioned score is not inconsistent with other measures of the candidate's abilities." Thus, Dalton's material fell within ETS' own definition of relevancy, as expressed in its manual and letter to Dalton.

. . .

issue

Where . . . ETS refuses to exercise its discretion in the first instance by declining even to consider relevant material submitted by the test-taker, the legal question is whether this refusal breached an express or implied term of the contract, not whether it was arbitrary or irrational. Here, the courts below agreed that ETS did not consider the relevant information furnished by Dalton. By doing so, ETS failed *holding)* to comply in good faith with its own test security procedures, thereby breaching its contract with Dalton.

. . .

EASTERN AIR LINES, INC.
v.
GULF OIL CORP.

2

U.S. District Court, Southern District of Florida
415 F. Supp. 429
1975

KING, J.

. . .

On June 27, 1972, an agreement was signed by the parties which, as amended, was to provide the basis upon which Gulf was to furnish jet fuel to Eastern at certain specific cities in the Eastern system. . . .

The parties agreed that this contract, as its predecessor, should provide a reference to reflect changes in the price of the raw material from which jet fuel is processed, i.e., crude oil, in direct proportion to the cost per gallon of jet fuel.

Accordingly, the parties selected an indicator (West Texas Sour); a crude which is bought and sold in large volume and was thus a reliable indicator of the market value of crude oil. From June 27, 1972 to the fall of 1973, there were in effect various forms of U.S. government imposed price controls which at once controlled the price of crude oil generally, West Texas Sour specifically, and hence the price of jet fuel. As the government authorized increased prices of crude those increases were in turn reflected in the cost of jet fuel. Eastern has paid a per gallon increase under the contract from 11 cents to 15 cents (or some 40%).

The indicator selected by the parties was "the average of the posted prices for West Texas sour crude, 30.0-30.9 gravity of Gulf Oil Corporation, Shell Oil Company, and Pan American Petroleum Corporation." The posting of crude prices under the contract "shall be as listed for these companies in Platts Oilgram Service-Crude Oil Supplement. . . ."

. . .

During 1970 domestic United States oil production "peaked"; since then it has declined while the percentage of imported crude oil has been steadily increasing. Unlike domestic crude oil, which has been subject to price control since August 15, 1971, foreign crude oil has never been subject to price control by the United States Government. Foreign crude oil prices, uncontrolled by the Federal Government, were generally lower than domestic crude oil prices in 1971 and 1972; during 1973 foreign prices "crossed" domestic prices; by late 1973 foreign prices were generally several dollars per barrel higher than controlled domestic prices. It was during late 1973 that the Mid-East exploded in another war, accompanied by an embargo (at least officially) by the Arab oil-producing nations against the United States and certain of its allies. World prices for oil and oil products increased.

Mindful of that situation and for various other reasons concerning the nation's economy, the United States government began a series of controls affecting the oil industry culminating, in the fall of 1973, with the implementation of price controls known as "two-tier." In practice "two-tier" can be described as follows: taking as the bench mark the number of barrels produced from a given well in May of 1972, that number of barrels is deemed "old" oil. The price of "old" oil then is frozen by the government at a fixed level. To the extent that the productivity of a given well can be increased over the May, 1972, production, that increased production is deemed "new" oil. For each barrel of "new" oil produced, the government authorized the release from price controls of an equivalent number of barrels from those theretofore designated "old" oil. For example, from a well which in May of 1972, produced 100 barrels of oil; all of the production of that well would, since the imposition of "two-tier" in August of 1973, be "old" oil. Increased productivity to 150 barrels would result in 50 barrels of "new" oil and 50 barrels of "released" oil; with the result that 100 barrels of the 150 barrels produced from the well would be uncontrolled by the "two-tier" pricing system, while the 50 remaining barrels of "old" would remain government price controlled.

The implementation of "two-tier" was completely without precedent in the history of government price control action. Its impact, however, was nominal, until the imposition of an embargo upon the exportation of crude oil by certain Arab countries in October, 1973. Those countries deemed sympathetic to Israel were embargoed from receiving oil from the Arab oil producing countries. The United States was among the principal countries affected by that embargo, with the result that it experienced an immediate "energy crisis."

Following closely after the embargo, OPEC (Oil Producing Export Countries) unilaterally increased the price of their crude to the world market some 400% between September, 1973, and January 15, 1974. Since the United States domestic production was at capacity, it was dependent upon foreign crude to meet its requirements. New and released oil (uncontrolled) soon reached parity with the price of foreign crude, moving from approximately $5 to $11 a barrel from September, 1973 to January 15, 1974.

Since imposition of "two-tier," the price of "old oil" has remained fixed by government action, with the oil companies resorting to postings reflecting prices they will pay for the new and released oil, and subject to government controls. Those prices, known as "premiums," are the subject of supplemental bulletins which are likewise posted by the oil companies and furnished to interested parties, including Platts Oilgram.

Platts, since the institution of "two-tier," has not published the posted prices of any of the premiums offered by the oil companies in the United States, including those of Gulf Oil Corporation, Shell Oil Company and Pan American Petroleum, the companies designated in the agreement. The information which has appeared in Platts since the implementation of "two-tier" with respect to the price of West Texas Sour crude oil has been the price of "old" oil subject to government control.

Under the court's restraining order, entered in this cause by agreement of the parties, Eastern has been paying for jet fuel from Gulf on the basis of the price of "old" West Texas Sour crude oil as fixed by government price control action, i.e., $5 a barrel. Approximately 40 gallons of finished jet fuel product can be refined from a barrel of crude.

. . .

The contract talks in terms of fuel "requirements." The parties have interpreted this provision to mean that any aviation fuel purchased by Eastern at one of the cities covered by the contract, must be bought from Gulf. Conversely, Gulf must make the necessary arrangements to supply Eastern's reasonable good faith demands at those same locations. This is the construction the parties themselves have placed on the contract and it has governed their conduct over many years and several contracts.

Gulf suggests that Eastern violated the contract between the parties by manipulating its requirements through a practice known as "fuel freighting" in the airline industry. Requirements can vary from city to city depending on whether or not it is economically profitable to freight fuel. This fuel freighting practice in accordance with price could affect lifting from Gulf stations by either raising such liftings or lowering them. If the price was higher at a Gulf station, the practice could have reduced liftings there by lifting fuel in excess of its actual operating requirements at a prior station, and thereby not loading fuel at the succeeding high price Gulf station. Similarly where the Gulf station was comparatively cheaper, an aircraft might load more heavily at the Gulf station and not load at other succeeding non-Gulf stations.

holding

The court however, finds that Eastern's performance under the contract does not constitute a breach of its agreement with Gulf and is consistent with good faith and established commercial practices as required by U.C.C. §2-306.

"Good Faith" means "honesty in fact in the conduct or transaction concerned" U.C.C. §1-201(19). Between merchants, "good faith" means "honesty in fact and the observance of reasonable commercial standards of fair dealing in the trade"; U.C.C. §2-103(1)(b) and Official Comment 2 of U.C.C. §2-306. The relevant commercial practices are "courses of performance," "courses of dealing" and "usages of trade."

Throughout the history of commercial aviation, including 30 years of dealing between Gulf and Eastern, airlines' liftings of fuel by nature have been subject to substantial daily, weekly, monthly and seasonal variations, as they are affected by weather, schedule changes, size of aircraft, aircraft load, local airport conditions, ground time, availability of fueling facilities, whether the flight is on time or late, passenger convenience, economy and efficiency of operation, fuel taxes, into-plane fuel service charges, fuel price, and ultimately, the judgment of the flight captain as to how much fuel he wants to take.

All these factors are, and for years have been, known to oil companies, including Gulf, and taken into account by them in their fuel contracts. Gulf's witnesses at trial pointed to certain examples of numerically large "swings" in monthly liftings by Eastern at various Gulf stations. Gulf never complained of this practice and apparently accepted it as normal procedure. Some of the "swings" were explained by the fueling of a single aircraft for one flight, or by the addition of one schedule in mid-month. The evidence establishes that Eastern, on one occasion, requested 500,000 additional gallons for one month at one station, without protest from Gulf, and that Eastern increased its requirements at another station more than 50 percent year to year, from less than 2,000,000 to more than 3,000,000 gallons, again, without Gulf objection.

The court concludes that fuel freighting is an established industry practice, inherent in the nature of the business. The evidence clearly demonstrated that the practice has long been part of the established courses of performance and dealing between Eastern and Gulf. As the practice of "freighting" or "tankering" has gone on unchanged and unchallenged for many years accepted as a fact of life by Gulf without complaint, the court is reminded of Official Comment 1 to U.C.C. §2-208:

> "The parties themselves know best what they have meant by their words of agreement and their action under that agreement is the best indication of what that meaning was."

From a practical point of view, "freighting" opportunities are very few, according to the uncontradicted testimony, as the airline must perform its schedules in consideration of operating realities. There is no suggestion here that Eastern is operating at certain Gulf stations but taking no fuel at all. The very reason Eastern initially desired a fuel contract was because the airline planned to take on fuel, and had to have an assured source of supply.

If a customer's demands under a requirements contract become excessive, U.C.C. §2-306 protects the seller and, in the appropriate case, would allow him to refuse to deliver unreasonable amounts demanded (but without eliminating his basic contract obligation); similarly, in an appropriate case, if a customer repeatedly had no requirements at all, the seller might be excused from performance if the buyer suddenly and without warning should descend upon him and demand his entire inventory, but the court is not called upon to decide those cases here.

Rather, the case here is one where the established courses of performance and dealing between the parties, the established usages of the trade, and the basic contract itself all show that the matters complained of for the first time by Gulf after commencement of this litigation are the fundamental given ingredients of the aviation fuel trade to which the parties have accommodated themselves successfully and without dispute over the years.

The practical interpretation given to their contracts by the parties to them while they are engaged in their performance, and before any controversy has arisen concerning them, is one of the best indications of their true intent, and courts that adopt and enforce such a construction are not likely to commit serious error.

The court concludes that Eastern has not violated the contract.

CARMICHAEL
v.
ADIRONDACK BOTTLED GAS CORP.
Supreme Court of Vermont
161 Vt. 200
1993

Morse, J.

A jury awarded plaintiffs Carmichael $160,000 against defendant Adirondack Bottled Gas for breaching an implied covenant of good faith and fair dealing in the termination of their business relationship. On appeal, Adirondack claims that (1) Janet Carmichael was precluded from bringing this action because her claims were resolved either in arbitration or in a federal antitrust case, both of those proceedings having become final; (2) the trial court should have directed a verdict in Adirondack's favor; (3) the court erroneously instructed the jury on the law of breach of good faith; (4) the plaintiffs waived their claim for punitive damages and the facts did not warrant punitive damages to be considered by the jury; (5) the court erred in refusing to instruct the jury on the defense of accord and satisfaction; and (6) the award and calculation of interest in the judgment order were erroneous. We affirm.

The evidence supports the jury's concluding that the parties began and ended their business relationship in the following manner: In September 1981, Philip and Janet Carmichael bought an existing petroleum gas distributorship from Allen and Sharon Granger. The transaction required Philip Carmichael to enter into a contractor's agreement with Adirondack. In general, the agreement described the terms under which Adirondack would supply the Carmichaels with the product which they, in turn, would retail to their customers. Furthermore, the agreement contained a "key man" clause, which provided in part:

> This Agreement shall automatically terminate without written notice upon the sale or assignment of Contractor's business, the death of Philip Carmichael or upon any change in the capital structure, management or ownership of contractor.

(Emphasis added.)

After experiencing ups and downs, the Carmichaels' business turned modestly profitable, but in the summer of 1987, the couple had grown "sick of the gas business" and explored with Adirondack the possibility of selling their distributorship for $60,000. Adirondack was interested in acquiring the Carmichael business in order to convert it from a distributorship to a retail outlet. Adirondack offered the Carmichaels $38,500. The Carmichaels declined the offer.

Six months later, on December 24, 1987, Philip Carmichael died in a snowmobile accident, triggering the "key man" termination provision of the 1981 contractor's agreement. A few days later, David Johnson, Adirondack's district manager, attended Philip Carmichael's funeral. As he paid his respects, Johnson asked Janet Carmichael about her intentions toward the business. Carmichael indicated an intention to stay in business, and Johnson replied that they would get together at a future time to discuss how she would operate the distributorship. Shortly thereafter, Johnson reported the gist of this conversation to his supervisor, James Harrison. Harrison testified he would not have been opposed to Janet Carmichael continuing in the business, provided she sign a contract in her own right with Adirondack, but Harrison did not communicate that to her. Instead, on January 5, 1988, Adirondack sent a letter to Carmichael's attorney, again offering to purchase the business for $38,500. The letter gave no acceptance deadline, but Carmichael promptly instructed her attorney to inform Adirondack that she still wished to stay in business.

On January 13, 1988, Adirondack corresponded with Janet Carmichael's attorney, instructing him to tell her that the offer would be withdrawn in five days. Two days later, on Friday, January 15, Adirondack's attorney asked Carmichael if she was going to accept Adirondack's offer. She replied, "I'm not going to sell. I'm not going out of business. I want to keep this business." According to Carmichael, the attorney became "very upset with me and he told me at the end of the conversation that no matter what, whether I sold the assets to them or not, I was out of business Monday at noon." Concluding that Adirondack would no longer supply her with fuel as of Monday, Carmichael laid off her employees Friday afternoon. During the weekend, Carmichael sold much of her business equipment for $35,000 to Blue Flame Gas, a local competitor. She did not want to sell to Adirondack because "they wanted to take my business away from me that we had worked hard for."

On Monday, January 18, she returned to her work place and began closing up shop. The phone rang repeatedly that morning with calls from customers needing fuel deliveries. The calls were attended to either on site or by relaying the calls to Adirondack's business phone in Bolton, Vermont. Later that morning, David Johnson stopped by to see Carmichael, who told him she had sold her trucks and discharged her employees. She then handed him a list of customers who required immediate attention from Adirondack.

Shortly after Johnson's departure, Carmichael had another telephone conversation with Adirondack's attorney. According to Carmichael, the attorney again became upset, this time because "I wasn't going to deliver that day. That I had taken him on his word that I was done at noon." The attorney began yelling so loudly that Carmichael held the receiver up so that others who were in the office with her could hear it.

After that phone call, Adirondack arranged a meeting for the next day, January 19, to transfer vital business records and to tie up loose ends as provided for under the distributorship agreement. Fifteen minutes before the meeting, Carmichael was notified that her attorney could not be present. She elected to attend, but announced upon her arrival that she would not discuss legal questions without her lawyer present. Despite this statement, Adirondack repeatedly asked Carmichael to accept and sign a written agreement that had been drafted and signed by Adirondack prior to the meeting. The agreement provided for the transfer of Carmichael's remaining business assets. Carmichael repeatedly refused to sign the document then and there, although she did sign it after the meeting. Adirondack also asked at the meeting to review all of her records, including her customer list, route cards, accounts receivable and other records. Concerned that her customers not be left without fuel in the dead of winter, Carmichael handed over the requested documents. Adirondack then immediately began servicing the customers formerly serviced by the Carmichaels.

The winding down of remaining business affairs between Carmichael and Adirondack was not smooth. Carmichael had claims against Adirondack for the return of deposits, payments under the January 19 agreement, collection of accounts receivable, and other items. Adirondack had claims against Carmichael for inventory that was not returned or otherwise accounted for, fuel that had been supplied but not paid for, and other items. In March 1989, all of these issues were submitted to arbitration by order of the Washington Superior Court, where Carmichael had filed suit against Adirondack. The court ordered that "[c]laims raised by Plaintiff in Civil Action Docket Number S-12-89 WnC which do not arise out of the Contractor Agreement are not subject to arbitration and are properly within the jurisdiction of the Washington Superior Court."

On September 24, 1990, the parties stipulated to the entry of an arbitration award. The award set the various claims of the parties off one against another and concluded that "the adoption of the 'account resolution' set forth herein and the monetary award to Carmichael in the amount of $4,922.26 fully resolves all of the disputes which either of the parties has raised, or could have raised, arising under the Contractor Agreement, as amended, between the parties."

The arbitration proceedings, however, did not address any claim regarding bad faith and unfair dealing. It dealt only with accounting disputes. While the parties were in arbitration, Carmichael initiated suit against Adirondack in federal district court on January 5, 1990, alleging federal antitrust violations by Adirondack. Eight months later, Carmichael was granted a stay of the state court proceedings pending the outcome of her federal antitrust suit. Adirondack neither opposed the stay nor attempted to remove Carmichael's state claims to the federal forum.

In December 1991, the district court dismissed Carmichael's antitrust suit with prejudice. Arguing that Carmichael's remaining complaints were now barred by the res judicata effect of the federal court's dismissal, Adirondack moved for summary judgment in state court. In April of 1992, the state court denied summary judgment and the parties proceeded to trial.

After a seven-day jury trial, the trial court directed a verdict in Adirondack's favor on all but one count of Janet Carmichael's complaint. That count, alleging that

Adirondack's conduct toward Carmichael following Philip's death amounted to a breach of the implied covenant of good faith and fair dealing, was submitted to the jury, which returned a verdict against Adirondack in the amount of $60,000 compensatory and $100,000 punitive damages. Thereafter, Adirondack filed several post-verdict motions, all of which were denied.

. . .

II.

We treat together Adirondack's claims that the jury instruction on Carmichael's claim was erroneous and that, in any event, it was entitled to a directed verdict. Adirondack argues that it could not have violated "good faith and fair dealing" because no contract existed between the parties as of Philip Carmichael's death. We disagree that the duty of good faith and fair dealing expired abruptly on December 24, 1987, when Philip died. The very nature of their business relationship contemplated that, after the contract termination, the parties owed each other duties with respect to winding down their affairs as long as the post-termination conduct was related to the contractual relationship. See deTreville v. Outboard Marine Corp., 439 F.2d 1099, 1100 (4th Cir. 1971) ("[R]egardless of broad unilateral termination powers, the party who terminates a contract commits an actionable wrong if the manner of termination is contrary to equity and good conscience.").

The definition of the "covenant of good faith and fair dealing" is broad. An underlying principle implied in every contract is that each party promises not to do anything to undermine or destroy the other's rights to receive the benefits of the agreement. Shaw v. E.I. DuPont de Nemours & Co., 126 Vt. 206, 209, 226 A.2d 903, 906 (1966). The implied covenant of good faith and fair dealing exists to ensure that parties to a contract act with "faithfulness to an agreed common purpose and consistency with the justified expectations of the other party." Restatement (Second) of Contracts §205 comment a (1981). The factual question in this case was whether Adirondack so acted toward Janet Carmichael after her husband died.

Other than stating the underlying principles, little can be said in general as to what constitutes a breach of the covenant. Although we have stated that a covenant of good faith is implied in every contract, an action for its breach is really no different from a tort action, because the duty of good faith is imposed by law and is not a contractual term that the parties are free to bargain in or out as they see fit. Cf. Ainsworth v. Franklin County Cheese Corp., 156 Vt. 325, 331-32, 592 A.2d 871, 874-75 (1991).

We note that "good faith" is a concept that "varies . . . with the context" in which it is deemed an implied obligation. Restatement (Second) of Contracts §205 comment a (1981). Contextual and fact-specific, the implied good-faith covenant has been the subject of many decisions that have informed the substance of this cause of action. The implied promise by its nature protects against "a variety of types of conduct characterized as involving 'bad faith' because they violate community standards of decency, fairness or reasonableness." Id. As the Restatement points out,

> [a] complete catalogue of types of bad faith is impossible, but the following types are among those which have been recognized in judicial decisions: evasion of the spirit of the bargain, lack of diligence and slacking off, willful rendering of imperfect performance, abuse of a power to specify terms, and interference with or failure to cooperate in the other party's performance.

Id. §205 comment d. Further, bad faith inheres in "harassing demands for assurances of performance, rejection of performance for unstated reasons, willful failure to mitigate damages, and abuse of a power to determine compliance or to terminate the contract." Id. §205 comment e. Additionally, "[s]ubterfuges and evasions violate the obligation of good faith in performance even though the actor believes his conduct to be justified." Id. §205 comment d. Finally, the covenant of good faith "also extends to dealing which is candid but unfair, such as taking advantage of the necessitous circumstances of the other party." Id. §205 comment e.

In the end, good faith is ordinarily a question of fact, one particularly well-suited for juries to decide. J. Calamari & J. Perillo, Contracts §11-38(c) (1987). It follows that a jury instruction on point will feature few precise analytical elements. Rather, such an instruction will ask the jurors to judge the context within which the alleged offensive conduct occurred.

Adirondack argues that the jury was improperly instructed when the trial court explained the implied covenant of good faith and fair dealing as follows:

> While the contracts between the parties provided that they terminated upon the death of Philip Carmichael, Adirondack was under a duty to treat Plaintiffs fairly and in good faith. Adirondack had a duty to advise Plaintiffs whether it would agree to enter into a new contract with them or to allow Plaintiffs a reasonable opportunity to find a buyer for the distributorship or to decide to sell their interest in the distributorship to Adirondack.

Adirondack claims for the first time on appeal that the instruction in effect created substantive duties that the parties had not bargained for in their original contract. Not only did Adirondack waive any objection it had to the language of the instruction, we believe the "duties" specified in the instructions, given the nature of the business relationship, arose under the termination provision of the parties' contract by the implication of fair dealing and good faith.

The context in which the jury was asked to judge involved a contract featuring a "key man" termination clause and a number of post-termination obligations demanding reasonable accommodations in winding up the parties' affairs and accounting for assets. For instance, the contract provided for returning deposits, cooperating in locating equipment in the field, turning over business records, and implementing a covenant not to compete. All of these activities contemplated continued interaction of the parties after the "key man" provision had triggered the termination of the existing contractual arrangement. All of this post-termination activity was subject to good faith and fair dealing. Although the "key man" provision may have spelled an end to the parties' contractually contemplated business-as-usual, the provision did not extinguish the context of prior dealings between the parties. These dealings might have legitimately led Janet Carmichael to expect that Adirondack might negotiate a new agreement with her, or that it might arrange to buy her out at a fair price, or that it might allow her sufficient time to negotiate a sale of the business to a third party. Specific facts were presented at trial that evidenced the relational context within which the termination clause went into effect. The trial court's instruction simply asked the jurors to decide whether good faith and fair dealing were observed in this context. The evidence showed that Adirondack knew Carmichael had just lost her husband and thus had incurred the sole responsibility for running the business and supporting her family; that Adirondack knew that Carmichael wanted to stay in business and arguably did not discourage her from thinking she could; that Adirondack knew that the price it was offering for the distributorship had previously been rejected; and that Adirondack imposed unreasonably short deadlines on Carmichael for making an important and complex business decision. The court's instruction captured the substance of the implied promise of good faith and fair dealing described in the Restatement. We see no error in the instruction.

It is settled law that "[g]eneral verdicts should be construed to give them effect, if that can reasonably be done." Vineyard Brands, Inc. v. Oak Knoll Cellar, 155 Vt. 473, 481, 587 A.2d 77, 81 (1990). On appeal, we view the facts in the light most favorable to Janet Carmichael, who prevailed at trial. The relevant question before us, however, is whether a jury reasonably could have found that Adirondack's conduct amounted to a breach of the implied covenant of good faith and fair dealing. In our opinion, the trial record contained sufficient evidence to support the jury's verdict, provided that it chose to believe Janet Carmichael's testimony. "[I]f the verdict is justified by 'any reasonable view of the evidence, it must stand.'" Claude G. Dern Elec., Inc. v. Bernstein, 144 Vt. 423, 426, 479 A.2d 136, 138 (1984) (quoting Crawford v. State Highway Bd., 130 Vt. 18, 25, 285 A.2d 760, 764 (1971)). It was not error to deny Adirondack's motion for a directed verdict.

. . .

Affirmed.

BRUNSWICK HILLS RACQUET CLUB, INC.
v.
ROUTE 18 SHOPPING CENTER ASSOCIATES

Supreme Court of New Jersey
182 N.J. 210
2005

Albin, J.

In the highly competitive world of commercial transactions, sophisticated business entities operate according to the impersonal laws of the marketplace in which self-interest, not altruism, is the dominating principle. We must decide to what extent the covenant of good faith and fair dealing, which is implicit in every contract, governs the arms-length business transactions of such entities.

. . .

I.

A.

Plaintiff Brunswick Hills Racquet Club, Inc. owns and operates a tennis club in East Brunswick on property that it leases from defendant Route 18 Shopping Center Associates. . . .

The agreement provided for an initial twenty-five-year term and permitted plaintiff to construct and operate an indoor tennis center on the leased premises. . . .

The agreement also provided plaintiff with the option of purchasing the leased property or entering into a ninety-nine-year lease, both on very favorable financial terms.[2] In order to exercise the option either to purchase the property or to lease the property over a ninety-nine-year term, the contract required plaintiff both to notify defendant of its intention and to pay $150,000 no later than September 30, 2001, six months before the expiration of the original lease term. Otherwise, the option would be lost. Additionally, if plaintiff did not exercise the option or terminate the lease by that date, the rent would increase to more than triple what plaintiff had been paying during the original lease term. During the period leading up to the option deadline, plaintiff repeatedly expressed in writing its intent to exercise the option. The heart of the controversy concerns defendant's nineteen-month posture of silence, which was punctuated by written and verbal evasions and delay, and plaintiff's failure to pay the option price of $150,000 to defendant before the deadline.

---

2. The terms for exercising the option are set forth in paragraph 42 of the contract.

> 42. *OPTION TO PURCHASE DEMISED PREMISES*
>
> 42.1 In lieu of the right to extend the original term of this Lease as provided in Article 41 above, *Tenant shall have the right, exercisable by written notice to Landlord communicated not later than six (6) months prior to the expiration of the original term hereof, to purchase the Demised Premises or otherwise convert this Lease into a fully vested ninety-nine (99) year land lease, upon and subject to the following express conditions:*
>
> . . .
>
> C. That with respect to either purchase or lease of the Demised Premises, *Tenant shall pay to Landlord, upon the exercise of its right hereunder, a purchase price or rental (fully paid in advance) of an amount equal to the product of the minimum annual rental then being paid by Tenant times twelve (12).*
>
> . . .
>
> 42.2 Should Tenant fail to exercise the right herein granted at the time and in the manner herein provided, or should Tenant fail to comply with the conditions herein set forth, this Article 42 and the right herein granted to Tenant shall automatically become null and void and of no further force and effect on the date corresponding to the 180th day prior to the expiration of the original Lease term. [Emphasis added.]

B.

We now review the series of letters that have led to this litigation. On February 23, 2000—nineteen months before the option deadline—plaintiff's attorney, Gabriel E. Spector, wrote to Rosen Associates Management Corporation, defendant's property management company, informing it that plaintiff intended to exercise its option to purchase the ninety-nine-year lease. That letter, in pertinent part, read:

> On behalf of my clients, this letter is written to exercise the option to purchase the ninety-nine year lease effective March 31, 2002. In accordance with the lease, the purchase price will be $150,000.00 representing the base annual rent of $12,500 times twelve.
>
> Prior to the closing on the lease, we will obtain a title search to verify the status of title and supply you or your attorney with a copy of same.
>
> Further, pursuant to Paragraph 42 of the original lease, the ninety-nine year lease will be subject to the terms and conditions of the original lease.
>
> Please advise whether your attorney or you will be preparing the ninety-nine year lease. I would like to receive it well in advance of the closing date in order to review same. If you know who will be representing you in this matter, please advise.

Plaintiff did not tender the required payment of $150,000 with that letter or at any time before the option deadline.

On March 8, 2000, Florence Rosen of Rosen Associates responded to Spector, stating that she had forwarded his letter to "our" attorney and would "be in touch with [Spector] within a week or two." One month later, on April 3, 2000, Spector wrote again to Rosen:

> "[Y]ou wrote to me on March 8 and advised that I would hear from you in a week or two. I have heard nothing and I would appreciate receiving a response."

Two months later, on June 9, 2000, Spector wrote yet again to Rosen, enclosing his previous letters:

> "I have not heard from you. . . . I would appreciate hearing from either you or your attorney concerning the matter."

On June 19, 2000, defendant's attorney wrote to Spector, advising him that he represented Rosen Associates and that Spector's June 9 letter had been referred to him for reply. The lawyer invited Spector to call him "at [Spector's] convenience." One month later, Spector forwarded a letter to the attorney reminding him about their telephone conversation two weeks earlier, in which he told Spector that he "would review the file and get back to [Spector]." Spector concluded by stating that he "would appreciate hearing from [him] as soon as possible."

When several weeks passed without a reply, Spector wrote once more to defendant's attorney stating that he had yet to hear from him. In an effort to move forward with the closing on the ninety-nine-year lease, Spector requested that the lawyer provide information concerning common area billing charges and real estate taxes for the previous year. Spector closed by writing, "I would like to resolve this matter as soon as possible and I would appreciate hearing from you." Five days later, defendant's attorney tersely replied: "I acknowledge receipt of your letter dated August 3, 2000 and have forwarded same to my client for its review."

Four-and-one-half months later, on December 28, 2000, Thomas Cuming, one of plaintiff's corporate officers, received a letter from defendant's property management company demanding that plaintiff complete an estoppel certificate in support of defendant's application for a bank loan. Cuming signed and returned the estoppel certificate for plaintiff, making two substantive changes. First, Cuming crossed out a portion of one paragraph that read: "Tenant has no right of first refusal or option to purchase the Premises." In its place, he inserted: "Tenant has exercised its option to convert the lease to a fully prepaid 99 year lease effective March 31st 2002." Second, Cuming added the following statement to another paragraph of the certificate: "Tenant has given notice of its exercise of the option to convert lease to a 99 year prepaid lease." Defendant neither responded to nor commented on Cuming's changes.

On January 16, 2001, Spector wrote yet again to defendant's attorney, noting that he had not received the information sought in his August 2000 letter. As he had in prior letters, Spector requested the opportunity "to receive and review the ninety-nine year lease as soon as possible." The lawyer never replied to Spector's letter. After a long illness, Spector died on May 28, 2001.

Seven months after Spector's final letter, and with little more than a month remaining before the option deadline of September 30, 2001, Spector's law partner, Arnold B. Levin, forwarded a letter to Rosen Associates via certified mail:

> You will recall the letter from my late partner, Gabriel E. Spector, Esq., to you of February 23, 2000 (copy attached). In Mr. Spector's letter, he had told you that our client, Brunswick Hills Racquet Club, Inc., was exercising the option contained in the Lease to purchase the 99 year Lease effective March 31, 2002.
>
> Mr. Spector's letter had requested a response as to whether you or your attorney would be preparing the 99 year Lease and requested that it be submitted well in advance of the closing so that it could be reviewed in the proper manner.

Levin then set forth the history of Spector's correspondence and contacts with Rosen Associates and defendant's attorney, and concluded by stating:

> The purpose of this letter is to serve as a courtesy advice that I am now handling this matter in behalf of our client and that we would like to have a copy of the proposed Lease forwarded to us as quickly as possible so that we can address any issues that may require attention. As a courtesy to you and [your attorney], I have sent [him] a copy of this

letter as well. It would be appreciated if you or [your attorney] would respond to our office upon your receipt of this letter.

There was no response to Levin's letter, and the option deadline passed.

Four months later, on December 17, 2001, still looking to finalize the option terms with a willing agent acting on defendant's behalf, Levin wrote again to Rosen Associates. Levin enclosed a copy of Spector's almost two-year-old original letter "exercising the option to purchase the 99 year lease effective March 31, 2002. . . ." Levin requested "a copy of the proposed lease for review and approval so that [they could] be prepared to proceed with the execution of the lease." A copy of the letter was sent to defendant's attorney.

On January 14, 2002, Levin finally received a telephone response from the attorney, and the two discussed details concerning plaintiff's expected purchase of the ninety-nine-year lease. During their conversation, the attorney questioned the need to draft a new lease. In a letter forwarded to him the next day, Levin memorialized their discussions and made further proposals about preparing and recording the ninety-nine-year lease.

On February 5, 2002, two years after Spector first communicated plaintiff's intent to exercise the option, defendant's attorney dropped the hammer. In a letter to Levin, the lawyer, for the first time, took the position that plaintiff had not properly executed the option and that defendant would not honor plaintiff's attempt to do so:

> . . .
>
> The original term hereof expires March 31, 2002. Accordingly, under the plain terms of the Lease, conversion of the Lease into a fully vested 99-year Land Lease would have required that the Tenant provide written notice of the exercise of the option to convert the Lease into a 99-year Land Lease *and* pay to Landlord an amount equal to the product of the minimum annual rental then being paid by Tenant times 12 no later than September 30, 2001. Inasmuch as the payment was not made within the time frame required, any rights granted pursuant to Article 42 automatically became null and void and of no further force and effect as of that date.
>
> Accordingly, any attempt to exercise any of the rights of the Tenant pursuant to Article 42 is hereby rejected. Please be guided accordingly.
>
> . . .

Soon thereafter, defendant rejected plaintiff's tender of the $150,000 option price. Plaintiff then deposited that amount in escrow and filed suit in the Law Division to compel specific performance of the option and to obtain damages on a common law claim alleged in the complaint.

C.

At the conclusion of a bench trial[,] the trial court determined . . . that the contract clearly required plaintiff to exercise the option and pay the $150,000 in a timely manner. According to the court, a written notice exercising the lease option without tendering payment before the deadline did not satisfy the terms of the contract. The court ruled that defendant had no duty to inform plaintiff that it had not properly exercised the option and that defendant had not misrepresented any fact causing plaintiff harm.

. . .

The Appellate Division, in a *per curiam* opinion, affirmed the trial court's decision, holding that plaintiff failed to act in "strict accordance" with the contract terms governing the option. Because plaintiff did not tender payment until after the option deadline, the panel determined that the "attempt to exercise the option was nugatory." The lease terms, the panel ruled, provided plaintiff with no right to cure its mistake. The panel agreed with the trial court that defendant had no "affirmative duty" to disclose to plaintiff that it had fumbled in exercising the option. As such, it found that defendant did not breach a duty of candor or the covenant of good faith and fair dealing inherent in every contract. Finally, in noting that the parties were sophisticated business entities represented by counsel, the panel declined to write a more favorable contract for plaintiff than the one it had signed.

. . .

II.

A.

[P]laintiff did not abide by the strict terms governing the exercise of the option and, ordinarily, would suffer the consequences of its default. Courts generally should not tinker with a finely drawn and precise contract entered into by experienced business people that regulates their financial affairs. Equitable relief is not available merely because enforcement of the contract causes hardship to one of the parties. *Dunkin' Donuts of America, Inc. v. Middletown Donut Corp.,* 100 N.J. 166, 183-84 (1985). A court cannot "abrogate the terms of a contract" unless there is a settled equitable principle, such as fraud, mistake, or accident, allowing for such intervention. *Id.* at 183. Plaintiff claims that this is a case for equitable intervention because defendant breached its duty to act in good faith and to deal fairly with plaintiff in fulfilling the terms of the contract.

B.

Every party to a contract, including one with an option provision, is bound by a duty of good faith and fair dealing in both the performance and enforcement of the contract. *See Wilson v. Amerada Hess Corp.,* 168 N.J. 236, 241, 244 (2001) (holding that "[a] covenant of good faith and fair dealing is implied in every contract," including contract granting party unilateral discretion over pricing); *see also Sons of Thunder, Inc. v. Borden, Inc.,* 148 N.J. 396, 420-21 (1997) (holding same for contract granting party unilateral right of termination); Restatement (Second) of Contracts §205 (1981) ("Every contract imposes upon each party a duty of good faith and fair dealing in its performance and its enforcement."); 23 Williston on Contracts §63:22, at 506 (Lord ed. 2002) (same).

Good faith is a concept that defies precise definition. The Uniform Commercial Code, as codified in New Jersey, defines good faith as "honesty in fact and the observance of reasonable commercial standards of fair dealing in the trade." N.J.S.A. 12A:2-103(1)(b). Good faith conduct is conduct that does not "'violate community standards of decency, fairness or reasonableness.'" *Wilson, supra,* 168 N.J. at 245, 773 A.2d 1121 (quoting Restatement (Second) of Contracts, *supra* §205 comment a) "'Good faith performance or enforcement of a contract emphasizes faithfulness to an agreed common purpose and consistency with the justified expectations of the other party.'" *Ibid.* (quoting Restatement (Second) of Contracts, *supra,* §205 comment a). The covenant of good faith and fair dealing calls for parties to a contract to refrain from doing "anything which will have the effect of destroying or injuring the right of the other party to receive" the benefits of the contract. *Palisades Props., Inc. v. Brunetti,* 44 N.J. 117, 130, 207 A.2d 522 (1965) (internal quotations omitted); *see also Wade v. Kessler Institute,* 172 N.J. 327, 340, 798 A.2d 1251 (2002) (same).

Proof of "bad motive or intention" is vital to an action for breach of the covenant. *Wilson, supra,* 168 N.J. at 251. The party claiming a breach of the covenant of good faith and fair dealing "must provide evidence sufficient to support a conclusion that the party alleged to have acted in bad faith has engaged in some conduct that denied the benefit of the bargain originally intended by the parties." *Williston, supra,* §63:22, at 513-14 (footnotes omitted); *see also Wilson, supra,* 168 N.J. at 251; *Sons of Thunder, supra,* 148 N.J. at 420. As a general rule, "[s]ubterfuges and evasions" in the performance of a contract violate the covenant of good faith and fair dealing "even though the actor believes his conduct to be justified." Restatement (Second) of Contracts, *supra,* §205 comment d.

C.

. . .

Our review of the undisputed facts of this case leads us to the inescapable conclusion that defendant breached the covenant of good faith and fair dealing. Nineteen months in advance of the option deadline, plaintiff notified defendant in writing of its intent to exercise the option to purchase the ninety-nine-year lease. We will never know whether plaintiff's original attorney, Gabriel Spector, who died after a lengthy illness and who generated most of the correspondence, intended to close the deal and make the option payment before the deadline. However, we do know that plaintiff mistakenly believed that the purchase price was not due until the time of closing. As a result of plaintiff's failure to tender the purchase price, as required by the contract, execution of the option remained unperfected.

During a nineteen-month period, defendant, through its agents, engaged in a pattern of evasion, sidestepping every request by plaintiff to discuss the option and ignoring plaintiff's repeated written and verbal entreaties to move forward on closing the ninety-nine-year lease. Over the course of nineteen months, plaintiff's attorneys reached out to defendant and its representatives in repeated letters and telephone calls regarding exercising the lease option, all to no avail. Moreover, in support of defendant's application for a bank loan, plaintiff averred in an estoppel certificate that it had "exercised its option to convert lease to a fully prepaid 99 year lease. . . ." Defendant never challenged that formal declaration. After Spector's death, defendant's attorney continued to "play possum" despite the impending option deadline and obvious potential harm to plaintiff.

Defendant never requested the purchase price of the lease. Indeed, as defendant's attorney candidly admitted at oral argument, defendant did not want the purchase price because the successful exercise of the option was not in defendant's economic interest. Defendant preferred to watch the option die and did not break its silence until after the deadline had passed. In the first complete response to plaintiff's many letters, defendant advised plaintiff that the option was off the table. Defendant, apparently, never intended to dispel plaintiff's misapprehension until plaintiff was fatally prejudiced.

Defendant submits that a landlord does not waive its right to demand strict compliance with the terms of an option in a lease agreement absent an affirmative misrepresentation. Defendant also insists that it did not engage in "delaying tactics" and that its "continued silence, in the face of repeated requests by plaintiff for affirmative action, could not reasonably have been construed as anything other than an implicit rejection." The record speaks otherwise.

We are not eager to impose a set of morals on the marketplace. Ordinarily, we are content to let experienced commercial parties fend for themselves and do not seek to "introduce intolerable uncertainty into a carefully structured contractual relationship" by balancing equities. *Brick Plaza, supra,* 218 N.J. Super. at 105. But as our good faith and fair dealing jurisprudence reveals, there are ethical norms that apply even to the harsh and sometimes cutthroat world of commercial transactions. Gamesmanship can be taken too far, as in this case. We do not expect a landlord or even an attorney to act as his brother's keeper in a commercial transaction. We do expect, however, that they will act in good faith and deal fairly with an opposing party. Plaintiff's repeated letters and telephone calls to defendant concerning the exercise of the option and the closing of the ninety-nine-year lease obliged defendant to respond, and to respond truthfully.

In concluding that defendant violated the covenant, we do not establish a new duty for commercial landlords to act as calendar clerks for their tenants. We do not propose that attorneys must keep watch over and protect their adversaries from the mishaps and missteps that occur routinely in the practice of law. The breach of the covenant of good faith and fair dealing in this case was not a landlord's failure to cure a tenant's lapse. Instead, the breach was a demonstrable course of conduct, a series of evasions and delays, that lulled plaintiff into believing it had exercised the lease option properly. Defendant acted in total disregard of the harm caused to plaintiff, unjustly enriching itself with a windfall increase in rent at plaintiff's expense. In the circumstances of this case, defendant's conduct amounted to a clear breach of the implied covenant of good faith and fair dealing.

III.

In light of defendant's breach of the covenant of good faith and fair dealing, we hold that plaintiff is entitled to specific performance of the lease option in accordance with the terms of the contract. We reverse the Appellate Division and remand to the trial court for proceedings consistent with this opinion.

JORDAN
v.
DUFF & PHELPS, INC.

U.S. Court of Appeals, Seventh Circuit
815 F.2d 429
1987

EASTERBROOK, J.

. . . Jordan started work at Duff & Phelps in May 1977 and was viewed as a successful securities analyst. In 1981 the firm offered Jordan the opportunity to buy some stock. By November 1983 Jordan had purchased 188 of the 20,100 shares outstanding. He was making installment payments on another 62 shares. Forty people other than Jordan held stock in Duff & Phelps.

Jordan purchased his stock at its "book value" (the accounting net worth of Duff & Phelps, divided by the number of shares outstanding). Before selling him any stock, Duff & Phelps required Jordan to sign a "Stock Restriction and Purchase Agreement" (the Agreement). This provided in part:

> Upon the termination of any employment with the Corporation . . . for any reason, including resignation, discharge, death, disability or retirement, the individual whose employment is terminated or his estate shall sell to the Corporation, and the Corporation shall buy, all Shares of the Corporation then owned by such individual or his estate. The price to be paid for such Shares shall be equal to the adjusted book value (as hereinafter defined) of the Shares on the December 31 which coincides with, or immediately precedes, the date of termination of such individual's employment.

. . .

While Jordan was accumulating stock, Hansen, the chairman of the board, was exploring the possibility of selling the firm. Between May and August 1983 Hansen and Francis Jeffries, another officer of Duff & Phelps, negotiated with Security Pacific Corp., a bank holding company. The negotiators reached agreement on a merger, in which Duff & Phelps would be valued at $50 million, but a higher official within Security Pacific vetoed the deal on August 11, 1983. As of that date, Duff & Phelps had no irons in the fire.

Jordan, however, was conducting a search of his own—for a new job. . . . His search took him to Houston, where Underwood Neuhaus & Co., a broker-dealer in securities, offered him a job at a salary ($110,000 per year) substantially greater than his compensation ($67,000) at Duff & Phelps. . . .

On November 16, 1983, Jordan told Hansen that he was going to resign and accept employment with Underwood. Jordan did not ask Hansen about potential mergers; Hansen did not volunteer anything. Jordan delivered a letter of resignation, which Duff & Phelps accepted the same day. By mutual agreement, Jordan worked the rest of the year for Duff & Phelps even though his loyalties had shifted. He did this so that he could receive the book value of the stock as of December 31, 1983—for under the Agreement a departure in November would have meant valuation as of December 31, 1982. Jordan delivered his certificates on December 30, 1983, and the firm mailed him a check for $23,225, the book value (at $123.54 per share) of the 188 shares of stock. Jordan surrendered, as worthless under the circumstances, the right to buy the remaining 62 shares.

Before Jordan cashed the check, however, he was startled by the announcement on January 10, 1984, of a merger between Duff & Phelps and a subsidiary of Security Pacific. Under the terms of the merger Duff & Phelps would be valued at $50 million. If Jordan had been an employee on January 10, had quickly paid for the other 62 shares, and the merger had closed that day, he would have received $452,000 in cash and the opportunity to obtain as much as $194,000 more in "earn out" (a percentage of Duff & Phelps's profits to be paid to the former investors—an arrangement that keeps the employees' interest in the firm keen and reduces the buyer's risk if profits fall short). Jordan refused to cash the check and demanded his stock back; Duff & Phelps told him to get lost. He filed this suit in March 1984, asking for damages measured by the value his stock would have had under the terms of the acquisition.

. . .

[E]mployment at will is still a contractual relation, one in which a particular duration ("at will") is implied in the absence of a contrary expression. E. Allan Farnsworth, *Contracts* 532 n.29 (1982). The silence of the parties may make it necessary to imply other terms—those we are confident the parties would have bargained for if they had signed a written agreement. One term implied in every written contract and therefore, we suppose, every unwritten one, is that neither party will try to take opportunistic advantage of the other. "[T]he fundamental function of contract law (and recognized as such at least since Hobbes's day) is to deter people from behaving opportunistically toward their contracting parties, in order to encourage the optimal timing of economic activity and to make costly self-protective measures unnecessary." Richard A. Posner, *Economic Analysis of Law* 81 (3d ed. 1986). See also, e.g., *Morin Building Products Co. v. Baystone Construction, Inc.,* 717 F.2d 413, 414-15 (7th Cir. 1983); *Martindell v. Lake Shore National Bank,* 15 Ill. 2d 272, 286, 154 N.E.2d 683, 690 (1958); Restatement (Second) of Contracts §205 (1979).

Employment creates occasions for opportunism. A firm may fire an employee the day before his pension vests, or a salesman the day before a large commission becomes payable. Cases of this sort may present difficult questions about the reasons for the decision (was it opportunism, or was it a decline in the employee's performance?). The difficulties of separating opportunistic conduct from honest differences of opinion about an employee's performance on the job may lead firms and their employees to transact on terms that keep such disputes out of court—which employment at will usually does. But no one, not even Professor Epstein, doubts that an *avowedly* opportunistic discharge is a breach of contract, although the employment is at-will. E.g., *Coleman v. Graybar Electric Co.,* 195 F.2d 374 (5th Cir. 1952), discussed with approval in Epstein, 51 U. Chi. L. Rev. at 980-82. See also, e.g., *Wilkes v. Springside Nursing Home, Inc.,* 370 Mass. 842, 353 N.E.2d 657 (1976). The element of good faith dealing implied in a contract "is not an enforceable legal duty to be nice or to behave decently in a general way." *Zick,* 623 F. Supp. at 929. It is not a version of the Golden Rule, to regard the interests of one's contracting partner the same way you regard your own. An employer may be thoughtless, nasty, and mistaken. Avowedly opportunistic conduct has been treated differently, however.

The stock component in Jordan's package induced him to stick around and work well. Such an inducement is effective only if the employee reaps the rewards of success as well as the penalties of failure. We do not suppose for a second that if Jordan had not resigned on November 16, the firm could have fired him on January 9 with a little note saying: "Dear Mr. Jordan: There will be a lucrative merger tomorrow. You have been a wonderful employee, but in order to keep the proceeds of the merger for ourselves, we are letting you go, effective this instant. Here is the $23,000 for your shares." Had the firm fired Jordan for this stated reason, it would have broken an implied pledge to avoid opportunistic conduct. It may well be that Duff & Phelps could have fired Jordan without the slightest judicial inquiry; it does not follow that an opportunistic discharge would have allowed Duff & Phelps to cash out the stock on the eve of its appreciation.

. . .

The timing of the sale and the materiality of the information Duff & Phelps withheld on November 16 are for the jury to determine.

REVERSED AND REMANDED.

POSNER, J. (dissenting).

. . . The target of the complaint is not misrepresentation or even misleading half-truths; it is Hansen's omission to tell Jordan that he should think twice about quitting since the company might soon be sold at a price that would increase the value of Jordan's stock almost 30-fold. The statement that Hansen failed to make may have been material, since it might have caused Jordan to change his mind about resigning. I say "may have been material" rather than "was material" because Hansen need not have allowed Jordan to change his mind about resigning. But I shall pass this point and assume materiality, in order to reach the more fundamental question, which is duty. "[O]ne who fails to disclose material information prior to the consummation of a transaction commits fraud only when he is under a duty to do so." *Chiarella v. United States,* 445 U.S. 222, 228 (1980).

We should ask why liability for failing to disclose, as distinct from liability for outright misrepresentation, depends on proof of duty. The reason is that information is a valuable commodity, and its production is discouraged if the producer must share it with the whole world. Hence an inventor is not required to blurt out his secrets, and a skilled investor is not required to disclose the results of his research and insights before he is able to profit from them. See Kronman, *Mistake, Disclosure, Information, and the Law of Contracts,* 7 J. Legal Stud. 1 (1978). But one who makes a contract, express or implied, to disclose information to another acts wrongfully if he then withholds the information. The question is whether Duff and Phelps made an undertaking, and therefore assumed a duty, to disclose to any stockholding employee who announced his resignation information regarding the prospects for a profitable sale of the company.

. . .

Jordan's deal with Duff and Phelps required him to surrender his stock at book value if he left the company. It didn't matter whether he quit or was fired, retired or died; the agreement is explicit on these matters. My brethren hypothesize "implicit parts of the relations between Duff & Phelps and its employees." But those relations are totally defined by (1) the absence of an employment contract, which made Jordan an employee at will; (2) the shareholder agreement, which has no "implicit parts" that bear on Duff and Phelps' duty to Jordan, and explicitly ties his rights as a shareholder to his status as an employee at will; (3) a provision in the stock purchase agreement between Jordan and Duff and Phelps (signed at the same time as the shareholder agreement) that "nothing herein contained shall confer on the Employee any right to be continued in the employment of the Corporation." There is no occasion to speculate about "the implicit understanding" between Jordan and Duff and Phelps. The parties left nothing to the judicial imagination. The effect of the shareholder and stock purchase agreements (which for simplicity I shall treat as a single "stockholder agreement"), against a background of employment at will, was to strip Jordan of any contractual protection against what happened to him, and indeed against worse that might have happened to him. Duff and Phelps points out that it would not have had to let Jordan withdraw his resignation had he gotten wind of the negotiations with Security Pacific and wanted to withdraw it. On November 14 Hansen could have said to Jordan, "I accept your resignation effective today; we hope to sell Duff and Phelps for $50 million but have no desire to see you participate in the resulting bonanza. You will receive the paltry book value of your shares as of December 31, 1982." The "nothing herein contained" provision in the stockholder agreement shows that this tactic is permitted. Equally, on November 14, at the board meeting before Hansen knew that Jordan wanted to quit, the board could have decided to fire Jordan in order to increase the value of the deal with Security Pacific to the remaining shareholders.

These possibilities eliminate any inference that the stockholder agreement obligated Duff and Phelps to inform Jordan about the company's prospects. Under the agreement, if Duff and Phelps didn't want to give him the benefit of the information all it had to do to escape any possible liability was to give him the information and then fire him. . . .

Was Jordan a fool to have become a shareholder of Duff and Phelps on such disadvantageous terms as I believe he agreed to? (If so, that might be a reason for doubting whether those were the real terms.) He was not. Few business executives in this country have contractual entitlements to earnings, bonuses, or even retention of their jobs. They would rather take their chances on their employer's good will and interest in reputation, and on their own bargaining power and value to the firm, than pay for contract rights that are difficult and costly to enforce. See *Miller v. International Harvester Co.,* 811 F.2d 1150, 1151 (7th Cir. 1987); *Tyson v. International Brotherhood of Teamsters, Local 710 Pension Fund,* 811 F.2d 1145, 1147 (7th Cir. 1987); *Kumpf v. Steinhaus,* 779 F.2d 1323, 1326 (7th Cir. 1985); Epstein, *In Defense of the Contract at Will,* 51 U. Chi. L. Rev. 947 (1984). If Jordan had had greater rights as a shareholder he would have had a lower salary; when he went to work for a new employer in Houston and received no stock rights he got a higher salary.

I go further: Jordan was protected by Duff and Phelps' own self-interest from being exploited. The principal asset of a service company such as Duff and Phelps is good will. It is a product largely of its employees' efforts and skills. . . .

My brethren are well aware that Duff and Phelps faced market constraints against exploiting its employee shareholders, but seem to believe that this implies that the company also assumed contractual duties. Businessmen, however, are less enthusiastic about contractual duties than lawyers are, see Macauley, *Non-Contractual Relations in Business: A Preliminary Study,* 28 Am. Sociological Rev. 55, 64 (1963), so it is incorrect to infer from the existence of market constraints against exploitation that the parties also imposed a contractual duty against exploitation. Contractual obligation is a source of uncertainty and cost, and is therefore an expensive way of backstopping market forces. That is why employment at will is such a common form of employment relationship. It is strange to infer that firms invariably assume a legal obligation not to do what is not in their self-interest to do, and stranger to suppose—in the face of an explicit disclaimer—that by "allow[ing] employees to time their departures to obtain the maximum advantage from their stock," Duff and Phelps obligated itself to allow them to do this.

. . .

. . . [I]f Duff and Phelps had fired Jordan (or refused to let him withdraw his resignation), this would not necessarily have been opportunistic. One might equally well say (in the spirit of *Villada*) that by trying to stick around merely to participate in an unexpectedly lucrative sale of Duff and Phelps, Jordan would have been the opportunist. The majority says that "understandably Duff & Phelps did not want a viper in its nest, a disgruntled employee remaining only in the hope of appreciation of his stock." I call that "viper" an opportunist.

Problems

1. A Fortune in Cash Registers. Orville Fortune worked as a salesman for The National Cash Register Company (NCR) for 25 years under a contract that was terminable at will by either party. NCR paid Fortune a weekly salary plus a bonus based on sales in his territory, payable in part at the time a sales contract was signed and in part at the time the case registers were delivered. In 1968, First National, a regular customer, signed an order to purchase $5 million worth of registers over the next four years, which would be worth a total bonus of $92,079.99. In a letter dated the next business day, NCR terminated Fortune. NCR retracted the termination when it realized his continued employment would help with the First National order, and kept Fortune in the job until June 1970, at which time it terminated him. NCR did not pay Fortune any bonus payments for the First National cash registers delivered after he was fired. Fortune sued NCR for breach of contract on the ground that the company breached the implied duty of good faith and fair dealing in the contract. Is there sufficient evidence to support a finding that NCR breached?

2. Payment for Popcorn. In 1973, Baker Popcorn Company agreed to buy farmer James Ratzlaff's entire popcorn crop for $4.75 per hundredweight. The popcorn was to be shipped in multiple installments, and the contract specified that "if Baker, for any reason, fails, neglects, or refuses to pay [Ratzlaff] for said popcorn . . . at the time of delivery, then, and in that event, the remaining undelivered popcorn in [Ratzlaff's] possession shall, at [Ratzlaff's] option, be released by Baker for [Ratzlaff] to retain or dispose of as he sees fit." Ratzlaff shipped popcorn twice under the agreement, and Baker did not pay nor did Ratzlaff request payment on either occasion. When deliveries stopped, Baker called about the delay and Ratzlaff claimed to have equipment problems, never mentioning Baker's failure to pay or requesting payment. One week later, Ratzlaff terminated the agreement on the grounds that Baker had failed to make payments at the time of the deliveries. Ratzlaff then sold the remaining crop for nearly twice the amount he would have received under the contract with Baker. In a suit by Baker against Ratzlaff for breach of contract, what result?

3. The Los Angeles Angels of Anaheim (Reprise). In addition to claiming that changing the name of the Anaheim Angels to the Los Angeles Angels of Anaheim violated section 11(f) of the contract in question (see Section D, Problem 4), the City of Anaheim alleged that the name change and Angels Baseball's systematic removal of the name "Anaheim" from the team's road jerseys, tickets, merchandise, and souvenirs breached the implied covenant of good faith and fair dealing. Should the court treat this claim differently than Anaheim's claim that the name change breached the express provision of section 11(f)?

4. Dealer Tank Wagon Price. Donald Casserlie leased a Cleveland gas station from Shell Oil Company and operated the station as a franchisee. Casserlie's contract provided that he would buy gas only from Shell and would pay Shell a price, including delivery costs, set by Shell at the time of delivery. Shell set the price (known as the "dealer-tank-wagon" price (DTW) because it included delivery costs) based on market factors, including competitor prices, and charged all Cleveland franchisees the same price. Shell also sold its gasoline to independent gas stations in Cleveland. Independent station owners obtained gasoline at Shell's terminal and, consequently, the "rack" price that they were charged did not include delivery costs. The rack price was often substantially lower than the DTW price. Casserlie and other Cleveland-area franchisees sued Shell, alleging that the company had violated the UCC's good faith requirement by setting prices too high for its franchisees to profitably compete with independent stations and did so with the intent of driving the franchisees out of business so that it could take over operations of the leased stations. Are the franchisees entitled to a jury trial?

Chapter 5

Defining Performance Obligations: Conditions and Excuses

When a contract obliges a party (the obligor) to perform an act, the obligor is said to have a "duty." Failure to perform a duty constitutes a breach of the contract, which in turn gives the obligee the right to a remedy. Rest. (2d) Contracts §235. The cases in Chapter 4 illustrated the standard tools of contract interpretation that courts use to determine whether duties exist and, if so, their content. For example, in the famous case of *Frigaliment Importing Company v. B.N.S. International Sales Corporation*, Judge Friendly easily determines that the seller has a duty to provide the buyer with poultry but struggles with the question of whether the seller's duty is to provide broilers and frying chickens specifically. If the seller had such a duty, then its delivery of stewing chickens would have constituted a breach of contract.

Chapter 5 considers two distinct but related ways in which parties' contractual duties might be circumscribed. Section A concerns the nature and implications of contractual conditions. In many circumstances, a duty is not absolute in nature, but rather is conditional on the occurrence of an event. If the event does not occur, then performance of the duty does not become due. Thus, a condition can be defined as an event that triggers a duty. Rest. (2d) Contracts §224. Section B turns to circumstances that excuse the failure of the obligor to perform a duty that has become due. The doctrines of mistake, impracticability, and frustration of purpose recognize that parties enter into contracts with certain assumptions about events, and that the non-occurrence of those events should affect the legal status of their duties. Rest. (2d) Contracts §§152, 153, 261, 265.

A. CONDITIONS

Understanding the role played by conditions in contract law requires learning both when conditions limit obligations to perform duties and when conditions themselves are (and are not) strictly enforced. Subsection 1 considers the first topic, illustrating how courts go about identifying conditions and exploring the difference between "ordinary" and "promissory" conditions and the difference between "express" and "constructive" conditions. Subsection 2 concerns how the similar doctrines of "material breach" and "substantial performance" can sometimes render duties enforceable even when conditions of those duties have not been completely satisfied. Subsection 3 describes several specific types of events that can excuse the satisfaction of conditions and thus require the performance of conditional duties.

1. Identifying Conditions and Their Type

As noted above, although some duties described in contracts are absolute, others become due only if a condition occurs. Some conditions, called "ordinary" conditions, are events beyond the control of either party and thus are not obligations of either. An example is an insurance contract that obligates the insurer to pay to rebuild the customer's home if it is destroyed by fire during the policy period. Under such a contract, the insurer's duty to pay is triggered only if the house burns down, but it is obviously neither party's obligation to destroy the home so that the insurer's duty to pay will arise. Other conditions, called "promissory" conditions, are a duty of one party as well as being a condition of the other party's duty. An example is a contract that calls for a landlord to furnish property to a tenant when the tenant posts a security deposit. Under such a contract, the tenant has a duty to provide the deposit, and this performance is also a condition of the landlord's duty to perform. See Rest. (2d) Contracts §225.

The distinction between ordinary and promissory conditions is critical because the consequences of a failure of the condition are dependent on the condition's type. When an ordinary condition is not satisfied, the conditional duty never becomes due, but neither party has a legal cause of action against the other. For example, if a fire does not destroy the insured's home during the policy period, the insurer has no duty to pay, but neither the insured nor the insurer has grounds to sue the other. The failure of a promissory condition, in contrast, constitutes a breach of contract, which means that the conditional duty is not triggered and also that the non-breaching party has a cause of action for breach. For example, if the tenant does not provide the required security deposit, the landlord not only has no duty to hand over the premises, she may also sue for damages caused by the tenant's breach, such as the income lost during the time period it takes to re-let the premises to another tenant.

Whether the occurrence of an event constitutes a condition is a question of contract interpretation. Thus, like a duty, a condition might arise from contractual language or surrounding circumstances.

A condition created by the parties is often called "express." In the first two cases, *Irving v. Town of Clinton* and *Main Electric, Ltd. v. Printz Services Corporation*, the courts interpret contractual language in order to determine whether events identified in the text of the contracts constitute a condition of one party's duty. Notice that in these two cases if the events in question are conditions, they must be ordinary conditions, since it is clear that it is not the duty of either party to ensure that the events occur. As a general matter, however, express conditions may be either ordinary or promissory conditions.

Based on the temporal order of duties specified in a contract, courts will determine that the performance of some duties constitutes conditions of other duties, even when the contract does not expressly provide that this is the case. Events that constitute conditions by operation of law are called "constructive" conditions. *Kingston v. Preston* and *Goodisson v. Nunn* are two foundational decisions that establish when events that are clearly the duties of one party also constitute constructive conditions of duties of the other party. See also Rest. (2d) Contracts §§234, 237, 238.

IRVING
v.
TOWN OF CLINTON

Supreme Judicial Court of Maine
711 A.2d 141
1998

DANA, J.

Kenneth Irving, Jr. appeals from the summary judgment entered in the Superior Court (Kennebec County, Kravchuk, C.J.) in favor of the Town of Clinton on Irving's breach of contract claim. Because we conclude that an express condition precedent to the contract did not occur, we affirm the judgment.

The underlying facts in this case are not in dispute. On June 19, 1996, Irving and a majority of the Town's selectmen signed a document entitled "Snow Plowing and Road Sanding Contract" which provided that Irving would maintain the Town's roads from October 1996 to May 1997 in return for $107,723.96. Paragraph 13 of the document states:

> 13. VOTER APPROVAL:
>   This contract is contingent upon voter approval (Article 11, Highway Dept. Account dated June 25, 1996).

The Town held its 1996 annual town meeting on June 25, 1996, at which the residents voted on Article 11, which stated in full: "To see if the town will vote to raise and appropriate the sum of $236,503.00 for the Highway Department Account." The annual town report, which had been distributed to residents and was available at the meeting, contained a detailed breakdown of the highway department budget, including an appropriation for $107,860 for plowing. At the meeting a voter moved to amend Article 11 to reduce the snow removal line from $107,860 to $99,999. The amendment passed and the Article was approved as amended. The Town then offered Irving the snowplowing contract at the reduced amount, which he refused, opting instead to file the breach of contract lawsuit that is the subject of this appeal.

. . .

We need not address Irving's argument that the Town selectmen possess the authority to enter into contracts on behalf of the Town to carry out necessary governmental functions such as snowplowing. Even if such authority exists the contingency provided for in paragraph 13 of the parties' contract was never met. The contract was made expressly contingent on the approval of the voters at the annual town meeting. The voters did not approve the contract as written and appropriated a lesser amount of money for snow removal. An elementary rule of contract law is that the nonoccurrence of a condition discharges the parties from their duties under the contract. Restatement (Second) of Contracts §225 (1981). Because the Town's duty to pay Irving for his snowplowing services was discharged by the failure of the Town's voters to approve the contract as written, the court properly entered a summary judgment in favor of the Town.

MAIN ELECTRIC, LTD.
v.
PRINTZ SERVICES CORP.

Supreme Court of Colorado (En Banc)
980 P.2d 522
1999

∿

BENDER, J.

. . .

I. FACTS AND PROCEEDINGS BELOW

Respondent Printz Services Corporation was the general contractor on a casino construction project in Cripple Creek, Colorado. Petitioners C.J. Masonry and Main Electric were subcontractors on the project. The relationship between Printz and C.J. Masonry was governed by a preprinted form contract prepared by Printz, the general contractor. The form contains the following pertinent payment provisions:

> 3. SUBCONTRACT AMOUNT. In consideration of the faithful performance of the covenants and agreements herein, . . . Contractor agrees to pay, or cause to be paid, Subcontractor . . . at the times and in the manner following in Articles 4 and 5.

4. PROGRESS PAYMENTS.

. . .

D. Contractor shall make payment on or before the 25th day of the next month following receipt of the Payment Request provided like payment has been made by Owner to Contractor.

. . .

5. FINAL PAYMENT. Contractor shall make final payment to Subcontractor after work is complete and accepted by Owner and Architect provided like payment shall have been made by Owner to Contractor.

. . .

Before the project was complete, the owner became insolvent and lost the property in a deed of trust foreclosure. The owner failed to pay Printz, and Printz in turn failed to pay its subcontractors. C.J. Masonry and Main Electric both sought payment for breach of contract against the general contractor. Printz claimed in defense that it was obligated to pay its subcontractors only *if* it was first paid by the owner.

The trial court interpreted the payment clause "provided like payment shall have been made by Owner to Contractor" in C.J. Masonry's contract to be a promise by Printz to pay the subcontractor *when* and not *if* the general contractor was paid by the owner. In the trial court's view, the general contractor remained unconditionally obligated to pay the subcontractor provided the work was performed. The trial court ruled that Printz must pay C.J. Masonry regardless of the owner's insolvency.

. . .

The court of appeals reversed the trial court on both subcontractors' claims. *See Printz Servs. Corp.*, 949 P.2d at 79. It held that the contract between Printz and C.J. Masonry created a condition precedent rather than a promise to pay, relying substantially on language in *Orman v. Ryan*, 25 Colo. 383, 55 P. 168 (1897), in which a similarly worded clause in a construction contract was referred to as a condition precedent. *See id.* at 388, 55 P. at 170. Thus, the court of appeals ruled Printz was not obligated to pay C.J. Masonry. *See Printz Servs. Corp.*, 949 P.2d at 81-82.

. . .

III. THE PAYMENT PROVISION IN THIS CONTRACT IS NOT A PAY-IF-PAID CLAUSE

We now turn to address the interpretation of the payment clause in the contract between Printz and C.J. Masonry. Initially, we note that the interpretation of a contract is a question of law which we review de novo. *See Union Ins. Co. v. Houtz*, 883 P.2d 1057, 1061 (Colo. 1994).

We begin our analysis by reviewing basic principles of contract interpretation. The parties' intention when drafting a contract governs the interpretation of that contract. *See Centennial Enter. v. Mansfield Dev. Co.*, 193 Colo. 463, 464, 568 P.2d 50, 51 (1977). A contract term can be interpreted as either a condition precedent or a promise to perform depending on the parties' intent. *See Charles Ilfeld*

Co. v. Taylor, 156 Colo. 204, 209, 397 P.2d 748, 750 (1964). In other contexts we have followed the rule that a condition precedent in a contract is not favored and will not be given effect unless established by clear and unequivocal language. *See id.; Balzano v. Bluewater Insurance Ltd.*, 801 P.2d 1, 3 (Colo. App. 1990). If there is any doubt as to the parties' intention, we interpret a clause in a contract as a promise rather than a condition. *See Ilfeld*, 156 Colo. at 209, 397 P.2d at 750. This rule of contract interpretation expresses the recognized policy of avoiding the harsh results of forfeiture against a party who has no control over the occurrence of the condition. *See Rohauer v. Little*, 736 P.2d 403, 409 (Colo. 1987); *Ilfeld*, 156 Colo. at 209, 397 P.2d at 750. As we stated in *Ilfeld*:

> The intention of the parties in making a contract controls. . . . In cases of doubt as to the intention of the parties, courts resolve the doubt in favor of an interpretation making the engagement a promise rather than a condition. And such rule of construction is founded on a policy of avoiding, if possible, forfeitures. . . . To frown upon forfeitures is part of the judicial policy of this state, too. *Ilfeld*, 156 Colo. at 209, 397 P.2d at 750-751 (citations omitted).

Although we have not yet applied this reasoning to conditions precedent in payment clauses of a construction contract, we believe that our general rule of contract interpretation applies with equal force in that context. If a payment provision such as the one here creates a condition precedent, then the subcontractor will forfeit payment for work performed due to the occurrence of a condition—the owner's insolvency—over which the subcontractor has no control. *See R.N. Robinson & Son, Inc. v. Ground Improvement Techniques & Fireman's Fund Ins. Co.*, 31 F. Supp. 2d 881, 886 (D. Colo. 1998) (applying Colorado law) ("[C]onditions precedent create a risk of forfeiture, even when the party against whom the condition operates has no control over whether the condition is met.").

Typically, a subcontractor looks to the general contractor for payment and not the owner. *See Thomas J. Dyer Co. v. Bishop Int'l Eng'g Co.*, 303 F.2d 655, 660 (6th Cir. 1962). Therefore, the subcontractor need not factor in the risk of nonpayment by the owner. *See Robinson*, 31 F. Supp. 2d at 886; *Peacock Constr. Co. v. Modern Air Conditioning Inc.*, 353 So. 2d 840, 842 (Fla. 1977). If the risk of the owner's nonpayment is to be shifted from the general contractor to the subcontractor, then this shift must be clearly articulated in the agreement. Which it is not here

With the principle in mind that we will interpret a clause as a promise rather than a condition unless the language of the contract explicitly mandates otherwise, we analyze the relevant terms of this contract. Printz argues that the contract's terms, that the general contractor will pay its subcontractor "provided like payment shall have been made by owner to contractor," establishes a condition precedent requiring payment by the owner before payment to the subcontractor. We are not persuaded.

Although the payment clause may be read to support the argument that the parties intended the subcontractors to be paid only if the owner paid the general contractor first, this clause contains no language reflecting any intent of the parties to shift the risk of the owner's nonpayment from the general contractor to the subcontractor. There is no express acknowledgement by the subcontractor that it, rather than the general contractor, agrees to assume the risk of the owner's nonpayment. The "provided" clause does not indicate that the parties reasonably anticipated the possibility that the owner might not pay and therefore specifically addressed this contingency. The payment clause contains no specific language creating a contingency that must occur before payment must be made by the general contractor.

We conclude that the payment clause here leaves room for reasonable argument by both the general contractor and the subcontractor as to whether the parties intended to shift the risk of the owner's nonpayment from the general contractor to the subcontractor. Applying our rule interpreting a clause as a promise rather than a condition if there is any doubt of the parties' intention, we conclude that this payment clause is a pay-when-paid clause. It created a promise to pay the subcontractor that remains unconditional, although payment may be delayed because of the owner's failure to pay the general contractor. . . .

KINGSTON
v.
PRESTON

3

King's Bench
Cited at the Bar in Jones v. Barkley, 2 Doug. 685, 689,
99 Eng. Rep. 434 (1781)
1773

MANSFIELD, L.

It was an action of debt, for non-performance of covenants contained in certain articles of agreement between the plaintiff and the defendant. The declaration stated; That, by articles made the 24th of March, 1770, the plaintiff, for the considerations therein-after mentioned, covenanted, with the defendant, to serve him for one year and a quarter next ensuing, as a covenant-servant, in his trade of a silk-mercer, at £200 a year, and in consideration of the premises, the defendant covenanted, that at the end of the year and a quarter, he would give up his business of a mercer to the plaintiff, and a nephew of the defendant, or some other person to be nominated by the defendant, and give up to them his stock in trade, at a fair valuation; and that, between the young traders, deeds of partnership should be executed for 14 years, and from and immediately after the execution of the said deeds, the defendant would permit the said young traders to carry on the said business in the defendant's house.

Then the declaration stated a covenant by the plaintiff, that he would accept the business and stock in trade, at a fair valuation, with the defendant's nephew, or such other person, &c. and execute such deeds of partnership, and, further, that the plaintiff should, and would, at, and before, the sealing and delivery of the deeds, cause and procure good and sufficient security to be given to the defendant, to be approved of by the defendant, for the payment of £250 monthly, to the defendant, in lieu of a moiety of the monthly produce of the stock in trade, until the value of the stock should be reduced to £4000.

Then the plaintiff averred, that he had performed, and been ready to perform, his covenants, and assigned for breach on the part of the defendant, that he had refused to surrender and give up his business, at the end of the said year and a quarter.

The defendant pleaded, 1. That the plaintiff did not offer sufficient security; and, 2. That he did not give sufficient security for the payment of the £250, &c.

And the plaintiff demurred generally to both pleas.

On the part of the plaintiff, the case was argued by Mr. Buller, who contended, that the covenants were mutual and independant, and, therefore, a plea of the breach of one of the covenants to be performed by the plaintiff was no bar to an action for a breach by the defendant of one of which he had bound himself to perform, but that the defendant might have his remedy for the breach by the plaintiff, in a separate action. On the other side, Mr. Grose insisted, that the covenants were dependant in their nature, and, therefore, performance must be alleged: the security to be given for the money, was manifestly the chief object of the transaction, and it would be highly unreasonable to construe the agreement, so as to oblige the defendant to give up a beneficial business, and valuable stock in trade, and trust to the plaintiff's personal security, (who might, and, indeed, was admitted to be worth nothing,) for the performance of his part.

In delivering the judgment of the Court, Lord Mansfield expressed himself to the following effect: There are three kinds of covenants: 1. Such as are called mutual and independant, where either party may recover damages from the other, for the injury he may have received by a breach of the covenants in his favour, and where it is no excuse for the defendant, to allege a breach of the covenants on the part of the plaintiff. 2. There are covenants which are conditions and dependant, in which the performance of one depends on the prior performance of another, and, therefore, till this prior condition is performed, the other party is not liable to an action on his covenant. 3. There is also a third sort of covenants, which are mutual conditions to be performed at the same time; and, in these, if one party who is ready, and offered, to perform his part, and the other neglected, or refused, to perform his, he who was ready, and offered, has fulfilled his engagement, and may maintain an action for the default of the other; though it is not certain that either is obliged to do the first act.

His Lordship then proceeded to say, that the dependance, or independance, of covenants, was to be collected from the evident sense and meaning of the parties, and, that, however transposed they might be in the deed, their precedency must depend on the order of time in which the intent of the transaction requires their performance. That, in the case before the Court, it would be the greatest injustice if the plaintiff should prevail: the essence of the agreement was, that the defendant should not trust to the personal security of the plaintiff, but, before he delivered up his stock and business, should have good security for the payment of the money. The giving such security, therefore, must necessarily be a condition precedent.

Judgment was accordingly given for the defendant, because the part to be performed by the plaintiff was clearly a condition precedent.

GOODISSON
v.
NUNN   य

King's Bench
4 T.R. 762, 100 Eng. Rep. 1288
1792

This was an action of debt to recover 21£ on certain articles of agreement, the substance of which was stated in the declaration. The defendant craved oyer of the agreement; by which the plaintiff agreed that he would on or before the 2d of September then next, ". . . convey to the defendant all that copyhold tenement lying," &c. In consideration whereof the defendant covenanted to pay to the plaintiff the sum of 210£ on or before the 2d day of September next ensuing; on failure of complying with the before-mentioned agreement the defendant was to pay to the plaintiff the sum of 21£; and if the plaintiff did not deliver the estate according to the before-mentioned agreement, then he was to pay the defendant the sum of 21£. . . . The defendant then pleaded, 1st, non est factum; 2dly, that the plaintiff did not on or before the 2d day of September next, &c, . . . convey, to the defendant, the said premises, &c. . . . To the [] last plea[] the plaintiff demurred generally.

. . .

KENYON, L. Ch. J.

This case is extremely clear, whether considered on principles of strict law or of common justice. The plaintiff engaged to sell an estate to the defendant, in consideration of which the defendant undertook to pay 210£; and, if he did not carry the contract into execution, he was to pay 21£; and now not having conveyed his estate, or offered to do so, or taken one step; towards it, the plaintiff has brought this action for the penalty. Suppose the purchase-money of an estate was 40,000£ it would be absurd to say that the purchaser might enforce a conveyance without payment, and compel the seller to have recourse to him, who perhaps might be an insolvent person. The old cases, cited by the plaintiff's counsel, have been accurately stated; but the determinations in them outrage common sense. I admit the principle on which they profess to go: but I think that the Judges misapplied that principle. It is admitted in them all that where they are dependent covenants, no action will lie by one party unless he have performed, or offered to perform his covenant. Then the question is, whether these are, or are not, dependent covenants? I think they are; the one is to depend on the other; when the one party conveyed his estate he was to receive the purchase-money; and when the other parted with his money he was to have the estate. They were reciprocal acts, to be performed at the same time. . . . It is our duty when we see that principles of law have been misapplied in any case, to overrule it. The principle is admitted in all the cases alluded to, that, if they be dependent covenants, performance, or the offer to perform, must be pleaded on the one part, in order to found the action against the other. The mistake has been in the misapplication of that principle in the cases cited; and I am glad to find that the old cases have been over-ruled; and that we are now warranted by precedent as well as by principle to say that this action cannot be maintained.

BULLER, J.

The agreement was that the plaintiff should sell his estate, and that the defendant should buy it. In the nature of the thing therefore the two acts are to be done together. *Kingston v. Preston.* . . .

GROSE, J.

. . . [N]otwithstanding the old authorities, the Courts of later times have considered whether in reality the first act is not to be performed by the seller or at least whether they are not concurrent acts. There is so much good sense in the later decisions, that it is too much to say that they are not law. There being several precedents in support of our decision, and those being founded in good sense and justice, I think we ought to take advantage of them.

Judgment for the defendant.

Problems

1. Sour Grapes. Merritt Hill Vineyards contracted to purchase a vineyard owned by Windy Heights Vineyard and paid Windy Heights a $15,000 deposit. The contract provided that, if the sale did not close, Windy Heights could keep the $15,000 as liquidated damages unless Windy Heights failed to satisfy the conditions specified in Section 3 of the contract. Section 3 listed as "conditions precedent" of Merritt Hill's obligation to complete the purchase that Windy Heights obtain a title insurance policy and that Merritt Hill receive confirmation from Farmers Home Administration that the sale would not constitute a default of certain mortgages on the property. At the time of closing, Windy Heights had not obtained a title insurance policy and Merritt Hills had not heard from Farmers Home Administration, so Merritt Hills refused to close. When Windy Heights refused to refund the deposit, Merritt Hills sued for both the deposit and damages it suffered as a result of the sale not closing. Which party should prevail?

2. A G.I.'s Loan Contingency. In 1958, John DeFreitas agreed to buy Israel and Euphemie Cote's house for $16,720, with the following provision:

> This sale is subject to a G.I. Loan and in the event that said amount is not approved, the deposit will be returned in full. . . . It is further understood and agreed that should

the G.I. appraisal be less than requested and should the sellers refuse to sell for the amount of said appraisal, then this contract becomes null and void seven days after the bank receives said statement of appraisal.

The G.I. appraisal was less than the stated purchase price of the house, and the Cotes refused to accept the lesser price. Nevertheless, DeFreitas obtained a conventional loan and wrote to the Cotes that he intended to complete the purchase at the agreed-upon price. The Cotes refused to go through with the transaction. Were they legally justified?

3. Paying for Nuclear Power. The Massachusetts Municipal Wholesale Electric Company (MMWEC) pools the resources of small municipal utilities in order to purchase energy at lower cost than the utilities could obtain as individual entities. MMWEC entered contracts, called "power sales agreements," with a number of Massachusetts and Vermont utilities in order to create a consortium and then, on behalf of that consortium, raised capital through the issuance of bonds in order to purchase a six-percent interest in two nuclear power plants then being built in Seabrook, New Hampshire.

Each of MMWEC's power sales agreements contained an "execution and delivery" term, which provided that:

> This Agreement shall be effective upon execution and delivery of Power Sales Agreements by MMWEC and Participants whose Participant's shares total 100%.

Each of the power sales agreements also included a "step up" provision, which provided that, should one or more of the utilities in the consortium default on its obligations, the other members would be required to increase their participation pro rata to make up the difference.

After the power sales agreements had been signed and the bonds issued, the Vermont Supreme Court held that Vermont utilities, which collectively owned 15 percent of the consortium's investment, lacked authority to enter into the power sales agreements. Consequently, the power sales agreements between MMWEC and those utilities were void. The MMWEC subsequently invoked the "step up" provision. Several Massachusetts utilities, including the Town of Danvers, brought suit, claiming that the power sales agreements (and, thus, the "step up" provision) never became binding because the condition precedent provided by the "execution and delivery" term was never satisfied. Should the utilities be excused from performing according to the "step up" provision?

4. The Sale of Corn. Morton entered into a contract to purchase corn from Lamb. Lamb was to deliver the corn to Morton at Shardlow, a village in Derbyshire, England, one month from the date of the agreement. When Lamb failed to deliver the corn within that period of time, Morton brought suit. Lamb argued that Morton should not be permitted to recover because Morton had not tendered payment. Who should prevail?

5. Gassed. John Shaw leased a gas station from Mobil Oil Corporation under a contract that provided that Mobil would provide Shaw with his gasoline requirements and Shaw would pay a specified price per gallon but not less than a "minimum rental" of $470. If the per gallon charges totaled less than $470 at the end of any given month, Shaw was to "pay the deficiency promptly." As a consequence of oil shortages, the federal government in July 1973 limited the amount of gas Mobil could provide its lessees. Consequently, although Shaw requested an amount of gasoline that would have exceeded $470, Mobil delivered a lesser quantity, the contract price of which totaled less than $470. At the end of the month, Mobil demanded that Shaw pay the deficiency amount, and Shaw refused. For whom should a court rule?

2. Substantial Performance and Material Breach

When parties create an ordinary condition to allocate the risk of an uncertain event, the failure of the condition typically imposes no hardship on the party who otherwise would have been entitled to performance. In the typical case, the purpose of the parties was to use the condition as a means of allocating risk. For example, in the case of an insurance contract that requires the insurer to rebuild the customer's house if it burns down, the parties' clear intent is that, in the absence of a fire, the insurer will keep the premium paid by the homeowner and the homeowner will receive nothing from the insurer. In the absence of fire, the homeowner receives precisely what she bargained for: her home in its condition at the time of contracting, whether untouched by fire or repaired after a fire.

In some circumstances, however, the failure of a relatively minor condition—often but not always a promissory condition—may threaten to impose a significant hardship on the party expecting a subsequent performance. Imagine, for example, that the homeowner's insurance contract contains a promissory condition requiring the annual premium to be paid no later than January 1, that the homeowner's payment arrives on January 2, and that all other potential insurers charge far higher premiums than the contract price. If the failure of the condition means that the insurer need not provide coverage, the cost suffered by the customer might be viewed as incommensurate with his oversight.

When the material breach doctrine applies, the breach of a promissory condition is treated as the failure of the condition only if the breach is material. If the breach is not material, the non-breaching party retains the right to sue for any damages caused by the breach, but subsequent conditional duties must be performed. See Rest. (2d) Contracts §229. Similarly, under the doctrine of substantial performance, substantial but incomplete performance satisfies the constructive condition, although the injured party may still demand compensation for harm caused by the breach of duty. Rest. (2d) Contracts §237 cmt. d. Both doctrines are designed to avoid disproportionate forfeitures that might result in the case of a relatively minor breach if the non-breaching party is allowed to suspend performance.

The traditional rule is that these doctrines apply only to constructive conditions while express conditions are strictly enforced, but as a comparison of the first trio of cases—*Maxton Builders, Inc. v. Lo Galbo, Sahadi v. Continental Illinois National Bank and Trust Company of Chicago*, and *Jacob & Youngs v. Kent*—demonstrates, not all courts abide by this limitation. The subsequent pair of cases, *O.W. Grun Roofing and Construction Company v. Cope* and *Dove v. Rose Acre Farms, Inc.*, explores the factors that determine the "materiality" of a breach or the "substantiality" of performance along with the allocation of authority for making these determinations between judge and jury. See Rest. (2d) Contracts §241.

The UCC takes a somewhat different approach than the common law on the performance required to satisfy a condition. Under what is known as the "perfect tender" rule, the UCC grants the buyer the right to reject goods that do not conform to exact contractual requirements. U.C.C. §2-601. The UCC dilutes the potential harshness of the perfect tender rule, however, by allowing the seller an opportunity to correct any breach if time remains for performance on the contract. U.C.C. §§2-508, 2-602, 2-605. In addition, if a buyer does not reject imperfect goods within a reasonable time after delivery, the buyer must pay but can sue for damages due to any breach. U.C.C. §§2-606, 2-607.

MAXTON BUILDERS, INC.
v.
LO GALBO

Court of Appeals of New York
502 N.E.2d 184
1986

WATCHLER, C.J.

. . .

In 1983 the defendants contracted to purchase a newly constructed house from the plaintiff for $210,000. At the contract signing on August 3, the defendants gave the plaintiff a check for $21,000 as a down payment to be held in escrow. A handwritten rider, included in the contract at the defendants' request, provided: "If real estate taxes are in excess of $3,500 based on a full assessment of house sold for $210,000.00, buyer shall have the right to cancel this contract upon written notice to the seller within three days of date and escrow funds to be returned."

The following day defendant Cynthia Lo Galbo and plaintiff's president, Scott Seeman, went to the county tax assessor's office to obtain an estimate of the taxes on the new house. The assessment was in excess of $3,500.

The defendants' attorney then called the plaintiff's counsel and informed him that the defendants had decided to exercise their option to cancel. He also sent a certified letter to the defendants' attorney informing him in writing of the defendants' decision to cancel. The letter was mailed on Friday August 5 and was received by plaintiff's attorney on August 9. Several days later plaintiff's attorney also received a bank notice that defendants had stopped payment on their check.

On September 20, 1983, the plaintiff commenced this action against the defendants to recover the amount of the down payment claiming that the defendants breached the contract when they stopped payment on the check. . . .

On this appeal the defendants again urge that their refusal to perform did not constitute a breach because they had reserved and adequately exercised a right to terminate. Although the plaintiff did not receive written notice of termination within three days, as the contract required, the defendants contend that this is not fatal when, as here, the contract does not provide that time is of the essence. The defendants argue that under these circumstances all that is required is reasonable notice and that this requirement was met here when the defendants mailed the notice and gave the plaintiff's attorney actual oral notice within the three-day period. It is settled, however, that when a contract requires that written notice be given within a specified time, the notice is ineffective unless the writing is actually received within the time prescribed (*see, Peabody v. Satterlee*, 166 N.Y. 174, 59 N.E. 818; *Kantrowitz v. Dairymen's League Co-op. Assn.*, 272 App. Div. 470, 71 N.Y.S.2d 821, aff'd 297 N.Y. 991, 80 N.E.2d 366; *cf. Sy Jack Realty Co. v. Pergament Syosset Corp.*, 27 N.Y.2d 449, 318 N.Y.S.2d 720, 267 N.E.2d 462). In short, the defendants bargained for and obtained a limited right to cancel which they failed to exercise within the time agreed upon. The cancellation was, therefore, ineffective and the defendants' refusal to perform constituted a breach (*Morgan & Brother Manhattan Stor. Co. v. Balin*, 39 N.Y.2d 848, 386 N.Y.S.2d 100, 351 N.E.2d 748).

. . .

SAHADI
v.
 CONTINENTAL ILLINOIS NATIONAL BANK & TRUST CO. OF CHICAGO

U.S. Court of Appeals, Seventh Circuit
706 F.2d 193
1983

HARLINGTON WOOD, JR., J.

This is an appeal from the district court's order granting partial summary judgment in favor of the defendant-appellee Continental Illinois Bank (the Bank) in an action alleging that the Bank breached its agreement with the plaintiff-appellant's business, Great Lakes and European Lines, Inc. (GLE), by calling a $7 million loan when GLE tendered interest payments less than one day after they were due. . . .

I.

Viewing the facts in the light most favorable to the plaintiffs, as we must, there emerges a story of financial brinkmanship and opaque dealing in which neither side emerges wholly blameless. GLE, an international shipping line, began its relationship with the Bank in 1976 with a $3 million loan, personally guaranteed by the Sahadis. The Bank increased its loan commitment to $11 million in 1977, a commitment upon which GLE relied in expanding its business, but which was repudiated by the Bank, to the detriment of GLE, when personal and institutional friction developed between the parties. The parties quickly reached a stalemate, with GLE threatening to sue the Bank for breach of its loan commitment and the Bank threatening to call the loans already extended. Meanwhile, GLE successfully interested another lender which conditioned its backing on GLE's settlement of its differences with the Bank.

Negotiations ensued in which, the evidence indicated, the Bank primarily sought to obtain release from the Sahadis and GLE of their claims stemming from the Bank's purported breach of its loan commitment, and to obtain further collateral from the Sahadis to secure their guarantee of the outstanding loan. The Bank also sought to have GLE's outstanding interest payments, which had been withheld during the several months of the dispute, brought up to date.

The negotiations resulted in two agreements executed on October 25, 1977. One agreement [stated:]

> 1. [The Bank] hereby agrees to forbear from demanding payment of the Liabilities during the period ending December 31, 1977, except for payment of current interest thereon as more fully set forth in clause (i) of paragraph 3 below.

The agreement went on to state:

> 3. Notwithstanding the foregoing, [the Bank] may demand payment in full of the Liabilities prior to December 31, 1977 if . . . (i) [GLE] shall fail to make payment of interest accrued on the Liabilities through September 30, 1977 on or before November 15, 1977.

This latter paragraph, as initially drafted, provided for October 7, 1977 as the deadline for the payment of accrued interest. This date was changed to November 15, 1977 at Sahadi's request with no objection by the Bank; moreover, there was no evidence that the precise date on which accrued interest was to be paid was ever a point of contention in the negotiations.

. . .

Sahadi was reminded by a subordinate on November 14 of the November 15 interest payment date, but Sahadi responded that the payment should be delayed so that GLE monies in Chicago would be available to satisfy other immediate liabilities. As Sahadi noted in his affidavit, "There was no great significance attached to the payment of interest in this covenant; it did not occur to us that the bank would treat the interest payment date any differently than it had treated previous payment dates." On the morning of November 16, a GLE representative was queried by the Bank as to whether the interest payments had been made; when the GLE representative responded negatively but indicated that the payment would be made by the end of the week, the Bank representative responded that the matter could be discussed later that day. At that later meeting, the Bank presented the surprised GLE representative with notification that the loan was called. The GLE representative immediately offered to tender payment for the due interest from the company's account with the Bank, but the Bank refused. The calling of the loan destroyed GLE and subjected the Sahadis to liability on the personal guarantee.

The Sahadis, indirectly as assignees of GLE, thereafter filed this action against the Bank, seeking release from their personal guarantee agreement and damages for the destruction of GLE. Chiefly, they contended that GLE's brief delay in tender of the November 15 interest payment did not amount to a "material" breach of the October 25 agreements justifying the Bank's cessation of forbearance. . . .

   . . .

II.

  . . .

It is black letter law in Illinois and elsewhere that only a "material" breach of a contract provision by one party will justify non-performance by the other party. *See Janssen Bros. v. Northbrook Trust and Savings Bank*, 12 Ill. App. 3d 840, 299 N.E.2d 431, 434 (2d Dist. 1973); *Herbert Shaffer Associates, Inc. v. First Bank of Oak Park*, 30 Ill. App. 3d 647, 332 N.E.2d 703, 710 (1st Dist. 1975); *Anderson v. Long Grove Country Club Estates*, 111 Ill. App. 2d 127, 249 N.E.2d 343, 349 (2d Dist. 1969); *Wright v. Douglas Furniture Corp.*, 98 Ill. App. 2d 137, 240 N.E.2d 259, 262 (1st Dist. 1968); *See also C.G. Caster Co. v. Regan*, 88 Ill. App. 3d 280, 43 Ill. Dec. 422, 426, 410 N.E.2d 422-426 (1st Dist. 1980); *John Kubinski & Sons, Inc. v. Dockside Development Corp.*, 33 Ill. App. 3d 1015, 339 N.E.2d 529, 534 (1st Dist. 1975); 5 *Williston on Contracts* §§675, 805 (3d ed. 1961); Restatement (Second) of Contracts §229 (1979). Moreover, the determination of "materiality" is a complicated question of fact, involving an inquiry into such matters as whether the breach worked to defeat the bargained-for objective of the parties or caused disproportionate prejudice to the non-breaching party, whether custom and usage considers such a breach to be material, and whether the allowance of reciprocal non-performance by the non-breaching party will result in his accrual of an unreasonable or unfair advantage. *Wright*, 240 N.E.2d at 262; *Anderson*, 249 N.E.2d at 349; *C.G. Caster Co.*, 43 Ill. Dec. at 426, 410 N.E.2d at 426; *National Importing & Trading Co. v. E.A. Bear Co.*, 324 Ill. 346, 155 N.E. 343, 346 (1927); *Cantrell v. Kruck*, 25 Ill. App. 3d 1060, 324 N.E.2d 260, 263 (2d Dist.1975); *Janssen Bros.*, 299 N.E.2d at 433. All of these issues must be resolved with reference to the intent of the parties as evidenced in large part by the full circumstances of the transaction, thus making these issues especially unsuited to resolution by summary judgment. *Conrad v. Delta Airlines, Inc.*, 494 F.2d 914, 918 (7th Cir. 1974); *Janssen Bros.*, 299 N.E.2d at 433.

The need for a complete factual inquiry into the underlying circumstances and commercial custom is especially acute where, as here, the purportedly breaching party claims that time was not of the essence of the contract. Even where the contract contains a provision, not present here, explicitly stipulating that "time is of the essence," the Illinois courts will inquire into the situation of the parties and the underlying circumstances to determine whether a delay in performance resulted in a "material" breach. *Janssen Bros.*, 299 N.E.2d at 434; *John Kubinski & Sons, Inc.*, 339 N.E.2d at 531, 534; *Cantrell*, 324 N.E.2d at 263. *See also* 3A *Corbin on Contracts* §715 (1960); 6 *Williston on Contracts* §846 (1961); Restatement (Second) of Contracts §229 (1979). The record in the case at bar discloses evidence that would permit a trier of fact to find that payment of the interest due precisely on November 15 was *not* "of the essence" of the agreement from the Bank's point of view. For example, Sahadi himself was allowed unilaterally to choose the payment date, and there was no contention in negotiations over the fixing of that date; the prejudice to the Bank's rights stemming from a payment delay of several hours was *de minimis* in view of the Bank's retention of the enhanced collateralization, its retention of the complete release of legal claims stemming from the reneged-upon loan commitment, and the Bank's clear knowledge that GLE had on hand in the Bank, and tendered, funds sufficient to satisfy the interest requirement; the Bank had previously accepted late payments in its course of dealings with GLE; and there was evidence that calling a loan for such a brief delay was without precedent in the banking community. Significantly, even the Bank conceded at oral argument on appeal, "The important thing . . . is not the date of the fifteenth in that sense; it's the fact of the promise." Whether or not these facts would be sufficient to prove non-materiality in light of all the other evidence adduced at trial, they at least raise a genuine issue as to whether the "promise" was in any important way defeated by the hours of delay in tender of payment. Indeed, it would be difficult to posit a set of alleged facts making summary resolution of the issue of "materiality" in favor of the defendant less appropriate.

The Bank . . . argues, the contract before us presents a uniquely attractive case for the rigid and summary application of time requirements because it contains a specific provision allowing the cessation of the Bank's forbearance if interest was not paid on or before November 15, 1977. However, this argument merely assumes what it seeks to prove: that the payment of interest on precisely the named date was an essential part of that specific provision, and that whether the precise day of payment was essential can be determined without the benefit of a full inquiry at trial.

The Illinois courts have rightly spurned such conclusory logic. In *Janssen Bros. v. Northbrook Trust & Savings Bank*, 12 Ill. App. 3d 840, 299 N.E.2d 431 (2d Dist. 1973), for example, a real estate contract specifically provided that time was of the essence and that if certain payments were not made by the named date, certain deeds would be automatically recorded and the purchase price refunded. 299 N.E.2d at 432. Notwithstanding this explicit recitation of the consequences of late payment, the court refused to undertake a wooden reading of the provision, let alone to do so through a summary procedure. Noting that even where the parties clearly intended to regard a specific payment date as crucial, "equity will refuse to enforce such a provision when to do so would be unconscionable or would give one party an unfair advantage over the other," *id.* at 434, the court also underscored that "summary procedure is not . . . suited to situations in which substantial questions are present relating to the formation and terms of a settlement agreement or its construction, and evidence or testimony is required to satisfactorily resolve the issue," *id.* at 433. *Accord Elliott v. Snyder*, 246 S.C. 186, 143 S.E.2d 374, 375, 376 (1965). . . .

The Bank contends alternatively that no room for a "materiality" analysis and its concomitant factual inquiry exists here because the payment of the interest on or before November 15 was an "express condition" of the Bank's forbearance, and thus its terms were required to be exactly fulfilled. This second argument, like the Bank's first, suffers from its conclusory assumption of what it seeks to prove—that the payment of the interest on the precise named date rather than payment of the interest in a reasonably prompt manner was of threshold importance to the completion of the contract. In short, asking whether a provision is a "condition" is similar to stating the "materiality" question: both seek to determine whether its performance was a *sine qua non* of the contract's fulfillment. And that determination may not be made through a mechanical process.

In general, contractual terms are presumed to represent independent promises rather than conditions. 3A *Corbin on Contracts* §635 (1960); 5 *Williston on Contracts* §§665, 666 (1961). Determining whether this presumption may be upset entails a full inquiry into the "intention of the parties and the good sense of the case" including such factors as whether the protected party can achieve its principal goal without literal performance of the contractual provision. *Foreman State Trust and Savings Bank v. Tauber*, 348 Ill. 280, 180 N.E. 827, 831, 832 (1932); *Palmer v. Meriden Britannia Co.*, 188 Ill. 508, 59 N.E. 247, 252 (1900). So reluctant are courts to elevate a term to the status of a condition that the factual inquiry will often be undertaken in spite of the existence of explicit language, not present here, creating liability only "on condition" of the occurrence of a required, prior act. *Rooks Creek Evangelical Lutheran Church v. First Lutheran Church*, 290 Ill. 133, 129 N.E. 793, 795 (1919); 5 *Williston on Contracts* §665 (1961) ("Especially words literally appropriate for conditions have not been given their natural meaning where the consequence would lead to injustice and a violation of the probable intent of the parties."). The Bank points to a confirmatory telex message from Sahadi stating that the Bank's forbearance was to be "on condition" that interest was paid by the named date, but such evidence is but one tile in the evidentiary mosaic; the law requires that the Sahadis be given the opportunity to present evidence that the parties only considered the payment of the interest, not its payment by an exact hour, to be the relevant "condition," if, indeed, that term as used in the telex is to be given its formal legal meaning. The Sahadis have been denied this opportunity by the district court's summary disposition.

Moreover, even if the payment of interest by the named date could be summarily construed as a necessary "condition," the district court would *still* be required to conduct a full-ranging factual inquiry into whether that condition had been "materially" breached or whether the technical breach was without "pecuniary importance." 5 *Williston on Contracts* §805 at 839-40 (1961). Restatement (Second) of Contracts §229 (1979) ("To the extent that the non-occurrence of a condition would cause disproportionate forfeiture, a court may excuse the non-occurrence of that condition unless its occurrence was a material part of the agreed exchange."); *see also* Restatement (Second) of Contracts §229, Illustrations 3 and 4 (demonstrating that day-late payments are not "material" breaches). At either level of the "promise/condition" analysis, then, summary judgment would not be appropriate in this case.

. . .

REVERSED AND REMANDED.

JACOB & YOUNGS
v.
KENT ⌐

Court of Appeals of New York
230 N.Y. 239
1921

CARDOZO, J.

The plaintiff built a country residence for the defendant at a cost of upwards of $77,000, and now sues to recover a balance of $3,483.46, remaining unpaid. The work of construction ceased in June, 1914, and the defendant then began to occupy the dwelling. There was no complaint of defective performance until March, 1915. One of the specifications for the plumbing work provides that "all wrought iron pipe must be well galvanized, lap welded pipe of the grade known as 'standard pipe' of Reading manufacture." The defendant learned in March, 1915, that some of the pipe, instead of being made in Reading, was the product of other factories. The plaintiff was accordingly directed by the architect to do the work anew. The plumbing was then encased within the walls except in a few places where it had to be exposed. Obedience to the order meant more than the substitution of other pipe. It meant the demolition at great expense of substantial parts of the completed structure. The plaintiff left the work untouched, and asked for a certificate that the final payment was due. Refusal of the certificate was followed by this suit.

The evidence sustains a finding that the omission of the prescribed brand of pipe was neither fraudulent nor willful. It was the result of the oversight and inattention of the plaintiff's subcontractor. Reading pipe is distinguished from Cohoes pipe and other brands only by the name of the manufacturer stamped upon it at intervals of between six and seven feet. Even the defendant's architect, though he inspected the pipe upon arrival, failed to notice the discrepancy. The plaintiff tried to show that the brands installed, though made by other manufacturers, were the same in quality, in appearance, in market value and in cost as the brand stated in the contract—that they were, indeed, the same thing, though manufactured in another place. The evidence was excluded, and a verdict directed for the defendant. The Appellate Division reversed, and granted a new trial.

We think the evidence, if admitted, would have supplied some basis for the inference that the defect was insignificant in its relation to the project. The courts never say that one who makes a contract fills the measure of his duty by less than full performance. They do say, however, that an omission, both trivial and innocent, will sometimes be atoned for by allowance of the resulting damage, and will not always be the breach of a condition to be followed by a forfeiture. The distinction is akin to that between dependent and independent promises, or between promises and conditions. Some promises are so plainly independent that they can never by fair construction be conditions of one another. Others are so plainly dependent that they must always be conditions. Others, though dependent and thus conditions when there is departure in point of substance, will be viewed as independent and collateral when the departure is insignificant. Considerations partly of justice and partly of presumable intention are to tell us whether this or that promise shall be placed in one class or in another. The simple and the uniform will call for different remedies from the multifarious and the intricate. The margin of departure within the range of normal expectation upon a sale of common chattels will vary from the margin to be expected upon a contract for the construction of a mansion or a "skyscraper." There will be harshness sometimes and oppression in the implication of a condition when the thing upon which labor has been expended is incapable of surrender because united to the land, and equity and reason in the implication of a like condition when the subject-matter, if defective, is in shape to be returned. From the conclusion that promises may not be treated as dependent to the extent of their uttermost minutiae without a sacrifice of justice, the progress is a short one to the conclusion that they may not be so treated without a perversion of intention. Intention not otherwise revealed may be presumed to hold in contemplation the reasonable and probable. If something else is in view, it must not be left to implication. There will be no assumption of a purpose to visit venial faults with oppressive retribution.

Those who think more of symmetry and logic in the development of legal rules than of practical adaptation to the attainment of a just result will be troubled by a classification where the lines of division are so wavering and blurred. Something, doubtless, may be said on the score of consistency and certainty in favor of a stricter standard. The courts have balanced such considerations against those of equity and fairness, and found the latter to be the weightier. The decisions in this state commit us to the liberal view, which is making its way, nowadays, in jurisdictions slow to welcome it. Where the line is to be drawn between the important and the trivial cannot be settled by a formula. "In the nature of the case precise boundaries are impossible." Williston on Contracts. The same omission may take on one aspect or another according to its setting. Substitution of equivalents may not have the same significance in fields of art on the one side and in those of mere utility on the other. Nowhere will change be tolerated, however, if it is so dominant or pervasive as in any real or substantial measure to frustrate the purpose of the contract. There is no general license to install whatever, in the builder's judgment, may be regarded as "just as good." The question is one of degree. . . . We must weigh the purpose to be served, the desire to be gratified, the excuse for deviation from the letter, the cruelty of enforced adherence. Then only can we tell whether literal fulfilment is to be implied by law as a condition. This is not to say that the parties are not free by apt and certain words to effectuate a purpose that performance of every term shall be a condition of recovery. That question is not here. This is merely to say that the law will be slow to impute the purpose, in the silence of the parties, where the significance of the default is grievously out of proportion to the oppression of the forfeiture. The willful transgressor must accept the penalty of his transgression. For him there is no occasion to mitigate the rigor of implied conditions. The transgressor whose default is unintentional and trivial may hope for mercy if he will offer atonement for his wrong.

In the circumstances of this case, we think the measure of the allowance is not the cost of replacement, which would be great, but the difference in value, which would be either nominal or nothing. It is true that in most cases the cost of replacement is the measure. The owner is entitled to the money which will permit him to complete, unless the cost of completion is grossly and unfairly out of proportion to the good to be attained. When that is true, the measure is the difference in value. Specifications call, let us say, for a foundation built of granite quarried in Vermont. On the completion of the building, the owner learns that through the blunder of a subcontractor part of the foundation has been built of granite of the same quality quarried in New Hampshire. The measure of allowance is not the cost of reconstruction. "There may be omissions of that which could not afterwards be supplied exactly as called for by the contract without taking down the building to its foundations, and at the same time the omission may not affect the value of the building for use or otherwise, except so slightly as to be hardly appreciable." The rule that gives a remedy in cases of substantial performance with compensation for defects of trivial or inappreciable importance, has been developed by the courts as an instrument of justice. The measure of the allowance must be shaped to the same end.

The order should be affirmed, and judgment absolute directed in favor of the plaintiff upon the stipulation, with costs in all courts.

McLAUGHLIN, J. (dissenting).

I dissent. The plaintiff did not perform its contract. Its failure to do so was either intentional or due to gross neglect which, under the uncontradicted facts, amounted to the same thing, nor did it make any proof of the cost of compliance, where compliance was possible.

Under its contract it obligated itself to use in the plumbing only pipe (between 2,000 and 2,500 feet) made by the Reading Manufacturing Company. The first pipe delivered was about 1,000 feet and the plaintiff's superintendent then called the attention of the foreman of the subcontractor, who was doing the plumbing, to the fact that the specifications annexed to the contract required all pipe used in the plumbing to be of the Reading Manufacturing Company. They then examined it for the purpose of ascertaining whether this delivery was of that manufacture and found it was. Thereafter, as pipe was required in the progress of the work, the foreman of the subcontractor would leave word at its shop that he wanted a specified number of feet of pipe, without in any way indicating of what manufacture. Pipe would thereafter be delivered and installed in the building, without any examination whatever. Indeed, no examination, so far as appears, was made by the plaintiff, the subcontractor, defendant's architect, or any one else, of any of the pipe except the first delivery, until after the building had been completed. Plaintiff's architect then refused to give the certificate of completion, upon which the final payment depended, because all of the pipe used in the plumbing was not of the kind called for by the contract. After such refusal, the subcontractor removed the covering or insulation from about 900 feet of pipe which was exposed in the basement, cellar and attic, and all but 70 feet was found to have been manufactured, not by the Reading Company, but by other manufacturers, some by the Cohoes Rolling Mill Company, some by the National Steel Works, some by the South Chester Tubing Company, and some which bore no manufacturer's mark at all. The balance of the pipe had been so installed in the building that an inspection of it could not be had without demolishing, in part at least, the building itself.

I am of the opinion the trial court was right in directing a verdict for the defendant. The plaintiff agreed that all the pipe used should be of the Reading Manufacturing Company. Only about two-fifths of it, so far as appears, was of that kind. The question of substantial performance of a contract of the character of the one under consideration depends in no small degree upon the good faith of the contractor. If the plaintiff had intended to, and had complied with the terms of the contract except as to minor omissions, due to inadvertence, then he might be allowed to recover the contract price, less the amount necessary to fully compensate the defendant for damages caused by such omissions. But that is not this case. It installed between 2,000 and 2,500 feet of pipe, of which only 1,000 feet at most complied with the contract. No explanation was given why pipe called for by the contract was not used, nor was any effort made to show what it would cost to remove the pipe of other manufacturers and install that of the Reading Manufacturing Company. The defendant had a right to contract for what he wanted. He had a right before making payment to get what the contract called for. It is no answer to this suggestion to say that the pipe put in was just as good as that made by the Reading Manufacturing Company, or that the difference in value between such pipe and the pipe made by the Reading Manufacturing Company would be either "nominal or nothing." Defendant contracted for pipe made by the Reading Manufacturing Company. What his reason was for requiring this kind of pipe is of no importance. He wanted that and was entitled to it. It may have been a mere whim on his part, but even so, he had a right to this kind of pipe, regardless of whether some other kind, according to the opinion of the contractor or experts, would have been "just as good, better, or done just as well." He agreed to pay only upon condition that the pipe installed were made by that company and he ought not to be compelled to pay unless that condition be performed. The rule, therefore, of substantial performance, with damages for unsubstantial omissions, has no application.

HISCOCK, Ch. J., HOGAN and CRANE, JJ., concur with CARDOZO, J.; POUND and ANDREWS, JJ., concur with McLAUGHLIN, J.

O.W. GRUN ROOFING & CONSTRUCTION CO.
v.
COPE

Court of Civil Appeals of Texas
529 S.W.2d 258
1975

CADENA, J.

Plaintiff, Cope, sued defendant, O.W. Grun Roofing & Construction Co., to set aside a mechanic's lien filed by defendant and for damages in the sum of $1,500.00 suffered by plaintiff as a result of the alleged failure of defendant to perform a contract calling for the installation of a new roof on plaintiff's home. Defendant, in addition to a general denial, filed a cross-claim for $648.00, the amount which plaintiff agreed to pay defendant for installing the roof, and for foreclosure of the mechanic's lien on plaintiff's home.

The jury found (1) defendant failed to perform his contract in a good and workmanlike manner; (2) defendant did not substantially perform the contract; (3) plaintiff received no benefits from the labor performed and the materials furnished by defendant; the reasonable cost of performing the contract in a good and workmanlike manner would be . . . $770.60, and the award of $122.60 to plaintiff is based on the difference between $770.60 and the contract price of $648. It is from this judgment that defendant appeals.

We look only to the evidence supporting the verdict.

The written contract required defendant to install a new roof on plaintiff's home for $648.00. The contract describes the color of the shingles to be used as "russet glow," which defendant defined as a "brown varied color." Defendant acknowledges that it was his obligation to install a roof of uniform color.

After defendant had installed the new roof, plaintiff noticed that it had streaks which she described as yellow, due to a difference in color or shade of some of the shingles. Defendant agreed to remedy the situation and he removed the nonconforming shingles. However, the replacement shingles do not match the remainder, and photographs introduced in evidence clearly show that the roof is not of a uniform color. Plaintiff testified that her roof has the appearance of having been patched, rather than having been completely replaced. According to plaintiff's testimony, the yellow streaks appeared on the northern, eastern and southern sides of the roof, and defendant only replaced the non-matching shingles on the northern and eastern sides, leaving the southern side with the yellow streaks still apparent. The result is that only the western portion of the roof is of uniform color.

When defendant originally installed the complete new roof, it used 24 "squares" of shingles. In an effort to achieve a roof of uniform color, five squares were ripped off and replaced. There is no testimony as to the number of squares which would have to be replaced on the southern, or rear, side of the house in order to eliminate the original yellow streaks. Although there is expert testimony to the effect that the disparity in color would not be noticeable after the shingles have been on the roof for about a year, there is testimony to the effect that, although some nine or ten months have elapsed since defendant attempted to achieve a uniform coloration, the roof is still "streaky" on three sides. One of defendant's experts testified that if the shingles are properly applied the result will be a "blended" roof rather than a streaked roof.

The evidence is undisputed that the roof is a substantial roof and will give plaintiff protection against the elements.

The principle which allows recovery for part performance in cases involving dependent promises may be expressed by saying that a material breach or a breach which goes to the root of the matter or essence of the contract defeats the promisor's claim despite his part performance, or it may be expressed by saying that a promisor who has substantially performed is entitled to recover, although he has failed in some particular to comply with his agreement. The latter mode of expressing the rule is generally referred to as the doctrine of substantial performance and is especially common in cases involving building contracts, although its application is not restricted to such contracts.

It is difficult to formulate definitive rules for determining whether the contractor's performance, less than complete, amounts to "substantial performance," since the question is one of fact and of degree, and the answer depends on the particular facts of each case. But, although the decisions furnish no rule of thumb, they are helpful in suggesting guidelines. One of the most obvious factors to be considered is the extent of the nonperformance. The deficiency will not be tolerated if it is so pervasive as to frustrate the purpose of the contract in any real or substantial sense. The doctrine does not bestow on a contractor a license to install whatever is, in his judgment, "just as good." The answer is arrived at by weighing the purpose to be served, the desire to be gratified, the excuse for deviating from the letter of the contract and the cruelty of enforcing strict adherence or of compelling the promisee to receive something less than for which he bargained. Also influential in many cases is the ratio of money value of the tendered performance and of the promised performance. In most cases the contract itself at least is an indication of the value of the promised performance, and courts should have little difficulty in determining the cost of curing the deficiency. But the rule cannot be expressed in terms of a fraction, since complete reliance on a mathematical formula would result in ignoring other important factors, such as the purpose which the promised performance was intended to serve and the extent to which the nonperformance would defeat such purpose, or would defeat it if not corrected.

What was the general plan contemplated for the work in this case? What was the object and purpose of the parties? It is clear that, despite the frequency with which the courts speak of defects that are not "pervasive," which do not constitute a "deviation from the general plan," and which are "not so essential that the object of the parties in making the contract and its purpose cannot, without difficulty, be accomplished by remedying them," when an attempt is made to apply the general principles to a particular case difficulties are encountered at the outset. Was the general plan to install a substantial roof which would serve the purpose which roofs are designed to serve? Or, rather, was the general plan to install a substantial roof of uniform color? Was the object and purpose of the contract merely to furnish such a roof, or was it to furnish such a roof which would be of a uniform color? In the matter of homes and their decoration, as much as, if not more than, in many other fields, mere taste or preference, almost approaching whimsy, may be controlling with the homeowner, so that variations which might, under other circumstances, be considered trifling, may be inconsistent with that "substantial performance" on which liability to pay must be predicated. . . . [M]ere incompleteness or deviations which may be easily supplied or remedied after the contractor has finished his work, and the cost of which to the owner is not excessive and readily ascertainable, present less cause for hesitation in concluding that the performance tendered constitutes substantial performance, since in such cases the owner can obtain complete satisfaction by merely spending some money and deducting the amount of such expenditure from the contract price.

In the case before us there is evidence to support the conclusion that plaintiff can secure a roof of uniform coloring only by installing a completely new roof.

Finally, defendant argues that it was entitled to judgment at least on the theory of quantum meruit on its cross claim because the evidence establishes as a matter of law that defendant installed a good weatherproof roof which was guaranteed for 15 years, and that such roof was installed properly in accordance with factory specifications and was of use and benefit to plaintiff.

The evidence does not conclusively establish that plaintiff has received any benefit from defendant's defective performance. As already pointed out, there is evidence that plaintiff will have to install a completely new roof. Nor does the evidence conclusively establish that plaintiff accepted the claimed benefit. She complained immediately and has expressed dissatisfaction at all times. We cannot infer an acceptance from the fact that plaintiff continued to live in the house. She was living in the house before defendant installed the new roof, and we know of no rule which would require that, in order to avoid a finding of implied acceptance, plaintiff was obligated to move out of her home.

The judgment of the trial court is affirmed.

DOVE
v.
ROSE ACRE FARMS, INC. 9
Court of Appeals of Indiana, First District
434 N.E.2d 931
1982

Neal, J.

Plaintiff-appellant Mark Dove (Dove) appeals a negative judgment of the Decatur Circuit Court in favor of defendant-appellee Rose Acre Farms, Inc. in a trial before the court without the intervention of a jury.

We affirm.

STATEMENT OF THE FACTS

The evidence most favorable to support the judgment and the facts found specially by the trial court are as follows. Dove had been employed by Rose Acre Farms, operated by David Rust (Rust), its president and principal owner, in the summers and other times from 1972 to 1979. The business of Rose Acre was the production of eggs, and, stocked with 4,000,000 hens and staffed with 300 employees, it produced approximately 256,000 dozen eggs per day. Rust had instituted and maintained extensive bonus programs, some of which were for one day only, or one event or activity only. For example, one bonus was the white car bonus; if an employee would buy a new white car, keep it clean and undamaged, place a Rose Acre sign on it, commit no tardiness or absenteeism, and attend one management meeting per month, Rose Acre would pay $100 per month for 36 months as a bonus above and beyond the employee's regular salary, to apply on payments. Any slight viola-tion, such as being a minute late for work, driving a dirty or damaged car, or missing work for any cause, would work a forfeiture of the bonus. Other bonuses consisted of egg production bonuses, deed conversion bonuses, house management bonuses, and a silver feather bonus. This last bonus program required the participant to wear a silver feather, and a system of rewards and penalties existed for employees who participated. While the conditions of the bonuses varied, one condition existed in all bonus programs: during the period of the bonus, the employee must not be tardy for even a minute, and must not miss work any day for any cause whatever, even illness. If the employee missed any days during the week, he was sometimes permitted to make them up on Saturday and/or Sunday. Any missed work not made up within the same week worked a forfeiture of the bonus. These rules were explained to the employees and were stated in a written policy. The bonus programs were voluntary, and all the employees did not choose to participate in them. When a bonus was offered a card was issued to the participant stating his name and the terms and amount of the bonus. Upon completion of the required tasks, the card was attached to the pay sheet, and the bonus was added to the paycheck. Rust was strict about tardiness and absenteeism, whether an employee was on a bonus program or not. If an employee was tardy, his pay would be docked to the minimum wage, or he would be sent home and lose an entire day. A minute's tardiness would also deprive the employee of a day for pur-poses of seniority. As was stated in the evidence, bonuses were given for the "extra mile" or actions "above and beyond the call of duty." The purpose of the bonus programs and penalties was to discourage absenteeism and tardiness, and to pro-mote motivation and dependability.

In June 1979, Rust called in Dove and other construction crew leaders and offered a bonus of $6,000 each if certain detailed construction work was completed in 12 weeks. As Dove conceded in his own testimony, the bonus card indicated that in addition to completing the work, he would be required to work at least five full days a week for 12 weeks to qualify for the bonus. On the same day Dove's bonus agree-ment, by mutual consent, was amended to ten weeks with a bonus of $5,000 to enable him to return to law school by September 1. Dove testified that there was no ambiguity in the agreement, and he understood that to qualify for the bonus he would have to work ten weeks, five days a week, commencing at starting time and quitting only at quitting time. Dove testified that he was aware of the provisions concerning absenteeism and tardiness as they affected bonuses, and that if he missed any work, for any reason, including illness, he would forfeit the bonus. The evidence disclosed that no exception had ever been made except as may have occurred by clerical error or inadvertence.

In the tenth week Dove came down with strep throat. On Thursday of that week he reported to work with a temperature of 104 degrees, and told Rust that he was unable to work. Rust told him, in effect, that if he went home, he would forfeit the bonus. Rust offered him the opportunity to stay there and lay on a couch, or make up his lost days on Saturday and/or Sunday. Rust told him he could sleep and still qualify for the bonus. Dove left to seek medical treatment and missed two days in the tenth week of the bonus program.

Rust refused Dove the bonus based solely upon his missing the two days of work. While there was some question of whether the construction job was finished, Rust does not seem to have made that issue the basis of his refusal. Bonuses to other crew leaders were paid. The trial court denied Dove's recovery and, in the conclusions of law, stated that Dove had not shown that all of the conditions of the bonus contract had been met. Specifically, Dove failed to work five full days a week for ten weeks.

DISCUSSION AND DECISION

We are constrained to observe, in the case before us, that the bonus rules at Rose Acre were well known to Dove when he agreed to the disputed bonus contract. He certainly knew Rust's strict policies and knew that any absence for any cause whatever worked a forfeiture of the bonus. With this knowledge he willingly entered into this bonus arrangement, as he had done in the past, and under *Montgomery Ward*, he must be held to have agreed to all of the terms upon which the bonus was conditioned. If the conditions were unnecessarily harsh or eccentric, and the terms odious, he could have shown his disdain by simply declining to participate, for participation in the bonus program was not obligatory or job dependent.

Contrary to Dove's assertion that completion of a task was the central element of the bonus program, we are of the opinion that the rules regarding tardiness and absenteeism were a central theme. Rust stated that the purpose of the bonus program was to discourage tardiness and absenteeism and to promote motivation and dependability. Indeed, some of the bonus programs such as the white car bonus and the silver feather bonus were apparently an effort on the part of Rust to establish among the employees an identity with Rose Acre and to create an esprit de corps. The direct tangible benefits to Rose Acre would be unmeasurable, and the burden upon the employees would be equally unmeasurable. Yet, Rust was willing to pay substantial bonuses in the implementation of his program, and the employees, including Dove, were quite as willing to take the money.

No fraud or bad faith has been shown on the part of Rose Acre, and no public policy arguments have been advanced to demonstrate why the bonus contract should not be enforced as agreed between the parties. We are not at liberty to remake the contract for the parties.

Affirmed.

Problems

1. The Angry Farmers. In 1997, Elda Arnhold and John Argoudelis agreed to sell 280 acres of farmland southwest of Chicago to property developer Ocean Atlantic Woodland Corporation. As the parties squabbled over attempts to renegotiate the price of the parcel and other provisions of the agreement, the agreed-upon closing date for the transaction slipped on several occasions, angering the sellers. The relationship between the parties continued to sour, and litigation ultimately commenced. In 2000, the parties settled the litigation by agreeing to certain substantive terms concerning the sale of the property and the following provision concerning the closing of the sale:

> If Ocean Atlantic, for any reason whatsoever, fails to close on the property within 90 days from the execution of [the] settlement document, it shall forfeit any and all rights it may have to purchase the property.

Ocean Atlantic soon after provided notice that it intended to close on January 24, 2001, one day before the 90-day period would expire. Ocean Atlantic failed to tender the purchase price on January 24 or January 25 because its lender demanded last-minute documentation. Performance was tendered on the afternoon of January 26, the day after the expiration of the 90-day period. The sellers refused to tender the property and notified Ocean Atlantic that the contract was terminated. Ocean Atlantic filed suit. Were the sellers excused from performing, or was Ocean Atlantic entitled to judgment?

2. Hotel Fire. The Milner Hotel, located adjacent to a West Virginia railroad yard, contracted to provide rooms to the Norfolk and Western Railway Company's employees for a fixed price, with the railway guaranteeing occupancy of at least 60 rooms per night. The contract, which provided both parties with the right to terminate for any reason with 30-days' notice, specified that the Milner was responsible for:

> (d) Maintaining at all times good, clean, and sanitary conditions throughout the said hotel;
> (e) Observing and complying with all local, state, or federal laws and regulations pertaining to the operation of said hotel. . . .

In March 1991, a fire broke out at the hotel. There was no structural damage, but the hotel suffered smoke damage from the flames and water damage from efforts to extinguish the fire. A post-fire inspection by the local fire department revealed numerous violations of fire and electrical codes, as well as the presence of crumbling, friable asbestos in several locations inside the hotel.

The railway company then provided notice that it was terminating the contract, and it did not send any employees back to the hotel after the fire. The Milner sued for lost profits suffered during the 30-day period before the railway's termination became effective. Who should prevail?

3. A Misplaced Wall. Frank and Carol Jacobs entered into a contract with Eugene Plante, a builder, for the construction of a new house on a lot owned by the Jacobs family in Waukesha County, Wisconsin. The contract called for the builder to construct the house according to a "stock" floor plan and accompanying specifications. The Jacobses made periodic progress payments totaling approximately $20,000 during the course of construction, but they refused to make the final payment of more than $6,000, and the builder brought suit.

The Jacobses identified a number of imperfections in the construction work but primarily stressed the fact that the builder had misplaced the wall between the living room and the kitchen, which resulted in the narrowing of the width of the living room by more than one foot. The location of the wall was, in fact, inconsistent with the plans for the house. At the trial, the builder called as witnesses real estate experts who testified that the location of the wall would not affect the market value of the house. Were the Jacobses justified in withholding payment, or should the doctrine of substantial performance apply?

4. The Late Notice. Dentist George Murphy ran his practice in an office leased from Hopmeadow Professional Center Associates. After Murphy terminated the lease, Hopmeadow's insurer, Aetna Casualty and Surety Company, sued Murphy for alleged damage caused when Murphy dismantled his office. More than two years later, Murphy brought a claim against his liability insurance carrier, Chubb. Chubb moved to dismiss Murphy's claim on the ground that he failed to satisfy the notice provisions of his policy which provided, in part, "[i]n the event of an occurrence, written notice . . . shall be given by or for the insured to the company . . . as soon as practicable." Chubb has not alleged that Murphy's delay has caused any harm. Should the court grant Chubb's motion to dismiss?

3. Excusing Conditions: Prevention, Waiver, Divisibility, and Restitution

In addition to material breach and substantial performance, courts have developed several other doctrines that soften the harsh consequences that can stem from the failure of a condition. *Cantrell-Waind & Associates, Inc. v. Guillaume Motorsports, Inc.* illustrates the prevention doctrine (also called the hindrance doctrine), under which courts will consider a condition excused—and the duties dependent on the condition thus triggered—if the obligor of a duty interferes with the satisfaction of the condition. *Clark v. West* considers the parameters of the rule that a party may waive a condition of that party's duty. See also Rest. (2d) Contracts §84. *Gill v. Johnstown Lumber* and *Lowy v. United Pacific Insurance Company* explore when courts will consider a contract divisible, such that satisfaction of certain conditions will trigger associated duties of the non-breaching party. See also Rest. (2d) Contracts §240. Finally, *Stark v. Parker* and *Britton v. Turner* demonstrate a split of authorities as to whether a party who breaches a promissory condition can recover the value of benefits conferred on the non-breaching party under a theory of restitution. See also Rest. (2d) Contracts §374.

CANTRELL-WAIND & ASSOCIATES, INC.
v.
GUILLAUME MOTORSPORTS, INC.
Court of Appeals of Arkansas
968 S.W.2d 72
1998

BIRD, J.

On August 1, 1994, appellee [Guillaume Motorsports, Inc.], represented by its president and sole stock-holder Todd Williams, agreed to lease real property in Bentonville to Kenneth Bower and Kay Bower. The lease gave the Bowers an option to purchase and provided for the payment of a commission to appellant, the real estate broker in this transaction, as follows:

> In the event of the *exercise* of this option within the first twenty-four (24) month period, ten per cent (10%) of the monthly rental payments shall apply to the purchase price. Thereafter, this credit shall reduce two per cent (2%) per year until the expiration of the original lease term hereof, to the effect that the credit will be eight per cent (8%) during the third year, six per cent (6%) during the fourth year, and four per cent (4%) during the fifth year. The sales price shall be $295,000.00. GUILLAUME MOTORSPORTS, INC., agrees [to] pay CANTRELL-WAIND & ASSOCIATES, INC., a real estate commission of $15,200.00 upon closing of sale of the property under this Option to Purchase, provided the *closing* occurs within two (2) years from the date of execution of the Lease with Option to Purchase.

The Bowers' attorney, Charles Edward Young, III, notified Williams in writing on April 23, 1996, that the Bowers chose to exercise the option to purchase, and that they anticipated closing at the earliest possible date. Young also sent a copy of this letter to Samuel Reeves, appellee's attorney. Soon after this, Williams approached Mr. Bower and offered to credit him with one-half of the appellant's $15,200 commission if he would agree to delay closing until after August 1, 1996. Mr. Bower declined this offer.

Ruth Ann Whitehead, a loan officer at the Bank of Bentonville, notified Mr. Bower on July 19, 1996, that the loan had been approved and that she awaited notification of a closing date. In his deposition, Young said that he attempted to set a July closing date on behalf of the Bowers but had been told by Ms. Whitehead, Reeves, and a representative of the title company that Williams had told them he would be out of the country in late July and unavailable for closing until after August 1.

Young also said that he had asked Reeves if Williams would utilize a power of attorney for closing before August 1 but Williams refused. Williams did not leave the country and was in Bentonville July 22 through 25. Closing occurred on August 14, 1996, and the commission was not paid.

Appellant filed a complaint against Guillaume Motorsports, Inc., on August 12, 1996, for breach of contract. . . .

In a hearing on the motion for summary judgment, counsel for appellee argued that neither the corporation nor Williams was under any obligation to close prior to August 1. He contended there was no bad faith to be inferred by the deliberate avoidance of a real estate commission that is keyed to a "drop-dead" date. He said the real estate broker agreed to the terms of the contract and was bound by it. Counsel pointed out the two separate terms used in the contract when referring to the option to purchase and the closing. The contract stated that to get the maximum discount in the purchase price the Bowers had to *exercise* the option before August 1, 1996. However, the clause referring to the commission stated that the transaction had to *close* by August 1. Counsel stated, "I believe my client had every right to do anything within his power, short of breaching his contract with this buyer, to see that this closing didn't occur earlier than that date so he would not owe the commission."

In response to appellee's motion for summary judgment, appellant argued that appellee (by Williams) had a duty to act in good faith and that, in taking steps to prevent the transaction from closing before August 1, 1996, appellee had not acted in good faith. Appellant contended that all contingencies and requirements for the loan had been satisfied by July 19, 1996, and that Mr. and Ms. Bower had attempted to establish a closing date before August 1, but had been deliberately prevented from doing so by Williams's misrepresentations that he would be out of the country and unavailable to close until after August 1. Appellant attached as exhibits excerpts from the depositions of Ms. Whitehead, Mr. Young, Laura Tway (who assisted with closing), Mrs. Bower, Mr. Bower, Williams, and Mr. Carroll. Also attached was a copy of Mr. Young's May 28, 1996, letter to Mr. Reeves. In a supplemental response to the motion for summary judgment, appellant also requested summary judgment against appellee.

In his order granting summary judgment, the judge stated that appellee had no obligation to appellant to arrange for a closing date that would have entitled appellant to a commission and said that the real estate commission was "clearly avoidable" by appellee.

. . .

The term of the contract providing that a commission would be due appellant only if closing occurred before August 1, 1996, is a condition precedent. *See Stacy v. Williams*, 38 Ark. App. 192, 834 S.W.2d 156 (1992). When a contract term leaves a decision to the discretion of one party, that decision is virtually unreviewable; however, courts will become involved when the party making the decision is charged with bad faith. *Vigoro Indus., Inc. v. Crisp*, 82 F.3d 785 (8th Cir. 1996).

In *Willbanks v. Bibler*, 216 Ark. 68, 224 S.W.2d 33 (1949), the Arkansas Supreme Court held that "he who prevents the doing of a thing shall not avail himself of the nonperformance he has occasioned." *Id.* at 72, 224 S.W.2d at 35. *See also* Samuel Williston, *The Law of Contracts* §677 (3d ed. 1961). This principle is expressed in 17A Am. Jur. 2d *Contracts* §703 (1991):

> One who prevents or makes impossible the performance or happening of a condition precedent upon which his liability by the terms of a contract is made to depend cannot avail himself of its nonperformance. Even more broadly, where a promisor prevents or hinders the occurrence, happening, or fulfillment of a condition in a contract, and the condition would

have occurred except for such hindrance or prevention, the performance of the condition is excused and the liability of the promisor is fixed regardless of the failure to perform the condition. Moreover, while prevention by one party to a contract of the performance of a condition precedent excuses the nonperformance of the condition, it must be shown that the nonperformance was actually due to the conduct of such party; if the condition would not have happened whatever such conduct, it is not dispensed with.

A party has an implied obligation not to do anything that would prevent, hinder, or delay performance. *See Housing Auth. of the City of Little Rock v. Forcum-Lannom, Inc.*, 248 Ark. 750, 454 S.W.2d 101 (1970); *Dickinson v. McKenzie*, 197 Ark. 746, 126 S.W.2d 95 (1939); *Townes v. Oklahoma Mill Co.*, 85 Ark. 596, 109 S.W. 548 (1908); *Smith v. Unitemp Dry Kilns, Inc.*, 16 Ark. App. 160, 698 S.W.2d 313 (1985); *City of Whitehall v. Southern Mechanical Contracting, Inc.*, 269 Ark. 563, 599 S.W.2d 430 (Ark. App. 1980).

Comment b to section 225 of the Restatement (Second) of Contracts (1981) provides that the non-occurrence of a condition of a duty is said to be "excused" when the condition need no longer occur in order for performance of the duty to become due: "It may be excused by prevention or hindrance of its occurrence through a breach of the duty of good faith and fair dealing." The Restatement (Second) of Contracts §205 (1981) states: "Every contract imposes upon each party a duty of good faith and fair dealing in its performance and its enforcement." This legal principle also applies to contracts providing for the payment of commissions to real estate agents. *McKay and Co. v. Garland*, 17 Ark. App. 1, 701 S.W.2d 392 (1986). Accordingly, we hold that the circuit court erred in failing to recognize that a duty of good faith and fair dealing was included in this contract and, therefore, appellee was obligated to not deliberately avoid closing the transaction before August 1, 1996.

. . .

In our opinion, genuine issues of material fact remained for trial. Accordingly, we reverse the circuit judge's entry of summary judgment for appellee and remand this case for trial.

CLARK
v.
WEST

Court of Appeals of New York
193 N.Y. 349
1908

WERNER, J.

The contract before us, stripped of all superfluous verbiage, binds the plaintiff to total abstention from the use of intoxicating liquors during the continuance of the work which he was employed to do. The stipulations relating to the plaintiff's compensation provide that if he does not observe this condition he is to be paid at the rate of $2 per page, and if he does comply therewith he is to receive $6 per page. The plaintiff has written one book under the contract known as "Clark & Marshall on Corporations," which has been accepted, published and copies sold in large numbers by the defendant. The plaintiff admits that while he was at work on this book he did not entirely abstain from the use of intoxicating liquors. He has been paid only $2 per page for the work he has done. He claims that, despite his breach of this condition, he is entitled to the full compensation of $6 per page because the defendant, with full knowledge of plaintiff's non observance of this stipulation as to total abstinence, has waived the breach thereof and cannot now insist upon strict performance in this regard. This plea of waiver presents the underlying question which determines the answers to the questions certified.

Briefly stated, the defendant's position is that the stipulation as to plaintiff's total abstinence is the consideration for the payment of the difference between $2 and $6 per page and therefore could not be waived except by a new agreement to that effect based upon a good consideration; that the so-called waiver alleged by the plaintiff is not a waiver but a modification of the contract in respect of its consideration. The plaintiff on the other hand argues that the stipulation for his total abstinence was merely a condition precedent intended to work a forfeiture of the additional compensation in case of a breach and that it could be waived without any formal agreement to that effect based upon a new consideration.

The subject-matter of the contract was the writing of books by the plaintiff for the defendant. The duration of the contract was the time necessary to complete them all. The work was to be done to the satisfaction of the defendant, and the plaintiff was not to write any other books except those covered by the contract unless requested so to do by the defendant, in which latter event he was to be paid for that particular work by the year. The compensation for the work specified in the contract was to be $6 per page, unless the plaintiff failed to totally abstain from the use of intoxicating liquors during the continuance of the contract, in which event he was to receive only $2 per page. That is the obvious import of the contract construed in the light of the purpose for which it was made, and in accordance with the ordinary meaning of plain language. It is not a contract to write books in order that the plaintiff shall keep sober, but a contract containing a stipulation that he shall keep sober so that he may write satisfactory books. When we view the contract from this standpoint it will readily be perceived that the particular stipulation is not the consideration for the contract, but simply one of its conditions which fits in with those relating to time and method of delivery of manuscript, revision of proof, citation of cases, assignment of copyrights, keeping track of new cases and citations for new editions, and other details which might be waived by the defendant, if he saw fit to do so. This is made clear, it seems to us, by the provision that, "In consideration of the above promises," the defendant agrees to pay the plaintiff $2 per page on each book prepared by him, and if he "abstains from the use of intoxicating liquor and otherwise fulfills his agreements as hereinbefore set forth, he shall be paid an additional $4 per page in manner hereinbefore stated." The compensation of $2 per page, not to exceed $250 per month, was an advance or partial payment of the whole price of $6 per page, and the payment of the two-thirds which was to be withheld pending the performance of the contract, was simply made contingent upon the plaintiff's total abstention from the use of intoxicants during the life of the contract. It is possible, of course, by segregating that clause of the contract from the context, to give it a wider meaning and a different aspect than it has when read in conjunction with other stipulations. But this is also true of other paragraphs of the contract. The paragraph, for instance, which provides that after the publication of any of the books written by the plaintiff he is to receive an amount equal to one-sixth of the net receipts from the combined sales of all the books which shall have been published by the defendant under the contract, less any and all payments previously made, "until the amount of $6 per page of each book shall have been paid, after which the first party (plaintiff) shall have no right, title or interest in said books or the receipts from the sales thereof." That section of the contract standing alone would indicate that the plaintiff was to be entitled in any event to the $6 per page to be paid out of the net receipts of the copies of the book sold. The contract read as a whole, however, shows that it is modified by the preceding provisions making the compensation in excess of the $2 per page dependent upon the plaintiff's total abstinence, and upon the performance by him of the other conditions of the contract. It is obvious that the parties thought that the plaintiff's normal work was worth $6 per page. That was the sum to be paid for the work done by the plaintiff and not for total abstinence. If the plaintiff did not keep to the condition as to total abstinence, he was to lose part of that sum. Precisely the same situation would have risen if the plaintiff had disregarded any of the other essential conditions of the contract. The fact that the particular stipulation was emphasized did not change its character. It was still a condition which the defendant could have insisted upon, as he has apparently done in regard to some others, and one which he could waive just as he might have waived those relating to the amount of the advance payments, or the number of pages to be written each month. A breach of any of the substantial conditions of the contract would have entailed a loss or forfeiture similar to that consequent upon a breach of the one relating to total abstinence, in case of the defendant's insistence upon his right to take advantage of them. This, we think, is the fair interpretation of the contract, and it follows that the stipulation as to the plaintiff's total abstinence was nothing more nor less than a condition precedent. If that conclusion is well founded there can be no escape from the corollary that this condition could be waived; and if it was waived the defendant is clearly not in a position to insist upon the forfeiture which his waiver was intended to annihilate. The forfeiture must stand or fall with the condition. If the latter was waived, the former is no longer a part of the contract. Defendant still has the right to counterclaim for any damages which he may have sustained in consequence of the plaintiff's breach, but he cannot insist upon strict performance.

This whole discussion is predicated of course upon the theory of an express waiver. We assume that no waiver could be implied from the defendant's mere acceptance of the books and his payment of the sum of $2 per page without objection.

The theory upon which the defendant's attitude seems to be based is that even if he has represented to the plaintiff that he would not insist upon the condition that the latter should observe total abstinence from intoxicants, he can still refuse to pay the full contract price for his work. The inequity of this position becomes apparent when we consider that this contract was to run for a period of years, during a large portion of which the plaintiff was to be entitled only to the advance payment of $2 per page, the balance being contingent, among other things, upon publication of the books and returns from sales. Upon this theory the defendant might have waived the condition while the first book was in process of production, and yet when the whole work was completed, he would still be in a position to insist upon the forfeiture because there had not been strict performance. Such a situation is possible in a case where the subject of the waiver is the very consideration of a contract but not where the waiver relates to something that can be waived. In the case at bar, as we have seen, the waiver is not of the consideration or subject-matter, but of an incident to the method of performance. The consideration remains the same. The defendant has had the work he bargained for, and it is alleged that he has waived one of the conditions as to the manner in which it was to have been done. He might have insisted upon literal performance and then he could have stood upon the letter of his contract. If, however, he has waived that incidental condition, he has created a situation to which the doctrine of waiver very precisely applies.

A waiver has been defined to be the intentional relinquishment of a known right. It is voluntary and implies an election to dispense with something of value, or forego some advantage which the party waiving it might at its option have demanded or insisted upon.

It remains to be determined whether the plaintiff has alleged facts which, if proven, will be sufficient to establish his claim of an express waiver by the defendant of the plaintiff's breach of the condition to observe total abstinence. In the 12th paragraph of the complaint, the plaintiff alleges facts and circumstances which we think, if established, would prove defendant's waiver of plaintiff's performance of that contract stipulation. These facts and circumstances are that long before the plaintiff had completed the manuscript of the first book undertaken under the contract, the defendant had full knowledge of the plaintiff's non-observance of that stipulation, and that with such knowledge he not only accepted the completed manuscript without objection, but "repeatedly avowed and represented to the plaintiff that he was entitled to and would receive said royalty payments (i.e., the additional $4 per page), and plaintiff believed and relied upon such representations * * * and at all times during the writing of said treatise on corporations, and after as well as before publication thereof as aforesaid, it was mutually understood, agreed and intended by the parties hereto that notwithstanding plaintiff's said use of intoxicating liquors, he was nevertheless entitled to receive and would receive said royalty as the same accrued under said contract."

Under the modern rule pleadings are not to be construed against the pleader, but averments which sufficiently point out the nature of the plaintiff's claim are sufficient, if under them he would be entitled to give the necessary evidence. Tested by these rules, we think it cannot be doubted that the allegations contained in the 12th paragraph of the complaint, if proved upon the trial, would be sufficient to establish an express waiver by the defendant of the stipulation in regard to plaintiff's total abstinence.

The order of the Appellate Division reversed.

GILL
v.
ƺ ## JOHNSTOWN LUMBER CO.
Supreme Court of Pennsylvania
151 Pa. 534
1892

HEYDRICK, J.

The single question in this cause is whether the contract upon which the plaintiff sued is entire or severable. If it is entire, it is conceded that the learned court below properly directed a verdict for the defendant; if severable, it is not denied that the cause ought to have been submitted to the jury. The criterion by which it is to be determined to which class any particular contract shall be assigned is thus stated in Parsons on Contracts, 29-31: "If the part to be performed by one party consists of several and distinct items, and the price to be paid by the other is apportioned to each item to be performed, or is left to be implied by law, such a contract will generally be held to be severable. . . . But if the consideration to be paid is single and entire, the contract must be held to be entire, although the subject of the contract may consist of several distinct and wholly independent items." The rule thus laid down was quoted with approval and applied in Oil Co. v. Brewer, 66 Pa. St. 351, and followed in Rugg v. Moore, 110 Pa. St. 236, 1 Atl. Rep. 320. It was also applied in Ritchie v. Atkinson, 10 East, 295, a case not unlike the present. There the master and freighter of a vessel of 400 tons mutually agreed that the ship should proceed to St. Petersburgh, and there load from the freighter's factors a complete cargo of hemp and iron, and deliver the same to the freighter at London on being paid freight, for hemp £>5 per ton, for iron 5s. per ton, and certain other charges, one half to be paid on delivery and the other at three months. The vessel proceeded to St. Petersburgh, and when about half loaded was compelled by the imminence of a Russian embargo upon British vessels to leave, and returning to London delivered to the freighter so much of the stipulated cargo as had been taken on board. The freighter, conceiving that the contract was entire, and the delivery of a complete cargo a condition precedent to a recovery of any compensation, refused to pay at the stipulated rate for so much as was delivered. Lord Ellenborough said: "The delivery of the cargo is in its nature divisible, and therefore I think it is not a condition precedent; but the plaintiff is entitled to recover freight in proportion to the extent of such delivery; leaving the defendant to his remedy in damages for the short delivery."

Applying the test of an apportionable or apportioned consideration to the contract in question, it will be seen at once that it is severable. The work undertaken to be done by the plaintiff consisted of several items, viz., driving logs, first, of oak, and, second, of various other kinds of timber, from points upon Stony creek and its tributaries above Johnstown to the defendant's boom at Johnstown, and also driving cross-ties from some undesignated point or points, presumably understood by the parties, to Bethel, in Somerset county, and to some other point or points below Bethel. For this work the consideration to be paid was not an entire sum, but was apportioned among the several items at the rate of $1 per 1,000 feet for the oak logs; 75 cents per 1,000 feet for all other logs; 3 cents each for cross-ties driven to Bethel; and 5 cents each for cross-ties driven to points below Bethel. But while the contract is severable, and the plaintiff entitled to compensation at the stipulated rate for all logs and ties delivered at the specified points, there is neither reason nor authority for the claim for compensation in respect to logs that were swept by the flood to and through the defendant's boom, whether they had been driven part of the way by plaintiff, or remained untouched by him at the coming of the flood. In respect to each particular log the contract in this case is like a contract of common carriage, which is dependent upon the delivery of the goods at the designated place, and, if by casus the delivery is prevented, the carrier cannot recover *pro tanto* for freight for part of the route over which the goods were taken. Whart. Cont. §714. Indeed, this is but an application of the rule already stated. The consideration to be paid for driving each log is an entire sum per 1,000 feet for the whole distance, and is not apportioned to parts of the drive. The judgment is reversed, and a *venire facias de novo* is awarded.

LOWY
v.
UNITED PACIFIC INSURANCE CO.
Supreme Court of California
67 Cal. 2d 87
1967

McComb, J.

Plaintiffs, owners and subdividers, entered into a contract with defendant, a licensed contractor, for certain excavation and grading work on lots and streets, together with street improvement work consisting of paving the streets and installing curbs and gutters, in a subdivision containing 89 residential lots.

After defendant had performed 98 percent of the contracted excavation and grading work, a dispute arose between the parties regarding payment of $7,200 for additional work, consisting of importing dirt for fills, necessitated by changes made by plaintiffs in the plans.

Defendant ceased performance. Plaintiffs immediately employed others to do street improvement work called for by the contract and thereafter sued defendant and his bonding company for breach of contract. Defendant answered and cross-complained for damages for breach of contract and reasonable services rendered. The trial court determined that plaintiffs were entitled to nothing against defendant and his bonding company and allowed defendant recovery on his cross-complaint.

The contract provided, in part, as follows:

[Defendant] agrees to provide and pay for all materials, labor, tools, equipment, light, transportation and other facilities necessary for the execution, in a good and workmanlike manner, of all the following described work: Excavation, Grading and Street Improvements in Tracts No. 26589 and 19517 in accordance with plans and specifications . . . and Exhibit "A" attached hereto. . . .

The price which [plaintiffs] shall pay [defendant] for performing his obligations, as aforesaid or as hereunder set forth, is at the following prices indicated: . . .

See Exhibits *"A" and "B"* attached hereto. (Italics added.)

Exhibit "A" states in part:

[Defendant] agrees to furnish all equipment, labor and material necessary for street improvements, onsite and offsite grading, grade and excavation and erosion control on Tracts 26589 and 19517 . . . for the lump sum price of Seventy-Three Thousand, Five Hundred Dollars ($73,500.00) including, without limitation, *all grading, compaction, cleaning, grade and erosion control and dumping*, all of which are to be performed to satisfaction of [plaintiffs]. . . . (Italics added.)

The construction of pavement, curbs and gutters is not included in the list of specific items for which the sum of $73,500 is to be paid.

Exhibit "B" lists 45 unit prices ranging from $.04 to $4.50 per unit for use in the computation of the amount to be charged for the performance of that part of the street improvement work consisting of paving the streets and installing curbs and gutters. The unit prices are entirely unrelated to excavation and grading.

The contract further provides:

In invoicing [plaintiffs], multiply all the final quantities by the unit prices set forth in Exhibit "B." All quantities will be determined by Delta Engineering & Surveying Co. and approved by [defendant] and [plaintiffs], *with the exception of grading, etc., mentioned in Exhibit "A" of this Agreement, which is a lump sum price for a complete job without any limitations.* (Italics added.)

The latter paragraph of the contract shows clearly that the lump sum of $73,500 was not intended to include payment for paving the streets and installing curbs and gutters.

The trial court found that under the contract there were two phases of work to be performed, (1) grading and (2) street improvements; that defendant performed all the terms and conditions thereof relating to grading, except work which could be completed for $1,470, being 2 percent of the total grading cost contracted for; that defendant performed additional grading work, reasonably worth $7,200, necessitated by changes in plans on the part of plaintiffs and not attributable to defendant, which additional work was also authorized by plaintiffs through their superintendent; that plaintiffs breached the contract by employing others to do street improvement work and by not making payments to defendant for grading work done by him when due, thereby excusing further performance by defendant;

and that defendant was entitled to recover on his cross-complaint for damages, as follows:

Contract price for grading	$73,500.00
Additional work	7,200.00
	80,700.00
Less amount paid defendant	− 60,227.50
	20,472.50
Less credit for uncompleted work	− 1,470.00
	19,002.50
Less credit for items paid for defendant's account	− 1,166.00
Balance owing defendant	$17,836.50

The trial court further found that defendant had breached that portion of the contract relating to street improvement work and was not entitled to recover damages for loss of profits in connection therewith.

As indicated above, the contract required the performance of two kinds of work. First, certain excavation and grading work was to be done on lots and streets. Thereafter, street improvement work, consisting of paving the streets and installing curbs and gutters was required.

Plaintiffs agreed to pay defendant for the excavation and grading work (including street grading work) the sum of $73,500, as set forth in Exhibit "A" of the contract; and they agreed to pay defendant for the paving of the streets and the installation of curbs and gutters (all commonly called "street improvement work") pursuant to the unit prices set forth in Exhibit "B" of the contract.

Accordingly, since the consideration was apportioned, the contract was a severable or divisible one.[1]

Before defendant commenced the excavation and grading work, for which a lump sum price of $73,500 was set by the contract, he gave a surety bond for $73,500. When the excavation and grading work was nearing completion, and it was almost time for work under the second phase to begin, plaintiffs requested that defendant provide a surety bond for "street improvements" in the sum of $125,000, stating that "no work should be performed on any portion of the street improvement portion of the contract until such bond is furnished." Thus, it is clear that the parties treated the contract as a divisible one.

Under the circumstances, the fact that defendant did not perform the second phase of the contract does not prevent his recovering for work done under the first phase.

Defendant did not entirely perform under the first phase of the contract. However, the doctrine of substantial performance, ordinarily applied to building

---

1. Williston defines a divisible contract, as follows: "A contract under which the whole performance is divided into two sets of partial performance, each part of each set being the agreed exchange for a corresponding part of the set of performances to be rendered by the other promisor, is called a divisible contract. Or, as expressed in the cases: 'A contract is divisible where by its terms, 1, performance of each party is divided into two or more parts, and 2, the number of parts due from each party is the same, and 3, the performance of each part by one party is the agreed exchange for a corresponding part by the other party.'"

contracts, is here applicable, since the evidence shows that defendant completed 98 percent of the work under the first phase and was prevented from completing the balance through the fault of plaintiffs.

The judgment is affirmed.

STARK
v.
PARKER

Supreme Judicial Court of Massachusetts
19 Mass. 267
1824

LINCOLN, J.

This case comes before us upon exceptions filed, pursuant to the statute, to the opinion, in matter of law, of a judge of the Court of Common Pleas, before whom the action was tried by a jury; and we are thus called upon to revise the judgment which was there rendered. The exceptions present a precise abstract question of law for consideration, namely, whether upon an entire contract for a term of service for a stipulated sum, and a part-performance, without any excuse for neglect of its completion, the party guilty of the neglect can maintain an action against the party contracted with, for an apportionment of the price, or a *quantum meruit,* for the services actually performed. Whatever may be the view properly taken of the contract between the parties in the case at bar, the point upon which it was ruled in the court below embraced but this single proposition. The direction to the jury was, "that although proved to them, that the plaintiff agreed to serve the defendant for an agreed price for a year, and had voluntarily left his service before the expiration of that time, and without the fault of the defendant, and against his consent, still the plaintiff would be entitled to recover of the defendant, in this action, a sum in proportion to the time he had served, deducting therefrom such sum, (if any,) as the jury might think the defendant had suffered by having his service deserted." If this direction was wrong, the judgment must be reversed, and the case sent to a new trial, in which the diversity of construction given to the character and terms of the contract by the counsel for the respective parties may be a subject for distinct consideration.

It cannot but seem strange to those who are in any degree familiar with the fundamental principles of law, that doubts should ever have been entertained upon a question of this nature. Courts of justice are eminently characterized by their obligation and office to enforce the performance of contracts, and to withhold aid and countenance from those who seek, through their instrumentality, impunity or excuse for the violation of them. And it is no less repugnant to the well established rules of civil jurisprudence, than to the dictates of moral sense, that a party who deliberately and understandingly enters into an engagement and voluntarily breaks it, should be permitted to make that very engagement the foundation of a claim to compensation for services under it. The true ground of legal demand in all cases of contracts between parties is, that the party claiming has done all which on his part was to be performed *by the terms of the contract, to entitle him to enforce the obligation of the other party*. It is not sufficient that he has given to the party contracted with, a right of action against him. The ancient doctrine on this subject, which was carried to such an absurd extent as to allow an action for the stipulated reward for a specified service, under a total neglect of performance, leaving the other party to his remedy for this neglect, by an action in turn, has been long since wisely exploded, and the more reasonable rule before stated, in late decisions, is clearly established.

Upon examining the numerous authorities, which have been collected with great industry by the counsel for the plaintiff, it will be found, that a distinction has been uniformly recognised in the construction of contracts, between those in which the obligation of the parties is reciprocal and independent, and those where the duty of the one may be considered as a condition precedent to that of the other. In the latter cases, it is held, that the performance of the precedent obligation can alone entitle the party bound to it, to his action. Indeed the argument of the counsel in the present case has proceeded entirely upon this distinction, and upon the *petitio principii* in its application. It is assumed by him, that the service of the plaintiff for a year was not a condition precedent to his right to a proportion of the stipulated compensation for that entire term of service, but that upon a just interpretation of the contract, it is so far divisible, as that consistently with the terms of it, the plaintiff, having labored for any portion of the time, may receive compensation *pro tanto.* That this was the intention of the parties is said to be manifest from the fact found in the case, that the defendant from time to time did in fact make payments expressly toward this service. We have only to observe upon this point in the case, that how ever the parties may have intended between themselves, we are to look to the construction given to the contract by the court below. The jury were not instructed to inquire into the meaning of the parties in making the contract. They were instructed, that if the contract was entire, in reference alike to the service and the compensation, still by law it was so divisible in the remedy, that the party might recover an equitable consideration for his labor, although the engagement to perform it had not been fulfilled. . . . Nothing can be more unreasonable than that a man, who deliberately and wantonly violates an engagement, should be permitted to seek in a court of justice an indemnity from the consequences of his voluntary act; and we are satisfied that the law will not allow it.

. . .

The performance of a year's service was in this case a condition precedent to the obligation of payment. The plaintiff must perform the condition, before he is entitled to recover any thing under the contract, and he has no right to renounce his agreement and recover upon a *quantum meruit.* The cases of *McMillan v. Vanderlin*, 12 Johns R. 165, *Jennings v. Camp*, 13 Johns. R. 94, and *Reab v. Moor*, 19 Johns. R. 337, are analogous in their circumstances to the case at bar and are directly and strongly in point. The decisions in the English cases express the same doctrine, *Waddington v. Oliver*, 2 New Rep. 61; *Ellis v. Hamlen*, 3 Taunt. 52; and the principle is fully supported by all the elementary writers.

. . . The law indeed is most reasonable in itself. It denies only to a party an advantage from his own wrong. It requires him to act justly by a faithful performance of his own engagements, before he exacts the fulfilment of dependent obligations on the part of others. It will not admit of the monstrous absurdity, that a man may voluntarily and without cause violate his agreement, and make the very breach of that agreement the foundation of an action which he could not maintain under it. Any apprehension that this rule may be abused to the purposes of oppression, by holding out an inducement to the employer, by unkind treatment near the close of a term of service, to drive the laborer from his engagement, to the sacrifice of his wages, is wholly groundless. It is only in cases where the desertion is voluntary and without cause on the part of the laborer, or fault or consent on the part of the employer, that the principle applies. Wherever there is a reasonable excuse, the law allows a recovery. To say that this is not sufficient protection, that an excuse may in fact exist in countless secret and indescribable circumstances, which from their very nature are not susceptible of proof, or which, if proved, the law does not recognise as adequate, is to require no less than that the law should *presume* what can never legally be established, or should admit that as *competent*, which by positive rules is held to be wholly *immaterial*. We think well established principles are not thus to be shaken, and that in this commonwealth more especially, where the important business of husbandry leads to multiplied engagements of precisely this description, it should least of all be questioned, that the laborer is worthy of his hire, only upon the performance of his contract, and as the reward of fidelity.

The judgment of the Court of Common Pleas is reversed, and a new trial granted at the bar of this Court.

BRITTON
v.

TURNER

Superior Court of Judicature of New Hampshire
6 N.H. 481
1834

ASSUMPSIT for work and labour, performed by the plaintiff, in the service of the defendant, from March 9th, 1831, to December 27, 1831.

The declaration contained the common counts, and among them a count in *quantum meruit*, for the labor, averring it to be worth one hundred dollars.

At the trial in the C. C. Pleas, the plaintiff proved the performance of the labor as set forth in the declaration.

The defence was that it was performed under a special contract—that the plaintiff agreed to work one year, from some time in March, 1831, to March 1832, and that the defendant was to pay him for said year's labor the sum of one hundred and twenty dollars; and the defendant offered evidence tending to show that such was the contract under which the work was done.

Evidence was also offered to show that the plaintiff left the defendant's service without his consent, and it was contended by the defendant that the plaintiff had no good cause for not continuing in his employment.

There was no evidence offered of any damage arising from the plaintiffs departure, farther than was to be inferred from his non fulfilment of the entire contract.

The court instructed the jury, that if they were satisfied from the evidence that the labor was performed, under a contract to labor a year, for the sum of one hundred and twenty dollars, and if they were satisfied that the plaintiff labored only the time specified in the declaration, and then left the defendant's service, against his consent, and without any good cause, yet the plaintiff was entitled to recover, under his *quantum meruit* count, as much as the labor he performed was reasonably worth, and under this direction the jury gave a verdict for the plaintiff for the sum of $95.

The defendant excepted to the instructions thus given to the jury.

PARKER, J.

. . . It is clear . . . that he is not entitled to recover upon the contract itself, because the service, which was to entitle him to the sum agreed upon, has never been performed. But the question arises, can the plaintiff, under these circumstances, recover a reasonable sum for the service he has actually performed, under the count in *quantum meruit.* Upon this, and questions of a similar nature, the decisions to be found in the books are not easily reconciled.

It has been held, upon contracts of this kind for labor to be performed at a specified price, that the party who voluntarily fails to fulfil the contract by performing the whole labor contracted for, is not entitled to recover any thing for the labor actually performed, however much he may have done towards the performance, and this has been considered the settled rule of law upon this subject.

That such rule in its operation may be very unequal, not to say unjust, is apparent. A party who contracts to perform certain specified labor, and who breaks his contract in the first instance, without any attempt to perform it, can only be made liable to pay the damages which the other party has sustained by reason of such non performance, which in many instances may be trifling—whereas a party who in good faith has entered upon the performance of his contract, and nearly completed it, and then abandoned the further performance—although the other party has had the full benefit of all that has been done, and has perhaps sustained no actual damage—is in fact subjected to a loss of all which has been performed, in the nature of damages for the non fulfilment of the remainder, upon the technical rule, that the contract must be fully performed in order to a recovery of any part of the compensation.

By the operation of this rule, then, the party who attempts performance may be placed in a much worse situation than he who wholly disregards his contract, and the other party may receive much more, by the breach of the contract, than the injury which he has sustained by such breach, and more than he could be entitled to were he seeking to recover damages by an action.

The case before us presents an illustration. Had the plaintiff in this case never entered upon the performance of his contract, the damage could not probably have been greater than some small expense and trouble incurred in procuring another to do the labor which he had contracted to perform. But having entered upon the performance, and labored nine and a half months, the value of which labor to the defendant as found by the jury is $95, if the defendant can succeed in this defence, he in fact receives nearly five sixths of the value of a whole year's labor, by reason of the breach of contract by the plaintiff a sum not only utterly disproportionate to any probable, not to say possible damage which could have resulted from the neglect of the plaintiff to continue the remaining two and an half months, but altogether beyond any damage which could have been recovered by the defendant, had the plaintiff done nothing towards the fulfilment of his contract.

. . .

The party who contracts for labor merely, for a certain period, does so with full knowledge that he must, from the nature of the case, be accepting part performance from day to day, if the other party commences the performance, and with knowledge also that the other may eventually fail of completing the entire term.

If under such circumstances he actually receives a benefit from the labor performed, over and above the damage occasioned by the failure to complete, there is as much reason why he should pay the reasonable worth of what has thus been done for his benefit. . . .

We hold then, that where a party undertakes to pay upon a special contract for the performance of labor, or the furnishing of materials, he is not to be charged upon such special agreement until the money is earned according to the terms of it, and where the parties have made an express contract the law will not imply and raise a contract different from that which the parties have entered into, except upon some farther transaction between the parties.

. . .

This rule, by binding the employer to pay the value of the service he actually receives, and the laborer to answer in damages where he does not complete the entire contract, will leave no temptation to the former to drive the laborer from his service, near the close of his term, by ill treatment, in order to escape from payment; nor to the latter to desert his service before the stipulated time, without a sufficient reason; and it will in most instances settle the whole controversy in one action, and prevent a multiplicity of suits and cross actions.

. . .

Applying the principles thus laid down, to this case, the plaintiff is entitled to judgment on the verdict.

Judgment on the verdict.

Problems

1. The Dulles Toll Road. Brown & Root, Inc. was the general contractor for the construction of the Dulles Toll Road Extension, a 14-mile long private highway between Dulles Airport and Leesburg, Virginia. Brown & Root subcontracted a portion of the construction to Moore Brothers Company, and the subcontract included the following pay-when-paid provision:

> [P]ayment by Owner to General Contractor is a condition precedent to any obligation of General Contractor to make payment hereunder; General Contractor shall have no obligation to make payment to Subcontractor for any portion of the Sublet Work for which General Contractor has not received payment from Owner.

Brown & Root realized that some of the project specifications provided to it by the toll road's owner, the Toll Road Investors Partnership II (TRIP), and on which Brown & Root priced the job, were likely to be insufficient, which meant that future changes to the specifications ("change orders") were likely. One of the likely changes was to the thickness of the concrete for the road. TRIP and Brown & Root, however, sought to convince lenders, who would potentially provide financing for the project, that the total project costs were predictable and not subject to escalation. Thus, TRIP and Brown & Root intentionally left out several items from the principal general contract (which the lenders would review before agreeing to provide financing). These omitted provisions included the procedures by which TRIP would submit change orders for a number of potentially costly changes, including concrete thickness, and the procedures by which Brown & Root would be entitled to increase its charges for the construction work. The provisions omitted from the principal contract were spelled out in a separate side agreement between TRIP and Brown & Root that was not provided to the lenders.

During construction, the State of Virginia required TRIP to increase the thickness of the road's concrete, and TRIP submitted the necessary change order, which, under the side agreement, entitled Brown & Root to increase the price charged. Brown & Root told its subcontractors, including Moore Brothers, to install the thicker concrete. The lenders, surprised by the claim for significant additional costs, however, refused to provide funds to cover the costs of the change order, leaving TRIP unable to make the payment.

Having not been paid for the change order, Brown & Root refused to pay Moore Brothers for its portion of the increased costs. Moore Brothers sued Brown & Root for payment. Is Moore Brothers entitled to collect?

2. The Salesman's Quota. Wesley Pearce sold insurance for ELIC Corporation and earned commissions based on his sales performance. A 1978 contract provided that, in addition to his regular commissions, Pearce would be entitled to receive an additional 5 percent of sales of a particular line of automotive insurance (the "VIP commission") for each month in which his net sales of life and health insurance exceeded $67,500. Although Pearce did not meet this life and health insurance quota, ELIC paid him the VIP commission for all of 1978. In July 1979, ELIC wrote to him that his 5 percent VIP commission on $60,000 of automotive insurance sold through June 1, 1979, would be forthcoming, although it was never paid.

In July 1980, ELIC wrote to Pearce and requested that he return the VIP commissions that had been paid for 1978, which ELIC claimed was actually an "advance" on VIP commissions that Pearce had not earned. Pearce sued for the unpaid 1979 commissions, and ELIC counterclaimed for the return of the 1978 commissions. How should the court rule?

3. The Housing Development. James Carrig, the owner of a parcel of land in Watertown, Massachusetts, contracted for builder Gilbert-Varker Corporation to construct 35 houses on the parcel according to a set of plans and specifications. The contract specified which basic house plan would be used for each of the 35 lots, along with the basic price for each plan. Purchasers of the houses would be allowed to select variations on the standard house plans, and the contract also specified how much the builder would be paid for each of the various alterations or additions. The contract called for the houses to be built in groups of "not less than ten." Progress payments would be made to the builder on each house when certain milestones were achieved, with final payment due 40 days after completion of the house.

The builder constructed 20 houses and received progress payments on those houses but not the final payments. At that time, the builder claimed that it was losing money, and it refused to start work on the remaining 15 houses unless the owner agreed to an increase in the contract price. The owner refused and withheld the final payments on the 20 completed houses, and the builder never constructed the remaining 15 houses. The owner sued for the difference between the contract price of the 15 houses, which were not built, and the cost of hiring another builder to construct them ($9,935, according to the trial court). The builder countersued for the unpaid final payments on the first 20 houses ($3,143, according to the trial court). How should the court rule?

4. The Angry Farmers (Reprise). In preparing to purchase the sellers' 280-acre parcel of farmland in the Chicago exurbs (see Section A.2, Problem 1), plaintiff Ocean Atlantic Woodland Corporation spent $1.7 million over 4 years rezoning the property so that the property would be suitable for development, planning the subsequent development, conducting preliminary engineering studies, and marketing the property. Ocean Atlantic argued that termination of the contract for the sale caused a complete forfeiture of this investment and increased the value of the property to the sellers. Should Ocean Atlantic be awarded the value of the benefits its expenditures conferred on the sellers?

B. EXCUSE OF NON-PERFORMANCE OF DUTIES

Some authorities distinguish between conditions *precedent* and conditions *subsequent*. The former is an event that must occur before a duty is triggered, while the latter is an event that excuses a duty that would otherwise be due. "*A will pay B $1,000 for painting A's portrait if A is satisfied with the portrait*" exemplifies a condition precedent: *A* must be satisfied with the performance before *A*'s duty to pay arises. In contrast, "*A* will pay *B* $1,000 for painting *A*'s portrait *unless A* is dissatisfied with the portrait" demonstrates a condition subsequent: *A* has an unconditional duty to pay *B* for the portrait, but that duty is extinguished if *A* is not satisfied with the performance.

The distinction between conditions precedent and conditions subsequent is largely semantic, except to the extent that some courts hold that the difference determines which party bears the burden of proof concerning whether the condition was satisfied. Importantly, though, the distinction between the two varieties of conditions sheds light on a trio of doctrines — mistake, impracticability, and frustration of purpose—that operate to excuse parties from the obligation to perform contractual duties. Each of these doctrines can be understood to impose on contracts a constructive condition subsequent, even though the contracts include no such condition, either expressly or impliedly. By their terms, these doctrines become effective only when the risks of unanticipated developments are not explicitly or implicitly allocated by the parties' agreement. See Rest. (2d) Contracts §§154, 261, 263. Consequently, these doctrines should be understood as creating default conditions that the parties are free to contract around.

When these doctrines are successfully invoked, the harmed party is usually entitled to rescission of the contract, excusing both parties from further performance obligations and entitling them to restitution of benefits previously conferred. In some circumstances, however, the complaining party might be entitled only to temporarily suspend the performance of a duty.

1. Mistake

The doctrine of mutual mistake allows a party to avoid enforcement of a contract when three criteria are met. First, both parties must be mistaken at the time of contracting as to a basic assumption of the contract. Second, the mistake must have a material effect on the bargain. Third, the party who is adversely affected by the mistake must not "bear the risk" of that mistake. Rest. (2d) Contracts §152. The doctrine bears some similarities to the affirmative defense of misrepresentation covered in Chapter 3. A mistake is a belief that is not in accord with the facts, whereas a misrepresentation is an assertion not in accord with the facts.

While it might sound expansive, the excuse of mutual mistake can be successfully invoked only in limited circumstances. This is because the risk of mistake will be considered to be allocated to the adversely affected party whenever that party "is aware of limited knowledge but proceeds anyway." Rest. (2d) Contracts §154. A party cannot claim a "mistake" merely because a fact that seemed unlikely to be true at the time of contracting turns out to be true. The fundamental challenge in mastering the doctrine of mutual mistake, then, is recognizing when a fact about the world is sufficiently unanticipated and unforeseeable to excuse performance by one of the parties when a shared assumption about that fact turns out to be mistaken. The first five cases in this section—*West Coast Airlines v. Miner's Aircraft & Engine Service, Inc., City of Everett v. Estate of Oddmund Sumstad, Wood v. Boynton, Smith v. Zimbalist,* and *Beachcomber Coins v. Boskett*—provide some guideposts for mapping the dividing line.

As hard as it is for a disappointed party to avoid enforcement of a contract or win rescission on the basis of mutual mistake, it is even more difficult to establish an excuse based on his unilateral mistake. The party must meet all of the requirements for asserting mutual mistake and also must demonstrate that the other party knew about or caused the mistake or, alternatively, that enforcing the contract would be unconscionable. Rest. (2d) Contracts §153. The unilateral mistake doctrine imposes this additional burden to avoid providing an incentive to parties to under-invest in information that could help them to avoid mistakes of fact. The final case in this section, *Donovan v. RRL Corporation*, explores the contours of this doctrine.

WEST COAST AIRLINES, INC.
v.
MINER'S AIRCRAFT & ENGINE SERVICE, INC.

Supreme Court of Washington, Department 1
66 Wash. 2d 513
1965

STAFFORD, J.

Sometime prior to September of 1959, West Coast purchased aircraft engines "A" and "B" for $2,280 and $2,285 respectively. They were delivered with all existing logbooks, engine build-up and repair records, change records and other documents required by the United States Federal Aviation Agency (hereinafter called the FAA). As owner of the engines, West Coast was entitled to the exclusive possession of both engines and their associated records. . . .

In the course of its operation, West Coast accumulated unuseable scrap metal that was sold to junk dealers. At the time here in question, West Coast had collected an excessive number of sealed "cans" which had been placed along a fence near the hangar to get them out of the way.

Junk Traders is a commercial scrap metal company engaged exclusively in the purchase, sale and trade of scrap metal. In June, 1960, West Coast's purchasing agent asked Junk Traders to pick up the "cans" along the fence. The "cans" were constructed of 3/8-inch steel and were very heavy. It was necessary for Junk Traders to use a fork-lift truck to load them. When the job was completed, Junk Traders had salvaged four truck-loads of sealed "cans" and one truck-load of "can" halves and other miscellaneous scrap. Junk Traders paid West Coast 2 cents a pound for 20,370 pounds of scrap metal.

Through some inadvertence, and wholly unknown to either West Coast or Junk Traders, the two sealed "cans" containing engines "A" and "B" were loaded by Junk Traders' driver and delivered to their junk yard. However, West Coast continued in possession of all documents required by the FAA because the removal of the two engines had been in error.

. . .

The following year, it was brought to West Coast's attention that the engines had been taken by Junk Traders. . . . West Coast immediately called Junk Traders in an effort to correct the mistake.

. . .

The "cans" must be distinguished from their contents. West Coast intended to sell "cans" and Junk Traders intended to buy them. Their title passed to Junk Traders. However, neither party was aware of the contents. Neither the vendor nor the vendee intended that title to the engines would pass with the "cans."

A sale is a consensual transaction. The subject matter which passes is to be determined by the intent of the parties, as revealed by the terms of their agreement, in the light of the surrounding circumstances. 46 Am. Jur., Sales §§129, 142; 77 C.J.S. Sales §24, pp. 630, 631; RCW 63.04.040.

The engines were not part of an agreement between West Coast and Junk Traders. Unknown contents of the subject matter of a sale that are not essential to its existence or usefulness, but which are merely deposited therein, and which are not within the contemplation of or intention of the contracting parties, do not pass by the sale. Huthmacher v. Harris's Adm'rs, 38 Pa. 491, 80 Am. Dec. 502 (1861); Livermore v. White, 74 Me. 452, 43 Am. Rep. 600 (1883); Evans v. Barnett's Admr., 6 Pennewill's Del. Reports 44, 63 A. 770 (1906); 46 Am. Jur., Sales, Unknown Contents of Articles Sold, §147; 3 Williston on Sales (Rev. ed.), Mistake Rendering Agreement Void, §654, 1965 Supp. A contract of sale, like any other contract, must rest upon the mutual agreement of the parties on all essential elements of the sale. 77 C.J.S. Sales §24, Mutual Assent or Agreement, including the identity of the thing sold. American Nat. Bank of Nashville v. West, 31 Tenn. App. 85, 212 S.W.2d 683, 4 A.L.R.2d 314 (1948).

There was no meeting of the minds, no contract and thus no sale of the engines. Title to the two engines remained in West Coast. Huthmacher v. Harris's Adm'rs, supra; Livermore v. White, supra; Evans v. Barnett's Admr., supra.

. . .

Judgment affirmed.

---

2 # CITY OF EVERETT
v.
ESTATE OF ODDMUND SUMSTAD

Supreme Court of Washington (En Banc)
95 Wash. 2d 853
1981

DOLLIVER, J.

The City of Everett commenced an interpleader action against the seller (the Sumstad Estate) and the buyer (Al and Rosemary Mitchell) of a safe to determine who is entitled to a sum of money found in the safe. Both the Estate and the Mitchells moved for summary judgment. The trial court entered summary judgment in favor of the Estate. The Court of Appeals affirmed. *Everett v. Estate of Sumstad*, 26 Wash. App. 742 (1980).

Petitioners, Mr. and Mrs. Mitchell, are the proprietors of a small secondhand store. On August 12, 1978, the Mitchells attended Alexander's Auction, where they frequently had shopped to obtain merchandise for their own use and for use as inventory in their business. At the auction the Mitchells purchased a used safe with an inside compartment for $50. As they were told by the auctioneer when they purchased the safe, the Mitchells found that the inside compartment of the safe was locked. The safe was part of the Sumstad Estate.

Several days after the auction, the Mitchells took the safe to a locksmith to have the locked compartment opened. The locksmith found $32,207 inside. . . .

. . . The issue is whether there was in fact a sale of the safe and its unknown contents at the auction. In contrast to the Court of Appeals, we find that there was.

A sale is a consensual transaction. The subject matter which passes is to be determined by the intent of the parties as revealed by the terms of their agreement in light of the surrounding circumstances. *West Coast Airlines, Inc. v. Miner's Aircraft & Engine Serv., Inc.*, 66 Wash. 2d 513, 518, 403 P.2d 833 (1965). The objective manifestation theory of contracts, which is followed in this state (*Plumbing Shop, Inc. v. Pitts*, 67 Wash. 2d 514, 408 P.2d 382 (1965)), lays stress on the outward manifestation of assent made by each party to the other. The subjective intention of the parties is irrelevant.

. . .

The case upon which the Court of Appeals relies, *West Coast Airlines, Inc. v. Miner's Aircraft & Engine Serv., Inc.*, is inapposite. In that case, a commercial scrap metal company, Junk Traders, removed several containers of scrap metal from plaintiff West Coast Airlines' storage yard. Inadvertently, two containers in which aircraft engines were stored were removed by Junk Traders along with the scrap metal. . . .

In *West Coast Airlines*, the aircraft engines were clearly not intended to be sold to Junk Traders. The inclusion of the engines in the sale of scrap metal was inadvertent and wholly unknown to both parties. Neither party was aware the sealed containers might hold anything other than scrap metal. Furthermore, West Coast Airlines retained the Federal documents that must be transferred to the purchaser upon the sale of an aircraft engine, a clear indication it did not intend to pass title to the engines.

In the case before us, the purchasers stated in their affidavit:

> [W]e saw that the top outermost door with a combination lock was open, and that the inner door was locked shut. That inner door required a key to open, and we learned that the safe would have to be taken to a locksmith to get the inner door opened because no key was available. We also learned that the combination for the outer lock was unknown. The auctioneer told the bidders that both this and the other safe had come from an estate, that both were still locked, that neither had been opened, and that the required combinations and key were unavailable for either.

The auctioneer's affidavit stated that:

> I told the crowd at the auction that (the safes) were from an estate, that they were still locked and had never been opened by me and that I didn't have the combinations.

These affidavits are undisputed. In addition, the Mitchells were aware of the rule of the auction that all sales were final. Furthermore, the auctioneer made no statement reserving rights to any contents of the safe to the Estate. Under these circumstances, we hold reasonable persons would conclude that the auctioneer manifested an objective intent to sell the safe and its contents and that the parties mutually assented to enter into that sale of the safe and the contents of the locked compartment.

In the words of the dissenting judge in the Court of Appeals, 26 Wash. App. at 757, 614 P.2d 1294:

> The unique facts of this case make it one of those apparently rare instances in history in which the objective manifestations of the contracting parties reflected a mutual assent to the sale of the unknown contents of the object sold. The function of a safe is to provide a place for storing one's money or other valuables. When a locked safe is sold without the key, under all of the circumstances present in this case, the reasonable expectations of the buyer should be protected.

We concur in this view.

3

WOOD
v.
BOYNTON

Supreme Court of Wisconsin
64 Wis. 265
1885

TAYLOR, J.

This action was brought in the circuit court for Milwaukee county to recover the possession of an uncut diamond of the alleged value of $1,000. The case was tried in the circuit court, and after hearing all the evidence in the case, the learned circuit judge directed the jury to find a verdict for the defendants. The plaintiff excepted to such instruction, and, after a verdict was rendered for the defendants, moved for a new trial upon the minutes of the judge. The motion was denied, and the plaintiff duly excepted, and after judgment was entered in favor of the defendants, appealed to this court. The defendants are partners in the jewelry business. On the trial it appeared that on and before the twenty-eighth of December, 1883, the plaintiff was the owner of and in the possession of a small stone of the nature and value of which she was ignorant; that on that day she sold it to one of the defendants for the sum of one dollar. Afterwards it was ascertained that the stone was a rough diamond, and of the value of about $700. After hearing this fact the plaintiff tendered the defendants the one dollar, and ten cents as interest, and demanded a return of the stone to her. The defendants refused to deliver it, and therefore she commenced this action.

The plaintiff testified to the circumstances attending the sale of the stone to Mr. Samuel B. Boynton, as follows: "The first time Boynton saw that stone he was talking about buying the topaz, or whatever it is, in September or October. I went into the store to get a little pin mended, and I had it in a small box,—the pin,—a small ear-ring; . . . this stone, and a broken sleeve-button were in the box. Mr. Boynton turned to give me a check for my pin. I thought I would ask him what the stone was, and I took it out of the box and asked him to please tell me what that was. He took it in his hand and seemed some time looking at it. I told him I had been told it was a topaz, and he said it might be. He says, 'I would buy this; would you sell it?' I told him I did not know but what I would. What would it be worth? And he said he did not know; he would give me a dollar and keep it as a specimen, and I told him I would not sell it; and it was certainly pretty to look at. He asked me where I found it, and I told him in Eagle. He asked about how far out, and I said right in the village, and I went out. Afterwards, and about the twenty-eighth of December, I needed money pretty badly, and thought every dollar would help, and I took it back to Mr. Boynton and told him I had brought back the topaz, and he says, 'Well, yes; what did I offer you for it?' and I says, 'One dollar'; and he stepped to the change drawer and gave me the dollar, and I went out." In another part of her testimony she says: "Before I sold the stone I had no knowledge whatever that it was a diamond. I told him that I had been advised that it was probably a topaz, and he said probably it was. The stone was about the size of a canary bird's egg, nearly the shape of an egg,—worn pointed at one end; it was nearly straw color,—a little darker." . . .

The evidence on the part of the defendant is not very different from the version given by the plaintiff, and certainly is not more favorable to the plaintiff. Mr. Samuel B. Boynton, the defendant to whom the stone was sold, testified that at the time he bought this stone, he had never seen an uncut diamond; had seen cut diamonds, but they are quite different from the uncut ones; "he had no idea this was a diamond, and it never entered his brain at the time." . . .

This evidence clearly shows that the plaintiff sold the stone in question to the defendants, and delivered it to them in December, 1883, for a consideration of one dollar. By such sale the title to the stone passed by the sale and delivery to the defendants. How has that title been divested and again vested in the plaintiff? The contention of the learned counsel for the appellant is that the title became vested in the plaintiff by the tender to the Boyntons of the purchase money with interest, and a demand of a return of the stone to her. Unless such tender and demand revested the title in the appellant, she cannot maintain her action. The only question in the case is whether there was anything in the sale which entitled the vendor (the appellant) to rescind the sale and so revest the title in her. The only reasons we know of for rescinding a sale and revesting the title in the vendor so that he may maintain an action at law for the recovery of the possession against his vendee are (1) that the vendee was guilty of some fraud in procuring a sale to be made to him; (2) that there was a mistake made by the vendor in delivering an article which was not the article sold,—a mistake in fact as to the identity of the thing sold with the thing delivered upon the sale. This last is not in reality a rescission of the sale made, as the thing delivered was not the thing sold, and no title ever passed to the vendee by such delivery.

In this case, upon the plaintiff's own evidence, there can be no just ground for alleging that she was induced to make the sale she did by any fraud or unfair dealings on the part of Mr. Boynton. Both were entirely ignorant at the time of the character of the stone and of its intrinsic value. Mr. Boynton was not an expert in uncut diamonds, and had made no examination of the stone, except to take it in his hand and look at it before he made the offer of one dollar, which was refused at the time, and afterwards accepted without any comment or further examination made by Mr. Boynton. The appellant had the stone in her possession for a long time, and it appears from her own statement that she had made some inquiry as to its nature and qualities. If she chose to sell it without further investigation as to its intrinsic value to a person who was guilty of no fraud or unfairness which induced her to sell it for a small sum, she cannot repudiate the sale because it is afterwards ascertained that she made a bad bargain. *Kennedy v. Panama, etc., Mail Co.*, L. R. 2 Q. B. 580. There is no pretense of any mistake as to the identity of the thing sold. It was produced by the plaintiff and exhibited to the vendee before the sale was made, and the thing sold was delivered to the vendee when the purchase price was paid. *Kennedy v. Panama, etc., Mail Co., supra*, 587; *Street v. Blay*, 2 Barn. & Adol. 456; *Gompertz v. Bartlett*, 2 El. & Bl. 849; *Gurney v. Womersley*, 4 El. & Bl. 133; *Ship's Case*, 2 De G. J. & S. 544. Suppose the appellant had produced the stone, and said she had been told it was a diamond, and she believed it was, but had no knowledge herself as to its character or value, and Mr. Boynton had given her $500 for it, could he have rescinded the sale if it had turned out to be a topaz or any other stone of very small value? Could Mr. Boynton have rescinded the sale on the ground of mistake? Clearly not, nor could he rescind it on the ground that there had been a breach of warranty, because there was no warranty, nor could he rescind it on the ground of fraud, unless he could show that she falsely declared that she had been told it was a diamond, or, if she had been so told, still she knew it was not a diamond. See *Street v. Blay, supra.*

. . .

We can find nothing in the evidence from which it could be justly inferred that Mr. Boynton, at the time he offered the plaintiff one dollar for the stone, had any knowledge of the real value of the stone, or that he entertained even a belief that the stone was a diamond. It cannot, therefore, be said that there was a suppression of knowledge on the part of the defendant as to the value of the stone which a court of equity might seize upon to avoid the sale. The following cases show that, in the absence of fraud or warranty, the value of the property sold, as compared with the price paid, is no ground for a rescission of a sale. *Wheat v. Cross*, 31 Md. 99; *Lambert v. Heath*, 15 Mees. & W. 487; *Bryant v. Pember*, 45 Vt. 487; *Kuelkamp v. Hidding*, 31 Wis. 503-511. However unfortunate the plaintiff may have been in selling this valuable stone for a mere nominal sum, she has failed entirely to make out a case either of fraud or mistake in the sale such as will entitle her to a rescission of such sale so as to recover the property sold in an action at law.

The judgment of the circuit court is affirmed.

SMITH
v.
ZIMBALIST

District Court of Appeal, Second District, Division 1, California
2 Cal. App. 2d 324
1934

HOUSER, J.

From the "findings of fact" made pursuant to the trial of the action, it appears that plaintiff, who was of the age of 86 years, although not a dealer in violins, had been a collector of rare violins for many years; "that defendant was a violinist of great prominence, internationally known, and himself the owner and collector of rare and old violins made by the old masters"; that at the suggestion of a third person, and without the knowledge by plaintiff of defendant's intention in the matter, defendant visited plaintiff at the home of the latter and there asked plaintiff if he might see plaintiff's collection of old violins; that in the course of such visit and inspection, "plaintiff showed a part of his collection to defendant; that defendant picked up one violin and asked plaintiff what he would take for the violin, calling it a 'Stradivarius'; that plaintiff did not offer his violins, or any of them, for sale, but on account of his age, after he had been asked what he would take for them, said he would not charge as much as a regular dealer, but that he would sell it for $5,000; that thereafter defendant picked up another violin, calling it a 'Guarnerius,' and asked plaintiff what he would take for that violin, and plaintiff said if defendant took both violins, he could have them for $8,000; that the defendant said 'all right,' thereupon stating his financial condition and asking if he could pay $2,000 cash and the balance in monthly payments of $1,000." Thereupon a memorandum was signed by defendant as follows:

> "I hereby acknowledge receipt of one violin by Joseph Guarnerius and one violin by Stradivarius dated 1717 purchased by me from George Smith for the total sum of Eight Thousand Dollars toward which purchase price I have paid Two Thousand Dollars the

balance I agree to pay at the rate of one thousand dollars on the fifteenth day of each month until paid in full."

In addition thereto, a "bill of sale" in the following language was signed by plaintiff:

This certifies that I have on this date sold to Mr. Efrem Zimbalist one Joseph Guarnerius violin and one Stradivarius violin dated 1717, for the full price of $8,000.00 on which has been paid $2,000.00.

The balance of $6,000.00 to be paid $1,000.00 fifteenth of each month until paid in full, I agree that Mr. Zimbalist shall have the right to exchange these for any others in my collection should he so desire.

That at the time said transaction was consummated each of the parties thereto "fully believed that said violins were made one by Antonius Stradivarius and one by Josef Guarnerius"; that preceding the closing of said transaction "plaintiff made no representations and warranties as to said violins, or either of them, as to who their makers were, but believed them to have been made one by Antonius Stradivarius and one by Josef Guarnerius in the early part of the eighteenth century; that plaintiff did not fraudulently make any representations or warranties to defendant at the time of said purchase"; that there was "a preponderance of evidence to the effect that said violins are not Stradivarius or Guarnerius violins, nor made by either Antonius Stradivarius or Josef Guarnerius, but were in fact made as imitations thereof, and were not worth more than $300.00."

The action which is the foundation of the instant appeal was brought by plaintiff against defendant to recover judgment for the unpaid balance of the purchase price of the two violins.

As is shown by the conclusions of law reached by the trial court from such facts, the theory upon which the case was decided was that the transaction in question was the result of "a mutual mistake on the part of plaintiff and defendant," and consequently that plaintiff was not entitled to recover judgment. From a judgment rendered in favor of defendant, plaintiff has appealed to this court.

In urging a reversal of the judgment, it is the contention of appellant that the doctrine of caveat emptor should have been applied to the facts in the case; that is to say, that in the circumstances shown by the evidence and reflected in the findings of fact, the trial court should have held that defendant bought the violins at his own risk and peril.

. . .

The governing principle of law to the effect that an article described in a "bill of parcels," or, as in the instant case, in a "bill of sale," amounts to a warranty that such article in fact conforms to such description and that the seller is bound by such description, has been applied in this state in the case of Flint v. Lyon, 4 Cal. 17, wherein it was held that where the defendant purchased an entire cargo of flour which was described as "Haxall" flour, he was not required by the contract to accept the same flour which in reality was "Gallego" flour, but which was of as excellent quality as "Haxall" flour. Therein, in part, the court said:

"What the inducement was to the defendant to purchase Haxall, we know not; but having purchased that particular brand, he was entitled to it, and could not be compelled to accept any other as a substitute. The use of the word 'Haxall' in the sale-note amounted to a warranty that the flour was Haxall. How, then, stands the case? The contract was founded in mistake, both parties supposing they were contracting concerning a certain article which had no existence, consequently the contract was void for want of the substance of the thing contracted for. Could then the acceptance of a different article than the one sold by Gorham[,] the sub-vendee, conclude the defendant? Certainly not! . . ."

. . .

Although it may be that by some authorities a different rule may be indicated, it is the opinion of this court that, in accord with the weight of the later authorities to which attention hereinbefore has been directed, the strict rule of caveat emptor may not be applied to the facts of the instant case, but that such rule is subject to the exception thereto to the effect that on the purported sale of personal property the parties to the proposed contract are not bound where it appears that in its essence each of them is honestly mistaken or in error with reference to the identity of the subject-matter of such contract. In other words, in such circumstances, no enforceable sale has taken place. But if it may be said that a sale, with a voidable condition attached, was the outcome of the transaction in the instant case, notwithstanding the "finding of fact" by the trial court that "plaintiff made no representations and warranties as to said violins," from a consideration of the language employed by the parties in each of the documents that was exchanged between them (to which reference hereinbefore has been had), together with the general conduct of the parties, and particularly the acquiescence by plaintiff in the declaration made by defendant regarding each of the violins and by whom it was made, it becomes apparent that, in law, a warranty was given by plaintiff that one of the violins was a Guarnerius and that the other was a Stradivarius.

The findings of fact unquestionably show that each of the parties believed and assumed that one of said violins was a genuine Guarnerius and that the other was a genuine Stradivarius; the receipt given by defendant to plaintiff for said violins so described them, and the "bill of sale" given by plaintiff to defendant certifies that plaintiff "sold to Mr. Efrem Zimbalist (defendant) one Joseph Guarnerius violin and one Stradivarius violin dated 1717 for the full price of $8,000.00 on which has been paid $2,000.00. . . ."

Without burdening this opinion with the citation of additional authorities, it may suffice to state that, although the very early decisions may hold to a different rule, all the more modern authorities, including many of those in California to which attention has been directed (besides the provision now contained in section 1734, Civ. Code), are agreed that the description in a bill of parcels or sale note of the thing sold amounts to a warranty on the part of the seller that the subject-matter of the sale conforms to such description. See, generally, 22 Cal. Jur. 994; 55 Cor. Jur. 738 et seq.; 24 R. C. L. 171; and authorities respectively there cited.

It is ordered that the judgment be and it is affirmed.

BEACHCOMBER COINS, INC.
v.
BOSKETT

Superior Court of New Jersey, Appellate Division
166 N.J. Super. 442
1979

CONFORD, P.J.A.D.

Plaintiff, a retail dealer in coins, brought an action for rescission of a purchase by it from defendant for $500 of a dime purportedly minted in 1916 at Denver. Defendant is a part-time coin dealer. Plaintiff asserts a mutual mistake of fact as to the genuineness of the coin as Denver-minted, such a coin being a rarity and therefore having a market value greatly in excess of its normal monetary worth. Plaintiff's evidence at trial that the "D" on the coin signifying Denver mintage was counterfeited is not disputed by defendant. Although at trial defendant disputed that the coin tendered back to him by plaintiff was the one he sold, the implicit trial finding is to the contrary, and that issue is not raised on appeal.

The trial judge, sitting without a jury, held for defendant on the ground that the customary "coin dealing procedures" were for a dealer purchasing a coin to make his own investigation of the genuineness of the coin and to "assume the risk" of his purchase if his investigation is faulty. The judge conceded that the evidence demonstrated satisfaction of the ordinary requisites of the rule of rescission for mutual mistake of fact that both parties act under a mistake of fact and that the fact be "central" (material) to the making of the contract. The proofs were that the seller had himself acquired this coin and two others of minor value for a total of $450 and that his representative had told the purchaser that he would not sell the dime for less than $500. The principal of plaintiff firm spent from 15 to 45 minutes in close examination of the coin before purchasing it. Soon thereafter he received an offer of $700 for the coin subject to certification of its genuineness by the American Numismatic Society. That organization labelled it a counterfeit, and as a result plaintiff instituted the present action.

The evidence and trial judge's findings establish this as a classic case of rescission for mutual mistake of fact. As a general rule, ". . . where parties on entering into a transaction that affects their contractual relations are both under a mistake regarding a fact assumed by them as the basis on which they entered into the transaction, it is voidable by either party if enforcement of it would be materially more onerous to him than it would have been had the fact been as the parties believed it to be." (Restatement, Contracts, §502 at 961 (1932);[1] 13 Williston on Contracts (3 ed. 1970), §1543, 74-75).

---

1. No substantial change in the rule was effected by Restatement, Contracts 2d, §294(1), Tent. Dr. No. 10 (1975) at 10. This provides (1) Where a mistake of both parties at the time a contract was made as to a basic assumption on which the contract was made has a material effect on the agreed exchange of performances, the contract is voidable by the adversely affected party unless he bears the risk of the mistake under the rule stated in §296. The exceptions in §296 are not here applicable.

By way of example, the Restatement posits the following:

> A contracts to sell to B a specific bar of silver before them. The parties supposed that the bar is sterling. It has, however, a much larger admixture of base metal. The contract is voidable by B.

Moreover, "negligent failure of a party to know or to discover the facts as to which both parties are under a mistake does not preclude rescission or reformation on account thereof." Restatement, op. cit., §502 at 977. The law of New Jersey is in accord. In the *Riviere* case relief was denied only because the parties could not be restored to the Status quo ante. In the present case they can be. It is undisputed that both parties believed that the coin was a genuine Denver-minted one. The mistake was mutual in that both parties were laboring under the same misapprehension as to this particular, essential fact. The price asked and paid was directly based on that assumption. That plaintiff may have been negligent in his inspection of the coin (a point not expressly found but implied by the trial judge) does not, as noted above, bar its claim for rescission. Cf. *Smith v. Zimbalist*, 2 Cal. App. 2d 324, 38 P.2d 170 D. Ct. App. 1934.

Defendant's contention that plaintiff assumed the risk that the coin might be of greater or lesser value than that paid is not supported by the evidence. It is well established that a party to a contract can assume the risk of being mistaken as to the value of the thing sold. 13 Williston, Contracts, op. cit., §1543A at 85. The Restatement states the rule this way:

> Where the parties know that there is doubt in regard to a certain matter and contract on that assumption, the contract is not rendered voidable because one is disappointed in the hope that the facts accord with his wishes. The risk of the existence of the doubtful fact is then assumed as one of the elements of the bargain.

(§502, Comment f at 964. See also §296(b), Comment c at 4.)

However, for the stated rule to apply, the parties must be conscious that the pertinent fact may not be true and make their agreement at the risk of that possibility. 17 Am. Jur. 2d, Contracts, §145 at 492. In this case both parties were certain that the coin was genuine. They so testified. Plaintiff's principal thought so after his inspection, and defendant would not have paid nearly $450 for it otherwise. A different case would be presented if the seller were uncertain either of the genuineness of the coin or of its value of genuine, and had accepted the expert buyer's judgment on these matters.

The trial judge's rationale of custom of the trade is not supported by the evidence. It depended upon the testimony of plaintiff's expert witness who on cross-examination as to the "procedure" on the purchase by a dealer of a rare coin, stated that the dealer would check it with magnification and then "normally send it to the American Numismatic Certification Service for certification." This testimony does not in our opinion establish that practice as a usage of trade "having such regularity of observance in a . . . trade as to justify an expectation that it will be observed with respect to the transaction in question," within the intent of the Uniform Commercial Code, N.J.S.A. 12A:1-205(2).

The cited code provision contemplates that the trade usage is so prevalent as to warrant the conclusion that the parties contracted with reference to, and intended their agreement to be governed by it. Cf. *Manhattan Overseas Co. v. Camden Co. Beverage Co.*, 125 N.J.L. 239, 244, 15 A.2d 217 (Sup. Ct. 1940), aff'd 126 N.J.L. 421, 19 A.2d 828 (E. & A. 1941). Our reading of the testimony does not indicate any basis for findings either that this was a trade usage within the Code definition at all or that these parties in fact accepted it as such to the extent that they were agreeing that because of it the sale was an "as is" transaction. Indeed, the same witness testified there was a "normal policy" among coin dealers throughout the United States of a "return privilege" for altered coins.

. . .

Reversed.

DONOVAN
v.
RRL CORP.

Supreme Court of California
26 Cal. 4th 261
2001

GEORGE, C.J.

. . .

While reading the April 26, 1997, edition of the Costa Mesa Daily Pilot, a local newspaper, plaintiff noticed a full-page advertisement placed by defendant. The advertisement promoted a "Pre-Owned Coup-A-Rama Sale!/2-Day Pre-Owned Sales Event" and listed, along with 15 other used automobiles, a 1995 Jaguar XJ6 Vanden Plas. The advertisement described the color of this automobile as sapphire blue, included a vehicle identification number, and stated a price of $25,995. The name Lexus of Westminster was displayed prominently in three separate locations in the advertisement, which included defendant's address along with a small map showing the location of the dealership. The following statements appeared in small print at the bottom of the advertisement: "All cars plus tax, lic., doc., smog & bank fees. On approved credit. Ad expires 4/27/97[.]"

Also on April 26, 1997, plaintiff visited a Jaguar dealership that offered other 1995 Jaguars for sale at $8,000 to $10,000 more than the price specified in defendant's advertisement. The following day, plaintiff and his spouse drove to Lexus of Westminster and observed a blue Jaguar displayed on an elevated ramp. After verifying that the identification number on the sticker was the same as that listed in defendant's April 26 Daily Pilot advertisement, they asked a salesperson whether they could test drive the Jaguar. Plaintiff mentioned that he had seen the advertise-ment and that the price "looked really good." The salesperson responded that, as a Lexus dealer, defendant might offer better prices for a Jaguar automobile than would a Jaguar dealer. At that point, however, neither plaintiff nor the salesperson men-tioned the specific advertised price.

After the test drive, plaintiff and his spouse discussed several negative charac-teristics of the automobile, including high mileage, an apparent rust problem, and worn tires. In addition, it was not as clean as the other Jaguars they had inspected. Despite these problems, they believed that the advertised price was a very good price and decided to purchase the vehicle. Plaintiff told the salesperson, "Okay. We will take it at your price, $26,000." When the salesperson did not respond, plaintiff showed him the advertisement. The salesperson immediately stated, "That's a mistake."

After plaintiff asked to speak with an individual in charge, defendant's sales manager also told plaintiff that the price listed in the advertisement was a mistake. The sales manager apologized and offered to pay for plaintiff's fuel, time, and effort expended in traveling to the dealership to examine the automobile. Plaintiff declined this offer and expressed his belief that there had been no mistake. Plaintiff stated that he could write a check for the full purchase price as advertised. The sales manager responded that he would not sell the vehicle at the advertised price. Plaintiff then requested the sales price. After performing some calculations, and based upon defendant's $35,000 investment in the automobile, the sales manager stated that he would sell it to plaintiff for $37,016. Plaintiff responded, "No, I want to buy it at your advertised price, and I will write you a check right now." The sales manager again stated that he would not sell the vehicle at the advertised price, and plaintiff and his spouse left the dealership.

Plaintiff subsequently filed this action against defendant for breach of contract, fraud, and negligence. In addition to testimony consistent with the facts set forth above, the following evidence was presented to the municipal court, which acted as the trier of fact.

Defendant's advertising manager compiles information for placement in adver-tisements in several local newspapers, including the Costa Mesa Daily Pilot. Defen-dant's advertisement published in the Saturday, April 19, 1997, edition of the Daily Pilot listed a 1995 Jaguar XJ6 Vanden Plas but did not specify a price for that automobile; instead, the word "Save" appeared in the space where a price ordinarily would have appeared. The following Thursday afternoon, defendant's sales manager instructed the advertising manager to delete the 1995 Jaguar from all advertisements and to substitute a 1994 Jaguar XJ6 with a price of $25,995. The advertising man-ager conveyed the new information to a representative of the Daily Pilot that same afternoon.

Because of typographical and proofreading errors made by employees of the Daily Pilot, however, the newspaper did not replace the description of the 1995 Jaguar with the description of the 1994 Jaguar, but did replace the word "Save" with the price of $25,995. Thus, the Saturday, April 26, edition of the Daily Pilot erroneously advertised the 1995 Jaguar XJ6 Vanden Plas at a price of $25,995. The Daily Pilot acknowledged its error in a letter of retraction sent to defendant on April 28. No employee of defendant reviewed a proof sheet of the revised Daily Pilot advertisement before it was published, and defendant was unaware of the mistake until plaintiff attempted to purchase the automobile.

. . .

Having concluded that defendant's advertisement for the sale of the Jaguar automobile constituted an offer that was accepted by plaintiff's tender of the advertised price, and that the resulting contract satisfied the statute of frauds, we next consider whether defendant can avoid enforcement of the contract on the ground of mistake.

A party may rescind a contract if his or her consent was given by mistake. (Civ. Code, §1689, subd. (b)(1).) A factual mistake by one party to a contract, or unilateral mistake, affords a ground for rescission in some circumstances. (4) Civil Code section 1577 states in relevant part: "Mistake of fact is a mistake, not caused by the neglect of a legal duty on the part of the person making the mistake, and consisting in: [¶] 1. An unconscious ignorance or forgetfulness of a fact past or present, material to the contract. . . ."

. . .

Under the first Restatement of Contracts, unilateral mistake did not render a contract voidable unless the other party knew of or caused the mistake. (1 Witkin, *supra*, Contracts, §370, p. 337; see Rest., Contracts, §503.) In *Germain etc. Co. v. Western Union etc. Co.* (1902) 137 Cal. 598, 602 [70 P. 658], this court endorsed a rule similar to that of the first Restatement. Our opinion indicated that a seller's price quotation erroneously transcribed and delivered by a telegraph company contractually could bind the seller to the incorrect price, unless the buyer knew or had reason to suspect that a mistake had been made. Some decisions of the Court of Appeal have adhered to the approach of the original Restatement. (See, e.g., *Conservatorship of O'Connor* (1996) 48 Cal. App. 4th 1076, 1097-1098 [56 Cal. Rptr. 2d 386], and cases cited therein.) Plaintiff also advocates this approach and contends that rescission is unavailable to defendant, because plaintiff was unaware of the mistaken price in defendant's advertisement when he accepted the offer.

. . . [I]n *M.F. Kemper Const. Co. v. City of L.A.* (1951) 37 Cal. 2d 696, 701 [235 P.2d 7] (*Kemper*), we acknowledged but rejected a strict application of the foregoing Restatement rule regarding unilateral mistake of fact. The plaintiff in *Kemper* inadvertently omitted a $301,769 item from its bid for the defendant city's public works project—approximately one-third of the total contract price. After discovering the mistake several hours later, the plaintiff immediately notified the city and subsequently withdrew its bid. Nevertheless, the city accepted the erroneous bid, contending that rescission of the offer was unavailable for the plaintiff's unilateral mistake.

Our decision in *Kemper* recognized that the bid, when opened and announced, resulted in an irrevocable option contract conferring upon the city a right to accept the bid, and that the plaintiff could not withdraw its bid unless the requirements for rescission of this option contract were satisfied. (*Kemper, supra*, 37 Cal. 2d at pp. 700, 704.) We stated: "Rescission may be had for mistake of fact if the mistake is material to the contract and was not the result of neglect of a legal duty, if enforcement of the contract as made would be unconscionable, and if the other party can be placed in status quo. [Citations.]" (*Id.* at p. 701.) Although the city knew of the plaintiff's mistake before it accepted the bid, and this circumstance was relevant to our determination that requiring the plaintiff to perform at the mistaken bid price would be unconscionable (*id.* at pp. 702-703), we authorized rescission of the city's option contract even though the city had not known of or contributed to the mistake before it opened the bid.

. . .

. . . [T]he Restatement Second of Contracts authorizes rescission for a unilateral mistake of fact where "the effect of the mistake is such that enforcement of the contract would be unconscionable." (Rest. 2d Contracts, §153, subd. (a).) The comment following this section recognizes "a growing willingness to allow avoidance where the consequences of the mistake are so grave that enforcement of the contract would be unconscionable." (*Id.*, com. a, p. 394.) . . .

Because the rule in section 153, subdivision (a), of the Restatement Second of Contracts, authorizing rescission for unilateral mistake of fact where enforcement would be unconscionable, is consistent with our previous decisions, we adopt the rule as California law. As the author of one treatise recognized more than 40 years ago, the decisions that are inconsistent with the traditional rule "are too numerous and too appealing to the sense of justice to be disregarded." (3 Corbin, Contracts (1960) §608, p. 675, fn. omitted.) We reject plaintiff's contention and the Court of Appeal's conclusion that, because plaintiff was unaware of defendant's unilateral mistake, the mistake does not provide a ground to avoid enforcement of the contract.

Having concluded that a contract properly may be rescinded on the ground of unilateral mistake of fact as set forth in section 153, subdivision (a), of the Restatement Second of Contracts, we next consider whether the requirements of that provision, construed in light of our previous decisions, are satisfied in the present case. Where the plaintiff has no reason to know of and does not cause the defendant's unilateral mistake of fact, the defendant must establish the following facts to obtain rescission of the contract: (1) the defendant made a mistake regarding a basic assumption upon which the defendant made the contract; (2) the mistake has a material effect upon the agreed exchange of performances that is adverse to the defendant; (3) the defendant does not bear the risk of the mistake; and (4) the effect of the mistake is such that enforcement of the contract would be unconscionable. We shall consider each of these requirements below.

A significant error in the price term of a contract constitutes a mistake regarding a basic assumption upon which the contract is made, and such a mistake ordinarily has a material effect adverse to the mistaken party. (See, e.g., *Elsinore, supra*, 54 Cal. 2d at p. 389 [7 percent error in contract price]; *Lemoge Electric v. County of San Mateo* (1956) 46 Cal. 2d 659, 661-662 [297 P.2d 638] [6 percent error]; *Kemper, supra*, 37 Cal. 2d at p. 702 [28 percent error]; *Brunzell Const. Co. v. G. J. Weisbrod, Inc.* (1955) 134 Cal. App. 2d 278, 286 [285 P.2d 989] [20 percent error]; Rest. 2d Contracts, §152, com. b, illus. 3, p. 387 [27 percent error].) In establishing a material mistake regarding a basic assumption of the contract, the defendant must show that the resulting imbalance in the agreed exchange is so severe that it would be unfair to require the defendant to perform. (Rest. 2d Contracts, §152, com. c, p. 388.)

Ordinarily, a defendant can satisfy this requirement by showing that the exchange not only is less desirable for the defendant, but also is more advantageous to the other party. (*Ibid.*)

Measured against this standard, defendant's mistake in the contract for the sale of the Jaguar automobile constitutes a material mistake regarding a basic assumption upon which it made the contract. Enforcing the contract with the mistaken price of $25,995 would require defendant to sell the vehicle to plaintiff for $12,000 less than the intended advertised price of $37,995—an error amounting to 32 percent of the price defendant intended. The exchange of performances would be substantially less desirable for defendant and more desirable for plaintiff. Plaintiff implicitly concedes that defendant's mistake was material.

The parties and amici curiae vigorously dispute, however, whether defendant should bear the risk of its mistake. Section 154 of the Restatement Second of Contracts states: "A party bears the risk of a mistake when [¶] (a) the risk is allocated to him by agreement of the parties, or [¶] (b) he is aware, at the time the contract is made, that he has only limited knowledge with respect to the facts to which the mistake relates but treats his limited knowledge as sufficient, or [¶] (c) the risk is allocated to him by the court on the ground that it is reasonable in the circumstances to do so." Neither of the first two factors applies here. Thus, we must determine whether it is reasonable under the circumstances to allocate to defendant the risk of the mistake in the advertisement.

Civil Code section 1577, as well as our prior decisions, instructs that the risk of a mistake must be allocated to a party where the mistake results from that party's neglect of a legal duty. (*Kemper, supra*, 37 Cal. 2d at p. 701.) It is well established, however, that ordinary negligence does not constitute neglect of a legal duty within the meaning of Civil Code section 1577. (*Kemper, supra*, 37 Cal. 2d at p. 702.) For example, we have described a careless but significant mistake in the computation of the contract price as the type of error that sometimes will occur in the conduct of reasonable and cautious businesspersons, and such an error does not necessarily amount to neglect of legal duty that would bar equitable relief. (*Ibid.*; see also *Sun 'n Sand, Inc. v. United California Bank* (1978) 21 Cal. 3d 671, 700-701 [148 Cal. Rptr. 329, 582 P.2d 920] (plur. opn. of Mosk, J.); *Elsinore, supra*, 54 Cal. 2d at pp. 388-389.)

. . .

Defendant's erroneous advertisement in the Daily Pilot listed 16 used automobiles for sale. Each of the advertisements prepared for several newspapers in late April 1997, except for the one in the Daily Pilot, correctly identified the 1994 Jaguar XJ6 for sale at a price of $25,995. In May 1997, defendant's advertisements in several newspapers listed the 1995 Jaguar XJ6 Vanden Plas for sale at $37,995, and defendant subsequently sold the automobile for $38,399. Defendant had paid $35,000 for the vehicle.

Evidence at trial established that defendant adheres to the following procedures when an incorrect advertisement is discovered. Defendant immediately contacts the newspaper and requests a letter of retraction. Copies of any erroneous advertisements are provided to the sales staff, the error is explained to them, and the mistake is circled in red and posted on a bulletin board at the dealership. The sales staff informs customers of any advertising errors of which they are aware.

No evidence presented at trial suggested that defendant knew of the mistake before plaintiff attempted to purchase the automobile, that defendant intended to mislead customers, or that it had adopted a practice of deliberate indifference regarding errors in advertisements. [An employee of the defendant] regularly reviews proof sheets for the numerous advertisements placed by defendant, and representatives of the newspapers, including the Daily Pilot, also proofread defendant's advertisements to ensure they are accurate. Defendant follows procedures for notifying its sales staff and customers of errors of which it becomes aware. The uncontradicted evidence established that the Daily Pilot made the proofreading error resulting in defendant's mistake.

Defendant's fault consisted of failing to review a proof sheet reflecting the change made on Thursday, April 24, 1997, and/or the actual advertisement appearing in the April 26 edition of the Daily Pilot—choosing instead to rely upon the Daily Pilot's advertising staff to proofread the revised version. Although, as the Court of Appeal found, such an omission might constitute negligence, it does not involve a breach of defendant's duty of good faith and fair dealing that should preclude equitable relief for mistake. In these circumstances, it would not be reasonable for this court to allocate the risk of the mistake to defendant.

As indicated above, the Restatement Second of Contracts provides that during the negotiation stage of a contract "each party is held to a degree of responsibility appropriate to the justifiable expectations of the other." (Rest. 2d Contracts, §157, com. a, p. 417.) No consumer reasonably can expect 100 percent accuracy in each and every price appearing in countless automobile advertisements listing numerous vehicles for sale. The degree of responsibility plaintiff asks this court to impose upon automobile dealers would amount to strict contract liability for any typographical error in the price of an advertised automobile, no matter how serious the error or how blameless the dealer. We are unaware of any other situation in which an individual or business is held to such a standard under the law of contracts. Defendant's good faith, isolated mistake does not constitute the type of extreme case in which its fault constitutes the neglect of a legal duty that bars equitable relief. . . .

The final factor defendant must establish before obtaining rescission based upon mistake is that enforcement of the contract for the sale of the 1995 Jaguar XJ6 Vanden Plas at $25,995 would be unconscionable. Although the standards of unconscionability warranting rescission for mistake are similar to those for unconscionability justifying a court's refusal to enforce a contract or term, the general rule governing the latter situation (Civ. Code, §1670.5) is inapplicable here, because unconscionability resulting from mistake does not appear at the time the contract is made. (Rest. 2d Contracts, §153, com. c, p. 395; 1 Witkin, *supra*, Contracts, §370, pp. 337-338.)

An unconscionable contract ordinarily involves both a procedural and a substantive element: (1) oppression or surprise due to unequal bargaining power, and (2) overly harsh or one-sided results. (*Armendariz v. Foundation Health Psychcare Services, Inc.* (2000) 24 Cal. 4th 83, 114 [99 Cal. Rptr. 2d 745, 6 P.3d 669].) Nevertheless, " 'a sliding scale is invoked which disregards the regularity of the procedural process of the contract formation, that creates the terms, in proportion to the greater harshness or unreasonableness of the substantive terms themselves.' [Citations.]" (*Ibid.*) For example, the Restatement Second of Contracts states that "[i]nadequacy of consideration does not of itself invalidate a bargain, but gross disparity in the values exchanged may be an important factor in a determination that a contract is unconscionable and may be sufficient ground, without more, for denying specific performance." (Rest. 2d Contracts, §208, com. c, p. 108.) In ascertaining whether rescission is warranted for a unilateral mistake of fact, substantive unconscionability often will constitute the determinative factor, because the oppression and surprise ordinarily results from the mistake—not from inequality in bargaining power. Accordingly, even though defendant is not the weaker party to the contract and its mistake did not result from unequal bargaining power, defendant was surprised by the mistake, and in these circumstances overly harsh or one-sided results are sufficient to establish unconscionability entitling defendant to rescission.

. . .

In the present case, enforcing the contract with the mistaken price of $25,995 would require defendant to sell the vehicle to plaintiff for $12,000 less than the intended advertised price of $37,995—an error amounting to 32 percent of the price defendant intended. Defendant subsequently sold the automobile for slightly more than the intended advertised price, suggesting that that price reflected its actual market value. Defendant had paid $35,000 for the 1995 Jaguar and incurred costs in advertising, preparing, displaying, and attempting to sell the vehicle. Therefore, defendant would lose more than $9,000 of its original investment in the automobile. Plaintiff, on the other hand, would obtain a $12,000 windfall if the contract were enforced, simply because he traveled to the dealership and stated that he was prepared to pay the advertised price.

The judgment of the Court of Appeal is reversed.

Problems

1. Rose 2d. of Aberlone. T.C. Sherwood was interested in purchasing livestock and visited Hiram Walker, importer and breeder of Angus cattle, at Walker's farm. Walker told Sherwood to look over several cows being housed at another farm owned by Walker, but Walker warned Sherwood that they were "probably barren, and would not breed." Sherwood went and viewed the cows and several days later expressed an interest in purchasing one named "Rose 2d. of Aberlone." The parties agreed to the sale of Rose for 5.5 cents per pound, which was approximately 10 percent of what a breeding cow would cost. When Sherwood arrived to pick up Rose two weeks later, the Walkers refused to complete the exchange, claiming that in the intervening time period they had discovered that Rose, whom both parties believed to be barren, was actually with calf. Sherwood sued. Who should prevail?

2. A More Serious Injury. Henry Kruzich was seriously injured while working in a mine when an ore bucket struck him in the head. Kruzich was permanently disabled and required home care for a period of time. Old Republic Insurance Company, the mine's insurer, accepted liability and reached a settlement that provided Kruzich with the needed care. However, the agreement excluded any future home-care expenses. Kruzich recovered from his head injury to some degree: although he remained permanently disabled, he did not require constant monitoring, and as a result, his wife was able to return to work. Nearly 16 years after the accident, Kruzich began suffering motor-skills deterioration. Doctors diagnosed him as having Parkinson's disease caused by the mine accident. Apparently, Kruzich's Parkinson's developed as a result of the mine trauma, but he did not actually have the disease at the time the settlement was reached.

As the Parkinson's worsened, Kruzich once again required home care and was afraid his wife would have to leave work to care for him. He filed a lawsuit seeking to rescind the settlement agreement under the doctrine of mutual mistake. Should the court grant rescission?

3. A Zoning Restriction. In 1970, Northwestern Bell Telephone Company convinced the City of Duluth to rezone its property from "S" (suburban) to "M-1" (manufacturing) so that Northwestern Bell could build a distribution center, on the condition that only a single building could be built on the property. Years later, Northwestern Bell sold a portion of that property not containing the structure to Robert Eikill, who subsequently sold it to Jack Gartner for $40,000. Eikill's real estate agent told Gartner that the property was zoned M-1, and all concerned believed this meant that Gartner could use the property for industrial purposes. Gartner made no independent investigation of the property's zoning status. The standard form contract signed by both parties stated the seller's duty to deliver "marketable title to said premises subject only to the following exceptions: (a) building and zoning laws, ordinances, State and Federal regulations. . . ."

A year after the purchase, Gartner learned that, because of the original restriction, he could not construct any buildings on the property. Useful only for agricultural or open-use purposes, the property was appraised at a value of $15,000-$25,000. Gartner sought rescission of the purchase on grounds of mutual mistake. Should he prevail?

4. Arbitrate This. Blue Cross Blue Shield of Tennessee (BCBST), a health insurance corporation, purchased a Directors and Officer's Liability Insurance Policy from BCS Insurance Company. BCBST submitted claims related to a recently settled lawsuit to BCS, and BCS refused to pay. The parties' insurance contract called for arbitration in the event of this type of dispute, with the arbitrator to be chosen from a specified group of potential arbitrators. At this point in time, BCBST learned that virtually every potential arbitrator in the relevant pool had an inherent conflict of interest, which BCBST believed predisposed them to favor BCS's position. BCBST then claimed that it made a unilateral mistake in agreeing to the arbitration term in the contract on the ground that it did not know at the time of contracting that the potential arbitrators would be biased toward BCS. Assuming that all of the potential arbitrators at least appear to be biased, should the court grant BCBST's motion to rescind the arbitration clause?

5. Going Once, Going Twice, SOLD! Richard Limehouse and David Smith settled a property dispute in their real estate partnership by agreeing to sell the property at auction, although they each wanted to own the property individually. The two parties agreed that each would receive a 10 percent deposit from the auction purchaser, but only a 5 percent deposit if one of them obtained the property through the auction by making the highest bid. They also agreed that either of them could bid on the property through a surrogate.

On the day of the auction, only three people bid on the property: Smith, Gene Greeter (Limehouse's attorney), and Ann Kazel, a real estate developer. When Kazel had the highest bid and Greeter had stopped bidding, Smith decided to let Kazel win the auction because he wanted the 10 percent deposit to which he would then be entitled, and he believed he could subsequently work out a deal with Kazel to purchase the property back from her. It turned out, however, that Kazel was bidding on behalf of Limehouse, who ended up with the property. Smith not only lost the property to his former partner, but he only received the 5 percent deposit. Smith quickly moved to rescind the sale based on his unilateral mistake that Kazel was bidding on her own behalf (rather than as Limehouse's agent). Should the court grant Smith's motion?

2. Impracticability

Like the doctrines of mutual and unilateral mistake, the doctrine of impracticability (sometimes referred to as "impossibility") is invoked when facts that were unanticipated at the time of contracting prove to be detrimental to the interests of one of the parties. The primary difference between the mistake and impracticability doctrines is temporal: the mistake doctrines concern facts that were in existence at the time of contracting but were unknown; impracticability arises from an unexpected change in circumstances that occurs subsequent to contracting and renders performance by one party (usually the seller) actually impossible or far more difficult ("impracticable") than anticipated at the time of contracting. Rest. (2d) Contracts §261. On the margin, a distinction between the two categories of events can be difficult to maintain. If a contractor begins an excavation project and then unexpectedly discovers rock under the topsoil, it might be said that the problem is one of mistake concerning an existing fact (the rock did not develop overnight), or it might be said that the discovery of the rock constitutes a post-contractual change in circumstance.

Unexpected events regularly occur after contracts are formed, and these events often disappoint the expectations of one of the parties. If parties contract to sell a widget for a fixed price of $100, a subsequent increase in the price of the raw materials used to build widgets can easily cause distress or hardship for the seller. If the law is to encourage parties to rely on contractual commitments, however, such common events cannot be sufficient to release the seller from his obligation. By agreeing to accept a fixed price for a future performance, the seller is implicitly accepting the risk (and the financial consequences thereof) that the price of inputs might increase in the intervening time.

This means that, like the doctrine of mistake, the doctrine of impracticability is invoked only in a relatively circumscribed subset of situations in which a supervening event causes disappointment. In the language of the Restatement, the non-occurrence of the event in question must be a "basic assumption" of the contract, and, additionally, the occurrence of the event must not be the fault of the adversely affected party. Rest. (2d) Contracts §261; see also U.C.C. §§2-613, 2-614, 2-615. The following trio of cases provides guidance concerning what events are sufficient to justify an invocation of the doctrine. *Taylor v. Caldwell* is a prototype of a classic "impossibility" claim involving the physical destruction of the contract's subject matter. *U.S. Bancorp Equipment Finance, Inc. v. Ameriquest Holdings LLC* and *Bush v. ProTravel International, Inc.* concern the consequences of the same unforeseen event—the terrorist attacks of September 11, 2001—that sharply increased the difficulty of the adversely affected parties fulfilling their contractual duties.

TAYLOR
v.
CALDWELL
Court of Queen's Bench
3 B. & S. 826, 122 Eng. Rep. 309
1863

BLACKBURN, J.

In this case the plaintiffs and the defendants, on the 27th May 1861, entered into a contract by which the defendants agreed to let the plaintiffs have the use of The Surrey Gardens and Music Hall on four days then to come, viz., the 17th June, 15th July, 5th August and 19th August, for the purpose of giving a series of four grand concerts, and day and night fêtes at the Gardens and Hall on those days respectively; and the plaintiffs agreed to take the Gardens and Hall on those days, and pay 100£. for each day.

The parties inaccurately call this a "letting," and the money to be paid a "rent"; but the whole agreement is such as to shew that the defendants were to retain the possession of the Hall and Gardens so that there was to be no demise of them, and that the contract was merely to give the plaintiffs the use of them on those days. Nothing however, in our opinion, depends on this. The agreement then proceeds to set out various stipulations between the parties as to what each was to supply for these concerts and the entertainments, and as to the manner in which they should be carried on. The effect of the whole is to shew that the existence of the Music Hall in the Surrey Gardens in a state fit for a concert was essential for the fulfilment of the contract,—such entertainments as the parties contemplated in their agreement could not be given without it.

After the making of the agreement, and before the first day on which a concert was to be given, the hall was destroyed by fire. This destruction, we must take it on the evidence, was without fault of either party, and was so complete that in consequence the concerts could not be given as intended. And the question we have to decide is whether, under these circumstances, the loss which the plaintiffs have sustained is to fall upon the defendants. The parties when framing their agreement evidently had not present to their minds the possibility of such a disaster, and have made no express stipulation with reference to it, so that the answer to the question must depend on the general rules of law applicable to such a contract.

Issue

There seems no doubt that where there is a positive contract to do a thing, not in itself unlawful, the contractor must perform it or pay damages for not doing it, although in consequence of unforeseen accident, the performance of his contract has become unexpectodly burdensome, or even impossible. . . . But this rule is only applicable when the contract is positive and absolute, and not subject to any condition either expressed or implied; and there are authorities which, as we think, establish the principle that where, from the nature of the contract, it appears that the parties must from the beginning have known that it could not be fulfilled unless when the time for the fulfilment of the contract arrived some particular specified thing continued to exist, so that, when entering into the contract they must have contemplated such continuing existence as the foundation of what was to be done; there, in the absence of any expressed or implied warranty that the thing shall exist, the contract is not to be construed as a positive contract, but as subject to an implied condition that the parties shall be excused in case, before breach, performance becomes impossible from the perishing of the thing without default of the contractor.

rule

There seems little doubt that this implication tends to further the great object of making the legal construction such as to fulfil the intention of those who enter into the contract. For in the course of affairs men in making such contracts in general would, if it were brought to their minds, say that there should be such a condition.

. . . [T]he principle is adopted in the Civil law as applicable to every obligation of which the subject is a certain thing. The general subject is treated of by POTHIER who in his Traité des Obligations," partie 3, chap 6, art. 3, §668, states the result to be that the debtor corporis certi is freed from his obligation when the thing has perished, neither by his act, nor his neglect, and before he is in default, unless by some stipulation be has taken on himself the risk of the particular misfortune which has occurred.

rule

Although the Civil law is not of itself an authority in an English Court, it affords great assistance in investigating the principles on which the law is grounded. And it seems to us that the common law authorities establish that in such a contract the same condition of the continued existence of the thing is implied by English law.

There is a class of contracts in which a person binds himself to do something which requires to be performed by him in person, and such promises, e.g. promises to marry, or promises to serve for a certain time, are never in practice qualified by an express exception of the death of the party; and therefore in such cases, the contract is in terms broken if the promisor dies before fulfillment. Yet it was very early determined that, if the performance is personal, the executors are not liable; *Hyde v. The Dean of Windsor* (Cro. Eliz. 552, 553). See 2 Wms. Exers. 1560, 5th ed., where a very apt illustration is given. "Thus," says the learned author: "if an author undertakes to compose a work, and dies before completing it, his executors are discharged from this contract: for the undertaking is merely personal in its nature, and, by the intervention of the contractor's death, has become impossible to be performed."

For this, he cites a dictum of Lord Lyndhurst, in *Marshall v. Broadhurst* (1 Tyr. 348, 349), and a case mentioned by Patteson J. in *Wentworth v. Cock* (10 A. & E. 42, 45-46). In *Hall v. Wright* (E. B. & E. 746, 749,) Crompton J., in his judgment, puts another case. "Where a contract depends upon personal skill, and the act of God renders it impossible, as, for instance, in the case of a painter employed to paint a picture who is struck blind, it may be that the performance might be excused."

It seems that, in these cases, the only ground on which the parties or their executors, can be excused from the consequences of the breach of the contract is that from the nature of the contract there is an implied condition of the continued existence of the life of the contractor, and, perhaps, in the case of the painter of his eyesight. In the instances just given, the person, the continued existence of whose life is necessary to the fulfilment of the contract, is himself the contractor, but that does not seem in itself to be necessary to the application of the principle; as is illustrated by the following example. In the ordinary form of an apprentice deed the apprentice binds himself in unqualified terms to "serve until the full end and term of seven years to be fully complete and ended," during which term it is covenanted that the apprentice his master "faithfully shall serve," and the father of the apprentice in equally unqualified terms binds himself for the performance by the apprentice of all and every covenant on his part. (See the form, 2 Chitty on Pleading, 370, 7th ed. by Greening.) It is undeniable that if the apprentice dies within the seven years, the covenant of the father that he shall perform his covenant to serve for seven years is not fulfilled, yet surely it cannot be that an action would be against the father, yet the only reason why it would not, is, that he is excused because of the apprentice's death.

These are instances where the implied condition is of the life of a human being, but there are others in which the same implication is made as to the continued existence of a thing. . . .

It may, we think, be safely asserted to be now English law, that in all contracts of loan of chattels or bailments if the performance of the promise of the borrower or bailee to return the things lent or bailed, becomes impossible because it has perished, this impossibility (if not arising from the fault of the borrower or bailee from some risk which he has taken upon himself) excuses the borrower or bailee from the performance of his promise to redeliver the chattel.

The great case of *Coggs v. Bernard* (1 Smith's L. C. 171, 5th ed.; 2 L. Raym. 909) is now the leading case on the law of bailments, and Lord Holt, in that case, referred so much to the Civil law that it might perhaps be thought that this principle was there derived direct from the civilians, and was not generally applicable in English law except in the case of bailments; but the case of *Williams v. Lloyd* (W. Jones, 179) above cited, shows that the same law had been already adopted by the English law as early as The Book of Assizes. The principle seems to us to be that, in contracts in which the performance depends on the continued existence of a given person or thing, a condition is implied that the impossibility of performance arising from the perishing of the person or thing shall excuse the performance.

In none of these cases is the promise in words other than positive, nor is there any express stipulation that the destruction of the person or thing shall excuse the performance; but that excuse is by law implied, because from the nature of the contract it is apparent that the parties contracted on the basis of the continued existence of the particular person or chattel. In the present case, looking at the whole contract, we find that the parties contracted on the basis of the continued existence of the Music Hall at the time when the concerts were to be given, that being essential to their performance. *reasoning*

We think, therefore, that, the Music Hall having ceased to exist, without fault of either party, both parties are excused, the plaintiffs from taking the gardens and paying the money, the defendants from performing their promise to give the use of the Hall and Gardens and other things. Consequently the rule must be absolute to enter the verdict for the defendants. *disposition*

Rule absolute.

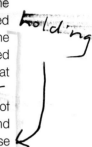

U.S. BANCORP EQUIPMENT FINANCE, INC.
v.
AMERIQUEST HOLDINGS LLC

U.S. District Court, District of Minnesota
2004 WL 2801601
2004

MONTGOMERY, J.

I. INTRODUCTION

On November 1, 2004, oral argument before the undersigned United States District Judge was heard on Plaintiff U.S. Bancorp Equipment Finance, Inc.'s ("USBEF") Motion for Summary Judgment. In its Complaint, USBEF seeks enforcement of loan agreements after alleged defaults by Defendants Ameriquest Holdings LLC ("Ameriquest"), Ananya Aviation LLC ("Ananya"), and Brad Gupta ("Gupta") (collectively, "Defendants"). For the reasons set forth below, Plaintiff's Motion is granted. *Summary J for P — disposition*

II. BACKGROUND[1]

In 1999, Brad Gupta formed Ameriquest Holdings LLC. Gupta and his brother-in-law are the sole shareholders of Ameriquest. In July 2000, Ameriquest purchased a Boeing 737 ("Ameriquest Airplane") from Bank of America Leasing and Capital. At the

---

1. For purposes of the instant Motion, the facts are viewed in the light most favorable to Defendants. *Ludwig v. Anderson*, 54 F.3d 465, 470 (8th Cir. 1995).

time of purchase, the plane was leased to U.S. Airways under a lease scheduled to expire in April 2003. In order to finance the plane, Ameriquest borrowed $3,858,000 from Firstar Equipment Finance ("Firstar"). The loan terms included quarterly payments during the life of the U.S. Airways lease, followed by a lump-sum "balloon" payment equal to the outstanding balance when the lease expired in April 2003. Ameriquest and Firstar entered into a Secured Loan Agreement which gave Firstar a security interest in the Ameriquest Airplane. The Secured Loan Agreement gave Firstar the right to repossess and sell the airplane in the event of default by Ameriquest. . . .

. . .

Following the closing of the above-described loans, USBEF acquired Firstar's rights under the relevant loan documents.

After the tragic events of September 11, 2001, all parties agree that the airline and airplane market was devastated. In August and September of 2002, Continental Airlines decided not to renew the leases on the Ananya Airplanes, and returned the aircraft to Ananya. Both planes were returned to Ananya in a damaged condition. Damages included an unserviceable engine and an inferior auxiliary power unit installed by Continental. Additionally, both airplanes required expensive inspections. Following the failure of Continental to renew the leases, Ananya did not make the balloon payment that came due in September 2002.

Meanwhile, U.S. Airways filed for bankruptcy following 9/11. As part of the bankruptcy proceedings, U.S. Airways terminated the lease and returned the Ameriquest Airplane to Ameriquest. U.S. Airways made its last lease payment in June 2002. Following the termination of the lease, Ameriquest failed to make its quarterly payments to USBEF, and also failed to make the balloon payment that came due in April 2003.

. . .

Ultimately, USBEF foreclosed on and sold the Ameriquest [airplane] for $450,000 [and] applied the [proceeds] . . . to the Ameriquest debt. . . .

After applying these payments, the principal balance on the Ameriquest note as of August 27, 2004 was $2,986,960.45, with $315,586.36 owed in interest. The interest on the Ameriquest note is accruing at the rate of $871.03 per day. . . .

. . .

3. Impossibility of Performance and *Force Majeure*

Defendants have . . . raised the defense of impossibility and *force majeure.* Under New York law, impossibility may be raised if one of two conditions is met: (1) the subject matter of the contract is destroyed; or (2) the means of performance is destroyed so as to make performance objectively impossible. *Kel Kim Corp. v. Central Markets, Inc.*, 519 N.E.2d 295, 296 (N.Y. 1987). However, "that performance should be excused only in extreme circumstances." Moreover, "financial difficulty or economic hardship, even to the extent of insolvency or bankruptcy," are not sufficient circumstances for a finding of impossibility. *407 East 61st Garage, Inc. v. Savoy Fifth Ave. Corp.*, 244 N.E.2d 37, 41 (N.Y. 1968).

Here, Defendants do not argue that the subject matter of the contract—the airplanes—was destroyed. Rather, Defendants contend performance was rendered impossible by the events of 9/11. Following 9/11, the airplane and airline market around the world suffered immense losses. Numerous airlines went bankrupt (including U.S. Airways), while other airlines simply ceased operations. While the Court is sympathetic to Defendants' plight, the crash of the airline and airplane industry does not rise to the level of impossibility demanded by New York law. Certainly, 9/11 radically depressed the market for airplanes. However, decreased value of collateral is not contemplated by New York law as an excuse for lack of performance based on impossibility. As New York courts have made plain, the fact that a contract proves to be unprofitable or onerous for one party does not excuse performance. *407 East 61st Garage*, 244 N.E.2d at 41; *Lowe v. Feldman*, 168 N.Y.S.2d 674, 685 (N.Y. Sup. 1957). Investments gone bad due to unforeseen market forces undoubtedly are also captured in this rubric.

. . .

Defendants also raise the defense of *force majeure*. However, for *force majeure* to apply under New York law, such a clause must be present in the contract which specifically covers the event in question. *Kel Kim*, 519 N.E.2d at 296-97. Here, the relevant loan agreements contain *force majeure* clauses, but only to protect USBEF from liability—not to protect Defendants. As a result, this defense cannot be employed by Defendants.

. . .

Based on the foregoing, and all the files, records and proceedings herein, IT IS HEREBY ORDERED that Plaintiff's Motion for Summary Judgment is GRANTED.

BUSH
v.
PROTRAVEL INTERNATIONAL, INC.

Civil Court, City of New York, Richmond County, New York
746 N.Y.S.2d 790
2002

Vitaliano, J.

Dreams of a honeymoon safari in East Africa dashed offers fresh evidence of how the terror attack on the World Trade Center of September 11, 2001 has shredded the lives of ordinary New Yorkers and has engendered still continuing reverberations in decisional law. What might have ordinarily warranted summary disposition in favor of the safari company and its travel agent, pinning on the traveler the economic burden of trip cancellation, cannot, in the wake of September 11th, be sustained here on their motion for summary judgment.

Defendant Taicoa Corporation, doing business as Micato Safaris ("Micato"), acknowledges that plaintiff Alexandra Bush contacted Micato about booking a safari. By its admission, Micato referred the plaintiff to defendant ProTravel International, Inc. ("ProTravel"), a retail travel agent, to arrange for a reservation on one of the various safaris offered by Micato. It is undisputed that, on or about May 8, 2001, the plaintiff booked an African safari travel package for herself and her fiancé through ProTravel with Micato. At that time, it is also undisputed, the plaintiff gave ProTravel an initial 20% deposit in the amount of $1,516.00. Micato admits that it received the plaintiff's deposit from ProTravel on May 15, 2001. The safari Alexandra Bush selected for husband to be and herself was scheduled to begin on November 14, 2001.

Sixty-four days before the safari's start, September 11, 2001, the world, as we knew it, came to an end. As a result of the attack on the World Trade Center, other terrorism alerts and airline scares, the plaintiff and her fiancé decided almost immediately to cancel their trip. Further, the plaintiff claims, she endeavored to notify ProTravel of her decision, but, as a result of the interruption of telephone service between Staten Island, where she had fled to safety, and Manhattan, where ProTravel maintained an office in Midtown, she was physically unable to communicate her cancellation order until September 27, 2001. ProTravel agrees that the plaintiff did contact it that day and avers it passed along her request to Micato orally and in writing. Micato acknowledged receiving a fax from ProTravel to that effect on October 4, 2001. Thereafter, when the defendants refused to return her deposit, Alexandra Bush sued in this action to get it back.

The defendants, by their Manhattan and Massachusetts counsel, now move for summary judgment dismissing this action. The Court notes that it has granted a separate motion permitting counsel from the Massachusetts firm of Rubin, Hay & Gould, P.C. to appear *pro hac vice* to argue this motion for summary judgment. In support of the motion, counsel have appeared for oral argument and submitted four affidavits and two memoranda of law. The Court notes that the second affidavit of Patricia Buffolano, dated June 7, 2002, and received by the Court on June 10, 2002, is clearly a late submission. Counsel appeared on the June 6, 2002 submission date and did not request an adjournment in order to submit further papers. Nevertheless, the Court has considered this affidavit in deciding the motion.

The defendants' motion hangs on a registration form. A copy of a completed form executed by Alexandra Bush was annexed to the moving affidavits of Joseph Traversa and Patricia Buffolano. Mr. Traversa, the employee of ProTravel who made the plaintiff's travel arrangements, states that the plaintiff completed and signed the form when she booked the safari on May 8, 2001. The form contained the following provision: "I confirm that I have read and agree to the Terms and Conditions as outlined in our brochure." Also annexed to the moving affidavits was an excerpt the defendants contend was in the "brochure" referenced in the registration form, and which the plaintiff claims she never received, setting forth Micato's cancellation policy for the safari booked by Ms. Bush. The policy imposes a $50 per person penalty for a cancellation occurring more than 60 days prior to departure. For a cancellation occurring between 30 and 60 days prior to departure, the traveler was subject to a penalty equal to 20% of the total retail tour rate. There is no disagreement that the deposit given by the plaintiff was in an amount equal to 20% of the tour rate.

With a departure date of November 14, 2001, for Alexandra Bush the days of moment under the cancellation policy were September 14, 2001 and October 15, 2001. A cancellation order given by her on or before September 14, 2001, the 61st day prior to departure, would have subjected her to, at worst, a $50 per person, *i.e.*, a $100 penalty. Any cancellation after that date but on or before October 15, 2001 would subject her to the greater 20% penalty under the cancellation policy. Using either the September 27, 2001 date Mr. Traversa admits ProTravel received Ms. Bush's notice of cancellation or the October 4, 2001 date Micato's general manager, Patricia Buffolano, claims in her affidavit that Micato received written confirmation of the cancellation from ProTravel, the plaintiff's trip cancellation came within the 30 to 60 day prior to departure window that would trigger a 20% penalty for cancellation. On the strength of those facts, neither defendant returned the deposit to Alexandra Bush and both now seek summary judgment dismissing her claim.

Without conceding that the cancellation policy the defendants advance as their sword and buckler is either valid or binding on her, Ms. Bush states in her affidavit submitted in opposition to the motion that, beginning on September 12, 2001 and continuing for days thereafter, she attempted to contact the travel agency and that due to difficulties with telephone lines, access to Manhattan and closures of its office, she was unable to speak to someone from ProTravel until September 27, 2001. All of the phone calls made by the plaintiff to ProTravel were placed from Staten Island. While ProTravel's reply affidavit protests that it was open for business from September 12th and onward and supplies phone records to show its phones were able to make and receive calls, no evidence is offered to dispute the plaintiff's claim that it was virtually impossible for many days after the terrorist attack to place a call from Staten Island if such call was transmitted via the telephone trunk lines in downtown Manhattan.

In any event, the defendants ultimately argue that all of the horror, heartbreak and hurdles for communications and commerce visited on Alexandra Bush and all New Yorkers in the aftermath of September 11th doesn't matter, for the thrust of their motion is that a contract is a contract, and that since the cancellation call was received, at best, 13 days late, the plaintiff is not entitled, as a matter of law, to her refund. In an equitable bolster to its position, the defendants also assert that Micato imposes the cancellation penalties to cover costs which it incurs in planning and preparing for a customer's safari. However, upon oral argument, defendants were unable to set forth what, if any, expenses had been incurred towards plaintiff's trip, nor when such expenses were incurred. Thereafter, the defendants submitted, in an untimely manner, the further affidavit of Patricia Buffolano, dated June 7, 2002 restating the contention that, prior to receiving notice that Ms. Bush wished to cancel her trip, Micato was required to pay certain expenses. The affidavit, nonetheless, is silent as to when these expenses, and more specifically, whether any such expenses were incurred on or before September 14, 2001, whether any were incurred between September 14 and September 27, 2001 or whether any were incurred during the one week delay between the time ProTravel received notification of the cancellation, September 27, 2001, and when Micato claims it received notification from ProTravel, October 4, 2001.

issue When the residue has been poured away, the issue distilled here is whether the attack on the World Trade Center and the civil upset of its aftermath in the days that immediately followed excuses Alexandra Bush's admittedly late notice of cancellation. More to the point, given that effective cancellation on or before September 14, 2001 would have absolved the plaintiff of the 20% cancellation penalty, does Ms. Bush's sworn statement that she attempted to phone her cancellation notice to ProTravel beginning on September 12, 2001 but did not get through until September 27, 2001 raise a triable issue of fact, which, if resolved in her favor, entitles her to relief from the cancellation penalty provision of the contract?

. . .

rule Though it is true that the black letter of the law establishes the rule that "once a party to a contract has made a promise, that party must perform or respond in damages for its failure, even when unforeseen circumstances make performance burdensome," *Kel Kim Corp. v. Central Markets, Inc.*, 70 N.Y.2d 900, 902, 524 N.Y.S.2d 384, 385, 519 N.E.2d 295 (1987), the rule is not an absolute. Where the "means of performance" have been nullified, making "performance objectively impossible," a party's performance under a contract will be excused. *Id.* at 902, 524 N.Y.S.2d at 385, 519 N.E.2d 295. See *Conversion Equities, Inc. v. Sherwood House Owners Corp.*, 151 App. Div. 2d 635, 636, 542 N.Y.S.2d 703, 705 (2d Dep't 1989).

D Counsel for the defendants at oral argument claimed to understand the difficulties encountered by literally every New Yorker in the wake of the disaster at the World Trade Center, but argue that those difficulties do not constitute a valid excuse for the failure of the plaintiff to cancel the safari before September 15, 2001. The delay until September 27, 2001, they contend, is inexcusable. Putting aside the sheer insensitivity of their argument, the argument fails to come to grips with Alexandra Bush's *P* sworn claim that the disaster in lower Manhattan, which was unforeseen, unforeseeable and, certainly, beyond her control, had effectively destroyed her ability and means to communicate a timely cancellation under the contract for safari travel she had booked through and with the defendants. To the point, Alexandra Bush claims she could not physically take the steps necessary to cancel on time. Micato and ProTravel, to the contrary, claim she was simply a traveler too skittish to travel *D* after September 11th, who wanted to stick the travel professionals she had retained with the bill for her faint heart. Should the defendants establish that to be the case to the satisfaction of the jury or at a bench trial, they will be entitled to judgment. See *Evanoski v. All Around Travel*, 178 Misc. 2d 693, 682 N.Y.S.2d 342 (App. T., 2d Dep't 1998). They certainly have not established that as a matter of law now.

P Furthermore, the plaintiff's claim of excuse because of the frustration of the means of performance is supported, underscored and punctuated by the official actions taken by civil authorities on September 11, 2001 and in the days that followed. On the day of the attack, a state of emergency had been declared by the Mayor of the City of New York, directing the New York City Commissioners of Police, Fire and Health and the Director of Emergency Management to "take whatever steps are necessary to preserve the public safety and to render all required and available assistance to protect the security, well-being and health of the residents of the City." *New York City Legislative Annual* at 355 (footnote omitted). Simultaneously, the Governor of the State of New York declared a State Disaster Emergency, directing state officials to "take all appropriate actions to . . . provide . . . assistance as necessary to protect the public health and safety." Executive Order of the Governor, 9 N.Y.C.R.R. §5.113 (2001) (footnote omitted).

. . .

Particularly on the days at the focal point of the argument here, September 12, 13 and 14, 2001, New York City was in the state of virtual lockdown with travel either forbidden altogether or severely restricted. Precedent is plentiful that contract performance is excused when unforeseeable government action makes such performance objectively impossible. See *A & S Transportation Co. v. County of Nassau*, 154 App. Div. 2d 456, 459, 546 N.Y.S.2d 109, 111 (2d Dep't 1989); *Metpath Inc. v. Birmingham Fire Ins. Co.*, 86 App. Div. 2d 407, 411-12, 449 N.Y.S.2d 986, 989 (1st Dep't 1982). Further, in the painful recognition of the obvious and extraordinary dimensions of the disaster that prevented the transaction of even the most time sensitive business during the days and weeks that followed the September 11th atrocities, the Governor even issued an executive order extending the statute of limitations for all civil actions in every court of our state for a period well-beyond the times Alexandra Bush claims to have communicated her cancellation and Micato acknowledges it received it. Executive Order of the Governor, 9 N.Y.C.R.R. §5.113.7 (2001) (footnote omitted). In such light, to even hint that Alexandra Bush has failed to raise a triable issue of fact by her argument that the doctrine of impossibility excuses her late cancellation of the safari she booked through ProTravel with Micato borders on the frivolous.

. . .

It is not hyperbole to suggest that on September 11, 2001, and the days that immediately followed, the City of New York was on a wartime footing, dealing with wartime conditions. The continental United States had seen nothing like it since the Civil War and, inflicted by a foreign foe, not since the War of 1812. Accordingly, it is entirely appropriate for this Court to consider and follow wartime precedents which developed the law of temporary impossibility. Stated succinctly, where a supervening act creates a temporary impossibility, particularly of brief duration, the impossibility may be viewed as merely excusing performance until it subsequently becomes possible to perform rather than excusing performance altogether. See generally *Modern Status of the Rules Regarding Impossibility of Performance in Action for Breach of Contract*, 84 A.L.R.2d 12 §14(a) (1962).

The law of temporary and/or partial impossibility flows from the theory that when a promisor has obligated himself to perform certain acts, which, when taken together are impossible, the promisor should not be excused from being "called upon to perform insofar as he is able to do so." *Miller v. Vanderlip*, 285 N.Y. 116, 124, 33 N.E.2d 51, 55 (1941). The First Department's opinion in the World War I era case of *Erdreich v. Zimmermann*, 190 App. Div. 443, 179 N.Y.S. 829 (1st Dep't 1920), is extremely instructive. In *Erdreich*, the plaintiff purchased German war bonds, which, at the time of purchase on December 14, 1916, was entirely lawful since the United States had not yet entered the conflict. Because of the war, however, the bonds could not be delivered due to a naval blockade. In April 1917, after a state of war had been declared between the United States and Germany, the plaintiff demanded his money back for the defendant seller's failure to deliver the bonds. Almost two years later, with the bonds essentially worthless, the plaintiff sued for rescission and return of his purchase payment. Appellate Term held that the delivery of the bonds, though legally contracted for, would have been unlawful under wartime rules and, therefore, the contract should have been rescinded for impossibility. The Appellate Division reversed, holding that "at most, performance of [the] contract was suspended during the existence of hostilities," at 452, 179 N.Y.S. at 835, and the performance, which had been temporarily excused for impossibility during hostilities, was now required. The plaintiff was entitled, therefore, to his worthless bonds, but not the return of his purchase payment. This holding is in harmony with even earlier precedents acknowledging the fog of war and its upset of civil society:

> Where performance can be had without contravening the laws of war, the existence of the contract is not imperiled and, even if performance is impossible, the contract may still, when partly executed, be preserved by in grafting necessary qualifications upon it, or suspending its impossible provisions, i.e., physical impossibility to cancel timely, if the contract can be saved while the war lasts, it should be. *Mutual Life Ins. Co. v. Hillyard*, 37 N.J. Law 444, 18 Am. Rep. 741.

So too here, if Alexandra Bush can establish objective impossibility of performance at trial, she is entitled to, at minimum, a reasonable suspension of her contractual obligation to timely cancel, if not outright excuse of her untimely cancellation.

Clearly, the plaintiff has raised, in any event, sufficient material issues of fact concerning both her inability to cancel by September 15, 2001 the safari she had booked and the reasonableness of her cancellation on September 27, 2001, all as a result of the terrorist attack on the World Trade Center, the damage the attack caused to communications and transportation in the City of New York and the actions of government in declaring and enforcing a state of emergency in the city and beyond. Moreover, the failure of the defendants to establish that they sustained any loss whatsoever on account of the plaintiff's failure to act in the 13 day intervening period between September 14 and September 27, 2001 further supports the reasonableness of the plaintiff's late cancellation as well as the Court's determination that triable issues of fact are present.

In the instant matter, the Court finds that the plaintiff has raised sufficient material issues of fact concerning her inability to cancel the contract by September 15, 2001, which would, if established, provide a defense to the argument of the defendants, so as to warrant denial of this motion. Accordingly, for the reasons stated in the opinion of the Court, the motion of defendants ProTravel and Micato for summary judgment dismissing this action is denied in its entirety.

Problems

1. Navy Fire. RNJ Interstate Corporation entered into a contract with the Navy to renovate a building at the Naval Air Station in Glenview, Illinois. The contract provided for the government to make progress payments to RNJ during the renovation and included a "Permits and Responsibilities" clause, which provided:

> The Contractor shall, without additional expense to the Government, be responsible for obtaining any necessary licenses and permits, and for complying with any Federal, State, and municipal laws, codes, and regulations applicable to the performance of the work. The Contractor shall also be responsible for all damages to persons or property that occur as a result of the Contractor's fault or negligence, and shall take proper safety and health precautions to protect the work, the workers, the public, and the property of others. The Contractor shall also be responsible for all materials delivered and work performed until completion and acceptance of the entire work, except for any completed unit or work which may have been accepted under the contract.

RNJ began work in September 1991, and the government made progress payments to RNJ as the work progressed. RNJ had completed more than half of the project when the building was completely destroyed by fire. RNJ demanded payment for the work completed prior to the fire (less the progress payments already made), and the government refused to pay. The parties agreed that the fire was the fault of neither and that the government had not accepted any portion of RNJ's work at the time of the blaze. In a lawsuit brought by RNJ, which party should prevail?

2. The Consumptive Fiancé. In the early 1850s, Mr. Wright and Miss Hall became engaged to be married. Prior to the appointed date for the nuptials, Wright broke off the engagement, and Hall sued for breach of contract. Wright responded to Hall's complaint by pleading that, after the two had become engaged, he was stricken with consumption, did and continued to suffer from frequent and severe bleeding from his lungs, and was unable to fulfill the commitments of marriage without placing his life in grave danger. Should Hall be entitled to judgment on the pleadings, or would the facts alleged by Wright, if proven, excuse his obligation to marry?

3. Nuclear Power. In 1966, Florida Light & Power Company (FL&P) hired Westinghouse Electric Corporation to construct a nuclear power plant. The contract gave FL&P the option, which could be exercised prior to the plant going into operation, to impose on Westinghouse the obligation to "remove the irradiated [i.e., spent] fuel [after processing] and dispose of it as Westinghouse sees fit."

In 1957, to spur development of civilian nuclear power, the U.S. Government had issued a formal assurance that, if commercial reprocessing facilities did not become available, the government would provide reprocessing of spent nuclear fuel at government facilities. In 1966, when the contract between FL&P and Westinghouse was signed, the government was doing just this, and commercial reprocessing facilities were about to come on line. The parties' expectation at that time was that, depending on FL&P's choice, either FL&P or Westinghouse would have the reactor's spent fuel reprocessed, and the economics of reprocessing were taken into account when setting the price at which Westinghouse would provide FL&P with nuclear power under the contract.

In 1971, FL&P provided notice of its decision to exercise its option, thus requiring Westinghouse to dispose of the spent fuel. By 1975, however, increasing environmental regulation and concerns about possible environmental hazards associated with the reprocessing of spent nuclear fuel drove commercial reprocessors out of business, and the government stopped providing reprocessing services. Policymakers began to favor the previously discounted option of providing long-term storage for spent nuclear fuel rather than reprocessing the spent fuel. Westinghouse estimated that it would have earned an $18 to $20 million profit by reprocessing the FL&P reactor's spent fuel, as it had contemplated, whereas obtaining long-term storage would cost it over $80 million, assuming that the government was to establish or certify a long-term storage facility.

Westinghouse refused to take responsibility for removing the spent fuel from the reactor. FL&P sued for breach of contract, and Westinghouse defended by invoking common law impossibility and commercial impracticability under the UCC. Which side should prevail?

3. Frustration of Purpose

When a supervening event renders performance difficult for sellers of goods or services, they may attempt to invoke the doctrine of impracticability. Although buyers also might argue impracticability in unusual cases—*U.S. Bancorp Equipment Finance, Inc. v. Ameriquest Holdings LLC* is one such example—unanticipated, supervening events are more likely to reduce the value of executing the contract to buyers than to render performance itself unusually difficult. Thus, although courts occasionally confuse the two doctrines, the proper claim for buyers is usually one of frustration of purpose: specifically, that their duty to perform should be discharged because the purpose for which they entered into an agreement to procure a good or service no longer exists.

As should be familiar by now, the central issue in frustration cases is whether the risk of the unanticipated event that disappointed a party's expectations is implicitly allocated to the adversely affected party by the circumstances in which the contract was formed (if not by express language). According to the language of the Restatement, discharge of the duty is proper if the non-occurrence of the event in question was a "basic assumption" of the contract unless the language or circumstances indicate otherwise, and the claimant bears no fault for the occurrence of the event. Rest. (2d) Contracts §265.

As in impracticability cases, the following question arises: when is an assumption about the state of the world sufficiently basic to a contract that the risk of non-occurrence is not implicitly allocated to the party who is harmed by that non-occurrence, thus excusing that party's duty? A person who rents an apartment from which to view the coronation parade of the new King of England would almost certainly not be excused from paying if it were to rain on parade day, thus reducing the pleasure of viewing the parade, even if both landlord and tenant assumed that sun was a near certainty at that time of year. An electric utility would not be excused from purchasing coal at the price fixed by contract because a more desirable energy source became available. A company that engaged a cruise ship would not be excused from its obligations if its employees decided they would prefer to vacation on land. The following set of cases—*Krell v. Henry, Northern Indiana Public Service Company v. Carbon County Coal Company*, and *Sub-Zero Freezer Company v. Cunard Line Limited*—assesses whether the outcomes should differ if the King becomes ill, regulators place limitations on the electric utility, or a terrorist attack spooks the company's employees.

KRELL
v.
HENRY

Court of Appeal
[1900-1903] All E.R. Rep. 20
1903

VAUGHAN WILLIAMS, L.J.

The real question in this case is the extent of the application in English law of the principle of the Roman law which has been adopted and acted on in many English decisions, and notably in *Taylor v. Caldwell*. That case at least makes it clear that "where, from the nature of the contract, it appears that the parties must from the beginning have known that it could not be fulfilled unless, when the time for the fulfilment of the contract arrived, some particular specified thing continued to exist, so that when entering into the contract they must have contemplated such continuing existence as the foundation of what was to be done; there, in the absence of any express or implied warranty that the thing shall exist, the contract is not to be construed as a positive contract, but as subject to an implied condition that the parties shall be excused in case, before breach, performance becomes impossible from the perishing of the thing without default of the contractor."

Thus far it is clear that the principle of the Roman law has been introduced into the English law. The doubt in the present case arises as to how far this principle extends. The Roman law dealt with *obligationes de certo corpore*. Whatever may have been the limits of the Roman law, *Nickoll* and *Knight v. Ashton, Edridge & Co.* makes it plain that the English law applies the principle not only to cases where the performance of the contract becomes impossible by the cessation of existence of the thing which is the subject-matter of the contract, but also to cases where the event which renders the contract incapable of performance is the cessation or non-existence of an express condition or state of things, going to the root of the contract, and essential to its performance. It is said, on the one side, that the specified thing, state of things, or condition the continued existence of which is necessary for the fulfilment of the contract, so that the parties entering into the contract must have contemplated the continued existence of that thing, condition, or state of things as the foundation of what was to be done under the contract, is limited to things which are either the subject-matter of the contract, or a condition or state of things, present or anticipated, which are expressly mentioned in the contract. But, on the other side, it is said that the condition or state of things need not be expressly specified, but that it is sufficient if such condition or state of thing, clearly appears by extrinsic evidence to have been assumed by the parties to be the foundation or basis of the contract and the event which causes the impossibility is of such a character that it cannot reasonably be supposed to have been in the contemplation of the contracting parties when the contract was made. In such a case the contracting parties will not be held bound by general words which, though large enough to include, were not used with reference to a possibility of a particular event rendering performance of the contract impossible.

I do not think that the principle of the civil law as introduced into the English law is limited to cases in which the event causing the impossibility of performance is the destruction or non-existence of some thing which is the subject-matter of the contract or of some condition or state of things expressly specified as a condition of it. I think that you first have to ascertain, not necessarily from the terms of the contract, but if necessary from necessary inferences, drawn from surrounding circumstances recognised by both contracting parties, what is the substance of the contract, and then to ask the question whether that substantial contract needs for its foundation the assumption of the existence of a particular state of things. If it does, this will limit the operation of the general words, and in such case if the contract becomes impossible of performance by reason of the non-existence of the state of things assumed by both contracting parties, as the foundation of the contract, there will be no breach of the contract thus limited.

What are the facts of the present case? The contract is contained in two letters of 20 June 1902, which passed between the defendant and the plaintiff's agent, Mr. Cecil Bisgood. These letters do not mention the coronation, but speak merely of the taking of Mr. Krell's chambers, or, rather, of the use of them, in the daytime of 26 and 27 June 1902, for the sum of 75 pounds, 25 pounds then paid, balance 50 pounds to be paid on the 24th. But the affidavits, which by agreement between the parties are to be taken as stating the facts of the case, show that the plaintiff exhibited on his premises, third floor, 56A, Pall Mall, an announcement to the effect that windows to view the royal coronation processions were to be let, and that the defendant was induced by that announcement to apply to the housekeeper on the premises, who said that the owner was willing to let the suite of rooms for the purpose of seeing the royal procession for both days, but not nights, of 26 and 27 June. In my judgment, the use of the rooms was let and taken for the purpose of seeing the royal processions. It was not a demise of the rooms or even an agreement to let and take the rooms. It was a licence to use rooms for a particular purpose and none other. And in my judgment the taking place of those processions on the days proclaimed along the proclaimed route, which passed 56A,

Pall Mall, was regarded by both contracting parties as the foundation of the contract. I think that it cannot reasonably be supposed to have been in the contemplation of the contracting parties, when the contract was made, that the coronation would not be held on the proclaimed days, or the processions not take place on those days along the proclaimed route; and I think that the words imposing on the defendant the obligation to accept and pay for the use of the rooms for the named days, although general and unconditional, were not used with reference to the possibility of the particular contingency which afterwards occurred.

It was suggested in the course of the argument that if the occurrence, on the proclaimed days, of the coronation and the processions in this case were the foundation of the contract, and if the general words are thereby limited or qualified, so that in the event of the non-occurrence of the coronation and processions along the proclaimed route they would discharge both parties from further performance of the contract, it would follow that if a cabman was engaged to take someone to Epsom on Derby-day at a suitable enhanced price for such a journey, both parties to the contract would be discharged in the contingency of the race at Epsom for some reason becoming impossible, but I do not think this follows, for I do not think that in the cab case the happening of the race would be the foundation of the contract. No doubt the purpose of the engager was to go to see the Derby, and that the price was proportionately high; but the cab had no special qualifications for the purpose which led to the selection of the cab for this particular occasion. Any other cab would have done as well. Moreover, I think that, under the cab contract, the hirer, even if the race went off, could have said: "Drive me to Epsom, I will pay you the agreed sum, you have nothing to do with the purpose for which I hired the cab"—and that if the cabman refused he would have been guilty of a breach of contract, there being nothing to qualify his promise to drive the hirer to Epsom on a particular day, whereas, in the case of the coronation, there is not merely the purpose of the hirer to see the coronation processions, but it is the coronation processions and the relative position of the rooms which is the basis of the contract as much for the lessor as the hirer; and I think that if the King, before the coronation day and after the contract, had died, the hirer could not have insisted on having the rooms on the days named. It could not in the cab case be reasonably said that seeing the Derby race was the foundation of the contract, as viewing the processions was of the licence in this case, whereas, in the present case, where the rooms were offered and taken, by reason of their peculiar suitability from the position of the rooms for a view of the coronation processions, surely the view of the coronation processions was the foundation of the contract, which is a very different thing from the purpose of the man who engaged the cab—viz, to see the race—being held to be the foundation of the contract.

Each case must be judged by its own circumstances. In each case one must ask oneself, first: What, having regard to all the circumstances, was the foundation of the contract?; secondly: Was the performance of the contract prevented?; and thirdly: Was the event which prevented the performance of the contract of such a character that it cannot reasonably be said to have been in the contemplation of the parties at the date of the contract? If all these questions are answered in the affirmative (as I think they should be in this case) I think both parties are discharged from further performance of the contract. I think that the coronation processions were the foundation of this contract, and that the non-happening of them prevented the performance of the contract; and, secondly, I think that the non-happening of the processions, to use the words of Sir James Hannen in *Baily v. De Crespigny* (LR 4 QB at p 185) was an event "of such a character that it cannot reasonably be supposed to have been in the contemplation of the contracting parties when the contract was made, and that they are not to be held bound by general words which, though large enough to include, were not used with reference to the possibility of the particular contingency which afterwards happened."

The test seems to be, whether the event which causes the impossibility was or might have been anticipated and guarded against. It seems difficult to say, in a case where both parties anticipate the happening of an event, which anticipation in the foundation of the contract, that either party must be taken to have anticipated, and ought to have guarded against, the event which prevented the performance of the contract. . . .

NORTHERN INDIANA PUBLIC SERVICE CO.
v.
CARBON COUNTY COAL CO.
U.S. Court of Appeals, Seventh Circuit
799 F.2d 265
1986

POSNER, J.

These appeals bring before us various facets of a dispute between Northern Indiana Public Service Company (NIPSCO), an electric utility in Indiana, and Carbon County Coal Company, a partnership that until recently owned and operated a coal mine in Wyoming. In 1978 NIPSCO and Carbon County signed a contract whereby Carbon County agreed to sell and NIPSCO to buy approximately 1.5 million tons of coal every year for 20 years, at a price of $24 a ton subject to various provisions for escalation which by 1985 had driven the price up to $44 a ton.

NIPSCO's rates are regulated by the Indiana Public Service Commission. In 1983 NIPSCO requested permission to raise its rates to reflect increased fuel charges. Some customers of NIPSCO opposed the increase on the ground that NIPSCO could reduce its overall costs by buying more electrical power from neighboring utilities for resale to its customers and producing less of its own power. Although the Commission granted the requested increase, it directed NIPSCO, in orders issued in December 1983 and February 1984 (the "economy purchase orders"), to make a good faith effort to find, and wherever possible buy from, utilities that would sell electricity to it at prices lower than its costs of internal generation. The Commission added ominously that "the adverse effects of entering into long-term coal supply contracts which do not allow for renegotiation and are not requirement contracts, is a burden which must rest squarely on the shoulders of NIPSCO management." Actually the contract with Carbon County did provide for renegotiation of the contract price—but one-way renegotiation in favor of Carbon County; the price fixed in the contract (as adjusted from time to time in accordance with the escalator provisions) was a floor. And the contract was indeed not a requirements contract: it specified the exact amount of coal that NIPSCO must take over the 20 years during which the contract was to remain in effect. NIPSCO was eager to have an assured supply of low-sulphur coal and was therefore willing to guarantee both price and quantity.

Unfortunately for NIPSCO, however, as things turned out it was indeed able to buy electricity at prices below the costs of generating electricity from coal bought under the contract with Carbon County; and because of the "economy purchase orders," of which it had not sought judicial review, NIPSCO could not expect to be allowed by the Public Service Commission to recover in its electrical rates the costs of buying coal from Carbon County. NIPSCO therefore decided to stop accepting coal deliveries from Carbon County, at least for the time being; and on April 24, 1985, it brought this diversity suit against Carbon County in a federal district court in Indiana, seeking a declaration that it was excused from its obligations under the contract either permanently or at least until the economy purchase orders ceased preventing it from passing on the costs of the contract to its ratepayers. In support of this position it argued that . . . NIPSCO's performance was excused or suspended—either under the contract's *force majeure* clause or under the doctrines of frustration or impossibility—by reason of the economy purchase orders. [The court's decision on Carbon County's request for specific performance of the contract is included in Chapter 6, Remedies, *infra*.—EDS.]

. . .

The contract permits NIPSCO to stop taking delivery of coal "for any cause beyond [its] reasonable control . . . including but not limited to . . . orders or acts of civil . . . authority . . . which wholly or partly prevent . . . the utilizing . . . of the coal." This is what is known as a *force majeure* clause. See, e.g., *Northern Illinois Gas Co. v. Energy Coop., Inc.*, 122 Ill. App. 3d 940, 949-52, 461 N.E.2d 1049, 1057-58, 78 Ill. Dec. 215 (1984). NIPSCO argues that the Indiana Public Service Commission's "economy purchase orders" prevented it, in whole or part, from using the coal that it had agreed to buy, and it complains that the district judge instructed the jury incorrectly on the meaning and application of the clause. The complaint about the instructions is immaterial. The judge should not have put the issue of *force majeure* to the jury. It is evident that the clause was not triggered by the orders.

All that those orders do is tell NIPSCO it will not be allowed to pass on fuel costs to its ratepayers in the form of higher rates if it can buy electricity cheaper than it can generate electricity internally using Carbon County's coal. Such an order does not "prevent," whether wholly or in part, NIPSCO from using the coal; it just prevents NIPSCO from shifting the burden of its improvidence or bad luck in having incorrectly forecasted its fuel needs to the backs of the hapless ratepayers. The purpose of public utility regulation is to provide a substitute for competition in markets (such as the market for electricity) that are naturally monopolistic. Suppose the market for electricity were fully competitive, and unregulated. Then if NIPSCO signed a long-term fixed-price fixed-quantity contract to buy coal, and during the life of the contract competing electrical companies were able to produce and sell electricity at prices below the cost to NIPSCO of producing electricity from that coal, NIPSCO would have to swallow the excess cost of the coal. It could not raise its electricity prices in order to pass on the excess cost to its consumers, because if it did they would buy electricity at lower prices from NIPSCO's competitors. By signing the kind of contract it did, NIPSCO gambled that fuel costs would rise rather than fall over the life of the contract; for if they rose then the contract price would give it an advantage over its (hypothetical) competitors who would have to buy fuel at the current market price. If such a gamble fails, the result is not *force majeure*.

This is all the clearer when we consider that the contract price was actually fixed just on the downside; it put a floor under the price NIPSCO had to pay, but the escalator provisions allowed the actual contract prices to rise above the floor, and they did. This underscores the gamble NIPSCO took in signing the contract. It committed itself to paying a price at or above a fixed minimum and to taking a fixed quantity at that price. It was willing to make this commitment to secure an assured supply of low-sulphur coal, but the risk it took was that the market price of coal or substitute fuels would fall. A *force majeure* clause is not intended to buffer a party against the normal risks of a contract. The normal risk of a fixed-price contract is that the market price will change. If it rises, the buyer gains at the expense of the seller (except insofar as escalator provisions give the seller some protection); if it falls, as here, the seller gains at the expense of the buyer. The whole purpose of a fixed-price contract is to allocate risk in this way. A *force majeure* clause interpreted to excuse the buyer from the consequences of the risk he expressly assumed would nullify a central term of the contract.

The Indiana Public Service Commission is a surrogate for the forces of competition, and the economy fuel orders are a device for simulating the effects in a competitive market of a drop in input prices. The orders say to NIPSCO, in effect: "With fuel costs dropping, and thus reducing the costs of electricity to utilities not burdened by long-term fixed-price contracts, you had better substitute those utilities' electricity for your own when their prices are lower than your cost of internal generation. In a freely competitive market consumers would make that substitution; if you do not do so, don't expect to be allowed to pass on your inflated fuel costs to those consumers." Admittedly the comparison between competition and regulation is not exact. In an unregulated market, if fuel costs skyrocketed NIPSCO would have a capital gain from its contract (assuming the escalator provisions did not operate to raise the contract price by the full amount of the increase in fuel costs, a matter that would depend on the cause of the increase). This is because its competitors, facing higher fuel costs, would try to raise their prices for electricity, thus enabling NIPSCO to raise its price, or expand its output, or both, and thereby increase its profits. The chance of this "windfall" gain offsets, on an ex ante (before the fact) basis, the chance of a windfall loss if fuel costs drop, though NIPSCO it appears was seeking a secure source of low-sulphur coal rather than a chance for windfall gains. If as is likely the Public Service Commission would require NIPSCO to pass on any capital gain from an advantageous contract to the ratepayers (which is another reason for thinking NIPSCO wasn't after windfall gains—it would not, in all likelihood, have been allowed to keep them), then it ought to allow NIPSCO to pass on to them some of the capital loss from a disadvantageous contract—provided that the contract, when made, was prudent. Maybe it was not; maybe the risk that NIPSCO took was excessive. But all this was a matter between NIPSCO and the Public Service Commission, and NIPSCO did not seek judicial review of the economy purchase orders.

If the Commission had ordered NIPSCO to close a plant because of a safety or pollution hazard, we would have a true case of *force majeure*. As a regulated firm NIPSCO is subject to more extensive controls than unregulated firms and it therefore wanted and got a broadly worded *force majeure* clause that would protect it fully (hence the reference to partial effects) against government actions that impeded its using the coal. But as the only thing the Commission did was prevent NIPSCO from using its monopoly position to make consumers bear the risk that NIPSCO assumed when it signed a long-term fixed-price fuel contract, NIPSCO cannot complain of *force majeure*; the risk that has come to pass was one that NIPSCO voluntarily assumed when it signed the contract.

The district judge refused to submit NIPSCO's defenses of impracticability and frustration to the jury, ruling that Indiana law does not allow a buyer to claim impracticability and does not recognize the defense of frustration. Some background (on which see Farnsworth, Contracts §§9.5-9.7 (1982)) may help make these rulings intelligible. In the early common law a contractual undertaking unconditional in terms was not excused merely because something had happened (such as an invasion, the passage of a law, or a natural disaster) that prevented the undertaking. See *Paradine v. Jane*, Aleyn 26, 82 Eng. Rep. 897 (K.B. 1647). Excuses had to be written into the contract; this is the origin of *force majeure* clauses. Later it came to be recognized that negotiating parties cannot anticipate all the contingencies that may arise in the performance of the contract; a legitimate judicial function in contract cases is to interpolate terms to govern remote contingencies—terms the parties would have agreed on explicitly if they had had the time and foresight to make advance provision for every possible contingency in performance. Later still, it was recognized that physical impossibility was irrelevant, or at least inconclusive; a promisor might want his promise to be unconditional, not because he thought he had superhuman powers but because he could insure against the risk of nonperformance better than the promisee, or obtain a substitute performance more easily than the promisee. See *Field Container Corp. v. ICC*, 712 F.2d 250, 257 (7th Cir. 1983); Holmes, The Common Law 300 (1881). Thus the proper question in an "impossibility" case is not whether the promisor could not have performed his undertaking but whether his nonperformance should be excused because the parties, if they had thought about the matter, would have wanted to assign the risk of the contingency that made performance impossible or uneconomical to the promisor or to the promisee; if to the latter, the promisor is excused.

Section 2-615 of the Uniform Commercial Code takes this approach. It provides that "delay in delivery . . . by a seller . . . is not a breach of his duty under a contract for sale if performance as agreed has been made impracticable by the occurrence of a contingency the non-occurrence of which was a basic assumption on which the contract was made. . . ." Performance on schedule need not be impossible, only infeasible—provided that the event which made it infeasible was not a risk that the promisor had assumed. Notice, however, that the only type of promisor referred to is a seller; there is no suggestion that a buyer's performance might be excused by reason of impracticability. The reason is largely semantic. Ordinarily all the buyer has to do in order to perform his side of the bargain is pay, and while one can think of all sorts of reasons why, when the time came to pay, the buyer might not have the money, rarely would the seller have intended to assume the risk that the buyer might, whether through improvidence or bad luck, be unable to pay for the seller's goods or services. To deal with the rare case where the buyer or (more broadly) the paying party might have a good excuse based on some unforeseen change in circumstances, a new rubric was thought necessary, different from "impossibility" (the common law term) or "impracticability" (the Code term, picked up in Restatement (Second) of Contracts §261 (1979)), and it received the name "frustration." Rarely is it impracticable or impossible for the payor to pay; but if something has happened to make the performance for which he would be paying worthless to him, an excuse for not paying, analogous to impracticability or impossibility, may be proper. See Restatement, *supra*, §265, comment a.

. . .

Since impossibility and related doctrines are devices for shifting risk in accordance with the parties' presumed intentions, which are to minimize the costs of contract performance, one of which is the disutility created by risk, they have no place when the contract explicitly assigns a particular risk to one party or the other. As we have already noted, a fixed-price contract is an explicit assignment of the risk of market price increases to the seller and the risk of market price decreases to the buyer, and the assignment of the latter risk to the buyer is even clearer where, as in this case, the contract places a floor under price but allows for escalation. If, as is also the case here, the buyer forecasts the market incorrectly and therefore finds himself locked into a disadvantageous contract, he has only himself to blame and so cannot shift the risk back to the seller by invoking impossibility or related doctrines. See Farnsworth, *supra*, at 680 and n. 18; White & Summers Handbook of the Law Under the Uniform Commercial Code 133 (2d ed. 1980). It does not matter that it is an act of government that may have made the contract less advantageous to one party. See, e.g., *Connick v. Teachers Ins. & Annuity Ass'n*, 784 F.2d 1018, 1022 (9th Cir. 1986); *Waegemann v. Montgomery Ward & Co.*, 713 F.2d 452, 454 (9th Cir. 1983). Government these days is a pervasive factor in the economy and among the risks that a fixed-price contract allocates between the parties is that of a price change induced by one of government's manifold interventions in the economy. Since "the very purpose of a fixed price agreement is to place the risk of increased costs on the promisor (and the risk of decreased costs on the promisee)," the fact that costs decrease steeply (which is in effect what happened here—the cost of generating electricity turned out to be lower than NIPSCO thought when it signed the fixed-price contract with Carbon County) cannot allow the buyer to walk away from the contract. *In re Westinghouse Electric Corp. Uranium Contracts Litigation*, 517 F. Supp. 440, 453 (E.D. Va. 1981); cf. *Neal-Cooper Grain Co. v. Texas Gulf Sulphur Co.*, 508 F.2d 283, 293 (7th Cir. 1974). . . .

SUB-ZERO FREEZER CO.
v.
CUNARD LINE LTD.

U.S. District Court, Western District of Wisconsin
2002 WL 32357103
2002

φ

CRABB, J.

. . .

ALLEGATIONS OF FACT

Plaintiff Sub-Zero Freezer Co., Inc. is a Wisconsin corporation with its principal place of business in Madison, Wisconsin. Defendant Cunard Line Limited is a Bahamian corporation with its principal place of business in Miami, Florida.

On May 3, 1999, plaintiff signed a Space Allotment Agreement with Cunard. The agreement provided for a seven-night cruise in the Eastern Mediterranean Ocean aboard a vessel named the "Seabourn Spirit." The "Seabourn Spirit" is owned and operated by a subsidiary of defendant named Seabourn Cruise Line, a foreign corporation with its principal place of business in Miami, Florida. The trip was scheduled to depart on October 2, 2001 from Piraeus, Greece, and to disembark in Istanbul, Turkey on October 9, 2001, with intermediate ports of call in Santorini, Rhodes, Bodrum and Kusadasi.

The agreement was for the entire vessel and specified a per-night hire price of $120,000, with a base price for the cruise of $840,000. After the addition of per-passenger and beverage charges, the total price of the cruise was $892,000. As specified in Schedule V of the agreement, plaintiff prepaid the entire cruise price of $892,000. It made the last installment payment of the prepayment to defendant on July 2, 2001.

The Space Allotment Agreement includes a provision (Clause 9) relating to a default by the contractor (in this case, plaintiff), under which the entire cruise hire price becomes payable to defendant if plaintiff cancels the agreement. Clause 10 (Force Majeure) of the agreement relieves defendant of any liability for failure to perform in the event of acts of God, war, fire, acts or threats of terrorism, or order or restraint by government authorities, among other things. Clause 26.1 is the integration clause. It incorporates into the agreement "[a]ll prior understandings and agreements heretofore entered into between [defendant] and [plaintiff] whether written or oral." Further it provides that "[n]o course of dealing between the parties shall operate as a waiver by either party . . . of any right of such party."

The cruise was arranged with the assistance of Burkhalter Travel & Cruise Shoppe, a travel agency located in Madison, Wisconsin. Before entering into the agreement, plaintiff asked defendant, through Burkhalter, how defendant would treat plaintiff in regard to refunds or rescheduling if there was an outbreak of terrorism or war at the time of the cruise. In response, defendant's director of charter sales at the time, Bruce Setoff, told Burkhalter that defendant would never put its vessels or guests in danger and would work with plaintiff to reschedule the location or dates of the cruise as necessary to assure safety and to satisfy the safety concerns of plaintiff's guests. Alternatively, Setoff said, defendant would give plaintiff a refund.

On April 29, 1999, Setoff sent a letter to plaintiff memorializing his response to plaintiff's inquiries. He stated in relevant part:

> It goes without saying that [defendant] would never go to an area where we have been officially advised not to go, as we would never place our guests, crew and vessel in harm's way.
>
> If we are advised not to go to a scheduled port, we would always work with our charterers to move (if operationally possible) to another port for the better of all involved. As you can see, there are quite a few behind the scenes professionals who monitor all security aspects of our operation.
>
> It should be noted that a charterer may decide on their own to cancel or reschedule their cruise, *but our agreement does not allow for any release of financial responsibility unless we have been officially directed by the government and can't perform.* (Emphasis added.)

On May 3, 1999, plaintiff signed the agreement with defendant for the cruise. Plaintiff completed the prepayment and the cruise was scheduled to occur until the intervention of the terrorist attacks destroying the World Trade Center in New York City and damaging the Pentagon in Washington, D.C. Several days after the attacks, the United States declared a "war on terrorism." The United States government mobilized substantial resources in and around the eastern Mediterranean and Middle East and elsewhere, and placed its military units on a high state of alert and battle readiness. During the scheduled time of the cruise the United States launched a major military action against Afghanistan.

In response to the September 11 attacks, the United States Department of State issued formal warnings to Americans abroad and to those who were considering traveling abroad, instructing them to exercise heightened caution and vigilance while traveling abroad and urging that Americans avoid such travel. However, the United States government did not issue any orders requiring defendant to cancel its October 2, 2001 cruise.

In the three-week period between the September 11 attacks and the scheduled cruise date, many of plaintiff's employees, guests and their spouses informed plaintiff that they would not go on the cruise because they believed it would be unsafe. Plaintiff and Burkhalter made repeated efforts to persuade defendant to work with plaintiff to reschedule the cruise dates or to refund some or all of the prepayment. Defendant refused to make any adjustment to the date or location of the cruise. In addition, defendant informed plaintiff that it would retain the entire amount of plaintiff's prepayment whether or not the cruise took place.

Plaintiff notified defendant formally before the scheduled departure date that it was cancelling the cruise and demanded that defendant mitigate its losses and provide plaintiff a return of money equal to the amount of cost savings effected by cancellation. Defendant refused to remit any refund or cost savings. Defendant relied upon clauses 9, 10, and 26.1 of the agreement to support its refusal to refund any of the money paid by plaintiff.

OPINION

A motion to dismiss under Fed. R. Civ. P. 12(b)(6) will be granted only if "it is clear that no relief could be granted under any set of facts that could be proved consistent with the allegations" of the complaint. *Cook v. Winfrey*, 141 F.3d 322, 327 (7th Cir. 1998) (citing *Hishon v. King & Spalding*, 467 U.S. 69, 73, 104 S. Ct. 2229, 81 L. Ed. 2d 59 (1984)). On a motion to dismiss for failure to state a claim under Rule 12(b)(6), the court must accept as true all well-pleaded allegations of the complaint and draw all inferences in favor of the non-movant. *Levenstein v. Salafasky*, 164 F.3d 345, 347 (7th Cir. 1998).

. . .

In its third claim, plaintiff argues that its performance under the contract was excused under the doctrines of impossibility of performance and commercial frustration. In arguing that its "performance" should be excused because of the unforeseeable attacks on September 11 and their aftermath, plaintiff misconstrues the performance that was required of it under the contract. The contract between the parties designated the duties of each party. Plaintiff's obligation was to pay the agreed-upon charter fee. The contract did not require that plaintiff's employees and guests had to embark on the cruise. Therefore, plaintiff's performance was complete when it made its last installment payment on July 2, 2001. Defendant stood ready to hold up its end of the bargain and provide the cruise.

Under Florida law, business entities are expected to cover foreseeable risks in their contract. *See, e.g., Home Design Center v. County Appliances of Naples*, 563 So. 2d 767, 770 (Fla. Dist. Ct. App. 1990) (holding that defense of frustration of purpose is not available for difficulties that are "basic business risks" unless substantial competent evidence establishes that risks were not foreseeable). *See also American Aviation v. Aero-Flight Serv.*, 712 So. 2d 809, 811 (Fla. Dist. Ct. App. 1998) (when plaintiff could have shifted business risk by contract and chose not to, it should not be allowed to accomplish same effect by claiming impossibility of performance resulting from foreseeable risk).

It is understandable that plaintiff's dealers were reluctant to cruise the eastern Mediterranean in the immediate aftermath of September 11. It does not follow, however, that plaintiff can rewrite the contract to insert provisions it failed to bargain for in the original agreement. The agreement states clearly that defendant is entitled to the entire Cruise Hire Price if plaintiff cancelled the cruise. Plaintiff argues correctly that it was not possible to predict the September 11 attacks, but fails to acknowledge that it anticipated the possibility of war or terrorist activity. Indeed, in its briefs it talks at length about its negotiations with defendant when it had planned a cruise that was to take place just after the Gulf War began in 1991. After that experience, plaintiff can hardly argue that the possibility of war or terrorism was not foreseeable. Less foreseeable perhaps was what happened here: a terrorism attack on the United States; military retaliation without an order restraining pleasure cruises; reluctant guests; and a refusal by defendant to change the cruise dates or itinerary. That the parties might not have foreseen the exact nature of the problem, however, does not make the risk unforeseeable under the law. Plaintiff knew of the risk of war and terrorism and knew that the agreement as written provided no recourse except in certain specified circumstances. . . .

Problems

1. A Car Dealer in Wartime. In 1941, prior to the entry of the United States into World War II, Harold Murphy leased a lot in Los Angeles from Caroline Lloyd for the purpose of selling new cars. After the country's entry into the war, wartime industrial production shifted toward military purposes, and the government restricted sales of cars to the small percentage of the population possessing preferential ratings of A-1-j or higher. These events made selling cars difficult and drastically reduced the profitability of Murphy's business. Murphy repudiated the lease and defended against Lloyd's subsequent lawsuit by arguing frustration of purpose. Is Murphy excused, or must he continue to pay Lloyd the lease rate for the lot?

2. The Bankrupt Football League. In 1974, the Birmingham Stallions of the World Football League signed Dallas Cowboys football star Larry Rayfield Wright to a contract obligating Wright to play for the Stallions for three years beginning in 1977. The Stallions paid Wright a $75,000 signing bonus at the time, with the rest of Wright's substantial salary to be paid between 1977 and 1979.

After the contract was signed but before Wright joined the team, the World Football League went bankrupt and ceased to exist. The Stallions sued Wright for the return of the $75,000 signing bonus. Wright argued that he already provided consideration for the bonus by signing the contract, by forbearing from negotiating with other teams, and by allowing the Stallions to publicize his affiliation with the team. Wright also counterclaimed for the salary specified in the contract, which the Stallions never paid. Who should prevail?

3. Concrete Barriers. The Commonwealth of Massachusetts hired general contractor J.J. Paonessa Company for a highway improvement project. The contract included a standard provision allowing the government to eliminate (and not pay for) portions of work from the original job specifications that it later determined were unnecessary. Paonessa subcontracted to Chase Precast Corporation the job of supplying concrete barriers for the road median. There was no similar provision in the subcontract covering changes the government might later make to the project.

Shortly after construction began, residents complained that concrete medians were being used to replace grassy strips between the two sides of the highway and filed a lawsuit against the Commonwealth to stop this improvement. Anticipating that the Commonwealth would issue a change order eliminating the concrete barriers, Paonessa told Chase to immediately stop building them. Paonessa paid Chase the contract price for the barriers already produced but refused to pay more. Chase sued and claimed that Paonessa breached its contract, entitling Chase to its expected profits on the remaining medians. Should Chase prevail?

4. A Change in the Law. Charles Boley was charged with manufacturing methamphetamine, which was a "level 1" drug felony under Kansas law. He entered into a plea agreement with the state that called for Boley to plead guilty and for the prosecutor to request the court to depart downward from the sentencing guidelines for level 1 drug felonies and sentence Boley to 48 months in prison. Boley understood that the court could choose to ignore the prosecutor's recommendation and that the plea was not contingent on the court actually sentencing him to 48 months. Boley pled guilty, the prosecutor recommended the downward departure, and the court did sentence Boley to 48 months.

Shortly before the plea agreement was signed, an individual (McAdams) in an unrelated case challenged his sentence for manufacturing methamphetamine on the ground that this crime should be classified as a lower level felony, meaning that conviction would carry a shorter sentence. Ultimately, McAdams prevailed. Based on the *McAdams* precedent, Boley challenged his sentence as based on the wrong felony classification, and the court of appeals ruled in his favor and remanded his case for a new, shorter sentence, expected to be 17 to 19 months. The prosecutor then sought to rescind the plea agreement on the ground of frustration of purpose. How should the court rule on the prosecutor's motion?

Chapter 6

Remedies

A breach of contract is defined as a party's failure to perform a duty that is due. Rest. (2d) Contracts §235. When a breach occurs, the non-breaching party is entitled to a remedy. The nature of that remedy is the subject of this chapter.

Remedies can be fashioned to serve different goals, including compensating the injured party or punishing the responsible party. As Section A describes, contract law remedies almost always seek to compensate the non-breaching party, with punishment limited to a narrowly circumscribed set of circumstances. As compensation for a breach of contract, courts can issue an injunction ordering a breaching party to perform its contractual obligations ("specific performance") or can require a breaching party to pay money in lieu of and as a substitute for performance ("damages"). Traditionally, contract law has favored damages, but injunctive relief is available in a broad range of circumstances in which damages are "inadequate." Section B considers the doctrinal contours of the specific-substitutional divide.

Parties injured by a breach of contract are entitled to damages adequate to satisfy the "expectation" that they had for contract performance, as explored in Section C. The financial award must be sufficient to make the non-breaching party indifferent as between the promised performance and damages for the breach of that performance, or at least sufficient to allow the non-breaching party to pay for a substitute performance that makes it indifferent. This goal of contract law is undermined to some degree—although perhaps justifiably—by the doctrinal requirements that the non-breaching party be treated as if she took reasonable steps to mitigate her damages (Section D), that the breaching party not be charged for damages not foreseeable at the time of contracting (Section E), and that the non-breaching party be entitled to recover only damages she can prove with reasonable certainty (Section F). Section G considers the extent to which parties may stipulate as part of their contract what damages are due in the event of breach, essentially opting out of these remedies doctrines.

A. PUNITIVE DAMAGES

Oliver Wendell Holmes, Jr. famously wrote in "The Path of the Law" that "[t]he duty to keep a contract at common law means a prediction that you must pay damages if you do not keep it—and nothing else." 10 Harv. L. Rev. 457, 462 (1897). The implication of this statement, with which most contemporary contract law scholars would agree, is that failing to perform a contractual duty should not invite condemnation, but only an obligation on the part of the breaching party to compensate the non-breaching party for harm caused by the breach. This view of breach as a morally neutral act is consistent with one of contract law's most clearly articulated bright-line rules, as stated in the first case in this chapter, *White v. Benkowski*: punitive (sometimes called "exemplary") damages—which by definition are intended to punish the defendant rather than to compensate the plaintiff—are not recoverable in actions for breach of contract. See Rest. (2d) Contracts §355.

As is true of many bright-line rules, exceptions to the general prohibition on punitive damages exist. *Delzer v. United Bank of Bismarck* and *Freeman & Mills, Inc. v. Belcher Oil* provide examples of situations in which courts have challenged the view that there is no moral distinction between performance and breach, resulting predictably in cracks in the edifice of the no-punitive-damages rule.

WHITE
v.
BENKOWSKI

Supreme Court of Wisconsin
155 N.W.2d 74
1967

This case involves a neighborhood squabble between two adjacent property owners.

Prior to November 28, 1962, Virgil and Gwynneth White, the plaintiffs, were desirous of purchasing a home in Oak Creek. Unfortunately, the particular home that the Whites were interested in was without a water supply. Despite this fact, the Whites purchased the home.

The adjacent home was owned and occupied by Paul and Ruth Benkowski, the defendants. The Benkowskis had a well in their yard which had piping that connected with the Whites' home.

On November 28, 1962, the Whites and Benkowskis entered into a written agreement wherein the Benkowskis promised to supply water to the White home for ten years or until an earlier date when either water was supplied by the municipality, the well became inadequate, or the Whites drilled their own well. The Whites promised to pay $3 a month for the water and one-half the cost of any future repairs or maintenance that the Benkowski well might require. As part of the transaction, but not included in the written agreement, the Whites gave the Benkowskis $400 which was used to purchase and install a new pump and an additional tank that would increase the capacity of the well.

Initially, the relationship between the new neighbors was friendly. With the passing of time, however, their relationship deteriorated and the neighbors actually became hostile. In 1964, the water supply, which was controlled by the Benkowskis, was intermittently shut off. Mrs. White kept a record of the dates and durations that her water supply was not operative. Her record showed that the water was shut off on the following occasions:

(1) March 5, 1964, from 7:10 P.M. to 7:25 P.M.
(2) March 9, 1964, from 3:40 P.M. to 4:00 P.M.
(3) March 11, 1964 from 6:00 P.M. to 6:15 P.M.
(4) June 10, 1964, from 6:20 P.M. to 7:03 P.M.

The record also discloses that the water was shut off completely or partially for varying lengths of time on July 1, 6, 7, and 17, 1964, and on November 25, 1964.

Mr. Benkowski claimed that the water was shut off either to allow accumulated sand in the pipes to settle or to remind the Whites that their use of the water was excessive. Mr. White claimed that the Benkowskis breached their contract by shutting off the water.

Following the date when the water was last shut off (November 25, 1964), the Whites commenced an action to recover compensatory and punitive damages for an alleged violation of the agreement to supply water. A jury trial was held. Apparently it was agreed by counsel that for purposes of the trial plaintiffs' case was based upon an alleged deliberate violation of the contract consisting of turning off the water at the times specified in the plaintiffs' complaint. Accordingly, in the special verdict the jury was asked:

QUESTION 1: Did the defendants maliciously, vindictively or wantonly shut off the water supply of the plaintiffs for the purpose of harassing the plaintiffs?

The jury was also asked:

QUESTION 2: If you answered Question 1 "Yes," then answer this question:

(a) What compensatory damages did the plaintiffs suffer?
(b) What punitive damages should be assessed?

The jury returned a verdict which found that the Benkowskis maliciously shut off the Whites' water supply for harassment purposes. Compensatory damages were set at $10 and punitive damages at $2,000. On motions after verdict, the court reduced the compensatory award to $1 and [voided the punitive damages award].

Judgment for plaintiffs of $1 was entered and they appeal.

WILKIE, J.

Two issues are raised on this appeal.

1. Was the trial court correct in reducing the award of compensatory damages from $10 to $1?

2. Are punitive damages available in actions for breach of contract? *issue*

REDUCTION OF JURY AWARD

The evidence of damage adduced during the trial here was that the water supply had been shut off during several short periods. Three incidents of inconvenience resulting from these shut-offs were detailed by the plaintiffs. Mrs. White testified that the lack of water in the bathroom on one occasion caused an odor and that on two other occasions she was forced to take her children to a neighbor's home to bathe them. Based on this evidence, the court instructed the jury that:

> * * * in an action for a breach of contract the plaintiff is entitled to such damages as shall have been sustained by him which resulted naturally and directly from the breach if you find that the defendants did in fact breach the contract. Such damages include pecuniary loss and inconvenience suffered as a natural result of the breach and are called compensatory damages. In this case the plaintiffs have proved no pecuniary damages which you or the Court could compute. In a situation where there has been a breach of contract which you find to have damaged the plaintiff but for which the plaintiffs have proven no actual damages, the plaintiffs may recover nominal damages.
>
> By nominal damages is meant trivial—a trivial sum of money.

Plaintiffs did not object to this instruction. In the trial court's decision on motions after verdict it states that the court so instructed the jury because, based on the fact that the plaintiffs paid for services they did not receive, their loss in proportion to the contract rate was approximately 25 cents. This rationale indicates that the court disregarded or overlooked Mrs. White's testimony of inconvenience. In viewing the evidence most favorable to the plaintiffs, there was some injury. The plaintiffs are not required to ascertain their damages with mathematical precision, but rather the trier of fact must set damages at a reasonable amount. Notwithstanding this instruction, the jury set the plaintiffs' damages at $10. The court was in error in reducing that amount to $1.

The jury finding of $10 in actual damages, though small, takes it out of the mere nominal status. The award is predicated on an actual injury. This was not the situation present in Sunderman v. Warnken. *Sunderman* was a wrongful entry action by a tenant against his landlord. No actual injury could be shown by the mere fact that the landlord entered the tenant's apartment, therefore damages were nominal and no punitory award could be made. Here there was credible evidence which showed inconvenience and thus actual injury, and the jury's finding as to compensatory damages should be reinstated.

PUNITIVE DAMAGES

"If a man shall steal an ox, or a sheep, and kill it, or sell it; he shall restore five oxen for an ox, and four sheep for a sheep." Exodus 22:1.

Over one hundred years ago this court held that, under proper circumstances, a plaintiff was entitled to recover exemplary or punitive damages. . . .

In Wisconsin compensatory damages are given to make whole the damage or injury suffered by the injured party. On the other hand, punitive damages are given "on the basis of punishment to the injured party not because he has been injured, which injury has been compensated with compensatory damages, but to punish the wrongdoer for his malice and to deter others from like conduct." [Malco, Inc. v. Midwest Aluminum Sales, 14 Wis. 2d 57, 66, 109 N.W.2d 516, 521 (1961).]

Thus we reach the question of whether the plaintiffs are entitled to punitive damages for a breach of the water agreement.

The overwhelming weight of authority supports the proposition that punitive damages are not recoverable in actions for breach of contract. In Chitty on Contracts, the author states that the right to receive punitive damages for breach of contract is now confined to the single case of damages for breach of a promise to marry.

Simpson states: "Although damages in excess of compensation for loss are in some instances permitted in tort actions by way of punishment * * * in contract actions the damages recoverable are limited to compensation for pecuniary loss sustained by the breach." Simpson, Contracts (2d ed. hornbook series), p. 394, sec. 195.

Corbin states that as a general rule punitive damages are not recoverable for breach of contract. 5 Corbin, Contracts, p.438, sec. 1077.

. . .

Persuasive authority from other jurisdictions supports the proposition (without exception) that punitive damages are not available in breach of contract actions. This is true even if the breach, as in the instant case, is willful.

Although it is well recognized that breach of a contractual duty may be a tort, in such situations the contract creates the relation out of which grows the duty to use care in the performance of a responsibility prescribed by the contract. Not so here. No tort was pleaded or proved.

Reversed in part by reinstating the jury verdict relating to compensatory damages and otherwise affirmed. Costs to appellant.

DELZER
v.
UNITED BANK OF BISMARCK
Supreme Court of North Dakota
559 N.W.2d 531
1997

MESCHKE, J.

Ray Delzer and Betty Jean Delzer . . . ranched near Bismarck. In 1979, Delzers and United Bank entered into a loan agreement for Delzers to pledge all of their assets and their son's equipment as collateral for repayment of money to be loaned by

United Bank. Delzers contend United Bank orally agreed to lend them $300,000—an operating loan of $150,000, to be followed by additional loans totaling $150,000 for the purchase of cattle. Delzers executed a promissory note for $150,000, and the Bank advanced that amount. The Bank never advanced any funds to purchase cattle. As a result, Delzers contend, they were unable to pay their debts, they lost their ranch when the holder of the first mortgage foreclosed, and they lost all of the other assets pledged as security for the United Bank loan.

Delzers sued United Bank. . . . The jury verdict found that (1) United Bank breached an "oral contract to lend $150,000 to [Delzers] for the purchase of cattle as part of an agreement to loan the total sum of $300,000"; and (2) "United Bank willfully deceived the Delzers by promising the Delzers $150,000 for cattle when United Bank had no intention of lending Delzers an additional $150,000 to purchase cattle." The jury awarded no damages for United Bank's breach of contract, awarded damages of $538,000 for its deceit, and awarded exemplary damages of $3,000,000.

United Bank moved for judgment as a matter of law on the deceit claim or, alternatively, for a new trial. . . . The court entered a judgment of dismissal, and Delzers appealed.

. . .

When someone fraudulently induces another to enter into a contract by making a promise with no intention of performing it, that conduct is actionable fraud. *Las Palmas Assoc. v. Las Palmas Center Assocs.*, 235 Cal. App. 3d 1220, 1 Cal. Rptr. 2d 301, 310 (1991). The law recognizes that fraud has such an adverse effect on commercial transactions that punitive damages "may be awarded where a defendant fraudulently induces the plaintiff to enter into a contract." *Id.* 1 Cal. Rptr. 2d at 311. As *Foster v. Dwire*, 51 N.D. 581, 199 N.W. 1017, 1021 (1924), explained, "[t]he real gist of the fraud in such a case is not the breach of the agreement to perform, but the fraudulent intent of the promisor and the false representation of an existing intention to perform, where such intent is in fact nonexistent."

Delzers' contract claim is, essentially, based upon the following elements: (1) When United Bank made Delzers a $150,000 operating loan, the Bank also promised to loan them an additional $150,000 for the purchase of cattle; (2) in reliance on that promise, Delzers pledged all of their assets and their son's equipment as collateral; (3) United Bank breached the contract by failing to loan the $150,000 for the purchase of cattle; and (4) Delzers were injured by the Bank's breach of the contract. Delzers' deceit claim is based upon the same elements as the contract claim, plus the additional element that when United Bank promised to loan Delzers an additional $150,000 for the purchase of cattle, the Bank did not intend to perform its promise.[3] That is an "additional, independent fact[ ] not connected to the manner of the breach of contract." *Delzer III*, 527 N.W.2d at 654. United Bank's promise to loan money for the purchase of cattle, made without any intention of performing it,

---

3. Kenneth Reno, Chief Executive Officer of United Bank, testified that on November 1, 1979, when Delzers executed the loan documents, United Bank did not "intend to provide the Delzers with money for cattle."

was "[t]ortious conduct . . . exist[ing] independently of the breach of contract." *Pioneer Fuels*, 474 N.W.2d at 710. . . .

We conclude that the trial court erred in granting United Bank judgment as a matter of law on Delzers' deceit and punitive damages claims. . . .

FREEMAN & MILLS, INC.
v.
BELCHER OIL CO.

Supreme Court of California
11 Cal. 4th 85
1995

3

LUCAS, C.J.

We granted review in this case to resolve some of the widespread confusion that has arisen regarding the application of our opinion in *Seaman's Direct Buying Service, Inc. v. Standard Oil Co.* (1984) 36 Cal. 3d 752 [206 Cal. Rptr. 354, 686 P.2d 1158] (*Seaman's*). We held in that case that a tort cause of action might lie "when, in addition to breaching the contract, [defendant] seeks to shield itself from liability by denying, in bad faith and without probable cause, that the contract exists." (*Id.* at p. 769.)

. . .

I. FACTS

We first review the underlying facts, taken largely from the Court of Appeal opinion herein. In June 1987, defendant Belcher Oil Company (Belcher Oil) retained the law firm of Morgan, Lewis & Bockius (Morgan) to defend it in a Florida lawsuit. Pursuant to a letter of understanding signed by Belcher Oil's general counsel (William Dunker) and a Morgan partner (Donald Smaltz), Belcher Oil was to pay for costs incurred on its behalf, including fees for accountants. In February 1988, after first obtaining Dunker's express authorization, Smaltz hired plaintiff, the accounting firm of Freeman & Mills, Incorporated (Freeman and Mills), to provide a financial analysis and litigation support for Belcher Oil in the Florida lawsuit.

. . .

Freeman & Mills billed Morgan, but no payment was forthcoming. Freeman & Mills then billed Belcher Oil directly and, for about a year, sent monthly statements and regularly called Bowman about the bill, but no payment was forthcoming. In August 1989, Smaltz finally told Freeman & Mills that Belcher Oil refused to pay their bill. . . .

Ultimately, Freeman & Mills filed this action against Belcher Oil, alleging (in its second amended complaint) causes of action for breach of contract, "bad faith denial of contract," and quantum meruit. . . .

The jury returned its first phase verdict. On Freeman & Mills's breach of contract claim, the jury found that Belcher Oil had authorized Morgan to retain Freeman & Mills on Belcher Oil's behalf, that Freeman & Mills had performed its obligations under the contract, that Belcher Oil had breached the contract, and that the amount of damages suffered by Freeman & Mills was $25,000. The jury also answered affirmatively the questions about whether Belcher Oil had denied the existence of the contract and had acted with oppression, fraud, or malice. Thereafter, the jury returned its verdict awarding $477,538.13 in punitive damages and judgment was entered consistent with the jury's verdicts.

. . .

II. THE *SEAMAN'S* DECISION

The tort of bad faith "denial of contract" was established in a per curiam opinion in *Seaman's, supra*, 36 Cal. 3d 752. These were the facts before the court in that case: In 1971, Seaman's Direct Buying Service, a small marine fueling station in Eureka, wanted to expand its operation by developing a marine fuel dealership in conjunction with a new marina under development by the City of Eureka. When Seaman's approached the city about a long-term lease of a large parcel of land in the marina, the city required Seaman's to obtain a binding commitment from an oil supplier. To that end, Seaman's negotiated with several companies and, by 1972, reached a tentative agreement with Standard Oil Company of California.

Both Seaman's and Standard Oil signed a letter of intent setting forth the basic terms of their arrangement, but that letter was subject to government approval of the contract, continued approval of Seaman's credit status, and future agreement on specific arrangements. Seaman's showed the letter to the city and, shortly thereafter, signed a 40-year lease with the city. (*Seaman's, supra*, 36 Cal. 3d at pp. 759-760.)

Shortly thereafter, an oil shortage dramatically reduced the available supplies of oil and, in November 1973, Standard Oil told Seaman's that new federal regulations requiring allocation of petroleum products to those that had been customers since 1972 precluded its execution of a new dealership agreement. In response, Seaman's obtained an exemption from the appropriate federal agency. Standard Oil appealed and persuaded the agency to reverse the order, but Seaman's eventually had the exemption reinstated contingent on a court determination that a valid contract existed between the parties. (36 Cal. 3d at pp. 760-761.)

Seaman's then asked Standard Oil to stipulate to the existence of a contract, stating that a refusal would force it to discontinue operations. Standard Oil's representative refused the request, telling Seaman's, "See you in court." Seaman's business collapsed and it sued Standard Oil for damages on four theories—breach of contract, fraud, breach of the implied covenant of good faith and fair dealing, and interference with Seaman's contractual relationship with the city. (36 Cal. 3d at pp. 761-762.)

The case was tried to a jury, which returned its verdicts in favor of Seaman's on all theories except fraud, awarding compensatory and punitive damages. Standard

Oil appealed. (36 Cal. 3d at p. 762.) We considered "whether, and under what circumstances, a breach of the implied covenant of good faith and fair dealing in a commercial contract may give rise to an action in tort." (*Id.* at p. 767.) For purposes of completeness, we quote from *Seaman's* at some length:

> It is well settled that, in California, the law implies in *every* contract a covenant of good faith and fair dealing. [Citations.] Broadly stated, that covenant requires that neither party do anything which will deprive the other of the benefits of the agreement. . . .
>
> . . . In holding that a tort action is available for breach of the covenant in an insurance contract, we have emphasized the "special relationship" between insurer and insured, characterized by elements of public interest, adhesion, and fiduciary responsibility. [Citation.] No doubt there are other relationships with similar characteristics and deserving of similar legal treatment.
>
> . . .
>
> For the purposes of this case it is unnecessary to decide the broad question which Seaman's poses. Indeed, it is not even necessary to predicate liability on a breach of the implied covenant. It is sufficient to recognize that *a party to a contract may incur tort remedies when, in addition to breaching the contract, it seeks to shield itself from liability by denying, in bad faith and without probable cause, that the contract exists.* [Italics added.] . . .

. . .

V. *SEAMAN'S* SHOULD BE OVERRULED

As previously indicated, the *Seaman's* decision has generated uniform confusion and uncertainty regarding its scope and application, and widespread doubt about the necessity or desirability of its holding. These doubts and criticisms, express or implied, in decisions from this state and from other state and federal courts, echoed by the generally adverse scholarly comment cited above, convince us that *Seaman's* should be overruled in favor of a general rule precluding tort recovery for noninsurance contract breach, at least in the absence of violation of "an independent duty arising from principles of tort law" (*Applied Equipment, supra*, 7 Cal. 4th at p. 515) other than the bad faith denial of the existence of, or liability under, the breached contract.

As set forth above, the critics stress, among other factors favoring *Seaman's* abrogation, the confusion and uncertainty accompanying the decision, the need for stability and predictability in commercial affairs, the potential for excessive tort damages, and the preference for legislative rather than judicial action in this area.

Even if we were unimpressed by the nearly unanimous criticism leveled at *Seaman's*, on reconsideration the analytical defects in the opinion have become apparent. It seems anomalous to characterize as "tortious" the bad faith denial of the existence of a contract, while treating as "contractual" the bad faith denial of liability or responsibility under an acknowledged contract. In both cases, the breaching party has acted in bad faith and, accordingly, has presumably committed acts offensive to "accepted notions of business ethics." (*Seaman's, supra*, 36 Cal. 3d at p. 770.) Yet to include bad faith denials of liability within *Seaman's* scope could potentially convert every contract breach into a tort. Nor would limiting *Seaman's* tort to incidents involving "stonewalling" adequately narrow its potential scope. Such conduct by the breaching party, essentially telling the promisee, "See you in court," could incidentally accompany *every* breach of contract.

For all the foregoing reasons, we conclude that *Seaman's* should be overruled. We emphasize that nothing in this opinion should be read as affecting the existing precedent governing enforcement of the implied covenant in insurance cases. Further, nothing we say here would prevent the Legislature from creating additional civil remedies for noninsurance contract breach, including such measures as providing litigation costs and attorney fees in certain aggravated cases, or assessing increased compensatory damages covering lost profits and other losses attributable to the breach, as well as restoration of the *Seaman's* holding if the Legislature deems that course appropriate. . . .

VII. CONCLUSION

The judgment of the Court of Appeal, reversing the trial court's judgment in plaintiff's favor and remanding the case for a retrial limited to the issue of damages under plaintiff's breach of contract cause of action, and for judgment in favor of defendant on plaintiff's bad faith denial of contract cause of action, is affirmed.

Mosk, J. (concurring and dissenting)

I concur in the judgment. I disagree, however, with the majority's conclusion that *Seaman's Direct Buying Service, Inc. v. Standard Oil Co.* (1984) 36 Cal. 3d 752 [206 Cal. Rptr. 354, 686 P.2d 1158] (*Seaman's*) was wrongly decided. Although in retrospect I believe its holding was too broad, our task, both for the sake of sound public policy and stare decisis, is to clarify rather than repudiate that holding.

. . .

The notion that a breach of contract might be tortious causes conceptual difficulty because of the fundamental difference between the objectives of contract and tort law. " ' " [Whereas] [c]ontract actions are created to protect the interest in having promises performed," "[t]ort actions are created to protect the interest in freedom from various kinds of harm. The duties of conduct which give rise to them are imposed by law, and are based primarily on social policy, not necessarily based upon the will or intention of the parties. . . ." ' " (*Applied Equipment Corp. v. Litton Saudi Arabia Ltd.* (1994) 7 Cal. 4th 503, 515 [28 Cal. Rptr. 2d 475, 869 P.2d 454] (*Applied Equipment Corp.*), quoting *Tameny v. Atlantic Richfield Co.* (1980) 27 Cal. 3d 167, 176 [164 Cal. Rptr. 839, 610 P.2d 1330, 9 A.L.R.4th 314].)

This difference in purpose has its greatest practical significance in the differing types of damages available under the two bodies of law. "Contract damages are generally limited to those within the contemplation of the parties when the contract was entered into or at least reasonably foreseeable by them at that time; consequential damages beyond the expectations of the parties are not recoverable." (*Applied*

Equipment Corp., supra, 7 Cal. 4th at p. 515.) Damages for emotional distress and mental suffering, as well as punitive damages, are also generally not recoverable. (*Id.* at p. 516.) "This limitation on available damages serves to encourage contractual relations and commercial activity by enabling parties to estimate in advance the financial risks of their enterprise." (*Id.* at p. 515.) "In contrast, tort damages are awarded to compensate the victim for injury suffered. [Citation.] 'For the breach of an obligation not arising from contract, the measure of damages . . . is the amount which will compensate for all the detriment proximately caused thereby, whether it could have been anticipated or not. (Civ. Code, §3333.)'" (*Applied Equipment Corp., supra*, 7 Cal. 4th at p. 516.) Both emotional distress damages and punitive damages are, under the proper circumstances, available to the tort victim.

Tort and contract law also differ in the moral significance that each places on intentional injury. Whereas an intentional tort is seen as reprehensible—the deliberate or reckless harming of another—the intentional breach of contract has come to be viewed as a morally neutral act, as exemplified in Justice Holmes's remark that "[t]he duty to keep a contract at common law means a prediction that you must pay damages if you do not keep it—and nothing else." (Holmes, *The Path of the Law* (1897) 10 Harv. L. Rev. 457, 462.) This amoral view is supported by the economic insight that an intentional breach of contract may create a net benefit to society. The efficient breach of contract occurs when the gain to the breaching party exceeds the loss to the party suffering the breach, allowing the movement of resources to their more optimal use. (See Posner, Economic Analysis of Law (1986) pp. 107-108.) Contract law must be careful "not to exceed compensatory damages if it doesn't want to deter efficient breaches." (*Id.* at p. 108.)

But while the purposes behind contract and tort law are distinct, the boundary line between the two areas of the law is neither clear nor fixed. As Justice Holmes also observed, "the distinction between tort and breaches of contract, and especially between the remedies for the two, is not found ready made." (Holmes, The Common Law (1881) p. 13.) Courts have long permitted a party to a contract to seek tort remedies if behavior constituting a contract breach also violates some recognized tort duty. The courts "have extended the tort liability for misfeasance to virtually every type of contract where defective performance may injure the promisee. An attorney or an abstractor examining a title, a physician treating a patient, a surveyor, an agent collecting a note or lending money or settling a claim, or a liability insurer defending a suit, all have been held liable in tort for their negligence. . . . The principle which seems to have emerged from the decisions in the United States is that there will be liability in tort for misperformance of a contract whenever there would be liability for gratuitous performance without the contract—which is to say, whenever such misperformance involves a foreseeable, unreasonable risk of harm to the interests of the plaintiff." (Prosser & Keeton on Torts (5th ed. 1984) Tort and Contract, pp. 660-661, fns. omitted.) Stated another way, " '[c]onduct which merely is a breach of contract is not a tort, but the contract may establish a relationship demanding the exercise of proper care and acts and omissions in performance may give rise to tort liability.' " (*Groseth Intern., Inc. v. Tenneco, Inc.* (S.D. 1981) 440 N.W.2d 276, 279.)

Nor are the rules that determine whether the action will sound in tort or contract, or both, clear-cut. When the breach of contract also involves physical injury to the promisee, or the destruction of tangible property, as opposed to damage to purely economic interests, then the action will generally sound in tort. Thus, a manufacturer that sells defective automobiles may be liable to an automobile dealer in contract for delivery of nonconforming goods, but will be liable in tort if one of the nonconforming automobiles leads to an accident resulting in physical injury. But society also imposes tort duties to protect purely economic interests between contracting parties—such as the duty of care imposed on accountants for malpractice (see *Lindner v. Barlow, Davis & Wood* (1962) 210 Cal. App. 2d 660, 665 [27 Cal. Rptr. 101]), or on banks for wrongfully dishonoring checks (see *Weaver v. Bank of America* (1953) 59 Cal. 2d 428, 431 [30 Cal. Rptr. 4, 380 P.2d 644])—as well as the recognition of intentional torts such as promissory fraud. The complete failure to perform a contractual obligation generally sounds in contract, but once a contractual obligation has begun, a failure to perform which injures the promisee may sometimes sound in tort. (Prosser & Keeton on Torts, *supra*, pp. 661-662.) Perhaps the most reliable manner to differentiate between actions that are purely contract breaches and those that are also tort violations is the following abstract rule: courts will generally enforce the breach of a contractual promise through contract law, except when the actions that constitute the breach violate a social policy that merits the imposition of tort remedies.

It is also true that public policy does not always favor a limitation on damages for *intentional* breaches of contract. The notion that society gains from an efficient breach must be qualified by the recognition that many intentional breaches are not efficient. . . . As Judge Posner explained in *Patton, supra*, 841 F.2d at page 751: "Not all breaches of contract are involuntary or otherwise efficient. Some are opportunistic; the promisor wants the benefit of the bargain without bearing the agreed-upon costs, and exploits the inadequacies of purely compensatory remedies (the major inadequacies being that pre- and post-judgment interest rates are frequently below market levels when the risk of nonpayment is taken into account and that the winning party cannot recover . . . attorney's fees." Commentators have also pointed to other "inadequacies of purely compensatory remedies" that encourage inefficient breaches (i.e. breaches that result in greater losses to the promisee than gains for the promisor): the lack of emotional distress damages, even when such damages are the probable result of the breach, and the restriction of consequential damages to those in the contemplation of the parties at the time the contract was formed. (See Diamond, *The Tort of Bad Faith Breach of Contract: When, If at All, Should It Be Extended Beyond Insurance Transactions?* (1981) 64 Marq. L. Rev. 425; 439-443; see also Sebert, *supra*, 33 U.C.L.A. L. Rev. at p. 1578.)

In addition to fully compensating contract plaintiffs and discouraging inefficient breaches, the imposition of tort remedies for certain intentional breaches of contract serves to punish and deter business practices that constitute distinct social wrongs independent of the breach. For example, we permit the plaintiff to recover exemplary damages in cases in which the breached contract was induced through promissory fraud, even though the plaintiff has incurred the same loss whether the contract was fraudulently induced or not. (See *Walker v. Signal Companies, Inc.* (1978) 84 Cal. App. 3d 982, 995-998 [149 Cal. Rptr. 119].) Our determination to allow the plaintiff to sue for fraud and to potentially recover exemplary damages is not justified by the plaintiff's greater loss, but by the fact that the breach of a fraudulently induced contract is a significantly greater wrong, from society's standpoint, than an ordinary breach. "We are aware of the danger of grafting tort liability on what ordinarily should be a breach of contract action. . . . However, no public policy is served by permitting a party who never intended to fulfill his obligations to fraudulently induce another to enter into an agreement." (*Las Palmas Associates v. Las Palmas Center Associates* (1991) 235 Cal. App. 3d 1220, 1238 [1 Cal. Rptr. 2d 301].)

As the above illustrate, the rationale for limiting actions for intentional breaches of contract to contract remedies—that such limitation promotes commercial stability and predictability and hence advances commerce—is not invariably a compelling one. Breaches accompanied by deception or infliction of intentional harm may be so disruptive of commerce and so reprehensible in themselves that the value of deterring such actions through the tort system outweighs the marginal loss in the predictability of damages that may result. But in imposing tort duties to deter intentionally harmful acts among contracting parties, courts must be cautious not to fashion remedies which overdeter the illegitimate and as a result chill legitimate activities. (See Posner, Economic Analysis of Law, *supra*, at p. 108.) Thus, courts should be careful to apply tort remedies only when the conduct in question is so clear in its deviation from socially useful business practices that the effect of enforcing such tort duties will be, as in the case of fraud, to aid rather than discourage commerce.

As observed above, not all tortious breaches of contract arise from conventional torts. Numerous courts have recognized types of intentionally tortious activity that occur exclusively or distinctively within the context of a contractual relationship. The most familiar type of tortious breach of contract in this state is that of the insurer, whose unreasonable failure to settle or resolve a claim has been held to violate the covenant of good faith and fair dealing. (*Egan v. Mutual of Omaha Ins. Co., supra,* 24 Cal. 3d 809.) Tort liability is imposed primarily because of the distinctive characteristics of the insurance contract: the fiduciary nature of the relationship, the fact that the insurer offers a type of quasi-public service that provides financial security and peace of mind, and the fact that the insurance contract is generally one of adhesion. (*Id.* at pp. 820-821.) In these cases, the special relationship between insurer and insured supports the elevation of the covenant of good faith and fair dealing, a covenant implied by law in every contract and generally used as an aid to contract interpretation (*Foley, supra,* 47 Cal. 3d at p. 684), into a tort duty.

Because the good faith covenant is so broad and all-pervasive, this court and others have been reluctant to expand recognition of the action for tortious breach of the covenant beyond the insurance context. (See *Foley, supra,* 47 Cal. 3d at p. 692 [no special relationship in the employment context]; but see *id.* at pp. 701, 715, 723 (separate conc. and dis. opns. of Broussard, J., Kaufman, J., and Mosk, J.).) Unfortunately, the preoccupation of California courts with limiting the potentially enormous scope of this tort has diverted attention away from the useful task of identifying *specific practices* employed by contracting parties that merit the imposition of tort remedies. Other jurisdictions not so preoccupied have made greater progress in developing a common law of tortious breach of contract. While the cases are not easily amenable to classification, they appear to fit into two broad categories.

The first category focuses on tortious *means* used by one contracting party to coerce or deceive another party into foregoing its contractual rights. . . . *Adam's v.*

Crater Well Drilling, Inc. (1976) 276 Ore. 789 [556 P.2d 679, 681] [punitive damages justified when contracting party uses threat of prosecution to obtain more than is owed under the contract]; *John A. Henry & Co., Ltd. v. T.G. & Y Stores Co.* (10th Cir. 1991) 941 F.2d 1068, 1072-1073 [punitive damages allowed under Oklahoma law when commercial tenant attempts to compel landlord to release it from its lease by fabricating defects in the landlord's maintenance and sending letters complaining of such defects to the landlord's lender, thereby disparaging the former's reputation]. . . .

. . .

A second type of tortious intentional breach has been found when the *consequences* of the breach are especially injurious to the party suffering the breach, and the breaching party intentionally or knowingly inflicts such injury. Cases of this type have generally occurred outside the commercial context, involving manifestly unequal contracting parties and contracts concerning matters of vital personal significance, in which great mental anguish or personal hardship are the probable result of the breach. In these cases, courts have permitted substantial awards of emotional distress damages and/or punitive damages, both as a means of providing extra sanctions for a defendant engaging in intentionally injurious activities against vulnerable parties, and as a way of fully compensating plaintiffs for types of injury that are neither readily amendable to mitigation nor generally recoverable as contract damages. For example, in *K Mart Corp. v. Ponsock* (1987) 103 Nev. 39 [732 P.2d 1364, 1370], disapproved on other grounds by *Ingersoll-Rand Co. v. McClendon* (1990) 498 U.S. 133, 137 [112 L. Ed. 2d 474, 482-483, 111 S. Ct. 478], the Nevada Supreme Court allowed a $50,000 award of punitive damages to stand when an employer discharged a long-term employee on a fabricated charge for the purpose of defeating the latter's contractual entitlement to retirement benefits. . . .

In other cases of this type, an intentional breach of a warranty of habitability by a landlord or building contractor has given rise to substantial emotional distress or punitive damages awards. For example, Missouri courts recognize that a wrongful eviction will sound in tort as well as contract. (*Ladeas v. Carter* (Mo. App. 1992) 845 S.W.2d 45, 52; see also *Emden v. Vitz* (1948) 88 Cal. App. 2d 313, 318-319 [198 P.2d 696]. . . .

. . .

In sum, the above cited cases show that an intentional breach of contract may be found to be tortious when the breaching party exhibits an extreme disregard for the contractual rights of the other party, either knowingly harming the vital interests of a promisee so as to create substantial mental distress or personal hardship, or else employing coercion or dishonesty to cause the promisee to forego its contractual rights. These cases illustrate the recognition by a number of jurisdictions that an intentional breach of contract outside the insurance context, and not accompanied by any conventional tortious behavior such as promissory fraud, may nonetheless be deemed tortious when accompanied by these kinds of aggravating circumstances.

. . .

Seaman's was . . . correctly decided, in my view, on narrower grounds than bad faith denial of the contract's existence. As discussed above, a number of cases allow tort damages for an intentional breach which the breaching party knows will probably result in significant emotional distress or personal hardship. In the commercial sphere, we do not as a rule permit such recovery for personal distress—the frustrations that attend breached contracts, unreliable suppliers, and the like are part of the realities of commerce. Society expects the business enterprise to go to the marketplace to seek substitutes to mitigate its losses, and to seek contract damages for those losses that cannot be mitigated. But there are some commercial cases in which the harm intentionally inflicted on an enterprise cannot be mitigated, and in which ordinary contract damages are insufficient compensation. *Seaman's* is such a case. In *Seaman's*, because of the unusual combination of market forces and government regulation set in motion by the 1973 oil embargo, Standard's conduct had a significance beyond the ordinary breach: its practical effect was to shut *Seaman's* out of the oil market entirely, forcing it out of business. In other words, Standard intentionally breached its contract with Seaman's with the knowledge that the breach would result in Seaman's demise. Having thus breached its contract with blithe disregard for the severe and, under these rare circumstances, unmitigatable injury it caused Seaman's, Standard was justly subject to tort damages.

In sum, I would permit an action for tortious breach of contract in a commercial setting when a party intentionally breaches a contractual obligation with neither probable cause nor belief that the obligation does *not* exist, *and* when the party intends or knows that the breach will result in severe consequential damages to the other party that are not readily subject to mitigation, and such harm in fact occurs. This rule is a variant of the more general rule of tort law that, as Holmes said, "the intentional infliction of temporal damage is a cause of action, which, as a matter of substantive law, . . . requires a justification if the defendant is to escape." (*Aikens v. Wisconsin* (1904) 195 U.S. 194, 204 [49 L. Ed. 154, 159, 25 S. Ct. 3].) A breach should not be considered tortious if the court determines that it was justified by avoidance of some substantial, unforeseen cost on the part of the breaching party, even if such cost does not excuse that party's nonperformance. (See 3A Corbin on Contracts (1994 Supp.) §654E, p. 109.) Nor should a tortious breach under these circumstances be recognized if it is clear that the party suffering the harm voluntarily accepted that risk under the contract. But the intentional or knowing infliction of severe consequential damages on a business enterprise through the unjustified, bad faith breach of a contract is reprehensible and costly both for the party suffering the breach and for society as a whole, and is therefore appropriately sanctioned through the tort system.

. . .

The present case, on the other hand, is essentially a billing dispute between two commercial entities. Belcher Oil Company claimed, apparently in bad faith and without probable cause, that it had no contractual agreement with Freeman & Mills. That is, Belcher Oil not only intentionally breached its contract, but then asserted a bad faith defense to its liability. [T]he solution which the Legislature has devised for this kind of transgression is the awarding of the other party's attorney fees, and this is precisely what occurred—Freeman & Mills was awarded $212,891 in attorney fees pursuant to Code of Civil Procedure sections 128.5 and 2033, subdivision (c). To permit the award of punitive damages in addition to this sum would upset the legislative balance established in the litigation sanctions statutes and make tortious actions—intentional breach of contract and the assertion of a bad faith defense—which we have consistently held not to be tortious.

On this basis, I concur in the majority's disposition in favor of Belcher Oil on the bad faith denial of contract cause of action.

Problems

1. Sleepless Nights. Neat Sawyer purchased a pick-up truck with financing by Bank of America. As part of the agreement with the bank, Sawyer was required to have insurance, but he could choose to get it himself or have the bank purchase it for him. Sawyer elected to delegate the responsibility to the bank. Some time later, the truck was badly damaged in a fire. The damage was estimated at $2,000. When Sawyer tried to collect the insurance money, he discovered that the bank had accidentally forgotten to pay the premium and so his coverage had been discontinued. Sawyer then asked the bank to pay the $2,000 for damages due to its breach of the contract. Bank of America refused and offered a $1,000 settlement without providing any rationale for the lower figure. Sawyer rejected the offer, and the stress of the damage to the truck and his inability to pay for the repairs caused him to suffer from insomnia for months. He sued Bank of America for breach of contract and sought $2,000 in compensatory damages plus punitive damages for the unnecessary stress the bank's refusal to pay caused him. Should the court award punitive damages?

2. The Dodgy Dodge. Robert Clark purchased a car from Boise Dodge for $2,400 that the dealership claimed was "new" and showed 165 miles on its odometer. In fact, the dealership knew that the car was used and that the odometer had been set back from 6,968 miles to disguise this fact. When Clark learned that the car was used, rather than seek rescission of the agreement, he sued for breach of contract. A jury awarded Clark $350 in compensatory damages—the difference between the $2,400 value of the car as represented and the $2,050 value of the car as it actually was. On the basis of the trial judge's instruction that the jury could award punitive damages if it found Boise's conduct to have been "willful, wanton, gross or outrageous," the jury also returned an award of $12,500 in punitive damages. Boise appealed the punitive damages award. How should the court rule?

3. The Unpaid Attorney. Claud Yeldell retained attorney John Goren to represent Yeldell's co-defendants in a property dispute and later to provide assistance in the sale of that property. Yeldell promised to pay Goren's fees out of the profits of the sale after closing. During the litigation of the property dispute and when he persuaded Goren to take on the property transaction, Yeldell repeated his promise.

Shortly after the sale closed, Goren contacted the title company to inquire after his fee. The title company told him that Yeldell had ordered that Goren not be paid. In fact, Yeldell had specifically instructed the title company, "Do not pay John Goren any money. He was not my attorney and has never represented me in any matter," and then withdrew all of the sale proceeds from his title company account. Goren sued for breach of contract. The trial court found Yeldell liable and awarded Goren $1,336 in unpaid fees and $2,400 in punitive damages. Yeldell appealed, claiming the punitive damages award was inappropriate and should be reversed. How should the appellate court rule?

B. SPECIFIC vs. SUBSTITUTIONAL PERFORMANCE

The specific performance versus substitutional performance divide in contract remedies may be traced to the English roots of American courts. Historically, English "law" courts were authorized to provide only monetary remedies. The power to provide specific relief—that is, to issue an injunction ordering a party to perform some act besides remuneration—was limited to special courts of equity. Although the American legal system does not distinguish between courts of law and courts of equity, the principle that damages are the standard remedy for contractual breach and that injunctive relief is extraordinary remains black letter contract law in this country to this day. According to the Restatement, courts will not order specific performance or other injunctive relief "if damages would be adequate to protect the expectation interest of the injured party." Rest. (2d) Contracts §359; see also §360 (listing factors affecting the adequacy of damages). Substitutional performance—the value of promised performance serving as a substitute for the performance itself—is the presumed remedy for breach of contract.

Specific performance—a court order requiring a breaching party to perform his contractual duties—must be justified. If "adequacy" of expectation damages were understood to mean that there must be some amount of money that would make the non-breaching party indifferent between performance and breach, specific performance would be exceedingly rare because some amount of damages would nearly always be sufficient (death or grievous bodily harm might be exceptions, but these harms are rarely the direct result of contract breach). The first three cases—*Van Wagner Advertising Corporation v. S & M Enterprises*, *Laclede Gas Company v. Amoco Oil Company*, and *Walgreen Company v. Sara Creek Property Company*—represent attempts by courts to distinguish circumstances in which damages are adequate from those in which they are not. *Laclede Gas Company* involves the UCC, which limits specific performance to "unique goods or in other proper circumstances." U.C.C. §2-716.

The availability of specific performance is further limited by considerations of the costs of judicial administration. The court's entry of an award of damages marks the end of its responsibility for the matter. By contrast, a court supervises implementation of a specific performance decree until such time as performance is complete (or the parties voluntarily agree to settle the suit). *[City of] Columbus v. Cleveland, Cincinnati, Chicago & St. Louis Railway Company* and *Ryan v. Ocean Twelve, Inc.* concern the question of when specific performance would be an improper remedy because the costs of judicial supervision are greater than the benefits of granting specific performance. See also Rest. (2d) Contracts §366.

VAN WAGNER ADVERTISING CORP.
v.
S & M ENTERPRISES

Court of Appeals of New York
492 N.E.2d 756
1986

Kaye, Judge.

. . .

By agreement dated December 16, 1981, Barbara Michaels leased to plaintiff, Van Wagner Advertising, for an initial period of three years plus option periods totaling seven additional years space on the eastern exterior wall of a building on East 36th Street in Manhattan. Van Wagner was in the business of erecting and leasing billboards, and the parties anticipated that Van Wagner would erect a sign on the leased space, which faced an exit ramp of the Midtown Tunnel and was therefore visible to vehicles entering Manhattan from that tunnel.

In early 1982 Van Wagner erected an illuminated sign and leased it to Asch Advertising, Inc. for a three-year period commencing March 1, 1982. However, by agreement dated January 22, 1982, Michaels sold the building to defendant S & M Enterprises. Michaels informed Van Wagner of the sale in early August 1982, and on August 19, 1982 S & M sent Van Wagner a letter purporting to cancel the lease as of October 18. . . .

. . .

Given defendant's unexcused failure to perform its contract, we next turn to a consideration of remedy for the breach: Van Wagner seeks specific performance of the contract, S & M urges that money damages are adequate but that the amount of the award was improper.

Whether or not to award specific performance is a decision that rests in the sound discretion of the trial court, and here that discretion was not abused. Considering first the nature of the transaction, specific performance has been imposed as the remedy for breach of contracts for the sale of real property (*Judnick Realty Corp. v. 32 W. 32nd St. Corp.*, 61 N.Y.2d 819, 823, 473 N.Y.S.2d 954, 462 N.E.2d 131; *Da Silva v. Musso*, 53 N.Y.2d 543, 545, 444 N.Y.S.2d 50, 428 N.E.2d 382; *S.E.S. Importers v. Pappalardo*, 53 N.Y.2d 455, 442 N.Y.S.2d 453, 425 N.E.2d 841), but the contract here is to lease rather than sell an interest in real property. While specific performance is available, in appropriate circumstances, for breach of a commercial or residential lease, specific performance of real property leases is not in this State awarded as a matter of course (*see, Gardens Nursery School v. Columbia Univ.*, 94 Misc. 2d 376, 378, 404 N.Y.S.2d 833).

Van Wagner argues that specific performance must be granted in light of the trial court's finding that the "demised space is unique as to location for the particular advertising purpose intended." The word "uniqueness" is not, however, a magic door to specific performance. A distinction must be drawn between physical difference and economic interchangeability. The trial court found that the leased property is physically unique, but so is every parcel of real property and so are many consumer goods. Putting aside contracts for the sale of real property, where specific performance has traditionally been the remedy for breach, uniqueness in the sense of physical difference does not itself dictate the propriety of equitable relief.

By the same token, at some level all property may be interchangeable with money. Economic theory is concerned with the degree to which consumers are willing to substitute the use of one good for another (*see*, Kronman, *Specific Performance*, 45 U. Chi. L. Rev. 351, 359), the underlying assumption being that "every good has substitutes, even if only very poor ones," and that "all goods are ultimately commensurable" (*id.*). Such a view, however, could strip all meaning from uniqueness, for if all goods are ultimately exchangeable for a price, then all goods may be valued. Even a rare manuscript has an economic substitute in that there is a price for which any purchaser would likely agree to give up a right to buy it, but a court would in all probability order specific performance of such a contract on the ground that the subject matter of the contract is unique.

The point at which breach of a contract will be redressable by specific performance thus must lie not in any inherent physical uniqueness of the property but instead in the uncertainty of valuing it: "What matters, in measuring money damages, is the volume, refinement, and reliability of the available information about substitutes for the subject matter of the breached contract. When the relevant information is thin and unreliable, there is a substantial risk that an award of money damages will either exceed or fall short of the promisee's actual loss. Of course this risk can always be reduced—but only at great cost when reliable information is difficult to obtain. Conversely, when there is a great deal of consumer behavior generating abundant and highly dependable information about substitutes, the risk of error in measuring the promisee's loss may be reduced at much smaller cost. In asserting that the subject matter of a particular contract is unique and has no established market value, a court is really saying that it cannot obtain, at reasonable cost, enough information about substitutes to permit it to calculate an award of money damages without imposing an unacceptably high risk of undercompensation on the injured promisee. Conceived in this way, the uniqueness test seems economically sound." (45 U. Chi. L. Rev., at 362.) This principle is reflected in the case law (*see, e.g., Erie R.R. Co. v. City of Buffalo*, 180 N.Y. 192, 200, 73 N.E. 26; *St. Regis Paper Co. v. Santa Clara Lbr. Co.*, 173 N.Y. 149, 160, 65 N.E. 967; *Dailey v. City of New York*, 170 App. Div. 267, 276-277, 156 N.Y.S. 124, *affd.* 218 N.Y. 665, 113 N.E. 1053), and is essentially the position of the Restatement (Second) of Contracts, which lists "the difficulty of proving damages with reasonable certainty" as the first factor affecting adequacy of damages (Restatement [Second] of Contracts §360[a]).

Thus, the fact that the subject of the contract may be "unique as to location for the particular advertising purpose intended" by the parties does not entitle a plaintiff to the remedy of specific performance.

. . . Van Wagner asserts that while lost revenues on the Asch contract may be adequate compensation, that contract expired February 28, 1985, its lease with S & M continues until 1992, and the value of the demised space cannot reasonably be fixed for the balance of the term.

. . . [I]t is hardly novel in the law for damages to be projected into the future. Particularly where the value of commercial billboard space can be readily determined by comparisons with similar uses—Van Wagner itself has more than 400 leases—the value of this property between 1985 and 1992 cannot be regarded as speculative.

LACLEDE GAS CO.
v.
AMOCO OIL CO.

U.S. Court of Appeals, Eighth Circuit
522 F.2d 33
1975

Ross, J.

The Laclede Gas Company (Laclede), a Missouri corporation, brought this diversity action alleging breach of contract against the Amoco Oil Company (Amoco), a Delaware corporation. It sought relief in the form of a mandatory injunction prohibiting the continuing breach or, in the alternative, damages. The district court held a bench trial on the issues of whether there was a valid, binding contract between the parties and whether, if there was such a contract, Amoco should be enjoined from breaching it. It then ruled that the "contract is invalid due to lack of mutuality" and denied the prayer for injunctive relief. The court made no decision regarding the requested damages. Laclede Gas Co. v. Amoco Oil Co., 385 F. Supp. 1332, 1336 (E.D. Mo. 1974). This appeal followed, and we reverse the district court's judgment.

On September 21, 1970, Midwest Missouri Gas Company (now Laclede), and American Oil Company (now Amoco), the predecessors of the parties to this litigation, entered into a written agreement which was designed to provide central propane gas distribution systems to various residential developments in Jefferson County, Missouri, until such time as natural gas mains were extended into these areas. The agreement contemplated that as individual developments were planned the owners or developers would apply to Laclede for central propane gas systems. If Laclede determined that such a system was appropriate in any given development, it could request Amoco to supply the propane to that specific development. This request was made in the form of a supplemental form letter, as provided in the September 21 agreement; and if Amoco decided to supply the propane, it bound itself to do so by signing this supplemental form.

Once this supplemental form was signed the agreement placed certain duties on both Laclede and Amoco. Basically, Amoco was to "(i)nstall, own, maintain and operate . . . storage and vaporization facilities and any other facilities necessary to provide (it) with the capability of delivering to (Laclede) commercial propane gas suitable . . . for delivery by (Laclede) to its customers' facilities." Amoco's facilities were to be "adequate to provide a continuous supply of commercial propane gas at such times and in such volumes commensurate with (Laclede's) requirements for meeting the demands reasonably to be anticipated in each Development while this Agreement is in force." Amoco was deemed to be "the supplier," while Laclede was "the distributing utility."

For its part Laclede agreed to "(i)nstall, own, maintain and operate all distribution facilities" from a "point of delivery" which was defined to be "the outlet of (Amoco) header piping." Laclede also promised to pay Amoco "the Wood River Area Posted Price for propane plus four cents per gallon for all amounts of commercial propane gas delivered" to it under the agreement.

Since it was contemplated that the individual propane systems would eventually be converted to natural gas, one paragraph of the agreement provided that Laclede should give Amoco 30 days written notice of this event, after which the agreement would no longer be binding for the converted development.

Another paragraph gave Laclede the right to cancel the agreement. However, this right was expressed in the following language:

> This Agreement shall remain in effect for one (1) year following the first delivery of gas by (Amoco) to (Laclede) hereunder. Subject to termination as provided in Paragraph 11 hereof (dealing with conversions to natural gas), this Agreement shall automatically continue in effect for additional periods of one (1) year each unless (Laclede) shall, not less than 30 days prior to the expiration of the initial one (1) year period or any subsequent one (1) year period, give (Amoco) written notice of termination.

There was no provision under which Amoco could cancel the agreement.

For a time the parties operated satisfactorily under this agreement, and some 17 residential subdivisions were brought within it by supplemental letters. However, for various reasons, including conversion to natural gas, the number of developments under the agreement had shrunk to eight by the time of trial. These were all mobile home parks.

During the winter of 1972-73 Amoco experienced a shortage of propane and voluntarily placed all of its customers, including Laclede, on an 80% Allocation basis, meaning that Laclede would receive only up to 80% of its previous requirements. Laclede objected to this and pushed Amoco to give it 100% of what the developments needed. Some conflict arose over this before the temporary shortage was alleviated.

Then, on April 3, 1973, Amoco notified Laclede that its Wood River Area Posted Price of propane had been increased by three cents per gallon. Laclede objected to this increase also and demanded a full explanation. None was forthcoming. Instead Amoco merely sent a letter dated May 14, 1973, informing Laclede that it was "terminating" the September 21, 1970, agreement effective May 31, 1973. It claimed it had the right to do this because "the Agreement lacks 'mutuality.'"

The district court felt that the entire controversy turned on whether or not Laclede's right to "arbitrarily cancel the Agreement" without Amoco having a similar right rendered the contract void "for lack of mutuality" and it resolved this question in the affirmative. We disagree with this conclusion and hold that settled principles of contract law require a reversal.

I.

A bilateral contract is not rendered invalid and unenforceable merely because one party has the right to cancellation while the other does not. . . .

The important question in the instant case is whether Laclede's right of cancellation rendered all its other promises in the agreement illusory so that there was a complete failure of consideration. This would be the result had Laclede retained the right of immediate cancellation at any time for any reason. 1 S. Williston, Law of Contracts §104, at 400-401 (3d ed. 1957). However, Professor Williston goes on to note:

> Since the courts . . . do not favor arbitrary cancellation clauses, the tendency is to interpret even a slight restriction on the exercise of the right of cancellation as constituting such legal detriment as will satisfy the requirement of sufficient consideration; for example, where the reservation of right to cancel is for cause, or by written notice, or after a definite period of notice, or upon the occurrence of some extrinsic event, or is based on some other objective standard.

Id. §105, at 418-419 (footnotes omitted). . . .

Here Laclede's right to terminate was neither arbitrary nor unrestricted. It was limited by the agreement in at least three ways. First, Laclede could not cancel until one year had passed after the first delivery of propane by Amoco. Second, any cancellation could be effective only on the anniversary date of the first delivery under the agreement. Third, Laclede had to give Amoco 30 days written notice of termination. These restrictions on Laclede's power to cancel clearly bring this case within the rule.

A more difficult issue in this case is whether or not the contract fails for lack of "mutuality of consideration" because Laclede did not expressly bind itself to order all of its propane requirements for the Jefferson County subdivisions from Amoco.

. . .

We are satisfied that, while Laclede did not expressly promise to purchase all the propane requirements for the subdivisions from Amoco, a practical reading of the contract provisions reveals that this was clearly the intent of the parties. . . .

Once Amoco had signed the supplemental letter agreement, thereby making the September 21 agreement applicable to any given Jefferson County development, it was bound to be the propane supplier for that subdivision and to provide a continuous supply of the gas sufficient to meet Laclede's reasonably anticipated needs for that development. It was to perform these duties until the agreement was cancelled by Laclede or until natural gas distribution was extended to the development.

For its part, Laclede bound itself to purchase all the propane required by the particular development from Amoco. This commitment was not expressly written out, but it necessarily follows from an intelligent, practical reading of the agreement.

Laclede was to "(i)nstall, own, maintain and operate all distribution facilities from the point of delivery as defined in Paragraph 3(b). . . ." Paragraph 3(b) provided: "the point of delivery shall be at the outlet of (Amoco) header piping." Also under Paragraph 3(b) Amoco was to own and operate all the facilities on the bulk side of that header piping. Laclede thus bound itself to buy all its requirements from Amoco by agreeing to attach its distribution lines to Amoco's header piping; and even if a change of suppliers could be made under the contract, Laclede could not own and operate a separate distribution system hooked up to some other supplier's propane storage tanks without substantially altering the supply route to its distribution system or making a very substantial investment in its own storage equipment and site. As a practical matter, then, Laclede is bound to buy all the propane it distributes from Amoco in any subdivision to which the supplemental agreement applies and for which the distribution system has been established.

When analyzed in this manner, it can be seen that the contract herein is simply a so-called "requirements contract." Such contracts are routinely enforced by the courts where, as here, the needs of the purchaser are reasonably foreseeable and the time of performance is reasonably limited. . . .

We conclude that there is mutuality of consideration within the terms of the agreement and hold that there is a valid, binding contract between the parties as to each of the developments for which supplemental letter agreements have been signed.

II.

Since he found that there was no binding contract, the district judge did not have to deal with the question of whether or not to grant the injunction prayed for by Laclede. He simply denied this relief because there was no contract.

Generally the determination of whether or not to order specific performance of a contract lies within the sound discretion of the trial court. However, this discretion is, in fact, quite limited; and it is said that when certain equitable rules have been met and the contract is fair and plain "specific performance goes as a matter of right." Miller v. Coffeen, 365 Mo. 204 (1955). . . .

With this in mind we have carefully reviewed the very complete record on appeal and conclude that the trial court should grant the injunctive relief prayed. We are satisfied that this case falls within that category in which specific performance should be ordered as a matter of right. Miller v. Coffeen, supra, 280 S.W.2d at 102.

Amoco contends that four of the requirements for specific performance have not been met. Its claims are: (1) there is no mutuality of remedy in the contract; (2) the remedy of specific performance would be difficult for the court to administer without constant and long-continued supervision; (3) the contract is indefinite and uncertain;

and (4) the remedy at law available to Laclede is adequate. The first three contentions have little or no merit and do not detain us for long.

There is simply no requirement in the law that both parties be mutually entitled to the remedy of specific performance in order that one of them be given that remedy by the court. Beets v. Tyler, 365 Mo. 895, 290 S.W.2d 76, 80 (1956). . . .

While a court may refuse to grant specific performance where such a decree would require constant and long-continued court supervision, this is merely a discretionary rule of decision which is frequently ignored when the public interest is involved. See, e.g., Joy v. St. Louis, 138 U.S. 1, 47 (1891). . . .

Here the public interest in providing propane to the retail customers is manifest, while any supervision required will be far from onerous.

Section 370 of the Restatement of Contracts (1932) provides: "Specific enforcement will not be decreed unless the terms of the contract are so expressed that the court can determine with reasonable certainty what is the duty of each party and the conditions under which performance is due."

We believe these criteria have been satisfied here. As discussed in part I of this opinion, as to all developments for which a supplemental agreement has been signed, Amoco is to supply all the propane which is reasonably foreseeably required, while Laclede is to purchase the required propane from Amoco and pay the contract price therefor. The parties have disagreed over what is meant by "Wood River Area Posted Price" in the agreement, but the district court can and should determine with reasonable certainty what the parties intended by this term and should mold its decree, if necessary accordingly. Likewise, the fact that the agreement does not have a definite time of duration is not fatal since the evidence established that the last subdivision should be converted to natural gas in 10 to 15 years. This sets a reasonable time limit on performance and the district court can and should mold the final decree to reflect this testimony.

It is axiomatic that specific performance will not be ordered when the party claiming breach of contract has an adequate remedy at law. Jamison Coal & Coke Co. v. Goltra, 132 F.2d 889, 894 (8th Cir.), *cert. denied*, 323 U.S. 769 (1944). This is especially true when the contract involves personal property as distinguished from real estate.

However, in Missouri, as elsewhere, specific performance may be ordered even though personalty is involved in the "proper circumstances." Mo. Rev. Stat. §400.2-716(1); Restatement of Contracts, supra, §361. . . .

One of the leading Missouri cases allowing specific performance of a contract relating to personalty because the remedy at law was inadequate is *Boeving v. Vandover*, 240 Mo. App. 117 (1949). In that case the plaintiff sought specific performance of a contract in which the defendant had promised to sell him an automobile. At that time (near the end of and shortly after World War II) new cars were hard to come by, and the court held that specific performance was a proper remedy since a new car "could not be obtained elsewhere except at considerable expense, trouble or loss, which cannot be estimated in advance."

We are satisfied that Laclede has brought itself within this practical approach taken by the Missouri courts. As Amoco points out, Laclede has propane immediately available to it under other contracts with other suppliers. And the evidence indicates that at the present time propane is readily available on the open market. However, this analysis ignores the fact that the contract involved in this lawsuit is for a long-term supply of propane to these subdivisions. The other two contracts under which Laclede obtains the gas will remain in force only until March 31, 1977, and April 1, 1981, respectively; and there is no assurance that Laclede will be able to receive any propane under them after that time. Also it is unclear as to whether or not Laclede can use the propane obtained under these contracts to supply the Jefferson County subdivisions, since they were originally entered into to provide Laclede with propane with which to "shave" its natural gas supply during peak demand periods.[4] Additionally, there was uncontradicted expert testimony that Laclede probably could not find another supplier of propane willing to enter into a long-term contract such as the Amoco agreement, given the uncertain future of worldwide energy supplies. And, even if Laclede could obtain supplies of propane for the affected developments through its present contracts or newly negotiated ones, it would still face considerable expense and trouble which cannot be estimated in advance in making arrangements for its distribution to the subdivisions.

Specific performance is the proper remedy in this situation, and it should be granted by the district court.

CONCLUSION

For the foregoing reasons the judgment of the district court is reversed and the cause is remanded for the fashioning of appropriate injunctive relief in the form of a decree of specific performance as to those developments for which a supplemental agreement form has been signed by the parties.

WALGREEN CO.
v.
SARA CREEK PROPERTY CO.
U.S. Court of Appeals, Seventh Circuit
966 F.2d 273
1992

POSNER, J.

This appeal from the grant of a permanent injunction raises fundamental issues concerning the propriety of injunctive relief. 775 F. Supp. 1192 (E.D. Wis. 1991). The essential facts are simple. Walgreen has operated a pharmacy in the Southgate Mall in Milwaukee since its opening in 1951. Its current lease, signed in 1971 and

---

4. During periods of cold weather, when demand is high, Laclede does not receive enough natural gas to meet all this demand. It, therefore, adds propane to the natural gas it places in its distribution system. This practice is called "peak shaving."

carrying a 30-year, 6-month term, contains, as had the only previous lease, a clause in which the landlord, Sara Creek, promises not to lease space in the mall to anyone else who wants to operate a pharmacy or a store containing a pharmacy. Such an exclusivity clause, common in shopping-center leases, is occasionally challenged on antitrust grounds—implausibly enough, given the competition among malls; but that is an issue for another day, since in this appeal Sara Creek does not press the objection it made below to the clause on antitrust grounds.

In 1990, fearful that its largest tenant—what in real estate parlance is called the "anchor tenant"—having gone broke was about to close its store, Sara Creek informed Walgreen that it intended to buy out the anchor tenant and install in its place a discount store operated by Phar-Mor Corporation, a "deep discount" chain, rather than, like Walgreen, just a "discount" chain. Phar-Mor's store would occupy 100,000 square feet, of which 12,000 would be occupied by a pharmacy the same size as Walgreen's. The entrances to the two stores would be within a couple of hundred feet of each other.

Walgreen filed this diversity suit for breach of contract against Sara Creek and Phar-Mor and asked for an injunction against Sara Creek's letting the anchor premises to Phar-Mor. After an evidentiary hearing, the judge found a breach of Walgreen's lease and entered a permanent injunction against Sara Creek's letting the anchor tenant premises to Phar-Mor until the expiration of Walgreen's lease. He did this over the defendants' objection that Walgreen had failed to show that its remedy at law—damages—for the breach of the exclusivity clause was inadequate. Sara Creek had put on an expert witness who testified that Walgreen's damages could be readily estimated, and Walgreen had countered with evidence from its employees that its damages would be very difficult to compute, among other reasons because they included intangibles such as loss of goodwill.

Sara Creek reminds us that damages are the norm in breach of contract as in other cases. Many breaches, it points out, are "efficient" in the sense that they allow resources to be moved into a more valuable use. Patton v. Mid-Continent Systems, Inc., 841 F.2d 742, 750-51 (7th Cir. 1988). Perhaps this is one—the value of Phar-Mor's occupancy of the anchor premises may exceed the cost to Walgreen of facing increased competition. If so, society will be better off if Walgreen is paid its damages, equal to that cost, and Phar-Mor is allowed to move in rather than being kept out by an injunction. That is why injunctions are not granted as a matter of course, but only when the plaintiff's damages remedy is inadequate. Northern Indiana Public Service Co. v. Carbon County Coal Co., 799 F.2d 265, 279 (7th Cir. 1986). Walgreen's is not, Sara Creek argues; the projection of business losses due to increased competition is a routine exercise in calculation. Damages representing either the present value of lost future profits or (what should be the equivalent, Carusos v. Briarcliff, Inc., 76 Ga. App. 346, 351-52, 45 S.E.2d 802, 806-07 (1947)) the diminution in the value of the leasehold have either been awarded or deemed the proper remedy in a number of reported cases for breach of an exclusivity clause in a shopping-center lease. Why, Sara Creek asks, should they not be adequate here?

Sara Creek makes a beguiling argument that contains much truth, but we do not think it should carry the day. For if, as just noted, damages have been awarded in some cases of breach of an exclusivity clause in a shopping-center lease, injunctions have been issued in others. The choice between remedies requires a balancing of the costs and benefits of the alternatives. Hecht Co. v. Bowles, 321 U.S. 321, 329 (1944); Yakus v. United States, 321 U.S. 414, 440 (1944). The task of striking the balance is for the trial judge, subject to deferential appellate review in recognition of its particularistic, judgmental, fact-bound character. . . .

The plaintiff who seeks an injunction has the burden of persuasion—damages are the norm, so the plaintiff must show why his case is abnormal. . . .

The benefits of substituting an injunction for damages are twofold. First, it shifts the burden of determining the cost of the defendant's conduct from the court to the parties. If it is true that Walgreen's damages are smaller than the gain to Sara Creek from allowing a second pharmacy into the shopping mall, then there must be a price for dissolving the injunction that will make both parties better off. Thus, the effect of upholding the injunction would be to substitute for the costly processes of forensic fact determination the less costly processes of private negotiation. Second, a premise of our free-market system, and the lesson of experience here and abroad as well, is that prices and costs are more accurately determined by the market than by government. A battle of experts is a less reliable method of determining the actual cost to Walgreen of facing new competition than negotiations between Walgreen and Sara Creek over the price at which Walgreen would feel adequately compensated for having to face that competition.

That is the benefit side of injunctive relief but there is a cost side as well. Many injunctions require continuing supervision by the court, and that is costly. . . . Some injunctions are problematic because they impose costs on third parties. A more subtle cost of injunctive relief arises from the situation that economists call "bilateral monopoly," in which two parties can deal only with each other: the situation that an injunction creates. The sole seller of widgets selling to the sole buyer of that product would be an example. But so will be the situation confronting Walgreen and Sara Creek if the injunction is upheld. Walgreen can "sell" its injunctive right only to Sara Creek, and Sara Creek can "buy" Walgreen's surrender of its right to enjoin the leasing of the anchor tenant's space to Phar-Mor only from Walgreen. The lack of alternatives in bilateral monopoly creates a bargaining range, and the costs of negotiating to a point within that range may be high. Suppose the cost to Walgreen of facing the competition of Phar-Mor at the Southgate Mall would be $1 million, and the benefit to Sara Creek of leasing to Phar-Mor would be $2 million. Then at any price between those figures for a waiver of Walgreen's injunctive right both parties would be better off, and we expect parties to bargain around a judicial assignment of legal rights if the assignment is inefficient. R.H. Coase, "The Problem of Social Cost," 3 J. Law & Econ. 1 (1960). But each of the parties would like to engross as much of the bargaining range as possible—Walgreen to press the price toward $2 million, Sara Creek to depress it toward $1 million. With so much at stake, both parties will have an incentive to devote substantial resources of time and money to the negotiation process. The process may even break down, if one or both parties want to create for future use a reputation as a hard bargainer; and if it does break down, the injunction will have brought about an inefficient result. All these are in one form or another costs of the injunctive process that can be avoided by substituting damages.

The costs and benefits of the damages remedy are the mirror of those of the injunctive remedy. The damages remedy avoids the cost of continuing supervision and third-party effects, and the cost of bilateral monopoly as well. It imposes costs of its own, however, in the form of diminished accuracy in the determination of value, on the one hand, and of the parties' expenditures on preparing and presenting evidence of damages, and the time of the court in evaluating the evidence, on the other.

The weighing up of all these costs and benefits is the analytical procedure that is or at least should be employed by a judge asked to enter a permanent injunction, with the understanding that if the balance is even the injunction should be withheld. . . .

. . . [H]ere damages would be a costly and inaccurate remedy; and on the other side of the balance some of the costs of an injunction are absent and the cost that is present seems low. . . .

The only substantial cost of the injunction in this case is that it may set off a round of negotiations between the parties. . . .

Affirmed.

CITY OF COLUMBUS
v.
CLEVELAND, CINCINNATI, CHICAGO & ST. LOUIS RAILWAY CO.

Circuit Court of Ohio
15 Ohio C.D. 663
1904

WILSON, J.

These actions [Columbus v. Cleveland, C.C. & St. Louis. Ry. Co., and Columbus v. Pittsburgh, C.C. & St. Louis. Ry. Co.] come into this court on appeal from a judgment in the court below, sustaining a general demurrer and dismissing the petition in each case (Columbus v. Railway Co. 12 Dec. 310). They are submitted together as involving the same questions of law.

The actions are brought to enforce the specific performance of a contract made by the defendants, respectively, with the plaintiff in and about the erection of the viaduct on High street in said city. The contract is attached to the petition. The particular stipulation which is brought into question is contained in what is designated as section fourteen of the contract. It reads as follows:

"In consideration of the first party (the city) constructing the viaduct at the elevation shown upon said plan hereto attached, said second and third parties will, at their own expense erect, or cause to be erected, on their property fronting on the viaduct and its

High street approaches, *neat and ornamental buildings* to obstruct from the part of said viaduct immediately opposite their said property the view of cars and engines; the construction of said buildings to be commenced within sixty days after the completion of said viaduct, prosecuted without unnecessary delay, and fully completed within two years from the completion of the viaduct. This stipulation shall not create any lien, charge or incumbrance on said fronting property, nor impair, in any wise, the right or power, of said second and third parties to lease, sell, convey or dispose of said property, or any part thereof, free from any claim or lien, of the first party, arising out of this agreement; nor shall such lease, sale, conveyance or disposition, release said second and third parties from their obligation to erect said buildings, or to cause them to be erected."

The city pleads compliance with all of the terms of the contract on its part and avers in the first case that the Cleveland, Cincinnati, Chicago & St. Louis Railway Company, owning property fronting on each side of the viaduct, and still being in possession of the same, has failed and refused, and still refuses, to erect the buildings as it has agreed to do; and in the second case that the Pittsburgh, Cincinnati, Chicago & St. Louis Railway Company, owning and in possession of property fronting on both sides, having complied with the contract to the satisfaction of the city, as to the property on the east side, has failed, and refused, and still refuses, to erect the buildings on the west side thereof.

The question raised upon the demurrer is, do the petitions state a case for specific performance? . . .

The general rule that a court of equity will not decree specific performance of a building contract does not apply, where it is not competent for the plaintiff, or any one for it, to enter upon the defendant's premises to build, and where a measurable money equivalent cannot be had.

In a footnote to the case of Mosely v. Virgin, 3 Ves. Jr. 184, the reason for the rule is said to be "If one will not build, another may, and there can be a full compensation in damages."

The exceptions to the rule, and the authorities sustaining them are collected in 3 Pomeroy, Eq. Jurisp. Sec. 1402, p. 445, n. From them we quote:

> "This court has jurisdiction to enforce the specific performance of a contract by a defendant to do defined work upon his property, in the performance of which the plaintiff has a material interest, and which is not capable of adequate compensation in damages." Storer v. Railway Co. 2 You. & Coll. Ch. 48.
>
> "Where, from the nature of the relief sought, performance of a covenant *in specie*, will alone answer the purpose of justice, the court of chancery will compel a specific performance instead of leaving the plaintiff to an inadequate remedy at law." Stuyvesant v. New York (Mayor), 11 Paige 414.

Another exception to the general rule, well sustained by authority is, where there has been a part performance, so that the defendant is enjoying the benefits *in specie*.

The cases at bar come clearly within the exceptions, if the work is sufficiently defined. The relief here sought is, in the language of the contract, the erection of "neat and ornamental buildings, to obstruct from the part of said viaduct immediately opposite their (the defendants') said property the view of cars and engines."

Nothing short of performance *in specie* will accomplish this purpose, and at the same time give to the viaduct the appearance and advantages of a continuous street. Nor is it perceivable how a rule in damages could be framed so as to give adequate relief.

But is the contract sufficiently definite?

In the case of Price v. Corporation of Penzance, 4 Hare 507, the contract was that "the corporation, having purchased the plaintiff's land, should, at their own expense, make a street, and also a market."

The vice chancellor said:

> "Under this contract the corporation have taken possession of the land and converted it; and having had the benefit of the contract *in specie* as far as they are concerned, I need not say that the court will go to any length which it can to compel them to perform the contract *in specie.*"

The court asked this question, however, "If I make a decree for the performance of the contract, how is the court to know when the contract is performed?"

Subsequently, the corporation having by resolution declared that the market should be one for the sale of fish and shoes, the court said, in a further hearing of the case: "This has gone far to remove the difficulty to which I have adverted." Thereafter the corporation performed the contract, leaving the case to be adjudged as to costs only.

In the case of Sanderson v. Railway Co. 11 Beav. 497, "A railway company about to sever the plaintiff's land by their railroad, agreed to purchase the necessary portion of land, subject to making such roads, ways, and slips for cattle as might be necessary." And, having taken possession, and severed the land, the court held that "though it was difficult to execute an agreement thus expressed, yet that the plaintiff was entitled to specific performance; that the word 'Necessary' must receive a reasonable interpretation." And it was held to mean "such roads, ways, and slips for cattle, as might be necessary and proper for convenient communication between the severed portions of the plaintiff's land."

In the case of Storer v. Railway Co. *supra*, "The defendants agreed to purchase so much land as was necessary for their purposes, at a price named, and to construct, and forever thereafter maintain, one neat archway, sufficient to permit a loaded carriage of hay to pass under the archway, at such place as the plaintiff, his heirs and assigns should think most convenient, in his pleasure grounds, and should form and complete the approaches to such archway."

The vice chancellor said: "There is no difficulty in enforcing such a decree. The court has to order the thing done, and then it is a question capable of solution whether the order has been obeyed."

In the case of Lawrence v. Railway Co. 36 Hun (N.Y.) 467, the contract provided among other things, that: "The defendant should simultaneously with the construction of said railroad, erect at or near Excelsior Spring, owned by the plaintiff, a *neat* and *tasteful* station building, for the accommodation of passengers to and from said spring, which shall be a regular station of the road, and all regular trains shall stop at said station, the name of which shall be Excelsior Spring Station: *Held*, that the defendant could, and should be compelled to specifically perform the said agreement."

This case is approvingly cited by the New York court of appeals in Prospect Park & C. I. Ry. Co. v. Railway Co. 1 Am. & Eng. Eq. Dec. 395. These cases are cited because the contracts might be said to be indefinite, and because they illustrate the length to which the courts of equity will go in order to do justice between the parties.

There is a class of cases holding that kindred contracts cannot be specifically performed. Port Clinton Ry. Co. v. Railway Co. 13 Ohio St. 544, 545, is a leading case in that class. In the nature of things, this must be so, for the reason that some such contracts are capable of being performed, while others are not. It is not, then, so much a question of authority as it is, to which class does the contract belong; always remembering that a doubtful case will be cast on the side where complete justice can be done.

In the light of all the authorities there are no insuperable difficulties in the contract sued upon here. The words "neat and ornamental" should receive a reasonable construction, looking to the purpose it is sought to accomplish. The contract specifies the purpose, in so far as the city is concerned. It is to obstruct the view of cars and engines, to persons and animals crossing the viaduct—a very useful purpose, and, it would seem, very easy of accomplishment, to the satisfaction of the city. The fact that one of the railroad companies has erected buildings on the east side of the viaduct satisfactory to the city, is a demonstration of this view of the contract.

The defendants should not be heard to complain of the latitude in the contract, which will permit them to erect buildings suitable otherwise to their own purposes, and within their discretion as to cost and material.

The court will not assume, for the purpose of defeating the contract, that they will use material they should not, or that they will build other than upon approved architectural lines. Nor will the court be without power to execute its decree. It could, under the contract, enjoin the erection of a building that was being made purposely grotesque and unsightly, or that was plainly fraudulent and evasive of the contract. The same power will execute the decree.

. . .

The demurrer to the petition will in each case be overruled.

5

RYAN
v.
OCEAN TWELVE, INC.

Court of Chancery of Delaware, Sussex County
316 A.2d 573
1973

BROWN, V.C.

This matter is before the Court upon the motion of the Defendant to dismiss for lack of jurisdiction. The basis for the motion is that Plaintiffs have an adequate remedy at law. 10 Del. C. §342.

Plaintiffs are the owners of record of the eight residential dwelling units in a condominium known as "Ocean Eight Condominium" located at Bethany Beach. Defendant Ocean Twelve, Inc., was the developer and builder of the condominium. It is alleged that at the time the titles to the units were transferred from the Defendant to the various Plaintiffs, the Defendant had not completed all construction work on the residential units. Plaintiffs were allegedly induced to proceed to final settlement, however, by the express representation of Defendant that a list of deficiencies would be compiled as to each unit and that subsequent to final settlement the incomplete work set forth on each list would be completed by Defendant in a timely manner. In addition, each of the purchasing Plaintiffs were provided with an "Agreement of Warranty" setting forth the guarantees of Defendant against defective material and workmanship.

The complaint goes on to allege that certain of the warranties have been breached and that, despite numerous oral and written complaints to Defendant, the incomplete work set forth on the various lists has not been finished and defects have not been corrected. Among the things complained of is that the air conditioning system is defective in that it does not maintain the required temperature range and leaks large quantities of water throughout the units causing damages to the walls and possessions of Plaintiffs. The roof, which was supposed to be utilized as a sun deck, is said to have developed blisters which prevents such use, and it also leaks. Appliances installed by Defendant were not covered by normal manufacturer's service warranties and Defendant is said to have refused to correct defects in them. The central sewage system is claimed to be faulty in that it emits excessive noise and foul and nauseating odors. It is also contended that Defendant has not installed the type of driveway promised and that the seawall was not properly secured to the pilings.

Each set of Plaintiffs has attached to the complaint a separate list setting forth the work felt to be unfinished by the Defendant. Collectively, these lists cover a myriad of ills, ranging from leaky windows and chipped formica to wobbly towel racks and a defective ice maker.

Plaintiffs seek an order of specific performance to require Defendant to perform its obligations under the agreement to complete as well as the warranty, or in the alternative a judgment for compensatory and punitive damages. As noted previously, Defendant contends that this Court has no jurisdiction because the Plaintiffs have an adequate remedy at law to recover their money damages, if in fact they are entitled to any.

From the foregoing it is obvious that Plaintiffs seek specific performance of various building and construction commitments and an agreement of warranty pertaining thereto. As a general rule, a court of equity will not order specific performance of a building contract in a situation in which it would be impractical to carry out such an order unless there are special circumstances or the public interest is directly involved. Northern Delaware Industrial Development Corporation v. E. W. Bliss Co., Del. Ch., 245 A.2d 431 (1968); Restatement, Contracts §371. See also 4 Pomeroy, Equity Jurisprudence §1402.

While there are exceptions to this general rule, it may be safely said that even where specific performance is ordered there is an implied condition precedent that the terms of the obligation be fixed and certain and that there is a construction plan "so precisely definite as to make compliance therewith subject to effective judicial supervision." Northern Delaware Industrial Development Corporation v. E. W. Bliss Co., supra; Wilmont Homes, Inc. v. Weiler, Del. Supr., 202 A.2d 576 (1964). Compare Lee Builders v. Wells, 33 Del. Ch. 315, 92 A.2d 710 (1952) where the builder sought specific performance to compel the purchasers to go through with the transaction and stood ready to complete the dwelling according to the existing construction plans and agreement.

Here, the owners of eight separate condominium units seek to have the developer fix or complete a variety of alleged defects which differ in degree, and no doubt complexity, as to each unit. It is an inescapable conclusion that in each case whether or not a defect is completed will depend greatly upon the eye and taste of a given Plaintiff. If all the allegations of defects and incomplete work are accurate, it would undoubtedly require a considerable period of time and involve a series of corrective acts on the part of the Defendant to effect satisfaction. When these elements are present, where compensatory damages to cover the costs of correcting the wrongs can bring about the same ultimate relief, and where there are no special circumstances existing which would render money damages inadequate, equity will generally not assume jurisdiction. 13 Am. Jur. 2d, 105 Building & Construction Contracts §112.

I am therefore of the opinion that it would be inappropriate to grant specific performance in this case in view of the apparent complexities of the situation and the disparity, duration and nature of the work to be performed if the allegations are true. Effective enforcement by the Court under such circumstances would be impractical, and, no doubt, improbable.

The motion to dismiss will be granted, subject to the right of the Plaintiffs to transfer their action to the Superior Court, if they so desire, pursuant to 10 Del. C. §1901. Order on notice.

Problems

1. Not a Harrier Jet. Eugene Klein retained a broker to help him locate and purchase a Gulfstream II corporate jet (GII), and entered into a contract to purchase such an aircraft from PepsiCo for $4.6 million. When the chairman of PepsiCo's Board of Directors decided he wanted to keep the airplane, PepsiCo breached, and Klein sought specific performance of the agreement. The trial court found that of the 21 other G-IIs available on the market, only 3 were roughly comparable, and Klein would have had to go to considerable expense to locate a replacement. Klein testified that he did not purchase a replacement plane because prices rose sharply following the breach. Ultimately, he purchased a Gulfstream III corporate jet (GIII). Should the court grant Klein's request for specific performance of the PepsiCo airplane?

2. The Pace Car. When Corvette was named the official pace car of the Indianapolis 500, Chevrolet announced that it would produce 6,000 special-edition models of the car to commemorate the event. Joseph Sedmak, a collector of Corvettes, contacted Charlie's Chevrolet to pre-order one. Charlie's Chevrolet learned it would be allotted one special-edition car from the manufacturer. Charlie's Chevrolet and Sedmak agreed to a sale at the manufacturer's suggested retail price, which had not yet been set. At the request of Sedmak, Charlie's Chevrolet ordered the car equipped with a special engine, a four-speed standard transmission, and an AM-FM radio with a cassette tape deck. When the car arrived, Charlie's Chevrolet told Sedmak that, given the high demand for the special-edition model, it could not sell its single allotted car for the manufacturer's suggested price (approximately $15,000), and that Sedmak would have to bid for the car in an auction. Charlie's Chevrolet received offers to buy the car for $24,000 and $28,000 from prospective purchasers as far away as Florida and Hawaii.

Sedmak immediately filed a lawsuit for breach of contract and requested specific performance. After a bench trial, the court found that Charlie's Chevrolet was in breach of contract and ordered it to make the car "available for delivery" to Sedmak. Charlie's Chevrolet appealed the grant of specific performance, arguing that, given the existence of 6,000 special-edition Corvettes, damages were a sufficient remedy. How should the court of appeals rule?

3. Purchased for Resale. Ace Equipment Company entered into a contract with Aqua Chem to purchase a used, 6,000 KVA General Electric Transformer—a very large piece of industrial equipment—for $1,800. At the time, Ace already had a deal in place to resell the transformer to Frank Lunney for $7,500. Ace loaded the transformer onto a truck on Aqua Chem's premises in order to transport it to Lunney, but Aqua Chem prohibited Ace from removing it and disavowed the contract. Ace filed suit against Aqua Chem for breach of contract and requested specific performance, asking the court to order Aqua Chem to turn over possession of the transformer. Aqua Chem argued that specific performance was improper because damages were an adequate remedy. Assuming that the court finds a breach of contract, should it grant Ace's request for specific performance?

4. Coal and Coal Miners. In a case excerpted in Chapter 5.B.3, the Northern Indiana Public Service Company unsuccessfully sought to be excused from its duty to purchase coal from Carbon County Coal Company due to a change in circumstances. Carbon County sought specific performance of the contract, arguing that damages would not help the coal miners who would be laid off if NIPSCO were to stop purchasing coal from Carbon County and the businesses in the mining town which would suffer indirectly from the layoffs. Should Carbon County be entitled to specific performance or should it be limited to damages?

5. Export Technology. Justina Falk worked as an export agent arranging commercial deals for Chinese producers. She contacted Axiam to order a steel skirt gauge, a technical piece of industrial equipment, for a client in China. As part of the arrangement, Falk required that representatives from Axiam travel to China to install the gauge, test the gauge, and train her client to correctly use the gauge.

Axiam manufactured the gauge and shipped it to the client in China. It did not, however, send personnel to install the gauge or train the client's workers. Falk filed a lawsuit for breach of contract and requested specific performance. Axiam argued that damages were sufficient and that it should not have to send an engineer to China to supervise the installation and training. Should the court grant specific performance?

C. EXPECTATION DAMAGES

Contract law achieves its goal of compensation in most cases by awarding damages based on the non-breaching party's expectation interest. Expectation damages are the amount of money necessary to make the non-breaching party as well off as she would have been had the contract been performed. See Rest. (2d) Contracts §347.

While money might never be a *perfect* substitute for an anticipated performance, it is a sufficient substitute in many commercial transactions. As demonstrated by the first case below, *J.O. Hooker & Sons v. Roberts Cabinet Company*, a monetary award usually will compensate fully a non-breaching seller. A money judgment often can enable a non-breaching buyer to obtain the expected performance from a third party, thus finding herself at the end of the transaction with exactly what she expected to receive under the contract. For example, assume a customer contracts with a car dealer to purchase a new Ford Taurus for $25,000, the dealer breaches, and another dealer is selling the same car for $29,000. The fact that no amount of cash will give the customer the feeling of freedom that she enjoys when speeding down the highway is irrelevant, because a judgment of $4,000—plus any "incidental" costs associated with having to form a new contract with the third party—will enable her to purchase the precise item she expected from the original deal at the same net out-of-pocket cost (and thus to experience that feeling, at least to the extent she would have gained it from the original deal). When available substitute performances vary from the promised performance—in attributes, quality, timing, or in some other material characteristic—determining a party's expectation damages becomes more complicated. *Egerer v. CSR West* provides an illustration of how the law attempts to deal with such circumstances. Although *Egerer* is decided under the UCC, the reasoning is applicable to non-Code cases as well.

In most cases, the cost of obtaining the promised performance at the time of breach is less than the subjective value of that performance to the non-breaching party. The reason is that a party's subjective value of the performance for which she bargains necessarily exceeds the cost (in money, goods, or services) she agrees to pay for that performance, absent a mistake in judgment. Otherwise, she would have no reason to agree to the terms because the contract would make her worse off rather than better off. In some unusual circumstances, however, changes in a party's preferences or market conditions between the time of contracting and the time of breach can result in the cost of obtaining a substitute performance exceeding the value of that performance to the non-breaching party. Suppose, for example, that the customer who contracted to purchase a Ford Taurus for $25,000 values the car at $27,000. At the time of breach, the market price of an identical car is $29,000. In this situation, should a court attempt to award expectation damages by ordering the breaching dealer to pay her the $4,000 necessary for her to purchase an identical car, or only the $2,000 necessary to make her indifferent between performance and breach? As the disparate rulings in *Groves v. John Wunder Company* and *Peevyhouse v. Garland Coal & Mining Company* suggest, courts have struggled mightily with this conceptual conundrum. See also Rest. (2d) Contracts §348(2).

J.O. HOOKER & SONS, INC.
v.
ROBERTS CABINET CO.
Supreme Court of Mississippi
683 So. 2d 396
1996

PRATHER, P.J.

. . .

[General contractor J.O. Hooker & Sons, Inc.] entered into a subcontract agreement with Roberts Cabinet Co., Inc. ("Roberts"), pursuant to which Roberts was required to "furnish cabinets, tops, plastic laminates on walls and down materials and fronts for hot water heaters as per plans and specs for the price listed below." The agreement also provided that "the price includes the cost of tear-out (sic) old cabinets and installation of new cabinets."

. . . Later, a dispute arose between Hooker and Roberts. . . . The parties were unable to resolve their dispute, and on December 13, 1991, Hooker sent Roberts a fax in which he stated that he had consulted with his lawyer and was considering the contract null and void.

On December 18, 1991, Roberts Cabinet Co., Inc. filed suit against J.O. Hooker & Sons, Inc., alleging that Hooker had wrongfully breached a subcontract agreement with Roberts after Roberts had already begun performance. On September 16, 1992, the trial court granted summary judgment in favor of Roberts, finding that Hooker had no legal right to unilaterally terminate the contract in the present case.

On December 10, 1992, a trial was held for the sole purpose of determining the amount of damages suffered by Roberts as a result of Hooker's actions, and a jury determined Robert's damages to be in the amount of $42,870. . . .

Plaintiff's Exhibit 6 listed the following damage

$ 5,117.28	Net Loss on Manufactured Cabinets
$ 3,775.04	Countertops
$ 886.25	Laminate
$ 72.38	Travel Expenses
$ 1,760.00	Administrative Time
$ 1,440.00	Storage of Cabinets
$30,000.00	Lost profit on job (lowerod)
$43,050.95	Total Damages

. . .

A. STORAGE AND ADMINISTRATIVE COSTS

With regard to the storage costs for the cabinets, it is clear that Roberts would have incurred said costs regardless of any breach on the part of Hooker, given that the cabinets were stored in space which Roberts had already leased. . . . Roberts is only entitled to recover damages for expenses in storing the cabinets that it would not otherwise have incurred absent Hooker's breach. As noted by Hooker, Roberts was not forced to rent additional space to store the cabinets, but merely utilized storage facilities that it had already leased. Roberts' rental fees were not raised a single penny by the storage of the cabinets in question, and it was not forced to rent additional space to store other materials as a result of a lack of space arising from the storage of the cabinets. Roberts' claim for recovery in this regard is based solely on the abstract economic value of previously empty storage space which it filled with the cabinets in question. Allowing Roberts to recover for the cost of storing the cabinets would place it in a better position than if the contract had been fully performed. Under these facts, Roberts' claimed damages of $1,440 for storage costs are disallowed in their entirety.

A somewhat similar analysis may appear to apply with regard to the "administrative time" damages of $1,760 which were cited by Roberts as having been incurred in paying Kevin Roberts for his time as general manager. . . . As with the expenses relating to storage space, Roberts' expenses in paying Kevin Roberts were exactly the same as they would have been if Hooker had not breached the contract. Kevin Roberts' salary, however, is not comparable to the storage costs in an important respect.

It is clear that the time which Kevin spent working on the Hooker project could, and presumably would, have been spent productively in other projects. As such, Roberts suffered an economic loss by having to pay an important employee his salary for working on a contract which would eventually be canceled. Kevin testified that he spent approximately forty percent of his working hours over a two-month period on the Hooker project. It is true that Roberts would have paid Kevin regardless of whether he had spent that time working on the Hooker project. However, the distinction is that, unless reimbursed for these expenses, the salary paid by Roberts for this time spent will have been paid for no resulting economic value. Given that Kevin Roberts was a salaried employee of Roberts who was directly engaged in working on the Hooker project, it can not be disputed that Roberts suffered expenses related to the contract in question by paying Kevin for his work.

The issue arises as to whether compensating Roberts for both its lost profits and for the salary of Kevin Roberts would amount to a double recovery. The answer to this question depends upon whether Kevin Roberts' salary was included in the $120,000 in expenses which Roberts estimated it would have incurred in completing the project. If said salary was included in the expenses, then the recovery would not amount to a double recovery, given that the amount of the salary would have already served to reduce the amount of profits in the calculation of damages.

The record does not reveal whether Roberts included an estimate of Kevin Roberts' salary allocable to the Hooker contract in his determination of his expenses. It is reasonable to assume, however, that a subcontractor includes in his bid estimate the salaries which he will be required to pay to all employees who will be directly involved in the project in question. It naturally adds to the expense of a project if a company is required to utilize the services of managerial personnel who may be unable to perform other tasks as a result of said project. Roberts suffered expenses by paying Kevin Roberts his salary without being able to utilize his expertise on other jobs for which they would be receiving the full amount of contract value. On these facts, it can not be said that the jury's awarding of these administrative costs was against the overwhelming weight of the evidence.

B. LOST PROFITS

. . .

It is clear that damages awarded by the jury were in the nature of expectation damages, and said damages included Roberts' lost profit from the deal, along with expenses that Roberts incurred in manufacturing the cabinets that it was unable to mitigate. The jury's awarding of Roberts' direct expenses in partially performing the contract in addition to lost profits was entirely proper, given that failing to do so would under-compensate Roberts by forcing him to pay for said expenses out of his net profits.

. . .

Hooker . . . argues that Roberts' lost profits should be measured by the four-day period during which production at Roberts' factory was shut down. However, the shut-down period at the factory would be much more relevant with regard to determining the amount of consequential damages resulting from the breach rather than measuring Roberts' amount of lost profits. The relevant inquiry is not the amount of profit that Roberts would have been able to make in the four days that the factory was shut down, but rather the amount of profit it would have been able to make on the *deal as a whole* had the contract not been breached by Hooker.

Roberts' daily manufacturing output would only be relevant in determining the amount of lost profits on the deal as a whole if it could be shown exactly how many days it would have taken for Roberts to manufacture the cabinets, and there was no exact proof in this regard at trial. Given the bid price of over $150,000, however, it is clear that it would have taken Roberts many more than four days to complete the contract, considering the daily manufacturing output of the factory of only $6,000/day. Kevin testified that the factory was capable of generating a daily production output considerably in excess of $6,000/day, but the completion of the contract would have taken weeks even at an increased rate of production.

Kevin testified that, in making his bid, he estimated the costs that his company would have incurred in manufacturing the cabinets to be approximately $120,000, and then factored in his desired profit margin of twenty-six percent, for a total of an approximately $151,000 total bid. Thus, Kevin testified that, had the contract been completed, Roberts expected to receive a profit of around thirty thousand dollars. Bids in construction situations are rarely susceptible of exact proof as to what the manufacturing costs and profits would have been, and, while the profit margin of twenty-six percent may appear high, Hooker's sole proof regarding the excessive nature of Roberts' claimed profit margin was his testimony regarding his own experiences as a general contractor, rather than a manufacturer/subcontractor.

This Court thus has only the conflicting testimony of Hooker and Roberts with which to determine the true profit margin, and, on these facts, it can not be said that the jury's verdict was against the overwhelming weight of the evidence. . . .

The only damages granted by the jury which this Court considers to be against the overwhelming weight of the evidence are the damages for the storage of the cabinets. While the storage costs constitute a rather insignificant portion of the damages, the fact remains that the awarding of the $1440 in storage costs was clearly erroneous and an abuse of discretion, given that Hooker suffered no real economic loss as a result of being forced to store the cabinets at his factory. Having established that a rather minor remittitur is in order, this Court's role is to reduce the damages to such an amount that the verdict is not in conflict with the overwhelming weight of the evidence.

Accordingly, this Court grants a remittitur of $1,260.00, which constitutes the difference between the $42,870.00 sum awarded by the jury and the sum of $41,610.00, which, this Court concludes, is not against the overwhelming weight of the evidence.

$ 5,117.28	Net Loss on Manufactured Cabinets
$ 3,775.04	Countertops
$ 886.25	Laminate
$ 72.38	Travel Expenses
$ 1,760.00	Administrative Time
$30,000.00	Lost profit on job
= $41,610.00	proper amount of damages

Affirmed on condition of remittitur; if remittitur refused, reversed and remanded for a new trial on damages only.

EGERER
v.
CSR WEST, LLC

Court of Appeals of Washington
67 P.3d 1128
2003

BECKER, C.J.

Appellant CSR West breached a contract to supply fill for land development. Issues on appeal include the calculation of damages based on "hypothetical cover"; the allowance of prejudgment interest; and the denial of the plaintiff's requests to include sales tax and consequential damages in the award of damages. We affirm in all respects.

MEASURE OF DAMAGES

According to unchallenged findings of fact entered after a bench trial, Robert Egerer owned a 10 acre parcel of land in Skagit County that he planned to develop into commercial property. The property required a considerable amount of fill to make it suitable for development.

Egerer first purchased fill material in 1995, when he contracted at the rate of $1.10 per cubic yard to have Wilder Construction haul to his property some material being excavated from the shoulders of Interstate 5 as a part of a highway improvement project. In its suitability to serve as structural fill, the shoulder material resembled a gravel known as "pit run," but it was cheaper than pit run because it contained asphalt grindings.

Beyond what Wilder Construction could supply, Egerer needed roughly 17,000 cubic yards of fill material. In May 1997, Egerer learned that CSR West had contracted with the Washington State Department of Transportation to excavate material from the shoulder areas of Interstate 5 near Lake Samish. He met with John Grisham, CSR's sales manager, and they reached an agreement to have CSR transport "all" the shoulder excavations from the project to Egerer's site at the rate of $.50 per cubic yard.

CSR brought fill material to Egerer's property on only two nights: July 9 and 10, 1997. Shortly thereafter, the Department of Transportation issued a change order that allowed CSR to use the excavated shoulder material in the reconstruction of the shoulder area. It was more profitable for CSR to supply the material for the State's use than to fulfill its contract with Egerer. CSR excavated a total of 16,750 cubic yards of material during its work on the shoulder project in 1997, and supplied virtually all of it to the Department of Transportation.

Egerer did not purchase replacement fill at the time of the breach in July 1997. Asked about this at trial, he explained that it would have been too expensive, and he also did not think there was time to find replacement fill and get it onto his property before the end of the summer. Egerer said that his window of opportunity to place fill on the property was June through September, before the weather became too wet. In January and February 1998, he obtained price quotes for pit run ranging from $8.25 per cubic yard to $9.00 per cubic yard. These prices exceeded Egerer's budget, and he did not contract for replacement fill at that time either.

In the summer of 1999, Egerer learned of an unexpected landslide at a gravel pit not far from his property. The company agreed to sell Egerer the unwanted slide material at a cost of $6.39 per cubic yard, including the cost of hauling and spreading.

Egerer filed suit in November 2000, alleging that CSR breached its contract by failing to deliver all the excavated shoulder material in the summer of 1997. After a bench trial, the court found breach. The court then turned to the Uniform Commercial Code to determine the measure of damages. CSR raises several legal issues with respect to the award of damages.

The findings, which are unchallenged, are deemed verities on appeal. We review conclusions of law de novo to see if they are supported by the trial court's findings of fact. *Bingham v. Lechner*, 111 Wash. App. 118, 127, 45 P.3d 562 (2002).

Where a seller fails to make delivery of goods sold to a buyer, the buyer has two alternative remedies under the Uniform Commercial Code. One is the remedy of "cover": the buyer may purchase substitute goods and recover as damages the difference between the cost of this cover and the contract price, provided the buyer covers in good faith and without unreasonable delay. RCW 62A.2-712. The other, a complete alternative, is damages for non-delivery, also known as "hypothetical cover": the buyer may recover as damages from the seller "the difference between the market price at the time when the buyer learned of the breach and the contract price." RCW 62A.2-713. This measure applies only when and to the extent that the buyer does not cover. Uniform Commercial Code Comment 5, RCWA 62A.2-713. "The general baseline adopted in this section uses as a yardstick the market in which the buyer would have obtained cover had he sought that relief." U.C.C. Comment 1, RCWA 62A.2-713. "The market or current price to be used in comparison with the contract price under this section is the price for goods of the same kind and in the same branch of trade." U.C.C. Comment 2, RCWA 62A.2-713.

The court determined that Egerer was limited to damages for non-delivery under section 2-713: "Mr. Egerer is limited to damages reflecting the difference between CSR contract price and the price he could have obtained replacement material for at the time of the breach in 1997. *See* RCW 62A.2-713(1) and Comment 3." The court found that Egerer could have obtained replacement material at the time of the breach for a cost of $8.25 per cubic yard—a price quoted to Egerer in early 1998. The court calculated his damages for the non-delivery of fill to be $129,812.50, which was the difference between the market price of $8.25 per cubic yard and the contract price of $.50 per cubic yard.

CSR accepts the trial court's decision to apply the remedy furnished by section 2-713, but contends the court erred by calculating damages based on a market price of $8.25 per cubic yard for pit run. CSR argues that $8.25 was not "the price for goods of the same kind" (as U.C.C. Comment 2 calls for) because pit run is a product superior to shoulder excavations containing asphalt grindings. CSR further argues that $8.25 was not "the market price at the time when the buyer learned of the breach" (as section 2-713 calls for) because the breach was in July 1997 and the $8.25 price was as of six months later—in January, 1998. CSR takes the position that the trial court should instead have used the $1.10 per cubic yard price reflected in Egerer's 1995 contract with Wilder Construction, because that was the only evidence in the record of a price for shoulder excavations. Use of the much higher price for pit run resulted in a windfall for Egerer, according to CSR.

The trial court expressly relied on Comment 3 to U.C.C. 2 713 in determining that $8.25 per cubic yard was the price for which Egerer could have obtained replacement material at the time of the breach. That comment states in part, "When the current market price under this section is difficult to prove the section on determination and proof of market price is available to permit a showing of a comparable market price or, where no market price is available, evidence of spot sale prices is proper." U.C.C. Comment 3, RCWA 62A.2-713. The section on determination and proof of market price provides,

> If evidence of a price prevailing at the times or places described in this Article is not readily available the price prevailing within any reasonable time before or after the time described or at any other place which in commercial judgment or under usage of trade would serve as a reasonable substitute for the one described may be used, making any proper allowance for the cost of transporting the goods to or from such other place.

RCW 62A.2-723(2).

A court is granted a "reasonable leeway" in measuring market price under section 2-723. *Sprague v. Sumitomo Forestry Co., Ltd.*, 104 Wash. 2d 751, 760, 709 P.2d 1200 (1985). Contrary to CSR's argument, a trial court may use a market price for goods different in quality from those for which the buyer contracted. That possibility is encompassed in the reference to "price . . . which in commercial judgment or under usage of trade would serve as a reasonable substitute for the one described." And section 2-723 expressly permits looking to a price "prevailing within any reasonable time before or after the time described."

We conclude the trial court did not misapply the law in concluding that the January 1998 price for pit run was the relevant market price. The court found the 1998 quotes for replacement material and hauling "were reasonable and customary," and noted that CSR "did not offer evidence that suitable replacement material was available at a lower price at the time of breach." There was testimony that shoulder excavation material, though cheap when available, is rarely available. John Grisham, CSR's sales manager, acknowledged that it would have been difficult for Egerer to locate an alternative supplier of shoulder excavations in 1997 because "quantities like that are few and far between." Grisham said he was unaware of any other pit in the area that would have had similar material available at a price anywhere near $.50 per cubic yard in the summer of 1997. Egerer's eventual purchase in 1999 was possible only because of the landslide that unexpectedly deposited unwanted fill material in a local gravel pit. If Egerer had covered at the time of the breach, higher-priced pit run would have been a reasonable substitute for the shoulder excavations.

Egerer, in his cross-appeal, argues that the relevant market price was much higher. He contends the trial court should have based its calculation of damages on figures showing that the Washington Department of Transportation was paying CSR between $33.33 and $46.80 per cubic yard for gravel pit material at that time. But the record does not indicate that Egerer made any argument below based on figures in CSR's contract with the State, and we will not consider it for the first time on appeal.

PREJUDGMENT INTEREST

The court determined that Egerer was entitled to prejudgment interest totaling $70,098.75, calculated at the statutory rate "beginning in July 1997 when CSR retained profits from the breach." The award was based on the court's conclusion that Egerer's damages were liquidated. CSR challenges this conclusion.

Prejudgment interest is awardable for a liquidated claim. *Prier v. Refrigeration Eng'g Co.*, 74 Wash. 2d 25, 32, 442 P.2d 621 (1968). A claim is liquidated "where the evidence furnishes data which, if believed, makes it possible to compute the amount with exactness, without reliance on opinion or discretion." *Prier*, 74 Wash. 2d at 32, 442 P.2d 621 (citing C. McCormick, *Damages* (Hornbook Series) §54, at 213 (1935)). A claim is unliquidated "where the exact amount of the sum to be allowed cannot be definitely fixed from the facts proved, disputed or undisputed, but must in the last analysis depend upon the opinion or discretion of the judge or jury as to whether a larger or a smaller amount should be allowed." *Prier*, 74 Wash. 2d at 33, 442 P.2d 621 (quoting C. McCormick, *Damages* (Hornbook Series) §54, at 213 (1935)).

CSR argues that Egerer's claim required the trial court, as fact-finder, to exercise discretion in deciding to use the January 1998 price of pit run as the market price, rather than the actual price Egerer paid for landslide gravel in the summer of 1999 or the Wilder contract price for shoulder excavations.

The fact that a claim is disputed does not render the claim unliquidated, so long as it may be determined by reference to an objective source such as fair market value. *Aker Verdal A/S v. Neil F. Lampson, Inc.*, 65 Wash. App. 177, 190, 828 P.2d 610 (1992). "However, when determining the *measure* of damages requires the exercise of discretion by the factfinder, the claim is unliquidated." *Aker Verdal A/S*, 65 Wash. App. at 191, 828 P.2d 610 (emphasis in original) (plaintiff made in-house repairs to part of damaged crane, and jury decided to measure damage as the internal cost of labor and materials rather than as the rate plaintiff could have charged the customer if crane had not collapsed; held, cost of in-house repair was unliquidated). *See also Maryhill Museum of Fine Arts v. Emil's Concrete Constr. Co.*, 50 Wash. App. 895, 903, 751 P.2d 866, *review denied*, 111 Wash. 2d 1009 (1988) (damages were unliquidated where finder of fact used discretion to determine that damages for breaching a contract to reconstruct a unique building would be the original cost of the contract).

Unlike in *Aker Verdal A/S* and *Maryhill Museum of Fine Arts*, here the measure of damages to be used was not left to the discretion of the fact-finder; it was fixed by statute as the difference between the contract price and the prevailing market price at the time of the breach. The facts are more like those in *Dautel v. Heritage Home Center, Inc.*, 89 Wash. App. 148, 948 P.2d 397 (1997), *review denied*, 135 Wash. 2d 1003, 959 P.2d 126 (1998). In that case, the plaintiff sued for back wages, including unpaid commissions. The trial court found the plaintiff was owed a 20 percent commission on two transactions rather than a 10 percent commission, as the employer contended. On appeal, this court held that the trial court had erroneously refused to award prejudgment interest.

. . .

CSR cites authority stating that a defendant should not be required to pay prejudgment interest in cases where the defendant is unable to ascertain the amount owed to the plaintiff. *Aker Verdal A/S*, 65 Wash. App. at 189, 828 P.2d 610, citing *Hansen v. Rothaus*, 107 Wash. 2d 468, 473, 730 P.2d 662 1986). But while CSR did not know precisely how much it would owe to Egerer until judgment was rendered, $8.25 per cubic yard was found to be a reasonable and customary rate and thus was within a range of market values readily ascertainable by CSR. That is enough to make the damages liquidated in cases where the measure of damage is market or current value:

> Where this is so, while the person who is charged with the duty of paying this valuation could probably not have known when the duty to pay arose, with entire exactness, the precise figure at which the value would be fixed, he could have estimated it within a narrow range of possible variation.

C. McCormick, *Damages* (Hornbook Series) §55, at 218 (1935).

That CSR proposed a lower market price does not render the claim unliquidated. The fact finder believed evidence showing that $8.25 was the market price, and that evidence made it possible to compute exact damages without reliance on opinion or discretion. *See Prier*, 74 Wash. 2d at 32, 442 P.2d 621.

CSR further argues that prejudgment interest, if awardable, should accrue from the time Egerer bought replacement fill in June 1999, not—as the trial court concluded—from the time of the breach in 1997. CSR cites authority stating that an injured party "should be compensated for the 'use value' of money it was forced to spend to cover its loss." *Aker Verdal A/S*, 65 Wash. App. at 189, 828 P.2d 610. CSR reasons that Egerer did not lose the use value of money until he actually made a replacement purchase in June of 1999, and that an award of prejudgment interest before that date constitutes a windfall for Egerer because it compensates him for the use of his money during a time when he still retained its use.

This is not, however, a case where damages were measured by the differences between the cost of cover and the contract price. Egerer's purchase in June 1999 was not cover. His damages were measured as "the difference between the market price *at the time the buyer learned of the breach* and the contract price." RCWA 62A.2-713 (emphasis added). Awarding prejudgment interest from the time of the breach is consistent with the section 2-713 measure of damages and with its purpose—to discourage sellers from repudiating their contracts as the market rises. *TexPar Energy, Inc. v. Murphy Oil USA, Inc.*, 45 F.3d 1111, 1114

(7th Cir. 1995). The award of prejudgment interest from the time of CSR's breach is also consistent with the Restatement of Contracts:

> If the breach consists of a failure to pay a definite sum in money or to render a performance with fixed or ascertainable monetary value, interest is recoverable from the time for performance on the amount due less all deductions to which the party in breach is entitled.

Restatement (Second) of Contracts §354, at 150 (1981). The comment to this section states:

> This Section deals with an injured party's right to interest as damages in compensation for the deprivation of a promised performance. Had the performance been rendered when it was due, the injured party would have been able to make use of it. Interest is a standardized form of compensation to the injured party for the loss of that use.

Restatement (Second) of Contracts §354, comment a, at 151 (1981).

CSR promised to supply fill to Egerer at a price he could afford. The breach deprived him of the opportunity to advance his development plans in the summer of 1997 because as the record indicates, cheap fill is rarely available. We conclude that the trial court properly selected July 1997, the date of breach, as the initiation point for the award of prejudgment interest.

GROVES
v.
JOHN WUNDER CO.
Supreme Court of Minnesota
286 N.W. 235
1939

STONE, J.

Action for breach of contract. Plaintiff got judgment for a little over $15,000. Sorely disappointed by that sum, he appeals.

In August, 1927, S. J. Groves & Sons Company, a corporation (hereinafter mentioned simply as Groves), owned a tract of 24 acres of Minneapolis suburban real estate. It was served or easily could be reached by railroad trackage. It is zoned as heavy industrial property. But for lack of development of the neighborhood its principal value thus far may have been in the deposit of sand and gravel which it carried. The Groves company had a plant on the premises for excavating and screening the gravel. Nearby defendant owned and was operating a similar plant.

In August, 1927, Groves and defendant made the involved contract. For the most part it was a lease from Groves, as lessor, to defendant, as lessee; its term seven years. Defendant agreed to remove the sand and gravel and to leave the property "at a uniform grade, substantially the same as the grade now existing at the roadway . . . on said premises, and that in stripping the overburden . . . it will use said overburden for the purpose of maintaining and establishing said grade."

Under the contract defendant got the Groves screening plant. The transfer thereof and the right to remove the sand and gravel made the consideration moving from Groves to defendant, except that defendant incidentally got rid of Groves as a competitor. On defendant's part it paid Groves $105,000. So that from the outset, on Groves' part the contract was executed except for defendant's right to continue using the property for the stated term. (Defendant had a right to renewal which it did not exercise.)

Defendant breached the contract deliberately. It removed from the premises only "the richest and best of the gravel" and wholly failed, according to the findings, "to perform and comply with the terms, conditions, and provisions of said lease . . . with respect to the condition in which the surface of the demised premises was required to be left." Defendant surrendered the premises, not substantially at the grade required by the contract "nor at any uniform grade." Instead, the ground was "broken, rugged, and uneven." Plaintiff sues as assignee and successor in right of Groves.

As the contract was construed below, the finding is that to complete its performance 288,495 cubic yards of overburden would need to be excavated, taken from the premises, and deposited elsewhere. The reasonable cost of doing that was found to be upwards of $60,000. But, if defendant had left the premises at the uniform grade required by the lease, the reasonable value of the property on the determinative date would have been only $12,160. The judgment was for that sum, including interest, thereby nullifying plaintiff's claim that cost of completing the contract rather than difference in value of the land was the measure of damages. The gauge of damage adopted by the decision was the difference between the market value of plaintiff's land in the condition it was when the contract was made and what it would have been if defendant had performed. The one question for us arises upon plaintiff's assertion that he was entitled, not to that difference in value, but to the reasonable cost to him of doing the work called for by the contract which defendant left undone.

1. Defendant's breach of contract was wilful. There was nothing of good faith about it. Hence, that the decision below handsomely rewards bad faith and deliberate breach of contract is obvious. That is not allowable. Here the rule is well settled, and has been since Elliott v. Caldwell, 43 Minn. 357, 45 N.W. 845, 9 L.R.A. 52, that, where the contractor wilfully and fraudulently varies from the terms of a construction contract, he cannot sue thereon and have the benefit of the equitable doctrine of substantial performance. That is the rule generally. See Annotation, "Wilful or intentional variation by contractor from terms of contract in regard to material or work as affecting measure of damages," 6 A.L.R. 137.

Jacob & Youngs, Inc. v. Kent, 230 N.Y. 239, is typical. It was a case of substantial performance of a building contract. (This case is distinctly the opposite.)

Mr. Justice Cardozo, in the course of his opinion, stressed the distinguishing features. "Nowhere," he said, "will change be tolerated, however, if it is so dominant or pervasive as in any real or substantial measure to frustrate the purpose of the contract." Again, "the willful transgressor must accept the penalty of his transgression."

2. In reckoning damages for breach of a building or construction contract, the law aims to give the disappointed promisee, so far as money will do it, what he was promised. . . .

Never before, so far as our decisions show, has it even been suggested that lack of value in the land furnished to the contractor who had bound himself to improve it any escape from the ordinary consequences of a breach of the contract.

. . .

Even in case of substantial performance in good faith, the resulting defects being remediable, it is error to instruct that the measure of damage is "the difference in value between the house as it was and as it would have been if constructed according to contract." The "correct doctrine" is that the cost of remedying the defect is the "proper" measure of damages. Snider v. Peters Home Building Co., 139 Minn. 413, 414, 416, 167 N.W. 108.

. . .

The owner's right to improve his property is not trammeled by its small value. It is his right to erect thereon structures which will reduce its value. If that be the result, it can be of no aid to any contractor who declines performance. As said long ago in Chamberlain v. Parker, 45 N.Y. 569: "A man may do what he will with his own, . . . and if he chooses to erect a monument to his caprice or folly on his premises, and employs and pays another to do it, it does not lie with a defendant who has been so employed and paid for building it, to say that his own performance would not be beneficial to the plaintiff." To the same effect is Restatement, Contracts, §346, p. 576, Illustrations of Subsection (1), par. 4.

Suppose a contractor were suing the owner for breach of a grading contract such as this. Would any element of value, or lack of it, in the land have any relevance in reckoning damages? Of course not. The contractor would be compensated for what he had lost, i.e., his profit. Conversely, in such a case as this, the owner is entitled to compensation for what he has lost, that is, the work or structure which he has been promised, for which he has paid, and of which he has been deprived by the contractor's breach.

To diminish damages recoverable against him in proportion as there is presently small value in the land would favor the faithless contractor. It would also ignore and so defeat plaintiff's right to contract and build for the future. To justify such a course would require more of the prophetic vision than judges possess. . . .

. . .

That is unquestioned law, but for its correct application there must be ascertainment of the loss for which compensation is to be reckoned. In tort, the thing lost is money value, nothing more. But under a construction contract, the thing lost by a breach such as we have here is a physical structure or accomplishment, a promised and paid for alteration in land. That is the "injury" for which the law gives him compensation. Its only appropriate measure is the cost of performance.

It is suggested that because of little or no value in his land the owner may be unconscionably enriched by such a reckoning. The answer is that there can be no unconscionable enrichment, no advantage upon which the law will frown, when the result is but to give one party to a contract only what the other has promised; particularly where, as here, the delinquent has had full payment for the promised performance.

3. It is said by the Restatement, Contracts, §346, comment b: "Sometimes defects in a completed structure cannot be physically remedied without tearing down and rebuilding, at a cost that would be imprudent and unreasonable. The law does not require damages to be measured by a method requiring such economic waste. If no such waste is involved, the cost of remedying the defect is the amount awarded as compensation for failure to render the promised performance."

The "economic waste" declaimed against by the decisions applying that rule has nothing to do with the value in money of the real estate, or even with the product of the contract. The waste avoided is only that which would come from wrecking a physical structure, completed, or nearly so, under the contract. The cases applying that rule go no further. Illustrative are Buchholz v. Rosenberg, 163 Wis. 312, 156 N.W. 946; Burmeister v. Wolfgram, 175 Wis. 506, 185 N.W. 517. Absent such waste, as it is in this case, the rule of the Restatement, Contracts, §346, is that "the cost of remedying the defect is the amount awarded as compensation for failure to render the promised performance." That means that defendants here are liable to plaintiff for the reasonable cost of doing what defendants promised to do and have wilfully declined to do.

. . .

The judgment must be reversed with a new trial to follow.
So ordered.

JULIUS J. OLSON, J. (dissenting).

. . .

Since there is no issue of fact we should limit our inquiry to the single legal problem presented: What amount in money will adequately compensate plaintiff for his loss caused by defendant's failure to render performance?

When the parties entered into this contract each had a right to rely upon the promise of full and complete performance on the part of the other. And by "performance" is meant "such a thorough fulfillment of a duty as puts an end to obligations by leaving nothing more to be done." McGuire v. J. Neils Lumber Co., 97 Minn. 293, 298, 107 N.W. 130, 132. . . .

Another principle, of universal application, is that a party is entitled to have that for which he contracted, or its equivalent. What that equivalent is depends upon the circumstances of each case. . . . [P]laintiff "is entitled to be placed, in so far as this can be done by money, in the same position he would have occupied if the contract had been performed." But "his recovery is limited to the loss he has actually suffered by reason of the breach; he is not entitled to be placed in a better position than he would have been in if the contract had not been broken." 15 Am. Jur., Damages, §43.

. . .

We have here then a situation where, concededly, if the contract had been performed, plaintiff would have had property worth, in round numbers, no more than $12,000. If he is to be awarded damages in an amount exceeding $60,000 he will be receiving at least 500 per cent more than his property, properly leveled to grade by actual performance, was intrinsically worth when the breach occurred. To so conclude is to give him something far beyond what the parties had in mind or contracted for. There is no showing made, nor any finding suggested, that this property was unique, specially desirable for a particular or personal use, or of special value as to location or future use different from that of other property surrounding it. Under the circumstances here appearing, it seems clear that what the parties contracted for was to put the property in shape for general sale. . . .

. . . I think the judgment should be affirmed.

PEEVYHOUSE
v.
 # GARLAND COAL & MINING CO.
Supreme Court of Oklahoma
382 P.2d 109
1962

Modified and Rehearing Denied March 26, 1963
Second Rehearing Denied May 28, 1963

JACKSON, J.

In the trial court, plaintiffs Willie and Lucille Peevyhouse sued the defendant, Garland Coal and Mining Company, for damages for breach of contract. Judgment was for plaintiffs in an amount considerably less than was sued for. Plaintiffs appeal and defendant cross-appeals.

In the briefs on appeal, the parties present their argument and contentions under several propositions; however, they all stem from the basic question of whether the trial court properly instructed the jury on the measure of damages.

Briefly stated, the facts are as follows: plaintiffs owned a farm containing coal deposits, and in November, 1954, leased the premises to defendant for a period of five years for coal mining purposes. A "stripmining" operation was contemplated in which the coal would be taken from pits on the surface of the ground, instead of from underground mine shafts. In addition to the usual covenants found in a coal mining lease, defendant specifically agreed to perform certain restorative and remedial work at the end of the lease period. It is unnecessary to set out the details of the work to be done, other than to say that it would involve the moving of many thousands of cubic yards of dirt, at a cost estimated by expert witnesses at about $29,000.00. However, plaintiffs sued for only $25,000.00.

During the trial, it was stipulated that all covenants and agreements in the lease contract had been fully carried out by both parties, except the remedial work mentioned above; defendant conceded that this work had not been done.

Plaintiffs introduced expert testimony as to the amount and nature of the work to be done, and its estimated cost. Over plaintiffs' objections, defendant thereafter introduced expert testimony as to the "diminution in value" of plaintiffs' farm resulting from the failure of defendant to render performance as agreed in the contract—that is, the difference between the present value of the farm, and what its value would have been if defendant had done what it agreed to do.

At the conclusion of the trial, the court instructed the jury that it must return a verdict for plaintiffs, and left the amount of damages for jury determination. On the measure of damages, the court instructed the jury that it might consider the cost of performance of the work defendant agreed to do, "together with all of the evidence offered on behalf of either party."

It thus appears that the jury was at liberty to consider the "diminution in value" of plaintiffs' farm as well as the cost of "repair work" in determining the amount of damages.

It returned a verdict for plaintiffs for $5000.00—only a fraction of the "cost of performance," *but more than the total value of the farm even after the remedial work is done.*

On appeal, the issue is sharply drawn. Plaintiffs contend that the true measure of damages in this case is what it will cost plaintiffs to obtain performance of the work that was not done because of defendant's default. Defendant argues that the measure of damages is the cost of performance "limited, however, to the total difference in the market value before and after the work was performed."

It appears that this precise question has not heretofore been presented to this court. In Ardizonne v. Archer, 72 Okl. 70, 178 P. 263, this court held that the measure of damages for breach of a contract to drill an oil well was the reasonable cost of drilling the well, but here a slightly different factual situation exists. The drilling of an oil well will yield valuable geological information, even if no oil or gas is found, and of course if the well is a producer, the value of the premises increases. In the case before us, it is argued by defendant with some force that the performance of the remedial work defendant agreed to do will add at the most only a few hundred dollars to the value of plaintiffs' farm, and that the damages should be limited to that amount because that is all plaintiffs have lost.

Plaintiffs rely on Groves v. John Wunder Co., 205 Minn. 163. In that case, the Minnesota court, in a substantially similar situation, adopted the "cost of performance" rule as-opposed to the "value" rule. The result was to authorize a jury to give plaintiff damages in the amount of $60,000, where the real estate concerned would have been worth only $12,160, even if the work contracted for had been done.

It may be observed that Groves v. John Wunder Co., supra, is the only case which has come to our attention in which the cost of performance rule has been followed under circumstances where the cost of performance greatly exceeded the diminution in value resulting from the breach of contract. Incidentally, it appears that this case was decided by a plurality rather than a majority of the members of the court.

. . .

The explanation may be found in the fact that the situations presented are arti-ficial ones. It is highly unlikely that the ordinary property owner would agree to pay $29,000 (or its equivalent) for the construction of "improvements" upon his property that would increase its value only about ($300) three hundred dollars. The result is that we are called upon to apply principles of law theoretically based upon reason and reality to a situation which is basically unreasonable and unrealistic.

. . .

. . . The primary purpose of the lease contract between plaintiffs and defendant was neither "building and construction" nor "grading and excavation." It was merely to accomplish the economical recovery and marketing of coal from the premises, to the profit of all parties. The special provisions of the lease contract pertaining to remedial work were incidental to the main object involved.

Even in the case of contracts that are unquestionably building and construction contracts, the authorities are not in agreement as to the factors to be considered in determining whether the cost of performance rule or the value rule should be applied. The American Law Institute's Restatement of the Law, Contracts, Volume 1, Sections 346(1)(a)(i) and (ii) submits the proposition that the cost of performance is the proper measure of damages "if this is possible and does not involve *unreason-able economic waste*"; and that the diminution in value caused by the breach is the proper measure "if construction and completion in accordance with the contract would involve *unreasonable economic waste*." (Emphasis supplied.) In an explana-tory comment immediately following the text, the Restatement makes it clear that the "economic waste" referred to consists of the destruction of a substantially com-pleted building or other structure. Of course no such destruction is involved in the case now before us.

On the other hand, in McCormick, Damages, it is said with regard to building and construction contracts that ". . . in cases where the defect is one that can be repaired or cured without *undue expense*" the cost of performance is the proper measure of damages, but where ". . . the defect in material or construction is one that cannot be remedied without *an expenditure for reconstruction disproportionate to the end to be attained*" (emphasis supplied) the value rule should be followed. The same idea was expressed in Jacob & Youngs, Inc. v. Kent:

> "The owner is entitled to the money which will permit him to complete, unless the cost of completion is grossly and unfairly out of proportion to the good to be attained. When that is true, the measure is the difference in value."

It thus appears that the prime consideration in the Restatement was "economic waste"; and that the prime consideration in McCormick and in Jacob & Youngs, was the relationship between the expense involved and the "end to be attained"—in other words, the "relative economic benefit."

. . .

We therefore hold that where, in a coal mining lease, lessee agrees to perform certain remedial work on the premises concerned at the end of the lease period, and thereafter the contract is fully performed by both parties except that the remedial work is not done, the measure of damages in an action by lessor against lessee for damages for breach of contract is ordinarily the reasonable cost of performance of the work; however, where the contract provision breached was merely incidental to the main purpose in view, and where the economic benefit which would result to lessor by full performance of the work is grossly disproportionate to the cost of performance, the damages which lessor may recover are limited to the diminution in value resulting to the premises because of the non-performance.

. . .

Under the most liberal view of the evidence herein, the diminution in value resulting to the premises because of non-performance of the remedial work was $300.00. After a careful search of the record, we have found no evidence of a higher figure, and plaintiffs do not argue in their briefs that a greater diminution in value was sustained. It thus appears that the judgment was clearly excessive, and that the amount for which judgment should have been rendered is definitely and satisfactorily shown by the record.

. . .

We are of the opinion that the judgment of the trial court for plaintiffs should be, and it is hereby, modified and reduced to the sum of $300.00, and as so modified it is affirmed.

WELCH, DAVISON, HALLEY, and JOHNSON, JJ., concur.

WILLIAMS, C.J., BLACKBIRD, V.C.J., and IRWIN and BERRY, JJ., dissent.

IRWIN, J. (dissenting).

By the specific provisions in the coal mining lease under consideration, the defendant agreed as follows:

> "* * *
>
> "7b Lessee agrees to make fills in the pits dug on said premises on the property line in such manner that fences can be placed thereon and access had to opposite sides of the pits.
>
> "c Lessee agrees to smooth off the top of the spoil banks on the above premises.
>
> "7d Lessee agrees to leave the creek crossing the above premises in such a condition that it will not interfere with the crossings to be made in pits as set out in 7b.
> "* * *
>
> "7f Lessee further agrees to leave no shale or dirt on the high wall of said pits. * * *"

Following the expiration of the lease, plaintiffs made demand upon defendant that it carry out the provisions of the contract and to perform those covenants contained therein.

Defendant admits that it failed to perform its obligations that it agreed and contracted to perform under the lease contract and there is nothing in the record which indicates that defendant could not perform its obligations. Therefore, in my opinion defendant's breach of the contract was wilful and not in good faith.

Although the contract speaks for itself, there were several negotiations between the plaintiffs and defendant before the contract was executed. Defendant admitted in the trial of the action, that plaintiffs insisted that the above provisions be included in the contract and that they would not agree to the coal mining lease unless the above provisions were included.

In consideration for the lease contract, plaintiffs were to receive a certain amount as royalty for the coal produced and marketed and in addition thereto their land was to be restored as provided in the contract.

Defendant received as consideration for the contract, its proportionate share of the coal produced and marketed and in addition thereto, the *right to use* plaintiffs' land in the furtherance of its mining operations.

The cost for performing the contract in question could have been reasonably approximated when the contract was negotiated and executed and there are no conditions now existing which could not have been reasonably anticipated by the parties. Therefore, defendant had knowledge, when it prevailed upon the plaintiffs to execute the lease, that the cost of performance might be disproportionate to the value or benefits received by plaintiff for the performance.

Defendant has received its benefits under the contract and now urges, in substance, that plaintiffs' measure of damages for its failure to perform should be the economic value of performance to the plaintiffs and not the cost of performance.

If a peculiar set of facts should exist where the above rule should be applied as the proper measure of damages, (and in my judgment those facts do not exist in the instant case) before such rule should be applied, consideration should be given to the benefits received or contracted for by the party who asserts the application of the rule.

Defendant did not have the right to mine plaintiffs' coal or to use plaintiffs' property for its mining operations without the consent of plaintiffs. Defendant had knowledge of the benefits that it would receive under the contract and the approximate cost of performing the contract. With this knowledge, it must be presumed that defendant thought that it would be to its economic advantage to enter into the contract with plaintiffs and that it would reap benefits from the contract, or it would have not entered into the contract.

Therefore, if the value of the performance of a contract should be considered in determining the measure of damages for breach of a contract, the value of the benefits received under the contract by a party who breaches a contract should also be considered. However, in my judgment, to give consideration to either in the instant action, completely rescinds and holds for naught the solemnity of the contract before us and makes an entirely new contract for the parties.

. . .

In the instant action defendant has made no attempt to even substantially perform. The contract in question is not immoral, is not tainted with fraud, and was not entered into through mistake or accident and is not contrary to public policy. It is clear and unambiguous and the parties understood the terms thereof, and the approximate cost of fulfilling the obligations could have been approximately ascertained. There are no conditions existing now which could not have been reasonably anticipated when the contract was negotiated and executed. The defendant could have performed the contract if it desired. It has accepted and reaped the benefits of its contract and now urges that plaintiffs' benefits under the contract be denied. If plaintiffs' benefits are denied, such benefits would inure to the direct benefit of the defendant.

Therefore, in my opinion, the plaintiffs were entitled to specific performance of the contract and since defendant has failed to perform, the proper measure of damages should be the cost of performance. Any other measure of damage would be holding for naught the express provisions of the contract; would be taking from the plaintiffs the benefits of the contract and placing those benefits in defendant which has failed to perform its obligations; would be granting benefits to defendant without a resulting obligation; and would be completely rescinding the solemn obligation of the contract for the benefit of the defendant to the detriment of the plaintiffs by making an entirely new contract for the parties.

I therefore respectfully dissent to the opinion promulgated by a majority of my associates.

SUPPLEMENTAL OPINION ON REHEARING

JACKSON, J.

In a Petition for Rehearing, plaintiffs Peevyhouse have raised certain questions not presented in the original briefs on appeal.

They insist that the trial court excluded evidence as to the total value of the premises concerned, and, in effect, that they have not had their "day in court". . . .

. . .

In their motion for new trial, plaintiffs did not complain that they had been prevented from offering evidence as to the diminution in value of their lands; on the contrary, they affirmatively complained of the trial court's action in admitting evidence of the defendant on that point.

. . .

The whole record in this case justifies the conclusion that plaintiffs tried their case upon the theory that the "cost of performance" would be the sole measure of damages and that they would recognize no other. In view of the whole record in this case and the original briefs on appeal, we conclude that they so tried it *with notice* that defendant would contend for the "diminution in value" rule. . . .

. . . [P]laintiffs offered no evidence on the question of "diminution in value" and objected to similar evidence offered by the defendant; their motion for new trial contained no allegation that they had been prevented from offering evidence on this question; in their reply brief they did not controvert the allegation in defendant's answer brief that the record showed a "diminution in value" of only $300.00; and their statement in petition for rehearing that the court's instructions on the measure of damages came as a "complete surprise" and "did not afford them the opportunity to prepare and introduce evidence under the 'diminution in value' rule" is not supported by the record.

We think plaintiffs' present position is that of a plaintiff in any damage suit who has failed to prove his damages—opposed by a defendant who has proved plaintiff's damages; and that plaintiffs' complaint that the record does not show the total "diminution in value" to their lands comes too late. It is well settled that a party will not be permitted to change his theory of the case upon appeal. Knox v. Eason Oil Co., 190 Okl. 627, 126 P.2d 247.

. . .

The petition for rehearing is denied.

HALLEY, V.C.J., and WELCH, DAVISON and JOHNSON, JJ., concur.

BLACKBIRD, C.J., and WILLIAMS, IRWIN and BERRY, JJ., dissent.

Problems

1. Insubstantial Performance. Paul Gould's contractor, Takis Argentinis, stopped work on Gould's house prior to completion. Gould sued Argentinis seeking the cost of completing performance, which was $73,000. Argentinis countered that Gould was entitled to only $30,000 because Gould had paid only $297,000 of the $340,000 contract price. If the court finds that Argentinis failed to substantially perform his obligations under the contract, what is the appropriate remedy for Gould?

2. Challenger Fallout. NASA contracted to launch a series of commercial satellites owned by Hughes Communications Galaxy into space from NASA's space shuttles. Following the explosion that destroyed the space shuttle Challenger in January 1986, President Reagan decided that NASA shuttles would no longer be used for commercial satellite launches. At that time, NASA was still contractually obligated to launch five of Hughes's HS-393 satellites over a period of several years. Without access to the space shuttles, Hughes turned to expendable launch vehicles (ELVs)—essentially, large rockets—to launch its satellites. Launching satellites using ELVs was more expensive than Hughes's contracted price with NASA. In addition, the HS-393 satellites were not well suited for ELV launches, so after launching three HS-393 satellites on ELVs, Hughes developed and launched HS-601 satellites, which were better suited to the ELV technology and, in addition, more powerful satellites.

At a trial on the issue of damages, Hughes calculated the difference in the cost of launching an HS-393 satellite using ELVs and the cost it would have paid under the NASA contract and requested five times that amount (for the five launches it had left on its contract with NASA at the time of breach). NASA contended that, because Hughes only launched three HS-393s, it was only entitled to three times the cost differential.

The NASA contract with Hughes included a "reflight" clause, which would provide Hughes with a free relaunch on a later space shuttle if a satellite was not deployed or its deployment deviated from the proper orbit. Such a term was not available in Hughes's contracts with the ELV providers, so Hughes purchased "launch insurance," which would have reimbursed the company for the cost of an unsuccessful launch. Hughes sought reimbursement for the cost of the launch insurance, and NASA objected on the ground that such insurance was not included in its contract with Hughes.

As a result of NASA's breach of contract and the subsequent increase in costs of launching satellites, Hughes increased the price it charged its customers for satellite space. NASA sought to have these revenues subtracted from the damages it owed to Hughes as "losses avoided." Hughes argued that it would be improper to consider price concessions obtained by Hughes subsequent to the breach as part of the damage calculation.

How should the court rule on these three issues concerning the calculation of damages?

3. Restricted Stock. According to the contract between TheraTx and holders of certain restricted shares of its stock, the stockholders would be permitted to trade their shares for a two-year period if TheraTx undertook a public offering of additional stock. (Otherwise, the restrictions would prevent those shareholders from trading their stock.) TheraTx did make a public offering, but prevented those stockholders from selling their shares for the first six months. During that six-month period, TheraTx's share price reached a high of $23 per share. When TheraTx lifted the restriction on the stockholders, the share price had declined to $13. The stockholders sued for breach of contract. Assuming that TheraTx's actions breached its agreement with the shareholders, how should their damages be calculated?

4. Hardwood Floors. Steven and Ana Marie Bray brought a suit for breach of contract against the builder of their new house, Founders C.D., for improperly installing the hardwood floors in their home. Visible sections of the kitchen floor were incorrectly installed, cracked, and/or faded, and the flooring under the kitchen cabinets was improperly installed as well. At trial, undisputed evidence was presented that replacing the floor, including removing the cabinets, installing flooring underneath, and then reinstalling the cabinets, would cost approximately $25,000. The Brays objected to this measure of damages, however, because it did not take into account the disruption that they would suffer as a result of the repairs. Instead, the Brays sought the diminished value of the home as a consequence of the mistakes in the flooring, which they and their real estate agent estimated to be $60,000. What amount of damages should the court award?

D. THE MITIGATION PRINCIPLE

As described in the introduction to the previous section, the law of contract damages assumes that non-breaching parties can and will use the proceeds of a monetary award to secure from a third party the performance expected under the contract. More broadly, under the mitigation principle, the law treats non-breaching parties as if they took whatever steps necessary, within reason, to minimize the extent of the damages suffered as a result of the breach. Although the non-breaching party may choose to suffer the full direct consequences of breach rather than take action to avoid them, courts will calculate her damages—and thus limit her award—on the assumption that she took reasonable steps to reduce the harm. See Rest. (2d) Contracts §350.

The following cases address three conceptual issues raised by the mitigation principle. The first pair of cases—*Rockingham County v. Luten Bridge Company* and *Bomberger v. McKelvey*—concern how to measure damages where there was some uncertainty as to what course of action would minimize total damages. The next case—*Parker v. Twentieth Century-Fox Film Corporation*—considers, in the context of an employment contract, when taking no action is reasonable under the circumstances. The final decision, *In re WorldCom, Inc.*, considers the non-breaching party's argument that entering into a substitute transaction would reduce his direct damages by cannibalizing his stream of future business opportunities, often referred to as the "lost volume seller" problem.

ROCKINGHAM COUNTY
v.
LUTEN BRIDGE CO.
U.S. Court of Appeals, Fourth Circuit
35 F.2d 301
1929

PARKER, J.

This was an action at law instituted in the court below by the Luten Bridge Company, as plaintiff, to recover of Rockingham county, North Carolina, an amount alleged to be due under a contract, but contends that notice of cancellation was given the bridge company before the erection of the bridge was commenced, and that it is liable only for the damages which the company would have sustained, if it had abandoned construction at that time. The judge below refused to strike out an answer filed by certain members of the board of commissioners of the county, admitting liability in accordance with the prayer of the complaint, allowed this pleading to be introduced in evidence as the answer of the county, excluded evidence offered by the county in support of its contentions as to notice of cancellation and damages, and instructed a verdict for plaintiff for the full amount of its claim. From judgment on this verdict the county has appealed.

The facts out of which the case arises, as shown by the affidavits and offers of proof appearing in the record, are as follows: On January 7, 1924, the board of commissioners of Rockingham county voted to award to plaintiff a contract for the construction of the bridge in controversy. Three of the five commissioners favored the awarding of the contract and two opposed it. Much feeling was engendered over the matter, with the result that on February 11, 1924, W.K. Pruitt, one of the commissioners who had voted in the affirmative, sent his resignation to the clerk of the superior court of the county. The clerk received this resignation on the same day, and immediately accepted same and noted his acceptance thereon. Later in the day, Pruitt called him over the telephone and stated that he wished to withdraw the resignation, and later sent him written notice to the same effect. The clerk, however, paid no attention to the attempted withdrawal, and proceeded on the next day to appoint one W.W. Hampton as a member of the board to succeed him.

After his resignation, Pruitt attended no further meetings of the board, and did nothing further as a commissioner of the county. Likewise Pratt and McCollum, the other two members of the board who had voted with him in favor of the contract, attended no further meetings. Hampton, on the other hand, took the oath of office immediately upon his appointment and entered upon the discharge of the duties of a commissioner. He met regularly with the two remaining members of the board, Martin and Barber, in the courthouse at the county seat, and with them attended to all of the business of the county. Between the 12th of February and the first Monday in December following, these three attended, in all, 25 meetings of the board.

At one of these meetings, a regularly advertised called meeting held on February 21st, a resolution was unanimously adopted declaring that the contract for the building of the bridge was not legal and valid, and directing the clerk of the board to notify plaintiff that it refused to recognize same as a valid contract, and that plaintiff should proceed no further thereunder. This resolution also rescinded action of the board theretofore taken looking to the construction of a hard-surfaced road, in which the bridge was to be a mere connecting link. The clerk duly sent a certified copy of this resolution to plaintiff.

At the regular monthly meeting of the board on March 3d, a resolution was passed directing that plaintiff be notified that any work done on the bridge would be done by it at its own risk and hazard, that the board was of the opinion that the contract for the construction of the bridge was not valid and legal, and that, even if the board were mistaken as to this, it did not desire to construct the bridge, and would contest payment for same if constructed. A copy of this resolution was also sent to plaintiff. At the regular monthly meeting on April 7th, a resolution was passed, reciting that the board had been informed that one of its members was privately insisting that the bridge be constructed. It repudiated this action on the part of the member and gave notice that it would not be recognized. At the September meeting, a resolution was passed to the effect that the board would pay no bills presented by plaintiff or any one connected with the bridge. At the time of the passage of the first resolution, very little work toward the construction of the bridge had been done, it being estimated that the total cost of labor done and material on the ground was around $1,900; but, notwithstanding the repudiation of the contract by the county, the bridge company continued with the work of construction.

On November 24, 1924, plaintiff instituted this action against Rockingham county, and against Pruitt, Pratt, McCollum, Martin, and Barber, as constituting its board of commissioners. Complaint was filed, setting forth the execution of the contract and the doing of work by plaintiff thereunder, and alleging that for work done up until November 3, 1924, the county was indebted in the sum of $18,301.07. . . .

. . .

As the county now admits the execution and validity of the contract, and the breach on its part, the ultimate question in the case is one as to the measure of plaintiff's recovery . . . whether plaintiff, if the notices are to be deemed action by the county, can recover under the contract for work done after they were received, or is limited to the recovery of damages for breach of contract as of that date.

. . .

Coming, then, to the [] question—i.e., as to the measure of plaintiff's recovery—we do not think that, after the county had given notice, while the contract was still executory, that it did not desire the bridge built and would not pay for it, plaintiff could proceed to build it and recover the contract price. It is true that the county had no right to rescind the contract, and the notice given plaintiff amounted to a breach on its part; but, after plaintiff had received notice of the breach, it was its duty to do nothing to increase the damages flowing therefrom. If A enters into a binding contract to build a house for B, B, of course, has no right to rescind the contract without A's consent. But if, before the house is built, he decides that he does not want it, and notifies A to that effect, A has no right to proceed with the building and thus pile up damages. His remedy is to treat the contract as broken when he receives the notice, and sue for the recovery of such damages, as he may have sustained from the breach, including any profit which he would have realized upon performance, as well as any other losses which may have resulted to him. In the case at bar, the county decided not to build the road of which the bridge was to be a part, and did not build it. The bridge, built in the midst of the forest, is of no value to the county because of this change of circumstances. When, therefore, the county gave notice to the plaintiff that it would not proceed with the project, plaintiff should have desisted from further work. It had no right thus to pile up damages by proceeding with the erection of a useless bridge.

The contrary view was expressed by Lord Cockburn in Frost v. Knight, L.R. 7 Ex. 111, but, as pointed out by Prof. Williston (Williston on Contracts, vol. 3, p. 2347), it is not in harmony with the decisions in this country. The American rule and the reasons supporting it are well stated by Prof. Williston as follows:

"There is a line of cases running back to 1845 which holds that, after an absolute repudiation or refusal to perform by one party to a contract, the other party cannot continue to perform and recover damages based on full performance. This rule is only a particular application of the general rule of damages that a plaintiff cannot hold a defendant liable for damages which need not have been incurred; or, as it is often stated, the plaintiff must, so far as he can without loss to himself, mitigate the damages caused by the defendant's wrongful act. The application of this rule to the matter in question is obvious. If a man engages to have work done, and afterwards repudiates his contract before the work has been begun or when it has been only partially done, it is inflicting damage on the defendant without benefit to the plaintiff to allow the latter to insist on proceeding with the contract. The work may be useless to the defendant, and yet he would be forced to pay the full contract price. On the other hand, the plaintiff is interested only in the profit he will make out of the contract. If he receives this it is equally advantageous for him to use his time otherwise."

The leading case on the subject in this country is the New York case of Clark v. Marsiglia, 1 Denio (N.Y.) 317, 43 Am. Dec. 670. In that case defendant had employed plaintiff to paint certain pictures for him, but countermanded the order before the work was finished. Plaintiff, however, went on and completed the work and sued for the contract price. In reversing a judgment for plaintiff, the court said:

> "The plaintiff was allowed to recover as though there had been no countermand of the order; and in this the court erred. The defendant, by requiring the plaintiff to stop work upon the paintings, violated his contract, and thereby incurred a liability to pay such damages as the plaintiff should sustain. Such damages would include a recompense for the labor done and materials used, and such further sum in damages as might, upon legal principles, be assessed for the breach of the contract; but the plaintiff had no right, by obstinately persisting in the work, to make the penalty upon the defendant greater than it would otherwise have been."

And the rule as established by the great weight of authority in America is summed up in the following statement in 6 R.C.L. 1029, which is quoted with approval by the Supreme Court of North Carolina in the recent case of Novelty Advertising Co. v. Farmers' Mut. Tobacco Warehouse Co., 186 N.C. 197, 119 S.E. 196, 198:

> "While a contract is executory a party has the power to stop performance on the other side by an explicit direction to that effect, subjecting himself to such damages as will compensate the other party for being stopped in the performance on his part at that stage in the execution of the contract. The party thus forbidden cannot afterwards go on and thereby increase the damages, and then recover such damages from the other party. The legal right of either party to violate, abandon, or renounce his contract, on the usual terms of compensation to the other for the damages which the law recognizes and allows, subject to the jurisdiction of equity to decree specific performance in proper cases, is universally recognized and acted upon."

This is in accord with the earlier North Carolina decision of Heiser v. Mears, 120 N.C. 443, 27 S.E. 117, in which it was held that, where a buyer countermands his order for goods to be manufactured for him under as executory contract, before the work is completed, it is notice to the seller that he elects to rescind his contract and submit to the legal measure of damages, and that in such case the seller cannot complete the goods and recover the contract price.

. . .

... The measure of plaintiff's damage, upon its appearing that notice was duly given not to build the bridge, is an amount sufficient to compensate plaintiff for labor and materials expended and expense incurred in the part performance of the contract, prior to its repudiation, plus the profit which would have been realized if it had been carried out in accordance with its terms.

Our conclusion, on the whole case, is that there was error in . . . directing a verdict for plaintiff. The judgment below will accordingly be reversed, and the case remanded for a new trial.

Reversed.

BOMBERGER
v.
McKELVEY

Supreme Court of California
35 Cal. 2d 607
1950

GIBSON, J.

Plaintiffs brought this action against D.P. McKelvey to recover a sum of money promised for the demolition and removal of a building which stood on real property purchased by McKelvey from plaintiffs. . . .

Early in 1946 defendants purchased 12 lots in the city of Modesto for the purpose of constructing a building and adjoining parking facilities for rental to a chain grocery store. Four of these lots, including Lots 15 and 16, were acquired from plaintiffs for $60,000. At this time Lots 15 and 16 were improved by a business structure. . . .

. . .

It was orally agreed that defendants would pay plaintiffs $3,500 upon the demolition and removal of the old building on Lots 15 and 16. During the various conversations relating to the transaction defendants stated that they did not want the old building or any part of it, and it appears that Lots 15 and 16 were to be used as a parking lot by the chain store. Plaintiffs informed defendants that they intended to use whatever material they could from the old building in constructing [a] new one [elsewhere in Modesto].

The oral agreement was confirmed by a letter from defendants to plaintiffs on March 11, 1946, wherein defendants recited that plaintiffs were to "remove the existing improvements therefrom" and that in consideration for this defendants would pay them $3,500. . . . In reliance upon this letter and the agreement to tear down the old building, plaintiffs changed the plans for the new building "to fit the possible use of salvage" from the old building, namely, plate glass and skylights, and for this reason did not order those items, which were then scarce and could be obtained only after a delay of at least 90 to 120 days. In addition sheet metal for skylights was under priority by reason of governmental restrictions. There is testimony that the new building could not be completed without the glass and sky-lights from the old one.

. . . [D]efendants were unable to get materials for the contemplated chain store and parking lot. Because of this delay defendants on August 2, 1946, notified plaintiffs that construction of the chain store building was not contemplated in the immediate future, that until further written notice plaintiffs were not to proceed with the demolition, and that notice would be given in ample time for plaintiffs to have the improvements "dismantled and removed." Plaintiffs answered by letter that they intended to proceed since the plate glass and skylights in the old building were needed for use in the construction of the new store. . . .

. . .

Toward the end of October plaintiffs removed the plate glass and skylights from the old building. . . .

Defendants refused to pay . . . the agreed price of $3,500 due upon demolition of the old building. . . .

. . .

. . . It is the general rule in California and in practically all other jurisdictions that either party to an executory contract has the power to stop performance of the contract by giving notice or direction to that effect, subjecting himself to liability for damages, and upon receipt of such notice the other party cannot continue to perform and recover damages based on full performance. (*Richardson v. Davis*, 116 Cal. App. 388 [2 P.2d 860]; *Atkinson v. District Bond Co.*, 5 Cal. App. 2d 738, 745 [43 P.2d 867]; see *Crawford v. Pioneer Box & Lumber Co.*, 105 Cal. App. 760, 765 et seq. [288 P. 694]; 5 Williston on Contracts [rev. ed. 1937], §1298, pp. 3693-3695; 12 Am. Jur. 979-980.) This is an application of the principle that a plaintiff must mitigate damages so far as he can without loss to himself. (See 5 Williston on Contracts [rev. ed. 1937], §1298, p. 3694.)

The reason for this rule is twofold: Ordinarily a plaintiff is interested only in the profit he will make from his contract, and if he receives this he obtains the full benefit of his bargain; on the other hand, performance by the plaintiff might be useless to the defendant, although he would have to pay the entire contract price if the plaintiff were permitted to perform, and this would inflict damage on the defendant without benefit to the plaintiff. (See 5 Williston on Contracts [rev. ed. 1937], §1298, p. 3694; *Dowling v. Whites Lumber & Supply Co.*, 170 Miss. 267 [154 So. 703, 705].) If these reasons are not present, the rule is not applied. For example, where the plaintiff is not interested solely in profit from the agreement but must proceed with the work in order to fulfill contract obligations to others, or where refraining from performance might involve closing a factory, damages may be inadequate and the plaintiff may have a right to continue performance. (*Southern Cotton-Oil Co. v. Heflin*, 99 F. 339 [39 C.C.A. 546]; 5 Williston on Contracts [rev. ed. 1937], §1299, p. 3696.) It has likewise been held that where a contractor has started work and has reached a point where it would be impracticable to attempt to make a reasonable estimate of damages, or where to complete the work will diminish damages or at least not enhance them, the contractor may go forward and complete performance. (*Dowling v. Whites Lumber & Supply Co.*, 170 Miss. 267 [154 So. 703].) In the Restatement of Contracts, comment a on section 336, it is said that "It is not reasonable to expect the plaintiff to avoid harm if at the time for action it appears that the attempt may cause other serious harm. He need not enter into other risky contracts, incur unreasonable inconvenience or expense, disorganize his business, or put himself in a humiliating position or in one involving loss of honor and respect."

The general rule is also subject to the jurisdiction of equity to order specific performance of the contract, and, apparently in recognition of this principle, it has been held that in cases where damages will not afford adequate compensation and where specific performance will lie, the plaintiff may continue to perform, in spite of a notice to stop, and thereafter recover on the basis of his continued performance. (*Marsh v. Blackman*, (N.Y. Supreme Court), 50 Barb. 329; *Fine Art Pictures Corp. v. Karzin*, (Mo. App.) 29 S.W.2d 170, 173; see *Woodman v. Blue Grass Land Co.*, 125 Wis. 489, 494 [103 N.W. 236, 237, 104 N.W. 920]; *Badger State Lumber Co. v. G.W. Jones Lumber Co.*, 140 Wis. 73 [121 N.W. 933, 934]; 17 C.J.S. 979; 12 Am. Jur. 980; *cf. La Salle Extension University v. Ogburn*, 174 N.C. 427 [93 S.E. 986, 988, Ann. Cas. 1918C 887].) In the *Fine Art Pictures* decision the court stated that this is one of the necessary exceptions to the rule. (29 S.W.2d at p. 173.)

. . .

. . . Unlike the situations presented in *Richardson v. Davis*, 116 Cal. App. 388 [P.2d 860], and *Crawford v. Pioneer Box & Lumber Co.*, 105 Cal. App. 760 [288 P. 694], relied upon by defendants, the agreement involved here did not provide simply for the payment of money in return for the performance of services. As we have seen, it was contemplated that plaintiffs were to keep all salvaged material. During the negotiations for the agreement they informed defendants that they planned to use as much of this material as they could in constructing the new building for the Hills, and, in reliance on the contract, they altered the plans for the new building to permit use of the glass and skylights from the old one. These materials were then scarce, and sheet metal for the skylights was under priority. There was testimony that it would take from 90 to 120 days to obtain new glass and skylights, and some other glass required for the new building did not arrive until about five months after it was ordered. Except for the glass and skylights the new building was completed sometime in October, and the lack of these materials left it exposed to the weather and apparently unsuitable for occupation by the Hills. Thus it is obvious that an essential element of the rule giving one party the power to stop performance by giving notice not to perform is lacking here since plaintiffs were not interested solely in the profit to be derived from tearing down the old building and selling the salvage, but they had an additional interest in obtaining actual performance of the agreement so that they could secure scarce materials and complete the new building.

The fact that the agreement involved property which was scarce and under priority is of particular importance in the present case. There are analogous decisions in other jurisdictions holding that a purchaser does not have an adequate remedy at law and may obtain specific performance of a contract to sell materials if he needs them in his business and cannot obtain them or their equivalent within the local marketing area. (*Oreland Equipment Co. v. Copco Steel & Engineering Corp.*, 310 Mich. 6 [16 N.W.2d 646]; *Eastern Rolling Mill Co. v. Michlovitz*, 157 Md. 51 [145 A. 378, 383-384] [steel scrap, not procurable in the area]; *Conemaugh Gas Co. v. Jackson Farm Gas Co.*, 186 Pa. 443 [40 A. 1000, 1001, 65 Am. St. Rep. 865], *Gloucester Isinglass & Glue Co. v. Russia Cement Co.*, 154 Mass. 92 [27 N.E. 1005, 1007, 26 Am. St. Rep. 214,

12 L.R.A. 563]; see *Campbell Soup Co. v. Wentz*, 172 F.2d 80, 82-83; 152 A.L.R. 4, 26-29.) Some of these cases were decided in states which, like California, have adopted the Uniform Sales Act provision authorizing specific performance, in the discretion of the court, of contracts to sell goods. (See, e.g., Civ. Code §1788.) Although the Uniform Sales Act may not be directly applicable here, since part of the consideration was the transfer of realty (Civ. Code, §1729, subd. 3), the cases are nevertheless in point insofar as they hold that damages do not afford an adequate remedy in such a situation. Moreover, the adoption of the Uniform Sales Act exemplifies a tendency to liberalize the requirements for specific performance of contracts to sell or transfer personal property. (See 3 Williston on Sales [rev. ed. 1948], §601; *cf. Sanford v. Boston Edison Co.*, 316 Mass. 631 [56 N.E.2d 1, 3, 156 A.L.R. 644], stating that there is a "growing tendency" to allow specific performance where damages are not the equivalent of the performance.)

Under these circumstances the trial court could properly conclude that inability to obtain the salvage from the old building would seriously interfere with completion of the new building, that equivalent materials could not then be secured by plaintiffs and that in an action for breach of contract damages would be difficult to ascertain and would be inadequate.

. . . Defendants argue that plaintiffs were not entitled to proceed with performance because they could have covered up the holes in the new building with boards to protect it from the weather until new glass and skylights could be obtained and, further, that the glass and skylights from the old building, even if required, could have been removed without tearing down the entire structure. Boarding up the new building, however, would have rendered it unusable for an indefinite period. Also, removal of part of the old building without demolition of the remainder was not authorized by the agreement, and there is nothing in the record to indicate that defendants had suggested or would have consented to such a step, even though they knew that the need for the glass and skylights was the principal reason for plaintiffs' insistence upon full performance of the contract. All of these factors were, of course, to be considered by the trial court in passing upon the propriety of plaintiffs' conduct, and we cannot say as a matter of law that plaintiffs were required to adopt one of the solutions now mentioned by defendants.

. . . Defendants introduced testimony that the value of the old building, if allowed to remain on the property for continued use, was $26,250, and they contend that demolition of such a valuable structure was not justified by plaintiffs' need for the salvage, which, it is asserted, could have been replaced for $540. Regardless of the weight to be given this testimony, however, the trial court could properly consider the facts that defendants had purchased the property for construction of a chain grocery store, that they had made a lease to the chain store operators by which they agreed to deliver possession of Lots 15 and 16 for use as a parking lot with all improvements removed, and that for this reason the building had little if any value for continued use on the property. On the other hand the value of the salvage to plaintiffs was enhanced by their need of materials for the new building.

. . .

. . . In view of the foregoing we conclude that the facts found by the trial court, supported by the evidence, are sufficient to justify the determination that plaintiffs acted within their rights in fully performing the agreement. . . . Defendants, on the other hand, became liable to pay plaintiffs the sum due under the contract upon completion of the demolition.

. . .

The judgment is affirmed.

PARKER
v.
TWENTIETH CENTURY-FOX FILM CORP.
Supreme Court of California
3 Cal. 3d 176
1970

Burke, J.

Defendant Twentieth Century-Fox Film Corporation appeals from a summary judgment granting to plaintiff [Shirley MacLaine Parker] the recovery of agreed compensation under a written contract for her services as an actress in a motion picture. As will appear, we have concluded that the trial court correctly ruled in plaintiff's favor and that the judgment should be affirmed.

Plaintiff is well known as an actress, and in the contract between plaintiff and defendant is sometimes referred to as the "Artist." Under the contract, dated August 6, 1965, plaintiff was to play the female lead in defendant's contemplated production of a motion picture entitled "Bloomer Girl." The contract provided that defendant would pay plaintiff a minimum "guaranteed compensation" of $53,571.42 per week for 14 weeks commencing May 23, 1966, for a total of $750,000. Prior to May 1966 defendant decided not to produce the picture and by a letter dated April 4, 1966, it notified plaintiff of that decision and that it would not "comply with our obligations to you under" the written contract.

By the same letter and with the professed purpose "to avoid any damage to you," defendant instead offered to employ plaintiff as the leading actress in another film tentatively entitled "Big Country, Big Man" (hereinafter, "Big Country"). The compensation offered was identical, as were 31 of the 34 numbered provisions or articles of the original contract. Unlike "Bloomer Girl," however, which was to have been a musical production, "Big Country" was a dramatic "western type" movie. "Bloomer Girl" was to have been filmed in California; "Big Country" was to be produced in Australia. Also, certain terms in the proffered contract varied from those of the original.[2] Plaintiff was

---

2. Article 29 of the original contract specified that plaintiff approved the director already chosen for "Bloomer Girl" and that in case he failed to act as director plaintiff was to have approval rights of any substitute director. Article 31 provided that plaintiff was to have the right of approval of the "Bloomer Girl" dance director, and Article 32 gave her the right of approval of the screenplay. Defendant's letter of April 4 to plaintiff, which contained both defendant's notice of breach of the "Bloomer Girl" contract and offer of the lead in "Big Country," eliminated or impaired each of those rights.

given one week within which to accept; she did not and the offer lapsed. Plaintiff then commenced this action seeking recovery of the agreed guaranteed compensation.

The complaint sets forth two causes of action. The first is for money due under the contract; the second, based upon the same allegations as the first, is for damages resulting from defendant's breach of contract. Defendant in its answer admits the existence and validity of the contract, that plaintiff complied with all the conditions, covenants and promises and stood ready to complete the performance, and that defendant breached and "anticipatorily repudiated" the contract. It denies, however, that any money is due to plaintiff either under the contract or as a result of its breach, and pleads as an affirmative defense to both causes of action plaintiff's allegedly deliberate failure to mitigate damages, asserting that she unreasonably refused to accept its offer of the leading role in "Big Country."

Plaintiff moved for summary judgment, the motion was granted, and summary judgment for $750,000 plus interest was entered in plaintiff's favor. This appeal by defendant followed.

The familiar rules are that the matter to be determined by the trial court on a motion for summary judgment is whether facts have been presented which give rise to a triable factual issue. The court may not pass upon the issue itself. Summary judgment is proper only if the affidavits or declarations in support of the moving party would be sufficient to sustain a judgment in his favor and his opponent does not by affidavit show facts sufficient to present a triable issue of fact. The affidavits of the moving party are strictly construed, and doubts as to the propriety of summary judgment should be resolved against granting the motion. Such summary procedure is drastic and should be used with caution so that it does not become a substitute for the open trial method of determining facts. . . .

As stated, defendant's sole defense to this action which resulted from its deliberate breach of contract is that in rejecting defendant's substitute offer of employment plaintiff unreasonably refused to mitigate damages.

The general rule is that the measure of recovery by a wrongfully discharged employee is the amount of salary agreed upon for the period of service, less the amount which the employer affirmatively proves the employee has earned or with reasonable effort might have earned from other employment. (W.F. Boardman Co. v. Petch (1921) 186 Cal. 476, 484; De Angeles v. Roos Bros., Inc. (1966) 244 Cal. App. 2d 434, 441-442; de la Falaise v. Gaumont-British Picture Corp. (1940) 39 Cal. App. 2d 461, 469, and cases cited; see also Wise v. Southern Pac. Co. (1970) 1 Cal. 3d 600, 607-608.) However, before projected earnings from other employment opportunities not sought or accepted by the discharged employee can be applied in mitigation, the employer must show that the other employment was comparable, or substantially similar, to that of which the employee has been deprived; the employee's rejection of or failure to seek other available employment of a different or inferior kind may not be resorted to in order to mitigate damages. (Gonzales v. Internat. Assn. of Machinists (1963) 213 Cal. App. 2d 817, 822-824; Harris v. Nat. Union etc. Cooks, Stewards (1953) 116 Cal. App. 2d 759, 761; Crillo v. Curtola (1949) 91 Cal. App. 2d 263, 275; de la Falaise v. Galumont-British Picture Corp., supra, 39 Cal. App. 2d 461, 469; Schiller v. Keuffel & Esser Co. (1963) 21 Wis. 2d 545; 28 A.L.R. 736, 749; 22 Am. Jur. 2d, Damages, §§71- 72, p. 106.)

In the present case defendant has raised no issue of *reasonableness of efforts* by plaintiffs to obtain other employment; the sole issue is whether plaintiff's refusal of defendant's substitute offer of "Big Country" may be used in mitigation. Nor, if the "Big Country" offer was of employment different or inferior when compared with the original "Bloomer Girl" employment, is there an issue as to whether or not plaintiff acted reasonably in refusing the substitute offer. Despite defendant's arguments to the contrary, no case cited or which our research has discovered holds or suggests that reasonableness is an element of a wrongfully discharged employee's option to reject, or fail to seek, different or inferior employment lest the possible earnings therefrom be charged against him in mitigation of damages.[5]

Applying the foregoing rules to the record in the present case, with all intendments in favor of the party opposing the summary judgment motion—here, defendant—it is clear that the trial court correctly ruled that plaintiff's failure to accept defendant's tendered substitute employment could not be applied in mitigation of damages because the offer of the "Big Country" lead was of employment both different and inferior, and that no factual dispute was presented on that issue. The mere circumstance that "Bloomer Girl" was to be a musical revue calling upon plaintiff's talents as a dancer as well as an actress, and was to be produced in the City of Los Angeles, whereas "Big Country" was a straight dramatic role in a "Western Type" story taking place in an opal mine in Australia, demonstrates the difference in kind between the two employments; the female lead as a dramatic actress in a western style motion picture can by no stretch of imagination be considered the equivalent of or substantially similar to the lead in a song-and-dance production.

Additionally, the substitute "Big Country" offer proposed to eliminate or impair the director and screenplay approvals accorded to plaintiff under the original "Bloomer Girl" contract (see fn. 2, ante), and thus constituted an offer of inferior employment. No expertise or judicial notice is required in order to hold that the deprivation or infringement of an employee's rights held under an original employment contract converts the available "other employment" relied upon by the employer to mitigate damages, into inferior employment which the employee need not seek or accept.

. . .

In view of the determination that defendant failed to present any facts showing the existence of a factual issue with respect to its sole defense—plaintiff's rejection of its substitute employment offer in mitigation of damages—we need not consider plaintiff's further contention that for various reasons, including the provisions of the original contract set forth in footnote 1, ante, plaintiff was excused from attempting to mitigate damages.

The judgment is affirmed.

McComb, J., Peters, J., Tobriner, J., Kaus, J., and Roth, J., concurred.

Sullivan, Acting C.J.

---

5. Instead, in each case the reasonableness referred to was that of the *efforts* of the employee to obtain other employment that was not different or inferior; his right to reject the latter was declared as an unqualified rule of law. . . .

The basic question in this case is whether or not plaintiff acted reasonably in rejecting defendant's offer of alternate employment. The answer depends upon whether that offer (starring in "Big Country, Big Man") was an offer of work that was substantially similar to her former employment (starring in "Bloomer Girl") or of work that was of a different or inferior kind. To my mind this is a factual issue, which the trial court should not have determined on a motion for summary judgment. The majority have not only repeated this error but have compounded it by applying the rules governing mitigation of damages in the employer-employee context in a misleading fashion. Accordingly, I respectfully dissent.

The familiar rule requiring a plaintiff in a tort or contract action to mitigate damages embodies notions of fairness and socially responsible behavior which are fundamental to our jurisprudence. Most broadly stated, it precludes the recovery of damages which, through the exercise of due diligence, could have been avoided. Thus, in essence, it is a rule requiring reasonable conduct in commercial affairs. This general principle governs the obligations of an employee after his employer has wrongfully repudiated or terminated the employment contract. Rather than permitting the employee simply to remain idle during the balance of the contract period, the law requires him to make a reasonable effort to secure other employment. He is not obliged, however, to seek or accept any and all types of work which may be available. Only work which is in the same field and which is of the same quality need be accepted.

Over the years the courts have employed various phrases to define the type of employment which the employee, upon his wrongful discharge, is under an obligation to accept. Thus in California alone it has been held that he must accept employment which is "substantially similar"; "comparable employment"; employment "in the same general line of the first employment"; "equivalent to his prior position"; "employment in a similar capacity"; employment which is "not . . . of a different or inferior kind. . . ."

For reasons which are unexplained, the majority cite several of these cases yet select from among the various judicial formulations which they contain one particular phrase, "Not of a different or inferior kind," with which to analyze this case. I have discovered no historical or theoretical reason to adopt this phrase, which is simply a negative restatement of the affirmative standards set out in the above cases, as the exclusive standard. Indeed, its emergence is an example of the dubious phenomenon of the law responding not to rational judicial choice or changing social conditions, but to unrecognized changes in the language of opinions or legal treatises. However, the phrase is a serviceable one and my concern is not with its use as the standard but rather with what I consider its distortion.

The relevant language excuses acceptance only of employment which is of a different kind. It has never been the law that the mere existence of differences between two jobs in the same field is sufficient, as a matter of law, to excuse an employee wrongfully discharged from one from accepting the other in order to mitigate damages. Such an approach would effectively eliminate any obligation of an employee to attempt to minimize damage arising from a wrongful discharge. The only alternative job offer an employee would be required to accept would be an offer of his former job by his former employer.

Although the majority appear to hold that there was a difference "in kind" between the employment offered plaintiff in "Bloomer Girl" and that offered in "Big Country," an examination of the opinion makes crystal clear that the majority merely point out differences between the *two films* (an obvious circumstance) and then apodically assert that these constitute a difference in the *kind of employment*. The entire rationale of the majority boils down to this; that the *"mere circumstances"* that "Bloomer Girl" was to be a musical revue while "Big Country" was a straight drama "demonstrates the difference in kind" since a female lead in a western is not "the equivalent of or substantially similar to" a lead in a musical. This is merely attempting to prove the proposition by repeating it. It shows that the vehicles for the display of the star's talents are different but it does not prove that her employment as a star in such vehicles is of necessity different *in kind* and either inferior or superior.

I believe that the approach taken by the majority (a superficial listing of differences with no attempt to assess their significance) may subvert a valuable legal doctrine. The inquiry in cases such as this should not be whether differences between the two jobs exist (there will always be differences) but whether the differences which are present are substantial enough to constitute differences in the *kind* of employment or, alternatively, whether they render the substitute work employment of an *inferior kind*.

. . .

I believe that the judgment should be reversed so that the issue of whether or not the offer of the lead role in "Big Country, Big Man" was of employment comparable to that of the lead role in "Bloomer Girl" may be determined at trial.

IN RE WORLDCOM, INC.
U.S. Bankruptcy Court, Southern District of New York
361 B.R. 675
2007

GONZALEZ, Bankruptcy Judge:

On or about July 10, 1995, [Michael] Jordan and the Debtors entered into an endorsement agreement (the "Agreement"). At that time, Jordan was considered to be one of the most popular athletes in the world. The Agreement granted MCI a ten-year license to use Jordan's name, likeness, "other attributes," and personal services to advertise and promote MCI's telecommunications products and services beginning in September 1995 and ending in August 2005. The Agreement did not prevent Jordan from endorsing most other products or services, although he could not endorse the same products or services that MCI produced. In addition to a $5 million signing bonus, the Agreement provided an annual base compensation of $2 million for Jordan. The Agreement provided that Jordan would be treated as an independent contractor and that MCI would not withhold any amount from Jordan's compensation for tax purposes. The Agreement provided that Jordan was to make himself available for four days, not to exceed four hours per day, during each contract year to produce television commercials and print advertising and for promotional appearances. The parties agreed that the advertising and promotional materials would be submitted to Jordan for his approval, which could not be unreasonably withheld, fourteen days prior to their release to the general public. From 1995 to 2000, Jordan appeared in several television commercials and a large number of print ads for MCI.

On July 1, 2002, MCI commenced a case under chapter 11 of title 11 of the United States Code (the "Bankruptcy Code") in the Bankruptcy Court for the Southern District of New York . . . . On July 18, 2003, the Debtors rejected the Agreement. . . . As of the rejection in July 2003, two years remained under the Agreement.

. . . MCI argues that Jordan had an obligation to mitigate his damages and failed to do so. . . . MCI argues that it is under no obligation to pay Jordan for contract years 2004 and 2005. . . . Jordan argues that the objection should be overruled and dismissed for three independent reasons (1) Jordan was a "lost volume seller" and thus mitigation does not apply, (2) there is no evidence that Jordan could have entered into a "substantially similar" endorsement agreement, and (3) Jordan acted reasonably when he decided not to pursue other endorsements after MCI's rejection of the Agreement.

. . .

C. MITIGATION

The doctrine of avoidable consequences, which has also been referred to as the duty to mitigate damages, "bars recovery for losses suffered by a non-breaching party that could have been avoided by reasonable effort and without risk of substantial loss or injury." *Edward M. Crough, Inc. v. Dep't of Gen. Servs. of D.C.*, 572 A.2d 457, 466 (D.C. 1990). The burden of proving that the damages could have been avoided or mitigated rests with the party that committed the breach. *See Obelisk Corp. v. Riggs Nat'l Bank of Washington, D.C.*, 668 A.2d 847, 856 (D.C. 1995); *see also Norris v. Green*, 656 A.2d 282, 287 (D.C. 1995) ("The failure to mitigate damages is an affirmative defense and the [breaching party] has the burden of showing the absence of reasonable efforts to mitigate"). The efforts to avoid or mitigate the damages do not have to be successful, as long as they are reasonable. *See Edward M. Crough*, 572 A.2d at 467.

. . .

1. Whether Jordan Was a "Lost Volume Seller"

Jordan argues that MCI's mitigation defense does not apply here because Jordan is akin to a "lost volume seller." Jordan points to testimony demonstrating that he could have entered into additional endorsement contracts even if MCI had not rejected the Agreement. Thus, he argues, any additional endorsement contracts would not have been substitutes for the Agreement and would not have mitigated the damages for which MCI is liable.

"A lost volume seller is one who has the capacity to perform the contract that was breached in addition to other potential contracts due to unlimited resources or production capacity." *Precision Pine & Timber, Inc. v. United States*, 72 Fed. Cl. 460, 490 (Fed. Cl. 2006). A lost volume seller does not minimize its damages by entering into another contract because it would have had the benefit of both contracts even if the first were not breached. *See Jetz Service Co. v. Salina Props.*, 19 Kan. App. 2d 144, 865 P.2d 1051, 1055-56 (1993). The lost volume seller has two expectations, the profit from the breached contract and the profit from one or more other contracts that it could have performed at the same time as the breached contract. *See Snyder v. Herbert Greenbaum & Assocs.*, 38 Md. App. 144, 380 A.2d 618, 624 (1977). "The philosophical heart of the lost volume theory is that the seller would have generated a second sale irrespective of the buyer's breach" and that "[i]t follows that the lost volume seller cannot possibly mitigate damages." D. Matthews, *Should the Doctrine of Lost Volume Seller Be Retained? A Response to Professor Breen*, 51 U. Miami L. Rev. 1195, 1214 (July 1997); *see also Snyder*, 380 A.2d at 625 (under this theory, "the original sale and the second sale are independent events").

The lost volume seller theory is recognized in the Restatement (2d) of Contracts, §§347, 350 (1981) (the "Restatement (2d)").[8] The lost volume seller theory applies to contracts for services as well as goods. *See* Restatement (2d), §347, ill. 16; *see also Jetz Service*, 865 P.2d at 1055-56 (applying theory to seller of services); *Gianetti v. Norwalk Hosp.*, 64 Conn. App. 218, 779 A.2d 847, 853 (2001) (applying theory to provider of medical services), *aff'd in part, rev'd in part*, 266 Conn. 544, 833 A.2d 891 (2003).

This case offers a twist on the typical lost volume seller situation. In what the Court regards as the typical situation, the non-breaching seller has a near-inexhaustible supply of inventory. *See, e.g., Katz Commc'ns, Inc. v. Evening News Ass'n*, 705 F.2d 20, 26 (2d Cir. 1983). In the typical situation, when a buyer breaches an agreement to buy a good or service from the seller, the item is returned to inventory and the lost volume seller continues in its efforts to sell its goods or services. However, the transactions that occur following the breach are not necessarily the result of the breach but fundamentally the result of the seller continuing efforts to market its goods and services. It is this continuous effort

---

8. Comment f to §347 states in part

"Lost volume." Whether a subsequent transaction is a substitute for the broken contract sometimes raises difficult questions of fact. If the injured party could and would have entered into the subsequent contract, even if the contract had not been broken, and could have had the benefit of both, he can be said to have "lost volume" and the subsequent transaction is not a substitute for the broken contract. The injured party's damages are then based on the net profit that he has lost as a result of the broken contract.

Comment d to §350 states

"Lost volume." The mere fact that an injured party can make arrangements for the disposition of the goods or services that he was to supply under the contract does not necessarily mean that by doing so he will avoid loss. If he would have entered into both transactions but for the breach, he has "lost volume" as a result of the breach. See Comment f to §347. In that case the second transaction is not a "substitute" for the first one. See Illustrations 9 and 10.

coupled with a virtually limitless supply that warrants the lost volume exception to mitigation. As stated above, the transactions that may occur after the breach would in the context of the lost volume seller have occurred independent of the breach. Here, Jordan lacked a nearly limitless supply and had no intention of continuing to market his services as a product endorser.

Although not addressed by a D.C. court, the majority of cases hold that Jordan bears the burden of proving that he is a lost volume seller. *See generally Precision Pine*, 72 Fed. Cl. at 495 ("The case law demonstrates that . . . plaintiff bears the burden of demonstrating that it should be compensated as a lost volume seller"); *Snyder*, 380 A.2d at 624; *Ullman-Briggs, Inc. v. Salton, Inc.*, 754 F. Supp. 1003, 1008-09 (S.D.N.Y. 1991); *R.E. Davis Chemical Corp. v. Diasonics, Inc.*, 826 F.2d 678, 684 (7th Cir. 1987); *Green Tree Fin. Corp. v. ALLTEL Info. Servs., Inc.*, No. Civ. 02-627 JRTFLN, 2002 WL 31163072, at *9 (D. Minn. Sept. 26, 2002).

To claim lost volume seller status, Jordan must establish that he would have had the benefit of both the original and subsequent contracts if MCI had not rejected the Agreement. *See Ullman-Briggs*, 754 F. Supp. at 1008. Although there is no definitive set of elements that the non-breaching party must show, many cases seem to follow the language from the Restatement (2d), Section 347, that the non-breaching party must show that it "could and would have entered into" a subsequent agreement. *See, e.g., Donald Rubin, Inc. v. Schwartz*, 191 A.D.2d 171, 172, 594 N.Y.S.2d 193, 194-95 (1st Dep't 1993); *Precision Pine*, 72 Fed. Cl. at 496-97; *Gianetti*, 833 A.2d at 897; *Jetz Service*, 865 P.2d at 1056; *see also Green Tree Financial*, 2002 WL 31163072, at *9 ("[t]o recover lost profits under this theory, a non-breaching party must prove three things: (1) that the seller of services had the capability to perform both contracts simultaneously; (2) that the second contract would have been profitable; and (3) that the seller of service would have entered into the second contract if the first contract had not been terminated").

In his arguments, Jordan focuses primarily on his *capacity* to enter subsequent agreements, arguing that the loss of MCI's sixteen-hour annual time commitment hardly affected his ability to perform additional endorsement services. On this prong alone, Jordan likely would be considered a lost volume seller of endorsement services because he had sufficient time to do multiple endorsements. Although he does not have the "infinite capacity" that some cases discuss, a services provider does not need unlimited capacity but must have the requisite capacity and intent to perform under multiple contracts at the same time. *See Gianetti*, 266 Conn. at 561-62, 833 A.2d 891 (plastic surgeon could be considered a lost volume seller if it were determined that he had the capacity and intent to simultaneously work out of three or four hospitals profitably).

Contrary to Jordan's analysis, courts do not focus solely on the seller's capacity. The seller claiming lost volume status must also demonstrate that it *would* have entered into subsequent transactions. *See Diasonics*, 826 F.2d at 684; *Green Tree Financial*, 2002 WL 31163072, at *9; *Gianetti*, 779 A.2d at 853 ("for sellers of personal services to come within the purview of the Restatement's lost volume seller theory . . . , they must establish," in addition to capacity, that additional sales would have been profitable and that they would made the additional sale regardless of the buyer's breach). Jordan has not shown he could and *would have* entered into a subsequent agreement. Rather, the evidence shows that Jordan did not have the "subjective intent" to take on additional endorsements. *See Ullman-Briggs*, 754 F. Supp. at 1008. The testimony from Jordan's representatives establishes that although Jordan's popularity enabled him to obtain additional product endorsements in 2003, Jordan desired to scale back his level of endorsements. Jordan's financial and business advisor, Curtis Polk ("Polk"), testified that at the time the Agreement was rejected, Jordan's desire was "not to expand his spokesperson or pitchman efforts with new relationships." *See* Debtors' Mot. Summ J., App. 6, at 02. Polk testified that had Jordan wanted to do additional endorsements after the 2003 rejection, he could have obtained additional deals. *See id.* at 64-65. Jordan's agent, David Falk ("Falk"), testified that "there might have been twenty more companies that in theory might have wanted to sign him" but that Jordan and his representatives wanted to avoid diluting his image. *See* Debtors' Mot. Summ J., App. 6, at 24. Jordan's Memorandum for Summary Judgment stated that at the time the Agreement was rejected, Jordan had implemented a strategy of not accepting new endorsements because of a belief that new deals would jeopardize his ability to achieve his primary goal of National Basketball Association ("NBA") franchise ownership.

. . .

One of the classic examples of the lost volume seller is found in *Neri v. Retail Marine Corp.*, 30 N.Y.2d 393, 399-400, 334 N.Y.S.2d 165, 169-70, 285 N.E.2d 311 (N.Y. 1972)[:]

> [I]f a private party agrees to sell his automobile to a buyer for $2,000, a breach by the buyer would cause the seller no loss (except incidental damages, i.e., expense of a new sale) if the seller was able to sell the automobile to another buyer for $2,000. But the situation is different with dealers having an unlimited supply or standard-priced goods. Thus, if an automobile dealer agrees to sell a car to a buyer at the standard price of $2,000, a breach by the buyer injures the dealer, even though he is able to sell the automobile to another for $2,000. If the dealer has an inexhaustible supply of cars, the resale to replace the breaching buyer costs the dealer a sale, because, had the breaching buyer performed, the dealer would have made two sales instead of one. The buyer's breach, in such a case, depletes the dealer's sales to the extent of one, and the measure of damages should be the dealer's profit on one sale.

This example would surely have a different result if the car dealership was winding down its business and had agreed to sell one of its last cars to a buyer. If that buyer subsequently breached the contract and did not purchase the car, the dealership could hardly be expected to recover lost profits damages if the dealer put the car back onto a deserted car lot, made no attempts to sell it, and kept the dealership shuttered to new customers. Those modifications are analogous to Jordan's situation, with his stated desire to withdraw his services from the endorsement marketplace, and the lost volume seller theory accordingly does not apply to his circumstances.

Jordan states that it is a "red herring" to speculate under the lost volume analysis on what he *would* have done because that ignores the central point of the lost volume principle: if Jordan had . . . accepted a substantially similar endorsement opportunity—exactly what [MCI] argues he was required to do to mitigate damages—the damages for which [MCI] is liable would not have been reduced by one penny because the lost volume principle would allow Jordan to retain the benefits of both the [MCI] Agreement and the hypothetical additional endorsement. *See* Michael Jordan's Reply Brief, at 14-15.

Jordan overlooks an important point about the lost volume seller theory—that the "original sale and the second sale are independent events," *Snyder*, 380 A.2d at 625, because the lost volume seller's intent to enter into new contracts is the same before and after a purchaser's breach. The lost volume seller's desire to sell more units of goods or services is virtually unaffected by the loss of a single sale or agreement.

Next, even if Jordan had mitigated damages by entering one subsequent endorsement agreement, this, without more, does not mean that Jordan was a lost volume seller. The lost volume seller has the intent and capacity to sell multiple units despite the breach of a contract for one transaction.

Finally, if Jordan had entered into a subsequent agreement or agreements, and if he had showed both the capacity and the intent to make subsequent sales, that might have had the effect of helping him to establish his status as a lost volume seller, which generally would relieve him of the duty to mitigate. This would not be a novel situation but it ignores the fact that he did not do so. *See, e.g., Storage Tech. Corp. v. Trust Co. of N.J.*, 842 F.2d 54, 57 (3d Cir. 1988) ("The lost volume seller theory is a response to a breaching buyer's right to have a non-breaching seller mitigate damages. In other words, a seller can avoid the effect of its failure to mitigate by proving that it was a lost volume seller."); *Chicago Title Ins. Corp. v. Magnuson*, No. 2:03-CV-368, 2005 WL 2373430, at *23 (S.D. Ohio Sept. 26, 2005) (when there is no evidence in the record that plaintiff "turned away or would have turned away business during the relevant period" and the "only evidence on the issue supports that the [plaintiff] could and would have completed such transactions," the consequent instructions to the jury that the plaintiff was a lost volume seller and therefore had no duty to mitigate its damages were not erroneous).

Because the evidence establishes, among other things, that Jordan would not have entered into subsequent agreements, Jordan has not established that he is a lost volume seller. This theory thus does not relieve Jordan from the duty to mitigate damages.

. . .

The Court finds that Jordan failed to mitigate damages but a further evidentiary hearing is necessary to determine what Jordan could have received had he made reasonable efforts to mitigate, a determination that consequently will affect the Claim.

Problems

1. Family Help. Frank Gironda, Jr. ("Junior") contracted with Schiavi Mobile Homes to purchase a two-bedroom mobile home for $23,029 and paid a $1,000 deposit. When personal difficulties caused Junior to breach the contract, Schiavi contacted Gironda's father, Frank Gironda, Sr. ("Senior"), to try to learn if Junior was planning to go through with the purchase. Senior said that he didn't know, but that he would be willing to purchase the mobile home if his son could not be found and would otherwise lose his deposit.

Two months later, Schiavi sold the mobile home to a third party for $22,000 and sued Junior for lost profits and interest. At trial, Senior testified that while he did not have sufficient cash available to buy the mobile home at the time of the telephone conversation with Schiavi, he stood ready to mortgage his house to raise the money. What damages may Schiavi collect?

2. Fair Employment. Patricia Fair delivered room service at a Red Lion Inn hotel. After suffering a non-work-related accident, Fair took a medical leave of absence (during which she learned and informed Red Lion that she was pregnant). Red Lion fired Fair two weeks before her doctor believed she could safely return to work. Fair's lawyer contacted Red Lion, asserting that the firing constituted a breach of contract and threatening a lawsuit. In response, Red Lion offered Fair the opportunity to return to her room service position. Fair responded that she would return if she could work at the hotel's front desk, Red Lion would agree to additional restrictions on its ability to terminate her in the future, and she be guaranteed the right to transfer to another Red Lion in the future under the same terms. Red Lion declined and reiterated its offer to reinstate her to her old job under the same terms. Fair refused and sued Red Lion for breach of contract.

At trial, Fair testified that she did not accept Red Lion's reinstatement offer because she was concerned about the possibility of retaliatory termination, she was concerned about the physical demands of the job in light of her pregnancy, and she was uncertain about whether her reinstated medical benefits would cover the period during which she had been fired. Red Lion argued that Fair failed to mitigate her damages and moved to have damages limited to those suffered prior to the offer of reinstatement. The trial judge denied the motion, and the jury awarded Fair damages that included losses suffered after the offer of reinstatement. Red Lion appealed. How should the appellate court rule?

3. Can the Collection Agency Collect? Sprint Spectrum hired Penncro Associates to staff a call center with employees, who would try to collect unpaid charges from Sprint's cell phone customers. The contract called for Penncro to provide 500 dedicated employees for Sprint's business, but it continually had problems retaining enough employees to satisfy this requirement (although Sprint never complained about this because its call volume was never high enough to require the contractually specified number of employees), and the service quality of its employees was poor enough that Penncro ranked last among Sprint's contract collection agents in performance quality measures specified in the contract.

Sprint breached the contract, and Penncro sought damages of $53 million due under the contract minus $28 million that it would save in "costs avoided," which netted out to approximately $25 million. Sprint argued that $6.5 million, which Penncro earned from contracts with AT&T and American Water after the end of its work for Sprint, should be subtracted from that amount as "losses avoided." Penncro won its contract with AT&T on the basis of its experience working for Sprint and based on the understanding that employees who had serviced the Sprint contract would service the AT&T contract. The American Water contract required immediate staffing at the time it was awarded. Penncro conceded that it used employees who had previously serviced the Sprint account to service the AT&T and American Water accounts. It argued, however, that it was a lost volume seller because it could have hired additional workers and profitably serviced the AT&T and American Water accounts even if it were still servicing the Sprint account. The trial court ruled for Sprint, and Penncro appealed. How should the appellate court rule?

E. THE FORESEEABILITY REQUIREMENT

When no substitute transaction is available to the non-breaching party, the compensation principle suggests that the breaching party is liable for the difference between the contract price and the full value of performance expected by the non-breaching party. Complete fidelity to the compensation principle, however, could create unpredictable liability, which in turn could chill desirable commercial activity to the detriment of both buyers and sellers of goods and services. Following the decision in *Hadley v. Baxendale*, contract law deals with this problem by limiting the breaching party's liability to damages that are foreseeable at the time of contracting. See Rest. (2d) Contracts §351. But what features render a particular type of damages "foreseeable," and how likely must it be that a breach will cause a particular type of damage? *C. Czarnikow Ltd. v. Koufos, Allen v. Jones*, and *Jackson v. Royal Bank of Scotland* wrestle with these questions.

HADLEY
v.
BAXENDALE
Court of Exchequer
156 Eng. Rep. 1220
1854

. . .

At the trial before Crompton, J., at the last Gloucester Assizes, it appeared that the plaintiffs carried on an extensive business as millers at Gloucester; and that, on the 11th of May, their mill was stopped by a breakage of the crank shaft by which the mill was worked. The steam-engine was manufactured by Messrs. Joyce & Co., the engineers, at Greenwich, and it became necessary to send the shaft as a pattern for a new one to Greenwich. The fracture was discovered on the 12th, and on the 13th the plaintiffs sent one of their servants to the office of the defendants, who are the well-known carriers trading under the name of Pickford & Co., for the purpose of having the shaft carried to Greenwich. . . . [I]n answer to the inquiry when the shaft would be taken, the answer was, that if it was sent up by twelve o'clock any day, it would be delivered at Greenwich on the following day. . . . The delivery of the shaft at Greenwich was delayed by some neglect; and the consequence was, that the plaintiffs did not receive the new shaft for several days after they would otherwise have done, and the working of their mill was thereby delayed, and they thereby lost the profits they would otherwise have received.

On the part of the defendants, it was objected that these damages were too remote, and that the defendants were not liable with respect to them. The learned Judge left the case generally to the jury, who found a verdict with 25£ damages beyond the amount paid into Court.

. . .

ALDERSON, B.

We think that there ought to be a new trial in this case; but, in so doing, we deem it to be expedient and necessary to state explicitly the rule which the Judge, at the next trial, ought, in our opinion, to direct the jury to be governed by when they estimate the damages.

It is, indeed, of the last importance that we should do this; for, if the jury are left without any definite rule to guide them, it will, in such cases as these, manifestly lead to the greatest injustice. . . .

"There are certain established rules," this Court says, in *Alder v. Keighley* (15 M. & W. 117), "according to which the jury ought to find." And the Court, in that case, adds: "and here there is a clear rule, that the amount which would have been received if the contract had been kept, is the measure of damages if the contract is broken."

Now we think the proper rule in such a case as the present is this: Where two parties have made a contract which one of them has broken, the damages which the other party ought to receive in respect of such breach of contract should be such as may fairly and reasonably be considered either arising naturally, i.e., according to the usual course of things, from such breach of contract itself, or such as may reasonably be supposed to have been in the contemplation of both parties, at the time they made the contract, as the probable result of the breach of it. Now, if the special circumstances under which the contract was actually made were communicated by the plaintiffs to the defendants, and thus known to both parties, the damages resulting from the breach of such a contract, which they would reasonably contemplate, would be the amount of injury which would ordinarily follow from a breach of contract under these special circumstances so known and communicated. But, on the other hand, if these special circumstances were wholly unknown to the party breaking the contract, he, at the most, could only be supposed to have had in his contemplation the amount of injury which would arise generally, and in the great multitude of cases not affected by any special circumstances, from such a breach of contract. For, had the special circumstances been known, the parties might have specially provided for the breach of contract by special terms as to the damages in that case; and of this advantage it would be very unjust to deprive them.

Now the above principles are those by which we think the jury ought to be guided in estimating the damages arising out of any breach of contract. . . . Now, in the present case, if we are to apply the principles above laid down, we find that the only circumstances here communicated by the plaintiffs to the defendants at the time the contract was made, were, that the article to be carried was the broken shaft of a mill, and that the plaintiffs were the millers of that mill. But how do these circumstances shew reasonably that the profits of the mill must be stopped by an unreasonable delay in the delivery of the broken shaft by the carrier to the third person? Suppose the plaintiffs had another shaft in their possession put up or putting up at the time, and that they only wished to send back the broken shaft to the engineer who made it; it is clear that this would be quite consistent with the above circumstances, and yet the unreasonable delay in the delivery would have no effect upon the intermediate profits of the mill. Or, again, suppose that, at the time of the delivery to the carrier, the machinery of the mill had been in other respects defective, then, also, the same results would follow. Here it is true that the shaft was actually sent back to serve as a model for a new one, and that the want of a new one was the only cause of the stoppage of the mill, and that the loss of profits really arose from not sending down the new shaft in proper time, and that this arose from the delay in delivering the broken one to serve as a model. But it is obvious that, in the great multitude of cases of millers sending off broken shafts to third persons by a carrier under ordinary circumstances, such consequences would not, in all probability, have occurred; and these special circumstances were here never communicated by the plaintiffs to the defendants.

It follows, therefore, that the loss of profits here cannot reasonably be considered such a consequence of the breach of contract as could have been fairly and reasonably contemplated by both the parties when they made this contract. For such loss would neither have flowed naturally from the breach of this contract in the great multitude of such cases occurring under ordinary circumstances, nor were the special circumstances, which, perhaps, would have made it a reasonable and natural consequence of such breach of contract, communicated to or known by the defendants. The Judge ought, therefore, to have told the jury, that, upon the facts then before them, they ought not to take the loss of profits into consideration at all in estimating the damages. There must therefore be a new trial in this case.

Rule absolute.

C. CZARNIKOW, LTD.
v.
KOUFOS
House of Lords
2 Lloyd's Rep. 457
1967

LORD REID.

My Lords, by a charter-party of Oct. 15, 1960, the respondents chartered the appellant's vessel, *Heron II*, to proceed to Constantza, there to load a cargo of 3000 tons of sugar; and to carry it to Basrah, or, in the charterers' option, to Jeddah. The vessel left Constantza on Nov. 1. The option was not exercised and the vessel arrived at Basrah on Dec. 2. The umpire has found that "a reasonably accurate prediction of the length of the voyage was 20 days." But the vessel had in breach of contract made deviations which caused a delay of nine days.

It was the intention of the respondents to sell the sugar "promptly after arrival at Basrah and after inspection by merchants." The appellant did not know this but he was aware of the fact that there was a market for sugar at Basrah. The sugar was in fact sold at Basrah in lots between Dec. 12 and 22 but shortly before that time the market price had fallen partly by reason of the arrival of another cargo of sugar. It was found by the umpire that if there had not been this delay of nine days the sugar would have fetched £32 10s. per ton. The actual price realized was only £31 2s. 9d. per ton. The respondents claim that they are entitled to recover the difference as damage for breach of contract. The appellant admits that he is liable to pay interest for nine days on the value of the sugar and certain minor expenses but denies that fall in market value can be taken into account in assessing damages in this case.

Mr. Justice McNair, following the decision in The Parana, (1877) 2 P.D. 118, decided this question in favour of the appellant. He said ([1966] 1 Lloyd's Rep., at p. 274):

> . . . In those circumstances, it seems to me almost impossible to say that the shipowner must have known that the delay in prosecuting the voyage would probably result, or be likely to result, in this kind of loss.

The Court of Appeal by a majority (Lord Justice Diplock and Lord Justice Salmon; Lord Justice Sellers, dissenting) reversed the decision of the trial Judge. The majority . . . applying the rule (or rules) in Hadley and Another v. Baxendale and Others, (1854) 9 Ex. 341, as explained in Victoria Laundry (Windsor), Ltd. v. Newman Industries, Ltd.; Coulson & Co., Ltd. (Third Parties), [1949] 2 K.B. 528, they held that the loss due to fall in market price was not too remote to be recoverable as damages.

It may be well first to set out the knowledge and intention of the parties at the time of making the contract so far as relevant or argued to be relevant. The charterers intended to sell the sugar in the market at Basrah on arrival of the vessel. They could have changed their minds, and exercised their option to have the sugar delivered at Jeddah but they did not do so. There is no finding that they had in mind any particular date as the likely date of arrival at Basrah or that they had any knowledge or expectation that in late November or December there would be a rising or a falling market. The shipowner was given no information about these matters by the charterers. He did not know what the charterers intended to do with the sugar. But he knew there was a market in sugar at Basrah, and it appears to me that, if he had thought about the matter, he must have realized that at least it was not unlikely that the sugar would be sold in the market at market price on arrival[,] and he must be held to have known that in any ordinary market prices are apt to fluctuate from day to day: but he had no reason to suppose it more probable that during the relevant period such fluctuation would be downwards rather than upwards—it was an even chance that the fluctuation would be downwards.

So the question for decision is whether a plaintiff can recover as damages for breach of contract a loss of a kind which the defendant, when he made the contract, ought to have realized was not unlikely to result from a breach of contract causing delay in delivery. I use the words "not unlikely" as denoting a degree of probability considerably less than an even chance but nevertheless not very unusual and easily foreseeable.

For over a century everyone has agreed that remoteness of damage in contract must be determined by applying the rule (or rules) laid down by a Court including Lord Wensleydale (then Baron Parke), Baron Martin and Baron Alderson in Hadley v. Baxendale. But many different interpretations of that rule have been adopted by Judges at different times. So I think that one ought first to see just what was decided in that case, because it would seem wrong to attribute to that rule a meaning which, if it had been adopted in that case, would have resulted in a contrary decision of that case.

In Hadley v. Baxendale, the owners of a flour mill at Gloucester which was driven by a steam engine delivered to common carriers, Messrs. Pickford & Co., a broken crankshaft to be sent to engineers in Greenwich. A delay of five days in delivery there was held to be in breach of contract and the question at issue was the proper measure of damages. In fact the shaft was sent as a pattern for a new shaft and until it arrived the mill could not operate. So the owners claimed £300 as loss of profit for the five days by which resumption of work was delayed by this breach of contract. But the carriers did not know that delay would cause loss of this kind.

Baron Alderson delivering the judgment of the Court said:

> . . . we find that the only circumstances here communicated by the plaintiffs to the defendants at the time the contract was made, were, that the article to be carried was the broken shaft of a mill, and that the plaintiffs were the millers of that mill. But how do these circumstances shew reasonably that the profits of the mill must be stopped by an unreasonable delay in the delivery of the broken shaft by the carrier to the third person? Suppose the plaintiffs had another shaft in their possession put up or putting up at the time, and that they only wished to send back the broken shaft to the engineer who made it; it is clear that this would be quite consistent with the above circumstances, and yet the

unreasonable delay in the delivery would have no effect upon the intermediate profits of the mill. Or, again, suppose that at the time of the delivery to the carrier, the machinery of the mill had been in other respects defective, then, also, the same results would follow. . . .

Then, having said that in fact the loss of profit was caused by the delay, he continued:

> . . . But it is obvious that, in the great multitude of cases of millers sending off broken shafts to third persons by a carrier under ordinary circumstances, such consequences would not, in all probability, have occurred . . .

Baron Alderson clearly did not and could not mean that it was not reasonably foreseeable that delay might stop the resumption of work in the mill. He merely said that in the great multitude—which I take to mean the great majority—of cases this would not happen. He was not distinguishing between results which were foreseeable or unforeseeable, but between results which were likely because they would happen in the great majority of cases, and results which were unlikely because they would only happen in a small minority of cases. He continued:

> . . . It follows, therefore, that the loss of profits here cannot reasonably be considered such a consequence of the breach of contract as could have been fairly and reasonably contemplated by both the parties when they made this contract. . . .

He clearly meant that a result which will happen in the great majority of cases should fairly and reasonably be regarded as having been in the contemplation of the parties, but that a result which, though foreseeable as a substantial possibility, would only happen in a small minority of cases should not be regarded as having been in their contemplation. He was referring to such a result when he continued:

> . . . For such loss would neither have flowed naturally from the breach of this contract in the great multitude of such cases occurring under ordinary circumstances, nor were the special circumstances, which, perhaps, would have made it a reasonable and natural consequence of such breach of contract, communicated to or known by the defendants. . . .

I have dealt with the latter part of the judgment before coming to the well-known rule because the Court were there applying the rule and the language which was used in the latter part appears to me to throw considerable light on the meaning which they must have attached to the rather vague expressions used in the rule itself. The rule is that the damages

> . . . should be such as may fairly and reasonably be considered either arising naturally, i.e., according to the usual course of things, from such breach of contract itself, or such

> as may reasonably be supposed to have been in the contemplation of both parties, at the time they made the contract as the probable result of the breach of it. . . .

I do not think that it was intended that there were to be two rules or that two different standards or tests were to be applied. The last two passages which I quoted from the end of the judgment applied to the facts before the Court which did not include any special circumstances communicated to the defendants; and the line of reasoning there is that because in the great majority of cases loss of profit would not in all probability have occurred, it followed that this could not reasonably be considered as having been fairly and reasonably contemplated by both the parties, for it would not have flowed naturally from the breach in the great majority of cases.

I am satisfied that the Court did not intend that every type of damage which was reasonably foreseeable by the parties when the contract was made should either be considered as arising naturally, i.e., in the usual course of things, or be supposed to have been in the contemplation of the parties. Indeed the decision makes it clear that a type of damage which was plainly foreseeable as a real possibility but which would only occur in a small minority of cases cannot be regarded as arising in the usual course of things or be supposed to have been in the contemplation of the parties: the parties are not supposed to contemplate as grounds for the recovery of damage any type of loss or damage which on the knowledge available to the defendant would appear to him as only likely to occur in a small minority of cases.

In cases like Hadley v. Baxendale or the present case it is not enough that in fact the plaintiff's loss was directly caused by the defendant's breach of contract. It clearly was so caused in both. The crucial question is whether, on the information available to the defendant when the contract was made, he should, or the reasonable man in his position would, have realized that such loss was sufficiently likely to result from the breach of contract to make it proper to hold that the loss flowed naturally from the breach or that loss of that kind should have been within his contemplation.

The modern rule in tort is quite different and it imposes a much wider liability. The defendant will be liable for any type of damage which is reasonably foreseeable as liable to happen even in the most unusual case, unless the risk is so small that a reasonable man would in the whole circumstances feel justified in neglecting it and there is good reason for the difference. In contract, if one party wishes to protect himself against a risk which to the other party would appear unusual, he can direct the other party's attention to it before the contract is made, and I need not stop to consider in what circumstances the other party will then be held to have accepted responsibility in that event. But in tort there is no opportunity for the injured party to protect himself in that way, and the tortfeasor cannot reasonably complain if he has to pay for some very unusual but nevertheless foreseeable damage which results from his wrongdoing. I have no doubt that to-day a tortfeasor would be held liable for a type of damage as unlikely as was the stoppage of Hadley's mill for lack of a crankshaft: to anyone with the knowledge the carrier had that may have seemed unlikely but the chance of it happening would have been seen to be far from negligible. But it does not at all follow that Hadley v. Baxendale would today be differently decided.

. . .

But then it has been said that the liability of defendants has been further extended by Victoria Laundry (Windsor), Ltd. v. Newman Industries, Ltd.; Coulson & Co., Ltd. (Third Parties), [1949] 2 K.B. 528. I do not think so. The plaintiffs bought a large boiler from the defendants and the defendants were aware of the general nature of the plaintiffs' business and of the plaintiffs' intention to put the boiler into use as soon as possible. Delivery of the boiler was delayed in breach of contract and the plaintiffs claimed as damages loss of profit caused by the delay. A large part of the profits claimed would have resulted from some specially lucrative contracts which the plaintiffs could have completed if they had had the boiler: that was rightly disallowed because the defendants had no knowledge of these contracts. But Lord Justice Asquith then said:

> . . . It does not, however, follow that the plaintiffs are precluded from recovering some general (and perhaps conjectural) sum for loss of business in respect of dyeing contracts to be reasonably expected, any more than in respect of laundering contracts to be reasonably expected.

It appears to me that this was well justified on the earlier authorities. It was certainly not unlikely on the information which the defendants had when making the contract that delay in delivering the boiler would result in loss of business: indeed it would seem that that was more than an even chance. And there was nothing new in holding that damages should be estimated on a conjectural basis. This House had approved of that as early as 1813 in Hall v. Ross, (1813) 1 Dow. 201.

. . .

It appears to me that . . . the loss of profit claimed in this case was not too remote to be recoverable as damages. So it remains to consider whether the decision in The Parana, *sup.*, established a rule which, though now anomalous, should nevertheless still be followed. In that case owing to the defective state of the ship's engines a voyage which ought to have taken 65 to 70 days took 127 days, and as a result a cargo of hemp fetched a much smaller price than it would have done if there had been no breach of contract. But the Court of Appeal held that the plaintiffs could not recover this loss as damages. The vital part of their judgment is (1877) 2 P.D. 118, at p. 123:

> . . . In order that damages may be recovered, we must come to two conclusions—first, that it was reasonably certain that the goods would not be sold until they did arrive; and, secondly, that it was reasonably certain that they would be sold immediately after they arrived, and that that was known to the carrier at the time when the bills of lading were signed. . . .

If that was the right test then the decision was right, and I think that that test was in line with a number of cases decided before or about that time (1877). But, as I have already said, so strict a test has long been obsolete. And, if one substitutes for "reasonably certain" the words "not unlikely" or some similar words denoting a much smaller degree of probability, then the whole argument in the judgment collapses. I need not consider whether there were other facts which might be held to justify the decision, but I must say that I do not see why the mere duration of the voyage should make much difference.

For the reasons which I have given I would dismiss this appeal.

LORD MORRIS OF BORTH-Y-GEST.

. . . The appellant could and should at the very least have contemplated that if his ship was nine days later in arriving than she could and should have arrived some financial loss to the respondents or to an indorsee of the bill of lading might result. I use the words "at the very least" and the word "might" at this stage so as to point to the problem which is highlighted in this case. It is here that words and phrases begin to crowd in and to compete. Must the loss of the respondents be such that the appellant could see that it was certain to result? Or would it suffice if the loss was probable or was likely to result or was liable to result? In the present context what do these words denote? If there must be selection as between them which one is to be employed to convey the intended meaning?

I think that it is clear that the loss need not be such that the contract breaker could see that that it was certain to result. The question that arises concerns the measure of prevision which should fairly and reasonably be ascribed to him.

My Lords, in applying the guidance given in Hadley v. Baxendale, I would hope that no undue emphasis would be placed upon any one word or phrase. If a party has suffered some special and peculiar loss in reference to some particular arrangements of his which were unknown to the other party and were not communicated to the other party and were not therefore in the contemplation of the parties at the time when they made their contract, then it would be unfair and unreasonable to charge the contract breaker with such special and peculiar loss. If, however, there are no "special and extraordinary circumstances beyond the reasonable prevision of the parties" (see the speech of Lord Wright in Monarch Steamship Company, Ltd. v. Karlshamns Oljefabriker (A/B), [1949] A.C. 196, at p. 221) then it becomes very largely a question of fact as to whether in any particular case a loss can "fairly and reasonably" be considered as arising in the normal course of things. Though in these days commercial cases are not tried with Juries, in his speech in the Monarch Steamship Case, Lord du Parcq pointed out that in the end what has to be decided is a question of fact and therefore a question proper for a Jury and he added:

> . . . Circumstances are so infinitely various that, however carefully general rules are framed, they must be construed with some liberality, and not too rigidly applied. It was necessary to lay down principles lest juries should be persuaded to do injustice by imposing an undue, or perhaps an inadequate, liability on a defendant. The court must be careful, however, to see that the principles laid down are never so narrowly interpreted as

to prevent a jury, or judge of fact, from doing justice between the parties. So to use them would be to misuse them. . . .

. . . I regard the illuminating judgment of the Court of Appeal in Victoria Laundry (Windsor), Ltd. v. Newman Industries Ltd.; Coulson & Co., Ltd. (Third Parties), [1949] 2 K.B. 528, as a most valuable analysis of the rule. It was there pointed out (at p. 540) that in order to make a contract breaker liable under what was called "either rule" in Hadley v. Baxendale it is not necessary that he should actually have asked himself what loss is liable to result from a breach but that it suffices that if he had considered the question he would as a reasonable man have concluded that the loss in question was liable to result. Nor need it be proved, in order to recover a particular loss, that upon a given state of knowledge he could, as a reasonable man, foresee that a breach must necessarily result in that loss.

. . .

If the problem in the present case is that of relating accepted principle to the facts which have been found, I entertain no doubt that if at the time of their contract the parties had considered what the consequences would be if the arrival of the ship at Basrah was delayed they would have contemplated that some loss to the respondents was likely or was liable to result. The appellant at the time that he made his contract must have known that if in breach of contract his ship did not arrive at Basrah when she ought to arrive he would be liable to pay damages. He would not know that a loss to the respondents was certain or inevitable but he must, as a reasonable business man, have contemplated that the respondents would very likely suffer loss, and that it would be or would be likely to be a loss referable to market price fluctuations at Basrah. I cannot think that he should escape liability by saying that he would only be aware of a possibility of loss but not of a probability or certainty of it. He might have used any one of many phrases. He might have said that a loss would be likely[:] or that a loss would not be unlikely[:] or that a loss was liable to result[:] or that the risk that delay would cause loss to the respondents was a serious possibility[:] or that there would be a real danger of a loss[:] or that the risk of his being liable to have to pay for the loss was one that he ought commercially to take into account. As a practical business man he would not have paused to reflect on the possible nuances of meaning of any one of these phrases. Nor would he have sent for a dictionary.

The carriage of sugar from the Black Sea to Iraqi ports (including Basrah) is a recognized trade. The appellant knew that there was a sugar market at Basrah. When he contracted with the respondents to carry their sugar to Basrah, though he did not know what were the actual plans of the respondents, he had all the information to enable him to appreciate that a delay in arrival might in the ordinary course of things result in their suffering some loss. He must have known that the price in a market may fluctuate. He must have known that if a price goes down someone whose goods are late in arrival may be caused loss.

Since in awarding damages the aim is to award a sum which as nearly as possible will put the injured party into the position in which he would have been in if the breach of contract had not caused him loss and if in all the circumstances he had acted reasonably in an effort to mitigate his loss, I think that it must follow that, where there is delay in arrival, in many cases the actual loss suffered (above the amount of which there ought not to be recovery) can be measured by comparing the market price of the goods at the date when they should have arrived and the market price when they did arrive. That *prima facie* is the measure of the damages. . . .

I would dismiss the appeal.

. . .

LORD PEARCE.

. . .

The underlying rule of the common law is that

> . . . where a party sustains a loss by reason of a breach of contract, he is, so far as money can do it, to be placed in the same situation, with respect to damages, as if the contract had been performed. . . . [Baron Parke in Robinson v. Harman, (1848) 1 Ex. 850, at p. 855.]

But since so wide a principle might be too harsh on a contract breaker in making him liable for a chain of unforeseen and fortuitous circumstances the law limited the liability in ways which crystallized in the rule in Hadley v. Baxendale, *sup.* This was designed as a direction to Juries but it has become an integral part of the law.

. . .

I do not think that Baron Alderson was directing his mind to whether something resulting in the natural course of events was an odds-on chance or not. A thing may be a natural (or even an obvious) result even though the odds are against it. Suppose a contractor was employed to repair the ceiling of one of the Law Courts and did it so negligently that it collapsed on the heads of those in Court. I should be inclined to think that any tribunal (including the learned Baron himself) would have found as a fact that the damage arose "naturally, i.e., according to the usual course of things." Yet if one takes into account the nights, week-ends, and vacations, when the ceiling might have collapsed, the odds against it collapsing on top of anybody's head are nearly 10 to one. I do not believe that this aspect of the matter was fully considered and worked out in the judgment. He was thinking of causation and type of consequence rather than of odds. . . .

. . .

The facts of the present case lead to the view that the loss of market arose naturally, i.e., according to the usual course of things, from the shipowner's deviation. The sugar was being exported to Basrah where, as the respondents knew, there was a sugar market. It was sold on arrival and fetched a lower price than it would have done had it arrived on time. The fall in market price was not due to any unusual or unpredictable factor.

. . .

In the United States the Corpus Juris Secundum states that

> In the ordinary case of deviation or delay, the measure of damages is the difference in the market value of the goods at the time when actually delivered and when they should have been delivered, with interest [80 C.J.S. 124].

. . .

In my opinion the line of approach in . . . the United States is correct. In most cases the loss of market will be found to be within the contemplation of the parties in carriage of goods by sea. It is however ultimately a question of fact and it may be that in some unusual cases it will be found that the situation between the parties showed that the shipper was indifferent to the time of arrival and that the parties did *not* contract on the basis that in case of deviation or delay the shipowner should be liable for loss of market. But the absence of an express clause (which could easily be inserted) to that effect will obviously make it hard to establish. I have not dealt with the various particular facts in this case by which Mr Kerr's able argument occks to show that these particular parties did not contemplate damage by loss of market. For I agree with the remarks of the majority of the Court of Appeal on this subject.

. . .

I would dismiss the appeal.

Lord Upjohn.

. . .

It is perfectly true that at the time of the contract nothing was said as to the purpose for which the charterers wanted the sugar delivered at Basrah; they might have wanted to do so to stock up their supply of sugar or to carry out a contract already entered into which had nothing to do with the market at Basrah; or they might sell it during the voyage, but all that is pure speculation. It seems to me that on the facts of this case the parties must be assumed to have contemplated that there would be a punctual delivery to the port of discharge and that port having a market in sugar there was a real danger that as a result of a delay in breach of contract the charterers would miss the market and would suffer loss accordingly. It being established that the goods were in fact destined for the market the shipowner is liable for that loss.

. . .

For these reasons I would dismiss this appeal.

3

ALLEN
v.
JONES

California Court of Appeal, Fourth District
104 Cal. App. 3d 207
1980

Tamura, J.

Plaintiff sued defendants, individually and as a partnership doing business under the name of Miller Jones Valley Mortuary, to recover damages for mental distress suffered upon learning that the cremated remains of plaintiff's brother, which defendants had undertaken to ship to Illinois, were lost in transit. Plaintiff appeals from a judgment of dismissal following the sustaining of defendants' demurrer to plaintiff's second amended complaint.

The factual allegations of the second amended complaint, which are deemed true for purposes of this review (Guess v. State of California (1979) 96 Cal. App. 3d 111, 114 [157 Cal. Rptr. 618]), are as follows: Plaintiff is the brother and nearest living relative of Ralph Allen, who died on December 2, 1976. On or about December 4, 1976, plaintiff entered into an oral agreement with defendants under which defendants agreed to cremate the body of Ralph Allen and to ship the cremated remains to Rantoul, Illinois. Plaintiff agreed to pay, and did pay, $516 for defendants' services. As a result of defendants' negligence in packaging the remains, the package arrived empty and the remains were lost, causing plaintiff to suffer great nervous shock, mental anguish and humiliation.

. . .

The second amended complaint was framed in causes of action for negligent performance of a contract, intentional infliction of emotional distress and deceit. In the negligence cause of action, plaintiff sought damages for emotional distress only. In the other two causes of action, plaintiff sought both emotional distress damages and punitive damages. The court below, in the minute order announcing its ruling, stated that the demurrers were sustained on the ground that the complaint failed to plead "recognized damages." . . .

. . .

In an action for breach of contract the measure of damages is "the amount which will compensate the party aggrieved for all the detriment proximately caused thereby, or which, in the ordinary course of things would be likely to result therefrom" (Civ. Code, §3300), provided, however, that the damages are "clearly ascertainable in both their nature and origin" (Civ. Code, §3301). These statutory provisions have been interpreted by our courts to mean that damages for breach of contract are ordinarily confined to those which would naturally arise from the breach or which might have been reasonably contemplated or foreseen by the parties at the time they contracted, as the probable result of the breach.

The great majority of contracts involve commercial transactions in which it is generally not foreseeable that breach will cause significant mental distress as distinguished from mere mental agitation or annoyance. Accordingly, the rule has developed that damages for mental suffering or injury to reputation are generally not recoverable in an action for breach of contract.

There are, however, certain contracts which so affect the vital concerns of the individual that severe mental distress is a foreseeable result of breach. For many years, our courts have recognized that damages for mental distress may be recovered for breach of a contract of this nature. (Crisci v. Security Ins. Co. (1967) 66 Cal. 2d 425, 434 [58 Cal. Rptr. 13, 426 P.2d 173]; Chelini v. Nieri (1948) 32 Cal. 2d 480, 482 [196 P.2d 915]; Windeler v. Scheers Jewelers (1970) 8 Cal. App. 3d 844, 851 [88 Cal. Rptr. 39]; Westervelt v. McCullough (1924) 68 Cal. App. 198, 208-209 [228 P. 734].)

A contract whereby a mortician agrees to prepare a body for burial is one in which it is reasonably foreseeable that breach may cause mental anguish to the decedent's bereaved relations. "One who prepares a human body for burial and conducts a funeral usually deals with the living in their most difficult and delicate moments. . . . The exhibition of callousness or indifference, the offer of insult and indignity, can, of course, inflict no injury on the dead, but they can visit agony akin to torture on the living. So true is this that the chief asset of a mortician and the most conspicuous element of his advertisement is his consideration for the afflicted. A decent respect for their feelings is implied in every contract for his services." (Fitzsimmons v. Olinger Mortuary Assn. (1932) 91 Colo. 544.) In a similar vein, another court has stated: "The tenderest feelings of the human heart center around the remains of the dead. When the defendants contracted with plaintiff to inter the body of her deceased husband in a workmanlike manner they did so with the knowledge that she was the widow and would naturally and probably suffer mental anguish if they failed to fulfill their contractual obligation in the manner here charged. The contract was predominantly personal in nature and no substantial pecuniary loss would follow its breach. Her mental concern, her sensibilities, and her solicitude were the prime considerations for the contract, and the contract itself was such as to put the defendants on notice that a failure on their part to inter the body properly would probably produce mental suffering on her part. It cannot be said, therefore, that such damages were not within the contemplation of the parties at the time the contract was made." (Lamm v. Shingleton (1949) 231 N.C. 10.)

. . .

The leading case on the same subject in this state is Chelini v. Nieri, in which the plaintiff recovered $10,000 general damages for a mortician's breach of contract to preserve the body of the plaintiff's mother. The only significant distinction between *Chelini* and the instant case is that in *Chelini* the plaintiff's emotional suffering was manifested in physical illness, whereas in the present case plaintiff has alleged only mental distress.

To date all of the cases in this state in which mental distress damages have been awarded for breach of contract have been cases in which the mental distress caused physical illness, and it is not clear whether mental distress damages alone can ever support an action for breach of contract in this state. We need not address that question in the present case, however, because plaintiff alleged that the cremated remains were lost because of defendants' negligence in preparing them for shipment. Plaintiff has thereby pleaded an action in tort as well as in contract. (Crisci v. Security Ins. Co., supra, 66 Cal. 2d 425, 432; Eads v. Marks (1952) 39 Cal. 2d 807, 811 [249 P.2d 257]; Jarchow v. Transamerica Title Ins. Co. (1975) 48 Cal. App. 3d 917, 939-940 [122 Cal. Rptr. 470]; Prosser, Law of Torts (4th ed. 1971) pp. 617-618.)

In tort actions courts have traditionally been reluctant to allow recovery for mental distress not accompanied by physical injury. However, as Prosser states: "It is now more or less generally conceded that the only valid objection against recovery for mental injury is the danger of vexatious suits and fictitious claims, which has loomed very large in the opinions as an obstacle." (Prosser, Law of Torts (4th ed.) p. 328, fns. omitted.) Prosser observes that the majority of jurisdictions now permit recovery for negligent mishandling of corpses, and explains that this particular situation presents "an especial likelihood of genuine and serious mental distress, arising from the special circumstances, which serves as a guarantee that the claim is not spurious." (Ibid., at pp. 329-330. See also, Leavitt, *The Funeral Director's Liability for Mental Anguish*, 15 Hastings L.J. 464, 482-494.)

Section 868 of the Restatement Second of Torts recognizes a cause of action for intentional, reckless, or negligent conduct which prevents proper interment of a dead body.[2] The official comment to the section states: "The technical basis of the cause of action is the interference with the exclusive right of control of the body, which frequently has been called by the courts a 'property' or a 'quasi-property' right. This does not, however, fit very well into the category of property, since the body ordinarily cannot be sold or transferred, has no utility and can be used only for the one purpose of interment or cremation. In practice the technical right has served as a mere peg upon which to hang damages for the mental distress inflicted upon the survivor; and in reality the cause of action has been exclusively one for the mental distress. . . . There is no need to show physical consequences of the mental distress."

. . .

We conclude that damages are recoverable for mental distress without physical injury for negligent mishandling of a corpse by a mortuary. Public policy requires that mortuaries adhere to a high standard of care in view of the psychological devastation likely to result from any mistake which upsets the expectations of the decedent's bereaved family. As mental distress is a highly foreseeable result of such conduct and in most cases the only form of damage likely to ensue, recovery for mental distress is a useful and necessary means to maintain the standards of the profession and is the only way in which the victims may be compensated for the wrongs they have suffered. The nature of the wrongful conduct that must be present in this type of case provides sufficient assurance of the genuineness of a claim for emotional distress. As to this form of negligence action, therefore, we hold that plaintiff may recover for mental distress without accompanying physical injury.

It is neither necessary nor appropriate for us in this case to take that giant leap for mankind espoused by the concurring opinion. We need only take the modest step, consistent with common law tradition, of declaring the law applicable to the case at hand. Our decision today hopefully clarifies California law on liability for negligent mishandling of corpses by bringing it into conformity with the views expressed by Professor Prosser, the Restatement and modern decisions from sister states.

. . .

We conclude that the court below erred in sustaining the demurrer to the cause of action for negligent breach of contract, but we conclude also that the ruling was correct as to plaintiff's other causes of action. It follows, of course, that plaintiff may not recover punitive damages. (See Walker v. Signal Companies, Inc. (1978) 84 Cal. App. 3d 982, 996.)

The judgment of dismissal is reversed with directions to overrule defendants' demurrer to plaintiff's first cause of action.

---

2. Section 868 provides: "One who intentionally, recklessly, or negligently removes, withholds, mutilates or operates upon the body of a dead person or prevents its proper interment or cremation is subject to liability to a member of the family of the deceased who is entitled to the disposition of the body."

[Presiding Justice Gardner, concurring, advocated the recovery of damages for "purely mental and emotional" distress caused by the negligent mishandling of a corpse, whether or not there was an accompanying physical manifestation, and in ordinary negligence actions.]

JACKSON
v.
ROYAL BANK OF SCOTLAND

House of Lords
2005 UKHL 3
2005

LORD HOPE OF CRAIGHEAD.

My Lords, this is an appeal about the damages to be awarded to the former partners of a business partnership for a breach of contract as a result of which the relationship of that business with its principal customer was terminated. The claim is for the loss of the opportunity to earn further profits from that relationship. It raises issues about the proper approach to remoteness where damages are claimed for breach of contract and about the quantum of the damages.

The claimants are James Jackson and the late Barrie Stewart Davies, who carried on business in partnership. They traded under the name of Samson Lancastrian ("Samson"). Samson imported goods from the Far East, including Thailand, and sold them to customers in the United Kingdom. Its principal customer in this country was another business partnership which traded under the name Economy Bag. The partners in this business were Mr. Taylor and Mr. Holt. The products which Economy Bag sold to its wholesale and retail customers included dog chews. By coincidence the bankers to both Samson and Economy Bag were the Royal Bank of Scotland plc ("the Bank"). The Bank is the respondent in this appeal.

THE FACTS

Economy Bag had previously purchased various varieties of dog chews in bulk and packed them itself for supply to its customers. By 1990 it had decided to eliminate the packing operation and obtain pre-packed dog chews in packaging bearing its trade name. It was introduced to Samson, who found a potential supplier of dog chews in Thailand. Mr. Jackson showed samples of these dog chews to Mr. Taylor and quoted prices for their supply cif Manchester which were acceptable to Economy Bag. Mr. Jackson and Mr. Taylor agreed to do business with each other by means of transferable letters of credit. The letters of credit were to be issued by the Bank to Economy Bag, and Samson was to be named as the beneficiary. The intention was to provide Samson with security in the event of a default by Economy Bag. The bags of dog chews were to be labelled specifically for Economy Bag.

They would have been difficult to dispose of in the open market to other customers.

Economy Bag placed an order for dog chews with Samson in September 1990. At its request the Bank issued a transferable letter of credit in favour of Samson which provided for payment of the agreed sum on production of a commercial invoice, evidence of insurance and a packing list. Economy Bag was relatively inexperienced in these matters. So it agreed with Samson that Samson would deal with the import formalities and arrange carriage from Manchester to Economy Bag's premises in Preston. . . . Samson placed an order for the dog chews ordered by Economy Bag with the supplier in Thailand who had provided the samples. The supplier failed to fulfil the contract, so Samson placed an order with an alternative Thai supplier named Pet Products Ltd. Its transaction with Economy Bag was completed successfully on this basis. Samson retained part of the price paid by Economy Bag for itself as a mark-up. It transferred the remainder of the credit which had been provided to it by the Bank under the letter of credit to Pet Products as the second beneficiary.

A substantial number of transactions according to the same pattern for the supply by Samson of pre-packed dog chews to Economy Bag followed thereafter on an increasing scale until March 1993. During this period there were 33 such contracts. Payment was almost invariably made by transferable letters of credit issued by the Bank. Samson charged a different percentage mark-up on each transaction depending on the variety of the items sold. It did not disclose the amount of the mark-up to Economy Bag. Samson kept this information to itself. The insurance policy identified Pet Products as the insured, but the amount insured was the amount shown on Samson's invoice to Economy Bag plus 10%. The packing list was typed on Pet Products' stationery. This showed its address and its telephone and fax numbers in Thailand. It did not show the price on Pet Products' invoice to Samson or the unit price charged by Pet Products for each item.

The effect of these arrangements was that Economy Bag knew the identity of the supplier in Thailand and its contact details. These facts were known by its partners from the outset. But it did not know the extent of Samson's mark-up on the first or any of the subsequent transactions. . . . One of the advantages of the transferable credit arrangements from [Samson's] point of view was that they concealed the amount of its mark-up on its transactions with Pet Products.

The relationship came to an end unexpectedly as a result of a breakdown in these arrangements for which the Bank were responsible. In January 1993 Economy Bag asked the Bank to open a transferable letter of credit in favour of Samson in the sum of US$50,976 for a consignment of dog chews that it had ordered on 7 January 1993. The bank complied with this request. They issued the letter of credit to Samson on 22 January 1993. On 1 February 1993 Samson instructed the Bank to transfer the credit to Pet Products in the sum of US$43,932.50 and to debit its account with the Bank with the transfer charges. The transaction proceeded normally until 15 March 1993, when the Bank in error sent a completion statement and other documents including Pet Products' invoice to Economy Bag instead of to Samson. The effect of the Bank's error was to reveal to Economy Bag the substantial profit that

Samson was making on these transactions. On this occasion it amounted to a mark-up of 19% on the amount payable to Pet Products. . . .

Mr. Taylor was angry when he discovered the size of the mark-up. He decided to cut Samson out of Economy Bag's system for importing the dog chews from Thailand. He terminated their relationship. Four contracts that were already on foot were performed. But thereafter Economy Bag bought its dog chews from Pet Products direct. In the year ending March 1994 it purchased 15 shipments from Pet Products worth US$257,944. Between March 1994 and March 1995 it purchased 28 shipments worth US$468,296. Between March 1995 and March 1996 it purchased 23 shipments worth US$462,467. Between March 1996 and March 1997 it purchased 25 shipments worth US$645,429. Mr Taylor's evidence at the trial in 1998 was that its business was still continuing on that scale, and that it also did business with other suppliers in the Far East which would have been done through Samson if their relationship had continued.

As for Samson, the loss of its business with Economy Bag had disastrous consequences. It deprived it of its principal source of income. It had to cease trading. The partnership was dissolved.

THE ISSUES

The judge, His Honour Judge Kershaw, Q.C., held that the Bank was in breach of an obligation of confidence under its contract with Samson not to disclose to Economy Bag any of the documents relating to its purchase of goods from Pet Products. These documents included the invoice by Pet Products to Samson. It was the disclosure of this document to Economy Bag that revealed the amount of the profit that Samson was making on the transaction. There was no appeal against that part of his judgment. It was common ground in the Court of Appeal that the Bank was in breach of its contract with Samson when it disclosed the invoice to Economy Bag.

The Judge then found that Samson was entitled to damages for loss of the opportunity to earn profits from its trading relationship. He held that there was a significant chance that Samson's trading relationship with Economy Bag would have continued for a further four years. But in view of the uncertainties he reduced the profit which had been projected by Samson for each of these years for the purposes of his award, and he increased the amount of the reduction year by year. The implication of his judgment was that after the end of the fourth year Samson's chance of obtaining repeat business was so speculative as not to sound in damages.

Three points were in issue in the Court of Appeal. . . .

The second point . . . remains in issue. It is whether the Judge was correct in his findings on causation, remoteness and quantum. . . .

Lord Justice Potter, with whom Lord Justice Nourse and Mr. Justice Ferris agreed, said, in par. 33 of his judgment that there was no sufficient basis on which the Judges could have awarded damages for a period anything like as long as four years. He said that the Judge should have focused on the Bank's limited knowledge of the facts at the date of the breach. Had he done so he would have concluded that the Bank could reasonably foresee a substantial loss of business in relation to orders likely to be placed by Economy Bag in the near future but with a cut-off point far shorter than the four year period. In par. 34 he said that the award of damages should be limited to a period of one year from the date of the breach, all other loss being regarded as too remote.

[Samson] submitted that the decision of the Court of Appeal to limit the award to a period of one year was based on an error of principle and that it should be set aside. But she said that the [trial] judge too was in error, as there was no real justification for his finding that Samson's trading relationship with Economy Bag would have lasted for only four years. The bank's liability, she said, was open-ended. It ought not to have been subjected to an arbitrary cut-off point. Figures had been submitted which would have justified an award extending over a period of six years, and the Judge ought to have made an award for loss of repeat orders over that entire period. [The Bank] said that the proper conclusion from the facts was that there was no foreseeable loss at all. . . .

THE BREACH OF CONTRACT

. . .

The relationship between the Bank and Samson which gave rise to the breach of contract arose from the issue of the transferable letter of credit in favour of Samson on 22 January 1993. . . .

. . . [T]he Judge's finding that the Bank owed a duty of confidence to Samson was not challenged in the Court of Appeal. As Lord Justice Potter said in par. 27 of his judgment, the duty of confidence arises from the acknowledged need for the issuing bank to protect its customer from disclosure of his level of profit and from the danger that if that level of profit is disclosed his purchaser will go instead direct to the customer's own supplier. As *Paget's Law of Banking* observes in the passage mentioned above, the right of the first beneficiary to substitute his own invoice for that of the second beneficiary and draw on the credit according to its pre-transfer terms is an important part of the transfer regime. It enables the first beneficiary to keep confidential from the applicant the amount of his profit from the transaction. For sound commercial reasons he is entitled to keep the amount of that profit secret. The information is confidential to the first beneficiary. It is the duty of the issuing bank to protect that confidentiality.

. . .

The situation in this case was that Economy Bag knew the identity of the seller of the goods from the outset. . . . There is no doubt that [Economy Bag's president] was in a position from the outset, or at least well before January 1993, to ask Pet Products for a direct quotation for the dog chews which were being sent to Samson from Thailand if it had occurred to him to do so. . . . He told the judge that he knew that Samson was making a profit on the transaction. But it was the amount of it that was hurtful, and this was what caused him to terminate the relationship. No doubt he could have discovered this earlier, and done something about it, if he had been more streetwise and more energetic. But this did not happen.

. . .

THE ISSUES RELATING TO DAMAGES

The way in which the Court of Appeal dealt with the case suggests it misunderstood the effect of the rules that were identified in Hadley v. Baxendale, (1854) 9 Exch 341, 354. They are very familiar to every student of contract law. Most would claim to be able to recite them by heart. But it may be helpful, as background to the discussion that follows, if I were to set out the rules again here:

> Where two parties have made a contract which one of them has broken, the damages which the other party ought to receive in respect of such breach of contract should be such as may fairly and reasonably be considered either arising naturally, i.e. according to the usual course of things, from such breach of contract itself, or such as may reasonably be supposed to have been in the contemplation of both parties, at the time they made the contract, as the probable result of the breach of it.

The first rule, prefaced by the word "either," is the rule that applies in this case. It is the ordinary rule. Everyone is taken to know the usual course of things and consequently to know what loss is liable to result from a breach of the contract if things take their usual course. But the way the second rule is expressed, prefaced by the word "or," shows the principle that underlies both limbs. It refers to what was in the contemplation of the parties at the time they made their contract.

As Lord Justice Asquith said in Victoria Laundry (Windsor) Ltd v. Newman Industries Ltd, [1949] 2 KB 528, 539[,] in cases of breach of contract the aggrieved party is only entitled to recover such part of the loss actually resulting as was at the time of the contract reasonably foreseeable as likely to result from the breach. In tort, the question whether loss was reasonably foreseeable is addressed to the time when the tort was committed. In contract, the question is addressed to the time when the parties made their contract. Where knowledge of special circumstances is relied on, the assumption is that the defendant undertook to bear any special loss which was referable to those special circumstances. It is assumed too that he had the opportunity to seek to limit his liability under the contract for ordinary losses in the event that he was in breach of it.

The Bank's primary argument on damages was that the loss of the repeat business on which Samson based its claim was too remote. This was because it was not in the Bank's reasonable contemplation that the disclosure of the profit that Samson was making would lead to the termination by Economy Bag of its trading relationship with Samson. Their relationship, it was said, was based on mutual trust and confidence. There was no reason for the Bank to think that breach of its duty of confidence to Samson would result in any loss at all. The real reason for the loss of repeat business was [the president of Economy Bag's] anger when he detected the amount of the mark-up. This was something that could not have been predicted.

The trial Judge rejected that argument, and the Court of Appeal did so too for the reasons explained by Lord Justice Potter LJ in pars. 25 and 26 of his judgment. The [trial] judge proceeded to examine the figures for the profit which Samson projected on the basis of the figures relating to Economy Bag's trade in dog chews for the four years from March 1993 to March 1997 which I have set out in par. 10 above. Holding that there was a significant chance that Samson's business relationship with Economy Bag would have continued for some time, but that the likelihood of its coming to an end would have increased as time passed, he attributed what he said was an appropriate sum by way of each year in which the claimants had shown that damages should be awarded as follows: 1993-1994 $27,000; 1994-1995 $42,000; 1995-1996 $29,000; 1996-1997 $26,500. His total award, prior to the addition of interest, was $124,500.

The Court of Appeal applied the first rule in Hadley v. Baxendale, (1954) 9 Exch 341 as explained by Lord Justice Asquith in the *Victoria Laundry*, [1949] 2 KB 528. Lord Justice Potter said that loss of the chance or opportunity of repeat business should in principle be available, and that the issue in this case was for how long it was or should have been in the reasonable contemplation of the parties that the trading relationship would continue. In par. 29 he referred to the statement by Lord Justice Evans in Kpohraror v. Woolwich Building Society, [1996] 4 All ER 119, 127j-128a that the starting point for any application of Hadley v. Baxendale is the extent of the shared knowledge of both parties when the contract was made. In par. 31 he observed that the claim, as presented at the trial, was one for loss of business profits made up of specific transactions none of which had yet been concluded at the time of the Bank's breach. It depended on the chance or contingency that Economy Bag would act so as to enable Samson to make that profit as explained in Allied Maples Group Ltd v Simmons & Simmons [1995] 1 WLR 1602 where, at p 1614c, Lord Justice Stuart-Smith said that the plaintiff must prove as a matter of causation that he had a real substantial chance as opposed to a speculative one. Thus far the judgment proceeded on orthodox lines, and there are no grounds for criticism.

But at the end of par. 31 and the beginning of par. 32, in a passage where he identified the approach that he then took to this issue, Lord Justice Potter said:

> . . . [w]hatever the judge's view of the percentage chance that, but for the bank's breach, Samson would in fact have been Economy Bag's supplier in the respect of the transactions in the following years, the cut-off point for the bank's liability was the end of such period as was within the reasonable contemplation of the bank at the time of breach.
>
> "32. As to that, the bank's knowledge of the background and details of Samson's trading relationship was limited to the period of time and the individual transactions conducted *prior to breach*." (Emphasis added.)

In par. 33 Lord Justice Potter said that it seemed to him that there was no sufficient basis on which the judge could or should have predicated his award covering a period anything like as long as four years. In par. 34 he said that the judge could and should have approached the case on the broad basis that, while it could reasonably be contemplated that the established relationship of Samson and Economy Bag would have continued for a time, and thus that some award of damages for future business fell to be made, that time should in all the circumstances be limited to a period of one year from the date of the breach, all loss thereafter being regarded as too remote. In par. 35 he said:

> On the assumption that the evidence (as I read it) showed that, but for the bank's error, Samson was virtually certain to have retained Economy Bag's business in dog chews for the year 1993/94, the loss of profit on the figures adopted by the judge would have been $38,831, to which should be added 5% commission, less overheads, giving a total of $47,278.15. I would round down that figure to $45,000 to reflect the small degree of uncertainty inherent in even the closest of trading relationships and would award that sum together with interest by way of general damages for loss of profit.

[Samson] submitted that the Court of Appeal fell into error at this point. All that the claimant had to show was that at the time of the contract the contract-breaker should have contemplated that damage of the kind suffered would have occurred as a result of his breach. Once it had decided, correctly, that it was a natural and probable consequence of the Bank's breach that Samson would suffer a loss of repeat business, there was no cut-off point. The bank's liability was open-ended, as it had not limited its liability by the contract to any particular period. . . .

WAS THE LOSS OF REPEAT BUSINESS TOO REMOTE?

. . .

The effect of the contract that the Bank entered into was that it was obliged not to pass this information on, and Samson had an obvious and legitimate commercial interest in maintaining its confidentiality. There is no reason at all to suppose that, if it had been asked at the time of the contract, Samson would have agreed to the release of this information by the Bank to Economy Bag. I would hold in agreement both with the trial judge and the Court of Appeal, whose concurrent findings on the relevant facts I would regard as conclusive on this issue, that the loss of repeat orders from Economy Bag was not too remote. As soon as the confidential information was released there was no repeat business. The claimants are entitled to an award of damages to put them in the same position as they would have been if there had been no breach of contract. . . .

HOW IS THAT LOSS TO BE QUANTIFIED?

The first question is whether the Court of Appeal was wrong to limit the period for which damages were recoverable by reference to what was within the reasonable contemplation of the Bank at the time of the breach. Lord Justice Potter LJ said[,] par. 31, that, whatever the Judge's view was of the percentage chance that Samson would in fact in the following years have been Economy Bag's supplier of dog chews, the Bank's reasonable contemplation at the date of the breach introduced a cut-off point beyond which the Bank was not liable. He said that this was the effect of the rule as to remoteness in Hadley v. Baxendale 9 Exch 341.

In my opinion there are two errors in this approach to the assessment of damages. This first may appear to be the somewhat technical point, that it is the date of the making of the contract, not the date of the breach, that was identified as the relevant date in Hadley v. Baxendale. I say that it may appear to be somewhat technical because in this case the date of the making of the contract and the date of the breach were only about two months apart. There is no evidence that the facts that were relevant to what the Bank had in reasonable contemplation changed to any significant extent between 22 January 1993 when the letter of credit was issued and 15 March 1993 when the Bank sent Pet Products' invoice to Economy Bag. But the error was an error of principle. The choice of dates is more important than the differences, if any, in those facts. The parties have the opportunity to limit their liability in damages when they are making their contract. They have the opportunity at that stage to draw attention to any special circumstances outside the ordinary course of things which they ought to have in contemplation when entering into the contract. If no cut-off point is provided by the contract, there is no arbitrary limit that can be set to the amount of the damages once the test of remoteness according to one or other of the rules in Hadley v. Baxendale has been satisfied.

The second error flows from the first. The bank did not include any provision in the letter of credit limiting its liability for the loss of repeat business to any particular period. So the only limit on the period of its liability is that which the trial judge identified. This is when, on the facts, the question whether any loss has been sustained has become too speculative to permit the making of any award. He held that as time passed it was increasing likely that Economy Bag would have acquired the motive and the means to squeeze Samson's profit margins and would ultimately have ended their business relationship. . . .

These errors lie at the heart of the Court of Appeal's decision to limit the Bank's liability to a period of one year. For this reason I would hold that its decision cannot stand. I would allow the appeal and set aside its assessment of the amount to be awarded to the appellants as damages.

. . .

CONCLUSION

. . . I would restore the order which the trial judge made as to the principal sum to be awarded to the claimants as damages.

Problems

1. A Faulty Soil Assessment. Maine Rubber International planned to relocate its main manufacturing plant and paid Environmental Management Group (EMG) $1,900 to test the proposed site for contaminants. EMG is in the business of performing environmental site assessments for companies. At the time Maine Rubber hired EMG, Maine Rubber's president told an EMG representative about Maine Rubber's business and that it was contemplating a purchase of the property in question. The president did not provide any specific information about the company's plans to relocate to the property.

EMG's assessment determined that the property was clean, and Maine Rubber made extensive preparations for a phased move to the new location that would allow it to slowly shift production from the old site to the new one without suffering declines in productivity. Just before the phased move was about to begin, government regulators discovered significant environmental hazards on the new site. Because the toxins could not be remediated before the closing date, Maine Rubber canceled the purchase and completed an expedited, and much more expensive, move to another site.

Maine Rubber sued EMG for breach of contract, and a jury returned a verdict for Maine Rubber. Maine Rubber sought $200,000 in damages as compensation for the costs of preparing for the phased move and $500,000 for lost profits during the period in which its plant had to be shut down in order to effectuate the last-minute move to a new location. How should the court rule on Maine Rubber's damages claim?

2. The "1031 Exchange." The United States Tax Code (section 1031) enables the seller of an investment property to defer taxes due on the sale by purchasing a similar property with the proceeds within a short period of time. When a 1031 exchange is accomplished, the tax basis of the original property is shifted to the replacement property, and taxes are not due until the replacement property is eventually sold. To complete a 1031 exchange, the taxpayer must designate a replacement property within 45 days of selling the original property, and the purchase of the replacement property must be completed within 180 days of the original sale.

In January 2003, Lillian Logan sold a piece of investment property that had appreciated considerably and sought to take advantage of section 1031. Her real estate brokers told the owner of a shopping mall, D.W. Sivers Company, that Logan was a "motivated 1031 buyer." In March, Logan entered into a letter of intent agreement with Sivers to purchase the mall for $5 million with a closing date of June 30. The letter of intent listed several conditions of the purchase and stated that the parties "acknowledge that this Letter of Intent proposal is not a binding agreement and that it is intended solely to establish the principal terms of the purchase and as a basis for the preparation of a binding Purchase and Sale Agreement." It also provided that, in return for Logan's good faith efforts to review all the relevant information concerning the shopping mall, Sivers would not sell the property to any other party for 60 days. Logan then designated the mall as her "exchange" property under section 1031, just in time to meet the 45-day designation requirement.

Twenty-one days later, Sivers sold the mall to a third party. At this point, it was too late for Logan to designate another property under section 1031. Consequently, she sued Sivers for the $900,000 of federal taxes that would now be due as a result of her January sale, in addition to out-of-pocket costs associated with conducting due diligence on the shopping mall purchase. Is Logan entitled to collect?

3. When Shamu Attacks. Jonathan Smith, an animal trainer at Sea World in San Diego, was attacked by an orca (or "killer whale") during a live performance at the park. A member of the audience, who happened to catch the attack on film, gave Smith the tape, and Smith permitted two television networks to air the footage, accompanied by interviews with him, in return for $300 and $500, respectively.

A decade later, a Fox television show, *The Extraordinary*, aired 37 seconds of the footage without Smith's permission. Smith sued for copyright violation, and the case was settled out of court with Fox and the show's producer paying Smith $40,000 and promising not to duplicate, display, distribute, or perform the offending footage again. The producer later breached the settlement agreement by selling the rights to rebroadcast ten episodes of *The Extraordinary*, including the episode that included the Smith footage, to Universal Television Networks (which then broadcast the episode) for $200,000. Smith testified that, since the settlement agreement, he had not attempted to license the video, and he intended not to do so in order to protect his privacy.

Smith sued for breach of contract and sought damages both for mental suffering and emotional distress that he claimed he suffered as a result of the unauthorized rebroadcast, and for lost profits. Assuming Smith can prove he suffered emotional distress as a result of the breach, should he be entitled to recover an amount necessary to compensate for it as consequential damages? Should he be entitled to recover lost profits as consequential damages?

F. THE "REASONABLE CERTAINTY" REQUIREMENT

Both the compensation principle, which forms the basis of contract law damages, and the need for predictability, which underlies the foreseeability limitation, imply that non-breaching parties should not be permitted to recover for speculative losses. Imagine, for example, a disappointed buyer of a $1 widget, who, in the absence of a substitute widget seller, claimed that only a $100,000 gold bar would allow him to capture as much happiness as would the prized widget. On the other hand, requiring non-breaching parties to prove the precise dollar value of their damages would be too exacting a standard in any case in which there was no perfect substitute available for the failed performance and would often result in significant undercompensation. Contract law might be viewed as seeking a middle ground between these two problematic positions, requiring non-breaching parties to prove damages with "reasonable certainty." Rest. (2d) Contracts §352.

Like foreseeability, the requirement of reasonable certainty presents courts with a vague standard that invites a fact-specific inquiry rather than a bright-line rule subject to clear triggering facts. In the following quartet of cases—*Kenford Company, Inc. v. County of Erie, Florafax International, Inc. v. GTE Market Resources, Inc., Deitsch v. The Music Company*, and *Sullivan v. O'Connor*—courts applying this standard reach different outcomes. The first pair of cases concerns lost business profits; the second pair concerns lost subjective employment.

KENFORD CO.
v.
COUNTY OF ERIE
Court of Appeals of New York
67 N.Y.2d 257
1986

PER CURIAM.

The issue in this appeal is whether a plaintiff, in an action for breach of contract, may recover loss of prospective profits for its contemplated 20-year operation of a domed stadium which was to be constructed by defendant County of Erie (County).

On August 8, 1969, pursuant to a duly adopted resolution of its legislature, the County of Erie entered into a contract with Kenford Company, Inc. (Kenford) and Dome Stadium, Inc. (DSI) for the construction and operation of a domed stadium facility near the City of Buffalo. The contract provided that construction of the facility by the County would commence within 12 months of the contract date and that a mutually acceptable 40-year lease between the County and DSI for the operation of said facility would be negotiated by the parties and agreed upon within three months of the receipt by the County of preliminary plans, drawings and cost estimates. It was further provided that in the event a mutually acceptable lease could not be agreed upon within the three-month period, a separate management contract between the County and DSI, as appended to the basic agreement, would be executed by the parties, providing for the operation of the stadium facility by DSI for a period of 20 years from the completion of the stadium and its availability for use.

Although strenuous and extensive negotiations followed, the parties never agreed upon the terms of a lease, nor did construction of a domed facility begin within the one-year period or at any time thereafter. A breach of the contract thus occurred and this action was commenced in June 1971 by Kenford and DSI.

Prolonged and extensive pretrial and preliminary proceedings transpired throughout the next 10 years, culminating with the entry of an order which affirmed the grant of summary judgment against the County on the issue of liability and directed a trial limited to the issue of damages (*Kenford Co. v. County of Erie*, 88 AD2d 758, *lv dismissed*, 58 NY2d 689). The ensuing trial ended some nine months later with a multimillion dollar jury verdict in plaintiffs' favor. An appeal to the Appellate Division resulted in a modification of the judgment. That court reversed portions of the judgment awarding damages for loss of profits and for certain out-of-pocket expenses incurred, and directed a new trial upon other issues (*Kenford Co. v. County of Erie*, 108 AD2d 132). On appeal to this court, we are concerned only with that portion of the verdict which awarded DSI money damages for loss of prospective profits during the 20-year period of the proposed management contract, as appended to the basic contract. That portion of the verdict was set aside by the Appellate Division and the cause of action dismissed. The court concluded that the use of expert opinion to present statistical projections of future business operations involved the use of too many variables to provide a rational basis upon which lost profits could be calculated and, therefore, such projections were insufficient as a matter of law to support an award of lost profits. We agree with this ultimate conclusion, but upon different grounds.

Loss of future profits as damages for breach of contract have been permitted in New York under long-established and precise rules of law. First, it must be demonstrated with certainty that such damages have been caused by the breach and, second, the alleged loss must be capable of proof with reasonable certainty. In other words, the damages may not be merely speculative, possible or imaginary, but must be reasonably certain and directly traceable to the breach, not remote or the result of other intervening causes (*Wakeman v. Wheeler & Wilson Mfg. Co.*, 101 NY 205). In addition, there must be a showing that the particular damages were fairly within the contemplation of the parties to the contract at the time it was made (*Witherbee v. Meyer*, 155 NY 446). If it is a new business seeking to recover for loss of future profits, a stricter standard is imposed for the obvious reason that there does not exist a reasonable basis of experience upon which to estimate lost profits with the requisite degree of reasonable certainty (*Cramer v. Grand Rapids Show Case Co.*, 223 NY 63; 25 CJS, Damages, §42[b]).

These rules must be applied to the proof presented by DSI in this case. We note the procedure for computing damages selected by DSI was in accord with contemporary economic theory and was presented through the testimony of recognized experts. Such a procedure has been accepted in this State and many other jurisdictions (*see, De Long v. County of Erie*, 60 NY2d 296). DSI's economic analysis employed historical data, obtained from the operation of other domed stadiums and related facilities throughout the country, which was then applied to the results of a comprehensive study of the marketing prospects for the proposed facility in the Buffalo area. The quantity of proof is massive and, unquestionably, represents business and industry's most advanced and sophisticated method for predicting the probable results of contemplated projects. Indeed, it is difficult to conclude what additional relevant proof could have been submitted by DSI in support of its attempt to establish, with reasonable certainty, loss of prospective profits. Nevertheless, DSI's proof is insufficient to meet the required standard.

The reason for this conclusion is twofold. Initially, the proof does not satisfy the requirement that liability for loss of profits over a 20-year period was in the contemplation of the parties at the time of the execution of the basic contract or at the time of its breach (*see, Chapman v. Fargo*, 223 NY 32; 36 NY Jur 2d, Damages, §§39, 40, at 66-70). Indeed, the provisions in the contract providing remedy for a default do not suggest or provide for such a heavy responsibility on the part of the County. In the absence of any provision for such an eventuality, the commonsense rule to apply is to consider what the parties would have concluded had they considered the subject. The evidence here fails to demonstrate that liability for loss of profits over the length of the contract would have been in the contemplation of the parties at the relevant times.

Next, we note that despite the massive quantity of expert proof submitted by DSI, the ultimate conclusions are still projections, and as employed in the present day commercial world, subject to adjustment and modification. We of course recognize that any projection cannot be absolute, nor is there any such requirement, but it is axiomatic that the degree of certainty is dependent upon known or unknown factors which form the basis of the ultimate conclusion. Here, the foundations upon which the economic model was created undermine the certainty of the projections. DSI assumed that the facility was completed, available for use and successfully operated by it for 20 years, providing professional sporting events and other forms of entertainment, as well as hosting meetings, conventions and related commercial gatherings. At the time of the breach, there was only one other facility in this country to use as a basis of comparison, the Astrodome in Houston. Quite simply, the multitude of assumptions required to establish projections of profitability over the life of this contract require speculation and conjecture, making it beyond the capability of even the most sophisticated procedures to satisfy the legal requirements of proof with reasonable certainty.

The economic facts of life, the whim of the general public and the fickle nature of popular support for professional athletic endeavors must be given great weight in attempting to ascertain damages 20 years in the future. New York has long recognized the inherent uncertainties of predicting profits in the entertainment field in general (*see, Broadway Photoplay Co. v. World Film Corp.*, 225 NY 104) and, in this case, we are dealing, in large part, with a new facility furnishing entertainment for the public. It is our view that the record in this case demonstrates the efficacy of the principles set forth by this court in *Cramer v. Grand Rapids Show Case Co.* (223 NY 63), principles to which we continue to adhere. In so doing, we specifically reject the "rational basis" test enunciated in *Perma Research & Dev. Co. v. Singer Co.* (542 F2d 111, *cert denied* 429 US 987) and adopted by the Appellate Division.

Accordingly, that portion of the order of the Appellate Division being appealed from should be affirmed.

FLORAFAX INTERNATIONAL, INC.
v.
GTE MARKET RESOURCES, INC.

Supreme Court of Oklahoma
933 P.2d 282
1997

LAVENDER, J.

Florafax is generally a flowers-by-wire company acting as a clearinghouse to allow the placement and receipt of orders between florists throughout the United States and internationally. Basically the system works as follows: retail florists become members of the Florafax network (apparently, thousands of retail florists join Florafax's wire service). Florafax maintains a list of the members and circulates a directory to them. The members are then able to send and receive orders among each other throughout the system. In other words, a consumer orders flowers at a retail florist at a certain location (e.g. Oklahoma City) to be delivered to someone in another location (e.g. Los Angeles). Florafax assists the transactions by collecting money from the florist taking the order from the customer and guarantying payment to the florist delivering the flowers. It processes the credit card activity on the transactions and charges a fee or fees for this service. Florafax also maintains a computer network whereby member florists can send and receive orders by computer—if they have such technology—without using the telephone. It also has a division that advertises floral products by the use of brochures, and other sales and promotional materials, allowing consumers to place a telephone order for floral products directly without going through a florist in their hometowns.

Evidence at trial showed at the time the agreements giving rise to this dispute were entered that Florafax was one of the largest floral wire services of its kind in the nation, and, in fact, certain evidence placed it third world-wide behind Florists' Transworld Delivery Association (FTD) and a company known as Teleflora. Evidence also showed Florafax had been headquartered in Tulsa, Oklahoma since, at least, 1979.

In addition to the above activities, Florafax solicits agreements with third party clients such as supermarket chains, American Express and other entities that advertise the sale of floral products by various methods (e.g. television, radio, newspapers, billing circulars, mass mailings to consumers) which allow a consumer to order floral arrangements via the use of a 1-800 telephone call, with Florafax agreeing to handle the actual inbound and outbound communication aspects of the transactions. In other words, when a consumer responds to an advertisement, it is not the advertiser that answers the telephone call to take the order, or that makes a telephone call or computer communication to a retail florist for fulfillment, but it is Florafax who handles these activities. Such orders would, of course, be fulfilled, if possible, by retail florist members taken from the Florafax directory maintained by it and, again, Florafax would handle the mechanics of processing the transactions, e.g. credit card processing. The advertiser would pay Florafax a certain fee or fees for its services.

One client that signed up for an arrangement like that described immediately above was Bellerose Floral, Inc., d/b/a Flora Plenty, a leading marketer of floral products advertising sales through use of the telephone number 1-800-FLOWERS. Florafax and Bellerose entered a contract in early October 1989 whereby Florafax and/or its designee would accept direct consumer orders (i.e. inbound calls and orders) placed via the 1-800-FLOWERS number and, of course, it also agreed to handle the outbound placement of orders either by telephone or computer transmission. The Florafax/Bellerose contract provided Florafax would be paid certain fee(s) per order. As we read the contract its initial term was for one year, to be automatically renewed from month to month thereafter, but that either party, with or without cause, could terminate the agreement upon sixty (60) days written notice.

GTE, on the other hand, was a company providing telecommunication and/or telemarketing services for other businesses. It provided for other businesses a call answering center where telemarketing sales representatives (TSRs) physically answered telephones when orders from promotional activities came in from consumers and took care of transmitting the orders by telephone or computer for fulfillment. For certain management and business-related reasons Florafax subcontracted out much of the telecommunication and telemarketing services of its business.

In mid-October 1989, about two weeks after Florafax signed its agreement with Bellerose, the Florafax/GTE contract was entered. In essence it provided GTE would via a call answering center (apparently located in the Dallas, Texas area) handle much, if not all, of the activities connected with taking incoming orders and placing outgoing calls or computer transmissions directed to it by Florafax associated with the purchase and fulfillment of floral orders throughout the United States and internationally. The agreement required Florafax to pay GTE certain fees for this service depending on the type of order.

The Florafax/GTE contract generally ran for a term of three years from the effective date the parties anticipated Florafax would begin directing calls to GTE for floral orders—a date anticipated to be in early December 1989. It also contained certain provisions that in essence might result in termination after a two year period based upon application of a price/fee renegotiation clause. In answer to one of the questions submitted via a special verdict form, the jury determined the Florafax/GTE contract could be terminated after two years based on this clause.

. . .

[The evidence produced at trial indicated that GTE breached its agreement with Florafax and, as a consequence, Bellarose terminated its contract with Florafax.] The jury . . . , in addition to other damages, awarded Florafax $750,000.00 in lost profits that would have been earned under the Florafax/Bellerose contract over a two year period of time.

. . .

Generally speaking, this Court has long espoused the view that loss of future or anticipated profit—i.e. loss of expected monetary gain—is recoverable in a breach of contract action: 1) if the loss is within the contemplation of the parties at the time the contract was made, 2) if the loss flows directly or proximately from the breach—i.e. if the loss can be said to have been caused by the breach—and 3) if the loss is capable of reasonably accurate measurement or estimate. *Groendyke Transport, Inc. v. Merchant*, 380 P.2d 682 *Second Syllabus* (Okla. 1962).

. . .

. . . When a breach of a contractual obligation with resulting damages has been established, although the amount of damages may not be based on mere speculation, conjecture and surmise alone, the mere uncertainty as to the exact amount of damages will not preclude the right of recovery. *Larrance Tank Corporation v. Burrough*, 476 P.2d 346, 350 (Okla. 1970). It is sufficient if the evidence shows the extent of damage by just and reasonable inference. *Id.* We believe sufficient evidence was presented so that Florafax carried its burden to prove the fact, cause and amount of its lost profit damages with the requisite degree of reasonable certainty.

The fact of lost profit damage beyond merely a sixty (60) day period is shown by the testimony of Bellerose's President. Although not absolute, his testimony was, in essence, he considered the relationship with Florafax a long-term one had things worked out and that the most important issues to him in making the decision to terminate were issues concerning performance. This testimony showed the relationship in all probability would have continued long after it was terminated had GTE adequately performed. Although it is true—given the existence of the sixty (60) day notice provision—Bellerose might have terminated the Florafax/Bellerose contract at some point in time even had GTE performed, the state of this record does not require a conclusion Bellerose would have exercised its right of termination for some other reason.

We are also of the view the fact of damage is partially shown by the projections for profits of both the damage experts presented by the parties. Although they differed in their ultimate conclusions as to the extent or amount of lost profits, both presented estimates that Florafax could have made profits from the Florafax/Bellerose relationship had it survived.

. . .

As to the exact extent or amount of damages, the record contains sufficient evidence to take the matter out of the realm of mere speculation, conjecture or surmise. A track record existed which showed the calls coming to GTE from Bellerose during the five to seven months Bellerose business was actually being routed to GTE. There was also evidence that although the business relationship between Florafax and Bellerose was relatively new, Bellerose had been in business for a number of years, and it had experienced 100,000-200,000 orders annually. Such evidence clearly was appropriate to consider on the issue of the extent of lost profits. Although this case is not exactly like our cases dealing with the destruction of an established business by a breach of contract, it is sufficiently close to be analogized to the established business situation, where we have allowed the recovery of lost profits. *See e.g. Firestone Tire & Rubber Co. v. Sheets, supra*, 62 P.2d at 93; *See also Hardesty v. Andro Corporation-Webster Division*, 555 P.2d 1030, 1034-1035 (Okla. 1976), *disapproved on other grounds; Old Albany Estates, Ltd. v. Highland Carpet Mills, Inc.*, 604 P.2d 849 (Okla. 1979); and *City of Collinsville v. Brickey*, 115 Okla. 264, 242 P. 249, 249-250 *Fifth Syllabus* (1925) (tort case where nuisance resulted in destruction of established business).

Evidence also existed which showed that Bellerose, after terminating its relationship with Florafax, experienced a substantial increase in its sales volume in 1991. In other words, there was not only evidence tending to show a certain volume of orders prior to the breach, but evidence tending to show that level of sales would have in all probability increased substantially during part of the term of the Florafax/GTE contract had Bellerose continued its relationship with Florafax. This post-breach evidence is proper to be considered at arriving at a reasonable estimate of the loss caused by a breach of contract [*Ft. Smith & Western Railroad Co. v. Williams, supra*, 121 P. at 278] because all facts which would reasonably tend to make certain the amount of injury inflicted are admissible. *Cloe v. Rogers*, 31 Okla. 255, 121 P. 201, 208 (1912). Although the jury apparently did not totally credit the testimony or documentation presented by either Florafax's or GTE's experts as to their projections of profits lost, the $750,000.00 awarded for the two year period was within the range of the estimates of the two experts. Accordingly, not only was the fact and causation of lost profit damages adequately shown to a reasonable certainty, but the amount of lost profit damages awarded was sufficiently shown through competent evidence contained in this record to take the matter out of the realm of mere speculation, conjecture and surmise.

3

DEITSCH
v.
THE MUSIC CO.

Hamilton County Municipal Court, Ohio
453 N.E.2d 1302
1983

PAINTER, J.

This is an action for breach of contract. Plaintiffs and defendant entered into a contract on March 27, 1980, whereby defendant was to provide a four-piece band at plaintiffs' wedding reception on November 8, 1980. The reception was to be from 8:00 p.m. to midnight. The contract stated "wage agreed upon—$295.00," with a deposit of $65, which plaintiffs paid upon the signing of the contract.

Plaintiffs proceeded with their wedding, and arrived at the reception hall on the night of November 8, 1980, having employed a caterer, a photographer and a soloist to sing with the band. However, the four-piece band failed to arrive at the wedding reception. Plaintiffs made several attempts to contact defendant but were not successful. After much wailing and gnashing of teeth, plaintiffs were able to send a friend to obtain some stereo equipment to provide music, which equipment was set up at about 9:00 P.M.

This matter came on to be tried on September 28, 1982. Testimony at trial indicated there were several contacts between the parties from time to time between March and November 1980. The testimony of plaintiff Carla Deitsch indicated that she had taken music to the defendant several weeks prior to the reception and had received a telephone call from defendant on the night before the wedding confirming the engagement. Defendant's president testified that he believed the contract had been cancelled, since the word "cancelled" was written on his copy of the contract. There was no testimony as to when that might have been done, and no one from defendant-company was able to explain the error. There was also testimony that defendant's president apologized profusely to the mother of one of the plaintiffs, stating that his "marital problems" were having an effect on his business, and it was all a grievous error.

The court finds that defendant did in fact breach the contract and therefore that plaintiffs are entitled to damages. The difficult issue in this case is determining the correct measure and amount of damages.

Counsel for both parties have submitted memoranda on the issue of damages. However, no cases on point are cited. Plaintiffs contend that the *entire* cost of the reception, in the amount of $2,643.59, is the correct measure of damages. This would require a factual finding that the reception was a total loss, and conferred no benefit at all on the plaintiffs. Defendant, on the other hand, contends that the only measure of damages which is proper is the amount which plaintiffs actually lost, that is, the $65 deposit. It is the court's opinion that neither measure of damages is proper; awarding to plaintiffs the entire sum of the reception would grossly overcompensate them for their actual loss, while the simple return of the deposit would not adequately compensate plaintiffs for defendant's breach of contract.

Therefore, we have to look to other situations to determine whether there is a middle ground, or another measure of damages which would allow the court to award more than the deposit, but certainly less than the total cost of the reception.

It is hornbook law that in any contract action, the damages awarded must be the natural and probable consequence of the breach of contract or those damages which were within the contemplation of the parties at the time of making the contract. *Hadley v. Baxendale* (1854), 9 Exch. 341, 156 Eng. Rep. 145.

Certainly, it must be in the contemplation of the parties that the damages caused by a breach by defendant would be greater than the return of the deposit—that would be no damages at all.

The case that we believe is on point is *Pullman Company v. Willett* (Richland App. 1905), 7 Ohio C.C. (N.S.) 173, affirmed (1905), 72 Ohio St. 690, 76 N.E. 1131. In that case, a husband and wife contracted with the Pullman Company for sleeping accommodations on the train. When they arrived, fresh from their wedding, there were no accommodations, as a result of which they were compelled to sit up most of the night and change cars several times. The court held that since the general measure of damages is the loss sustained, damages for the deprivation of the comforts, conveniences, and privacy for which one contracts in reserving a sleeping car space are not to be measured by the amount paid therefor. The court allowed compensatory damages for the physical inconvenience, discomfort and mental anguish resulting from the breach of contract, and upheld a jury award of $125. The court went on to state as follows:

> "It is further contended that the damages awarded were excessive. We think not. The peculiar circumstances of this case were properly [a] matter for the consideration of the jury. The damages for deprivation of the comforts, conveniences and privacy for which he had contracted and agreed to pay *are not to be measured by the amount to be paid therefor.* He could have had cheaper accommodations had he so desired, but that he wanted these accommodations under the circumstances of this case was but natural and commendable, and we do not think that the record fails to show any damages, but, on the contrary it fully sustains the verdict and would, in our opinion, sustain even a larger verdict had the jury thought proper to fix a larger amount."

(Emphasis added.) *Pullman Company v. Willett, supra*, at 177-78; see, also, 49 Ohio Jurisprudence 2d 191, Sleeping Car Companies, Section 6.

Another similar situation would be the reservation of a room in a hotel or motel. Surely, the damages for the breach of that contract could exceed the mere value of the room. In such a case, the Hawaii Supreme Court has held the plaintiff was "not limited to the narrow traditional contractual remedy of out-of-pocket losses alone." *Dold v. Outrigger Hotel* (1972), 54 Haw. 18, 22, 501 P.2d 368, at 371-372.

The court holds that in a case of this type, the out-of-pocket loss, which would be the security deposit, or even perhaps the value of the band's services, where another band could not readily be obtained at the last minute, would not be sufficient to compensate plaintiffs. Plaintiffs are entitled to compensation for their distress, inconvenience, and the diminution in value of their reception. For said damages, the court finds that the compensation should be $750. Since plaintiffs are clearly entitled to the refund of their security deposit, judgment will be rendered for plaintiffs in the amount of $815 and the costs of this action. Judgment accordingly.

SULLIVAN
v.
O'CONNOR

Supreme Judicial Court of Massachusetts
363 Mass. 579
1973

KAPLAN, J.

The plaintiff patient secured a jury verdict of $13,500 against the defendant surgeon for breach of contract in respect to an operation upon the plaintiff's nose.

In the first count, the plaintiff alleged that she, as patient, entered into a contract with the defendant, a surgeon, wherein the defendant promised to perform plastic surgery on her nose and thereby to enhance her beauty and improve her appearance; that he performed the surgery but failed to achieve the promised result; rather the result of the surgery was to disfigure and deform her nose, to cause her pain in body and mind, and to subject her to other damage and expense. The second count, based on the same transaction, was in the conventional form for malpractice, charging that the defendant had been guilty of negligence in performing the surgery. Answering, the defendant entered a general denial.

On the plaintiff's demand, the case was tried by jury. At the close of the evidence, the judge put to the jury, as special questions, the issues of liability under the two counts, and instructed them accordingly. The jury returned a verdict for the plaintiff on the contract count, and for the defendant on the negligence count. The judge then instructed the jury on the issue of damages.

. . . The plaintiff was a professional entertainer, and this was known to the defendant. . . . The plaintiff's nose had been straight, but long and prominent; the defendant undertook by two operations to reduce its prominence and somewhat to shorten it, thus making it more pleasing in relation to the plaintiff's other features. Actually the plaintiff was obliged to undergo three operations, and her appearance was worsened. Her nose now had a concave line to about the midpoint, at which it became bulbous; viewed frontally, the nose from bridge to midpoint was flattened and broadened, and the two sides of the tip had lost symmetry. This configuration evidently could not be improved by further surgery. The plaintiff did not demonstrate, however, that her change of appearance had resulted in loss of employment. Payments by the plaintiff covering the defendant's fee and hospital expenses were stipulated at $622.65.

The judge instructed the jury, first, that the plaintiff was entitled to recover her out-of-pocket expenses incident to the operations. Second, she could recover the damages flowing directly, naturally, proximately, and foreseeably from the defendant's breach of promise. These would comprehend damages for any disfigurement of the plaintiff's nose—that is, any change of appearance for the worse—including the effects of the consciousness of such disfigurement on the plaintiff's mind, and in this connection the jury should consider the nature of the plaintiff's profession. Also consequent upon the defendant's breach, and compensable, were the pain and suffering involved in the third operation, but not in the first two. As there was no proof that any loss of earnings by the plaintiff resulted from the breach, that element should not enter into the calculation of damages.

By his exceptions the defendant contends that the judge erred in allowing the jury to take into account anything but the plaintiff's out-of-pocket expenses (presumably at the stipulated amount). The defendant excepted to . . . the judge's refusal of a charge that the plaintiff could not recover for pain and suffering connected with the third operation or for impairment of the plaintiff's appearance and associated mental distress.

The plaintiff on her part excepted to the judge's refusal of a request to charge that the plaintiff could recover the difference in value between the nose as promised and the nose as it appeared after the operations. However, the plaintiff in her brief expressly waives this exception and others made by her in case this court overrules the defendant's exceptions; thus she would be content to hold the jury's verdict in her favor. We conclude that the defendant's exceptions should be overruled.

It has been suggested on occasion that agreements between patients and physicians by which the physician undertakes to effect a cure or to bring about a given result should be declared unenforceable on grounds of public policy. . . . It is not hard to see why the courts should be unenthusiastic or skeptical about the contract theory. Considering the uncertainties of medical science and the variations in the physical and psychological conditions of individual patients, doctors can seldom in good faith promise specific results. . . . On the other hand, if these actions were outlawed, leaving only the possibility of suits for malpractice, there is fear that the public might be exposed to the enticements of charlatans, and confidence in the profession might ultimately be shaken. The law has taken the middle of the road position of allowing actions based on alleged contract, but insisting on clear proof. . . .

If an action on the basis of contract is allowed, we have next the question of the measure of damages to be applied where liability is found. Some cases have taken the simple view that the promise by the physician is to be treated like an ordinary commercial promise, and accordingly that the successful plaintiff is entitled to a standard measure of recovery for breach of contract—"compensatory" ("expectancy") damages, an amount intended to put the plaintiff in the position he would be in if the contract had been performed, or, presumably, at the plaintiff's election, "restitution" damages, an amount corresponding to any benefit conferred by the plaintiff upon the defendant in the performance of the contract disrupted by the defendant's breach. See Restatement: Contract §329 and comment a, §§347, 384(1). Thus in *Hawkins v. McGee*, 84 N.H. 114, the defendant doctor was taken to have promised the plaintiff to convert his damaged hand by means of an operation into a good or perfect hand, but the doctor so operated as to damage the hand still further. The court, following the usual expectancy formula, would have asked the jury to estimate and award to the plaintiff the difference between the value of a good or perfect hand, as promised, and the value of the hand after the operation. (The same formula would apply, although the dollar result would be less, if the operation had neither worsened nor improved the condition of the hand.) If the plaintiff had not yet paid the doctor his fee, that amount would be deducted from the recovery. There could be no recovery for the pain and suffering of the operation, since that detriment would have been incurred even if the operation had been successful; one can say that this detriment was not "caused" by the breach. But where the plaintiff by reason of the operation was put to more pain that he would have had to endure, had the doctor performed as promised, he should be compensated for that difference as a proper part of his expectancy recovery.

Other cases . . . have indicated that a different and generally more lenient measure of damages is to be applied in patient-physician actions based on breach of alleged special agreements to effect a cure, attain a stated result, or employ a given medical method. This measure is expressed in somewhat variant ways, but the substance is that the plaintiff is to recover any expenditures made by him and for other detriment (usually not specifically described in the opinions) following proximately and foreseeably upon the defendant's failure to carry out his promise. . . . [T]he tendency of the formulation is to put the plaintiff back in the position he occupied just before the parties entered upon the agreement, to compensate him for the detriments he suffered in reliance upon the agreement. . . . Fuller and Perdue, [in] "The Reliance Interest in Contract Damages," 46 Yale L.J. 52, 373, . . . show that, although not attaining the currency of the standard measures, a "reliance" measure has for special reasons been applied by the courts in a variety of settings, including noncommercial settings.

For breach of the patient-physician agreements under consideration, a recovery limited to restitution seems plainly too meager, if the agreements are to be enforced at all. On the other hand, an expectancy recovery may well be excessive. The factors, already mentioned, which have made the cause of action somewhat suspect, also suggest moderation as to the breadth of the recovery that should be permitted. . . . As a general consideration, Fuller and Perdue argue that the reasons for granting damages for broken promises to the extent of the expectancy are at their strongest when the promises are made in a business context, when they have to do with the production or distribution of goods or the allocation of functions in the market place; they become weaker as the context shifts from a commercial to a noncommercial field. 46 Yale L.J. at 60-63.

There is much to be said, then, for applying a reliance measure to the present facts, and we have only to add that our cases are not unreceptive to the use of that formula in special situations. We have, however, had no previous occasion to apply it to patient-physician cases.

The question of recovery on a reliance basis for pain and suffering or mental distress requires further attention. We find expressions in the decisions that pain and suffering (or the like) are simply not compensable in actions for breach of contract. The defendant seemingly espouses this proposition in the present case. True, if the buyer under a contract for the purchase of a lot of merchandise, in suing for the seller's breach, should claim damages for mental anguish caused by his disappointment in the transaction, he would not succeed; he would be told, perhaps, that the asserted psychological injury was not fairly foreseeable by the defendant as a probable consequence of the breach of such a business contract. See Restatement: Contracts, §341, and comment a. But there is no general rule barring such items of damage in actions for breach of contract. It is all a question of the subject matter and background of the contract, and when the contract calls for an operation on the person of the plaintiff, psychological as well as physical injury may be expected to figure somewhere in the recovery, depending on the particular circumstances. . . . These remarks seem unduly sweeping. Suffering or distress resulting from the breach going beyond that which was envisaged by the treatment as agreed, should be compensable on the same ground as the worsening of the patient's condition because of the breach. Indeed it can be argued that the very suffering or distress "contracted for"—that which would have been incurred if the treatment achieved the promised result—should also be compensable on the theory underlying the New York cases. For that suffering is "wasted" if the treatment fails. Otherwise stated, compensation for this waste is arguably required in order to complete the restoration of the status quo ante.

In the light of the foregoing discussion, all the defendant's exceptions fail: the plaintiff was not confined to the recovery of her out-of-pocket expenditures; she was entitled to recover also for the worsening of her condition,[7] and for the pain and suffering and mental distress involved in the third operation. These items were compensable on either an expectancy or a reliance view. We might have been required to elect between the two views if the pain and suffering connected with the first two operations contemplated by the agreement, or the whole difference in value between the present and the promised conditions, were being claimed as elements of damage. But the plaintiff waives her possible claim to the former element, and to so much of the latter as represents the [difference] in value between the promised condition and the condition before the operations.

---

7. That condition involves a mental element and appraisal of it properly called for consideration of the fact that the plaintiff was an entertainer. . . .

Problems

1. The Frustrated Professor. Professor Philip Freund entered into a contract with Washington Square Press, according to which Washington Square would publish Freund's manuscript on modern drama first in a hardbound edition and later in a paperback edition and pay Freund an advance of $2,000 and royalties of 10 percent of retail sales proceeds. Washington Square soon stopped publishing hardbound books and, although it paid Freund the advance, it never printed his book. Freund sued. At trial, Freund presented expert testimony that it would have cost Washington Square $10,000 to publish the book. He presented no evidence of any reliance damages incurred in performance of his contractual obligations. What damages should the court award?

2. When Shamu Attacks (Reprise). Review the facts of "When Shamu Attacks" above (see Section E, Problem 3). In addition to emotional damages, Smith sought to recover for lost profits resulting from the breach, calculated by multiplying the percentage of the episode of *The Extraordinary* containing his footage by the amount the producer received for selling the episode in violation of the contract. Should Smith be entitled to recover this amount?

3. Poor Service. In 1989, the owner of the Cheshire Lodge in a St. Louis suburb leased its adjoining restaurant, the Cheshire Inn, to L&S Properties Limited for a term of 25 years on the condition that the restaurant provide Lodge guests with room and breakfast service. After ten years, the restaurant's service deteriorated. Guests began to complain about slow or nonexistent room service, and there was often no breakfast available. From 1999 to 2004, the Cheshire Lodge experienced a significant increase in room vacancies.

The owner of the Lodge, Apted-Hulling, sued L&S for breach of contract in 2004. Without contradiction, the Lodge's business manager, Margaret Piot, testified that the Lodge rented 6,263 fewer single-occupancy rooms in 2003 and 6,543 fewer in 2004 than in 1991. She also testified that, using a conservative estimate of revenue per guest and the Lodge's profit margin of 40 percent, the reduction in occupancy resulted in a $244,000 reduction in profit for those two years compared with 1991 levels. Piot testified that the Lodge had received numerous complaints about the restaurant's service, and that the reduction in occupancy was due entirely to the actions of L&S. On cross examination, Piot testified that the Lodge had no direct competitors for business travelers within three miles of its location and, when the L&S attorney listed several hotels within that distance, admitted that at least two were competitors. She also testified that she did not know if the number of corporate headquarters had increased or decreased in St. Louis during the time period in question or whether the demolition of a nearby sports venue could have affected occupancy rates.

The trial judge, sitting as the trier of fact, awarded the plaintiff $244,000 in lost profits, and L&S Properties appealed. Assuming L&S breached, how should the appellate court rule on the issue of damages?

G. STIPULATED DAMAGES

Is the expectation damages rule, with its mitigation requirement and foreseeability and reasonable certainty limitations, immutable—applicable to all contract breaches—or is it a default rule that applies only when the parties have not specified their own measure of damages? The latter answer is consistent with both the Holmesian view that paying damages is a type of alternative performance that a contracting party may substitute for his primary duty or duties and the modern economic view that stipulated damages can be understood as the price of an option that entitles a party to exchange contractual performances if it chooses to do so. With few exceptions, of course, parties may specify their own duties by contract, reducing the role of courts to interpretation and gap filling, and they may agree on any price they wish for an option.

Despite these comparisons, contract law does not treat stipulated damages provisions like it treats most other contract terms. Stipulated damages are enforceable as "liquidated damages" only if they constitute a reasonable approximation of either anticipated or actual damages. In contrast, stipulated damages that exceed reasonable estimates of damages are labeled penalty clauses and are unenforceable. Rest. (2d) Contracts §356. The following pair of cases—*TAL Financial Corporation v. CSC Consulting, Inc.* and *NPS, LLC v. Minihane*—decided by the same court within a two-year period, explores this distinction.

TAL FINANCIAL CORP.
v.
𝒮 CSC CONSULTING, INC.

Supreme Judicial Court of Massachusetts
844 N.E.2d 1085
2006

GREANEY, J.

. . . TAL is a boutique finance company, located in Framingham, that specializes in extending credit to small companies through equipment leasing. TAL's president and sole shareholder is Howard D. Siegel. CSC is a company with headquarters in Waltham that provides information technology consulting services for businesses. In the summer of 1997, Onward was a start-up company, located in Natick, engaged in the business of website development.

On July 28, 1997, TAL and Onward entered into an agreement for the lease of computer hardware, telephone equipment, software, and office furniture needed by Onward to start its business. The agreement consisted of a master lease and the first of what would be a series of three schedules incorporating the terms of the master lease. The first schedule (schedule one) identified computer hardware, telephone equipment, and software licensed to Onward, and provided for monthly payments from Onward to TAL of $1,692.55, including taxes, for thirty-six months. On September 3, 1997, Onward and TAL executed a second schedule (schedule two) which identified additional computer hardware, used furniture, and software licensed to Onward. Schedule two provided for monthly payments of $2,587.55, including taxes, for thirty-six months. On January 28, 1998, Onward and TAL executed a third and final schedule (schedule three) to the master lease, also identifying computer hardware, used furniture, and software licensed to Onward. Schedule three provided for monthly payments of $716.07, including taxes, for thirty-six months.

The master lease provided that each schedule would begin as of the first day of the month following Onward's acceptance of the leased equipment and end as of the last day of the calendar month in which the schedule was executed. Thus, schedule one began on August 1, 1997, and was to end July 31, 2000; schedule two began on October 1, 1997, and was to end September 30, 2000; and schedule three began on February 1, 1998, and was to end on January 31, 2001. The schedules provided for TAL to receive a total of $179,862.12 over thirty-six months. At the time each schedule was executed, Onward paid TAL in advance the first, thirty-fifth, and thirty-sixth payments due.

TAL paid a total of $140,433.62 for all of the items listed in the schedules, including $76,590.15 for computer hardware and telephone equipment, $33,305.40 for used furniture, and $30,538.07 for software. . . .

. . . Section 20 of the master lease provides that, in the event of a default by Onward, then TAL "at its sole option" may elect one or more of several alternatives, including (1) declaring a default and demanding payment of the entire amount of rent remaining to be paid over the balance of the lease, and (2) recovering "as liquidated damages for loss of a bargain and not as a penalty (X) an amount equal to the present value of all moneys to be paid by [Onward] during the remaining Initial Term or any renewal period then in effect . . . discounted at the rate of six percent (6.0%) . . . plus (Y) eighteen percent (18%) of the Acquisition Cost to [TAL] of such Equipment and/or any Other Equipment." Section 20 additionally provides that Onward's failure to return any of the leased items would entitle TAL to recover "as liquidated damages for breach of this Lease, and not as a penalty, an amount equal to the sum of the amounts specified in items (X) and (Y) [set forth] above." . . .

On or about March 31, 1998, CSC acquired the stock of Onward, which merged into CSC. . . . CSC continued to make monthly payments set forth in the schedules. On or about August, 1999, Onward's employees moved from Natick to CSC's Waltham offices. Either before or during the move, CSC discarded most of the equipment and furniture covered by the master lease. CSC also misplaced the lease documents.

The case proceeded to trial on TAL's claim that . . . CSC's failure to return any of the leased items constituted a default entitling TAL to liquidated damages in the amount of eighteen per cent of its acquisition costs. In sum, TAL claimed damages in the amount of $112,156 (the remaining rental payments it claimed were due on a sixty-month lease, plus late charges, plus liquidated damages). [CSC questioned] whether the liquidated damages provision in the master lease calling for eighteen per cent of TAL's acquisition costs was enforceable as a reasonable estimate of actual damages under principles set forth in *Kelly v. Marx,* 428 Mass. 877, 880, 705 N.E.2d 1114 (1999), or void as an unconscionable penalty.

. . .

The judge determined that the liquidated damages provision calling for the present value of all future rent, plus eighteen per cent of the acquisition costs of all the items listed in the schedules, was an unreasonable estimate of any actual damage that could have been anticipated at the time the schedules were executed and, therefore, unenforceable. The judge's reasoning incorporated her findings that (a) the majority of items to be leased were not yet identified at the time the parties agreed to the provision in the master lease; (b) the lease did not provide for the reduction of the liquidated payment if the lease extended beyond the original thirty-six month term; and (c) it could have been anticipated that the leased items had little or no residual value after three years and, thus, the eighteen per cent figure was "grossly disproportionate" to a reasonable estimate of actual damages at the time of contract formation. We agree with the judge's conclusion and much of her reasoning. Before elaborating, however, we consider a matter intrinsically related to our resolution of the liquidated damages issue, but one not raised by the parties, or mentioned by the judge, at trial: which party bears the burden of proof when a clause in a contract providing for payment of liquidated damages is challenged as unenforceable.

. . .

Under freedom of contract principles, generally, parties are held to the express terms of their contract, and the burden of proof is on the party seeking to invalidate an express term. The burden of proof regarding the enforceability of a liquidated damages clause, therefore, should rest squarely on the party seeking to set it aside. See *Town Planning & Eng'g Assocs., Inc. v. Amesbury Specialty Co.*, 369 Mass. 737, 744, 342 N.E.2d 706 (1976); *Hastings Assocs., Inc. v. Local 369 Bldg. Fund, Inc.*, 42 Mass. App. Ct. 162, 173, 675 N.E.2d 403 (1997). Any reasonable doubt as to whether a provision constitutes a penalty or a legitimate liquidated damages clause should be resolved in favor of the aggrieved party. We thus join the majority of courts in other States that have considered the question.

. . .

It has long been the rule in Massachusetts that a contract provision that clearly and reasonably establishes liquidated damages should be enforced, so long as it is not so disproportionate to anticipated damages as to constitute a penalty. See *Kaplan v. Gray*, 215 Mass. 269, 270-273, 102 N.E. 421 (1913). There is no bright line separating an agreement to pay a reasonable measure of damages from an unenforceable penalty clause. In *Kelly v. Marx, supra*, we provided guidance as to how a judge should analyze the enforceability of a liquidated damages clause in a purchase and sale agreement. We squarely rejected the "second look" approach, where actual damages resulting from the breach are measured to determine whether enforcement of the agreement for liquidated damages would serve unfairly to punish one party rather than compensate the other "who suffered no loss from the [first party's] breach." *Id.* at 879, 705 N.E.2d 1114. Generally, a liquidated damages provision will be enforced when, at the time the agreement was made, potential damages were difficult to determine and the clause was a reasonable forecast of damages expected to occur in the event of a breach. Conversely, "[l]iquidated damages will not be enforced if the sum is 'grossly disproportionate to a reasonable estimate of actual damages' made at the time of contract formation." *Id.* at 880, 705 N.E.2d 1114, quoting *Lynch v. Andrew*, 20 Mass. App. Ct. 623, 628, 481 N.E.2d 1383 (1985). This approach, we concluded, will most accurately reflect the expectations of the parties when they contracted for liquidated damages. See *Kelly v. Marx, supra* at 880-881, 705 N.E.2d 1114.

. . . We conclude that CSC carried its burden of establishing that this provision called for damages that were "grossly disproportionate" to a reasonable estimate of anticipated damages at the time the schedules were executed. A reasonable estimate of such damages, occurring after a lease term of thirty-six months (a term guaranteed under the lease), would have been a negligible amount. Failing to provide any recognition for the type, or timing, of the default, while by no means determinative, tends to indicate that the provision's intended purpose was not to estimate the different types of damages that might arise from a future default, but to penalize for any failure, however immaterial. Although we cautioned in *Kelly v. Marx, supra* at 879, 705 N.E.2d 1114, against use of the "second look approach," the disparity between the stipulated sum (eighteen per cent of acquisition costs, or $25,278) and actual damages (here, none) cannot be ignored in this case, because that disparity was known at the time of the agreement. The set figure of eighteen per cent of acquisition costs bears no rational relation to the parties' expectation of the true value of the leased items[13] and, moreover, does not take into account TAL's independent ability to collect all future monthly payments still due under the lease. . . .

NPS, LLC
v.
MINIHANE

b

Supreme Judicial Court of Massachusetts
886 N.E.2d 670
2008

COWIN, J.

In this case we decide whether an acceleration clause in a ten-year license agreement for luxury seats for New England Patriots professional football games at Gillette Stadium is enforceable. The agreement requires the purchaser of the license to pay, upon default, the amounts due for all years remaining on the license. The plaintiff

---

13. CSC submitted evidence, through the testimony of an expert appraiser, that software that is licensed, typically, has no resale value, and that computer hardware, after three years, would have little or no resale value. The expert conceded, on cross-examination, that the software might have "some value" if the particular software at issue were transferable. We reject TAL's claim that the judge's findings with respect to the anticipated value of the leased items were not supported by the expert's testimony.

contends that the clause is a lawful liquidated damages provision; the defendant, who defaulted in the first year of the agreement, argues that it is an unlawful penalty. A judge in the Superior Court agreed with the defendant and refused to enforce the provision. Because we conclude the provision is enforceable, we modify the judgment accordingly.

. . . The plaintiff, NPS, LLC (NPS), is the developer of Gillette Stadium (stadium), the home field of the New England Patriots professional football team (Patriots). In 2002, while the stadium was still under construction, NPS entered into an agreement with the defendant, Paul Minihane, for the purchase of a ten-year license for two luxury seats in the Club Level III section. The agreement called for the defendant to pay $3,750 per seat annually for each of the ten seasons from 2002 to 2011. The agreement included a liquidated damages provision, set forth in the margin,[2] which provides that in the event of a default, including failure to pay any amount due under the license agreement, the payments would be accelerated so that the defendant would be required to pay the balance for all the years remaining on the contract. Upon executing the agreement, the defendant paid a $7,500 security deposit; he later made a payment of $2,000 toward the license fee for the 2002 season. Although he or his guests attended all but one of the 2002 preseason and regular season Patriots games at the stadium using the tickets for the Club Seats, he made no further payments.

After giving notice to the defendant, NPS accelerated the payments and filed a complaint in the Superior Court seeking the full amount due under the contract. After a bench trial, the judge ruled that the liquidated damages provision was unenforceable because the amount due was "grossly disproportionate to a reasonable estimate of actual damages made at the time of contract formation." After taking further evidence on the issue of actual damages, the judge issued a memorandum of decision and order in which he awarded damages to NPS in the amount of $6,000. This appeal followed, and we transferred the case to this court on our own motion.

. . .

It is well settled that "a contract provision that clearly and reasonably establishes liquidated damages should be enforced, so long as it is not so disproportionate to anticipated damages as to constitute a penalty." *TAL Fin. Corp. v. CSC Consulting, Inc., supra* at 431, 844 N.E.2d 1085. A liquidated damages provision will usually be enforced, provided two criteria are satisfied: first, that at the time of contracting the actual damages flowing from a breach were difficult to ascertain; and second, that

---

2. "15. *Default.* The following shall constitute an 'Event of Default' under this Agreement: (i) Licensee fails to pay when due any amounts to be paid by Licensee pursuant to the Agreement. . . . In the event of any such Event of Default, Owner may, at its option: (a) withhold distribution of tickets to Licensee for games and/or other Stadium Events until such time as such default is cured; and/or (b) terminate the rights of Licensee under the Agreement after giving Licensee not less than twenty (20) prior written notice of such default or breach. . . . In the event that Licensee shall not have cured the default or breach specified in said notice by the date specified in said notice, Owner may terminate the right of Licensee to the use and possession of the Club Seats and all other rights and privileges of Licensee under the Agreement and declare the entire unpaid balance of the License Fee (which for the purposes hereof shall include the total aggregate unpaid balance of the annual License Fees for the remainder of the Term) immediately due and payable, whereupon Owner shall have no further obligation of any kind to Licensee. Owner shall have no duty to mitigate any damages incurred by it as a result of a default by Licensee hereunder. . . ."

the sum agreed on as liquidated damages represents a "reasonable forecast of damages expected to occur in the event of a breach." *Cummings Props., LLC v. National Communications Corp., supra* at 494, 869 N.E.2d 617. Where damages are easily ascertainable, and the amount provided for is grossly disproportionate to actual damages or unconscionably excessive, the court will award the aggrieved party no more than its actual damages. *A-Z Servicenter, Inc. v. Segall*, 334 Mass. 672, 675, 138 N.E.2d 266 (1956). Since there is "no bright line separating an agreement to pay a reasonable measure of damages from an unenforceable penalty clause," *TAL Fin. Corp. v. CSC Consulting, Inc., supra*, the reasonableness of the measure of anticipated damages depends on the circumstances of each case. *A-Z Servicenter, Inc. v. Segall, supra.* In assessing reasonableness, we look to the circumstances at the time of contract formation; we do not take a "second look" at the actual damages after the contract has been breached. *Kelly v. Marx*, 428 Mass. 877, 878, 705 N.E.2d 1114 (1999).

In this case, the trial judge found that, at the time the parties entered into the license agreement, the harm resulting from a possible breach was difficult to ascertain. That finding was supported by the evidence, which indicated that the damages sustained by NPS would vary depending on the demand for tickets at the time of breach. Although the Patriots had won their first Super Bowl championship in 2002, shortly before the parties entered into their agreement, the demand for luxury stadium seats was then and remains variable and depends, according to the evidence, on the current performance of the team, as well as other factors, such as the popularity of the players and the relative popularity of other sports, that are unpredictable at the time of contract. Therefore, to predict at the time of contract how long it would take NPS to resell the defendant's seat license would be extremely difficult, if not impossible.

The judge went on to find, however, that the sum provided for in the agreement—acceleration of all payments for the remaining term of the contract—was "grossly disproportionate to a reasonable estimate of actual damages made at the time of contract formation." That finding was not supported by the evidence. It is the defendant's burden to show that the amount of liquidated damages is "unreasonably and grossly disproportionate to the real damages from a breach" or "unconscionably excessive." See *TAL Fin. Corp. v. CSC Consulting, Inc., supra* at 423, 844 N.E.2d 1085; *A-Z Servicenter, Inc. v. Segall, supra* at 675, 138 N.E.2d 266. Having presented little evidence beyond his assertion that the contract as a whole was unconscionable, the defendant in this case has not sustained that burden.

The liquidated damages provision here is similar to one we upheld in *Cummings Props., LLC v. National Communications Corp., supra* (*Cummings*). In that case, a tenant who defaulted on a commercial lease was required by the terms of the agreement to pay the entire amount of rent remaining under the lease. *Id.* at 491-492, 869 N.E.2d 617. . . . In upholding the liquidated damages provision in *Cummings*, we noted that "to the extent that the liquidated damages amount represented the agreed rental value of the property over the remaining life of the lease, decreasing in amount as the lease term came closer to expiration, it appears to be a reasonable anticipation of damages that might accrue from the nonpayment of rent." *Id.* at

496-497, 869 N.E.2d 617. The same is true here. This, like *Cummings*, is a case where the damages were difficult to estimate at the outset, and the defendant is required to pay no more than the total amount he would have paid had he performed his obligations under the agreement. The sum provided for therefore bears a reasonable relationship to the anticipated actual damages resulting from a breach. It anticipates a worst-case scenario, that is, NPS's inability to resell the seat for the remaining term of the license.[7] However, the defendant has not shown that this outcome is sufficiently unlikely that it renders the amount grossly disproportionate to a reasonable estimate of actual damages.

The defendant stood to receive a substantial benefit from this agreement: guaranteed luxury seating for all Patriots home games, as well as a hedge against future price increases over ten years. He was not deprived of an opportunity to learn and consider the terms of the agreement. Those terms may be harsh, especially when, as here, the breach occurred early in the life of the agreement. But the defendant has not shown that in the circumstances they are "unreasonably and grossly disproportionate to the real damages from a breach." *A-Z Servicenter, Inc. v. Segall*, 334 Mass. 672, 675, 138 N.E.2d 266 (1956).

On appeal, the parties have not raised the issue whether, if the liquidated damages provision is enforced, mitigation should be considered. . . . [W]e consider the issue, which appears to be one of first impression in Massachusetts.

We will follow the rule in many other jurisdictions[9] and hold that, in the case of an enforceable liquidated damages provision, mitigation is irrelevant and should not be considered in assessing damages. When parties agree in advance to a sum certain that represents a reasonable estimate of potential damages, they exchange the opportunity to determine actual damages after a breach, including possible mitigation, for the "peace of mind and certainty of result" afforded by a liquidated damages clause. *Kelly v. Marx*, 428 Mass. 877, 881, 705 N.E.2d 1114 (1999), quoting *Kelly v. Marx*, 44 Mass. App. Ct. 825, 833, 694 N.E.2d 869 (1998) (Spina, J., dissenting). In such circumstances, to consider whether a plaintiff has mitigated its damages not only is illogical, but also defeats the purpose of liquidated damages provisions. See *Barrie School v. Patch*, 401 Md. 497, 513-514, 933 A.2d 382 (2007) (sum that stipulates damages in advance "replaces any determination of actual loss," so that if liquidated damages provision is enforceable, court need not consider mitigation). Since the liquidated damages provision at issue here is enforceable, the question is irrelevant.

Conclusion. The ruling of the Superior Court that the liquidated damages provision of the license agreement is unenforceable is set aside, and the judgment

7. We note in passing that there was evidence at trial that NPS in fact had not been able to resell the defendant's seat, some four years after the defendant committed a breach of the agreement. Although *Kelly v. Marx*, 428 Mass. 877, 878, 705 N.E.2d 1114 (1999), prevents our consideration of this fact, it suggests that it was not unduly pessimistic to think that NPS might have difficulty reselling the defendant's seat in the event of breach.
9. See, e.g., *Federal Realty Ltd. Partnership v. Choices Women's Med. Ctr., Inc.*, 289 A.D.2d 439, 442, 735 N.Y.S.2d 159 (N.Y. 2001); *Lake Ridge Academy v. Carney*, 66 Ohio St. 3d 376, 385, 613 N.E.2d 183 (1993); *Cady v. IMC Mtge. Co.*, 862 A.2d 202, 219 (R.I. 2004) (applying Florida law). See also 24 S. Williston, Contracts §65.31, at 364 (4th ed. 2002) ("Since the effect of a stipulated damages provision is to substitute a predetermined amount for actual damages . . . , the existence of an enforceable liquidated damages provision has the effect of making the mitigation of damages irrelevant").

is modified to award NPS the total amount of unpaid license fees due under the agreement, $65,500, plus interest. . . .

So ordered.

Problems

1. A Monument Made of Italian Marble. In the 1880s, defendant Margaret Lynch contracted with plaintiff M. Muldoon for Muldoon to improve the San Francisco cemetery plot in which Lynch's husband was interred and to construct on the site a monument built out of Ravaccioni Italian marble. Seven thousand dollars of the $18,887 contract price was to be paid when the preparation work was complete, with the remaining $11,887 due after the completion of the monument. The contract provided that:

> All the work, with the exception of monument, to be completed within four months from date of contract, and the balance in twelve months from the date of this contract, under forfeiture of ten dollars per day for each and every day beyond the stated time for completion.

The preparation work proceeded on schedule and the first $7,000 was paid, but the monument was nearly two years late. Lynch claimed she was entitled to $7,820 in liquidated damages, which in turn meant she owed Muldoon only $4,067 of the outstanding $11,887. Muldoon sued for the full amount, testifying that the delay was due to the lack of a suitable ship to carry the marble from its Italian sea port and the $10 per day figure constituted an unenforceable penalty. Assuming that Muldoon's duty was not excused on grounds of impracticability, is he entitled to $11,887, or only $4,067?

2. A Double Deposit. Donald Leeber contracted to purchase a condominium from the Deltona Corporation for $150,200, with a 15-percent down payment ($22,530) made at the time the agreement was signed. The contract provided that if Leeber failed to close on the purchase, Deltona would retain the full deposit as liquidated damages. When Leeber failed to close on the appointed date, Deltona notified him that it was retaining the deposit. Four days later, it sold the same condominium unit to another buyer for $167,500 (including a $25,125 deposit). The evidence indicated that Deltona incurred costs of $5,704 as a result of the breach in the form of commission to the selling real estate agent and administrative costs. Leeber claimed that the liquidated damages term was unenforceable and sued for the return of his $22,530. What result?

3. Public Infrastructure. The City of Coffeeville, Kansas, hired Hutton Contracting Company to construct a power and fiber-optic cable line for the city within a 45-day period, with extensions for bad weather, for the price of approximately $1,132,000. The contract included the following stipulated damages clause:

> The time of the Completion of Construction of the Project is of the essence of the Contract. Should [Hutton] neglect, refuse or fail to complete the construction within the time herein agreed upon, after giving effect to extensions of time, if any, herein provided, then, in that event and in view of the difficulty of estimating with exactness damages caused by such delay, the [City] shall have the right to deduct from and retain out of such monies which may be then due, or which may become due and payable to [Hutton], the sum of **FIVE HUNDRED DOLLARS ($500.00)** per day for each and every day that such construction is delayed on its completion beyond the specified time, as liquidated damages and not as a penalty.

Hutton was nearly six months late in completing the project, and the city withheld $85,500 from the final payment as stipulated damages for the delay. Hutton sued. At trial, the city presented uncontroverted evidence that the delay had cost the city approximately $76,000 in increased engineering and inspection costs. How should the court rule?

4. Full Tuition. In March 1989, John Carney entered into a contract with Lake Ridge Academy to enroll his son, Michael, in the fourth grade of the private school for the following academic year, at a cost of $6,240 for tuition, books, and supplies. The contract allowed Carney to cancel the agreement in writing prior to August 1, and provided that Carney would be obligated to pay the full charge if enrollment were canceled after that date. On August 7, Carney notified Lake Ridge that Michael would not be enrolling that fall. When Carney refused to pay, Lake Ridge sued, and Carney defended on the ground that the contract provision constituted a penalty clause. At trial, the Lake Ridge headmaster testified that "we feel that August 1st is as far as we want to go prior to the start of the school year in order for us to be able to collect our revenue for expenses that are ongoing regarding the operations of the school." The only testimony concerning damages actually suffered by the school was the headmaster's testimony that, if the school enjoyed any savings from Michael's withdrawal, they were "minuscule." Should Lake Ridge be permitted to recover the full $6,240?

Chapter 7

Alternative Bases for Liability: Non-Contract Claims

In Chapter 1, we observed that there is no single, incontrovertible definition of what constitutes a "contract." There also is no undisputed delineation of which legal disputes fall within the discrete category termed "contract law" and which exist outside its subject-matter borders. To this point, we have taken a conservative position, limiting our scope to doctrinal categories that all experts would agree fall safely within the borders of contract law. In this final chapter, we expand our scope to consider disputes that arise at the far reaches of the domain of contract law, on the border of—or, arguably, within—the realm of tort law (a subject that all of you will study) or restitution (a subject that most of you will not, although it once was a staple of legal education).

The cases in this chapter involve disputes that, on first reading, are similar to those we saw in earlier chapters: a promisor fails to keep his word; family members or friends have a falling out; a business person violates the customs of her industry; one person benefits from another person's loss. The difference is that, in these cases, the traditional doctrinal requirements of contract law such as consideration or mutual assent are arguably, or in some cases clearly, lacking. Yet, rather than slam the courthouse door, judges have attempted to construct doctrines that enable aggrieved parties to recover, at least under some conditions. As you consider the cases in this chapter, you should consider whether each allegedly injured party could make a successful claim for breach of contract, as traditionally understood, and, if not, whether courts are justified in granting relief under alternative theories.

This chapter divides the collection of what we conservatively call "non-contract claims" into three categories: promissory estoppel, pre-contractual negotiations, and quasi-contract. The lines between these categories, like the line between "contract" and "non-contract" claims, sometimes blur, but this division reflects the way practitioners, scholars, and, most importantly, judges generally parse the subject matter.

A. PROMISSORY ESTOPPEL

In the early nineteenth-century case of *Kirksey v. Kirksey*, included in Chapter 2, the widow Antillico Kirksey moved to her brother-in-law's land in reliance on his promise to provide her with a place to raise her family. When brother Kirksey's actions failed to live up to Antillico's expectations, she sued, but the court held she was unable to recover for breach of contract because the promise at issue lacked consideration. The doctrine of promissory estoppel, which began to evolve many years after *Kirksey*, may have provided a remedy for Antillico.

The first pair of cases in this section—*Ricketts v. Scothorn* and *Feinberg v. Pfeiffer*—illustrates the doctrinal evolution from a somewhat clumsy attempt to employ the doctrine of equitable estoppel (which can prevent parties from claiming in court a fact that they previously denied) to enforce a gratuitous promise to the development of a substantive claim for breach of promise that induced detrimental reliance in the absence of consideration. Promissory estoppel is now recognized as an independent basis for recovery by the Restatement. Rest. (2d) Contracts §90. *Maryland National Bank v. United Jewish Appeal Federation* provides an example of the arguably perverse results that can arise from a doctrine that distinguishes between enforceable and unenforceable promises on the basis of actual reliance. *Alaska Airlines, Inc. v. Stephenson* explores the issue of whether defenses to the enforcement of *contracts* should also apply to promissory estoppel claims. *Grouse v. Group Health Plan, Inc.* raises difficult issues concerning the appropriate remedy for a promissory estoppel cause of action.

RICKETTS (D)
v.
SCOTHORN (P)

Supreme Court of Nebraska
77 N.W. 365
1898

SULLIVAN, J.

In the district court of Lancaster county the plaintiff, Katie Scothorn, recovered judgment against the defendant, Andrew D. Ricketts, as executor of the last will and testament of John C. Ricketts, deceased. The action was based upon a promissory note, of which the following is a copy: "May the first, 1891. I promise to pay to Katie Scothorn on demand, $2,000, to be at 6 per cent. per annum. J. C. Ricketts." In the petition the plaintiff alleges that the consideration for the execution of the note was that she should surrender her employment as bookkeeper for Mayer Bros., and cease to work for a living. She also alleges that the note was given to induce her to abandon her occupation, and that, relying on it, and on the annual interest, as a means of support, she gave up the employment in which she was then engaged. These allegations of the petition are denied by the administrator.

The material facts are undisputed. They are as follows: John C. Ricketts, the maker of the note, was the grandfather of the plaintiff. Early in May—presumably on the day the note bears date—he called on her at the store where she was working. What transpired between them is thus described by Mr. Flodene, one of the plaintiff's witnesses: "A. Well, the old gentleman came in there one morning about nine o'clock, probably a little before or a little after, but early in the morning, and he unbuttoned his vest, and took out a piece of paper in the shape of a note; that is the way it looked to me; and he says to Miss Scothorn, 'I have fixed out something that you have not got to work any more.' He says, none of my grandchildren work, and you don't have to. Q. Where was she? A. She took the piece of paper and kissed him, and kissed the old gentleman, and commenced to cry." It seems Miss Scothorn immediately notified her employer of her intention to quit work, and that she did soon after abandon her occupation. The mother of the plaintiff was a witness, and testified that she had a conversation with her father, Mr. Ricketts, shortly after the note was executed, in which he informed her that he had given the note to the plaintiff to enable her to quit work; that none of his grandchildren worked, and he did not think she ought to. For something more than a year the plaintiff was without an occupation, but in September, 1892, with the consent of her grandfather, and by his assistance, she secured a position as bookkeeper with Messrs. Funke & Ogden.

On June 8, 1894, Mr. Ricketts died. He had paid one year's interest on the note, and a short time before his death expressed regret that he had not been able to pay the balance. In the summer or fall of 1892 he stated to his daughter, Mrs. Scothorn, that if he could sell his farm in Ohio he would pay the note out of the proceeds. He at no time repudiated the obligation.

We quite agree with counsel for the defendant that upon this evidence there was nothing to submit to the jury, and that a verdict should have been directed peremptorily for one of the parties. The testimony of Flodene and Mrs. Scothorn, taken together, conclusively establishes the fact that the note was not given in consideration of the plaintiff pursuing, or agreeing to pursue, any particular line of conduct. There was no promise on the part of the plaintiff to do, or refrain from doing, anything. Her right to the money promised in the note was not made to depend upon an abandonment of her employment with Mayer Bros., and future abstention from like service. Mr. Ricketts made no condition, requirement, or request. He exacted no quid pro quo. He gave the note as a gratuity, and looked for nothing in return. So far as the evidence discloses, it was his purpose to place the plaintiff in a position of independence, where she could work or remain idle, as she might choose. The abandonment of Miss Scothorn of her position as bookkeeper was altogether voluntary. It was not an act done in fulfillment of any contract obligation assumed when she accepted the note. The instrument in suit, being given without any valuable consideration, was nothing more than a promise to make a gift in the future of the sum of money therein named. Ordinarily, such promises are not enforceable, even when put in the form of a promissory note. Kirkpatrick v. Taylor, 43 Ill. 207; Phelps v. Phelps, 28 Barb. 121; Johnston v. Griest, 85 Ind. 503; Fink v. Cox 18 Johns. 145. But it has often been held that an action on a note given to a church, college, or other like institution, upon the faith of which money has been expended or obligations incurred, could not be successfully defended on the ground of a want of consideration. Barnes v. Perine, 12 N.Y. 18. In this class of cases the note in suit is nearly always spoken of as a gift or donation, but the decision is generally put on the ground that the expenditure of money or assumption of liability by the donee on the faith of the promise constitutes a valuable and sufficient consideration. It seems to us that the true reason is the preclusion of the defendant, under the doctrine of estoppel, to deny the consideration. Such seems to be the view of the matter taken by the supreme court of Iowa in the case of Simpson Centenary College v. Tuttle, 71 Iowa, 596, 33 N.W. 74, where Rothrock, J., speaking for the court, said: "Where a note, however, is based on a promise to give for the support of the objects referred to, it may still be open to this defense [want of consideration], unless it shall appear that the donee has, prior to any revocation, entered into engagements, or made expenditures based on such promise, so that he must suffer loss or injury if the note is not paid. This is based on the equitable principle that, after allowing the donee to incur obligations on the faith that the note would be paid, the donor would be estopped from pleading want of consideration." . . .

Under the circumstances of this case, is there an equitable estoppel which ought to preclude the defendant from alleging that the note in controversy is lacking in one of the essential elements of a valid contract? We think there is. An estoppel in pais is defined to be "a right arising from acts, admissions, or conduct which have induced a change of position in accordance with the real or apparent intention of the party against whom they are alleged." . . . According to the undisputed proof, as shown by the record before us, the plaintiff was a working girl, holding a position in which she earned a salary of $10 per week, Her grandfather, desiring to put her in a position of independence, gave her the note, accompanying it with the remark that his other grandchildren did not work, and that she would not be obliged to work any longer. In effect, he suggested that she might abandon her employment, and rely in the future upon the bounty which he promised. He doubtless desired that she should give up her occupation, but, whether he did or not, it is entirely certain that he contemplated such action on her part as a reasonable and probable consequence of his gift. Having intentionally influenced the plaintiff to alter her position for the worse on the faith of the note being paid when due, it would be grossly inequitable to permit the maker, or his executor, to resist payment on the ground that the promise was given without consideration. The petition charges the elements of an equitable estoppel, and the evidence conclusively establishes them. If errors intervened at the trial, they could not have been prejudicial. A verdict for the defendant would be unwarranted. The judgment is right, and is affirmed.

FEINBERG
v.
PFEIFFER CO.

2

St. Louis Court of Appeals, Missouri
322 S.W.2d 163
1959

DOERNER, C.

. . .

The parties are in substantial agreement on the essential facts. Plaintiff began working for the defendant, a manufacturer of pharmaceuticals, in 1910, when she was but 17 years of age. By 1947 she had attained the position of bookkeeper, office manager, and assistant treasurer of the defendant, and owned 70 shares of its stock out of a total of 6,503 shares issued and outstanding. Twenty shares had been given to her by the defendant or its then president, she had purchased 20, and the remaining 30 she had acquired by a stock split or stock dividend. Over the years she received substantial dividends on the stock she owned, as did all of the other stockholders. Also, in addition to her salary, plaintiff from 1937 to 1949, inclusive, received each year a bonus varying in amount from $300 in the beginning to $2,000 in the later years.

On December 27, 1947, the annual meeting of the defendant's Board of Directors was held at the Company's offices in St. Louis, presided over by Max Lippman, its then president and largest individual stockholder. The other directors present were George L. Marcus, Sidney Harris, Sol Flammer, and Walter Weinstock, who, with Max Lippman, owned 5,007 of the 6,503 shares then issued and outstanding. At that meeting the Board of Directors adopted the following resolution, which, because it is the crux of the case, we quote in full:

> "The Chairman thereupon pointed out that the Assistant Treasurer, Mrs. Anna Sacks Feinberg, has given the corporation many years of long and faithful service. Not only has she served the corporation devotedly, but with exceptional ability and skill. The President pointed out that although all of the officers and directors sincerely hoped and desired that Mrs. Feinberg would continue in her present position for as long as she felt able, nevertheless, in view of the length of service which she has contributed provision should be made to afford her retirement privileges and benefits which should become a firm obligation of the corporation to be available to her whenever she should see fit to retire from active duty, however many years in the future such retirement may become effective. It was, accordingly, proposed that Mrs. Feinberg's salary which is presently $350.00 per month, be increased to $400.00 per month, and that Mrs. Feinberg would be given the privilege of retiring from active duty at any time she may elect to see fit so to do upon a retirement pay of $200.00 per month for life, with the distinct understanding that the retirement plan is merely being adopted at the present time in order to afford Mrs. Feinberg security for the future and in the hope that her active services will continue

with the corporation for many years to come. After due discussion and consideration, and upon motion duly made and seconded, it was—

"Resolved, that the salary of Anna Sacks Feinberg be increased from $350.00 to $400.00 per month and that she be afforded the privilege of retiring from active duty in the corporation at any time she may elect to see fit so to do upon retirement pay of $200.00 per month, for the remainder of her life."

At the request of Mr. Lippman his sons-in-law, Messrs. Harris and Flammer, called upon the plaintiff at her apartment on the same day to advise her of the passage of the resolution. Plaintiff testified on cross-examination that she had no prior information that such a pension plan was contemplated, that it came as a surprise to her, and that she would have continued in her employment whether or not such a resolution had been adopted. It is clear from the evidence that there was no contract, oral or written, as to plaintiff's length of employment, and that she was free to quit, and the defendant to discharge her, at any time.

Plaintiff did continue to work for the defendant through June 30, 1949, on which date she retired. In accordance with the foregoing resolution, the defendant began paying her the sum of $200 on the first of each month. Mr. Lippman died on November 18, 1949, and was succeeded as president of the company by his widow. Because of an illness, she retired from that office and was succeeded in October, 1953, by her son-in-law, Sidney M. Harris. Mr. Harris testified that while Mrs. Lippman had been president she signed the monthly pension check paid plaintiff, but fussed about doing so, and considered the payments as gifts. After his election, he stated, a new accounting firm employed by the defendant questioned the validity of the payments to plaintiff on several occasions, and in the Spring of 1956, upon its recommendation, he consulted the Company's then attorney, Mr. Ralph Kalish. Harris testified that both Ernst and Ernst, the accounting firm, and Kalish told him there was no need of giving plaintiff the money. He also stated that he had concurred in the view that the payments to plaintiff were mere gratuities rather than amounts due under a contractual obligation, and that following his discussion with the Company's attorney plaintiff was sent a check for $100 on April 1, 1956. Plaintiff declined to accept the reduced amount, and this action followed. . . .

. . . [A]t the time of trial [plaintiff] was sixty-five and a half years old, and . . . was no longer able to engage in gainful employment because of the removal of a cancer. . . .

Appellant's [] complaint is that there was insufficient evidence to support the court's findings that plaintiff would not have quit defendant's employ had she not known and relied upon the promise of defendant to pay her $200 a month for life, and the finding that, from her voluntary retirement until April 1, 1956, plaintiff relied upon the continued receipt of the pension installments. The trial court so found, and, in our opinion, justifiably so. Plaintiff testified, and was corroborated by Harris, defendant's witness, that knowledge of the passage of the resolution was communicated to her on December 27, 1947, the very day it was adopted. She was told at that time by Harris and Flammer, she stated, that she could take the pension as of that day, if she wished. She testified further that she continued to work for another year and a half, through June 30, 1949; that at that time her health was good and she could have continued to work, but that after working for almost forty years she thought she would take a rest. Her testimony continued:

> "Q: Now, what was the reason—I'm sorry. Did you then quit the employment of the company after you—after this year and a half? A. Yes.
>
> "Q: What was the reason that you left? A. Well, I thought almost forty years, it was a long time and I thought I would take a little rest.
>
> "Q: Yes. A. And with the pension and what earnings my husband had, we figured we could get along.
>
> "Q: Did you rely upon this pension? A. We certainly did.
>
> "Q: Being paid? A. Very much so. We relied upon it because I was positive that I was going to get it as long as I lived.
>
> "Q: Would you have left the employment of the company at that time had it not been for this pension? A. No.
>
> "Mr. Allen: Just a minute, I object to that as calling for a conclusion and conjecture on the part of this witness.
>
> "The Court: It will be overruled.
>
> "Q: (Mr. Agatstein continuing): Go ahead, now. The question is whether you would have quit the employment of the company at that time had you not relied upon this pension plan? A. No, I wouldn't.
>
> "Q: You would not have. Did you ever seek employment while this pension was being paid to you—A. (interrupting): No.
>
> "Q: Wait a minute, at any time prior—at any other place? A. No, sir.
>
> "Q: Were you able to hold any other employment during that time? A. Yes, I think so.
>
> "Q: Was your health good? A. My health was good."

It is obvious from the foregoing that there was ample evidence to support the findings of fact made by the court below.

. . .

It is defendant's contention, in essence, that the resolution adopted by its Board of Directors was a mere promise to make a gift, and that no contract resulted either thereby, or when plaintiff retired, because there was no consideration given or paid by the plaintiff. It urges that a promise to make a gift is not binding unless supported by a legal consideration; that the only apparent consideration for the adoption of the foregoing resolution was the "many years of long and faithful service" expressed therein; and that past services are not a valid consideration for a promise. Defendant argues further that there is nothing in the resolution which made its effectiveness conditional upon plaintiff's continued employment, that she was not under contract to work for any length of time but was free to quit whenever she wished, and that she had no contractual right to her position and could have been discharged at any time.

Plaintiff concedes that a promise based upon past services would be without consideration, but contends that there were two other elements which supplied the required element: First, the continuation by plaintiff in the employ of the defendant for the period from December 27, 1947, the date when the resolution was adopted, until the date of her retirement on June 30, 1949. And, second, her change of position, i.e., her retirement, and the abandonment by her of her opportunity to continue in gainful employment, made in reliance on defendant's promise to pay her $200 per month for life.

We must agree with the defendant that the evidence does not support the first of these contentions. There is no language in the resolution predicating plaintiff's right to a pension upon her continued employment. She was not required to work for the defendant for any period of time as a condition to gaining such retirement benefits. She was told that she could quit the day upon which the resolution was adopted, as she herself testified, and it is clear from her own testimony that she made no promise or agreement to continue in the employ of the defendant in return for its promise to pay her a pension. Hence there was lacking that mutuality of obligation which is essential to the validity of a contract. Middleton v. Holecraft, Mo. App., 270 S.W.2d 90.

But as to the second of these contentions we must agree with plaintiff. By the terms of the resolution defendant promised to pay plaintiff the sum of $200 a month upon her retirement. Consideration for a promise has been defined in the Restatement of the Law of Contracts, Section 75, as:

> "(1) Consideration for a promise is
> > (a) an act other than a promise, or
> > (b) a forbearance, or
> > (c) the creation, modification or destruction of a legal relation, or
> > (d) a return promise, bargained for and given in exchange for the promise.

As the parties agree, the consideration sufficient to support a contract may be either a benefit to the promisor or a loss or detriment to the promisee. Industrial Bank & Trust Co. v. Hesselberg, Mo., 195 S.W.2d 470.

Section 90 of the Restatement of the Law of Contracts states that: "A promise which the promisor should reasonably expect to induce action or forbearance of a definite and substantial character on the part of the promisee and which does induce such action or forbearance is binding if injustice can be avoided only by enforcement of the promise." This doctrine has been described as that of "promissory estoppel," as distinguished from that of equitable estoppel or estoppel in pais, the reason for the differentiation being stated as follows:

> "It is generally true that one who has led another to act in reasonable reliance on his representations of fact cannot afterwards in litigation between the two deny the truth of the representations, and some courts have sought to apply this principle to the formation of contracts, where, relying on a gratuitous promise, the promisee has suffered detriment. It is to be noticed, however, that such a case does not come within the ordinary definition of estoppel. If there is any representation of an existing fact, it is only that the promisor at the time of making the promise intends to fulfill it. As to such intention there is usually no misrepresentation and if there is, it is not that which has injured the promisee. In other

words, he relies on a promise and not on a misstatement of fact; and the term 'promissory' estoppel or something equivalent should be used to make the distinction." Williston on Contracts, Rev. Ed., Sec. 139, Vol. 1.

. . .

Was there such an act on the part of plaintiff, in reliance upon the promise contained in the resolution, as will estop the defendant, and therefore create an enforceable contract under the doctrine of promissory estoppel? We think there was. One of the illustrations cited under Section 90 of the Restatement is: "2. A promises B to pay him an annuity during B's life. B thereupon resigns a profitable employment, as A expected that he might. B receives the annuity for some years, in the meantime becoming disqualified from again obtaining good employment. A's promise is binding." This illustration is objected to by defendant as not being applicable to the case at hand. The reason advanced by it is that in the illustration B became "disqualified" from obtaining other employment *before* A discontinued the payments, whereas in this case the plaintiff did not discover that she had cancer and thereby became unemployable until *after* the defendant had discontinued the payments of $200 per month. We think the distinction is immaterial. The only reason for the reference in the illustration to the disqualification of A is in connection with that part of Section 90 regarding the prevention of injustice. The injustice would occur regardless of when the disability occurred. Would defendant contend that the contract would be enforceable if the plaintiff's illness had been discovered on March 31, 1956, the day before it discontinued the payment of the $200 a month, but not if it occurred on April 2nd, the day after? Furthermore, there are more ways to become disqualified for work, or unemployable, than as the result of illness. At the time she retired plaintiff was 57 years of age. At the time the payments were discontinued she was over 63 years of age. It is a matter of common knowledge that it is virtually impossible for a woman of that age to find satisfactory employment, much less a position comparable to that which plaintiff enjoyed at the time of her retirement.

The fact of the matter is that plaintiff's subsequent illness was not the "action or forbearance" which was induced by the promise contained in the resolution. As the trial court correctly decided, such action on plaintiff's part was her retirement from a lucrative position in reliance upon defendant's promise to pay her an annuity or pension. . . .

The Commissioner therefore recommends, for the reasons stated, that the judgment be affirmed.

PER CURIAM.

The foregoing opinion by DOERNER, C., is adopted as the opinion of the court. The judgment is, accordingly, affirmed.

WOLFE, P.J., and ANDERSON and RUDDY, JJ., concur.

MARYLAND NATIONAL BANK
v.
UNITED JEWISH APPEAL FEDERATION
OF GREATER WASHINGTON, INC.

Court of Appeals of Maryland
286 Md. 274
1979

ORTH, J.

The issue in this case is whether a pledge to a charitable institution survives the death of the pledgor and is an enforceable obligation of his estate.

I

Milton Polinger pledged $200,000 to the United Jewish Appeal Federation of Greater Washington, Inc. (UJA) for the year 1975. He died on 20 December 1976. His last will and testament was admitted to probate in the Orphans' Court for Montgomery County and letters were issued to Melvin R. Oksner and Maryland National Bank as personal representatives. At the time of Polinger's death $133,500 was unpaid on his pledge. The personal representatives disallowed the claim for the balance of the pledge. UJA filed a petition praying that the claim be allowed and moved for summary judgment. The personal representatives answered and filed a cross-motion for summary judgment. The court granted UJA's motion for summary judgment, denied the personal representatives' motion for summary judgment, allowed UJA's claim against the estate in the amount of $133,500, and assessed the costs against the personal representatives. The personal representatives noted an appeal to the Court of Special Appeals and petitioned this Court to issue a writ of certiorari to that court before decision by it. We did so.

II

The facts before the court were undisputed in material part. They showed the nature of UJA and its relationship with its beneficiaries. UJA, chartered in the District of Columbia, is a public non-profit corporation. In general, its objective is to solicit, collect and receive funds and property for the support of certain religious, charitable, philanthropic, scientific and educational organizations and institutions, and it enjoys tax exempt status federally and in Maryland, Virginia and the District of Columbia. Based on monies received and pledged, it makes allocations to tax exempt organizations. No formal commitment agreement is executed with respect to the allocations, but UJA undertakes to pay pursuant to the allocation and the beneficiary organizations "go ahead to act as though they are going to have the money and they spend it." In other words, UJA makes allocations to various beneficiary organizations based upon pledges made to it, and the beneficiary organizations incur liabilities based on the allocations. Historically 95% of the pledges are collected over a three year period, and allowance for the 5% which may be uncollected is made in determining the amount of the allocations. So, according to Meyer Brissman, Executive Vice-President Emeritus of UJA: "We always pay (the allocated amount). I don't know of any case where we haven't paid." Pledges to "emergency funds" are not paid on the basis of an allocation by UJA. All monies actually collected on those pledges are paid to the emergency funds.

The facts before the court showed the circumstances surrounding the pledge of Polinger with which we are here concerned. It was evidenced by a card signed by Polinger under date of 9 November 1974. It recited:

> In consideration of the obligation incurred based upon this pledge, I hereby promise to pay to the United Jewish Appeal the amount indicated on this card.

The amount indicated as his "1975 pledge" was $100,000 for "UJA including local national and overseas," and $100,000 for "Israel Emergency Fund."

. . .

III

We find that the law of Maryland with regard to the enforcement of pledges or subscriptions to charitable organizations is the rule thus expressed in the Restatement of Contracts §90 (1932):

> A promise which the promisor should reasonably expect to induce action or forbearance of a definite and substantial character on the part of the promisee and which does induce such action or forbearance is binding if injustice can be avoided only by enforcement of the promise.

We reach this conclusion through opinions of this Court in four cases, Gittings v. Mayhew, 6 Md. 113 (1854); Erdman v. Trustees Eutaw M. P. Ch., 129 Md. 595, 99 A. 793 (1917); Sterling v. Cushwa & Sons, 170 Md. 226, 183 A. 593 (1936); and American University v. Collings, 190 Md. 688, 59 A.2d 333 (1948).

Gittings concerned the building of an Atheneum. The subscription contract authorized the calling of payment of installments by the subscribers when a certain amount had been pledged. The amount was reached, installments were called for and paid, contracts to erect the building were made and the Atheneum was completed. It was in these circumstances that the Court said:

> In whatever uncertainty the law concerning voluntary subscriptions of this character may be at this time, in consequence of the numerous decisions pronounced upon the subject, it appears to be settled, that where advances have been made, or expenses or liabilities incurred by others, in consequence of such subscriptions, before notice of withdrawal, this should, on general principles, be deemed sufficient to make them obligatory.

provided the advances were authorized by a fair and reasonable dependence on the subscriptions. . . . The doctrine is not only reasonable and just, but consistent with the analogies of the law. (6 Md. at 131-132.)

This statement of the law appeared to be Obiter dictum in *Gittings*, but if it were, it became the law in *Erdman*.

Erdman dealt with a suit on a promissory note whereby there was a promise to pay the Eutaw Methodist Protestant Church the sum of $500 four years after date with interest. The consideration for the note was a subscription contract made with the trustees of the church for the purpose of paying off a building debt, which had been incurred for the erection of a new church building. It had been entered on the books of the church, the trustees had subsequently borrowed $2,000 on that subscription and other subscriptions to pay off the indebtedness for the erection of the church building. The Court held that in such circumstances the subscription contract was a valid and binding one and constituted a sufficient consideration to support the note, Id. 129 Md. at 602, 99 A. 793, observing that "(t)he policy of the law, to sustain subscription contracts of the character of the one here in question, is clearly stated by this court, and by other appellate courts, in a number of cases," Id. at 600, 99 A. at 795. The only Maryland case cited was *Gittings*. The holding in *Gittings* was said to be "that as the party had authorized others by the subscription to enter into engagements for the accomplishment of the enterprise, the law requires that he should save them harmless to the extent of his subscription." *Erdman*, 129 Md. at 601, 99 A. at 795. One case in another appellate court was discussed, Trustees v. Garvey, 53 Ill. 401 (1870) and two cited as to like effect, McClure v. Wilson, 43 Ill. 356 (1867) and United Presbyterian Church v. Baird, 60 Iowa 237, 14 N.W. 303 (1882). In *Garvey* the court noted that "(a)s a matter of public policy, courts have been desirous of sustaining the legal obligation of subscriptions of this character, and in some cases . . . have found a sufficient consideration in the mutuality of the promises, where no fraud or deception has been practiced." Id. at 403. "But," the court continued, "while we might be unwilling to go to that extent, and might hold that a subscription could be withdrawn before money had been expended or liability incurred, or work performed on the strength of the subscriptions, and in furtherance of the enterprise," the church trustees had, on the faith of the subscriptions, borrowed money, relying on the subscription as a means of payment and incurred a specific liability. Id. Thus, it seems that *Erdman* made law of the dictum in *Gittings*, but that law was that charitable subscriptions to be enforceable require reliance on the subscriptions by the charity which would lead to direct loss to the organization or its officers if the subscriptions were not enforced.

. . .

IV

UJA would have us "view traditional contract law requirements of consideration liberally" in order to maintain what it believes to be a judicial policy of favoring charities.

We deeply appreciate the fact that private philanthropy serves a highly important function in our society. This was well expressed by the Court some hundred and twenty-five years ago in observing that the maintenance of charitable institutions was "certainly of the highest merit":

> Whether projected for literary, scientific or charitable purposes, they address themselves to the favorable consideration of those whose success in life may have enabled them, in this way, to minister to the wants of others, and at the same time promote their own interests, by elevating the character of the community with whose prosperity their fortunes may be identified. (*Gittings*, 6 Md. at 131.)

But we are not persuaded that we should, by judicial fiat, adopt a policy of favoring charities at the expense of the law of contracts which has been long established in this state. We do not think that this law should be disregarded or modified so as to bestow a preferred status upon charitable organizations and institutions. It may be that there are cases in which judgments according to the law do not appear to subserve the purposes of justice, but this, ordinarily, the courts may not remedy. "It is safer that a private right should fail, or a wrong go unredressed, than that settled principles should be disregarded in order to meet the equity of a particular case." *Gittings* at 134. If change is to be made it should be by legislative enactment, as in the matter of the tax status of charitable organizations.

. . .

Restatement (Second) of Contracts (Tent. Draft No. 2, 1965) proposes changes in §90. It would read:

> A promise which the promisor should reasonably expect to induce action or forbearance on the part of the promisee or a third person and which does induce such action or forbearance is binding if injustice can be avoided only by enforcement of the promise. The remedy granted for breach may be limited as justice requires.

This deletes from the existing section the qualification "of a definite and substantial character" with regard to the inducement of action or forbearance and has the inducement of forbearance apply to "a third person" as well as the promisee. It also adds the discretionary limitation as to the remedy. Comment c to the proposed Section concerns "(c)haritable subscriptions, marriage settlements, and other gifts." It begins:

> One of the functions of the doctrine of consideration is to deny enforcement to a promise to make a gift. Such a promise is ordinarily enforced by virtue of the promisee's reliance only if his conduct is foreseeable and reasonable and involves a definite and substantial change of position which would not have occurred if the promise had not been made.

This reflects the previous section and the Maryland rule. The comment then notes that "(i)n some cases, however, other policies reinforce the promisee's claim." It states:

> American courts have traditionally favored charitable subscriptions and marriage settlements, and have found consideration in many cases where the element of exchange was

doubtful or nonexistent. Where recovery is rested on reliance in such cases, a probability of reliance is likely to be enough, and no effort is made to sort out mixed motives or to consider whether partial enforcement would be appropriate.

Illustration 7 is of a charitable subscription:

> A orally promises to pay B, a university, $100,000 in five annual installments for the purposes of its fund-raising campaign then in progress. The promise is confirmed in writing by A's agent, and two annual installments are paid before A dies. The continuance of the fund-raising campaign by B is sufficient reliance to make the promise binding on A and his estate.

Section 90 of the tentative draft No. 2 of the Restatement (Second) of Contracts, 1965, has not been adopted by the American Law Institute, and we are not persuaded to follow it.

"Cases throughout the country clearly reflect a conflict between the desired goal of enforcing charitable subscriptions and the realities of contract law. The result has been strained reasoning which has been the subject of considerable criticism." Salsbury v. Northwestern Bell Telephone Company, 221 N.W.2d 609, 611-612 (Iowa, 1974). When charitable subscriptions, even though clearly gratuitous promises, have been held either contracts or offers to contract, the "decisions are based on such a great variety of reasoning as to show the lack of any really sufficient consideration." Williston on Contracts, §116 (3d ed. 1957) (footnotes omitted). "Very likely, conceptions of public policy have shaped, more or less subconsciously, the rulings thus made. Judges have been affected by the thought that 'defenses of (the) character (of lack of consideration are) breaches of faith towards the public, and especially towards those engaged in the same enterprise, and an unwarrantable disappointment of the reasonable expectations of those interested.'" Allegheny College v. National Chautauqua County Bank, 246 N.Y. 369, 159 N.E. 173, 175 (1927). Therefore, "(c)ourts have . . . purported to find consideration on various tenuous theories. . . . (The) wide variation in reasoning indicates the difficulty of enforcing a charitable subscription on grounds of consideration. Yet, the courts have generally striven to find grounds for enforcement, indicating the depth of feeling in this country that private philanthropy serves a highly important function in our society." Calamari & Perillo, The Law of Contracts, §6-5 (1977) (footnotes omitted). Some courts have forthrightly discarded the facade of consideration and admittedly held a charitable subscription enforceable only in respect of what they conceive to be the public policy. See, for example, Salsbury v. Northwestern Bell Telephone Company, supra; More Game Birds in America, Inc. v. Boettger, 125 N.J.L. 97, 14 A.2d 778, 780-781 (1940).

We are not convinced that such departure from the settled law of contracts is in the public interest. . . .

V

When the facts concerning the charitable subscription of Polinger are viewed in light of the Maryland law, it is manifest that his promise was not legally enforceable. There was no consideration as required by contract law. The incidents on which *Gittings* indicated a charitable pledge was enforceable, and on which *Erdman* and *Sterling* held the subscriptions in those cases were enforceable are not present here. The consideration recited by the pledge card was "the obligation incurred based upon this pledge. . . ." But there was no legal obligation incurred in the circumstances. Polinger's pledge was not made in consideration of the pledges of others, and there was no evidence that others in fact made pledges in consideration of Polinger's pledge. No release was given or binding agreement made by the UJA on the strength of Polinger's pledge. The pledge was not for a specific enterprise; it was to the UJA generally and to the Israel Emergency Fund. With respect to the former, no allocation by UJA to its beneficiary organization was threatened or thwarted by the failure to collect the Polinger pledge in its entirety, and, with respect to the latter, UJA practice was to pay over to the Fund only what it actually collected, not what was pledged. UJA borrowed no money on the faith and credit of the pledge. The pledge prompted no "action or forbearance of a definite and substantial character" on the part of UJA. No action was taken by UJA on the strength of the pledge that could reasonably be termed "definite and substantial" from which it should be held harmless. There was no change shown in the position of UJA made in reliance on the subscription which resulted in an economic loss, and, in fact, there was no such loss demonstrated. UJA was able to fulfill all of its allocations. Polinger's pledge was utilized as a means to obtain substantial pledges from others. But this was a technique employed to raise money. It did not supply a legal consideration to Polinger's pledge. On the facts of this case, it does not appear that injustice can be avoided only by enforcement of the promise.

. . .

We hold that Polinger's pledge to UJA was a gratuitous promise. It had no legal consideration, and under the law of this State was unenforceable. The Orphans' Court for Montgomery County erred in allowing the claim for the unpaid balance of the subscription, and its order of 5 January 1979 is vacated with direction to enter an order disallowing the claim filed by UJA.

ALASKA AIRLINES, INC.
v.
STEPHENSON

U.S. Court of Appeals, Ninth Circuit
217 F.2d 295
1954

CHAMBERS, J.

Arthur W. Stephenson, plaintiff-appellee, is the discharged general manager of Alaska Airlines, Inc. . . . Stephenson seems to have had through the years a varied career in the airlines. One day he is a pilot. The next day he is an executive.

In September, 1950, he was a pilot regularly employed by Western Airlines. At Western he had certain rights to continued employment. But he could take a leave of absence therefrom for a period of not to exceed six months without prejudice to his rights of continued employment with Western.

Alaska Airlines, Inc., herein called Alaska, Inc., in 1950 was a small airline operating in the Territory of Alaska. It was living from day to day in the hope of obtaining a certificate to operate from the states, probably from Seattle, Washington, to Alaska. When that day should come, it was to be a big airline.

The financial headquarters of the company, at least, was in the City of New York. There R. W. Marshall, chairman of the board, had his office.

Stephenson went to New York on September 15, 1950, at the request of an aviation consultant company to be interviewed by Marshall. Then and there Stephenson was employed as general manager. He took leave of absence from Western and rather promptly commenced his duties. He eventually in mid-winter moved his family to Anchorage, Alaska, from Redondo Beach, California. In the winter of 1950-1951, with Stephenson's six months' leave with Western about to expire, he was in and out of New York pressing for a written contract of definite duration and of substantial length. He had one drawn up and conferred not only with Marshall but with the company's lawyer. He could not get it signed. The company wasn't signing any contracts, we take it, until it found out whether it was to have its certificate. Later on we shall advert to some of the discussions.

The certificate apparently was granted in May, 1951. It seems strange that with the granting of the certificate there followed no negotiations or steps to put the agreement in writing, if Alaska, Inc., had agreed to do so. But we do get the impression that by this time Stephenson had lost favor with the company. It appears that he was relieved of his duties about September 1, 1951, and was continued on the payroll until October 15, 1951.

Then Stephenson filed suit against Alaska, Inc. . . .

But what of the statute of frauds and a contract clearly not to be performed fully within one year? Alaska, Inc., relied on the statute of frauds.[2]

. . .

Stephenson's version of his employment may be summed up as follows:

1. When he was hired by Marshall the agreement was that he would go to work at $1,300 a month and that they would get together in six weeks to three months and work out a long-range agreement; that he was to have a raise when the certificate of convenience and necessity was granted for Alaska, Inc., to fly to and from the states.

2. Negotiations were had for the "contract" about January 6, 1951, in New York, with Marshall. At that time about all that was agreed definitely was that Stephenson should

---

2. [The court concludes that Alaska law controls on this question.—EDS.] . . . The Alaska statute reads:

Alaska Compiled Laws, Section 58-2-2[:]
    "In the following cases an agreement is void unless the same or some note or memorandum thereof expressing the consideration be in writing and subscribed by the party to be charged or by his lawfully authorized agent: First. An agreement that by its terms is not to be performed within a year from the making thereof; * * *."

take his family with him to the Territory of Alaska. This he did. Then, about March 15, 1951, Stephenson, his leave with Western about to expire, was in New York at the company office, pressing Marshall for the contract. He made clear to Marshall that because of this contingency the employment had to be made definite and formalized. (The testimony wobbles, but the jury could have found that on March 16 or 17 Marshall orally hired Stephenson for a period of two years at a salary of $1,300 per month, with the further understanding that on the granting of the certificate Stephenson was to have an increase in salary and a written contract.) Thereupon, Stephenson let his right to return to Western expire.

. . .

Turning to the Alaska statute, what is it? Where did it come from? What history does it have behind it?

It would appear that it went to Alaska from Oregon. Oregon may have taken it from Iowa or New York. We find nothing in the decisions made by the Alaska courts (or by this court) or in Oregon prior to Alaska's adoption of the statute that will help us.

Section 90 of the Restatement of the Law of Contracts provides as follows:

"Promise reasonably inducing definite and substantial action.

"A promise which the promisor should reasonably expect to induce action or forbearance of a definite and substantial character on the part of the promisee which does induce such action or forbearance is binding if injustice can be avoided only by enforcement of the promise."

The foregoing section, not mentioning promissory estoppel, is addressed not to the statute of frauds but to promissory estoppel as a substitute for consideration. However, when one considers the part Samuel Williston took in the formulation of the Restatement of Contracts and then examines Section 178, Comment f., one must conclude that there was an intention to carry promissory estoppel (or call it what you will) into the statute of frauds if the additional factor of a promise to reduce the contract to writing is present. Williston on Contracts, 1936 Ed., Sec. 533A.

The circumstance of Stephenson's relinquishing his rights with Western and the promise to make a written contract on the future condition, we think, meets the test of the Restatement.

Parenthetically, we observe that California courts probably would reach the same result. Seymour v. Oelrichs, 156 Cal. 782, 106 P. 88. True it is that under earlier decisions where one gave up job A to take job B on an oral promise of long time employment on job B, no exception to the statute of frauds was made. But we believe with the growth of tenure rights and fringe benefits on a given job, the pendulum has swung the other way and that Seymour v. Oelrichs, supra, will generally be followed throughout the country.

. . .

[T]he judgment is affirmed.

GROUSE
v.
GROUP HEALTH PLAN, INC.

Supreme Court of Minnesota
306 N.W.2d 114
1981

Oᴛɪs, J.

Plaintiff John Grouse appeals from a judgment in favor of Group Health Plan, Inc., in this action for damages resulting from repudiation of an employment offer. The narrow issue raised is whether the trial court erred by concluding that Grouse's complaint fails to state a claim upon which relief can be granted. In our view, the doctrine of promissory estoppel entitles Grouse to recover and we, therefore, reverse and remand for a new trial on the issue of damages.

The facts relevant to this appeal are essentially undisputed. Grouse, a 1974 graduate of the University of Minnesota School of Pharmacy, was employed in 1975 as a retail pharmacist at Richter Drug in Minneapolis. He worked approximately 41 hours per week earning $7 per hour. Grouse desired employment in a hospital or clinical setting, however, because of the work environment and the increased compensation and benefits. In the summer of 1975 he was advised by the Health Sciences Placement office at the University that Group Health was seeking a pharmacist.

Grouse called Group Health and was told to come in and fill out an application. He did so in September and was, at that time, interviewed by Cyrus Elliott, Group Health's Chief Pharmacist. Approximately 2 weeks later Elliott contacted Grouse and asked him to come in for an interview with Donald Shoberg, Group Health's General Manager. Shoberg explained company policies and procedures as well as salary and benefits. Following this meeting Grouse again spoke with Elliott who told him to be patient, that it was necessary to interview recent graduates before making an offer.

On December 4, 1975, Elliott telephoned Grouse at Richter Drug and offered him a position as a pharmacist at Group Health's St. Louis Park Clinic. Grouse accepted but informed Elliott that 2 week's notice to Richter Drug would be necessary. That afternoon Grouse received an offer from a Veteran's Administration Hospital in Virginia which he declined because of Group Health's offer. Elliott called back to confirm that Grouse had resigned.

Sometime in the next few days Elliott mentioned to Shoberg that he had hired, or was thinking of hiring, Grouse. Shoberg told him that company hiring requirements included a favorable written reference, a background check, and approval of the general manager. Elliott contacted two faculty members at the School of Pharmacy who declined to give references. He also contacted an internship employer and several pharmacies where Grouse had done relief work. Their responses were that they had not had enough exposure to Grouse's work to form a judgment as to his capabilities. Elliott did not contact Richter because Grouse's application requested that he not be contacted. Because Elliott was unable to supply a favorable reference for Grouse, Shoberg hired another person to fill the position.

On December 15, 1975 Grouse called Group Health and reported that he was free to begin work. Elliott informed Grouse that someone else had been hired. Grouse complained to the director of Group Health who apologized but took no other action. Grouse experienced difficulty regaining full time employment and suffered wage loss as a result. He commenced this suit to recover damages; the trial judge found that he had not stated an actionable claim.

In our view the principle of contract law applicable here is promissory estoppel. Its effect is to imply a contract in law where none exists in fact. Del Hayes & Sons, Inc. v. Mitchell, 304 Minn. 275, 230 N.W.2d 588 (1975). On these facts no contract exists because due to the bilateral power of termination neither party is committed to performance and the promises are, therefore, illusory. The elements of promissory estoppel are stated in Restatement of Contracts §90 (1932):

> A promise which the promisor should reasonably expect to induce action or forbearance . . . on the part of the promisee and which does induce such action or forbearance is binding if injustice can be avoided only by enforcement of the promise.

Group Health knew that to accept its offer Grouse would have to resign his employment at Richter Drug. Grouse promptly gave notice to Richter Drug and informed Group Health that he had done so when specifically asked by Elliott. Under these circumstances it would be unjust not to hold Group Health to its promise.

The parties focus their arguments on whether an employment contract which is terminable at will can give rise to an action for damages if anticipatorily repudiated. Group Health contends that recognition of a cause of action on these facts would result in the anomalous rule that an employee who is told not to report to work the day before he is scheduled to begin has a remedy while an employee who is discharged after the first day does not. We cannot agree since under appropriate circumstances we believe section 90 would apply even after employment has begun.

When a promise is enforced pursuant to section 90 "(t)he remedy granted for breach may be limited as justice requires." Relief may be limited to damages measured by the promisee's reliance.

The conclusion we reach does not imply that an employer will be liable whenever he discharges an employee whose term of employment is at will. What we do hold is that under the facts of this case the appellant had a right to assume he would be given a good faith opportunity to perform his duties to the satisfaction of respondent once he was on the job. He was not only denied that opportunity but resigned the position he already held in reliance on the firm offer which respondent tendered him. Since, as respondent points out, the prospective employment might have been terminated at any time, the measure of damages is not so much what he would have earned from respondent as what he lost in quitting the job he held and in declining at least one other offer of employment elsewhere.

Reversed and remanded for a new trial on the issue of damages.

Problems

1. A Very Bad Break-Up. Cecilia Barnes broke up with her boyfriend, who responded by posting unauthorized profiles of Barnes, including her contact information and nude photographs taken without her knowledge, on a Yahoo website. The ex-boyfriend, posing as Barnes, corresponded with men using Yahoo's online chat rooms and directed them to the false profiles. Barnes learned of the ex's actions when strangers began contacting and visiting her without invitation. Barnes sent proof of identity and a signed statement disavowing any role in the profiles to Yahoo, requesting Yahoo remove the profiles from its website. After months of inaction despite repeated communications from Barnes, a local news program prepared to broadcast a report of the incident. A day before the broadcast, Yahoo's director of communication called Barnes and promised to "personally walk the statements over to the division responsible for stopping unauthorized profiles and they would take care of it." Two more months passed. Barnes filed a lawsuit against Yahoo, and shortly thereafter the profiles disappeared. Does Barnes have a viable promissory estoppel claim against Yahoo?

2. The Surviving Spouse. In 1983, Jackson National sold a life insurance policy to Carl and Patricia Green, in which Mrs. Green was the primary beneficiary. In 1991, the Greens separated, and Mr. Green changed the primary beneficiary to two sons from a previous marriage. When Mr. Green became seriously ill in 1992, the couple reconciled, and Mrs. Green took substantial responsibility for caring for Mr. Green until his death in 2003. She incurred $20,000 worth of debt for his medical expenses. In 2002, Mr. Green told Mrs. Green that he wanted her to get the life insurance proceeds to cover the costs she incurred, and he contacted Jackson National to ask who was listed as the beneficiary on the policy. Jackson National sent a reply stating that it could not provide a duplicate copy of the policy but its policy summary listed Mrs. Green as the beneficiary on the date of issue. Mr. Green reported to Mrs. Green in front of two witnesses that Jackson National had confirmed that Mrs. Green was the beneficiary. But, when Mrs. Green contacted Jackson National after Mr. Green's death, the company informed her that the sons were in fact the beneficiaries of the policy. Mrs. Green sued Jackson National for breach of contract and promissory estoppel. What result?

3. Order of the Coif. Meyer Blatt attended the night program at the University of Southern California School of Law. While in school, he inquired about the requirements for induction to the Order of the Coif, a prestigious national legal honor society, and was told that he would be eligible if he was in the top 10 percent of his class. Later, but while Blatt was still a student, the law school added a requirement that students serve on the law review to be chosen for Coif. Blatt had started work on the law review but chose to quit after he was told that the requirement did not apply to him because he was a night student. Blatt graduated fourth in his class of 135, but was not selected for Coif because he did not continue with law review. He has brought breach of contract and promissory estoppel claims against USC. Should either claim survive a motion to dismiss?

4. Discarded Evidence. Bryan Cooper was involved in a single car accident caused by tread separation of the right rear tire. His insurer, State Farm Mutual Automobile Insurance Company, acquired possession of the car (including the right rear tire) as part of the collision damage settlement with Cooper. State Farm informed Cooper that its expert concluded that the tread separated because the tire was defectively manufactured. Cooper sued the tire manufacturer, and his attorney notified State Farm of the importance of the tire to Cooper's case. After State Farm informed Cooper that it would retain the tire, State Farm disposed of the car including the defective tire. Cooper has sued State Farm. On what claim(s), if any, is Cooper likely to succeed?

5. A Scenic View. Ken Nelson sold a lot to Karen and Alan Nicol, who planned to build a vacation home there. The property offered scenic views across an undeveloped piece of land. Prior to closing the deal, the Nicols expressed concern that the open land would be developed, cutting off their view. Nelson assured them that the property would remain undeveloped, and told them that, although he did not own the land, he had an option to purchase it. This representation was never memorialized in writing. Nelson later purchased the open land and started to build on it. The Nicols sued to enjoin the construction, asserting promissory estoppel. How should the court rule?

~

B. PRE-CONTRACTUAL NEGOTIATIONS LIABILITY

The traditional rules of contract law draw a clear line between the moment before a contract is formed, at which point either party may walk away without responsibility, and the moment after, at which point both parties are committed to the terms of the bargain. One cost of such clarity is that a party induced to make significant expenditures in the hope of obtaining a contract can find itself left worse off if the prospective deal is never finalized. Should the rule of *caveat emptor* ("buyer beware") prevail in these situations, or should the law offer protection for parties who rely to their detriment on the hopes of facilitating a deal? The following trio of cases considers the claims of parties who were allegedly harmed by relying on pre-contractual communications made by their negotiating counterparts—offers in the cases of *Drennan v. Star Paving Company* and *Corbin-Dykes Electric Company v. Burr* (see also Rest. (2d) Contracts §87(2)), and pre-contractual assertions in *Hoffman v. Red Owl Stores*—but who arguably have no valid cause of action under contract law.

DRENNAN
v.
STAR PAVING CO.

Supreme Court of California
51 Cal. 2d 409
1958

Traynor, J.

Defendant appeals from a judgment for plaintiff in an action to recover damages caused by defendant's refusal to perform certain paving work according to a bid it submitted to plaintiff.

On July 28, 1955, plaintiff, a licensed general contractor, was preparing a bid on the "Monte Vista School Job" in the Lancaster school district. Bids had to be submitted before 8 p.m. Plaintiff testified that it was customary in that area for general contractors to receive the bids of subcontractors by telephone on the day set for bidding and to rely on them in computing their own bids. Thus on that day plaintiff's secretary, Mrs. Johnson, received by telephone between 50 and 75 subcontractors' bids for various parts of the school job. As each bid came in, she wrote it on a special form, which she brought into plaintiff's office. He then posted it on a master cost sheet setting forth the names and bids of all subcontractors. His own bid had to include the names of subcontractors who were to perform one-half of one per cent or more of the construction work, and he had also to provide a bidder's bond of 10 per cent of his total bid of $317,385 as a guarantee that he would enter the contract if awarded the work.

Late in the afternoon, Mrs. Johnson had a telephone conversation with Kenneth R. Hoon, an estimator for defendant. He gave his name and telephone number and stated that he was bidding for defendant for the paving work at the Monte Vista School according to plans and specifications and that his bid was $7,131.60. At Mrs. Johnson's request he repeated his bid. Plaintiff listened to the bid over an extension telephone in his office and posted it on the master sheet after receiving the bid form from Mrs. Johnson. Defendant's was the lowest bid for the paving. Plaintiff computed his own bid accordingly and submitted it with the name of defendant as the subcontractor for the paving. When the bids were opened on July 28th, plaintiff's proved to be the lowest, and he was awarded the contract.

On his way to Los Angeles the next morning plaintiff stopped at defendant's office. The first person he met was defendant's construction engineer, Mr. Oppenheimer. Plaintiff testified: "I introduced myself and he immediately told me that they had made a mistake in their bid to me the night before, they couldn't do it for the price they had bid, and I told him I would expect him to carry through with their original bid because I had used it in compiling my bid and the job was being awarded them. And I would have to go and do the job according to my bid and I would expect them to do the same."

Defendant refused to do the paving work for less than $15,000. Plaintiff testified that he "got figures from other people" and after trying for several months to get as low a bid as possible engaged L & H Paving Company, a firm in Lancaster, to do the work for $10,948.60.

The trial court found on substantial evidence that defendant made a definite offer to do the paving on the Monte Vista job according to the plans and specifications for $7,131.60, and that plaintiff relied on defendant's bid in computing his own bid for the school job and naming defendant therein as the subcontractor for the paving work. Accordingly, it entered judgment for plaintiff in the amount of $3,817 (the difference between defendant's bid and the cost of the paving to plaintiff) plus costs.

Defendant contends that there was no enforceable contract between the parties on the ground that it made a revocable offer and revoked it before plaintiff communicated his acceptance to defendant.

There is no evidence that defendant offered to make its bid irrevocable in exchange for plaintiff's use of its figures in computing his bid. Nor is there evidence that would warrant interpreting plaintiff's use of defendant's bid as the acceptance thereof, binding plaintiff, on condition he received the main contract, to award the subcontract to defendant. In sum, there was neither an option supported by consideration nor a bilateral contract binding on both parties.

Plaintiff contends, however, that he relied to his detriment on defendant's offer and that defendant must therefore answer in damages for its refusal to perform. Thus the question is squarely presented: Did plaintiff's reliance make defendant's offer irrevocable?

(1) Section 90 of the Restatement of Contracts states: "A promise which the promisor should reasonably expect to induce action or forbearance of a definite and substantial character on the part of the promisee and which does induce such action or forbearance is binding if injustice can be avoided only by enforcement of the promise." This rule applies in this state. (*Edmonds v. County of Los Angeles*, 40 Cal. 2d 642 [255 P.2d 772]; *Frebank Co. v. White*, 152 Cal. App. 2d 522 [313 P.2d 633]; *Wade v. Markwell & Co.*, 118 Cal. App. 2d 410 [258 P.2d 497, 37 A.L.R.2d 1363]; *West v. Hunt Foods, Inc.*, 101 Cal. App. 2d 597 [225 P.2d 978]; *Hunter v. Sparling*, 87 Cal. App. 2d 711 [197 P.2d 807]; see 18 Cal. Jur. 2d 407-408; 5 Stan. L. Rev. 783.)

(2) Defendant's offer constituted a promise to perform on such conditions as were stated expressly or by implication therein or annexed thereto by operation of law. (See 1 Williston, Contracts [3d ed.], §24A, p. 56, §61, p. 196.) Defendant had reason to expect that if its bid proved the lowest it would be used by plaintiff. It induced "action . . . of a definite and substantial character on the part of the promisee."

Had defendant's bid expressly stated or clearly implied that it was revocable at any time before acceptance we would treat it accordingly. It was silent on revocation, however, and we must therefore determine whether there are conditions to the right of revocation imposed by law or reasonably inferable in fact. In the analogous problem of an offer for a unilateral contract, the theory is now obsolete that the offer is revocable at any time before complete performance. Thus section 45 of the Restatement of Contracts provides: "If an offer for a unilateral contract is made, and part of the consideration requested in the offer is given or tendered by the offeree in response thereto, the offeror is bound by a contract, the duty of immediate performance of which is conditional on the full consideration being given or tendered within the time stated in the offer, or, if no time is stated therein, within a reasonable time." In explanation, comment *b* states that the "main offer includes as a subsidiary promise, necessarily implied, that if part of the requested performance is given, the offeror will not revoke his offer, and that if tender is made it will be accepted. Part performance or tender may thus furnish consideration for the subsidiary promise. Moreover, merely acting in justifiable reliance on an offer may in some cases serve as sufficient reason for making a promise binding (see §90)."

(3) Whether implied in fact or law, the subsidiary promise serves to preclude the injustice that would result if the offer could be revoked after the offeree had acted in detrimental reliance thereon. Reasonable reliance resulting in a foreseeable prejudicial change in position affords a compelling basis also for implying a subsidiary promise not to revoke an offer for a bilateral contract.

(4) The absence of consideration is not fatal to the enforcement of such a promise. It is true that in the case of unilateral contracts the Restatement finds consideration for the implied subsidiary promise in the part performance of the bargained-for exchange, but its reference to section 90 makes clear that consideration for such a promise is not always necessary. The very purpose of section 90 is to make a promise binding even though there was no consideration "in the sense of something that is bargained for and given in exchange." (See 1 Corbin, Contracts 634 et seq.) Reasonable reliance serves to hold the offeror in lieu of the consideration ordinarily required to make the offer binding. In a case involving similar facts the Supreme Court of South Dakota stated that "we believe that reason and justice demand that the doctrine [of section 90] be applied to the present facts. We cannot believe that by accepting this doctrine as controlling in the state of facts before us we will abolish the requirement of a consideration in contract cases, in any different sense than an ordinary estoppel abolishes some legal requirement in its application. We are of the opinion, therefore, that the defendants in executing the agreement [which was not supported by consideration] made a promise which they should have reasonably expected would induce the plaintiff to submit a bid based thereon to the Government, that such promise did induce this action, and that injustice can be avoided only by enforcement of the promise." (*Northwestern Engineering Co. v. Ellerman*, 69 S.D. 397, 408 [10 N.W.2d 879]; see also *Robert Gordon, Inc. v. Ingersoll-Rand Co.*, 117 F.2d 654, 661; cf. *James Baird Co. v. Gimbel Bros.*, 64 F.2d 344.)

(5) When plaintiff used defendant's offer in computing his own bid, he bound himself to perform in reliance on defendant's terms. Though defendant did not bargain for this use of its bid neither did defendant make it idly, indifferent to whether it would be used or not. On the contrary it is reasonable to suppose that defendant submitted its bid to obtain the subcontract. It was bound to realize the substantial possibility that its bid would be the lowest, and that it would be included by plaintiff in his bid. It was to its own interest that the contractor be awarded the general contract; the lower the subcontract bid, the lower the general contractor's bid was likely to be and the greater its chance of acceptance and hence the greater defendant's chance of

getting the paving subcontract. Defendant had reason not only to expect plaintiff to rely on its bid but to want him to. Clearly defendant had a stake in plaintiff's reliance on its bid. Given this interest and the fact that plaintiff is bound by his own bid, it is only fair that plaintiff should have at least an opportunity to accept defendant's bid after the general contract has been awarded to him.

(6) It bears noting that a general contractor is not free to delay acceptance after he has been awarded the general contract in the hope of getting a better price. Nor can he reopen bargaining with the subcontractor and at the same time claim a continuing right to accept the original offer. (See *R.J. Daum Const. Co. v. Child*, 122 Utah 194 [247 P.2d 817, 823].) In the present case plaintiff promptly informed defendant that plaintiff was being awarded the job and that the subcontract was being awarded to defendant.

Defendant contends, however, that its bid was the result of mistake and that it was therefore entitled to revoke it. It relies on the rescission cases of *M.F. Kemper Const. Co. v. City of Los Angeles*, 37 Cal. 2d 696 [235 P.2d 7], and *Brunzell Const. Co. v. G.J. Weisbrod, Inc.*, 134 Cal. App. 2d 278 [285 P.2d 989]. (See also *Lemoge Electric v. San Mateo County*, 46 Cal. 2d 659, 662 [297 P.2d 638].) In those cases, however, the bidder's mistake was known or should have been to the offeree, and the offeree could be placed in status quo.

(7) Of course, if plaintiff had reason to believe that defendant's bid was in error, he could not justifiably rely on it, and section 90 would afford no basis for enforcing it. (*Robert Gordon, Inc. v. Ingersoll-Rand Co.*, 117 F.2d 654, 660.) Plaintiff, however, had no reason to know that defendant had made a mistake in submitting its bid, since there was usually a variance of 160 per cent between the highest and lowest bids for paving in the desert around Lancaster. He committed himself to performing the main contract in reliance on defendant's figures. Under these circumstances defendant's mistake, far from relieving it of its obligation, constitutes an additional reason for enforcing it, for it misled plaintiff as to the cost of doing the paving. Even had it been clearly understood that defendant's offer was revocable until accepted, it would not necessarily follow that defendant had no duty to exercise reasonable care in preparing its bid. It presented its bid with knowledge of the substantial possibility that it would be used by plaintiff; it could foresee the harm that would ensue from an erroneous underestimate of the cost. Moreover, it was motivated by its own business interest. Whether or not these considerations alone would justify recovery for negligence had the case been tried on that theory (see *Biakanja v. Irving*, 49 Cal. 2d 647, 650 [320 P.2d 16]), they are persuasive that defendant's mistake should not defeat recovery under the rule of section 90 of the Restatement of Contracts.

(8) As between the subcontractor who made the bid and the general contractor who reasonably relied on it, the loss resulting from the mistake should fall on the party who caused it.

. . .

The judgment is affirmed.

CORBIN-DYKES ELECTRIC CO.
v.
BURR

Court of Appeals of Arizona, Division 1, Department B
18 Ariz. App. 101
1972

EUBANK, J.

This appeal from a summary judgment questions whether a contractual relationship results from a situation where a subcontractor submits a bid for the electrical sub-contract to the general contractor, who in turn includes it within his bid for the general construction contract which is subsequently awarded the general contractor.

The facts are as follows:

General Motors Corporation requested bids from general contractors to construct the central air-conditioning plant at its proving grounds located east of the city of Mesa. The defendant-appellee Walter Burr, et al., a general contractor, hereafter "Burr," was interested in obtaining the contract and as a result received bids for the electrical subcontract solicited by Lowry & Sorensen, the consulting engineers on the project. One of the bids received by Burr was from the plaintiff-appellant Corbin-Dykes Electric Company, hereafter "Corbin-Dykes." Burr incorporated Corbin-Dykes' subcontract bid, which was the low bid, into his general contract bid and submitted it to General Motors Corporation. All bids were rejected by General Motors because they exceeded the cost estimate; and the project was rebid on October 14, 1969. The second bid submitted by Burr also included the Corbin-Dykes subcontract bid; however, prior to submitting the second bid, Burr had received another bid from Sands Electric Company which matched the Corbin-Dykes bid but also provided that, in the event Sands could work the proposed project in conjunction with its current project at the proving grounds, they would reduce their subcontract bid by $4000. When the second round of bids was opened, Burr was awarded the general contract, and since Sands Electric's other project at the proving grounds was not yet completed, Burr accepted Sands' bid for the electric subcontract as the low bid.

Corbin-Dykes objected to this selection of Sands as the subcontractor and sued Burr for breach of their alleged subcontract. The subcontract was denied by Burr in his answer; and following several depositions, Burr moved for summary judgment, which was granted. Corbin-Dykes appeals from that summary judgment.

Two questions are raised by Corbin-Dykes for review. First, whether taking all inferences in a light most favorable to Corbin-Dykes the trial court was justified in granting the summary judgment to Burr; Second, whether there remains a genuine issue as to a material fact which would preclude granting the summary judgment.

Both of these questions are based upon Corbin-Dykes' contention that a custom and usage exists in the trade to the effect that a subcontractor who is listed in the general contractor's bid will receive the subcontract, if the general contractor is successful and is awarded the general contract. This custom and usage would be introduced at the trial, according to Corbin-Dykes, in order to prove the contract existed between it and Burr, or in other words to prove the acceptance by Burr of Corbin-Dykes' bid offer. The record shows that there was no other evidence of acceptance by Burr of the subcontract offer.

In Arizona the law is clear that Corbin-Dykes' bid to Burr was nothing more than an offer to perform the subcontract under specified terms, and that it did not ripen into a contract until it was voluntarily accepted by Burr. Universal Construction Co. v. Arizona Consolidated Masonry & Plastering Contractors Ass'n, 93 Ariz. 4, 377 P.2d 1017 (1963). The law and its related problems are well stated in the 53 Virginia L. Rev. 1720 (1967), Law note: Another Look at Construction Bidding and Contracts at Formation, which states:

> From the time a general contractor (general) receives bids from subcontractors (subs) until he formally accepts one of those bids, the parties are not adequately protected by the common law. Although they are forced by the commercial context to rely upon each other during this period, at common law their relationship cannot be contractual until the general responds with the requisite promise of acceptance. To some extent the promissory estoppel doctrine has alleviated the general's problems by binding the sub to perform according to the terms of his bid. But this protection is one-sided, and despite the view of some courts that promissory estoppel is a panacea, it appears that in confining the scope of protection to the general, the doctrine in fact raises serious problems. (53 Virginia L. Rev. at 1720).

The serious problems referred to relate primarily to "bid shopping," for an excellent discussion of which see 18 U.C.L.A. L. Rev. 389 (1970), Law Comment: Bid Shopping and Peddling In the Subcontract Construction Industry. See also, 17 C.J.S. Contracts §48, p. 695.

If the law requires an actual voluntary acceptance of Corbin-Dykes' bid by Burr, can this acceptance be established solely by custom and usage in the trade evidence as offered by Corbin-Dykes? We think not.

In order for there to be any contract between Corbin-Dykes and Burr there must be a manifestation of mutual assent thereto by both, and the acts by which their mutual assent is manifested must show that they intended to do those acts. 1 Restatement of Contracts, §20 (1932). This manifestation of intent, i.e., offer or acceptance, is determined by the words used and the other manifestations of intent having reference to the contract. 1 Restatement of Contracts, §§226, 227 (1932). Custom or usage is defined as an habitual or customary practice, more or less widespread, which prevails within a geographical or sociological area. Sam Levitz Furniture Co. v. Safeway Stores, Inc., 10 Ariz. App. 225, 457 P.2d 938 (1969). Usage is a course of conduct based upon a series of actual occurrences. Coyner Crop Dusters v. Marsh, 90 Ariz. 157, 175, 367 P.2d 208, 220 (1961), rehearing granted on other grounds[,] 91 Ariz. 371, 372 P.2d 708 (1962) (footnote omitted). However, evidence of custom or usage is admissible only where an existing agreement between the parties is ambiguous, to show what the parties intended by their agreement. Coury Bros.

Ranches, Inc. v. Ellsworth, 103 Ariz. 515, 446 P.2d 458 (1968); Lenslite Co. v. Zocher, 95 Ariz. 208, 388 P.2d 421 (1964); Gray v. Headley, 35 Ariz. 232, 276 P. 523 (1929). Primarily this is limited to proving the meaning of words or phrases used in the agreement. Sam Levitz Furniture Co. v. Safeway Stores, Inc., 10 Ariz. App. 225, 457 P.2d 938 (1969); Pioneer Constructors v. Symes, 77 Ariz. 107, 267 P.2d 740 (1954). M. Udall, Ariz. Law of Evidence, §157, pp. 328-330 (1960).

Corbin-Dykes relies on no evidence of the acceptance of their offer by Burr except the above referred to custom and usage. As we have seen, a "voluntary acceptance" is required to bind Burr. It is also clear from the cited case law that such custom and usage evidence cannot be used to initially establish acceptance or the manifestation of mutual assent. Since there was no evidence presented by Corbin-Dykes from which to draw an inference that a genuine issue as to a material fact exists which would preclude the granting of the summary judgment complained of (Rule 56(c), Rules of Civil Procedure, 16 A.R.S.), and since the question of "acceptance" is one of law, it was properly disposed of by the trial court by summary judgment.

In our opinion the record shows no evidence of a voluntary acceptance of the offer involved, since the inclusion of Corbin-Dykes' subcontract bid as a part of the general contract bid did not constitute such an acceptance, and the offer never was accepted by Burr in any other manner. Universal Construction Co. v. Arizona Consolidated Masonry & Plastering Contractors Ass'n, supra.

The summary judgment is affirmed.

HOFFMAN
v.
RED OWL STORES, INC.
Supreme Court of Wisconsin
26 Wis. 2d 683
1965

The complaint alleged that Lukowitz, as agent for Red Owl, represented to and agreed with plaintiffs that Red Owl would build a store building in Chilton and stock it with merchandise for Hoffman to operate in return for which plaintiffs were to put up and invest a total sum of $18,000; that in reliance upon the above mentioned agreement and representations plaintiffs sold their bakery building and business and their grocery store and business; also in reliance on the agreement and representations Hoffman purchased the building site in Chilton and rented a residence for himself and his family in Chilton; plaintiffs' actions in reliance on the representations and agreement disrupted their personal and business life; plaintiffs lost substantial amounts of income and expended large sums of money as expenses. Plaintiffs demanded recovery of damages for the breach of defendants' representations and agreements.

The action was tried to a court and jury. The facts hereafter stated are taken from the evidence adduced at the trial. Where there was a conflict in the evidence the version favorable to plaintiffs has been accepted since the verdict rendered was in favor of plaintiffs.

Hoffman assisted by his wife operated a bakery at Wautoma from 1956 until sale of the building late in 1961. The building was owned in joint tenancy by him and his wife. Red Owl is a Minnesota corporation having its home office at Hopkins, Minnesota. It owns and operates a number of grocery supermarket stores and also extends franchises to agency stores which are owned by individuals, partnerships and corporations. Lukowitz resides at Green Bay and since September, 1960, has been divisional manager for Red Owl in a territory comprising Upper Michigan and most of Wisconsin in charge of 84 stores. Prior to September, 1960, he was district manager having charge of approximately 20 stores.

In November, 1959, Hoffman was desirous of expanding his operations by establishing a grocery store and contacted a Red Owl representative by the name of Jansen, now deceased. Numerous conversations were had in 1960 with the idea of establishing a Red Owl franchise store in Wautoma. In September, 1960, Lukowitz succeeded Jansen as Red Owl's representative in the negotiations. Hoffman mentioned that $18,000 was all the capital he had available to invest and he was repeatedly assured that this would be sufficient to set him up in business as a Red Owl store. About Christmastime, 1960, Hoffman thought it would be a good idea if he bought a small grocery store in Wautoma and operated it in order that he gain experience in the grocery business prior to operating a Red Owl store in some larger community. On February 6, 1961, on the advice of Lukowitz and Sykes, who had succeeded Lukowitz as Red Owl's district manager, Hoffman bought the inventory and fixtures of a small grocery store in Wautoma and leased the building in which it was operated.

After three months of operating this Wautoma store, the Red Owl representatives came in and took inventory and checked the operations and found the store was operating at a profit. Lukowitz advised Hoffman to sell the store to his manager, and assured him that Red Owl would find a larger store from him elsewhere. Acting on this advice and assurance, Hoffman sold the fixtures and inventory to his manager on June 6, 1961. Hoffman was reluctant to sell at that time because it meant losing the summer tourist business, but he sold on the assurance that he would be operating in a new location by fall and that he must sell this store if he wanted a bigger one. Before selling, Hoffman told the Red Owl representatives that he had $18,000 for "getting set up in business" and they assured him that there would be no problems in establishing him in a bigger operation. The makeup of the $18,000 was not discussed; it was understood plaintiff's father-in-law would furnish part of it. By June, 1961, the towns for the new grocery store had been narrowed down to two, Kewaunee and Chilton. In Kewaunee, Red Owl had an option on a building site. In Chilton, Red Owl had nothing under option, but it did select a site to which plaintiff obtained an option at Red Owl's suggestion. The option stipulated a purchase price of $6,000 with $1,000 to be paid on election to purchase and the balance to be paid within 30 days. On Lukowitz's assurance that everything was all set plaintiff paid $1,000 down on the lot on September 15th.

On September 27, 1961, plaintiff met at Chilton with Lukowitz and Mr. Reymund and Mr. Carlson from the home office who prepared a projected financial statement. Part of the funds plaintiffs were to supply as their investment in the venture were to be obtained by sale of their Wautoma bakery building.

On the basis of this meeting Lukowitz assured Hoffman: ". . . [E]verything is ready to go. Get your money together and we are set." Shortly after this meeting Lukowitz told plaintiffs that they would have to sell their bakery business and bakery building, and that their retaining this property was the only "hitch" in the entire plan. On November 6, 1961, plaintiffs sold their bakery building for $10,000. Hoffman was to retain the bakery equipment as he contemplated using it to operate a bakery in connection with his Red Owl store. After sale of the bakery Hoffman obtained employment on the night shift at an Appleton bakery.

The record contains different exhibits which were prepared in September and October, some of which were projections of the fiscal operation of the business and others were proposed building and floor plans. Red Owl was to procure some third party to buy the Chilton lot from Hoffman, construct the building, and then lease it to Hoffman. No final plans were ever made, nor were bids let or a construction contract entered. Some time prior to November 20, 1961, certain of the terms of the lease under which the building was to be rented by Hoffman were understood between him and Lukowitz. The lease was to be for 10 years with a rental approximating $550 a month calculated on the basis of 1 percent per month on the building cost, plus 6 percent of the land cost divided on a monthly basis. At the end of the 10-year term he was to have an option to renew the lease for an additional 10-year period or to buy the property at cost on an instalment basis. There was no discussion as to what the instalments would be or with respect to repairs and maintenance.

On November 22nd or 23rd, Lukowitz and plaintiffs met in Minneapolis with Red Owl's credit manager to confer on Hoffman's financial standing and on financing the agency. Another projected financial statement was there drawn up entitled, "Proposed Financing For An Agency Store." This showed Hoffman contributing $24,100 of cash capital of which only $4,600 was to be cash possessed by plaintiffs. Eight thousand was to be procured as a loan from a Chilton bank secured by a mortgage on the bakery fixtures, $7,500 was to be obtained on a 5 percent loan from the father-in-law, and $4,000 was to be obtained by sale of the lot to the lessor at a profit.

A week or two after the Minneapolis meeting Lukowitz showed Hoffman a telegram from the home office to the effect that if plaintiff could get another $2,000 for promotional purposes the deal could go through for $26,000. Hoffman stated he would have to find out if he could get another $2,000. He met with his father-in-law, who agreed to put $13,000 into the business provided he could come into the business as a partner. Lukowitz told Hoffman the partnership arrangement "sounds fine" and that Hoffman should not go into the partnership arrangement with the "front office." On January 16, 1962, the Red Owl credit manager teletyped Lukowitz that the father-in-law would have to sign an agreement that the $13,000 was either a gift or a loan subordinate to all general creditors and that he would prepare the agreement. On January 31, 1962, Lukowitz teletyped the home office that the father-in-law would sign one or other of the agreements. However, Hoffman testified that it was not until the final meeting some time between January 26th and February 2nd, 1962, that he was told that his father-in-law was expected to sign an agreement that the $13,000 he was advancing was to be an outright gift. No mention was then made by the Red Owl representatives of the alternative of the father-in-law signing a subordination agreement. At this meeting the Red Owl agents presented Hoffman with the following projected financial statement:

"Capital required in operation:

"Cash	$ 5,000.00	
"Merchandise	20,000.00	
"Bakery	18,000.00	
"Fixtures	17,500.00	
"Promotional Funds	1,500.00	
"TOTAL:		$62,000.00

"Source of funds:

"Red Owl 7-day terms	$ 5,000.00	
"Red Owl Fixture contract (Term 5 years)	14,000.00	
"Bank loans (Term 9 years Union State Bank of Chilton)	8,000.00	
"(Secured by Bakery Equipment)		
"Other loans (Term No-pay) No interest	13,000.00	
"Father-in-law (Secured by None)		
"(Secured by Mortgage on Wautoma Bakery Bldg.)	2,000.00	
"Resale of land	6,000.00	
"Equity Capital: $ 5,000.00—Cash		
"Amount owner has 17,500.00—Bakery Equip. to invest	22,500.00	
"TOTAL:		$70,500.00"

Hoffman interpreted the above statement to require of plaintiffs a total of $34,000 cash made up of $13,000 gift from his father-in-law, $2,000 on mortgage, $8,000 on Chilton bank loan, $5,000 in cash from plaintiff, and $6,000 on the resale of the Chilton lot. Red Owl claims $18,000 is the total of the unborrowed or unencumbered cash, that is, $13,000 from the father-in-law and $5,000 cash from Hoffman himself. Hoffman informed Red Owl he could not go along with this proposal, and particularly objected to the requirement that his father-in-law sign an agreement that his $13,000 advancement was an absolute gift. This terminated the negotiations between the parties.

The case was submitted to the jury on a special verdict with the first two questions answered by the court. This verdict, as returned by the jury, was as follows:

Question No. 1: Did the Red Owl Stores, Inc. and Joseph Hoffman on or about mid-May of 1961 initiate negotiations looking to the establishment of Joseph Hoffman as a franchise operator of a Red Owl Store in Chilton? Answer: Yes. (Answered by the Court.)

Question No. 2: Did the parties mutually agree on all of the details of the proposal so as to reach a final agreement thereon? Answer: No. (Answered by the Court.)

Question No. 3: Did the Red Owl Stores, Inc., in the course of said negotiations, make representations to Joseph Hoffman that if he fulfilled certain conditions that they would establish him as franchise operator of a Red Owl Store in Chilton? Answer: Yes.

Question No. 4: If you have answered Question No. 3 "Yes," then answer this question: Did Joseph Hoffman rely on said representations and was he induced to act thereon? Answer: Yes.

Question No. 5: If you have answered Question No. 4 "Yes," then answer this question: Ought Joseph Hoffman, in the exercise of ordinary care, to have relied on said representations? Answer: Yes.

Question No. 6: If you have answered Question No. 3 "Yes" then answer this question: Did Joseph Hoffman fulfill all the conditions he was required to fulfill by the terms of the negotiations between the parties up to January 26, 1962? Answer: Yes.

. . .

CURRIE, C.J.

The instant appeal and cross-appeal present these questions:

(1) Whether this court should recognize causes of action grounded on promissory estoppel as exemplified by sec. 90 of Restatement, 1 Contracts?
(2) Do the facts in this case make out a cause of action for promissory estoppel?
(3) Are the jury's findings with respect to damages sustained by the evidence?

APPLICABILITY OF DOCTRINE TO FACTS OF THIS CASE

The record here discloses a number of promises and assurances given to Hoffman by Lukowitz in behalf of Red Owl upon which plaintiffs relied and acted upon to their detriment.

Foremost were the promises that for the sum of $18,000 Red Owl would establish Hoffman in a store. After Hoffman had sold his grocery store and paid the $1,000 on the Chilton lot, the $18,000 figure was changed to $24,100. Then in November, 1961, Hoffman was assured that if the $24,100 figure were increased by $2,000 the deal would go through. Hoffman was induced to sell his grocery store fixtures and inventory in June, 1961, on the promise that he would be in his new store by fall. In November, plaintiffs sold their bakery building on the urging of defendants and on the assurance that this was the last step necessary to have the deal with Red Owl go through.

We determine that there was ample evidence to sustain the answers of the jury to the questions of the verdict with respect to the promissory representations made by Red Owl, Hoffman's reliance thereon in the exercise of ordinary care, and his fulfillment of the conditions required of him by the terms of the negotiations had with Red Owl.

There remains for consideration the question of law raised by defendants that agreement was never reached on essential factors necessary to establish a contract between Hoffman and Red Owl. Among these were the size, cost, design, and lay-out of the store building; and the terms of the lease with respect to rent, mainte-nance, renewal, and purchase options. This poses the question of whether the promise necessary to sustain a cause of action for promissory estoppel must embrace all essential details of a proposed transaction between promisor and prom-isee so as to be the equivalent of an offer that would result in a binding contract between the parties if the promisee were to accept the same.

issue

Originally the doctrine of promissory estoppel was invoked as a substitute for consideration rendering a gratuitous promise enforceable as a contract. See Williston, Contracts (1st ed.), p. 307, sec. 139. In other words, the acts of reli-ance by the promisee to his detriment provided a substitute for consideration. If promissory estoppel were to be limited to only those situations where the promise giving rise to the cause of action must be so definite with respect to all details that a contract would result were the promise supported by consideration, then the defen-dants' instant promises to Hoffman would not meet this test. However, see. 90 of Restatement, 1 Contracts, does not impose the requirement that the promise giving rise to the cause of action must be so comprehensive in scope as to meet the requirements of an offer that would ripen into a contract if accepted by the promisee. Rather the conditions imposed are:

rule
test

(1) Was the promise one which the promisor should reasonably expect to induce action or forbearance of a definite and substantial character on the part of the promisee?
(2) Did the promise induce such action or forbearance?
(3) Can injustice be avoided only by enforcement of the promise? . . .

We deem it would be a mistake to regard an action grounded on promissory estoppel as the equivalent of a breach of contract action. As Dean Boyer points out, it is desirable that fluidity in the application of the concept be maintained. 98 University of Pennsylvania Law Review (1950), 459, at page 497. While the first two of the above listed three requirements of promissory estoppel present issues of fact which ordinarily will be resolved by a jury, the third requirement, that the remedy can only be invoked where necessary to avoid injustice, is one that involves a policy decision by the court. Such a policy decision necessarily embraces an element of discretion.

holding

We conclude that injustice would result here if plaintiffs were not granted some relief because of the failure of defendants to keep their promises which induced plaintiffs to act to their detriment.

DAMAGES

Defendants attack all the items of damages awarded by the jury.

The bakery building at Wautoma was sold at defendants' instigation in order that Hoffman might have the net proceeds available as part of the cash capital he was to invest in the Chilton store venture. The evidence clearly establishes that it was sold at a loss of $2,000. Defendants contend that half of this loss was sustained by Mrs. Hoffman because title stood in joint tenancy. They point out that no dealings took place between her and defendants as all negotiations were had with her husband. Ordinarily only the promisee and not third persons are entitled to enforce the remedy of promissory estoppel against the promisor. However, if the promisor actually foresees, or has reason to foresee, action by a third person in reliance on the promise, it may be quite unjust to refuse to perform the promise. 1A Corbin, Contracts, p. 220, sec. 200. Here not only did defendants foresee that it would be necessary for Mrs. Hoffman to sell her joint interest in the bakery building, but defendants actually requested that this be done. We approve the jury's award of $2,000 damages for the loss incurred by both plaintiffs in this sale.

Defendants attack on two grounds the $1,000 awarded because of Hoffman's payment of that amount on the purchase price of the Chilton lot. The first is that this $1,000 had already been lost at the time the final negotiations with Red Owl fell through in January, 1962, because the remaining $5,000 of purchase price had been due on October 15, 1961. The record does not disclose that the lot owner had foreclosed Hoffman's interest in the lot for failure to pay this $5,000. The $1,000 was not paid for the option, but had been paid as part of the purchase price at the time Hoffman elected to exercise the option. This gave him an equity in the lot which could not be legally foreclosed without affording Hoffman an opportunity to pay the balance. The second ground of attack is that the lot may have had a fair market value of $6,000, and Hoffman should have paid the remaining $5,000 of purchase price. We determine that it would be unreasonable to require Hoffman to have invested an additional $5,000 in order to protect the $1,000 he had paid. Therefore, we find no merit to defendants' attack upon this item of damages.

We also determine it was reasonable for Hoffman to have paid $125 for one month's rent of a home in Chilton after defendants assured him everything would be set when plaintiff sold the bakery building. This was a proper item of damage.

Plaintiffs never moved to Chilton because defendants suggested that Hoffman get some experience by working in a Red Owl store in the Fox River Valley. Plaintiffs, therefore, moved to Neenah instead of Chilton. After moving, Hoffman worked at night in an Appleton bakery but held himself available for work in a Red Owl store. The $140 moving expense would not have been incurred if plaintiffs had not sold their bakery building in Wautoma in reliance upon defendants' promises. We consider the $140 moving expense to be a proper item of damage.

We turn now to the damage item with respect to which the trial court granted a new trial, i.e., that arising from the sale of the Wautoma grocery store fixtures and inventory for which the jury awarded $16,735. The trial court ruled that Hoffman could not recover for any loss of future profits for the summer months following the sale on June 6, 1961, but that damages would be limited to the difference between the sales price received and fair market value of the assets sold, giving consideration to any goodwill attaching thereto by reason of the transfer of a going business. There was no direct evidence presented as to what this fair market value was on June 6, 1961. The evidence did disclose that Hoffman paid $9,000 for the inventory, added $1,500 to it and sold it for $10,000 or a loss of $500. His 1961 federal income tax return showed that the grocery equipment had been purchased for $7,000 and sold for $7,955.96. Plaintiffs introduced evidence of the buyer that during the first eleven weeks of operation of the grocery store his gross sales were $44,000 and his profit was $6,000 or roughly 15 percent. On cross-examination he admitted that this was gross and not net profit. Plaintiffs contend that in a breach of contract action damages may include loss of profits. However, this is not a breach of contract action.

The only relevancy of evidence relating to profits would be with respect to proving the element of goodwill in establishing the fair market value of the grocery inventory and fixtures sold. Therefore, evidence of profits would be admissible to afford a foundation for expert opinion as to fair market value.

Where damages are awarded in promissory estoppel instead of specifically enforcing the promisor's promise, they should be only such as in the opinion of the court are necessary to prevent injustice. Mechanical or rule of thumb approaches to the damage problem should be avoided. In discussing remedies to be applied by courts in promissory estoppel we quote the following views of writers on the subject:

"Enforcement of a promise does not necessarily mean Specific Performance. It does not necessarily mean Damages for breach. Moreover the amount allowed as Damages may be determined by the plaintiff's expenditures or change of position in reliance as well as by the value to him of the promised performance. Restitution is also an 'enforcing' remedy, although it is often said to be based upon some kind of a rescission. In determining what justice requires, the court must remember all of its powers, derived from equity, law merchant, and other sources, as well as the common law. Its decree should be molded accordingly." 1A Corbin, Contracts, p. 221, sec. 200.

"The wrong is not primarily in depriving the plaintiff of the promised reward but in causing the plaintiff to change position to his detriment. It would follow that the damages should not exceed the loss caused by the change of position, which would never be more in amount, but might be less, than the promised reward." Seavey, Reliance on Gratuitous Promises or Other Conduct, 64 Harvard Law Review (1951), 913, 926.

"There likewise seems to be no positive legal requirement, and certainly no legal policy, which dictates the allowance of contract damages in every case where the defendant's duty is consensual." Shattuck, Gratuitous Promises—A New Writ? 35 Michigan Law Review (1936), 908, 912.[3]

At the time Hoffman bought the equipment and inventory of the small grocery store at Wautoma he did so in order to gain experience in the grocery store business. At that time discussion had already been had with Red Owl representatives that Wautoma might be too small for a Red Owl operation and that a larger city might be more desirable. Thus Hoffman made this purchase more or less as a temporary experiment. Justice does not require that the damages awarded him, because of selling

---

3. For expression of the opposite view, that courts in promissory estoppel cases should treat them as ordinary breach of contract cases and allow the full amount of damages recoverable in the latter, see note, 13 Vanderbilt Law Review (1960), 705.

these assets at the behest of defendants, should exceed any actual loss sustained measured by the difference between the sales price and the fair market value.

Since the evidence does not sustain the large award of damages arising from the sale of the Wautoma grocery business, the trial court properly ordered a new trial on this issue.

Order affirmed. . . .

Problems

1. Bid Shopping.   Pavel Enterprises, Inc., a general contractor, planned to submit a proposal for a National Institutes of Health (NIH) construction project and solicited bids from mechanical subcontractors. A.S. Johnson Company called with a quote of $898,000. Pavel used Johnson's sub-bid in computing its own bid of $1,585,000 for the project. A month later when the original winning bidder was disqualified, NIH informed Pavel that it was the successful bidder. Pavel met with Johnson to discuss Johnson's proposed role in the work, and then faxed all prospective mechanical subcontractors to ask them to resubmit their bids. None of the subcontractors submitted a bid below Johnson's original. When Pavel sought to accept, Johnson withdrew its bid because of a mistake in its calculation. Pavel has sued, seeking the difference between Johnson's bid and the next lowest bid ($32,000). What result?

2. Losing the Bet.   Pop's Cones operated a TCBY frozen yogurt franchise in Margate, New Jersey. From May through July 1994, Pop's President Brenda Taube had numerous discussions with The Players Club Casino Resort on the Atlantic City boardwalk about moving Pop's business there. Pop's obtained approval from TCBY to change its franchise site and delivered a written proposal to the resort on August 18. Three weeks later, Taube pressed the resort's executive director for a decision, explaining that Pop's option to renew its Margate lease expired October 1. He responded that "we are 95% there, we just need the COO's signature on the deal" and advised her "to pack up the Margate store and plan on moving." Taube did just that, storing the yogurt shop's equipment and preparing to relocate. On December 1, the resort's general counsel made a written offer to Pop's proposing slightly different terms. In early December, Taube met with the resort's general counsel to finalize lease terms. The resort put off a planned meeting to close the deal until January 1995, but assured Pop's that the Resort "wanted TCBY . . . on the boardwalk for the following season." In January, Pop's received a letter from the resort withdrawing its December 1 offer. (Simultaneously, the resort pursued, ultimately successfully, a lease with Host Marriott to operate a TCBY franchise in the space.) Pop's immediately began looking for another space (the Margate location was now unavailable), but was unable to reopen for business until July 1996. Pop's is now considering a suit against the resort. What are its prospects for success?

3. Meals to Go. Babyback's International, which sells ready-to-eat barbeque meat products, had a co-marketing agreement with the Indianapolis distributor of Coke products ("Coke Indy"). Coke Indy paid Babyback's to arrange and place coolers in grocery stores with their products displayed side by side. Based on the success of this "meals to go" concept, Babyback's met with Coke's national office to discuss expanding to other markets, including Atlanta. After the meeting, Coke faxed a multi-page memo to Babyback's, reviewing numerous terms on which the parties had agreed and discussing specific steps that had already been taken in an Atlanta grocery store chain. The first page of the fax stated, "We enjoyed our meeting yesterday with you and believe we have made further strides toward coming to agreement. As we have stated several times, we do agree that compl[e]mentary merchandising of Babyback's with Coca-Cola does make sense." Based on plans made in the meeting, Babyback's spent approximately $500,000 on coolers and advertising for the Atlanta stores. After doubts arose about the quality of Babyback's products, Coke withdrew from the deal, and Babyback's brought suit. Does it have a successful promissory estoppel claim?

C. QUASI-CONTRACT

The causes of action considered in the previous two sections arise from promises, either explicit or implicit, that fail to meet the formal requirements of contract. In contrast, quasi-contract claims do not require any type of promise at all. Instead, a party seeks to recover for the value of an unsolicited benefit conferred on another. Courts, not surprisingly, are skeptical of such claims for fear that it rewards or encourages parties who thrust benefits on the unwilling, so the critical question is whether the claimant acted reasonably in conferring a benefit without first obtaining a contractually enforceable promise of compensation.

A quasi-contract claim falls within the category of claims for specific or monetary restitution to prevent unjust enrichment, a doctrinal category known as the law of restitution that is traditionally considered distinct from both contract and tort. The subject of restitution boasts its own Restatement of Law (currently, the Restatement (3d) of Restitution), and is taught as its own upper-level course at some law schools. To recover on a quasi-contract theory, the plaintiff must demonstrate that she conferred a cognizable benefit on the defendant and it would be unjust for the defendant to retain the benefit without compensating her.

In the first case of the following trio, *Cotnam v. Wisdom*, the court considers when a claimant is justified in providing a service and expecting payment without first advancing an offer of a contract and procuring an acceptance. *Pyeatte v. Pyeatte* and *Farese v. McGarry*, in contrast, concern instances in which claimants thought that they had secured contractually enforceable promises but, in fact, had failed to do so. All three cases implicate the challenging, secondary question of how courts should measure the damages suffered by a harmed party for purposes of granting remedies in the absence of an enforceable promise.

Note that courts often use different terms, often interchangeably although they technically have slightly different meanings, to refer to what we call quasi-contract claims, including implied-in-law contract or constructive contract (both of which can be understood as the basis of a quasi-contract claim), quantum meruit (a common law term for a claim to recover for services rendered), unjust enrichment (the doctrinal basis for a quasi-contract claim), and restitution (the more general body of law of which quasi-contract is one part).

COTNAM
v.
WISDOM

Supreme Court of Arkansas
83 Ark. 601
1907

Action by F.L. Wisdom and another against T.T. Cotnam, administrator of A.M. Harrison, deceased, for services rendered by plaintiffs as surgeons to defendant's intestate. Judgment for plaintiffs. Defendant appeals. Reversed and remanded.

Instruction[] 1 . . . , given at the instance of plaintiffs, [is] as follows: "(1) If you find from the evidence that plaintiffs rendered professional services as physicians and surgeons to the deceased, A.M. Harrison, in a sudden emergency following the deceased's injury in a street car wreck, in an endeavor to save his life, then you are instructed that plaintiffs are entitled to recover from the estate of the said A.M. Harrison such sum as you may find from the evidence is a reasonable compensation for the services rendered. . . ."

HILL, C.J. (after stating the facts).

. . .

The first question is as to the correctness of this instruction. As indicated therein the facts are that Mr. Harrison, appellant's intestate, was thrown from a street car, receiving serious injuries which rendered him unconscious, and while in that condition the appellees were notified of the accident and summoned to his assistance by some spectator, and performed a difficult operation in an effort to save his life, but they were unsuccessful, and he died without regaining consciousness. The appellant says: "Harrison was never conscious after his head struck the pavement. He did not and could not, expressly or impliedly, assent to the action of the appellees. He was without knowledge or will power. However merciful or benevolent may have been the intention of the appellees, a new rule of law, of contract by implication of law, will have to be established by this court in order to sustain the recovery." Appellant is right in saying that the recovery must be sustained by a contract by implication of law, but is not right in saying that it is a new rule of law, for such contracts are almost as old as the English system of jurisprudence. They are usually called "implied contracts." More properly they should be called "quasi contracts" or "constructive contracts." See 1 Page on Contracts, §14; also 2 Page on Contracts, §771.

The following excerpts from *Sceva v. True*, 53 N.H. 627, are peculiarly applicable here:

> We regard it as well settled that an insane person, an idiot, or a person utterly bereft of all sense and reason by the sudden stroke of an accident or disease may be held liable, in assumpsit, for necessaries furnished to him in good faith while in that unfortunate and helpless condition. And the reasons upon which this rest are too broad, as well as too sensible and humane, to be overborne by any deductions which a refined logic may make from the circumstances that in such cases there can be no contract or promise, in fact, no meeting of the minds of the parties. The cases put it on the ground of an implied contract; and by this is not meant, as the defendant's counsel seems to suppose, an actual contract—that is, an actual meeting of the minds of the parties, an actual, mutual understanding, to be inferred from language, acts, and circumstances by the jury—but a contract and promise, said to be implied by the law, where, in point of fact, there was no contract, no mutual understanding, and so no promise. The defendant's counsel says it is usurpation for the court to hold, as a matter of law, that there is a contract and a promise, when all the evidence in the case shows that there was not a contract, nor the semblance of one. It is doubtless a legal fiction, invented and used for the sake of the remedy. If it was originally usurpation, certainly it has now become very inveterate, and firmly fixed in the body of the law. Illustrations might be multiplied, but enough has been said to show that when a contract or promise implied by law is spoken of, a very different thing is meant from a contract in fact, whether express or tacit. The evidence of an actual contract is generally to be found either in some writing made by the parties, or in verbal communications which passed between them, or in their acts and conduct considered in the light of the circumstances of each particular case. A contract implied by law, on the contrary, rests upon no evidence. It has no actual existence. It is simply a mythical creation of the law. The law says it shall be taken that there was a promise, when in point of fact, there was none. Of course this is not good logic, for the obvious and sufficient reason that it is not true. It is a legal fiction, resting wholly for its support on a plain legal obligation, and a plain legal right. If it were true, it would not be a fiction. . . .
>
> . . .
>
> . . . In its practical application [implied-in-law contract] sustains recovery for physicians and nurses who render services for infants, insane persons, and drunkards. And services rendered by physicians to persons unconscious or helpless by reason

of injury or sickness are in the same situation as those rendered to persons incapable of contracting, such as the classes above described. Raoul v. Newman, 59 Ga. 408; Maeyer v. K. of P., 70 N.E. 111, 178 N.Y. 63, 64 L.R.A. 839. The court was therefore right in giving the instruction in question.

2. The defendant sought to require the plaintiff to prove, in addition to the value of the services, the benefit, if any, derived by the deceased from the operation, and alleges error in the court refusing to so instruct the jury. The court was right in refusing to place this burden upon the physicians. The same question was considered in *Ladd v. Witte*, 116 Wis. 35, where the court said: "That is not at all the test. So that a surgical operation be conceived and performed with due skill and care, the price to be paid therefore does not depend upon the result. The event so generally lies with the forces of nature that all intelligent men know and understand that the surgeon is not responsible therefor. In absence of express agreement, the surgeon, who brings to such a service due skill and care, earns the reasonable and customary price therefore, whether the outcome be beneficial to the patient or the reverse."

3. The court permitted to go to the jury the fact that Mr. Harrison was a bachelor, and that his estate would go to his collateral relatives, and also permitted proof to be made of the value of the estate. . . . There is a conflict in the authorities as to whether it is proper to prove the value of the estate of a person for whom medical services were rendered, or the financial condition of the person receiving such services. . . .

There was evidence in this case proving that it was customary for physicians to graduate their charges by the ability of the patient to pay. . . . While the law may admit such evidence as throwing light upon the contract and indicating what was really in contemplation when it was made, yet a different question is presented when there is no contract to be ascertained or construed, but a mere fiction of law creating a contract where none existed in order that there might be a remedy for a right. This fiction merely requires a reasonable compensation for the services rendered. The services are the same be the patient prince or pauper, and for them the surgeon is entitled to fair compensation for his time, service, and skill. It was therefore error to admit this evidence. . . .

Judgment is reversed, and cause remanded.

Battle and Wood, JJ., concur in sustaining the recovery, and in holding that it was error to permit the jury to consider the fact that his estate would go to collateral heirs; but they do not concur in holding that it was error to admit evidence of the value of the estate, and instructing that it might be considered in fixing the charge.

PYEATTE
v.
PYEATTE

Court of Appeals of Arizona, Division 1
135 Ariz. 346
1982

CORCORAN, J.

. . .

The husband, H. Charles Pyeatte (appellant), and the wife, Margrethe May Pyeatte (appellee), were married in Tucson on December 27, 1972. At the time of the marriage both had received bachelors degrees. Appellee was coordinator of the surgical technical program at Pima College. Appellant was one of her students. In early 1974, the parties had discussions and reached an agreement concerning postgraduate education for both of them.

Appellee testified that they agreed she "would put him through three years of law school without his having to work, and when he finished, he would put [her] through for [her] masters degree without [her] having to work."

. . .

Appellant attended law school in Tucson, Arizona, from 1974 until his graduation. He was admitted to the State Bar shortly thereafter.

During appellant's first two years of law school appellee supported herself and appellant on the salary she earned at Pima College. During the last year, appellee lost her job, whereupon savings were used to support the couple. Although each spouse contributed to the savings, a significant amount was furnished by appellee.

After appellant's admission to the Bar, the couple moved to Prescott, Arizona, where appellant was employed by a law firm. Both parties realized that appellant's salary would not be sufficient to support the marriage and pay for appellee's education for a masters degree simultaneously. Appellee then agreed to defer her plans for a year or two until her husband got started in his legal career. In the meantime, she obtained part-time employment as a teacher.

In April, 1978, appellant told appellee that he no longer wanted to be married to her, and in June of 1978, she filed a petition for dissolution. Trial was had in March of 1979, and a decree of dissolution was granted. At the time of the trial, there was little community property and no dispute as to division of any community or separate property. Spousal maintenance was neither sought by nor granted to appellee.

The trial court determined that there was an agreement between the parties, that appellee fully performed her part of that agreement, that appellant had not performed his part of the agreement, and that appellee had been damaged thereby.

Based on appellee's expert testimony on the cost of furthering *her* education, in accordance with the agreement, the trial court awarded judgment of $23,000 against appellant as damages for breach of contract, with additional directions that the judgment be payable through the court clerk on a quarterly basis in a sum of not less than ten percent of appellant's net quarterly income.

. . .

On appeal, appellant argues that the agreement did not rise to the level of a binding contract because, among other things, the terms thereof were not definite and could not be legally enforced.

Appellee advances three theories as grounds upon which the trial court's award should be upheld [Two are retained here.—Eds.]:

1. The agreement between the parties was a binding contract. Appellant's failure to perform after appellee had fully performed her obligations renders appellant liable in damages.

. . .

3. If the agreement is not enforceable as a binding contract, appellee is nevertheless entitled to restitution in quantum meruit to prevent appellant's unjust enrichment because he received his education at appellee's expense.

We will address each argument in turn.

THE CONTRACT CLAIM

Although the terms and requirements of an enforceable contract need not be stated in minute detail, it is fundamental that, in order to be binding, an agreement must be definite and certain so that the liability of the parties may be exactly fixed. Terms necessary for the required definiteness frequently include time of performance, place of performance, price or compensation, penalty provisions, and other material requirements of the agreement. 17 C.J.S. *Contracts* §36(2) at 647-61 (1963); 17 Am. Jur. 2d *Contracts* §75 at 413-15 (1964). . . .

Upon examining the parties' agreement in this instance, it is readily apparent that a sufficient mutual understanding regarding critical provisions of their agreement did not exist. For example, no agreement was made regarding the time when appellee would attend graduate school and appellant would be required to assume their full support. Both parties concede that appellee could not have begun her masters program immediately after appellant's graduation because his beginning salary was not sufficient to provide both for her education and the couple's support. Appellee told appellant she was willing to wait a year or two until he "got on his feet" before starting her program. Nothing more definite than that was ever agreed upon. Furthermore, although appellee agreed to support appellant while he attended law school for three years, no corresponding time limitation was placed upon her within which to finish her education. Even if we assume that the agreement contemplated appellee's enrolling as a full-time student, the length of time necessary to complete a masters degree varies considerably depending upon the requirements of the particular program and the number of classes an individual elects to take at one time. Such a loosely worded agreement can hardly be said to have fixed appellant's liability with certainty.

. . .

Appellee urges us to enforce this agreement because contracts should be interpreted, whenever reasonable, in such a way as to uphold the contract, and that this is particularly true where there has been performance by one party. We are aware of these general legal concepts, and also note that reasonableness can be implied by the courts when interpreting agreements. *Shattuck v. Precision-Toyota, Inc.*, 115 Ariz. 586, 566 P.2d 1332 (1977).

The court's function, however, cannot be that of contract maker. *Savoca Masonry Co. v. Homes and Son Construction Co., supra.* Nor can the court create a contract simply to accomplish a purportedly good purpose. *Stearns-Roger Corp. v. Hartford Accident and Indemnity Co.*, 117 Ariz. 162, 571 P.2d 659 (1977). Our review of the record persuades us that the essential terms and requirements of this agreement were not sufficiently definite so that the obligations of the parties to the agreement could be determined. . . .

. . . On the basis of our determination that the agreement in this case is unenforceable, there can be no recovery for amounts necessary to further appellee's education.

. . .

THE RESTITUTION CLAIM

Appellee's last contention is that the trial court's award should be affirmed as an equitable award of restitution on the basis of unjust enrichment. She argues that appellant's education, which she subsidized and which he obtained through the exhaustion of community assets constitutes a benefit for which he must, in equity, make restitution. This narrow equitable issue is one of first impression in this court. We first addressed the broad outlines of the problem in *Wisner*, but in the context of significantly different facts and legal theories. Our recognition of the disparate considerations involved in a case such as the one before us led us to limit our holding in *Wisner* to its facts. 129 Ariz. at 341, 631 P.2d at 123.

Restitution is available to a party to an agreement where he performs services for the other believing that there is a binding contract.

> When Restitution for Services is Granted.
> A person who has rendered services to another or services which have inured to the benefit of another . . . is entitled to restitution therefor if the services were rendered
>
> . . .
>
> (b) To obtain the performance of an agreement with the other therefor, not operative as a contract, or voidable as a contract and avoided by the other party after the services were rendered, the one performing the services erroneously believing because of a mistake of fact that the agreement was binding upon the other. . . .

Restatement of Restitution §40(b) at 155 (1937).

In order to be granted restitution, appellee must demonstrate that appellant received a benefit, that by receipt of that benefit he was unjustly enriched at her expense, and that the circumstances were such that in good conscience appellant should make compensation. *John A. Artukovich & Sons v. Reliance Truck Co.*, 126

Ariz. 246, 614 P.2d 327 (1980); Restatement of Restitution §1 at 13 (1937). In *Artukovich*, the Supreme Court discussed unjust enrichment[:]

> Contracts implied-in-law or quasi-contracts, also called constructive contracts, are inferred by the law as a matter of reason and justice from the acts and conduct of the parties and circumstances surrounding the transactions . . . and are imposed for the purpose of bringing about justice without reference to the intentions of the parties. . . .
>
> Restatement of Restitution §1 provides, "A person who has been unjustly enriched at the expense of another is required to make restitution to the other." Comment (a) to that section notes that a person is enriched if he received a benefit and is unjustly enriched if retention of that benefit would be unjust. Comment (b) defines a benefit as being any form of advantage. . . .
>
>   . . .
>
> Unjust enrichment does not depend upon the existence of a valid contract, . . . nor is it necessary that plaintiff suffer a loss corresponding to the defendant's gain for there to be valid claim for an unjust enrichment. . . .

126 Ariz. at 248, 614 P.2d at 329.

A benefit may be any type of advantage, including that which saves the recipient from any loss or expense. *See Artukovich, supra.* Appellee's support of appellant during his period of schooling clearly constituted a benefit to appellant. Absent appellee's support, appellant may not have attended law school, may have been forced to prolong his education because of intermittent periods of gainful employment, or may have gone deeply into debt. Relieved of the necessity of supporting himself, he was able to devote full time and attention to his education.

The mere fact that one party confers a benefit on another, however, is not of itself sufficient to require the other to make restitution. Retention of the benefit must be unjust.

Historically, restitution for the value of services rendered has been available upon either an "implied-in-fact" contract or upon quasi-contractual grounds. D. Dobbs, *Remedies* §4.2 at 237 (1973); 1 Williston, *Contracts* §3 and 3A at 10-15 (3d ed. 1957). An implied-in-fact contract is a true contract, differing from an express contract only insofar as it is proved by circumstantial evidence rather than by express written or oral terms. *United States v. O. Frank Heinz Construction Co.*, 300 F. Supp. 396 (D.C. Ill. 1969); *Plumbing Shop, Inc. v. Pitts*, 67 Wash. 2d 514, 408 P.2d 382, 383 (1965). In contrast, a quasi-contract is not a contract at all, but a duty imposed in equity upon a party to repay another to prevent his own unjust enrichment. The intention of the parties to bind themselves contractually in such a case is irrelevant. 1 Williston, *Contracts* §3A at 12-15 (3d ed. 1957). To support her claim for restitution on the basis of an implied-in-fact contract, appellee must demonstrate the elements of a binding contract. For the reasons we have previously discussed, we cannot find the necessary mutual assent or certainty as to the critical terms of the agreement sufficient to establish such a contract. *See also Osborn v. Boeing Airplane Co.*, 309 F.2d 99 (9th Cir. 1962).

Restitution is nevertheless available in quasi-contract absent any showing of mutual assent. While a quasi-contractual obligation may be imposed without regard to the intent of the parties, such an obligation will be imposed only if the circumstances are such that it would be unjust to allow retention of the benefit without compensating the one who conferred it. *See* Williston, *supra.* One circumstance under which a duty to compensate will be imposed is when there was an expectation of payment or compensation for services at the time they were rendered.

. . .

Although we found that the spousal agreement failed to meet the requirements of an enforceable contract, the agreement still has importance in considering appellee's claim for unjust enrichment because it both evidences appellee's expectation of compensation and the circumstances which make it unjust to allow appellant to retain the benefits of her extraordinary efforts.

We next address the question of whether restitution on the basis of unjust enrichment is appropriate in the context of the marital relationship. No authority is cited to the court in support of the proposition that restitution as a matter of law is inappropriate in a dissolution proceeding. . . . Where both spouses perform the usual and incidental activities of the marital relationship, upon dissolution there can be no restitution for performance of these activities. . . . Where, however, the facts demonstrate an agreement between the spouses and an extraordinary or unilateral effort by one spouse which inures solely to the benefit of the other by the time of dissolution, the remedy of restitution is appropriate.

. . .

A number of jurisdictions have addressed the issue of restitution in the context of the marital relationship. The cases which have dealt with the issue involve two factual patterns: (1) The first group consists of those cases in which the couples had accumulated substantial marital assets over a period of time from which assets the wife received large awards of property, maintenance and child support. The courts have refused to apply the theory of restitution on the basis of unjust enrichment in each of these cases. (2) The second group consists of those cases in which the parties are divorced soon after the student spouse receives his degree or license and there is little or no marital property from which to order any award to the working spouse.

In the first group the courts have consistently refused to find a property interest in the husband's education, degree, license or earning capacity or to order restitution in favor of the wife. Because restitution is a matter of equity, the circumstances of these cases preclude at the outset any basis for a finding of inequitable circumstances sufficient to support restitution inasmuch as the wife in each case had received substantial awards of the marital assets and was seeking, in addition to those assets, a property interest in the husband's education, degree, license or earning capacity. Because the property award itself is largely the product of the education, degree, license or earning capacity in which the wife sought a monetary interest, the courts hold that the wife realized her "investment" in the husband's education by having received the benefits of his increased earning capacity during marriage and by receipt of an award of property upon its dissolution. *Wisner, supra; Lucas v. Lucas*, 27 Cal. 3d 808, 166 Cal. Rptr. 853, 614 P.2d 285 (1980), overruling in part on other grounds, *Aufmuth v. Aufmuth*, 89 Cal. App. 3d 446, 152 Cal. Rptr. 668 (1979) [citations omitted].

. . .

The second group presents the more difficult problem of the "working spouse" claiming entitlement to an equitable recovery where there is little or no marital property to divide and therefore the conventional remedies of property division or spousal maintenance are unavailable. The emerging consensus among those jurisdictions faced with the issue in this factual context is that restitution to the working spouse is appropriate to prevent the unjust enrichment of the student spouse. *See Inman v. Inman*, 578 S.W.2d 266 (Ky. 1979); *De La Rosa v. De La Rosa*, 309 N.W.2d 755 (Minn. 1981); *Hubbard v. Hubbard*, 603 P.2d 747 (Okl. 1979); *Lundberg v. Lundberg*, 107 Wis. 2d 1, 318 N.W.2d 918 (1982); *Contra, In re Marriage of Graham*, 194 Colo. 429, 574 P.2d 75 (1978).

. . .

The Oklahoma Supreme Court in *Hubbard* held that, while a degree is not "property" subject to valuation and division upon dissolution, equitable relief is not thereby precluded. The court then ordered that the wife be reimbursed in quasi-contract for the amounts she expended during the 12 years in which she supported her husband while he obtained his medical training.

> While it is true that Dr. Hubbard's license to practice medicine is his own to do with as he pleases, it is nonetheless also true that Ms. Hubbard has an equitable claim to repayment for the investment she made in his education and training. To hold otherwise would result in the unjust enrichment of Dr. Hubbard. He would leave the marriage with an earning capacity increased by $250,000 which was obtained in substantial measure through the efforts and sacrifices of his wife. She on the other hand would leave the marriage without either a return on her investment or an earning capacity similarly increased through joint efforts. . . . All the resources of the marriage had been dissipated on Dr. Hubbard's education. There is no reason in law or equity why Dr. Hubbard should retain the only valuable asset which was accumulated through joint efforts . . . free of claims for reimbursement by his wife.

603 P.2d at 750.

. . .

The record shows that the appellee conferred benefits on appellant—financial subsidization of appellant's legal education—with the agreement and expectation that she would be compensated therefor by his reciprocal efforts after his graduation and admission to the Bar. Appellant has left the marriage with the only valuable asset acquired during the marriage—his legal education and qualification to practice law. It would be inequitable to allow appellant to retain this benefit without making restitution to appellee. However, we need not decide what limits or standards would apply in the absence of an agreement. Commentators have discerned in various statutory enactments and the developing case law a renewed and expanded recognition of marriage's economic underpinnings. *See* Comment, *The Interest of the Community in a Professional Education*, 10 Calif. W. L. Rev. 590 (1974); Erickson, *Spousal*

Support Toward the Realization of Educational Goals: How the Law Can Ensure Reciprocity, 1978 Wis. L. Rev. 947. By our decision herein, we reject the view that the economic element necessarily inherent in the marital institution (and particularly apparent in its dissolution) requires us to treat marriage as a strictly financial undertaking upon the dissolution of which each party will be fully compensated for the investment of his various contributions. When the parties have been married for a number of years, the courts cannot and will not strike a balance regarding the contributions of each to the marriage and then translate that into a monetary award. To do so would diminish the individual personalities of the husband and wife to economic entities and reduce the institution of marriage to that of a closely held corporation.

THE MEASURE OF RECOVERY

Generally, where claims are made by the working spouse against the student spouse, the trial court in each case must make specific findings as to whether the education, degree or license acquired by the student spouse during marriage involved an unjust enrichment of that spouse, the value of the benefit, and the amount that should be paid to the working spouse. A variety of methods of computing the unjust enrichment may be employed in ascertaining the working spouse's compensable interest in the attainment of the student spouse's education, degree or license.

The award to appellee should be limited to the financial contribution by appellee for appellant's living expenses and direct educational expenses. *See De La Rosa v. De La Rosa*, 309 N.W.2d 755.

Under the agreement between the parties, the anticipated benefit to appellee may involve a monetary benefit in a lesser amount than the benefit conferred by appellee on appellant. In that event, the award to appellee should be limited to the amount of the anticipated benefit to appellee. Appellee should not recover more than the benefit of her bargain. Restatement of Restitution, §107, Comment b, at 449 (1937).

. . .

The relief granted to appellee is equitable in nature. The rule regarding equitable awards is set forth in *Mason v. Ellison*, 63 Ariz. 196, 160 P.2d 326 (1945) in which the Arizona supreme court stated:

> In an equity case the court ". . . adapts its relief and molds its decrees to satisfy the requirements of the case and to conserve the equities of the parties litigant. The court has such plenary power since its purpose is the accomplishment of justice amid all of the vicissitudes and intricacies of life. . . ."

63 Ariz. at 203, 160 P.2d at 329 (quoting 19 Am. Jur. *Equity* §123 at 123-24 (1939)).

The fact that this case presents a novel resolution of a difficult issue, without precedent, will not prevent this court from ordering relief in an amount and manner appropriate to the circumstances.

> It is the distinguishing feature of equity jurisdiction that it will apply settled rules to unusual conditions and mold its decrees so as to do equity between the parties.

30 C.J.S. *Equity* §12 at 798-99 (1965). . . .

. . .

The portion of the judgment in the amount of $23,000 is reversed and remanded for proceedings in accordance with this opinion.

FARESE
v.
McGARRY

Superior Court of New Jersey, Appellate Division
237 N.J. Super. 385
1989

Brochin, J.A.D.

Defendant James M. McGarry, Jr. rented a one-family house from plaintiff Frank Farese pursuant to a written lease. Despite a notice to vacate, the tenant continued in possession for approximately six and a half months after the expiration of the term of the lease. After the tenant had moved out, the landlord sued him, seeking compensation for damage which the tenant had allegedly caused to the property, twice the monthly rent pursuant to N.J.S.A. 2A:42-6 for the period during which he had remained in the house after the expiration of his lease, and an attorney's fee.

The tenant counterclaimed for specific performance or damages. He claimed a breach of his option to purchase the property, and he sought damages for the breach and compensation for the amount by which the landlord had allegedly been unjustly enriched as the result of improvements made by the tenant to the property in anticipation of his acquiring it under what he believed was his purchase option.

The case was tried to a jury which returned its verdict on special interrogatories. It rejected the landlord's claims that he was entitled to damages because the tenant had continued in possession beyond the term of his lease or because the premises had been injured by the tenant's neglect. The jury also found that the landlord had not breached his contractual obligation to sell the property to the tenant. However, the jury returned a verdict awarding the tenant $13,000 as the reasonable value of improvements which the tenant had made to the property.

The landlord appealed. He contends that the trial court erred in permitting the jury to return a verdict based on "an implied contract or quasi-contract.". . .

. . . Both counts are predicated on a single theory of the landlord's liability, that he gave his tenant an option to purchase the leased premises and breached his option agreement by refusing to convey. The difference between the two counts is the measure of damages which each asserts or implies. The first count does not specify a measure of damages. Under that count, a counterclaimant would be entitled to prove general damages measured by the difference between the option price of the property and its fair market value at the time that the option was exercisable. If there was no surprise to his adversary, he would also be entitled to prove other measures of damages; for example, expenditures which he reasonably incurred in reliance on being able to exercise the option agreement. The second count alleges, apparently as an alternative measure of damages, that the landlord "has been unjustly enriched in the improvements made to his property to the extent of the value of said improvements." . . . If the issue before the trial court or before this court were, as the landlord seems to be arguing that it is, whether the tenant could properly offer evidence in support of both counts, the answer would clearly be that he could.

. . . The court instructed the jury as follows:

> . . . a quasi contract is an obligation created by the law, for reasons of justice, without regard to the expression of . . . assent by either words or acts. Quasi-contractual obligations rest upon the equitable principles that a person shall not be allowed to enrich himself unjustly, at the expense of another, and that a man is deemed to have performed that which he ought to do.
>
> In other words, if you determine that the improvements made by this defendant on the premises were in reliance on an option he thought he had, which he attempted to exercise, as opposed to being done pursuant to the lease agreement, whereby he was going to be reimbursed only for materials, and as opposed to being done solely to make the premises occupiable by himself during a lease term because he was getting a favorable rent, then you will determine what if any amount he is entitled to receive for those alleged improvements.

> . . .

The lease between the parties clearly confers a right of first refusal on the tenant, not an option. However, the language of the right of first refusal clause could very well have been confusing to someone who, like the tenant in this case, was not a lawyer nor otherwise experienced in interpreting leases. A provision of the lease itself refers to a prior oral agreement between the parties which they intended should survive the execution of the lease. The lease indicates that that prior agreement dealt with improvements which the tenant was to make to the house and, perhaps, with other matters as well. The lease was drafted by the landlord's attorney who negotiated directly with the tenant. From all of the circumstances, the jury could reasonably have concluded that the tenant had an honest belief that he had an absolute contractual right to purchase the property, and that the landlord, directly or through his attorney, contributed to the tenant's misapprehension.

The principle upon which the trial court correctly submitted this case to the jury is analogous to the rule that "where one erects a building upon the lands of another in the mistaken belief that he is the owner thereof, and the true owner, having knowledge of the improvement, does nothing to apprise the builder of the true situation," the builder is entitled to relief. *See Riggle v. Skill*, 9 N.J. Super. 372, 378, 74 A.2d 424 (Ch. Div. 1950), aff'd 7 N.J. 268, 81 A.2d 364 (1951), and cases cited therein. In such a case, the courts have conditioned return of possession to the owner upon his paying adequate compensation for the reasonable cost of the improvements or, in an appropriate case, they have permitted the builder of the improvements to retain the property upon paying its reasonable value to the true owner. *See Brick Tp. v. Vannell*, 55 N.J. Super. 583, 593, 151 A.2d 404 (App. Div. 1959).

In the present case, the tenant made improvements to the landlord's house as the result of a mistake, which the landlord encouraged or at least did not dispel, not about the location of boundary lines, but about whether he had a valid option to purchase the property for an agreed price. Upon those facts, we hold that the tenant was entitled to recover under a theory of *quasi-contract* or unjust enrichment. *Cf. Power-Matics, Inc. v. Ligotti*, 79 N.J. Super. 294, 305-307, 191 A.2d 483 (App. Div. 1963); *Heim v. Shore*, 56 N.J. Super. 62, 74-75, 151 A.2d 556 (App. Div. 1959); Shapiro v. Solomon, 42 N.J. Super. 377, 383-385, 126 A.2d 654 (App. Div. 1956).

. . .

However, the amount of the award to the tenant was without support in the evidence. The proper measure of damages was the value of the improvements to the landlord. The only evidence submitted on the issue was the testimony by the tenant that the reasonable value of the work which he did on the house was $3,150. He calculated that amount by valuing his labor at $15 an hour for 210 hours. In the absence of any contrary testimony, that is the best evidence available of the value which the renovations had to the landlord.

. . .

The judgment is modified in accordance with this opinion to award defendant-counterclaimant $3,150 rather than $13,000 on his counterclaim. It is affirmed in all other respects. No costs are allowed.

Problems

1. Working on the Railroad. Azmina Weatherby and her husband were employees of Burlington Northern & Santa Fe Railway Co. (BNSF). She held a salaried crew planner position, and he held an hourly engineering position. When BNSF transferred her husband from Fort Worth to Kansas City, Weatherby applied for an open crew planner position in Kansas City to accompany him. At the time, she asked whether she would receive relocation benefits. She knew that other employees at her level had received relocation benefits when they had moved within the company. The Kansas City superintendent told her that he would "check on" it. After Weatherby accepted the Kansas City position and had arrived at her new job, she asked the superintendent again, and he again said he would find out. The employee handbook states:

> The BNSF Salaried Employee Relocation Policy provides coverage for most travel, living and moving expenses associated with your relocation. This policy applies to all *salaried* employees who are transferred from one location to another at the request of the Company, provided that the distance between your departure residence and the new work location must be 50 miles greater than the distance between your departure residence and your former work location. This policy is subject to revision by the Company at any time, without notice, as necessary, and is not to be construed as conferring any contractual right or becoming a part of any employment contract. Furthermore, BNSF does not assume any liability for relocation services provided by or arising out of any of the activities of the individual service providers, their agents, representatives, or employees.

Weatherby subsequently sought relocation expenses, which BNSF refused to pay. (BNSF did not pay any relocation expenses to her husband because he was an hourly employee.) Weatherby then sued BNSF asserting contract and quasi-contract claims. Which party should prevail?

2. Capping Fees. Elizabeth Rosenbaum, a private attorney, was appointed by the juvenile court as guardian ad litem for a minor in October 2003. The guardianship statute sets a $1,000 cap on fees, but allows a guardian to exceed fee limitations if she proves good cause and obtains approval prior to exceeding the limits. Despite the statutory language, Rosenbaum in the past had been permitted to obtain any necessary orders to exceed statutory fee limitations at the time she submitted her fee claim. In March 2004, Rosenbaum submitted a fee claim for $2,200 along with an application to exceed fee limitations. Her fee claim was reduced to $1,000 on the ground that she did not obtain prior approval for exceeding the fee limitations. The reasonableness of her fee claim is undisputed. Rosenbaum filed suit asking for payment on quasi-contract grounds. What result?

3. Sharing in the Winnings Redux. Wo Sin Chiu was seriously injured in an auto collision on March 27, 1998. Chiu signed a retention agreement with attorney Richard Shapero on April 1, which provided that Shapero would represent Chiu in exchange for a 40 percent contingency fee. Shapero immediately began working on the matter. On May 7, Chiu discharged Shapero, but rehired him four days later. On July 14, Chiu discharged Shapero for the last time and retained the services of Kenneth Baker. With Baker's assistance, Chiu ultimately obtained a settlement of $175,000. Shapero filed an attorney's lien against the settlement, claiming the 40 percent contingency fee. Can Shapero recover in quasi-contract? If so, what is the proper measure of his damages?

4. Subcontractor's Claim. Hy-Brasil Restaurants entered into a contract with Howell Management for the construction of a restaurant and bar, and in September, Howell hired Mike Glynn & Company as a subcontractor to do the plumbing, heating, and air-conditioning work. Mike Glynn had known Hy-Brasil's

President, Liam Tiernan, for over 30 years. On October 27, Howell breached its contract with Glynn by failing to pay an invoice in full within ten days, and Glynn threatened to walk off the job. Glynn and Tiernan dispute the exact content of their conversation. Glynn claims that Tiernan told him that it was most important that the job be finished before the holidays and promised Glynn that either Tiernan personally, or Hy-Brasil, would pay him if he completed the job. Tiernan denied making any promises to pay Glynn if Howell failed to do so, but admits that he encouraged Glynn to continue to work and explained that a delay past the holidays would work a terrible hardship on Hy-Brasil. Glynn did continue to work and hired additional workers and worked overtime to complete the job before the holidays. If Glynn had left the job when Howell stopped making payment, he would have incurred roughly $5,000 in costs. By remaining, he incurred $42,000. After Howell failed to pay him, Glynn demanded payment from Tiernan and Hy-Brasil, and Tiernan refused to make any payment. Are Tiernan and Hy-Brasil liable in quasi-contract to Glynn?

Table of Cases

641